Man and mind

Man and Mind

Collected papers of Jeanne Lampl-De Groot M.D.

1985
International Universities Press, New York, USA
Van Gorcum, Assen/Maastricht, The Netherlands

© 1985, International Universities Press, 315 Fifth Avenue, NEW YORK, NY 10016
Van Gorcum & Comp. B.V., P.O. Box 43, 9400 AA Assen, The Netherlands

ISBN 0 8236 3087 0

CIP-GEGEVENS KONINKLIJKE BIBLIOTHEEK, DEN HAAG

Lampl-de Groot, Jeanne

Man and mind : collected papers of Jeanne Lampl-de Groot M.D. – Assen [etc.]: Van Gorcum; New York: International Universities Press
Met index, lit. opg.
SISO 410.3 UDC 159.9(081.2)
Trefw.: psychologie; opstellen.

ISBN 90 232 2138 9

Printed in The Netherlands by Van Gorcum, Assen

Contents

Preface

Twenty years ago articles by Jeanne Lampl-de Groot which had already been published were collected in "The Development of the Mind". For years this book was almost unobtainable. It is of eminent importance for the development of psychoanalysis that not only these works, but also Jeanne Lampl-de Groot's later publications remain accessible.

The aim of this volume is to publish the work which she wrote from 1927 until early in 1985. With the help of many friends and pupils we have succeeded in publishing these articles on the occasion of Jeanne Lampl-de Groot's 90th birthday.

Her views have been of essential significance for the progress of psychoanalytic science. Her independent approach in supplementing Freud's work was apparent from the very first article. She is the first author to describe in "The Evolution of the Oedipus Complex in Women" the oedipal complex in a girl during the process of growing up. The essential part of this view is that the oedipal complex as the nuclear complex of the neurosis not only comprises this constellation but also that which has preceeded its development. This defines to a high degree the development of a future love life. The author elaborates on this theme in later publications. Along with other publications, the article "Female Psychology" which appeared as recently as 1982, includes an analysis of opinions about female sexuality.

Her familiarity with psychoanalytic literature from the earliest writings of Freud to the present is encyclopedic and her understanding is penetrating. There is an obvious link between her work from 1936 "Inhibition and Narcissism" and 1937 "Masochism and Narcissism" and Freud's "On Narcissism: An Introduction" and "The Economic Problem in Masochism". In this work Jeanne Lampl-de Groot elaborates on Freud's theories, using newly gained insights in the functioning of the ego and the role of omnipotence in narcissism. She also integrated these ideas in her articles describing defense as a function of the ego and its importance for character development. There is a parallel between the 1957 publication about defense and development on the one hand and the outstanding paper on Multiple Personality, published in 1981, on the other hand. The content of this article presents a clear picture of the personality as conceived by psychoanalysis. Jeanne Lampl-de Groot expresses her ideas in beautifully simple and lucid prose, always emphasizing the enormous complexity of the psyche. She never neglects the powerful force of the drives. In 1953 and 1965 she contributed articles on the theory of the drive and at an early stage she raised the question of the aggression in its destructive phase which arises when the analysis has liberated repressed forces and the patient learns how to handle these. However, her starting point continues to be the interaction between the drives, the ego, and the various forces which influence the interaction between these agencies. She stresses identification with the analyst's tolerance and empathy but also with his quiet mastery and control of his own affects and impulses, even under the patient's provoking acting out as important factors in the non-verbal part of the healing process. In later contributions she often returns to these non-verbal aspects of the psychoanalytic cure and the consequence of these insights for training analyses.

Jeanne Lampl-de Groot carefully describes the consequences of the expansion of our theoretical knowledge on the technique of psychoanalysis to which she has contributed so much. Her studies "On Obstacles Standing in the Way of Psychoanalytic Cure (1967) and "On the Influence of Early Development upon the Oedipal Constellation" (1980) of the working alliance (1975) and of the significance of insight in early child development (1971) have had international impact on psychoanalytic technique. As a co-founder of psychoanalytic training in the Netherlands and the Psychoanalytic Institute connected with it, this training has a special place in her heart. In the course of the years, she has expounded her views on this subject in a number of articles.

In her historical essays she reports the early revolutionary elan of psychoanalysis in her Berlin and Vienna periods. As early as 1950 she wrote about the development of psychoanalysis and to the present she is still actively involved. She is continuously differentiating between that which is detrimental. to the essential part and that where observations might lead to a deeper understanding.

Anna Freud wrote in the preface of The Development of the Mind about Jeanne Lampl-de Groot's position:
"The author of this book belongs to a small but prominent group of psychoanalysts who served their apprenticeship in Vienna in the twenties of the century and who are now, one after the other, approaching, celebrating, or looking back on their 70th birthday". That was 20 years ago. Anna Freud continues: "The members of this group were fortunate in their professional career in several respects. They entered the analytic field late enough to be spared many of the setbacks, hardships and attacks by a hostile world to which the pioneering generation had been subjected. They were early enough, on the other hand, to be taught by the originator of psychoanalysis himself, and to develop their ideas in lively interchange with him.
They entered the Vienna Society when scientific life there was at its height. And, when this Society broke up, they dispersed all over the world, to become the mainstay of analytic branches elsewhere, valued teachers in new analytic

Institutes, editors of or contributors to analytic journals, and guiding figures in the International Psychoanalytic Association".

Jeanne Lampl-de Groot herself has called these circumstances a privilege. We, in our turn as friends and colleagues, have the privilege to be able to preserve these experiences as far as she has published them now through this collection of essays. For us, as for everybody who is interested in the evolution of psychoanalysis, the publication of this book is a memorable event.

E. C. M. Frijling-Schreuder
P. J. van der Leeuw
N. Treurniet
E. Verhage-Stins
F. Verhage

1. The Evolution of the Oedipus Complex in Women

(1927)

One of the earliest discoveries of psychoanalysis was the existence of the oedipus complex. Freud found the libidinal relations to the parents to be the center and the acme of the development of infantile sexuality and soon recognized in them the nucleus of the neuroses. Many years of psychoanalytic work greatly enriched his knowledge of the developmental processes in this period of childhood; it gradually became clear to him that in both sexes there are a positive and a negative oedipus complex and that at this time the libido finds a physical outlet in the practice of masturbation. Hence the oedipus complex makes its appearance only when the phallic phase of libido development is reached and when the tide of infantile sexuality recedes, that complex must pass in order to make way for the period of latency, during which the instinctual tendencies are inhibited in their aim. Nevertheless, in spite of the many observations and studies by Freud and other authors, it is remarkable how many obscure problems have for years remained unsolved (Abraham, 1920; Alexander, 1923; H. Deutsch, 1925; Horney, 1923, 1926; Van Ophuijsen, 1918).

It seemed that one very important factor was the connection between the oedipus and the castration complexes, and there were many points about this which were obscure. Moreover, understanding of the processes in male children had been carried much further than with the analogous processes in females. Freud ascribed the difficulties in elucidating the early infantile love relations to the difficulty of getting at the material relating to them: he thought that this was due to the profound repression to which these impulses are subjected. The greater difficulty of understanding these particular mental processes in little girls may arise, on the one hand, from the fact that they are in themselves more complicated that the analogous processes in boys and, on the other hand, from the greater intensity with which the libido is repressed in women. Horney thinks that another reason is that, so far, analytical observations have been made principally by men.

In 1924 and 1925 Freud published two works which threw much light on the origin of the oedipus complex and its connection with the castration complex. The first of these, "The Dissolution of the Oedipus Complex" (1924b), shows what happens to that complex in little boys. It is true that several years previously, in "From the History of an Infantile Neurosis" (1918), and again in 1923 in "A Seventeenth-Century Demonological Neurosis" (1923a), its fate in

See Chapters 7, 14, and 27 for further considerations of the topics discussed here.

certain individual cases had been described. But in "The Dissolution of the Oedipus Complex" we have the general application and the theoretical appreciation of this discovery and also the further conclusions to be deduced from it. The conclusion arrived in this paper is as follows: the oedipus complex in male children receives its death blow from the castration complex, that it is to say, in both the positive and the negative oedipal attitudes the boy has to fear castration by his father, whose strenght is superior to his own. In the first, castration is the punishment for the inadmissible incest wish and, in the second, it is the necessary condition of the boy's adopting the feminine role in relation to his father. Thus, in order to escape castration and to retain his genital he must renounce his love relations with both parents. We see the peculiarly important part which this organ plays in boys and the enormous psychic significance it acquires in their mental life. Furthermore, analytic experience has shown how extraordinarily difficult it is for a child to give up the possession of the mother, who has been his love object ever since he was capable of object love. This reflection leads us to wonder whether the victory of the castration complex over the oedipus complex, together with the narcissistic interest in the highly prized organ, may not be due to still another factor, namely, the tenacity of the first love relation. The following train of thought may also have some significance: if the boy gives up the ownership of his penis, it means that the possession of the mother (or mother substitute) becomes forever impossible to him. If, however, forced by the superior power of that far stronger rival, his father, he renounces the fulfillment of his desire, the way remains open to him at some later period to fight his father more successfully and to return to his first love object, or, more correctly, to her substitute. It does not seem impossible that this knowledge of a future opportunity to fulfill his wish (a knowledge probably phylogenetically acquired and, of course, unconscious) may be a contributing motive in the boy's temporary renunciation of the prohibited love craving. This would also explain why before, or just at the beginning of, the latency period a little boy longs so intensely to be "big" and "grown-up."

In this work, then, Freud in large part explains the connection between the oedipus and the castration complexes in little boys, but he does not tell us much that is new about the same process in little girls. However, his paper, "Some Psychical Consequences of the Anatomical Distinction between the Sexes" (1925), does throw more light on the fate of the early infantile love impulses of the little girl. Freud holds that in girls the oedipus complex (he is speaking of the attitude which for the girl is possitive: love for the father and rivalry with the mother) is a secondary formation, first introduced by the castration complex; that is to say, it arises after the little girl has become aware of the difference between the sexes and has accepted the fact of her own castration. This theory throws a new light on many hitherto obscure problems. With this assumption Freud explains many later developmental characteristics, various differences in the further vicissitudes of the oedipus complex in girls and in boys and in the superego formation in the two sexes, and so forth.

Nevertheless, even after the discovery of this connection, several problems remain unsolved. Freud mentions that when the castration complex has become operative in the girl, that is, when she has accepted her lack of a penis and therefore become a victim of penis envy, "a loosening of the girl's relation with her mother as a love-object" (p. 254) begins to take place. He thinks that one possible reason for this may be the fact that the girl ultimately holds her mother responsible for her own lack of a penis and he further cites a historical factor in the case, namely, that often jealousy is conceived later on against a second child who is more beloved by the mother. But, Freud says, "The situation as a whole is not very clear" (p. 254). According to him, another remarkable effect of penis envy is the girl's struggle against masturbation, a struggle which is more intense than that of the boy and which, in general, makes itself felt at a later age. Freud's view is that the reason why the little girl revolts so strongly against phallic masturbation is the blow dealt to her narcissism in connection with her penis envy: she suspects that in this matter it is useless to compete with the boy and therefore it is best not to enter into rivalry with him. This statement gives rise to the involuntary thought: Why should the little girl who never possessed a penis, and therefore never knew its value from her own experience, regard it as so precious? Why has the little girl's discovery of this lack in herself such far-reaching mental consequences? And, above all, why should it begin to produce a mental effect at a particular moment when it is possible that the physical difference between herself and little boys has been perceived countless times previously without any reaction? Probably the little girl produces pleasurable physical sensations in the clitoris in the same way and presumably with the same degree of intensity as the boy does in the penis, and perhaps she feels them in the vagina too. On this latter point I received a communication from Josine Müller of the German Psychoanalytic Society; I have also been told of it by an acquaintance, the mother of two little girls. Why, then, should the little girl have this mental reaction to the discovery that her own member is smaller than the boy's or is lacking altogether? I should like to present the following considerations, which have been suggested to me by experiences in my analytic practice, in the hope that they will bring us a little nearer to answering these questions.

I think that several points will be clearer to us if we consider the previous history of the castration complex or penis envy in little girls, but before doing so it is advisable to re-examine the analogous process in boys. As soon as the little boy is capable of an object relation, he takes as his first love object the mother who feeds and tends him. As he passes through the pregenital phases of libidinal development, he retains the same object. When he reaches the phallic stage, he adopts the typical oedipal attitude, i.e., he loves his mother and desires to possess her and to get rid of his rival, the father. Throughout this development his love object remains the same. An alteration in his love attitude, an alteration characteristic of his sex, occurs at the moment when he accepts the possibility of castration as a punishment threatened by his powerful father for these libidinal desires of his. It is not impossible, indeed it is very probable, that even before the boy reaches the phallic stage and adopts the oedipal attitude which coincides with it, he has perceived the difference between the sexes by observing either a sister or girl playmate, but we assume that he attributed little significance to this perception. If, however, such a perception occurs when he is already in the oedipal situation and is experiencing castration anxiety, we know how great an impact this may have on his mind. The child's first reaction is an endeavor to deny the actuality of castration and to hold very tenaciously to his first love object. After violent inward struggles, however, the little boy makes a virtue of necessity; he renounces his love object in order to retain his penis. Possibly he thus ensures for himself the chance of a renewed and more successful battle with his father at some later date − a possibility which I suggested earlier in this paper. As we know, when the young man reaches maturity, he does succeed in wresting the victory from his father, normally with a mother substitute.

But what happens in the little girl? She, too, takes as her first love object the mother who feeds and tends her. She, too, retains the same love object as she passes through the pregenital phases of libidinal evolution. She, too, enters the phallic stage of libido development. Moreover, the little girl has a body organ analogous to the little boy's penis, namely, the clitoris, which gives her pleasurable feelings in masturbation. Physically she behaves exactly like the little boy. We may suppose that in the psychic realm too children of both sexes develop in a similar manner up to this point; that is to say, girls and boys both enter into an oedipal situation when they reach the phallic stage. However, for the girl it is a negative situation − she wants to conquer the mother for herself and to get rid of the father. Up to this point, too, a chance observation by the little girl of the difference between the sexes may have been without significance; now, however, a perception of this sort is fraught with serious consequences for her. It strikes her that the boy's genital is larger, stronger, and more visible than her own, and that he can use it actively in urinating, a process which for the child has a sexual significance. When she makes this comparison, the little girl must feel her own organ to be inferior. She imagines that hers was once like the boy's and that it has been taken from her as a punishment for her prohibited love cravings toward the mother. At first the little girl tries, as does the boy, to deny the fact of castration or to comfort herself with the idea that she will still grow a genital. The acceptance of castration has for her the same consequences as for the boy: not only does her narcissism suffer a blow on account of her physical inferiority, but she is forced to renounce the fulfillment of her first love longings. It is at this point that the difference in the psychic development of the two sexes sets in in connection with the perception of the anatomical difference between male and female. To the boy castration is only a threat, which can be escaped by a suitable modification of behavior. To the girl it is an accomplished fact, which is irrevocable, but the recognition of which compels her finally to renounce her first love object and to taste to the full the bitterness of its loss. Normally, the female child is bound at some time to come to this recognition: she is thereby forced to abandon completely her negative oedipal attitude, and with it the masturbation which is its accompaniment. The object-libidinal relation to the mother is transformed into an identification with her; the father is chosen as a love object; the enemy becomes the beloved. Now there also arises, in place of the wish for a penis, the desire for a child. A child of her own acquires for the girl a narcissistic value similar to that which the penis possesses for the boy; for only a woman, and never a man, can have children. The little girl, then, has now adopted the positive oedipal attitude, with the very far-reaching afterresults with which we are so familiar. Freud has explained more than once that there is no motive for the shattering of the positive oedipus complex in the girl such as we have in the threat of castration in the case of the boy. Therefore the female oedipus complex vanishes gradually, is largely incorporated in the normal development of the woman, and explains many of the differences between the mental lives of women and men.

We may now now sum up by saying that the little girl's castration complex (or her discovery of the anatomical difference between the sexes) which, according to Freud, ushers in and renders possible her normal, positive oedipal attitude, has its psychic correlative just like that of the boy, and it is only this correlative which lends it its enormous significance for the mental evolution of the female child. In the first years of her development as an individual (leaving out of consideration the phylogenetic influences which, of course, are undeniable) the little girl behaves exactly like a boy, not only in the matter of masturbation but in other aspects of her mental life: in her love aim and object choice she is actually a little man. When she has discovered and fully accepted the fact that castration has taken place, the little girl is forced once and for all to renounce her mother as love object and therewith to give up the active, conquering tendency of her love aim as well as the practice of clitoral masturbation. Perhaps here we also have the explanation of a fact with which we have long been familiar, namely, that the woman who is wholly feminine does not know object love in the true sense of the word — she can only "let herself be loved." Thus it is to the mental accompaniments of phallic masturbation that we must ascribe the fact that the little girl normally represses this practice much more energetically than the boy and has a far more intense struggle. For she has to forget with it the first love-disappointment, the pain of the first loss of a love object.

We know how often this repression of the little girl's negative oedipal attitude is wholly or partly unsuccesful. For the female as well as for the male child it is very hard to give up the first love object: in many cases the little girl clings to it for an abnormally long time. She tries to deny the punishment (castration) which would inevitably convince her of the forbidden nature of her desire. She firmly refuses to give up her masculine position. If later her love longing is disappointed a second time, this time in relation to the father who does not give way to her passive wooing of his love, she often tries to return to her former situation and to resume a masculine attitude. In extreme cases this leads to the manifest homosexuality of which Freud gives so excellent and clear an account in "The Psychogenesis of a Case of Homosexuality in a Woman" (1920b). The patient about whom Freud tells us in this work made a faint effort, on entering puberty, to adopt a feminine love attitude but later in the period of puberty she behaved toward an older woman whom she loved exactly like a young man in love. At te same time she was a pronounced feminist, denying the difference between men and women; thus she had gone right back to the first, negative phase of the oedipus complex.

There is another process which is perhaps commoner. The girl does not entirely deny the fact of castration but seeks overcompensation for her body inferiority on some plane other than the sexual (in her work, her profession). However, in so doing she represses sexual desire altogether, that is, she remains sexually unmoved. It is as if she wished to say: "I may not and cannot love my mother, and so I must give up any further attempt to love at all." Her belief in her possession of a penis has thus been shifted to the intellectual sphere; there she can be masculine and compete with men.

We may observe as a third possible outcome that a woman may form relationships with a man yet remain inwardly attached to the first object of her love, her mother. She is obliged to be frigid in coitus because she does not really desire the father or his substitute, but the mother. Now these considerations place in a somewhat different light the fantasies of prostitution so common among women. According to this view, they are an act of revenge not so much against the father as against the mother. The fact that prostitutes are so often manifest or disguised homosexuals might be explained in an analogous fashion: the prostitute turns to the man out of revenge against the mother, but she is not motivated by a wish for passive feminine surrender; rather she displays masculine activity: she captures the man on the street, castrates him by taking his money, and thus makes herself the masculine and him the feminine partner in the sexual act.

I think that in considering these disturbances in the woman's development to complete feminity we must keep two possibilities in view. Either the little girl has never been able wholly to give up her longing to possess her mother and thus has formed only a weak attachment to her father, or she has made an energetic attempt to substitute her father for her mother as love object but, after suffering a fresh disappointment at his hands, has returned to her first position.

In the paper "Some Psychical Consequences of the Anatomical Distinction between the Sexes" (1925), Freud draws attention to the fact that jealousy plays a far greater part in the mental life of women than in that of men. He thinks that the reason for this is that in women jealousy is reinforced by the deflected penis envy. Perhaps one might add that a woman's jealousy is stronger than a man's because she can never succeed in securing her first love object, while the man, when he grows up, can do so.

In another paragraph (1925, p. 254) Freud traces the fantasy of "a child is being beaten" ultimately to the masturbation of the little girl during the phallic phase. The child who is beaten or caressed is at bottom the clitoris (i.e., the penis); the being beaten is on the one hand the punishment for the forbidden genital relation and on the other a regressive substitute for it. But in this phase the pubishment for prohibited libidinal relations is precisely castration. Thus the formula "a child is being beaten" means "a child is being castrated." In the fantasies in which the child being beaten is a stranger, the idea of its being castrated is intelligible at first glance. It means: "No one else shall have what I have not got." Now we know that in the fantasies of puberty, which are often greatly metamorphosed and condensed, the child beaten by the father always represents the girl herself as well. Thus she is constantly subjecting herself to castration, for this is the necessary condition for being loved by the father; she is making a fresh effort to get clear of her old love relations and to reconcile herself to her womanhood. In spite of the many punishments, pains, and tortures which the hero has to undergo, "the fantasies always end happily" (see A. Freud, 1922), i.e., after the sacrifices have been made, the passive, feminine love is allowed to be victorious. Sometimes this immolation permits the return to masturbation, the first forbidden love tendency having been duly expiated. Often, however, masturbation remains none the less prohibited, or it becomes unconscious and is practiced in some disguised form, sometimes accompanied by a deep sense of guilt. It seems as if the repeated submission to the punishment of castration signifies not only the expiation due to the feelings of guilt but also a form of wooing the father, whereby the subject also experiences masochistic pleasure.

To sum up what I have said above: in little boys who develop normally, the positive oedipal attitude is by far the more prevalent because, by adopting it, the child, through his temporary renunciation of the mother object, can retain his genital and perhaps thereby ensure for himself the possibility of winning later in life a mother substitute; if he adopted the negative attitude, it would mean that he must renounce both from the outset. Little girls, however, normally pass through both situations in the oedipus complex: first the negative, which occurs under precisely the same conditions as in boys, but which they are finally compelled to abandon when they discover and accept the fact of their castration. Then the girl's attitude changes: she identifies herself with the lost love object and puts in its place her former rival, the father, thus passing into the positive oedipal situation. Thus in female children the castration complex deals a deathblow to the negative oedipal attitude and ushers in the positive oedipus complex.

This view confirms Freud's hypothesis that the (positive) oedipus complex in women is made possible and ushered in by the castration complex. But, in contradistinction to Freud, we are assuming that the castration complex in female children is a secondary formation and that its precursor is the negative oedipal situation; further, that it is only from the latter that the castration complex derives its greater psychic significance, and it is probably this negative attitude which enables us to explain in greater detail many peculiarities subsequently met with in the mental life of women.

I am afraid there will be objections that this hypothesis looks like spectulation and lacks an empirical basis. I must reply that this objection may be just in regard to part of what I have said, but that nevertheless the whole argument is built on a foundation of practical experience, although unfortunately this is still meager. I shall now give a short account of the material which has led me to my conclusions:

Some time ago I was treating a young girl who had been sent to me by a male collaegue. He had analyzed her for some years, but there were certain difficulties connected with the transference which resisted solution. This girl had sufferend from a rather severe hysterical neurosis. Her analysis had already been carried a good way. The normal, positive oedipus complex, her rivalry with her sister, and her envy of her younger brothers's penis had been dealt with thouroughly, and the patient had understood and accepted them. Many of her symptoms had disappeared but to her great regret she remained unfit for work. When she came to me, the unresolved, ambivalent transference to the male analyst was playing a principal part in the situation. It was difficult to determine which was the stronger, her passionate love or her no less passionate hate. I knew this patient personally before she came to me for treatment and the analysis began with a strong positive transference to me. Het attitude was rather like that of a child who goes to his mother for protection. But after a short time a profound change began to take place. The patient's behavior became first rebellious and hostile and soon, behind this attitude, there was revealed a deep-seated and wholly active tendency to woo my love. She behaved just like a young man in love, displaying, for instance, violent jealousy of a young man whom she suspected of being her rival in real life. One day she came to analysis with the idea that she would like to read all Freud's writings and become an analyst herself. The obvious interpretation which we tried first, namely, that she wanted to identify herself with me, proved inadequate. A series of dreams showed an unmistakable desire to get rid of my own analyst, to "castrate" him and take place, so as to be able to analyze (possess) me.

In this connection the patient remembered various situations in her childhood when her parents quarreled and she assumed a defensive and protective attitude toward her mother, and also times when they displayed mutual affection and she detested her father and wished to have her mother to herself. The analysis had long ago revealed both a strong positive attachment to the father and the experience which put an end to it. As a child the patient slept in a room next to her parents and was in the habit of calling them at night when she had to urinate; of course the intention was to disturb them. At first she generally demanded that her mother come, but later on, she demanded her father.

She said that when she was five years old, this happened once more and her father came to her and quite unexpectedly boxed her ears. From that moment the child resolved to hate him. The patient produced yet another recollection: when she was four years old she dreamed that she was lying in bed with her mother beside her and that she had a sense of supreme bliss. In her dream her mother said: "That is right, that is how it ought to be." The patient awoke and found that she had passed urine in bed; she was greatly disappointed and felt very unhappy.

She had various recollections of the time when she still slept in her parents' room. She said that she often used to awake in the night and sit up in bed. These recollections are a fairly certain indication that she observed her parents' coitus. The dream she had as a child may very well have been dreamed after such an observation. It clearly represented coitus with her mother, accompanied by a sense of bliss. Even in later life urethral erotism played a particularly important part in this patient. Her disappointment on awaking showed that she was already conscious of her inability to possess her mother: she had long ago discovered the male genital in her younger brother. The bed wetting can be construed as either a substitute for or a continuation of masturbation; the dream shows how intense must have been her emotional relation to her mother at that time. Hence is it clear that the patient, after her disappointement with her father (the box on the ears), tried to return to the earlier object, whom she had loved at the time of the dream, i.e., her mother. When she grew up she made a similar attempt. After an unsuccessful love affair with a younger brother of her father, she had, for a short time, a homosexual relation. This situation was repeated in her analysis when she came from the male analyst to me.

This patient stated that she had had a special form of the beating fantasy when she was from eight to ten years old. She described it as "the hospital fantasy." The gist of it was as follows. A large number of patients went to a hospital to get well, but they had to endure the most frightful pains and tortures. One of the most frequent practices was that they were flayed alive. The patient had a feeling of shuddering pleasure when she imagined their painful, bleeding wounds. Her associations brought recollections of how her younger brother sometimes pushed back the foreskin of his penis, whereupon she saw something red, which she thought of as a wound. The method of cure in her fantasy was therefore obviously a representation of castration. She identified herself on one occasion with the patients, who at the end always got well and left the hospital with great gratitude, but generally she had a different role. She was the protecting, compassionate Christ, who flew over the beds in the ward in order to bring relief and comfort to the sick people. In this fantasy, which reveals its sexual-symbolic character in the detail of *flying*, the patient is the man who alone possesses his mother (for Christ was born without a father), but who finally, to atone for the guilt and to be able to reach God the Father, offered the sacrifice of crucifixion (castration). After we broke off the analysis, which the patient gave up in a state of negative transference, a reaction to the disappointment of her love, she tried to translate this fantasy into reality by deciding to become a nurse. After a year, however, she abondoned this new profession for her earlier one, which was more masculine in character and much more suited to her temperament. Gradually her feelings of hate toward me also disappeared.

I had a second patient in whom I discovered similar processes with regard to the transference. In the first two months of treatment this patient produced very strong resistances. She acted the part of a naughty, defiant child and would utter nothing but monotonous complaints to the effect that she was forsaken and that her husband treated her badly. After we had succeeded in discovering that her resistance arose from feelings of hatred toward me, due to envy and jealousy, the full, positive, feminine oedipal attitude gradually developed in her-there entered into it both love for the father and the wish for a child. Soon, too, penis envy began to show itself. She produced a recollection from her fifth or sixth year. She said that she had once put on her elder brother's clothes and displayed herself proudly to all and sundry. Besides this she had made repeated efforts to urinate like a boy. At a later period she always felt that she was very stupid and inferior and thought that the other members of her family treated her as if this were the case. During puberty she conceived a remarkably strong aversion to every sort of sexual interest. She would listen to none of the mysterious conversations in which her girl friends engaged. She was interested only in intellectual subjects, literature, etc. When she married she was frigid. During

9

her analysis she experienced a desire to have some profession; to her, this stood for being male. But her feelings of inferiority forbade any real attempt to achieve this ambition. Up to this point the analysis had made splendid progress. The patient had one peculiarity: she remembered very little, instead she acted out a good deal. Envy and jealousy and the desire to do away with the mother were repeated in the most diverse guises in the transference. After this position had been worked through, a new resistance presented itself; we discovered behind it deep homosexual desires related to me. The patient now began to woo my love in a thoroughly masculine manner. The occasions of these declarations of love, during which in her dreams and fantasies she always pictured herself with a male genital, invariably coincided with some active behavior in real life. They alternated, however, with periods in which her behavior was wholly passive, At such times the patient was once more incapable of anything; she failed at everything, suffered from her inferiority, and was tortured by feelings of guilt. The meaning of this was that every time she conquered the mother, she was impelled to castrate herself in order to get free from her sense of guilt. Her attitude toward masturbation was also noteworthy. Before analysis she had never consciously practised this habit; during the period when she was being treated she began clitoral masturbation. At first this masturbation was accompanied by a strong sense of guilt; later, at times when her love wishes toward her father were most vehemently manifested, the feelings of guilt abated. They were succeeded by the fear that the masturbation might do her some physical harm: "weaken her genitals." At the stage when she was in love with me, the sense of guilt reappeared and she gave up masturbating because this fear became a certainty in her mind. This "weakening" of the genital organs signified castration. Thus the patient constantly oscillated between homosexual and heterosexual love. She had a tendency to regress to her first love relation – with the mother – and at this stage tried to deny the fact of castration. To make up, however, she had to refrain from masturbation and sexual gratification of any kind. She could not derive satisfaction from her husband, because she herself really wanted to be a man in order to be able to possess the mother.

Thus in both of the cases which I have discussed it was plain that behind the woman's positive oedipal attitude there lay a negative attitude, with the mother as love object, which revealed itself later in the analysis and therefore had been experienced at an earlier stage of development. Whether this evolution is typical cannot, of course, be asserted with any certainty from the observation of two cases. I should be inclined to believe that in other female patients the oedipus complex has had a similar previous history, but I have not been able to gahter enough material from their analyses to establish this beyond question. The phase of the negative oedipal attitude, lying, as it does, so far back in the patient's mental history, cannot be reached until the analysis has made very considerable progress. Perhaps it is very hard to bring this period to light with a male analyst for it is difficult for a female patient to enter rivalry with the father analyst; possibly treatment under these conditions cannot get beyond the analysis of the positive oedipal attitude. The homosexual tendency, which can hardly be missed in any analysis, may then merely give the impression of a later reaction to the disappointment experienced at the father's hands. In the cases described above, however, it was clearly a regression to an earlier phase – a circumstance which may help us to understand better the enormous psychic significance that the lack of a penis has in the erotic life of women. I do not know whether in the future it will turn out that my exposition in this paper explains the development of only these two patients of mine. I think it is not impossible that it may be found to have a more general significance. Only the gathering of further material will enable us to decide this question.

This Chapter also appeared in *The Psychoanalytic Reader*, edited by Robert Fliess (1948). His editorial comments follow (pp. 207-208):

> In his paper "On Female Sexuality" Freud has expressed agreement with the essentials of this contribution, published first in 1927, "Here," he comments, "the complete identity of the preoedipal phase in the boy and the girl is recognized, the sexual (phallic) activity in the little girl's attitude towards the mother is stated and proven by observation. The turning-away from the mother is traced back to the influence of the child's acknowledgment of castration, which forces it to abandon the sexual object, and often at the same time the practice of masturbation. The whole development is epitomized in the formula, that the little girl has to pass through a phase of the 'negative' oedipus complex before arriving at the positive one . . ."
> One inadequacy is found by Freud in Dr. Lampl's report: the author has failed to describe the hostility which accompanies the girl's turning-away from the mother.
> Dr. Lampl, upon editorial request, has put the following note at our disposal:
> "In the nineteen years since the appearance of my paper, the observations recorded in it have been fully confirmed by many colleagues as well as by myself. Their full significance, however, was brought our through Freud's magnificent formulation of the preoedipal mother-attachment. The negative oedipal attitude, described by me, is the terminal phase in the female child's early attachment to her mother; it introduces the oedipal father-attachment. The latter is indeed made possible only through the little girl's becoming inimical towards her mother, in other words, through the hostility, referred to by Freud in his criticism of my paper.
> "In the meaning reference has also been made occasionally to the significance for the development of the boy of this preoedipal attachment to the mother, in particular to the conditioning of his passive feminine attitude (homosexuality) by it. I hope to describe the influence of this early object-relation upon the ego development of both sexes in the near future."

Amsterdam, Holland [1947]   J. L. de G.

2. Problems of Femininity

(1933)

Though I started this paper from observations on female patients, some of which I had already presented in Chapter I, I gradually came to some hypothetical ideas. Many people may call them no more than mere speculations and reject them completely. Perhaps this paper is partly a youthful sin; perhaps I should have changed more than only a few of the formulations. Be that as it may, I have decided to publish it with only slight differences in wording because I myself cannot reject it altogether, though I am quite aware of its speculative side and am prepared to abandon it wherever different and better hypotheses are presented.

I

Implicit in Freud's doctrine of bisexually is the warning against too schematic an apposition of femininity in woman and masculinity in man. It is well recognized that no man exists whose masculine traits are not accompanied by more or less obviously feminine characteristics, and that likewise there are no women who fail to show masculine tendencies. Physical examination of the male reveals female residuals, while the female body shows vestigial male characteristics. Psychological investigations demonstrate bisexual elements even more strikingly; these are not only present, but are of important functional sifnificance. Analytic experience reveals many feminine characteristics that man must confront in the course of his psychic development, and many masculine traits complicating or disturbing the development of feminity. This psychic struggle takes place in the development of every man and woman, whereas the presence of physical rudiments of the opposite sex has little recognizable effect except in rare cases of hermaphoditism where the reproductive function is impaired.

Demonstration of the processes and forces which affect the differentiation of the sexes in their embryonic development admittedly belongs to the field of biology. Freud pointed out many years ago that the discovery of the organic basis of psychic forces is also one of the tasks of biology. At present, Bernfeld and Feitelberg are attempting experiments from which they hope to be able to deduce a physicobiological concept of psychic energy and of the drive theory as well. For the present, however, psychology must satisfy itself with hypotheses concerning the correspondences and differences in physical and psychic development. Nevertheless, we should guard against overlooking those psychological differences in men and women which are caused by a different physical setup (Anlage), and against underestimating the possibility of similar development of both sexes during a given period.

Although the child is provided at birth with masculine of feminine genitals, it is only after the passage of years, in puberty, that the ultimate physical developments and functioning are attained. The final psychic forms of masculinity and femininity are achieved even later, after the completion of physical maturity. We know, however, that the instinctual life has had a flourishing development much earlier and that the patterns attained then serve as models for the reactions at puberty. Infantile sexuality shows all the psychic characteristics to be found in the later love life. The child falls in love, desires the exclusive possession of the love object, defends this object with the same jealousy, hate, and revenge manifestations found among adults. The child has fantasies, sexual wishes, and aims similar to those of adults. Infantile sexuality is, however, doomed to frustration from the beginning, since the genital apparatus cannot yet perform its ultimate functions. The incestuous love object must be abandoned. Masturbation, the form of physical discharge of sexual tension, which is appropriate to the infantile period, has to be replaced by an adult love life. All these characteristics appear in children of both sexes. Even the first love object, the nurturing mother, is the same for both. This correspondence persists until that period of infantile sexuality when the oedipus complex is in the process of formation. At this time a difference manifests itself, not only in respect to the drive itself, but in respect to the object choice as well, thus preparing for later adolescent processes. If a normal development ensues at this time, a satisfactory final pattern is laid for the love life of maturity in respect to body function and object choice. The youth is then capable of securing a wife whom he can love and fertilize in a completely masculine fashion; the girl becomes capable of motherhood and yields herself in a feminine manner to the man from whom she can receive a child.

II

Before discussing this development it seems imperative to attempt a more exact description of the concepts of "masculinity" and "femininity." The words "masculine" and "feminine" are not scientifically precise concepts, but have been borrowed from colloquial speech. When Freud uses the word "masculine," it seems clear that he does not mean to designate a quality or a characteristic of behavior which belongs exclusively to men. In Freud's later works masculinity is more and more definitely made analogous to activity, while femininity and passivity appear to be identical. If one accepts this designation, one must next consider the meaning of "activity" and "passivity." The concepts of activity and passivity are borrowed from the sexual behavior of men and animals. One calls active the individual who approaches his sexual object and conquers it. The partner who submits to the approach and yields is passive. The first procedure is generally attributed to man, while woman usually plays the latter role. This general rule may have caused the apposition masculine-active, feminine-passive, as found in current speech. However, since Freud's doctrine recognizes that men and women each have active and passive drive impulses, it immediately becomes obvious that, in the analytic sense, the concepts of masculinity and femininity have no exclusive reference to either sex. Correspondingly, one may not impute to either of the concepts an appreciative or depreciative evaluation. The terms merely describe forms of expression or directions of the libido. In his article on "Female Sexuality" (1931b) Freud speaks of libidinal strivings with active and passive goals.

Active and passive behaviors occur outside the love life as well. In the above-mentioned article (1931b, p. 236) Freud says, "It can easily be observed that in every field of mental experience, not merely that of sexuality, when a child receives a passive impression if has a tendency to produce an active reaction." In the newborn, all libido is originally lodged in the person; this is the condition known as primary narcissism (Freud, 1914). If a person loves an object actively, he cathects that object with libido. This cathexis occurs at the expense of the amount of narcissistic energy, an impoverishment of this source ensues, and this condition can be endured by the person only when a sufficient narcissistic supply is available or when there is compensation for this loss through love received from objects. Frustrations induce the person to withdraw object love into the self, thus reinforcing narcissistic cathexis (secondary narcissism). A certain amount of narcissism is indispensable for enabling the person to cathect an object representation actively. An impairment of his narcissism leads him to strive for object love by surrendering to the object libido strivings with a passive aim, therefore serving the restoration of narcissistic cathexis. This demand to be loved, calculated to increase narcissism, at the same time creates a particularly strong dependence upon the object. An intense anxiety occurs at the prospect of a possible loss of love, since every disappointment constitutes a narcissistic insult.

On the other hand, someone who has achieved real object love suffers, if disappointed or disillusioned, an actual object loss. If development has been normal, the person knows how to help himself by withdrawing his libido into his self (as already mentioned above) preparatory to making a new love attempt with another object. This mechanism, which permits him to recover his narsiss-ism intact, makes him less dependent upon his former love object than in the case of the person whose love has been passive (Freud, 1931a). In summary, an adequate amount of narcissism enables the person to accomplish object love, whereas an insufficient supply of self-love or narcissistic injury incapacitates the person for cathecting an object. If narcissism is severely depleted, the person attempts to restore it by permitting himself to be loved. Activity, then, in contrast to passivity, denotes object cathexis. A person loves his object with his "masculinity," and permits himself to be loved with his "femininity."

III

We now turn to two questions:
1 How do we meet with the active and passive strivings alongside each other in a particular person?

2 How can we explain the differences and the similarities in the love lives of the two sexes?

As usual, we shall look into pathology to learn more about these matters.

An especially impressive instance of the apposition of actively and passively directed libido strivings came to my attention during the analysis of a strongly impulsive young man. At first sight it was completely impossible to understand how this exceptionally virile, masculine-looking young man had been severely paralyzed in his love life and his work, and how he had attained such marked feminine behavior. During a lengthy analysis it was discovered that as a small boy, feeling himself unloved by his parents, he had reacted to each disappointment in love with intense rage and spitefulness. The governess, whom he soon attempted to love in place of his mother, punished him for these attacks with physical blows, which he regarded as monstrously degrading. This new insult, this new lack of love, increased his need to be loved and caused him to become a "good little boy" for the sake of inducing love when he assumed his obedient attitude, he did not immediatly abandon his aggressive behavior; he did so only later, in response to violent reactions to castration threats from his governess and father regarding his masturbatory activities. These threats were vivified during sexual play instigated by an older brother, who recounted the most creepy tales of castration until finally the patient was convinced that he would lose his penis in any case and consequently might as well forfeit it. A surrender of the active role in his love life accompanied his renunciation of his penis. This sacrifice created an acute need to be loved, which the boy sought by becoming completely good and obedient. At the same time his aggression was turned inward and procured for him masochistic pleasure, shown in many diversified fantasies, and he became inhibited, shy, and incapacitated in his studies.

Summarizing, we might say, (1) disappointment in love and narcisstic insults diminished the patient's ability to play the active role in his love life and established a preference for passively directed libido strivings; (2) actual paralysis of activity occurred only when the boy, under the pressure of extremely vivid castration threats, saw the necessity for renouncing his penis; (3) the increase in passivity was accompanied by a turning inward of his aggressiveness, which became fixated in later life (masochism).

From this extreme case we turn now to the state of affairs in normal development. Every child suffers frustration in love and narcisstic insults, and every child becomes aware of sex differences. Anxiety concerning the genital is, therefore, never completely lacking. It is inevitable too, that a certain portion of the aggressive tendency should be turned inward. Nevertheless, the vigorous little boy who undergoes what is called normal development manages to surmount these difficulties. He becomes a man, capable of playing the active role in love life, having such a large store of libido that he is in a position to cathect his actual love object. From this store of narcisstic libido in the self surge the forces peculiar to man, making it possible for him to fulfill his potentialities for marriage and reproduction. His aggressive tendencies find an outlet partly in the "sadism" necessary for approaching the love object and partly in the sublimated form necessary to the rest of his lifework, his profession, social interests and relationships. The passive strivings which the small boy does not lack are subordinated to the active tendency. Only in pathological cases in this subordination not achieved; in such cases the narcisstic insults produce an excessive effect, notably where there is immoderate castration anxiety.

The situation is different in the case of the woman. Achievement of adequate femininity requires a preference for passivity. The aggressive tendency finds an outlet in that form of aggression which is directed inward (masochism). Some of the most important processes in the sexual life of women, defloration and giving birth, are quite normally accompanied by the pleasure of pain (H. Deutsch, 1930). The passive, "feminine" woman exhibits few aggressive tendencies toward love partners or in other spheres of life. Karen Horney assumes that the aggressive tendency is a priori stronger in the man, that the libido in the case of the woman gives preference to passive goals from the beginning, and that this is a simple biological law which one can never explain psychologically. It is obvious that differences in physical make-up and in biological functions must necessarily be accompanied by different psychic expressions. However, one may be too easily satisfied by such an assumption and fail to pursue psychological investigation as far as possible. The psychoanalytic libido (drive) theory, though based upon biological factors, is aware of the fact that in psychological manifestations there is only *one* "libido" whose direction and aim can be changed, but which is essentially the same in men and in women. Therefore we have to pursue its vicissitudes in males and in females with psychological means. Moreover, no theory of phylogenetic inheritance relieves us of the necessity of investigating the time and occasion in the life of the person when the functioning of given tendencies becomes observable.

Besides these theoretical considerations, there is a whole series of empirical observations which require study. Analysis of adults as well as observations on little girls demonstrate that the female is not a passive yielding being who permits herself to be loved from the beginning, but that she reveals active as well as passive tendencies often not unlike those of the boy, even quantitatively. The little girl, like the boy, courts with actively directed love, as long as the mother is still the love object. It is necessary, then, to explain how it happens that the little girl, in the course of normal development, renounces her activity. Of course, the little girl, like the boy, knows of passive modes of satisfaction, and with disappointments she longs to be loved, as do boys. The length of the period in which the little girl displays activity varies in each individual. In one little girl an actively directed relation to the mother was predominant until her fifth year. Not until the sixth year did this situation change and the oedipal situation become perceptible. The father relation up to that time had been exactly the same as that to any other member of the family circle. It was often friendly, often distant, according to the little one's disposition. The passionate love attachment, with all the accompanying feelings of demand for exclusiveness, jealousy, envy, hate when disappointed, were retained for the mother, and secondarily for a nurse who often took the mother's place. One may assume with confidence that the turning to the father, and the accompanying preference for the passively directed libidinal drives, occurs in many little girls at an earlier age, about five, four, or perhaps even three. The duration of the preoedipal mother attachment is of the greatest significance for the later events in the life of the child. In all cases, however, the mother is the first object which the child cathects and this must leave traces in later life. What is the cause of this turning and of the preference for passively directed drives? We repeat that for the achievement of object cathexis (which occurs by means of active tendencies) the person requires a certain amount of free libido at his disposal, a superabundance of narcissism; and the person who is subjected to narcissistic wounds attempts to salve them by adopting passive behavior in the hope of inducing love. The little child suffers from disappointments in love and narcissistic blows even more than the adult; and there is a further difference — the little child is doomed not to succeed with his incestuous love objects. The child — both male and female — also suffers continuously from the stigma of being small, of being regarded by adults as not completely, as inadeaquate, even as an object of ridicule. Karen Horney describes the anxiety of the boy that his member may be too small or that the mother will laugh at him or ridicule him. The little girl fears that her vagina may be too small for her father's organ and has exactly the same feeling of insufficiency, of inferiority to her mother, and of anxiety lest she be ridiculed and set aside as wanting. Moreover, this experience of not being sufficient for father has an earlier pattern in not having been adequate for mother, the first love object, by whom the child was also frustrated. In my paper, "The Evolution of the Oedipus Complex in Women" (Chapter 1) I expressed the belief that the inevitability of this frustration is recognized as a corollary of the discovery of the anatomical sex differences. Freud confirms this opinion in his paper on "Female Sexuality" (1931b) and shows that the little girl always holds her mother responsible for her lack of a penis and that this is the most important motive of resentment toward her.

At this point the development of the girl begins to diverge from that of the boy in normal cases, and it is here that the psychological differences between the sexes have a definite beginning. As long as the children of both sexes have the same love object — the mother — the possibility of satisfying passive as well as active libidinal strivings exists to the same extent (in the oral, anal, and phallic phases), and both sexes are subject to the same disappointments in love and the same narcisstic blows. A certain fundamental identity in the development of boy and girl is present even if there should be a difference in the quantitative relationship between activity and passivity in the two cases. Not until the fact of anatomical differences in sex begins to play a role in the psyche does this fundamental difference in development begin to occur. If the little girl discovers that the boy has something which she lacks, that the little boy can accomplish deeds of which she is not capable (exhibitionism, visible masturbation, urina-tion, etc.), if the little girl comes to the conclusion that such an organ is really indispensable to the possession of the mother, she experiences, in addition to the narcissistic insults common to children of both sexes, still another blow, namely, a feeling of inferiority concerning her genitals. The absence of a penis cannot be regarded as a matter of secondary and trifling significance for the little girl, as Karen Horney does. Careful and complete analysis of women provide daily evidence of the significance of the phenomenon. Any simple observation of little girls leaves no ambiguity concerning the girl's wish for a penis, her feeling of being harmed not only by grownups but also by her brother or playmates, and her difficulty in reconciling herself to this status. A little girl, well informed about all sexual processes and already aware of the gratification she could derive from the clitoris or the vaginal entrance, who, moreover, knew that she was capable of motherhood which would be denied to the boy, nevertheless insisted with astonishing stubbornness, "But I want a little tassel right now." For the girl the possibility of bearing a child in the dim future furnishes cold comfort — she wishes to have what the boy has, and the discovery that the boy's organ is so much bigger, so much more tangible and more obviously capable of performance than her own, regularly arouses a feeling of envy and deprivation.

To be sure, in the analysis of feminine men one frequently finds the wish to bear a child. Karen Horney regards birth envy among men as analogous to the penis envy of the woman. Birth envy is part of an attempt to rival the mother in the passive object relation to the father. In contrast to the little girl, however, who suffers from the deprivation of something possessed at that very moment by her brother, the boy's envy of the sister is an envy of something obtainable by her only in the remote future and therefore an envy of much less intensity. The question, much discussed recently, whether the little girl masturbates on the clitoris, or the vulva, or the entrance of the vagina, has little to do with the fact of penis envy, however important it may be theoretically. Without a doubt the little girl is capable of masturbatory satisfaction; wheters more or less than the boy, one cannot decide. But no matter from what source the girl succeeds in obtaining satisfaction, the wish for a penis is actively present and has far-reaching consequences for further development. Freud (1925) demonstrated that the castration complex in the little girl appears before the oedipus complex and that the discovery that she lacks a penis leads her to adopt a passive love orientation to the father. In my above-mentioned work (Chapter 1), I was able to demonstrate an actively directed object love for the mother present in the girl before the appearance of the castration complex, and this was confirmed by Freud. It is possible now to understand these processes in more detail. The severe narcissistic insults which the little girl feels because of her genital inferiority, and the coincidental appearance of resentment toward her mother, who is made responsible for this inferiority, are the cause of the girl's surrender of active love and acceptance of the passive role. She must permit herself to be loved in order to augment her injured self-love. She gradually begins to turn her passively directed love wishes from her mother to her father. This complete change of object is accomplished with the aid of increased enmity toward the mother; hatred and rage complete the process of turning away from the first love object. Then, stimulationeously with the paralyzing of the little girl's activity, aggression is inhibited as well and that part of her aggression which may not be turned outward is directed inward and expresses itself in a variety of masochistic fantasies and modes of behavior which are normal for women. Should, however, the little boy give such preference to passively directed libido, this process would take place only as the result of excessive castration anxiety and his development would not continue normally.

IV

A few theoretical questions present themselves: (1) Why does the individual require such a high degree of narcissistic cathexis? (2) How is one to explain the fact that the individual's attempt to restore his injured narcissism is accompanied by turning aggression toward his own person? (3) What is the relationship of actively and passively directed libidinal strivings to the active and passive reactions outside the sphere of sexuality? (4) What does psychoanalytic theory contribute toward the explanation of the biological fact that male sexual life is accomplished with the help of actively directed libidinal strivings while the woman ulitizes libidinal strivings with a passive aim?

According to Freud's first views, in the very beginning of psychic existence there is an interaction of two different types of drive impulse-self-preservation and libidinal object love. It was discovered, however, that self-preservation is accomplished with the aid of a certain amount of libidinal cathexis, and the dualism between self-preservation and libidinal object love was redefined as one of libidinal drives (ego and object) and other ego drives, which at the time were not defined more specificallly. Further observations then revealed the existence of destructive drive impulses, striving in a direction opposed to the libido, which were evident in sadism. Biological considerations led Freud to the concepts of life and death impulses (drives) which reveal themselves in the biophyciological processes of the organism from the beginning of life and later also manifest themselves in psychic reactions, becoming perceptible as outwardly directed object libido and agression (1920a, 1923b).

The theory of instinctual drives attempts to indicate the relationship between psychological and biological events. Such an attempt seems necessary since the sources of the impulses functioning in the psyche are somatic. What are the biological functions of the life and death instincts? The general aim of an instinctual drive is, according to Freud, the reinstatement of an earlier condition. The death instinct tends to reduce the organic to the inorganic. When it is successful, the unity of the living being is assailed, there is disintegration, and death. The life instinct (drive) (Eros) works in the opposite direction – its function is to increase the stability of life by aggregating unities (cells). In this manner, the life instinct (drive) also strives for a restitution of a previous condition, inasmuch as the origin of life is conceived as a dispersion of lifeless substances into numerous particles. The conception, however, remains for the present an unprovable speculation. On the other hand, the aggregating tendency of the life instinct in its effort to preserve individual life, and thus the life of the species, is unmistakable. The acme of its potency is reached during the fusion of the germinal cells, which are laden with incomparable vital energy, when a new unity is formed and the problem of race preservation is solved. The death instinct present in the individual cells of the organism must be neutralized by the life instinct in order that the individual life may be maintained. Freud conceives of these processes as being analogous to the physiological processes of anabolism and catabolism.

As long as the individual is at one with his environment, as in the case of the foetus in utero, the contest between life and death instinctual drives occurs exclusively within the organism. Birth creates a change in the situation. As soon as the child is delivered, new problems must be met. It is now surrounded by a number of dangers, of which the most threatening is the cessation of the previously continuous source of nourishment. It is remarkable that the process of birth, which initiates the independent life of the person, is in the biological sense a victory of the death instinct: birth causes the disruption of the mother-child unity and threatens the child daily with vital dangers. It is patent that the life instinct is responsible for overcoming these dangers. The combining tendency of Eros causes the child to seek union with the mother. At first, physical union with the mother's breast is the only objective. The life instinct cathects this indispensable object with its energy and there arises a libidinal object relationship, at first, however, in the service of self-preservation. But it is necessary for the child that the mother, too, form an object relationship with the child, providing it with care as well as with nourishment. In the case of such animals as are born dependent upon care, the mother instinct is found to ensure food until such time as the offspring can provide for itself. In the case of man, mother love has become a form of libido development which persists throughout life.

The cathexis of the mother object with libido occasions changes in the relationship between the life and death instincts. By diverting portions of the death instinct (tendencies to destruction, aggression, and overpowering of objects) to the outside world (Freud, 1923b), the internal equilibrium of instincts may be restored. In addition, the life instinct forces the death instinct into service during the conquest of the needed object, at which time an extremely intense union with the object is produced. Moreover, the mechanism of turning drive components outward for the purpose of self-preservation also occurs in the service of Eros. In this process portions of the two kinds of drives merge and interrelate.

The newborn child has other tasks to perform besides that of defense against the danger of death. On entrance into the world he becomes subject to the greatest variety of stimuli, arising in part internally from his own organism, since, on separation from the mother, tensions of needs, hunger, etc., arise, and in part from stimuli and impressions which penetrate through the sense organs from the outside world. The death instinct, which seeks reduction of tension, must master these stimuli if possible (Fechner's principle of constancy).

The organism deals with these stimuli in a way which is actually in opposition to the unifying tendency of Eros and in harmony with the separating tendency of the death instinct. This process may be observed most clearly in the mastery of stimuli from the outside world when this is accomplished by direct motor flight. This method, however, while often useful in later life, is of value to the helpless infant. He must manage by means of another mechanism. He is separated from the stimuli of the outside world by a layer of the nervous apparatus organized in such a way that the stimuli are prevented from penetrating into the rest of it. This structured layer is rendered permeable to stimuli, however, only when cathected with energy which has been mobile (Freud, 1920a).

How is the mastery of inner tension accomplished? Apparently the organism attempts to meet this situation in a manner similar to that used against external stimuli. Motor flight and stimuli defense are, however, of no avail. A psychic mechanism similar to flight is nevertheless used, since the person attempts to ward off the disturbing inner stimuli by means of repression (or other psychic defense mechanisms). This psychic process also occurs by means of cathexis, consequently by means of binding mobile energy. Cathexis is necessary to prevent penetration of internal stimuli (the claims of the drives) into consciousness. Freud, in *The Ego and the Id* (1923b), regards the energy utilized in cathexis as desexualized Eros, or energy originating from the life instinct. This explanation sounds plausible, at least in regard to the energy used in cathecting the protective barrier against outer stimuli, since the energy used in this manner is unifying and binding, several cells being combined into a single structure entrusted with a definite fuction. If we accept this hypothesis, we discern in the process of mastering stimuli an instance of the death instinct making use of a part of its antagonist, Eros, for its own purposes. Incidentally, this process is doubtless chronologically the earlier one, since the task mastering stimuli occurs at the moment of entrance into the outside world, while the necessity of establishing a libidinal object relation for the purpose of satisfying hunger and other needs arises later. It seems that the two instinctual drives, usually in conflict with one another, may unite in the battle against their common enemy, the outside world. In the beginning the infant is threatened only with physical dangers from without. It seeks to protect itself on the one hand by separating itself from these stimuli by means of the protective nerve layer and on the other hand by binding itself libidinally to the object which is necessary for its preservation. However, in the course of the first years of life physical dependence on the mother becomes transformed into psychic dependence. The long-continued bodily helplessness appears to have necessitated a libidinal object cathexis. The intensity of psychic fixation to the object, as well as its frequent persistence beyond the time when the individual is physically independent, is unmistakable. This dependence upon object complicates human relationships enormously and may create a great variety of ties and fusions of the instinctual drives.

Psychic development proceeds not only by the addition of new psychic content to object relationships, but also by a modification of the stability principle. Although the tendency to reduce tensions remains through the whole life, the person soon discovers certain tensions which, in themselves, may give him the gratification of organ pleasure. An explanation of this phenomenon presents us with great difficulty, since we have assumed to date that pleasure ensues from the reduction of tension and not as a result of tension. The nature of instinctual tensions is an extremely elusive problem, and quantitative instances seem to play a role in the production of pleasure and pain, as well as rhythm and the intensity of excitement within a given time unit. Perhaps the relationship between the two types of instinctual drives is also of decisive significance.

The child's first pleasurable sensations arise through the excitation of erotogenic zones during the process of taking nourishment and of being cared for by the mother. This naturally increases the intensity of the mother tie. The constancy principle becomes modified by the pleasure-pain principle. At this time defense is directed only against pain-bringing tensions. Pleasure-bringing stimuli are not only tolerated but sought. The pleasure-pain principle, then, sometimes supersedes the constancy principle in the service of the sexual (life) instincts, necessitating a new and even more complicated interrelation of the two types of instinctual drives. Gradually pleasure and pain sensations extend to pure psychic object relationships. The mere presence of the object or slight contacts, which are not necesarily accompanied by stimulation of the erogenous zones, may produce pleasure. The absence of the mother, withdrawel of love, or any other type of disappointment occasion pain. Thus the object is not only a source of pleasure but also a possible source of pain and disappointment, a part of the inimical outside world against which the child must protect himself. He attempts to master these unpleasant psychic experiences in a manner similar to the one employed in dealing with disturbing body stimuli — by flight from or rejection of the object, or by turning aggression outward in an attempt to destroy the object. Libido withdrawn from the object is reinvested in the self in an attempt to render it more resistant to further pain and so creates secondary narcissism.

Freud in *The Ego and the Id* (1923b) regards these different processes as the dynamic forces which produce the various organizations in the psyche. The original inner struggle between Eros and the death instinct takes place in the id. The need to distinguish itself from the outside world (Freud, 1920a) causes the id to surround itself with a layer which will take over the business of intercourse with the outside world. This differentiation within the personality makes it possible to describe the above processes topographically. The ego is at first a body ego, concerning itself with perceptions and the mastery of external stimuli. As soon as the ego has achieved a certain independence from the id, it also receives stimuli from within, from the id. The ego is the agent for the object relationships of the id; however, if libido is withdrawn from objects, it is utilized to cathect the ego.[1] Thus secondary narcissism is a cathexis of the ego. Withdrawal of libido from the object frees the originally bound aggression. This freed aggression, tending to destroy the object, gradually comes to serve the feelings of hate and revenge. Naturally the defense mechanisms of flight from and destruction of the object appear only incompletely in the case of the small child, who is so extremely dependent upon the object and must make every effort to retain it. He becomes, therefore, inevitably involved in an ambivalence conflict, with both libidinal and aggressive tendencies directed toward one and the same object. We have seen that certain libidinal strivings which have been withdrawn from the object and which cannot be directed outward, turn themselves secondarily back again to the individual's own person. This is also true of the aggression freed in the process of withdrawal. It appears, then, that the

---

[1] We now would say "the self."

union which the two kinds of instinctual drives form in the battle against the outside world can be dissolved. A new battle between the life and deathinstincts within the selfensues as a result of redirecting libido and aggression toward the self, and during this process dissociation or defusion of the drives occurs. The contest between secondary narcissism and self-destruction parallels the original battle between the life and death instincts in the id. Since the processes by which both kinds of drive are directed toward objects and withdrawn again into the ego are repeated innumerable times with varying intensity and always with different degrees of fusion and defusion, it is obvious that these events gradually become extremely complicated. Changes in the cathexis of objects affect the general internal drive economy and changes in internal equilibrium have a corresponding effect upon object relationships. Indeed, since there is such an interlacing of relationships, and since it is impossible to determine the intensity of excitation and the relationship of fusion and defusion, there is at present little prospect of observing the exact manner in which this equilibrium is maintained in any individual case.

It becomes evident, however, from the previous discussion, that the ego requires a definite level of libido cathexis, a certain quantity of narcissism, for the purpose of neutralizing self-destructive tendencies. The relationships in the ego are comparable to the biological processes in the id, where sufficient energy of the life instinct must be present in order to neutralize the death instinct present in the cells. The danger of self-mutilation or self-destruction is incurred if there is an insufficient amount of narcissistic ego cathexis, or an unusual amount of destructive excitation directed toward the ego. In pathological cases self-damage may very often occur under the influence of the superego. The superego is a further differentiation of the psyche, a substructure of the ego, which arises from the necessity to renounce object relations at the time when the oedipus complex is pressing for a solution. The superego represents an introjection of the parental imagos into the ego which perhaps occurs because the alternative of complete emancipation from the object is still impossible for the dependent child. To repeat, the return of libido to the ego on surrender of an object is accomplished by desexualization of the libido, dissociation of the two kinds of drives, and direction of aggression inward. If the ego does not succeed in restoring the instinctual equilibrium, the superego may avail itself of the inwardly directed aggression to threaten the ego, in which case a masochistic relationship to the superego results. Further detail of superego formation will be considered later.

The second question will now be examined: Why is the attempt to restore wounded narcissism accompanied by the turning of aggression against the self? Raising the level of the narcissistic cathexis is accomplished by withdrawal of object libido into the ego. The desexualization of this libido causes dissociation (defusion) of the two kinds of drive whereby destructive tendencies are freed which cannot be directed outward and must therefore be turned inward. The dependence of the child on the object prevents complete emancipation, and therefore the object is maintained by means of a preference for a passive love orientation, which strengthens the narcissism and enhances mastery of the increased tendency to self-destruction. The child must abandon active object relationships more and more, since these would further impoverish the narcissistic cathexis, a state of affairs which cannot be tolerated because a rich supply of narcissism is required for neutralizing the self-destructive tendencies present.

This leads us to the problem of libido with active and passive aims. As we have seen, a person be driven to withdraw object cathexes that had previously been actively directed if his internal equilibrium is threatened by disappointment in love or by other severe narcissistic injuries, This withdrawal may also occur if the destructive excitations are prevented from being directed outward by an especially rigid upbringing, so that a turning inward occurs to such an extreme degree that drive equilibrium is threatened. Dependence upon the object and the necessity for increasing narsissism cause an increase in the passively directed libido strivings. When, as often occurs, withdrawal of love and suppression of aggression occur together, the conversion of activity to passivity is increased. In the case of the patient mentioned above, this is obviously what happened. But how can we understand the fact that in females passivity in love life is the normal outcome of development?

The problems of active and passive goals are ultimately biological ones. The procedure by which the ego seeks to keep narcissism on a definite level for the purpose of neutralizing self-destructive tendencies is analogous to the biological events in the cells where the life instinct seeks to bind the death instinct. It may be possible to find parallel processes in the establishment of passive goals by the libido. We have already noted that passivity in sexual life is one aspect of a general passivity of behavior toward the outside the outside world. This consideration leads us to the third question.

It was suggested at the beginning of this paper that the concepts of "activity" and "passivity" were derived from the different types of behavior of man and woman in love life. In general, the former wishes to seize his love object and conquer it, while the latter surrenders herself to the object. The reaction to the outside world, outside the sphere of sexuality, is a similar one. The person may simply permit stimuli and impressions from the outside world to be borne in upon him, in which case he behaves passively, or he may react actively to the outside world in attempting to seize and master it. It is obvious that in passive behavior inner reactions are always present. The terms "active" and "passive" merely describe the observed behavior toward the outside world and toward the love object. The phenomena of activity and passivity do not appear until the person comes to see himself in relation to an outside world. As long as the child is still one with his environment, such a distinction is impossible. At first, then, the two types of drives follow exclusively their inner biological tasks. The striving and the goal of the drives coincide. Only after birth, when the person can be differentiatied from the outside world, is it meaningful to make a distinction between striving and goal. The striving of the instinct always remains the same. The death instinct strives to shatter unity and to decrease tension, while the libido is binding and unifying. In so far as the drive is a force, there is always an element of activity (Freud, 1915). The drives seed differently directed goals only after the outside world enters as a factor compelling the person to send out portions of drive energies as well as to produce inner reactive instinctual processes.

Observing the reactions of the newborn child, we find that his first relationships to the outside world, from which he receives impressions and stimuli, are unquestionably of a passive nature. He reacts to these impressions and stimuli in accordance with the constancy principle; he attempts a defense against them. There are two methods of defense. The first is actual physical flight or, where this is impossible, an inner process, the formation of a protective nervous layer, comes into existence. This inner process is accomplished at the behest of the death instinct with the help of energy from the life instinct. The reaction to the outside world remains a purely passive one. The second procedure for mastering stimuli is the seizing of the outer world to serve the person's own purposes. This process occurs in the service of Eros which is striving for union with the outside world, aided by aggressive energy. The inner processes are accompanied by sending out portions of drive energies, resulting in active behavior toward the outside world. Every person makes use of both mechanisms and a passively received impression often calls forth active behavior. Nevertheless, the relationship between active and passive reactions varies greatly in each person. Even in infancy the passive flight mechanism takes precedence in one case, while the active, seizing mechanism predominates in another case. The explanation of this fact, in which disposition, the original peculiarities of the drives, plays a role, is not easy. It seems evident, however, that the preference for active behaviour is dependent upon the capacity to turn instinctual energy outward, and the problem, in the last analysis, consists of the dynamic relations between Eros and aggression.

The stimuli which the newborn child does not need to dispose of, since they are pleasurable, are those which rise through the excitation of erotogenic zones. A modification of the constancy principle by the pleasure principle takes place under the influence of these experiences. Inasmuch as the pleasure principle ultimately requires diminution of tension, it may be said to serve the death instinct. However, it also accommodates itself to the demands of Eros, since it not only tolerates libidinal tensions but in some circumstances even aspires to them. Extraordinarily little is known about the nature of feelings and emotions, but perhaps one may risk the suspicion that pleasure and pain feelings correspond to quantitative tension units or intensities of Eros energy. The first sexual feelings of pleasure which are conveyed to the child from the outside world (the mother) are received by the child pureley passively, as are all stimuli at first. The child's reactions, are, however, different from those toward unpleasant stimuli. The mechanism of stimuli protection is utilized only in relation to the latter, whereas the pleasant excitations are taken up and the child seeks to bring about their repetition, in cathecting the object with libido. This mother tie now no longer serves exclusively for the satisfaction of tension needs, such as hunger. It also provides the child with new sexual tensions perceived by the child's ego, which differentiates and conveys them to the id. The mother has thus become a valuable love object. The mode of satifaction continues to be passive, since sexual tensions are received quite accidentally in relation to the acts of taking nourishment and being cared for. Even here, however, passive experience releases an active reaction, the object is cathected with libido, Eros conquers it with the help of aggressive tendencies. The first signs of activity then introduce the consideration of goal. These processes appear very clearly in the first object relation of the infant to the mother's breast. The pleasure feelings originating in the act of nursing lead to active sucking and biting. Both types of drive are to be seen functioning in this oral object relation; taking the object to one's self represents intense union and at the same time annihilation of the object.

For the sake of completeness we must state that pleasurable organ excitations may also be aroused from parts of the person's own body. At first these are perceived as if they emanated from objects in the outside world. The development of body feelings permits the child to make the distinction between autoerotic satisfactions and those dependent upon the mother; the child becomes aware that the bodily sensations are always present, while the mother often disappears.

In summary: The first sexual satisfaction provided by the mother are of a passive nature, but they release an active reaction which leads to an object cathexis. The first object relation has an active goal. The passive experience are repeated, however, and since they are pleasurable are desired again. The once-established object relation is utilized for passively experienced satisfactions, and thus a passive goal is set up. The libido strives again toward the object, but demands from it passive modes of satisfaction (to be loved, as well as to be looked at, to be touched, to be beaten, and the like). In the service of the death instinct the stability principle seeks flight from external stimuli, while Eros, which aspires to a union with the surroundings for self-preservation and later for preservation of the species, encourages active reactions to these passive experiences. The sex instincs, originating in Eros, follow this example, preferring actively directed erotic object cathexis, but passive experiences are again aspired to, in so far as they are pleasurable, that is, in so far as they are of a sexual nature or are connected with direct or sublimated sexual strivings. From now on, libido strivings with active goals, as well as those with passive goals, often occur together.

What determines the relationship of these strivings to each other? Both seek sexual satisfaction and therefore oppose the tendency of the death instinct. The libido strivings with an active goal, however, confer libido upon objects, while aggressive energy is turned outward in an effort to master the objects. When a passive goal is instituted, libidinal tension is taken back into the ego, and now Eros and aggression oppose each other within the person. The preference for active object cathexes or for passive goals is a matter dependent upon the relative strenght of Eros vis-à-vis aggression, above all upon the capacity of Eros to expel destructive excitations from within. We have already seen that situations in the outside world may influence the relation between activity and passivity. Of course, there is one relation between the two which is present ipso facto, namely, the quantitative dynamic relation existing between libido and aggression. This is, to be sure, modifiable by external circumstances, but only within limits which vary for each person.

We now turn to the fourth question, that of the preference of the biological sex functions for activity in males and passivity in females. The greatest increase of sexual excitation is present in the act of reproduction, in which the unifying tendency of Eros culminates. In the case of the male, following this increase in tension, there is a release of it in the sex act, when the germinal cells laden with enormous vital energy are emitted. These are introduced into the woman, in whom there is a heightening of vital energy after the fusion of a spermatozoon with an ovum. The sex function of the man, subserving Eros and the preservation of the race, consists of bestowing some vital energy on an object. For the conquering of the object, aggression is utilized by Eros for its own purposes, and when the task is completed, Eros again abandons the temporarily associated instinct. (In the case of certain lower animals the victory of the death instinct is complete, since the male dies after sexual union [Freud, 1923b]). The function assigned to the woman by Eros consist of the reception of vital energy which has been introduced for the purpose of producing a new living being, in the service of race preservation. The psychic processes in love life partly reflect the biological ones, since the man loves actively and the woman lets herself be loved. The battle between Eros and the death instinct in relation to the sexual function, serving race preservation, is apportioned to two beings. In men it is turned to the outside world and manifests itself in relation to the partner. In woman it is internal and proceeds in the newly created life. The process of giving birth implies a temporary loss of vital energy, which is regained by loving the newborn.

It is clear that biological processes determine the relationship between Eros and aggression in the two sexes, perhaps by obscure physical and chemical processes within the sex organs. These processes reach their peak during sexual maturity and create the final shapes of masculinity and feminity. However, they have been in preparation from the beginning of life. Analytic observations reveal clearly the significance of bisexuality for the development of psychic life and the developmental complications during the preparatory phases.

V

Subordination of active to passive libidinal strivings, however, is seldom complete in women, and it behooves us to consider the fate of these various active strivings. Their metamorphosis is so varied, complicated, and intricately structured that I must confine myself at present to only a few considerations.

The purely feminine orientation of the woman to the man leaves no place for activity. Feminine love is passive, a narcisssitic proces; the purely feminine woman does not love, she lets herself be loved. When a woman does accomplish active object love, however, as in her relation to her child, she does so with actively directed libidinal components (Freud, 1914). It is well known that many women also retain some of this activity in their relations to men and love them with real object love, that is, with "masculinity."[2] Just as the little girl satisfies her activity in her play with dolls, so the woman utilizes part of her "masculinity" in nourishing and caring for her child and later in educating it. It is quite understandable that the narcissistic satisfaction which motherhood offers woman may so increase her self-love that she has sufficient active strivings for object cathexis. After all, the child satisfies the early infantile desire for a penis which was transformed into a wish for a child during the oedipal stage. This process is especially perceptible in the study of the psychic life of young girls and childless women who have chosen professions having to do with children (teachers, pedagogues, etc.). The children whom they teach are substitutes for their own children and at the same time satisfy their "masculinity" wishes. Their work requires activity. Feminine, narcissistic women are usually poor mothers. Children are a burden to them. On the other hand, there are very maternal women who are so devoted to their children that they are sometimes disturbed in their feminine sensations, have a poor relationship to their husbands, and suffer from frigidity or other disturbances. Normal development would consist of the attainment of a balance between passivity and activity in which a woman who is feminine in her sexual life develops a strong maternal feeling for the children. The role of the man in the act of reproduction is completed with conception. The womans' role, however, does not cease with the passively experienced impregnation; the woman must nourish the child, first inside her body, later outside, and then guard it, care for it, and train it. For this purpose she must establish an object relationship by means of active libido.

However, this use of active strivings is possible only in adult life. What does the little girl do, since she can find no place for activity in the oedipal orientation to her father? She renounces her active wishes with great difficulty, tries to deny the absence of a penis, and attempts to insists upon her masculinity. After a disappointment from the father she often returns to her old mother tie, using the original activity in homosexual strivings. Often some of her dependence upon her mother remains beside the father relation, in which case a continuous oscillation between the two may be observed. Further analytic research will throw light upon these extremely complicated relationships.

VI

It is nesessary to turn our attention to a process inaugurated at the time of the latency period when the child has given up the oedipal orientation to the parents, having repressed libidinal and aggressive strivings and replaced them by aim-inhibited, tender feelings. The original parent relationship disappears, although not completely, being moved away and incorporated in the psyche by a process known as introjection. The part of the ego thus modified becomes the superego. The introjection or the incorporation of an object is an oral process; it is therefore the first form of object relationship. The unpleasure of hunger and

---

[2] That is, impulses with active aims.

other dangers causes the infant to desire possession of the satisfaction-producing object, the mother. The aggression against the object called forth by Eros is accompanied by libidinal object cathexis in order to protect the object representation from destruction, while the passively experienced libidinal satisfactions which the infant is proffered simultaneously with feeding and bodily care serve to strengthen his narcissism and bind the aggression against his own person. The incorporation of the object representation during the formation of the superego represents a psychic possession of the object and must be accomplished by the same energies employed in the oral phase to conquer the mother's breast, namely aggresssion. Libido strivings which are actively directed and which accompany aggression secure the intrapsychic existence of the object representation. Passive libido components are not involved in the process of introjection.

Let us now see how this process takes place in the two sexes. The little boy has, let us assume, developed in a masculine manner, and who has therefore subordinated his passivity to his masculinity, forms a simple oedipus complex; he loves the mother and whishes to remove the father as a rival. He fears punishment (castration) by this powerful rival, so that narcissistic interest in retaining his organ forces him to renounce his oedipal desires. Desexualization of his sexual wishes and defusion of the drives takes place. The aggression which, as mentioned above, has gradually stepped into the service of the hostile feelings, is utilized to introject the hated paternal object representation, while the active libido strivings toward the father, since he is also loved and admired, assure the further existence of the father imago in the superego. The actual father relationship becomes characterized by tolerated tenderness. The love of the mother also becomes desexualized. However, since the mother is no rival, but only a love object (the hatred arising out of the preoedipal phase can be transferred in the oedipal situation to hatred of the father), there is no occasion to destroy, to intoject her image. She remains the tenderly loved object in the outside wirld while only the father image is concerned with the formation of the superego. The gross sexual desires undergo repression. The more completely the introjective process succeeds, the stronger, more energic, and active will the paternal superego be. Therefore such an individual would presumably be capable, in his mature years, of rendering important social and cultural contributions.

A complication occurs, however, if strong femininity has developed in the boy. A double oedipus complex ensues. In addition to loving the mother, in which case he regards the father as a rival, he permits himself to be loved passively by the father, in which case the mother becomes a competitor. Passive love for the father presupposes a renuncation of the penis, so that the boy must also renounce the negative oedipus complex, because his narcissism requires the preservation of the genital. In such a case introjection of both mother and father images must take place since both are to be disposed of as rivals. The superego will then show traits of both parents and correspondingly will be less uniform and less stable. In the case of my already mentioned effeminate patient, it was clear that his superego represented at times the demands of the father and at other times those of the mother. It is no wonder that such a discordant superego would exert an inhibiting and dissipating influence upon the adult man's accomplishments.

In so far as the different instinctual drives have not been repressed, in the boy, what has happened to them? The aggression directed against the two partly hated objects is responsible for the destructive introjection, while the libido accompanying the aggressive tendencies is concerned with the preservation of the object representations in the superego. The passively directed libido components play no role in the mechanism of superego formation. Their sexual aim is abandoned, but the real objects are retained, although tenderness replaces sexual interest. Great dependence upon the object persists, since the intensity of the desexualized relationship is still very strong. The aggression which has been turned inward, fixated by portions of repressed libido, gives rise to secondary masochism, which may lead to conscious or unconscious masochistic fantasies and behavior. It is precisely in such feminine personalities that the fear of loss of love plays an important role and brings about in extreme dependence upon the object. This condition makes the emancipation from the parents in later years difficult and threatens the achievement of independence.

What happens in the process of superego formation in the case of the little girl? The essential similarity of her first preoedipal period of development to that of the boy allows the assumption of a certain parallelism in the formation of the superego precursors. However, her oedipus complex, which is directly reponsible for the formation of the superego, differs greatly from that of the boy. The positive oedipal situation, in which the girl loves her father passively and hates her mother as a rival, occurs only when the negative oedipus complex (love for the mother and hatred toward the father as a rival) is given up. This renunciation takes place by virtue of hostility toward the mother, and by an increase of passivity and strong repression of masculinity. Let us assume for a moment that this process in the little girl was completely successful and that all sexual strivings had been directed into paths of femininity, or that she was originally endowed with merely passive strivings. Experience proves that the girl, too, must give up the oedipus complex. Her motives for doing so are different from those of the boy, whose main narcisstic motive is the preservation of the penis. However, fear of losing love and other possible dangers from the outside as well as from inner drive constellation prevail upon the little girl to renounce her sexual oedipal wishes, and she gradually converts her feelings into tender, aim-inhibitied ones. Secondary masochism, which had already arisen in the process of subordinating her activity to passivity, is now increased by the repressed portions of libido which ally themselves with the aggressive tendencies directed against her own person. Accordingly there arises a passive, tender object dependence with strong masochistic fantasies which may be either conscious or unconscious. Since we have assumed that in this case activity is lacking altogether, the process is herewith finished. In the case of a theoretically purely feminine, completely passive woman, superego formation does not occur.

However, this course of events practically never occurs in real life. There are no people without a bisexual Anlage, a fact which is of much greater significance to women than to men, because subordination of active libido to passively directed tendencies never completely succeeds. Even where complete femininity in love life is achieved, more or less vigorous active tendencies are demonstrable. We have already seen that maternity requires the use of active tendencies. It becomes clear, then, that the little girl, in giving up the oedipus complex, also forms a superego. The girl, like the boy, utilizes activity, that is, her "masculinity," to accomplish this process. This may be the reason why the female's superego resembles more closely that of a feminine man than that of a markedly masculine man. The little girl also has a double oedipus complex to overcome. She introjects both parental object images, and the superego receives a double character, rendering it less powerful, unified, and imperative. These peculiarities are also favored by the circumstance that the little girl only gradually renounces her oedipal wishes and achieves superego formation slowly and less completely than the boy. It is no wonder that the superego of the woman usually allows her less significant social and cultural achievements than the man. On the other hand, it is not surprising that the complexity of the early instinctual development of the little girl and the formation of her feminine oedipus complex cause the later development of the woman, as well as her superego formation, to show the greatest variations and differences of character. I shall attempt to describe some of the varieties in subsequent chapters.

3. Review of "Fear of Castration in Women," by Sandor Rado

(1934)

Rado's work is worth our attention for three reasons: (1) it is a contribution to the developmental history of women; (2) it proposes a new theory of anxiety; and (3) it tries to establish a new general theory of the neuroses.

It seems to be difficult to do justice to a work which touches upon such comprehensive problems. However, we may find relief in the facts first, that, Rado presents his theories of anxiety and neuroses in connection with his conception of the little girl's development, and second, that a single vicissitude of the instinctual drives, namely masochism, is considered to be the cornerstone of all three hypotheses. Psychoanalysis has never underestimated the significance of masochism in human psychic life. Freud pointed out repeatedly that masochism has a particular relation to feminity, and therefore plays an important role in female development as well as those phenomena in male mental life which are based on passive-feminine tendencies. Furthermore, we must pay due attention to masochism because it may reveal itself in a perversion and in a general kind of behavior in life which Freud called moral masochism. Analytic therapy convinces us time and again of the intensity of masochistic drive processes and of the difficulty of influencing them. We certainly have to give Rado credit for having drawn attention to these phenomena once again. Many of his delineations of female neuroses (phobia and anxiety hysteria), of character peculiarities of women, of expressions of the masculinity complex are very impressive, colorful, and stimulating. The simplicity of his theory of anxiety is highly attractive. However, if we consider the complexity of mental events, the many and various factors causing inner and outer conflicts, we feel somewhat surprised at an attempt to hold one single process, the ego's struggle against masochism, responsible for all these phenomena.

We shall follow Rado's statements in detail. To begin with, we shall examine his theory of the development of the little girl toward feminity. The title of the work does not seem to be very appropriate since Rado confirms Freud's finding that women cannot experience real castration anxiety, being already "castrated" and therefore not exposed to the danger of castration. Thus, the female's anxietes, though sometimes resembling the male's castration fear in some way

Rado's essay was first published in *Psychoanalytic Quarterly* 2:425-475, 1933. This work was subsequently published in German as *Die Kastrationsangst des Weibes* (Vienna: Internalionaler Psychoanalytischer Verlag, 1934). Though the original review was based on the German edition, the quotations are taken from the English 1933 edition.

or other, should be termed differently. This, however, is of only secondary importance.

In Rado's Introduction to his work, he confirms Freud's discovery that penis envy is in the center of the feminine castration complex. Further on Rado looks for an explanation of the female's anxieties about being damaged, which according to clinical experience, are connected with the castration complex but which cannot be understood through the existence of penis envy. In the first chapter Rado tries to solve this problem in the following way: he suggests that the little girl, after having discovered that other human beings possess a penis of which she is envious, "hallucinates" this organ as being part of her own body and genital. This hallucinated organ is called an "illusory penis" by Rado. He assumes this hallucination will be soon corrected. However, this done, the illusory penis is set up anew on another part of the body. The female's "castration anxiety" therefore should be a fear of losing this "illusory penis" or its "symbolic substitute." Here the first objection arises. Psychoanalysis has good reasons to assume that the infant hallucinates satisfaction whenever he is exposed to need tensions. However, a little child of three to six years old is not likely to hallucinate a body organ, even if he has first dreamed of having it. Furthermore, observartions on little girls contradict this. Rado states explicity that he himself has not made any observations in this connection. It is true that a little girl can produce a strong wish for a penis. She may imagine and play that she possesses a male organ. In later years fantasies of having a penis can be uncovered and brought to consciousness during the analysis of dreams and, for instance, neurotic sypmtoms of hysterical patients. However, we do not encounter Rado's construction of a "hallucinatory illusory penis." Freud's discovery that little girls may produce a strong wish for a penis, which incidentally may be retained in the unconscious for any length of time, seems to explain the observed facts sufficiently.

In the second chapter, Rado looks for a solution of the economic problem of these processes. He believes that his hypothesis of the "illusory penis" describes them, to be sure, but that it does not explain their dynamics. At this point Rado turns to his theory of "trauma." He says: ". . . the anatomical experience was for these girls [who later on are "plagued . . . by castration fantasies"] a psychic trauma. On perceiving the penis they lost self-esteem, suffered a severe emotional upset – and the sanguinary fantasies appeared as a consequence of this narcissistic shock" (pp. 432-433). He continues: "The little girl suddenly catches sight of a penis. She is startled and fascinated. . . . From her emotional chaos emerges the strident desire: 'I want it!' which is followed immediately in fantasy by, 'I have it'. Then comes the humiliating reflection, 'But I haven't'; – this knowledgde produces severe psychic pain, and terimtates in something like a paralysis of feeling" (p. 433).

And still further: "The narcissistic shock at once inhibits the girl's actively directed desire for gratification, which up to this time was discharged in masturbation. But the intense mental pain which she experienced excited her sexually and supplied her with a 'substitutive gratification'. This emotional experience teaches her that she may obtain a new pleasure in place of the one that was destroyed by the traumatic event-passive pleasure in pain" (pp. 433-434). According to Rado, we must assume that a traumatic experience produces a shock which causes a sudden renunciation af actively directed masturbation and the replacement of a libidibal satisfaction by a masochistic one.

During the discussion of Rado's work in the Vienna Psychoanalytic Society, one of the discussants drew attention to the fact that a trauma theory can be controlled. Though the author, in his Introduction, promises to prove his statements with observational experiences, he now admits the lack of material gained in observations of children. His theory was developed from a combination of watching children's reactions to "innocuous experiences that astonish children or bring them disillusion," impressions gained from them "through empathy," and conclusions drawn from analysis of adults (p. 433). Therefore the author could not produce direct proof of his trauma theory. The Viennese child analysts, in the just mentioned discussion, declared that neither of them had at any time observed the course of development described by Rado. Moreover, analysis of women reveal different outcomes. Reactions of little girls on the observation of the anatomical sex difference vary. However, it very often occurs that a girl does not give up masturbation after she has discovered the existence of the male organ. In those cases she continues to masturbate with strong opposition, rage, and tenacity; she clings to actively directed desires and their satisfaction; she may hold to the fantasy that a penis will grow on her sometime or other. Only very gradually will she finally give up this position. A variety of factors is responsible for this; for instance, a strong demand from outside, an ever-increasing disappointment in the mother, an inner dissatisfaction with her "inferior" genital, perhaps a fear of the intensity of her own rage and hate, and maybe also other still unknown factors, But time and again it has been confirmed that little girls usually have to go through a long and difficult struggle before they are able to part from their active position and to adopt finally their passive role.

Sometimes, in normal cases, the development toward femininity will run a much easier course. However, in just such cases as described by Rado, in which hysterical symptoms, severe anxieties, and masculine character deformities occur, the active sexual strivings are only abandoned after a long and hard struggle, and one does observe an "erotogenic masochism" becoming operative as a surrogate for masturbatory libidinal pleasure. It may happen in some little girls that masochism plays an important role in fantasies or in a neurosis. We have already given Rado credit for having described this proces in various neurotic disorders in a beautiful way. The origin of these masochistic fantasies and behavior was recorded by Freud some time ago and has been presented by Helene Deutsch in many convincing observations. A little girl with a strong wish for a penis produces intense aggressive impulses, strong feelings of hate and rage, which reach a peak when she can no longer deny her own "inferior" organ and therefore has to give up her activity. If she has finally accepted her passsive feminine role, she cannot get rid of her aggression in the outer world and has to turn it toward her own person. The turning inward of aggression coincides approximately with another process. namely the structuration of a part of the mind into ego and superego, with the consequence that the superego incorporates the aggression. A sadistic superego evolves and the ego becomes masochistically shaped.

Rado does not mention these processes, which are of paramount importance in understanding neurotic disorders. This secondary masochism is based on the original erotogenic form of masochism, the latter possibly providing the personality with its masochistic attitude. That is all we can say about erotogenic masochism in this connection.

The core of Rado's train of thought is the following idea: If drive satisfaction is interrupted, masochistic pleasure gain immediately comes to the fore as a substitute. The same process is the base of this theory of anxiety and of his theory of neurosis as well. One gains the impression that the theory of anxiety was the first to be developed and only later on transferred to the neuroses of women. However, Rado promised to study the latter in observations, with which unfortunately we are not presented.

As we have to discard the author's theory of masochistic deformation of the genital drive as the immediate consequence of the upsetting discovery of a penis, we cannot at the same time accept his concept of an "illusory penis" a reaction formation against the shock, as a "phallic complementation" in the service of the defence against masochism. In the last decade we have learned a good deal about a little girl's early development. The study of the preoedipal phase has revealed an intense and rich mother relationship long before the little girl enters the oedipal situation. In connection with man's bisexual disposition, drives with passive as well as with active aims come to the fore during the preoedipal phase (the oral, anal, and phallic stages of development). In the phallic period of the preoedipal phase, penis envy and a wish for a penis are of great significance and especially strong in little girls with a clear bisexual disposition (masculinity). The little girl's wish for a penis is a "primary" one, stimulated by active tendencies. It exists long before she turns toward the father in passive surrender, and even earlier than masochism is found to play a role in her fantasy life or in a neurosis. It goes without saying that in later times (in latency and adolescence) the original wish for a penis can be reawakened, especially in those girls who have suffered severe disappointments from the father, spoiling her female role and throwing her back into the earlier active position. The power of these secondary reactive processes should not be underestimated. However, they are built upon the earlier preoedipal experiences and draw their force from them.

Rado does not mention Freud's latest findings, laid down in his paper "Female Sexuality" (1931b), which appeared two years before Rado's work. Where Rado considers recent literature, he refers only to details and presents them in a distorted manner. I cite Rado (p. 460): "I do not share the view of those writers that *the little girl at first feels as a boy does,* directing her 'phallic' genital impulses to her mother, and passing through a 'negative oedipus complex' in a *genital* sense before she begins her female genital career" (italics added). Indeed, one could stress the improbability of a little boy's feeling himself to be a girl from the very start as well. Children of both sexes develop impulses with active as well as with passive aims directed to the mother in analogous ways though with individually different intensities. The sex difference is originally unknown to boys and girls. Therefore those desires do not include a wish to belong to the other sex. Children of both sexes desire to be loved by the mother and to love and to possesss her. When Rado relates a dream in which a woman dreams of having sexual intercourse with her mother, he is quite right in his assertion that the dream represents a wish of a later period. In *this shape* a desire to possess the mother can only come into existence after the person has learned about the nature of sexual intercourse. The desire itself stems from earlier times and is shaped in accordance with the infantile psychic representations present in infants of both sexes. Little boys and little girls have no knowledge of the existence of a vagina, and their fantasies of possessing the mother are born out of their fantasies about the adults' being together. These fantasies may vary, for instance, from mutual masturbation or mutual urinating to fantasies of urinating into the mouth or the anus, to other bodily contacts, to sadistic scences, etc. In any case, observation has taught us that the little girl's wish for a penis and her demand that the mother must present her with it have already entered into her desires and ideas in the preoedipal phase. The same is valid for her aggression, hate, and rage, which are reactions to her final disappointment. In his dream example Rado does not present us with historical data about the woman's childhood. His attempt to use this material to prove his theories of femininity, of masochistic deformation of the genital drive, and of the "illusory penis" is therefore not convincing. His explanation of the dream is based upon these theories and thus cannot be used to prove them.

There seems to be a similar misunderstanding in Rado's rejection of Freud's term "phallic phase" (p. 434). This term does *not* apply to the idea of a little girl's already differentiating between male and female. On the contrary, it means that both boys and girls do *not* have any knowledge of the female organ and that their sexual activities take place almost exclusively on the phallic organs, penis and clitoris (sometime labia and vulva). Rado's suggestion that the term "phallic phase" be replaced by "amorphous genital phase of the ego" (p. 434) seems to be superfluous and confusing.

One more point about Rado's conception of femininity should be considered. According to him, a pathological, masochistically deformed femininity develops if the discovery of the penis takes place in a period of masturbation and thus has a traumatic result. Normal femininity should emerge whenever the discovery of the penis coincides with a period of "genital latency." The simplicity of this theory is tempting. However, the complexity of the preoedipal mother attachment reveals to us how manifold are the fixation points of the drives in this period, causing a variety of starting points for neurotic reactions. Furthermore, we know that a seemingly uneventful experience in infancy can give rise to a traumatic reaction in later periods. The little girl's discovery of a penis may be without consequence at the time, whereas later on many disturbances may develop as an afterreaction without the girl's having had the opportunity of observing the male organ again. The moment of penis observation does not seem to be decisive.

36

We now turn our attention to Rado's theory of anxiety in the fourth chapter. The author attempts to fill a gap in Freud's theory of anxiety. In his first theory, Freud assumed that anxiety emerges from the suppression of a libidinal impulse the energy of which is discharged in anxiety. The later hypothesis reads that this kind of discharge may take place in a traumatic situation (as a breaking of the stimulus barrier), that, however, later on anxiety is used as a signal for the ego in order to take action upon a danger situation. In this case it is no longer of importance where the energy for the signal comes from. Rado, however, prefers to hold to the first theory and believes that anxiety is exclusively derived from masochistic instinctual drives. He argues in the following way: The ego itself is not the place where anxiety originates. Even language assigns the active role to anxiety and the passive one to the ego, because we say "we are beset, attacked, overcome, overwhelmed, or shaken by . . . anxiety" (p. 454). Here Rado neglects the fact that we often say "I am anxious." Furthermore, the author says that anxiety produces a constriction of breathing followed by a remedial acceleration of the heart (p. 455). Many physiologists, however, have observed that anxiety may equally frequently give rise to acceleration of breathing without "remedial" action of the heart. Rado's idea that the nucleus of the experience of anxiety is a paralysis caused by masochism (p. 455) is in contradiction to the opinion of physiologists as well as of psychologists. In the beginning anxiety does not have a paralyzing effect, it first leads to a mobilization of energies (see Freud, 1926). The latter promotes activity aiming at an attempt to fly in order to escape a danger situation. Masochism is not involved in this process. In cases of "anxiety paralysis" a second danger is added to the original one. It may be that here Rado's train of thought becomes valuable. This second danger could be a masochistic one. In a footnote in *Inhibitions, Symptoms and Anxiety* (1926, p. 168), which Rado uses without citing it, Freud writes:

> It may quite often happen that although a danger-situation is correctly estimated in itself, a certain amount of instinctual anxiety is added to the realistic anxiety. In that case the instinctual demand before whose satisfaction the ego recoils is a masochistic one: the instinct of destruction directed against the subject himself. Perhaps an addition of this kind explains cases in which reactions of anxiety are exaggerated, inexpedient, or paralysing. Phobias of heights (windows, towers, precipices and so on) may have some such origin. Their hidden feminine significance is closely connected with masochism.

These sentences comprise the essence of the psychic processes involved. It is the *additional* masochism which has a paralyzing effect in anxiety states. The hypothesis that anxiety (and signal anxiety) is masochism cannot be affirmed. Another of Rado's ideas, that anxiety in the socalled "actual neuroses" should be masochism because every suppression of genital excitation, each "Inhibition of a pleasure-giving activity is always reacted to by an unleashing of masochism" (p. 456), runs parallel to his theory of the traumatic shock-producing effect of the penis observation in little girls. Both hypotheses must be rejected in regard

37

to the psychic events as observed. A similar motive is made use of in Rado's bioanalytic speculation on the phylogenesis of signal anxiety. According to him, an injury of a primitive creature "restricts the animal's freedom of motion, lessens or frustrates his pleasure-giving acts, and thus compels the pleasure function to turn to pain-pleasure. In other words, the wound is elaborated masochistically by the ego" (p. 457). One of the participants in the above-mentioned discussion in Vienna suggested that if every restriction of freedom of action caused masochistic self-damaging reactions in living beings, the living world would have been reduced to an inorganic world millions of years ago.

We now come to Rado's theory of neuroses. We have already mentioned Freud's view that masochism plays a role in height phobias. However, this form of masochism is the secondary one, the result of inwardly turned destructive tendencies, playing a role in various neuroses. It can finally become dangerous and has to be warded off. However, the original danger situation, which may raise anxiety, defensive processes, and sometimes a neurotic disposition, is a real one (see Freud, 1933). One of the earliest real dangers is the danger of losing the love object (or its love). This danger continues to exist in females. In analytic treatment we invariably discover at the bottom of the socalled "castration anxieties" in women just this fear of losing love. In later life this fear may be colored and reshaped in (unconscious) fantasies in which the wish for a penis and its derivatives may in fact play a role. Similar fantasies may enter into hysterical conversion symptoms as well. Rado's descriptions of female neuroses and character deformations under the infuence of the masculinity complex are interesting. However, in tracing back every symptom and every character formation to the sole influence of the masochistic deformation of the genital drive and the reactive "illusionary penis," he is simplifying and distorting the observed material.

In the section on "The Choice of the Lesser Evil," Rado elaborates on physical as well as psychic self-damage, which he attributes solely to masochistic action. However, he forgets about self-destruction. Masochism is destruction bound by libido. In actual self-injuries a defusion of libido and destruction has occurred prior to the deed, and this Rado does not mention. Masochism indeed plays an important role in male neuroses and in passive-feminine tendencies in men. However, observation do *not* permit us to accept Rado's two final theses, that (1) "the danger from the masochistic genital instinct . . . determine[s] the pathogenicity of the oedipus conflicts and hence . . . health or neurosis" (p. 473), and (2) "the basic phenomenon of a neurosis is the deformation of the ego-inherent genital impulse into ego-adverse genital masochism" (p. 475). Neuroses are not the outcome of a struggle between a reduced personality and a single drive impulse. I cite the last sentences of Freud's "Libidinal Types":

> It is a familiar fact that the aetiological preconditions of neurosis are not yet known. The precipitating causes of it are frustrations and internal conflicts: conflicts between the three major psychical agencies, conflicts arising within the libidinal economy in consequence of our bisexual disposition and conflicts between the erotic and the aggresive instinctual

components. It is the endeavour of the psychology of the neuroses to discover what makes these processes, which belong to the normal course of mental life, become pathogenic [1931a, p. 220].

Rado's simplified theory neglects all of these inner conflicts as well as the significance of the frustrations the helpless and dependent little child suffers from the encironment.

In *Inhibitions, Symptoms and Anxiety* (1926, pp. 152-153), Freud says:

It is to be feared that our need to find a single, tangible 'ultimate cause' of neurotic illness will remain unsatisfied. The ideal solution, which medical men no doubt still yearn for, would be to discover some bacillus which could be isolated and bred in a pure culture and which, when injected into anyone, would invariably produce the same illness; or, to put it rather less extravagantly, to demonstrate the existence of certain chemical substances the administration of which would bring about or cure particular neuroses. But the probability of a solution of this kind seems slight. Psycho-analysis leads to less simple and satisfactory conclusions.

Apparently, Rado's hypothesis do not provide us with the desired solution either.

4. Inhibition and Narcissism

(1936)

The starting point of this paper is the investigation of a mental process which, though well known, is of general importance and perhaps occurs regularly. I would formulate this psychic process as follows:

A number of mental processes with different and sometimes opposite goals can run a course that finally leads to identical results. This means that they bring about similar conditions in ego organization. We can study these processes by examining the genesis of neurotic inhibitions, which represent restrictions of ego functions. We may then discover that in one patient a certain inhibition is the result of special instinctual processes, whereas in a second patient it is caused by just the opposite course of the drives involved. I will give some illustrations, but before doing so, I want to state explicitly that the similar outcomes in ego organization are reached in the most different ways, I will not go into these intermediate events for the time being.

The connection between neurotic work inhibitions and masturbation[1]

Psychoanalysis showed very early that work and learning inhibitions often originate in masturbatory processes. If a patient masturbates excessively, the phenomenon is not so difficult to explain: most of his psychic energy is being used for masturbatory satisfaction and there is not enough left for other activities. His work inhibition, a curtailment of ego achievements, is a direct consequence of the masturbatory activity. An additional factor can be derived from the accompanying guilt feelings, which demand self-punishment in the shape of inhibition of functioning. It is basically masturbation, with its accompanying psychic phenomena, which causes the neurotic inhibitions.

The analysis of adolescents and adults demonstrate that exessive masturbatory activity has a previous history in infantile masturbation, which was usually very intense as well. In the struggle against it the little child had achieved no success, or only a partial or temporary one. The excessive masturbation of adolescents is usually a direct continuation or a repetition of a childhood period in which drive tensions found discharge in masturbatory activities.

In these cases the analyst is satisfied if the analysis succeeds in freeing the patient of his excessive masturbation with the accompanying guilt feelings, thus

---

[1] I presented a paper on this theme at the Thirteenth Congress of the International Psycho-Analytical Association, Lucerne, August 31, 1934.

providing him with the necessary forces and energy to remove his work inhibition. As such cases are well known to every analyst, a more detailed description of the processes is superfluous.

However, I want to single out another group of patients suffering from work inhibitions who do not masturbate at all. These patients usually report that they cannot remember having masturbated at any period of life, or, if they did so, it was merely occasionally and of very short duration. However, a prolonged analysis reveals, with great regularity in my experience, a quite different picture. It gradually becomes clear that in early childhood these patients went through a period of intense masturbatory activity that was suppressed and completely abandoned, usually after a long and hard struggle. Such struggles occur within the personality between ego and id. In the fist-mentioned patients, who have continued masturbation either without or with short interruptions, the id has gained victory. In the last-mentioned cases the ego has proved to be the stronger. However, it had to pay for its triumph with the same curtailment that brought about its defeat in the first-mentioned group of patients. In both groups the ego has become inhibited in its functions.

Case 1

The significance of this connection strongly impressed me in the analysis of an intelligent young girl suffering from a work inhibition. The patient could not remember having masturbated at any time in her life. The analysis revealed that as a little girl she had gone through period of intense, passionate masturbation that lasted until her seventh year. This period came to an end with a complete suppression of masturbatory activities, accomplished without any help or interference from the environment. The little girl took great pride in this achievement. However, in later years the proud satisfaction was nullified by a tormenting workinhibition. A long and laborious analysis brought little relief until the moment when the patient became able to resume masturbating. This occurred only after certain connections, of which I will speak later, had been uncovered in the treatment. From this moment on, a significant release of energy and fading away of her inhibition occurred. I will report later on the cause of the rigorous suppression of the masturbation in childhood. I now want to summarize a tentative conclusion:

Disturbances of ego functions (for instance, work inhibitions) can be the result of an unsuccessful struggle against masturbation as well as of its successful suppression. In other words, the struggle between ego and id for masturbatory discharge of libidinal tensions may cause identical outcomes in ego organization whether the ego was victorious or was defeated. This is in accordance with our former statement that opposing using courses of psychic processes can lead to identical results in ego organization.

Outcomes of satisfaction and of frustration of demands for love

The fact that opposite vicissitudes of the child's libidinal demands made upon the object may lead to similar situations in ego organization is more generally known.

The little child who has undergone a very rigorous training in cleanliness whose anal libidinal and aggressive tendencies have received insuffent satisfaction, may acquire a developmental disturbance. His ego is unable to master his drive demands sufficiently and he falls ill with a neurosis. However, the child who was subject to overindulgence, whose every wish for tenderness was satisfied, whose aggressive impulses could be acted out to a great extent, is also likely to acquire a neurosis. Both situations-too much gratification as well as undue suppression of drive needs-may lead to similar ego disturbances. The ego, then, has to put up with a neurotic distortion. Here, too, we encounter the same outcomes of drive demands. However, we must not overlook a difference between the two examples described above. The patient suffering from a work inhibition gave up masturbation in consequence of an inner proces, without aid from the outside. In the second example, the suppression of drive demands was the result of an educational measure, an influence of the environment. However, the difference is lessened by the fact the neurosis of the rigorously educated child usually comes to the fore only at an age when the prohibitions and demands from outside are already internalized. This means that the repression of anal tendencies has already been accomplished by the ego and super-ego. On the other hand, even in cases where masturbation is given up without support from outside, past experiences conceived as a prohibition of masturbation always play a role.

The patient who ended her masturbation struggle alone, with a victorious result, had never received direct prohibitions. However, she remembered being put to bed by her mother as a very little child dressed in pajamas. Though at that time she had not yet stopped masturbating, the analysis revealed that afterward, in the period of her struggle against masturbation, the patient took her mother's dressing her in pajamas as a signal of an interdiction.

Apparently it is of great significance for further ego development whether the decisive struggle to give up masturbation occurs with or without help from outside. I shall return to this point in later attempts at clarification. I now turn to another restriction of an ego function.

Potency disturbance as an inhibition due to different outcomes of drive tendencies

Case 2

A young man, aged thirty, had been suffering from impotency for approximately ten years. There had been a very short period during which he seemed to have been potent. The patient suffered from a compulsion to look for perverse relations with prostitutes of an outspoken, manly type. His attitude toward these women was gentle, loving, indulging, but desperate at the same time. The analysis revealed that the strong castration anxiety hidden behind his impotene which allowed him only masturbatory and perverse satisfaction was in fact a fear of retaliation. In every encounter, powerful aggressive tendencies against women were unconsciously mobilized and the patient feared punishment through castration during coitus. The preshistory of these aggressive impulses was to be found in his early childhood when they were directed toward his parents, who had subjected the child to a very severe education. The tantrums of the little boy gradually acquired the significance of a love scene and so served as a discharge of libidinal tendencies as well. The suppression of his rage became identical with a giving up of his sexual wishes. Afterward, the passive homosexual attitude, the strenght of which was also a consequence of the castration anxiety, played an important role.

However, the successful suppression of the fused aggressive and libidinal impulses had to be paid for by the ego with a functional disturbance of the patient's sexual life. After he had recognized these connections, the patient expressed the idea that he would be potent if he succeeded in behaving energetically and even violently toward a woman, some time or other. In a certain phase of his analysis such a situation suddenly occurred. One evening the irritating attitude of his woman friend provoked violent rage in the patient. He allowed himself to express it. He flew into a tantrum; he raged and it came to blows and violence. Afterward he felt immensely relieved and freed; he was proud and content and convinced of his manly potency. The patient tried to have intercourse. However, he was still impotent, which surprised and horrified him at the same time. We understood that the last occurrence, the acting out of the patient's aggressive sexual impulses, could not be tolerated without impairment of function. Only a gradual working through of the analytic material was able to bring about a kind of regulation of the discharge of drive energy which allowed this severely neurotic patient to regain some potency from time to time and in special circumstances which will not be discussed.

In this case we observe again that opposite vicissitudes of drive impulses may lead to similar functional disturbances, even in the same person.

Attempts at clarifications

The problem of Quantity

We will now try to learn something about the nature of these processes through comparison of the similarities and differences in the examples mentioned. We will not go further into the fact that in some cases we have to do with a restriction of an ego function (work inhibition, potency disturbance) and in other cases with a neurotic disorder of the personality as the final outcome. A neurosis, too, starts with the restriction of a normal ego capacity as a consequence of the necessity to ward off a drive impulse. On the other hand, an inhibition may initiate a neurotic symptom as well. For our purpose it is not important whether a simple curtailment of the ego emerges or whether the process leads to a compromise between ego and id and to the formation of neurotic symptoms.

We have already stated that the unrestrained expression of drive impulses can cause an ego disturbance. The same disturbance can be the result of the prevention of drive discharge. In other words, we get the impression that there must be a situation in which the influence of a drive impulse upon the ego leads to an optimal effect. We may see a parallel to the influence of certain drugs upon the body. We know that small quantities of certain medicines and chemicals may stimulate certain bodily functions, whereas larger quantities can bring about a paralysis or even a complete cessation of the same functions. It seems likely that in the problem of psychic processes we also encounter a question of quantity, of intensity. It is decisive for the ego what intensity of an id impulse is satisfied.

The discharged quantity is in itself dependent upon different factors, in the first place upon the absolute intensity of the drives, in the second place upon the oppotunities given for a satisfactory discharge. The latter are determined by several factors; the environment as well as the inner conditions of the personality, the relative strength or weakness of ego and superego vis-à-vis the drive impulse, are decisive here. So in the final instance we are dealing with questions of (relative) quantities. The problems of quantity seem to open a wide and very important field for research. They seem to play a predominant role in the understanding of mental processes.[2]

Unfortunately, this knowledge does not carry us far for the moment. We do not have at our disposal any means of measuring drive intensities.[3] For the time we have to content ourselves with observation and description of the processes and with an assessment of the relations between the various forces *post factum*. In analytic work we always feel it to be an impediment that we cannot determine intensities and that we have to limit ourselves to impressions and estimations (valuations). We have already observed that abundant masturbatory discharge of drive intensities may lead to a work inhibition, because it can influence certain ego functions in a "toxic" way. However, this knowledge does not permit us to expect the lack of an inhibition where no masturbation took place. The patient with the work inhibition showed us that an excess of suppression of a drive impulse has the same paralyzing influence on ego capacities. We cannot yet decide where and when and with which quantitative relations between drives and ego demands an optimum of activities and freedom of the ego can come about. In our male patient, the severe suppression of his aggressive sexual impulses as well as their abundant discharge (which took place later on) caused a potency disturbance. It was impossible to decide beforehand which quantities had to be discharged in order to enable his ego to dispose freely of his potency. In analytic work, which aims at liberation of the ego functions, one is often impressed by the observation that mastery of drive processes, already made conscious, is a matter of the relation between is strength and egostrength. Apart from its significance for psychoanalytic practice, this aspect is of great importance for the study of child development and education.

---

[2] L. Eidelberg (1935) develops interesting ideas in discussing the problem of quantity in the theory of neurosis. However, his ideas scarcely touch upon the questions put forward here.

[3] Bernfeld's interesting attempt to establish a "libido metrics" has not so far provided us with workable results.

Some decades ago Freud (1905c) pointed out that severe spoiling of a child as well as suppression of drive impulses can cause neuroses.

Anna Freud warned explicitly against the danger in psychoanalytically oriented education of concluding from analytic findings that a child could be protected from developmental disturbances by avoiding prohibitions and demands. She pointed out that too much indulgence may cause neurotic and character disturbances in the little child. Analytic pedagogy had to take refuge in a compromise and advised the educators to choose a middle path between indulgence and frustration. In this endeavor, however, it meets with the same limitations as did the psychoanalyst, namely, with the impossibility of measuring quantities. In education it is equally difficult to assess the intensity of the drive impulse which is to be allowed satisfaction or prevented from discharge. Consequently it is impossible to predict the outcome of an educational measure in a satisfactory way. Only the result teaches us something about the processes involved.

Waelder[4] proposed a very fine and correct formulation, namely, that education has to maintain "a maximum of love and a maximum of burdening of the child's ego." However, it is very limited in its practical consequences. How can we determine the maximum of love and the maximum of deprivation which the child is able to endure without impairment? We can never know beforehand, and every educator has encountered many difficulties and is aware of how often our expectations have proved to be erroneous.

Summarizing, we may say: Analytic experience teaches us that the intensity of a drive impulse is highly important in its effect upon ego functions. We assume that an unmeasurable intensity (quantity) arouses an optimal result in ego functioning. Both more and less bring about disturbances or paralyses of the ego. It is a question not of absolute but of relative quantities, of the relation between ego strength and drive intensity. We do not forget that "strenght" and "weakness" of the ego, too, are unmeasurable concepts and that they are meaningful only in relation to other factors and agencies. A "less" of drive intensity does not imply an absolute drive weakness; it may mean that only a small quantity is discharged.

With our girl patient, mentioned above, the ego was in a certain respect stronger than the id because it was able to prevent the drive discharge, to repress. However, the ego revealed its weakness vis-à-vis the id in so far as it had to tolerate the work inhibition. It will be clear that in an opposite case, where there is a great deal of masturbation, the inability to master drive impulses points to a primary relative ego weakness versus drive quantities.

A related problem seems to be worth mentioning here: what is the reaction of an already-constituted ego organization upon an increase of drive intensity? Such events occur in normal circumstances, for instance, in puberty, in menopause, and perhaps in other periods of life, as a consequence of bodily processes of certain pharmacological influences. We know very little about these events, so we can only put forward some assumptions. We are acquainted

[4] Read at the Vierländertagung in Vienna, 1935.

45

with the observation that in puberty and menopause an augmentation of drive intensity leads to changes in ego organization.

Anna Freud (1936) described some modes of behavior in adolescents, for instance, an oscillation between complete asceticism (not only in sexual life, but also in regard to every enjoyment of life) and dissolute self-indulgence, which she explains by a similar increase of drive quantities. In the menopause an intensifying of drive demands can cause a violent change of behavior in a normal person. It may also be responsible for the fact that during those periods of life neurosis or psychosis tend to break out and already-existing mental disorders are worsened. The ego has to react toward the intensified impulses either with more indulgence at the cost of distortions of the personality, or with a stronger defense which may lead to the outbreak of a mental disease. The aspect of drive quantities seems to be of significance in the explanation of slight psychotic states which may emerge out of "health" or on the base of a neurosis without any demonstrable precipitation from outside. The analyst is acquainted with cases in which after a prolonged analysis a hidden psychotic mechanism suddenly comes to the fore. These are usually paranoid mechanisms. One gets the impression that the analytic work has loosened the repression and liberated a certain amount of drive energy that the ego cannot manage at that moment. The former way of repressing is no longer open and so the ego is overwhelmed by the drive impulses. It has to choose a new tactic in turning against the outer world. The ego misinterprets the environment, for instance, by the mechanism of projection (as in a paranoid psychosis). In so far as this event is the result of a rapid and intensive influence of the analytic process, we may wait and expect the situation to be of short duration and not to spread outside of the analysis. In this case we are not dealing with a psychosis in a clinical sense.

However, I once observed a fifty-year-old woman, suffering from a hysterical neurosis in whom a paranoid syndrome that came to the fore after two years of analysis and without an outer precipitation lasted much longer than usual. The patient produced an erotic delusion not restricted to the analytic situation and not completely soluble. Time and again the patient came back for an afteranalysis. A core of paranoid mechanisms continued to exist and the condition revived occasionally, though it never came into severe conflict with the outer world and the patient could maintain her position in society.

I think that in this case we are dealing with an intensification of the drives, in consequence of the menopause, which overwhelmed the ego and incapacitated it for healthy mastering as well as for neurotic repression. In such cases the analysis is sometimes able to take hold of the symptom and to ameliorate the situation even when it is unable to cure. Because of outer circumstances I could not follow the patient. Therefore I do not know whether the passing of the menopause brought about a change in her psychic situation or not. For the time being we cannot decide whether, in psychoses emerging in other periods when no physiological intensification of the drives occurs, we are also dealing with an increase of drive quantities, perhaps by somatic processes. It does not seem impossible. Rado (1926) and Simmel (1930) have discussed the effects of drugs upon the mental life, i.e., on addiction as well as on psychotic syndromes. Both authors present many important clarifications. They do not touch upon the problem of a possible increase of drives caused by drugs or of a "toxic" effect upon the ego.

We will now come back to our original theme and summarize our suppositions as follows: we assume that a given drive quantity exercises an optimal effect upon the ego organization when it is allowed discharge. A greater as well as a smaller quantity may cause a disturbance of ego functions. We do not forget that for the time being we are unable ro measure the drive quantities.

Topografhic aspects

First I will recapitulate our observations, clarifications, and hypotheses brought forward so far.

We start with the relation of masturbation and work inhibition. It has already been mentioned that a person suffering from complusive masturbation does not have enough libido (drive energy) available for other activities. This picture of ego paralysis does not change appreciably if the masturbatory act is replaced by conscious or unconscious fantasies. In addition to this simple explanation, we mentioned a second one concerning ego restriction through spoiling; i.e., overgratification of libidinal tendencies deprives the ego of every stimulus to activity. Freud repeatedly stated that the ego acquires impetus for higher cultural achievements through the tension of incompletely satisfied wishes. With overgratification this tension is lacking and therewith the stimulus to work as well. In the spoiled child still another factor is involved: the ego becomes fixated to the mode of overgratification, there is no more necessity for further development, a later emerging frustration encounters an unprepared ego, and an anxiety-provoking danger situation comes into existence. The latter, again, may lead to inhibition and neurosis.

If masturbation has become a symptom no longer sanctioned by ego or superego, the inhibition can be reinforced by anxiety and by a tendency toward self-punishment. Self-punishment may also occur if the individual has acted out aggressions to an extent intolerable to the super-ego.

In *"Inhibitions, Symptoms and Anxiety"* (1926) Freud explains a number of inhibitions of functions as being a punishment for sexual and aggressive impulses, which are *not* discharged in masturbation. In these case the drive repression is the consequence of a superego demand. An inhibition can be the punishment for a carried-out masturbatory act as well as for a fantasied but repressed drive satisfaction. In other words. an inhibition caused by suppression of masturbation may be the expression of self-punishent, too.

The problem of quantities is complicated by one more factor. Until now, we have examined the relative drive intensity, that is, the relation of drive strength to ego strength. We have to add here the relation of ego forces and superego forces. Even if the ego is relatively strong vis-à-vis the id and successful in repression, a relative weakness vis-à-vis the superego may be able to compel the ego to renounce its function. In Freud's words, the ego foregoes its achievements *"in order to avoid coming into conflict with the super-ego"* (1926, p. 90).

In the case of an erotization of function, the ego renounces its achievements "*in order to avoid a conflict with the id*" (1926, p. 90). However, the complication of the situation due to superego demands is less severe than it seemed to be at first sight, because the superego gets its severity from the id. The intensity of ego oppression by the superego is dependent upon the drive intensity. In summary: a relatively strong drive intensity (or a relative ego weakness) may inhibit ego functions. The way in which this happens is dependent on the topographical starting point. If the id is victorious in a direct way, "too much" drive discharge is observable. If the process makes a detour over the superego, we observe "too much" drive repression. A strong dependence on the superego has a prehistory in an extreme dependency on the objects and their love in early childhood. The little child's development, therefore, codetermines these processes. I shall come back to this point later. Freud described a second mechanism which leads to a general inhibition: the impoverishment of energy available to the ego. Here also two ways are possible: too much drive discharge (for instance, in frequent masturbation or in a fit of rage) deprives the ego of the energy necessary for work achievements; too intense repression of drive discharge (libido as well as aggression) demands so much ego energy that there is no more available for other activities. Here the same topographical aspect has to be applied. In the first instance, the starting point of the attack on the ego is the id; in the second instance it is the superego.

In the latter considerations we presupposed that the repression was demanded by the superego (with the little child, by the demands of the environment). In our analytic work we can often affirm this state of affairs. However, I think we sometimes meet with another complication. The superego (or its forerunner, the parental prohibitions) is not always the motor of repression.

In order to clarify this point I turn again to our girl patient with the work inhibition. I promised above to come back to the causes of the patient's complete renunciation of masturbation in her seventh year of life. I was able to learn of the following events. The patient did not remember any prohibition of masturbation. The analysis could not uncover one either. However, the attitude of the environment, the parents' secrecy regarding sexuality, had made the child feel that masturbation was something bad and prohibited. Her being dressed in pajamas had the same result. During treatment it became clear that these mild "prohibitions" were not sufficient to explain the child's desperate struggly against masturbation for such a lengthy period of time. After removal of guilt feelings and anxiety the masturbatory inhibition continued to exist. After prolonged analysis the deeper cause of this intense struggle emerged.

It proved to be the same motive which had led the little girl to renounce masturbation without any outside support, a motive described by Freud in "Female Sexuality" (1931b). It is the little girl's discontent with her own genital that brings about a devaluation of its function. In a number of analysis of female patients an inner animosity toward the genital because of the lack of a penis is found to be the ultimate cause for giving up masturbatory activities. It is always accompanied by feelings of inferiority. The analyst often gains the impression that an intense injury as a consequence of feeling incompetent paves the way for anxiety and guilt feelings.[5] According to Freud, the little girl in this respect behaves like a wife who, being unfaithful to her husband, enjoys the happiness with her friend without feeling guilty as long as the relationship is undisturbed. The slightest disappointment, however, gives rise to severe guilt feelings. Analytic work reveals one more connection. In cases where the ego inhibitions were the result of suppression of masturbation in consequence of feelings of incompetence, the inhibitions are more intense and much more difficult to remove than in cases where superego demands have caused the renunciation of masturbation. In the latter cases the superego can sometimes be softened and a therapeutic result can be achieved. In our girl patient, anxiety and guilt could be removed. However, the work inhibition seemed to resist every therapeutic influence. Only after many years of analysis could the deeper cause for the giving up of masturbation, the discontent with the clitoris, be made conscious. The historical circumstances became clear at the same time. The little girl was extremely envious of a little boy playmate and refused to respond to his attempt to seduce her into sexual play. She was then present when other little girls gave in to him and our little patient repented and competed for his favor. However, the boy now refused her. Jealousy and hurt made her turn to a new period of frequent, stubborn, rebellious masturbation. This masturbatory period finally ended because of her strong penis envy. She felt she could never equal the little boy and so turned away every masturbatory activity. In the unconscious the idea was maintained: "You cannot masturbate because you do not have a penis." Later on this notion was replaced by the following: "You cannot work because you do not have the real instrument for it". The uncovering of these ideas did not succeed in curing the patient of her work inhibition. During analysis she had to take up masturbation again after twenty years, though her female love life had already been restored and brought her satisfaction in an earlier analytic period. Only after she was able to experience a full orgasm through masturbation did her fantasy "You cannot work because you have no penis" disappear, and she became free to work.

In a number of cases such a result can not be achieved, and the fusion of work inhibition with masturbatory incompetence proves to be unresolvable. Sometimes we can make an interesting observation in these cases. The little girl's reaction upon renouncing masturbation by her own efforts provokes a strong pride: "I have performed this grand achievement completely alone." This pride sometimes has grown into feelings of grandeur, which seem to make reparation

---

[5] A personal remark of Freud's encourages me to point to a very often encountered fantasy of the little girl, i.e., "I was once in possession of a penis; however, I am deprived of it as a punishment for having masturbated." This fantasy is also encountered in cases where no direct castration threat was made. Many females cling to it tenaciously even after anxiety and guilt have been removed in analysis. The explanation is apparently that anxiety and guilt are easier to endure than the admission of being incompetent. A narcissistic injury seems much more difficult to master than the suffering of the masochistic fantasies of being castrated. Here we may perhaps find a way to a better understanding of the still unsolved problems of masochism.

49

and hide the "inferiority." It often alternates with depression and inferiority feelings. This self-aggrandizement is of course nullified by the work inhibition in later times.

We may summarize: The drive repression leading to disturbances of ego functions is not always due to superego (or environmental) demands. In certain circumstances it can start from the ego, namely, if the process threatens the ego with a narcissistic injury. Again, the topographic aspect proves to be very important. Freud (1926) mentions two motives for the coming into being of inhibitions of ego functions: the ego's prudence which leads to avoiding (1) a conflict with the id and (2) a conflict with the superego. We now want to add a third one: (3) to avoid the confrontation with its own incompentence, which means, to avoid a disturbance of the narcissistic equilibrium. Especially in cases where the latter motive is present, a therapeutic influence is very tenaciously counteracted.

Disturbances of the narcissistic equilibrium

We must now face more questions. In our girl patient it was the narcisstic injury following her discovery of the lack of a penis which caused her masturbation inhibition and later on her work inhibition. The first question is: Is this state of affairs the individual fate of our patient, or is it a general occurrence? The second question is: Can we find similar connections between narcissistic injuries and inhibitions of function in men, and if so, what are those injuries?

The uncovering of the early infantile masturbation period in analysis is a laborious and difficult piece of work. Freud recently pointed to the importance of the details of the struggle between masturbatory impulses and defensive forces. The influence on ego development is different according to whether the struggle is successful or not, whether the suppression is the result of outer prohibitions or of inner motives, whether it takes place with or without support from outside, etc. These differences leave their marks in neurotic manifestations and especially in character formation. They can stamp adult love life as well.

There are still many uncertainties in this field just because the study of the details is so difficult. I was able to affirm Freud's discovery that in little girls the renunciation of masturbation is very often caused by their discontent with the clitoris. I also found in some cases that the inhibition of masturbation was the cause of a later work inhibition. Nevertheless, the observations are still too scarce, and the following tentative hypotheses are in need of further research. I have the impression, however, that, in women suffering from a variety of inhibitions, in the end we always come upon severe narcissistic injuries in connection with the lack of a penis. The struggle of the ego with drive impulses regularly touches upon it and it is decisive for the development of the personality. If the ego is victorious, an independent, active, and strong personality may develop. If the victory is only an incomplete one, an ego impairment may emerge. This damage may be limited to certain areas (for instance, work or sexual life) or it may appear only intermittently. In these cases, periods of free activity can alternative with periods of disturbances of functions accompanied by depressive moods. If the fight with the impulses is completely unsuccesful, a strong dependence of the ego on the id is to be expected. We most often encounter a compromise formation, especially if strong impulses and a considerable amount of activity (masculinity) are present. Of course we do not forget that the influence of the environment-prohibitions, etc. – plays an important role as well. However, as already mentioned, fear of the demands of the environment and guilt feelings are more easily removed in treatment.

We come now to the second question: What are the connections between inhibition of function and narcissistic injuries in men?

The comparison of the development of male and female children has taught us much about the similarities and differences between the sexes. Inhibitions in male patients are equally connected with sexual development and with the outcome of masturbation. Here we are interested in the cases in which an intensive suppression of it has led to disturbances. A comparison with female cases reveals first and foremost that they are less frequent in men. Freud mentioned that complete suppression of masturbation in adolescence occurs much more often in girls than in boys. Boys who are subject to strong castration anxiety, awakened either by threats from the environment or by observation of females, may renounce masturbatory activities, but usually less completely and for a shorter time that do girls. The little boy experiences castration as being a real danger. A little girl, showing anxieties which seem to be similar to a boy's, cannot take them as reality. Her anxieties are a reaction to her desire for a penis (which later on can become a masochistic desire to be castrated). So they are secondary factors for repression.

The difference between the processes in boys and in girls could be roughly described as follows: in the boy it is anxiety in the face of the threatening danger of a narcissistic injury, in the girl it is a present narcissistic disturbance which leads to the relinquishing of genital activity.

In my experience this difference is expressed in the fact that in pathological outcomes the consequent inhibition in women is more intensive, tenacious, and more difficult to remove. The man can recuperate more easily because the castration threat finally proves to be no real danger and his sence of inferiority therefore depends only upon his fears. This state of affairs is affirmed in cases where in the first days of life a circumcision was performed. When the little boy discovers the lack of the foreskin, he perceives a real mutilation of his genital, a perception which may then have consequences similar to the lack of a penis in the female child, though usually they are less severe. An operation on the penis at a later age sometimes leads to the same results.

In this connection, we must expect criticism from those analysts who conceive of the wish for a penis and of penis envy as acquired reactions and of secondary importance (Horney, Jones, et. al.). We still have to wait for the final decision on who is right in this matter. However, in my opinion, analytic exploration in just these cases of inhibitions and impairments of function which are consequences of the fate of infantile genital activity show clearly how strongly and lastingly the narcissistic injury caused by the lack of a penis interferes with ego development. We should not forget that inborn or very early acquired bodily injuries have a lasting influence upon ego development and may lead to over-compensations and inhibitions. Adler's theory of organ inferiority is based on this observation. However, our observations teach us that the psychic reactions to these injuries are of much smaller significance than those to the narcissistic injury caused by the lack of a penis. I cite Freud: "The only bodily organ which is really regarded as inferior is the atrophied penis, a girl's clitoris" (1932, p. 65). So Adler has considered one motive, valid in female development, to be the basis for all mental processes *(pars pro toto)*. Here the question arises whether there are other forms of narcissistic injury beside the lack of a penis which may bring about a devaluation of genital activity and an ego restriction. The answer is yes. In the analysis of patients of both sexes we regularly encounter the same monotonous complaints about childhood: the painful disappointment of being unable to fulfill all libidinal wishes toward the objects, of feeling the immaturity of the genital apparatus which the child seems to be aware of in comparing himself with adults. The little child wants to be "grown up," to do and experience what the adults do, and he continually meets which his powerlessness to compete with them successfully.[6] This injury is a general one to which every human being is subject. It is a consequence of the biphasic onset of sexuality. The first flourishing period of the drives is destined to decline. In the analysis of male patients one often finds this devaluating disappointment at the bottom of castration anxiety as a factor causing renunciation of genital activity. The stronger it is, the more tenacious is the change in masturbation and the more inaccessible is the neurotic disturbance consequent on it. In women the same process is fused with the disillusionment of lacking a penis. Both sources of narcissistic injury seem to be of paramount importance.

Nevertheless, in this general character of the impossibility of satisfying infantile sexual desires we have found a factor which may provoke an impairment of narcissism in men as well and which may lead to an inhibition of functions. In these cases we also observe a renunciation of the ego in order to avoid the experience of its own helplessness.

However, there certainly exists still another life experience which may cause a narcissistic injury to children of both sexes and have severe aftereffects. It is a trivial, well-known, ordinary experience. However, its explanation embarrasses us. It is the privation of love of the object felt by the little child even when surrounded by loving and devoted parents. This phenomenon is to be observed by every analyst and educator. We have to consider how to explain why this feeling of loss of love (because every delay of satisfaction is experienced as a loss) can lead to a narcissistic injury. According to Freud's early presentations (for instance, an "Instincts and Their Viccissitudes," 1915), object love emerges from the narcisstic reservoir in which all libido is stored in the beginning. A renunciation of the love for the object causes the libido to withdraw and to recathect the narcissistic position. After superficial consideration one might

---

[6] See Horney (1932). In this paper Horney stresses a disturbance of the little boy's self-esteem. However, her view related to this point deviates considerably from mine.

52

conclude that hostility toward an object would strengthen the narcissistic cathexis. However, in the little child we encounter just the opposite; a disappoinment in object love disturbs the narcissistic equilibrium. This seeming contradiction is easily solved if we take into account the fact that the form of object love in a little child is different from its form in an adult potent man. The latter is a real, actively directed cathexis of the object representation. The little child's object attachment develops out of the infant's bodily dependence on the mother and is still a passively directed surrender. The child wants to be loved as it formerly was fed and cared for. In Chapter 2, I tried to point out that the inner struggle between libido and destructive drives forces the person to maintain his narcissism at a certain level in order to escape self-destruction. Apparently the child's narcissism, though quantavely strong, is still unstable and free-floating in connection with the as yet feebly established ego organization. Moreover, a certain amount of libido is used to bind aggression aroused by disappointments. I further suggested that being loved leads to a strengthening of narcissism and that the first object ties are of a passive nature. Every disappointment, then, damages the drive equilibrium, and a striving to be loved comes to the fore again. To avoid misunderstanding I want to stress that a desire to be loved can be pursued by active behavior. This behavior, however, does not change the passive *aim* and its satisfaction strengthens narcissism.

The special nature of infantile love explains part of the little child's demeanor. He is strongly dependent upon this special form of love as well as upon the first object, which provides him with the satisfactions accompanying feeding and caring procedures, that is, upon the mother (or her substitute). Observations of infants confirm this state of affairs. The object tie with the aim of being loved, admired, cared for is later solved and exchanged for a new object which promises more satisfaction. There is only one constant attachment, the one to the mother. The weaker the ego organization is, the stronger must be the tie to the mother. Only the gradual consolidation of the ego organization permits a loosening of the passive form of love and prepares the way for the active cathexis of a love object. The final shape of active love does not appear until adolescence, when the love partner is taken possession of in accordance with the maturing of the genital apparatus.

The form of infantile love described here is at the same time the exquisitely female one. This is in accordance with the popular saying that a feminine woman is childish in her love life. Anatomy and the productive function of the woman determine her passive attitude and she finds in it a compensation for her damaged narcissism as well. Of course, active love toward her partner is also present, depending on the masculine trend in her development. A certain passivity is also maintained in the man's adult love life.[7]

To come back to early infantile development: the strong, passively directed dependence on object love is partly due to the relative weakness of the ego. At

[7] It goes without saying that this sketchy picture of certain vicissitudes of human love life does not cover all of the complicated and many-sided manifestations of love. I mentioned only some peculiarities which are relevant to the influence of disappointments on narcissism.

the same time the ego weakness is the cause of an oversensititveness to disappointments, which may bring about intolerable narcissistic injuries. Frustrations are not merely painful losses of love, they may also disturb the inner drive equilibrium through narcissistic damage. As a consequence of lack of satisfaction from the side of the objects, drive processes may have a similar effect, for instance, the narcissistic injury connected with the discovery of the lack of a penis in little girls.

The point at which the drive frustration starts is highly important for the later development of the personality. If the disturbance occurs mainly between ego and object relation, we encounter anxiety about loss of love, which causes repression or renunciation. If the narcissistic ego cathexis is impaired, we have to expect more severe disturbances that are more resistive to any influence. It is a process similar to that of infantile masturbation. If masturbatory activity is given up under the impact of fear of the educators or of the superego, the ensuing inhibitions will be more accessible to therapeutic influence than in the case where masturbation is renounced as a consequence of the lack of a penis. We become aware of the fact that alongside the consideration of quantitative processes the topographic viewpoint is of equal significance.

This simple state of affairs seems to be more complicated in our analytic practice. There are only a few narcissistic injuries independent of object relations, namely, the inadequacy of the little child's genital satisfaction in general and the "inferiority" of the little girl's clitoris in particular.

The other narcissistic impairments already described are closely attached to object relations and often insolubly fused with them. During treatment we get the impression that the one group of impairments could come into existence only through the interference of the other group.

I come back once more to the history of my female patient. I want to stress again that the suppression of masturbation owing to her sense of having an inferior organ (the clitoris) became established only after a period of obstinate masturbation which followed her experience of being despised by her playmate. Here we have to ask a critical question: Are not those authors right who maintain that the little girl's penis is only secondary and overvalued in its significance by Freud and others? In our patient is not the feeling of being rejected the main motive for renouncing masturbation and not so much the penis envy as suggested by me? The question is rightly put. We know cases of little girls in whom the two groups of factors merge, for instance, a case in which the female child has acquired her penis envy in the observation of a younger brother who she thinks is more loved by the mother just because he possesses a penis. Here disappointment in love and disappointment in having an "inferior" genital blend and the effects of the two events are almost indistinguishable.

In the endeavor to decide this question I nevertheless have to agree with Freud's view. In the analysis of my girl patient, I was strongly impressed by the little girl's reaction to the little seducer's rejection. However, the continued investigation of her childhood period, and also the patient's reaction to the different discoveries during analysis, indicated clearly that the penis envy was the decisive factor in her neurosis. After the period in which the little girl was rejected she took refuge in an intensified masturbation in which her feminine wishes were repressed and her masculinity was reinforced. She gave up genital activity only after she had gradually succeeded in accepting the fact that she would not get a penis. These connections were completely affirmed by the therapeutic results. In the first period of the analysis the experiences of seduction and rejection were brought to consciousness and revived. The working through of this material freed the patient from her sexual inhibitions and led her to a normal feminine love life. However, as already described, the work inhibition resisted any therapeutic influence. Only after long and difficult work in the analysis did the details of her masturbation period and the painful experience of feeling her bodily "inferiority" come to the fore. This narcissistic injury could finally be mastered. Only after this could the patient take up masturbation again, and next her work inhibition disappeared.

There are other experiences which seem to prove the fundamental significance of the wish for a penis in the lives of women. In the development toward complete and full femininity, the wish for a penis soon loses its importance. Where there is a clear masculine tendency, it is of great significance. The penis is the exponent of masculine, active tendencies and the lack of this organ hinders their discharge and damages the ego organization through injury of its narcissistic cathexis. We must mention in this connection that aggressive impulses (which are close to activity) are discharged in masturbation as well. In the "masculine" childhood period of masturbation my patient could live out a number of hostile impulses and vengeful feelings. The renunciation of masturbation then closed these outlets for aggression. The little child could thereafter do no more than turn these inhibited aggressions toward her own person. As I pointed out in Chapter 2, the aggressive tendencies turned inward threaten the inner equilibrium and the narcissistic cathexis of the ego organization. The passive dependence on the object (or superego) then becomes stronger and the danger of a new narcissistic injury through disappointment (or guilt feelings) grows. Nunberg (1932) described similar processes in a different context.

A last, but important, question is: When does a frustration from an object lead only to the experience of loss of love and when does it result in a narcissistic injury as well?

Apart from the already-mentioned quantities of drive demands, an age factor comes into play. If the frustrations occur in the first weeks or months of life, when the infant's ego organization is still very unstable, a narcissistic disturbance seems to be unavoidable. These privations can be of a somatic nature, for instance, hunger, severe illness, etc., or of a psychic nature if there is a lack of care, love, or tenderness from the mother's side. If the earliest infantile period is relatively undisturbed, healty, and satisfying, a sufficiently strong narcissistically cathected ego organization and a sound ego development may come about. Frustrations and traumata occuring in later childhood are more likely to be experienced as loss of love and to be overcome more easily and more quickly.

Summary

In all mental processes a given though unmeasurable drive intensity seems to exercise an optimal influence upon ego organization. If this particular intensity is discharged, it allows the ego a maximum of functioning.

The discharge of a greater quantity of drive energy causes a "poisoning" of the ego, paralyzing a number of ego functions. The process is comparable to the poisoning of bodily functions through an overdose of pharmacological matter. On the other hand, the discharge of too small a quantity of drive energy may result in a similarly paralyzing influence upon ego activities. Here we find a somatic analogy as well. We must expect disturbances of ego functions in all cases where the optimal discharge of drive intensity does not occur. Whether this happens or not is dependent on a number of different factors.

The first factor is the absolute drive intensity. If it is augmented by normal or pathological bodily processes (e.g., puberty, menopause, somatic illnesses), an overwhelming of ego functions may be the result. If the absolute drive intensity remains from the very beginning under a certain level, we see that a normal development of ego functions is not possible at all.

The second factor is the relative drive intensity, that is, the relation between id strength and ego strength. If the ego organization is a relatively feeble one, it is easily overwhelmed by the id. If a relatively strong ego encounters the same id demand, we can observe two different results: (1) the ego is able to allow a discharge of drive energy that provides an optimum of ego functioning; (2) the ego overshoots its aim and represses too much drive energy, which causes disturbances of functions. The ego can be brought to such an excessive effort, first, in order to avoid a conflict with the id, for instance, in cases where the given drive impulse is blended with a prohibited or painful tendency; second, in order to avoid a conflict with the superego (because of guilt feelings, fear of conscience); and third, in order to forestall a narcissistic disturbance or to deny a narcissistic injury.

Here we become aware of the fact that it is not only a question of relative intensities that decides whether an optimal functioning of the ego organization comes about or not. A third factor is the topographic starting point of the reaction to a given drive activity. This factor is comparable to a somatic process as well. Several chemicals are poisonous only for special body parts, for instance, particular regions of the brain or the musculature of the heart, whereas they may be harmless for other organs. In the same way it may happen that a drive impulse could be mastered quantitatively by the ego if it did not starts its action on a special part of the ego organization, for instance, on the relation of the ego to an extremely severe superego, or on a point of special narcissistic vulnerability. According to our observations, this last occurrence is of particular significance. We saw, that a drive impulse that provokes a narcissistic injury has to be warded off by the ego with extraordinary force. Consequently it can be brought back to consciousness only with extreme difficulty and sometimes not at all. The ego often has to pay for its victory with a severe impairment of its achievements. Apparently a sound libidinal cathexis of the ego organization is the first and most important condition for mental health. Of course, narsissicm must not be fixed, immobile one (as, for instance, in psychoses). The ego has to have at its disposal a certain quantity of mobile energy in order to be able to communicate with the environment in an undisturbed way. If this condition is fulfilled, the ego's undamaged narcissism allows the personality inner and outer freedom and independence. These qualities can raise the person to great and important achievements, if certain talents are present.

5. Masochism and Narcissism

(1937)

It has always been difficult to understand masochistic behavior in men. The idea of pleasurable suffering is hard to accept. However, psychoanalytic observation reveals the fact that a pleasure gain from suffering does exist. It is inherent in masochistic experience. In the activities of masochistically perverted persons and in the masochistic fantasies of many neurotics, the pleasure gain is conscious. In persons suffering from unconscious guilt feelings and the need for punishment, we must conclude from their behavior that the chastisement is longed for and provides pleasure.

We may study the problem of masochism under two headings:

(1) The first centers on the question of what factors make a person look for unpleasure, suffering, and pain in order to find satisfaction.

(2) The second point is: how can we explain that unpleasure, suffering, and pain can become pleasurable; how can this phenomenon be consistent with the nature of the drives?

It may be that the latter problem will never completely lose its mystery. Freud elaborates it in "The Economic Problem of Masochism" (1924a). In that paper Freud assumes a primary erotogenic masochism to be the basis of every masochistic experience. The latter is seen as biologically and constitutionally founded, as "an infantile physiological mechanism which ceases to operate later on" (p. 163); its explanation cannot be achieved without profound consideration. In the same article Freud states his opinion that primary masochism may be "evidence of, and a remainder from, the phase of development in which the coalescence, which is so important for life, between the death instinct and Eros took place" (p. 164). According to this assumption masochism should be seen as a portion of the destructive drive, still active in the inner world and fused with libido. As a consequence of this fusion it should have become a representative of the pleasure principle. These assumptions about the origin of primary masochism follow from psychoanalytic drive theory. As we are, for the time being, ignorant of the organic nature of the drives, we have nothing to add to this hypothesis.

Primary masochism or self-destruction is not observable in analytic practice. According to Freud, it works inside, silent and soundless. Masochistic behavior in infants is seldom or never seen. The infant reacts to pain and frustration with obvious unpleasure and tries to escape them. If the baby damages himself, it is

See also Chapter 26.

usually because of his lack of knowledge about real dangers. Expressions of masochism which we can observe in analytic practice are outcomes of complicated mental processes. They belong to the so-called secondary masochism, in the shape of feminine and moral masochism. We many assume that the infantile form of primary erotogenic masochism, which Freud believed disappears later on, will not always or completely be subject to this fate. Apparently it can be preserved in a smaller or greater intensity. However, it is exclusively the secondary masochism which is open to observation by means of its psychic representations. The economic processes leading to secondary masochism are well known. Those portions of the destructive drive which are directed toward the outer world can be turned inward in certain circumstances, thus constituting secondary masochism. In what follows I will limit myself exclusively to phenomena of secondary masochism.

This leads us automatically to our first question: What factors make a person search for masochistic satisfaction, accompanied by unpleasure, suffering, and pain? In other words, at what moment and through what events does secondary masochism develop?

I propose to turn our attention to a masochistic fantasy often encountered in psychoanalytic work. Freud remarked that masochism has an especially intimate relation to femininity. It is therefore understandable that I choose a female's fantasy which we very often observe in little girls who have begun to notice the anatomical difference between the sexes. The fantasy accompanies masturbation, as I have pointed out in Chapter 4. It reads: "I was once in possession of a penis; however, I am deprived of it as a punishment for having masturbated." This fantasy can persist into puberty and often be retained long afterward. In the analysis of adult women it can resist every therapeutic influence with astonishing tenacity.

The devaluation of environmental prohibitions, the reduction of the superego's cruel severity, do not change the fantasy. We finally become aware of the fact that the masochistic fantasy, the painful idea of being punished for a misdeed, is less intolerable than the acceptance of a physical defect, of an always present inferiority of one's own personality. (Edoardo Weiss [1932] was concerned with the same problem.) The notion "I was deprived of my penis" restores the person's intactness in the past. This fantasy appears to provide some satisfaction. However, it is incapable of abolishing the present disappointment and the narcissistic injury resulting from the observation of the "defect." Apparently an additional pleasure gain is necessary for diminishing the unpleasure, and it is found in the pleasurable idea of punishment and suffering. Thus the little girl's masochistic fantasy has come into being to alleviate the pain of a narcissistic injury (the lack of a penis). In other words, the little girl gropes for pleasure gain from the idea of being punished in order to escape the much greater unpleasure of feeling injured. The drive process involved is the following: the narcissistic injury raises anger and rage, and these aggressions, which cannot be sufficiently employed in the outer world, are turned inward and used for masochistic pleasure gain.

This outcome is a very simple one. From the very beginning, psychoanalysis has observed a close relationship between narcissism and masochism on the one side and between masochism and femininity on the other side.

The study of the genesis of this masochistic fantasy provides the observer with still another very important insight: the significant role played by narcissistic injuries in mental development. The tenacity with which the fantasy of being punished is retained demonstrates the strength of the effect of a narcissistic injury and of the necessity to deny it or cover it up.

It seems to be significant in many respects that this injury originates in penis envy in little girls.

Here we must consider a critical question: Is not the origin of the little girl's masochistic fantasy simply the expression of a guilt feeling that results from prohibited aggressive and libidinal whishes discharging themselves in masturbatory activity? Many fantasies of being punished certainly serve the alleviation of guilt feelings. They were described by Freud many years ago in "A Child Is Being Beaten" (1919). In the little girl the fantasy reads. "I am beaten by my father." Here the idea of being beaten is the punishment for the libidinal oedipal wish as well as the regressive substitute for it. In analytic practice we learn that the effect of this masochistic fantasy, which may inhibit the love life of the adult woman, usually disappears if the analysis succeeds in lifting the repression of the oedipal strivings, in annulling the superego's prohibitions, and in removing the neurosis that is rooted in the oedipus complex.

The above-described fantasy, however, has a quite different origin, though it may happen that it provides the basis for the fantasy of being beaten by the father. The earlier fantasy of "I was deprived of my penis as a punishment for having masturbated" does *not* originate in the oedipal phase. It dates from the time of the preoedipal phase in which the superego was not yet established, and consequently fear of the superego was still lacking. At that time the conscience's forerunner, the fear of loss of love and of punishment, caused the drive restriction, and inner guilt feelings could scarcely play a role.

In the phallic phase of *pre*oedipal development, the little girl is concerned with her wish for a penis. Narcissistic needs are prevalent and the object which plays a role in this period is the mother. It is also the mother who is made reponsible for the lack of a penis, "I was deprived of my penis" properly reads, "My mother has taken it from me." In contradistinction to the oedipal situation in which the tender father attachement is preserved, the outcome of this preoedipal phase is characterized by a strong hostility toward the mother and an abandonment of the mother as a love object. It is the stage in which the libidinal wishes are transferred to the father, thus preparing for the oedipus complex.

The idea of being castrated as a punishment for masturbation still serves to do away with the unpleasurable idea of being a defective person, and is not yet the expression of a loving surrender to the father. We must now ask how the different genesis of the two forms of fantasy reveals itself in analytic practice. The answer is the following: in our therapeutic endeavor, we learn that the fantasies of being punished that stem from the oedipus complex are relatively easy to influence. But the masochistic castration fantasies that serve to avoid narcissistic injuries are clung to tenaciaously and often cannot be removed.

In Chapter 4 I came to a similar conclusion regarding therapeutic influence on neurotic inhibitions. There I pointed out that in cases where a neurotic inhibition emerged as a consequence of the ego's anxiety vis-à-vis superego demands or of the conflict between ego and id (for instance, in the case of sexualization of an ego activity), the changes for a therapeutic success are much greater than in cases where an inhibition comes about in order to avoid or to deny a narcissistic injury.

To summarize: A very early starting point (perhaps the first?) in the origin of masochistic behavior is the flight from a narcissistic injury. The unpleasure aroused by such an injury is greater than the unpleasure of punishment, suffering, and pain, and the former is softened by a masochistic pleasure gain. At the same time, this condition may be the reason for a tenacious clinging to masochistic behavior. Later on, when the superego has been established, the ego's need for punishment can reinforce the masochistic structure which originated earlier. In analytic treatment we discover how important it is to know which of the sources the masochistic phenomena are predominantly based on. I have already illustrated these events with the fantasy of being punished in little girls; this frequently encountered fantasy reads: "I once had a penis; I have lost it as a penalty for having masturbated." The emergence of this fantasy can also be described as "the use of aggression turned inward in order to gain masochistic pleasure and to flee from the greater unpleasure consequent upon damage of the narcissistic libido position and upon hostility and rage which cannot be discharged sufficiently." Here I want to make the point that these happenings are of general significance in the development of little girls. In normal development they may be present in small intensities and serve the mastering of penis envy. In this way they provide the necessary amount of masochism inherent in normal femininity. In cases where an excessive narcissistic vulnerability, perhaps combined with a strong "masculine," bisexual Anlage is present, this method of protection may fail to undo the injury. The outcome may be either a pathologically strengthened masochism followed by neurotic phenomena, sexual inhibition, perversions, and character disorders, or reaction formations like sadism and reinforced masculine behavior.

We now come to another question: Is it only in women that we meet with a narcissistic injury as an early source of masochistic phenomena? The origin of masochism in men is doubtless a more complicated process than in women. Masochism runs counter to normal male development. It is sadism that belongs to "masculinity." Nevertheless, we often observe masochistic fantasies, perversions, and behavior in men. We term it feminine masochism and connect it with feminine, homosexual tendencies. We are well acquainted with masochistic fantasies and acts developed out of the positive and negative oedipal constellation, especially in connection with passive homosexual love for the father. They express a need to be punished for prohibited libidinal and aggressive tendencies like the little girl's later fantasies of being beaten. However, in men we often find as a prestage of these oedipal fantasies an earlier narcissistic form, just as in girls. In one case I observed a male patient who experienced his circumcision as a severe narcissistic injury. The result was a flight into a feminine masochistic castration fantasy. We are not surprised to encounter the idea of a damaged penis as the starting point for the narcissistic injury. In other cases, different experiences, as for instance the boy's comparison of his penis and its erections with the father's penis or the unsuccesful rivalry with older boys in connection with urination and masturbation, may lead to a severe narcissistic injury. It is well known that similar painful events may cause feminine masochistic behavior in boys. The anxiety about not possessing a well-functioning genital, in short, "castration anxiety," is the factor which in its outcome runs parallel to the penis envy in little girls. It is possible that these processes are less common in men than in women. However, a third form of masochistic behavior, called moral masochism, can easily be observed in both sexes.

Moral masochism forces a person to behavior that leads to self-damage, to unsuccessful performances, to suffering and pain. In analytic treatment moral masochism causes the patient to react to a solution of a neurotic symptom with a worsening instead of an improvement of his condition. Freud called it the "negative therapeutic reaction." The patient is dominated by a need for punishment (an "unconscious guilt feeling"). It is a process which takes place between ego and superego. This need for punishment can be one of the most powerful enemies of therapeutic endeavor. It can resist every influence, notwithstanding the patient's brilliant understanding of the unconscious causes of his symptoms. I have observed that with analytic exploration of the deeper causes of moral masochism one encounters differences in various patients' reactions. There are cases in which a prolonged and laborious analysis succeeds in removing the greater part of this need for punishment, restoring, at least partly, the patient's health. On the other hand, we encounter patients who resist every therapeutic influence; they are unable to renounce even part of their suffering. We then find the following explanation for the difference in result: the need for punishment stems from a tension between ego and superego, as already mentioned. The superego (conscience) inflicts punishments on the person in taking over the role of the demanding and prohibiting parental figures. However, it may prove to be much more severe and cruel than the parents ever were. We know the cause of this occurrence to be the process of turning inward aggressions which the child cannot discharge in the outer world. They lead to secondary masochism. A part of these aggressions, however, is invested in the superego, which now becomes cruel, torturing, and sadistic in its relation to the ego. The latter reacts masochistically toward the superego. The two processes, sadism of the superego and masochism of the ego, supplement each other, and finally lead to a need for punishment, self-damage and, in analytic treatment, the negative therapeutic reaction.[1]

The way in which the aggression turned inward is distributed is of great significance. The differences can be studied by looking for the intensity and the tenacity of the resistance in analytic treatment. Cases in which the larger part of the aggression is invested in the superego will offer much better opportunities

---

[1] Nunberg (1932) has drawn attention to this connection on several occasions.

for therapeutic influence. Sometimes a patient accepts the analyst as a substitute for parental and environmental demands. If the analyst then succeeds in softening the severity and cruelty of the superego, it may become possible to restore some of the ego functions, and a change in the personality and a benefical influence on the patient's suffering may be the outcome. In cases where the inner aggressions are invested in the masochistically deformed ego, providing masochistic pleasure gain, every therapeutic attempt seems to be doomed to fail. Here the mitigation of superego demands and the removal of sexual prohibitions are unable to counteract the ego's masochistic pleasure gain. Therefore it is important to learn to distinguish between those circumstances which cause aggressions to produce a more sadistic superego and those which intensify the ego's masochism.

In some cases it might be a simple distribution in the following way: the superego's sadism emerges from the internalization of the parent's real cruelty and the masochistic ego comes into existence as a consequence of the child's own aggression turned inward. However, in other cases the process is a quite different one. I observed the case of a young man who had to spoil every success in his profession. The relentlessness of his superego in preventing any success did not correspond to parental severity. On the contrary, the parents had been full of understanding and very liberal with the little boy. His superego had doubtless absorbed a great deal of his own aggression and demanded the surrender of his ego. He had produced a fantasy in which the punishment was a regressive substitute for libidinal oedipal wishes (a process described by Freud in "The Economic Problem of Masochism"). Apart from surrender, the ego showed a strong opposition toward the superego as well. In the analysis the patient tried, with the analyst's support, to renounce the self-damaging attitude. The working through of both positive and negative oedipus complex finally brought about a change in the patient's behavior and a good deal of the longed-for success.

However, in two other cases which seemed to be similar ones, a male and a female case, I learned that although removal of guilt feelings attendant upon the oedipus was, to be sure, followed by the acceptance of generally more realistic moral demands, a change of the masochistic behavior did not occur. In the female patient I finally discovered the above-mentioned fantasy of the penis being cut off as a penalty for masturbatory activity, a fantasy which was adhered to in order to avoid the narcissistic injury of feeling that her body was defective. The ego's masochistic attitude toward the superego corresponded to the secret idea: "Unknown powers (or fate) punish and damage me; therefore I myself am not inferior or defective." The patient was, unconsciously, highly ambitious and tried to deny the painful failure of some of her daring plans in a way similar to her attempts to do away with her penis envy in childhood. In the male patient a similar process came to light. He suffered from a strong feeling of inferiority that had its origin in rivalry with an older brother in childhood. The brother already had erections at a time when the patient was not yet able to produce them. The patient never overcame this injury. Every failure of ambitious desires in later times caused equal pain, which could be alleviated only by imagining that he was maltreated by fate and by drawing masochistic pleasure from this idea.

In summary, I would like to say once more that in many cases of moral masochism we discover, behind the wish to be punished originating from the forbidden oedipal object relationship, a turning toward masochistic pleasure gain in order to escape an injury to the narcissistic libidinal position, with the accompanying rage impulses experienced as being dangerous. Renouncing this masochistic attitude would require a confrontation of these painful injuries and the realization of the powerlessness to undo them and to change reality. We know from analytic practice how difficult it is to achieve these requirements. In most cases the patient prefers keeping his painful masochistic behavior to exposing himself to the painful feeling of being powerless. His pleasure gain, then, is reduced to the dubious masochistic satisfactions.

We may conclude that a relation between masochism and narcissism is present not just in a single fantasy of little girls. We have to add that narcissistic disturbances are of etiological sifnificance in many forms of masochistic expression in both sexes.

However, we started our investigation of this subject with the study of the little girl's masochistic fantasy connected with her penis wish and penis envy. It becomes clear that in studying mental developmental processes we time and again come upon the basic importance of the castration complex. A critical objection is whether it is not a blind onesidedness to ascribe a central significance to penis envy in the woman's mental life. However, careful analytic observations invalidate this criticism. Of course a number of other narcissistic injuries befall the little child, for instance, situation in which jealousy is aroused, where feelings of not being loved and of being deserted emerge. All of them are highly important. The complicated object relationships of the preoedipal phase with its intense ambivalence are responsible for many developmental processes. However, the material invariably comes back to penis envy as a central point. It is from this point that the development into normal femininity begins. Its successful or unsuccessful solution determines whether the little girl will mature into a healty woman or whether neurotic disturbances, an unmastered masculinity complex, or a masochistic attitude in life will come into existence. The inherent difficulty of mastering the narcissistic injury of the lack of a penis emerges not only in the analyses of our female patients; it also seems to express itself in the analytic literature. There have been many attempts to diminish the importance of the penis wish and penis envy in female psychic life. It is given a secondary place, or is avoided by attaching a greater significance to earlier or later experiences. Not only women but men, too, have participated in these endeavors to interpret the phenomenon differently. The resistance of men to accepting the importance of penis envy may be explained by the already-mentioned fact that in male mental life a comparable concern is of equal importance to the penis wish in females. It is a man's concern about the intactness of his genital, the vulnerable narcissistic estimation of his masculinity, in other words, the castration complex and its aftereffects. Man's castration fear apparently enables him to understand empathically the woman's penis envy. In both sexes it seems to be the castration complex which inspires the misinterpretation of the outcomes of penis wish and penis envy. It goes without saying that these assumptions cannot prove the correctness or incorrectness of the different theories. Freud, in a footnote to "Female Sexuality" points to the fact that in such cases "The use of analysis as a weapon of controversy can clearly lead to no decision" (1931b, p. 230).

The question why many of the most important normal as well as pathological mental processes often crystallize around the activities performed with the genital apparatus seems to be answered in principle by Freud. The contradictory interests of the individual and the species are manifested in the functions of the genitals. The species is preserved by propagation, which requires tasks running counter to the individual's own striving for pleasure and for the diminution of tension. As Freud puts it, "making use of libido in the service of the female function is most difficult to achieve, libido being an active urge in itself." Perhaps here we come upon the explanation of the fact that the development of women towards femininity is a highly complicated and arduous task.

6. Considerations of Methodology in Relation to the Psychology of Children

(1939)

A little while ago an acquaintance of mine, the mother of a two-and-a-half-year-old boy, said to me: "I must tell you something quite extraordinary about my little son. For the last few days he has refused to put on his knickers and has kept saying that he wants to wear a dress-a pretty dress, like Lini and Evi." (Lini and Evi are two playmates of his.) "Yesterday I went into his room and found him with flushed cheeks and sparkling eyes, playing with his indiarubber doll, which he had not taken any notice of for some time. He was tucking it into his blouse so that his body looked quite fat and then squeezing and pushing it out again, to the accompaniment of straining movements and noises, as through he were trying to defaecate." His mother, who had a great deal of insight, added: "I know why he was doing it. A friend of mine is expecting a baby quite soon, and I have often said to her that I should like to have another baby too. On those occasions Walter will look at me with great attention, and, now I come to think of it, with a certain amount of concern as well."

I asked my acquaintance what the child's attitude to his environment was. She told me that he was very much attached to her and nearly always preferred being with her to being with anyone else, but that lately he had now and then suddenly left her side and run to other people. She said: "When he is annoyed with me or feels that I have neglected him, he will go to his father or to our maid and behave in a very affectionate way to them." She went on to express anxiety about whether such behavior was not "abnormal." She had always understood that little boys loved their mothers and were their fathers' rivals. But Walter was behaving not at all like a little man, but like a girl. Was it possible he would turn into a weak and effeminate person? All I could do was to tell her to be patient and to wait and see how the child's development progressed.

About three quarters of a year later the mother told me that Walter had changed to a remarkable degree. His games of pregnancy had completely stopped. He was ardently and passionately devoted to her, always wanting to escort her and to protect her. He behaved, in fact, like her *cavalier servant*. His father seemed to be merely a nuisance to him and he had lost all trace of his clinging tenderness toward him. He was disagreeable to him and hated him and was glad when he went away. As regards his body functions, he had become quite "grown-up." He despised the chamber pot and went to the water closet instead. The only thing was that he masturbated at night rather often.

Unfortunately, circumstances did not permit me to follow the further course of this little boy's history in a systematic way. I heard that he did well at school and

66

achieved independence quite early. He reacted to the birth of a little sister a good deal later, when he was nine, by having an accident which nearly cost him his life; but he was affectionate with her and took care of her.

My readers will by wondering why I have troubled to give this doubtless instructive but quite commonplace story of a child. I have done so because I think that it illustrates and confirms very clearly certain findings which we have been able to make only as a result of long and hard analytic work with adults and older children.

I have in mind, among other instances, the case of a young man of thirthy who came to me for analysis. He was highly intelligent and well educated, had had scientific training, and was very successful in his work, but he suffered from complete sexual impotence. He had never had sexual relations with a woman. After a long period of analysis and in the face of strong resistances, he produced the following recollection from his early childhood. When he was between two and a half and three years old he had a passion for putting on dresses belonging to his little girl cousins. He used to walk around in them with pride, and obviously not only behaved, but felt like a girl. On the night before his fourth birthday — he could fix the date exactly — he had a dream, followed by certain experiences, which showed that some time after his "girlish" behavior he had harbored very intense and bold feelings of love toward his mother, but that they had ended in disappointment. The dream consisted of his performing the sexual act with his mother, and ended with his urinating in bed. The experiences consisted of being laughed at and made to feel ashamed by the others when he woke up next day, and of being threatened with punishment by his nurse for having been dirty and having wet his bed "like a baby." This experience caused him to give up his "masculine" attitude once more and to become a quiet, passive, and shy child with a strong inclination toward his father. My suspicion that the experience had had a fateful effect upon his subsequent development was confirmed by the following remarkable therapeutic success which took place in him. On the day after the recollection of the events of his fourth birthday had come up in his analysis (and this did not happen until much long and difficult analytic work had been done) he attempted to perform coitus and was successful. His analysis had various further results; and in the end he got married. He acquitted himself well as a married man, felt happy, and was able to cope with the external world which at one time had seemed to be full of insurmountable difficulties and demands. His feminine passive attitude hardly interfered with his life at all.

The similarity between the history of my patient and that of Walter is quite obvious. Both children passed through a phase in which they wanted to be girls; and in both this was succeeded by a phase of true "masculine" behavior, which was followed in the case of my patient by a return to a passive attitude later on. I have presented these two accounts, which are not at all unusual, not only to describe the case history of an analytic patient with a parallel taken from direct observation of a child and to point out their similarities. My real reason for doing it is a different one and is connected with the occasion of the appearance of this birthday number of *The International Journal of Psycho-Analysis*. It seems to me that the best way of marking that occasion and of doing honor to Ernest Jones is to pursue a line of through which he himself has often followed in the course of his scientific studies.

Jones has made more than one important and felicitous contribution to our knowledge of the early developmental phases of the child. At the same time, he has been foremost in stressing the desirability of bringing out into the open as much as possible the differences which exist between our method of viewing the material which we obtain from the analysis and observation of children and the theories which we build upon that material; for in this way, he thinks, we shall be most likely to understand and clear up the points in dispute.

Accordingly, I should like in this paper to attempt to put before the reader a problem of this kind as plainly as I can. We are still, I think, very far from having solved every problem concerning the young child, and our knowledge is especially lacking in regard to the psychological events of the very first months of his life. We can, of course, find out somethings about the subject from a phenomenological point of view by means, for instance, of nonanalytical child psychology, which sets out to record and collect all the child's reactions to every kind of stimulus, and so on, But we can at most only guess at the sort of instinctual manifestations that go on in the young infant and the sort of way in which his ego, as yet quite unfinished, reacts to those stimuli. This is not only because the infant is incapable of telling us in words about his inner life, but because his range of bodily expression is so incomplete too that what he communicates by means of play and action is very little indeed. Bodily expressions of this kind, which in slighly older children can convey so much important knowledge about their instinctual and affective lives, are limited in the infant. I think that a tremendous quantity of detailed and persistent observation of babies in the earliest months of life is needed before we can obtain a trustworthy picture of the situation.

My present contribution, therefore, is intended to take up a certain standpoint in regard to the methodology of the subject rather than to add any new facts to our scanty knowledge of the affective life of the infant. Fenichel (1926) and Waelder (1936) have already made some very important attempts to work out the differences of opinion that exist in this field of research. And although it is the methodological aspect which will principally be emphasized in this paper, we shall find many points of contact between the views put forward by those two writers.

The question which I should like to take up first is that of the relation between what we call the oedipus complex and that period of development which is known as the "preoedipal phase." The idea of the oedipus complex was established by Freud many years ago. He described it as "the fateful combination of love for the one parent and simultaneous hatred for the other as a rival" (1931b, p. 229), and places it in the phallic phase of libidinal development, that is, in that period of expansion of the infant's instinctual life which occurs somewhere between his fourth and sixth years and which is governed by the primacy of genital excitations. We see that Freud is very precise in his characterization of the nature and content of the oedipus complex. But the importance which he attributes to the development of the person does not prevent him from attaching equal importance to the instinctual occurrences and to the object relationships belonging to the earlier, pregenital phases of the child. (These phases, when viewed more particularly from the point of view object relationships, were later on classed together as the pre-oedipal phase.) In those phase, in which the child's instinct obtains their main gratification from the oral and anal zones, he undergoes experiences which are equally important for his subsequent development. It is then, whitout doubt, that his relations to the objects prepare the way for that "fateful conjunction" of love and hate toward his parents as it appears in the oedipal attitude. The various phases are, of course, not sharply separated, with regard to time or the dominant themes. They merge into one another, each succeeding phase taking over something from the one before and each earlier one providing "precursors" for the next.

As we know, many analysts, in particular Jones and his colleagues (Melanie Klein and others), employ the idea of the oedipus complex in a different sense from Freud. They no longer mean by it the "fateful combination" of feelings in regard to the parents which represents the end product and climax of infantile sexual development, but assume that the oedipus complex starts much earlier than Freud supposed. They believe that it often appears as early as the first year of life-at a time, that is, when oral gratification still predominates and the primacy of the genitals has not yet set in, and when there is as yet no hint of the "fateful" fact of the simultaneous love for one parent and hatred of the other. In the opinion of these analysts, the story of little Walter which we have given above would signify that at the early age of two and a half the child was already in the oedipal phase-at a time when, although he certainly chose his mother as his love object, he very easily turned to his father or the maid whenever he felt displeased with her, and when there was as yet no question of genital primacy. According to their views, if I have understood them aright, there would be no radical difference between the little boy's attitude then and his attitude six months later, when, as his mother said, he had become "totally changed" and had assumed toward her the typical role of a young man in love. Moreover, they "transpose back" the oedipus complex to much earlier stages even than those described in the case of Walter. They take it as far back as those quite early object relationship which are a necessary outcome of the physiological dependence of the child upon his mother.

The question I want to put is this: Are we justified from a methodological point of view in alterning Freud's conception of the oedipus complex in the sense described above? My answer to this, I may say at once is "No," and for the following reasons.

Walter's behavior at the age of three was, to use his mother's own words, "totally different" from what it had been at two and a half, both in regard to his object relationships (witness his altered love attitude toward his mother and his new hatred toward his father as a rival) and in regard to the manifestations of his instinctual life. Now there is no doubt, as we have already said, that this typical position of the small boy will contain traces and relics of what he has experienced on earlier levels. It was psychoanalysis which from the very first took special interest in genetic development and was always at pains to explain what existed in the light of what had gone before. But I think it is an error in method to assume that when there is a genetic connection between various events, those events are identical. The fact that A follows B does not mean that A is the same as B.

I should like to give a very simple example here to show how inadmissible such a method of argument is.

A man happened to tell a friend of his that he was very fond of big, high-colored tulips with long stalks. The next day his friend brought him some large tulip bulbs as a present. The man was very much surprised, but his friend was still more surprised at his astonishment. He tried to justify himself by saying that the fine bulbs would turn into wonderful tulips and that having bulbs or flowers in the room came to the same thing. All comparisons are to some extent inadequate, but this one does illustrate one or two points. The hungry baby who wants his mother's breast in order to appease his hunger and to obtain sexual gratification at the oral zone is not, after all, identical with the three- or four-year-old boy who tries to do the same things with his mother as his father does, who would like to kill his father, and who finds an outlet for sexual excitation in masturbation. The tulip bulbs contain all the forces and the material which will enable the flower to grow out of it; but this will happen only if certain conditions are fulfilled, such as that there shall be enough water, earth, air, and light. In the same way, the oedipal boy develops from the infant, but that development, too, depends upon all sorts of circumstances in his external world. Any changes or peculiarities that occur in those circumstances will exert an influence on his development, although its main lines are laid down from the beginning, just as in the case of the tulip its character, color, size, etc., are already contained in the nature of the bulb.

This procedure of "transposing back," or of equating the precursory stage with the final state, has not been confined to the conception of the oedipus complex. It has, I think, been made use of in many theoretical arguments. This is not only inadmissible as a method of thought but has led to a good many mistakes and false conclusions.

Many analytic writers, for instance, tend to "transpose back" the emergence of the superego. They are inclined to deny the fact that the superego springs from the extinct oedipus complex, as described by Freud, and attribute a superego to little children between the ages of one and two, or perhaps even younger. I believe that this procedure too is the result of a tendency to confuse the thing itself with the earlier stages out of which it has evolved. It is doubtless true that in the preoedipal stage children exhibit certain reactions which are similar to the reactions caused by the superego. A child who is being trained in cleanliness may, for instance, show signs of apprehension and look guilty if he is discovered making a mess; and, again, he may give up playing with his excrement, as he used to do with great zest a few months before. But can we fairly ascribe this behavior to the intervention of the superego? Unless we are prepared to apply Freudian terminology indiscriminately to different mental processes, we must reply in the negative. What Freud means by the superego is an agency which has separated off from the ego and which has come into existence through the introjection of object representations and which is already set apart from the real objects. The superego is an endopsychic agency acting more or less independently of the reality demands being made at the particular moment by the objects which are actually present. It may cause the individual to renounce an instinctual gratification without being required to do so by any real person, and even if no one in the external world is noticing whether and how the individual is doing it. However, a little child in the preoedipal phase gives up a gratification not because a part of himself demands this renunciation but because he is afraid of the reactions of his parents-that is, because he is afraid of punishment or loss of love. He may do "wrong" if he knows he will not be found out or if he is on bad terms with his love objects, not needing their love at that particular moment. A command from the superego has to be obeyed without regard to the object, and any disobedience will be followed by an intence sense of guilt and internal torment. If an instinctual renunciation is made because of fear of loss of the object's love, the resulting state is of course a precurser of the subsequent formation of the superego, but an important process of development must still be gone through before the superego can emerge from this early reactive behavior.

We might go back still further. We know that in the fertilized ovum which lodges in the wall of the uterus all the forces and all the preconditions are present which are necessary for the production of an individual belonging to the species of *Homo sapiens*. But we shall not make the mistake of calling that fertilized cell a human being. The same principle applies to the separate parts of the body and the mind. As regards the latter, there exists in each embryo an inborn instinctual disposition which can, under the influence of a variety of internal and external factors, give rise to extremely complicated instinctual constellations. In the same way we must assume that the embryo brings with it into the world the nucleus of a future ego; that the attitudes and forms of reaction of the ego, as it emerges, are subjected to the influence of the environment, until a distinctive personality finally takes shape. But, to return to our simile of the tulip, there is a great difference in actual fact between whether the bulb has reached the bud stage or whether it has grown into a full-blown flower. If the necessary preconditions are lacking, the bud will never become a flower, but only an incomplete and stunted one.

There is a strong temptation to equate a finished psychological phenomenon with the earlier stages out of which it has developed, and to transpose mental products back to a period of life when their existence is not susceptible of proof or disproof. The strength of this temptation is demonstrated by the fact that a good many analysts are inclined to take it as an established event that babies, when they are only a few weeks − or is it days? − old entertain such fantasies as "robbing the mother's body" or "getting out of her father's penis which she has obtained from him in copulation" and other similar notions. Our analysis of children and adults have familiarized us with these and many other fantasies as they have told to us in words and actions, and, in the case of children, in play. What psychoanalysis has endeavored to do from the very first is precisely to trace back fantasies, whishes, and affective reactions like these to earlier periods of development. I think that analysis has succeeded in this complex task. However, Freud has always insisted that in making the attempt we should produce confirmatory evidence for our conclusions, and he has always done so himself. In adult analysis we obtain evidence of this kind from our patients' recollections; and in the observation of children from their play. The two sources of knowledge are complementary and bear each other out. It is true that with infants we can, as has already been said, observe their reactions to stimuli, but so far we have no empirical knowledge whatever upon which to base a judgement about whether any such fantasies as the ones mentioned above are already attached to those reactions or not. We can observe that out of the suckling's need for nourishment there develops later on a psychological attachment to his mother, and we may perhaps be justified in assuming that the unpleasurable stimuli which he experiences, such as deprivation, pain, etc., give rise to aggressive trends in subsequent life. But here, too, we must not confuse a precursory stage with the final state, and we are not justified in equating the child's later fantasy of taking something away from his mother with his earlier reaction to a disturbing stimulus. A very important process of development has to take place before the one stage can emerge from the other. Similar doubts and objections must be felt when we hear the affective states of little children given names that have hitherto been applied only to the gravest pathological conditions in adult persons. It seems to be more than a mere terminological inexactitude that the sorrow which a child shows when his mother leaves the room should be called a melancholia. Here again I think it is a question of confusing the rudiments or part of a thing with the completed whole. Melancholia is a very highly complicated pathological state of mind, which no doubt contains the affect of "mourning" and in which loss of love also plays a role. But nevertheless it is something quite different in its entity from the sadness of a lonely child.

Again, analysis may enable us to discover that a patient who is suffering from paranoia had, in the first years of his life, felt neglected by his mother and had thought her responsible for a great many of his troubles, but we should be making a great mistake if we said that the young child who brings unfair reproaches against his mother was suffering from paranoia or has a paranoid disposition. It seems to me that if we are not continually on our guard against equating later developments with their earlier stages we shall inevitably be led into imagining the existence of mental processes in early periods of life where we have no means of verifying our assumptions empirically. It is owing to this mistake that the genetic-dynamic method of research employed by psychoanalysis (which is legitimate in itself and has always been based on empirical principles) had been brought to a *reductio ad absurdum*, and that the Freudian discoveries concerning the development of the child's mental world have undergone distortions. It is quite evident that the described method of procedure must lead to similar consequences, for by equating early stages with later ones it passes over the developmental processes and thus proves to be a genetic-dynamic method only in appearance. When we study a developmental process we observe what happens to a given phenomenon under the influence of the most varied factors, both internal and external. To equate the initial product with the final one is to ignore the operation of those factors and of the dynamic process. As Waelder has pointed out, the adherents of that school of thought do not give due weight to the influence of reality. And I think we might add that they overlook the existence of a process of development within the individual himself. Just as preanalytic psychology denied that there exists an "unconscious," so do they deny the phenomenon of the dynamic developmental processes in the personality under the influence of external forces.

7. The Preoedipal Phase in the Development of the Male Child

(1946)

In the study of infantile development the data gained from the analysis of male and female patients were accorded different importance in the evolution of psychoanalysis. The first insight into neurotic mechanisms in general were derived from the treatment of women; in *Studies on Hysteria* (Breuer and Freud, 1895) only female patients were described. The case of Dora (Freud, 1905a) gave us the first insight into the impact of infantile events on development.

In a later phase, our knowledge of infantile sexuality was gained in the analysis of patients of both sexes; at that time, however, more was known about boys than about girls. The growth of the oedipus complex and its relation to the phases of pregenital libidinal development and the early object relation to the mother were first described in the male child, but the parallel processes in the girl remained obscure for some time. Similarly, the development of the superego as it relates to the termination of the oedipal conflict and the castration threat was understood as part of the boy's development before the sequence of analogous events in the development of the girl was understood.

In "Some Psychical Consequences of the Anatomical Distinction between the Sexes" Freud (1925) discussed some differences between male and female development and demonstrated that the latter is more complex. The castration complex of the little girl does not obliterate the oedipus complex; rather it proves to be its forerunner; the content of the castration complex of the girl, the penis envy, pushes her into her sexual position as a female. However, the earlier history of these developments remained obscure.

At this point in the history of psychoanalysis insight into the development of the girl came before that of the boy: the preoedipal phase was first studied in connection with female patients. In 1927 this author tried to point out that the female castration complex, and therefore the normal oedipus complex of the woman, was preceded by a negative oedipal constellation (Chapter 1). In these studies stress was laid on libidinal development, on the object relation toward the mother in so far as she is indispensable for the fulfillment of the needs and the desire for love of the child. Freud's study on female sexuality (1931b) taught

After the completion of this paper in Holland, I had the opportunity to read the interesting paper of Ruth Mack Brunswick, "The Pre-oedipal Phase of Libido Development" (1940), in which many similar problems are discussed. Since my own conslusions were arrived at independently during the war years, I did not try to discuss Brunswick's paper here.
See also Chapter 14.

us how full of content, how rich and decisive the pre-oedipal attachment to the mother is in the development of the little girl. We have since succeeded in gaining more detailed knowledge about this period, both in relation to the id of the little girl and to her ego development. In particular, many of the peculiarities of the woman's object relation and of her adult love life are now better understood.

This paper deals with the influence of the preoedipal relation to the mother on the development of the boy, especially from the point of view of the sexual life of the adult male. In approaching this subject we have two sets of expectations. First, since the earliest mother-child relationship is physically and mentally the closest possible between two individuals, traces of it must be found in adult life. Second, the difference between boy and girl must play a part in their development: the little girl has the more complicated development; she must abandon her early attachement to the mother in order to develop into womanhood, whereas the boy need not part from his original love object. Thus we may expect that the influence of the preoedipal phase on the development of female sexuality may be more decisive and overwhelming than on the development of male sexuality. However, we may well expect this influence on male sexuality to be important enough to justify its closer study.

All further considerations must start from one insight: the direct development of male sexuality from the infantile oedipal attachment to the mother to the love life of the adult is threatened by the fact that a negative oedipus complex regularly exists in childhood in addition to the positive one. At one time or other in their development all boys develop a more or less intense loving attachement to the father and a more or less intense rivalry with and hostility to the mother. In this position the boys tend to behave in a way similar to little girls in their normal development. The attachment to the father is, as a rule, a passive feminine one (we can also speak of a homosexual attachment).

The existence of these passive libidinal tendencies must have a prehistory. Our findings indicate that during the preoedipal stage of development these passive libidinal tendencies are satisfied by the mother, who at the same time satisfies the boy's active strivings. In normal development these active strivings predominate and the passive ones are subordinated to them; it is well known that they are of great importance in the social adjustment of the normal male. In cases of pathological development these passive tendencies manifest themselves in three ways. First, they may influence the adult's sexual life as potency disturbances, in the guise of feminine masochistic behavior; or, in extreme cases, they may lead to homosexuality. Second, they may lead to neurotic tendencies. Third, they may cause abnormal character formation.

The analytic exploration of such cases shows that the continuation of the passive relation to the father is due to a fixation in the negative oedipus complex. In prolonged analysis we reach the earlier history of this fixation and we are able to observe the residues of the original passive attachment to the mother. We may therefore say that the passive feminine relation to the father is in the male a second edition of his primitive passive love relation to the mother, in a way similar to that of the girl. The difference is obvious. In the girl, passive attachment falls within normal development; in the boy, it contributes to pathological trends which may later disturb his normal sexuality.

There is still another consequence of the early attachment of the little boy to the mother which can be of decisive importance. Not only the negative oedipus complex, but also the positive oedipal relation has its forerunner in the preoedipal phase: in the active turning of the little boy toward the mother. A fixation at this stage or a regression to it has equally important consequences in the later development of the boy. His sexual life does not become a truly active and manly one; rather, it repeats his early relationship with the mother. Various signs of this relationship can easily be discerned. Its stigmata are the infantile aggressive forms of object relation, which is less libidinal and more narcissistic, intensely ambivalent, generally fluctuating. When passivity plays a considerable part, potency disturbances may occur. Peculiarities of pregenital libidinal development may be persistent. Oral and anal gratifications may be preferred and may lead to perversions. Males of this type behave like infants, whose love for the mother is egoistic, and claim indulgence of their own needs without respecting the needs of the partner.

A specific form of sexual behavior, the separation of sexuality from tenderness, which Freud first described, now seems easier to understand. Men whose behavior takes this form worship a woman whom they dare not possess as a sexual partner; their sexual partner must always be degraded. Freud explained the genesis of this attitude in the following way: the revered and unreachable woman is the beloved mother; since sexual activity has become degraded through prohibition and has become bad and dirty through its link to masturbation, the sexual partner has to be a degraded person. We can now add to this explanation: the admired and honored woman is chosen according to the mother image of the period of the oedipus complex. She is the heiress to the great love of little Oedipus for Jocasta. The degraded sexual partner, on the other hand, is the heiress to the image of the mother of the preoedipal phase; she has inherited the intense hostility that the little boy may have felt for her. That hostility, in turn, stems from his early ambivalence toward the mother and is reinforced by the fact that the mother has later become his rival in his love for the father. The adult man can vent his anger against the degraded sexual object; he can mistreat her, can force her to satisfy all his needs and desires, even perverse ones, and can compel her to attend to his wants as he wished his mother to do when he was a little boy.

At this point we are confronted with a specific question. How can we differentiate in analysis between the material pertaining to the oedipal period and that pertaining to the preoedipal period? This differentiation meets with considerable difficulty under certain circumstances. There are two reasons for this. First, all phases of infantile development overlap; second, a subsequent phase of development is always to a greater or lesser extent used to suppress residues of previous phases. And yet, on more detailed and precise examination of the material we discover many differences in the way in which the material is brought forth. In some instances even the body posture of the patient may be expressive: he may – as was the case with a patient of Paul Federn[1] – actually imitate the posture of the infant.

A young man who had undergone a successful analysis, which to a considerable extent had relieved him of his neurotic work inhibitions, came to me several years later because of a potency disturbance. He gave me an excellent exposition of his case history and of the results of his former treatment, which had revealed the development of his oedipus complex in all details. After some months of treatment with me the patient's behavior in analysis began to change. During the first period of analysis he spoke easily and fluently, in a clear and loud voice, even when transference difficulties emerged, as, for instance, when he was compelled to re-experience his oedipal desires, and also when his transference resistance took other forms. In the second period of analysis his personality changed completely. He began to behave like an infant. His voice became high and childish. He no longer spoke as an adult does, but uttered incomplete and childish words and sentences. His emotions and his demands changed from one minute to another. He wept like a small child and clamored for my support and my love; the next morning he shouted and gave vent to the most intense hostility. This acting out in transference was amalgamated with bits of primitive fantasies, as ambivalent as we know the emotional life of the child to be. These fantasies had an extremely passive content: I should handle him, feed him, nurse him, and satisfy immediately all his needs. These passive fantasies were interspersed with reaction formations: aggressive tendencies appeared and a wealth of suppressed anger and hate crystallized into reproaches and accusations. The slightest change in the tone of my voice, or any movement I might make in my chair, were used in order to produce love fantasies or were taken as occasions for outbursts of invectives. The love fantasies expressed oral and anal tendencies, wishes to be nursed and touched, demands for tenderness and for the satisfaction of exhibitionistic needs.

I gradually succeeded in persuading him that this change was natural and unavoidable. He became interested in the meaning of the change and succeeded in overcoming his narcissistic pride. He thus surrendered to the material which came from deeper layers of the unconscious. In the course of analysis his acting out in the transference was discussed, yet the patient occasionally manifested similar behavior patterns in his relationships with female partners. At the time when I primarily represented the mother whom, in identification with his father, he wished to love but whom he was not permitted to possess, he attempted partially to satisfy his preoedipal wishes in a relationship with a young girl of lower social status. During the period in which, in the transference situation, his early ambivalent mother attachement was revived, he turned adoringly to a much older woman of his acquaintance for a short time. Thus, most of the time his transference relationship to me shifted from one extreme to the other. However, gradually some historical events began to enter into his awareness: at the age of two he used to sit on his mother's lap in order to make her tell him stories and show him pictures. He spoke of sensations or feelings of

---

[1] New york, personal communication.

warmth and delight, and expressed this in the childish manner that I have tried to characterize above; but he also remembered outbursts of hostility when his mother refused to repeat or to prolong situations which for him represented heavenly bliss. Memories from this period were scarce. However, the intensity and clarity of repetition in his acting out in the analysis made a convincing impression on both of us. The adult man who consciously had a strong desire to establish a family life was unconsciously seeking a woman who represented to him the preoedipal mother and who could revive all the details of his personal experience. Relationships that satisfied these unconscious perverse and hostile tendencies were to a certain extent disgusting to his adult personality. They disturbed the image of the adored mother of the later oedipal situation. It thus became impossible for him to reconcile love and sexuality. He had to prevent himself from marriage and even from potency with an approved sexual partner. Another type of man who, in spite of a normal sexual potency, is constantly compelled to search for new women demonstrates a somewhat similar developmental disturbace. Such men, too, have an urgent desire for a quiet family life as a repetition of the infantile family situation; however, they are always forced to exchange one love object for another. They generally have infantile personalities and are fixated at the preoedipal phase of development. They are always in search of the mother of the preoedipal age, the mother who nursed them and toward whom they can behave as the spoiled child does. Either the adult part of their personality is frustrated in its manly aspirations or the infantile part of their personality is dissatisfied in its hopes and expectations. When in marriage a woman is able to fulfill the wishes of both parts of his personality – and this is possible only with women who have strong bisexual tendencies and a high degree of activity – the marriage can be succesful. Otherwise divorces and changes of love objects follow each other. Needless to say, in the desires of these men oral and anal components play a considerable role, both directly in sexual behavior and indirectly in the urge to be fed and to be handled like a little child.

The case of another type of man, whom one might call the misogynist, is similar. Men of this type likewise show fixation points in the preoedipal phase; however, they usually have regressed to this phase because of the intensity of castration fear that they could not overcome. During the oedipal phase, in the eyes of the little boy the father is the castrator. In the analysis of this type of patient one discovers that in an earlier phase the boy was regularly extremely afraid of the mother. When he fails to free himself of his fear, he tends to make the mother responsible for it. The boys who cannot overcome castration fear are, as a rule, those whose fear of their own passive tendencies is related to their *wish* to be castrated. Their hostility remains derected toward the mother. She becomes the actively hated object. Moreover, it is the woman who reminds these boys of the possibility of 'being castrated''; she is feared and hated also because of this.

I should like to mention here a patient who had a good relationship with his wife, she being able to combine in her personality both mother images, the oedipal and the preoedipal one.

The patient came into analysis because of a work inhibition. After some time we discovered transient periods of disturbance in his relation to his wife. In the transference these disturbances expressed themselves in paranoid ideas; this proved to be a repetition of an experience that has occurred in infancy. As a little boy the patient had had a severe infection, and because of it had to be hospitalized for several months. During this period he developed the fantasy of being poisened, so that he did not dare to eat; he remembered an intense hate of his mother, whom he made responsible for his suffering. The acting out in analysis seemed to show that this event was the second edition of an earlier one that had taken place after the birth of a younger sister. The patient was then one and a half years old and showed the wellknown reaction of hostility to the unfaithful mother who had weaned him and given her milk to the other child. Because of his wife's behavior, which enabled the patient to act out the different tendencies towards her, his marriage had not suffered. But the patient developed his work inhibitions as a substitute through which to express his conflict.

The influence of the preoedipal phase can also be studied in the formation of the superego. Where the sexual development is disturbed, the superego has not been consolidated. Traces of both father and mother images can easily be isolated, as well as traces of the identifications that are forerunners of the true superego formation. I intend to discuss this problem in another context.

However, I should like to mention here a case that shows clearly the fluctuation between father- and mother-identification, in behavior as well as in the superego functions.

The patient was a business man, though he had studied to be an engineer. He was nearly forty years old, very successful in his job, married, and the father of three children. The reason he came for analysis was, as he said, an interest in psychology, which time and again forced him to consider the possibility of changing his career. In these periods he wanted to study psychology in order to become a psychotherapist. He himself was astonished by this fantasy because he enjoyed his work. He wanted to establish a business of his own and knew he would be able to do so.

In his job he cometimes felt very independent. He than had excellent ideas and invented new plans to increase profits-ideas which were nearly always success- ful. Thus he was very much appreciated by his superiors. In other periods, he suddenly became inactive and lost his initiative. He then felt very dependent on the attitude of his chief toward himself. He had to watch carefully each remark, each change in the facial expression or voice of the latter, and was very much afraid of losing the chief's appreciation and sympathy.

The patient's history soon showed that this behavior was a repetition of the oedipal relation to his father. The latter, being a rich and a successful business man also, was the patient's example. The patient competed with and wanted to surpass him; but the moment he was successful he became guilty and had to punish himself by undoing his success, losing his initiative, and perhaps even he appreciation of others. He then had to reconcile his chief − father − and so behaved like a good dependent child. Thus he turned from the rivalrous, active, oedipal attitude to the passive feminine position. Thus far the analysis proceeded in the usual well-know way. But how could his sudden interest in psychological and intellectual problems be explained?

The family history showed that the patient's mother was a person of a cultural level quite different from the father's. Whereas he was a simple, crude, uncomplicated person, she was a refined, nervous woman, interested in science and art. The patient's scientific interest derived from an identification with his mother. However, this mother identification proved *not* to be related to his passive love for the father. As a very little boy he had understood that his father had no feeling at all for his wife's interests, and in the passive father attachment the patient's psychological aspirations played no role. His intellectual interests derived from an early mother identification, a primitive form of love attachment to her.

This preoedipal mother identification had various aspects. The mother had been suffering from a severe mental desease, for which she sometimes had to be hospitalized for several weeks or months. The patient was the only person in the family who has any understanding for this illness. As in early puberty he had heard something about psychology and psychoanalysis, he had become interested in it and produced the fantasy of curing his mother by it. However, in this fantasy the mother became the little child who was handled and treated and loved by him. The psychotherapeutic fantasy obviously was a later edition of very early mother-baby fantasies in which the patient alternatively played the role of the active (loving and aggressive) mother, and the passive child who wants to be handled and loved. These fantasies were revived in detail in an intense acting out in the transference.

For many reasons I cannot here go into detail. I hope I have succeeded in showing how the oedipal active-passive father relation, as seen in the patient's business life, was based on a preoedipal active-passive mother attachment that motivated his intellectual, mainly fantasied, interests. The patient's emotional life fluctuated between these two positions, each of them with a double foundation. His ability to identify with the active mother image was the basis of his later oedipal identification with the father and led to the normal manly part of his personality. The residues and continuation of his early passive mother attachment were partly transferred to a passive father relation and produced the split in his adult personality.

The superego formation showed similar discord. Traits of both father images and mother images could easily be found. In his moral attitudes toward others, for example, the patient fluctuated between crude, rough, ruthless conduct on the one hand, and soft, fine, sensitive behavior on the other. However, as mentioned before, I shall discuss these problems in detail elsewhere.

8. On the Development of Ego and Superego

(1947)

In resuming contact with psychoanalytic writing in other countries after many years of separation enforced by the war, I am struck by the varieties of directions in which research work has been extended. One line of investigation, however, seems to me the most prevalant: there is an increasing interest in the development of the ego and superego. Many authors lay stress on the influence of environmental elements connected with the formation of the ego. Psychoanalysis has shown from the very beginning how important external experiences are for the development of personality. But unfortunately many authors who stress the importance of environmental factors seem to overemphasize their influence and neglect or underestimate the importance of internal psychic processes. Sometimes they even go so far as to deny the eminent significance of id drives,[1] especially of infantile sexuality, for the ego and superego formation (Horney, Fromm). Our daily analytic work regularly shows us the interplay of internal and external events on the ego. These experiences forse us to study the growth of personality as a biologically based dynamic process, which is certainly influenced by social circumstances.

As far as I can see, the psychology of the social development of groups, of nations, and even of mankind in general must be regarded from the same point of view. Highly influenced by climate, economics, social life, and political circumstances, the development of mankind and its culture can only be understood as a dynamic process on a biological basis (N. Elias, 1939). Freud often pointed out that sexuality is the best-known part of the id, the psychic agency comprising the biologically rooted drives. We know that the genital organization of the adult is the result of a developmental process reaching back into early childhood. The phases of infantile sexuality, the oral, anal, and phallic stages in the formation of which libido and aggression participate, are the earliest and best-studied areas of psychoanalysis.

Early research work proved that the ultimate shape of sexuality in every person emerges from an interplay between the inborn nature of the drives and the influence of the environment. When we study a patient suffering from an obsessional neurosis we find a fixation of his libido on the anal phase of development owing to some traumatic events in his early childhood, on account

See also chapter 23, 24, and 27.

[1] I use the English word "drive" for the German *Trieb*, reserving the word "instinct" for the inborn mechanisms observed in animals, as for instance the nesting instinct of birds, the food and fighting instincts of insects, etc. (see McDougall). I hope to speak of this matter in another essay.

of an anal disposition. Sometimes the first element is the more important, while the second is complementary (Freud's "complementary series").

We now turn to ego psychology. In the course of the development of psychoanalysis the ego was studied at a later period than the id. It is noteworthy that what attracts attention are the *functions* of the ego as they develop in dealing with the claims of the outer world. We spoke about a "weak" and a "strong" ego in its struggle with the id and the outer world, in its defense against inner and outer dangers. It was said by Freud and even more emphatically by Anna Freud (1936) that these defense mechanisms could become part of the character. However, the inner development of the ego has not been systematically taken into consideration. Yet we may observe in practice as well as in the study of the child that this inner development of the ego out of an inborn core actually takes place. This is parallel to the teaching of biology that in the fertilized ovum there lives the potential form of the whole highly complicated organism. In the id, which provides the mental power, the development of the drives is predetermined. We can expect the same from the ego. It is the task of the psychologist to study how the individual ego develops out of this inborn ego core. As a matter of fact, the investigation of the ego, or more precisely of the instrument with which the ego operates, the intelligence, has already been partially carried out. I refer to the developmenal psychologies of Werner, Stern, Karl and Charlotte Bühler, Spranger, Piaget, etc. First and foremost, the work of Piaget (1936, 1937) seems to me of lasting value. In a series of accurate experiments he observes how the intelligence evolues from hereditary reflex which is present at birth, as the sucking reflex, and shortly afterward in the form of the grasping reflex.

According to Piaget, the empirical intelligence is employed at the age of about one year; the systematic intelligence at one and a half to two years by the mechanisms of assimilation and accommodation. During this period real thinking in words begins; later on we see the constructive intelligence and the formation of judgement and reason. Psychologists differ in fixing the age when the child is able to judge logically, but certainly this function is not achieved before the third or fourth year (perhaps even much later). I do not intend to describe the whole of Piaget's research work. I only wish to point out the gradual autonomous development of intelligence.

I have just called "intelligence" the instrument with which the ego operates. The ego, it is true, uses it to get in touch with the outer world, groping for the environment and retaining its own observations as memory traces. We may say that the ego learns to observe by means of the intelligence and its forerunners; but at the same time it creates and develops them in executing its important function as an organ of perception. In later childhood and in adult life intelligence matures into different forms: one of them is the intellect, as for instance used in scientific work. However, other forms of intelligence are indispensable, e.g., common sense for judging situations, emotional processes in the inner and outer world, etc. There is still a large field of research work to be done in this direction. But now I will return to the study of the primitive ego. Its development − though partly an autonomous one − is at the same time highly dependent on the influences of the outer world as well as on the other parts of the person (id and later superego).

As I mentioned before, the functions of the ego are better known than its development. What are these functions? We have already spoken about the function of perception. A second function is the building up of the memory which enables the personality to progress toward the third and very important function of reality testing. Testing and judging reality, however, require intelligence of a certain degree, which, as we saw above, is only reached by the two- or three-year-old child. At an earlier age it exists only in a primitive form, as the environment and the knowledge of the infant are very limited. The ego functions of reality testing and building up of the memory, established during the first years, develop and grow during the whole life. A fourth important ego function is that of the "control of motility." The tendencies of the id try to find an outlet in actions which often come into conflict with environmental claims, so that the ego is forced to interfere. This intervention, however, is only possible if the child is able to master his muscular apparatus physically and mentally. In so far as the ego is a body ego, it has been formed in the earlier stage of childhood. The mental control of the motor discharge of tendencies and emotions follows and develops during the entire life, like other ego functions. The growing intelligence and reason play an important part in the maturing of this capacity. They also show their influence in the fifth function of the ego, the so-called "synthetic function."[2] Though not entirely dependent on the level of intelligence and intellect, it is without doubt influenced by it. While in the id there is no question of a synthetic function, it is inherent in the ego from the very beginning of life. It develops, however, with the growth of personality and is perhaps as a rule more or less unfinished. Later on we shall speak about its origin.

We called the intelligence the instrument of ego capacities. But where does it come from? The intelligence itself is a highly organized mental process. According to Piaget, it develops out of hereditary reflexes. Perhaps we have to consider the instincts of the animals (instincts in McDougall's sense; see also Brun) as being the phylogenetic forerunner of human intelligence. (See the above-mentioned organized instinctive behavior of animals such as birds, insects, etc.) But it is not the task of human psychology to state whether this idea is of any value or not.

We must now turn to another important question: what is the force or what are the forces which enable the ego to develop intelligence and its achievements? Piaget speaks about "activity." The psychoanalyst can answer this question less vaguely: the ego originates out of the id, and in consequence must draw its forces from the same source. So it must be the energy of the drives, of Eros and aggression, which is used by the ego for its functions.[3] Freud's libido theory

[2] I was very pleased to discover nearly the same ego functions mentioned in Anna Freud's "Indication for Child Analysis" (1945).

[3] Here I wish to mention a remark made to me personally by Heinz Hartmann. He considers that id and ego both originate from a primitive, still undifferentiated state. I think it is merely a question of terminology. Phylogenetically, the id is older than the ego. Moreover, the id contains the biologically based drives.

enables us to imagine the process. We know the ego is cathected with libido which we call narcissism, and it is taken for granted that the individual needs a certain amount of narcissism in order to function properly.

According to Freud, there must be a quantity of undifferentiated energy for the nonlibidinal mental processes, and he supposes this energy to be desexualized libido. Since we know the enormous role of aggression in mental life, we may amplify this opinion in describing a kind of sublimated aggression as the second contribution to this energy. The exploration and mastering of the outer world for the purposes of the ego take place through aggression sublimated into energic action and mixed with desexualized libidinal tendencies. However, in order to regulate this function a direct narcissistic cathexis is necessary as well as a balance between narcissistic and aggressive cathexis of the ego organization. This equilibrium is perceived as a satisfying feeling of self-esteem.

We may now summarize these questions in the following way: the ego as a part of the id develops out of an inborn ego core and has a development of its own. The process of the growth of the intelligence is well known to us (perhaps it is the basis of the "conflict-free sphere" of Hartmann). This autonomous development occurs under the influence of the contact with reality, with the id (and later on with the superego). In this development the ego functions arise, namely: (1) perception; (2) the building up of memory out of the traces of perception; (3) reality testing; (4) control of motility (in the physical and mental way); and finally, (5) the synthetic function. An optimal narcissistic cathexis enables the ego to accomplish this task, which is many-sided and very complicated.

It is well known that in consequence of these various differentiated functions the ego is threatened by a great many dangers.

The ego is the servant of the id, the outer world, and the superego and it has to satisfy these three masters, as Freud described it. As the claims of the environment and the id are often in conflict, the ego frequently has to mediate. As far as the outer world is concerned, it tries to do so by its knowledge and experience. In the period in which these capacities are still small, i.e., in childhood, the person is very dependent on the outer objects (primarily the mother). It learns from them how to master reality. Here the mechanism of identification with the objects is used, and this is a very important process that we shall discuss later on. If the help of the mother, however, does not suffice, or if the mother herself is a part of the outer world which makes all these demands, the child must defend himself against these claims. Then the ego mobilizes one of the well-known defense mechanisms (A. Freud, 1936). Here denial plays the most important role.

On the other hand, the satisfaction of the id claims is not less difficult. The id requires satisfaction according to the pleasure-pain principle. In many cases these demands run counter to the claims of the environments. The ego tries to modify the id wishes, but when it fails to do so it must defend itself against these tendencies too, and mobilizes various defense mechanisms against them. These mechanisms are known as repression, isolation, regression, reaction formation, undoing, projection, introjection, sublimation, etc., well described by Freud,

Anna Freud, and others. The ego is impressed by them. Thus, little by little, the ego organization becomes formed by these reactions and the child's character takes shape.

Observation teaches us that the choice of the special defense mechanisms is determined by an inborn factor, a tendency of the ego core, though also influenced by internal and external experiences of the child.

At a later period, when the superego is formed, its claims bring the ego into a third dependency, and, of course, equivalent actions and defense reactions become necessary and influence character development. Later on I shall speak about these processes. First I should like to turn to a fourth dependency of the ego, which has been less studied.

As I mentioned before, the ego organization needs a certain amount of narcissistic cathexis in order to function properly. Especially in the earlier stages of ego development, this libidinal position is very vulnerable. There are experiences, disappointments, and frustrations which are injurious to the ego's self-esteem and thus disturb the integrity of the ego cathexis. In chapter 4 I described the danger to the ego when it is forced to defend itself against them. If the ego cathexis is hurt by the exorbitant claims of the outer world or overwhelmed by strong urges of the id, the ego is unable to develop its capacities and to behave normally. When it is injured in its libidinal position it will be disturbed in its autonomic functions, as already described.

In clinical work we can observe these processes if we turn our attention to ego analysis. When we study a patient suffering from hysteria, we can see, in dissolving his symptoms, that he has rejected an id impulse, at the command of the superego, by the mechanism of repression; the id tendencies cannot find normal discharge; the libido is partly regressed to the phallic or perhaps oral phase. But what about the ego? It is unable to function normally. In the first place, the memory is disturbed. There are gaps in its functioning. Sometimes the mastery of movement is interrupted, e.g., in hysterical paralysis control of movement is inhibited. In other cases perception is disturbed, e.g., in hysterical scotomization. In all cases the synthetic function is deranged; there is no more harmony in the personality. In other diseases, e.g., the obsessional neurosis, intelligence – though its level may be high in general – has partially regressed to a primitive level such as the magic phase, a forerunner of logical thinking. Here the split in the personality is much more obvious than in hysteria. The most far-reaching regression of the ego can be observed in the so-called narcissistic neuroses and the psychoses. Here the ego is really split up, the synthetic function has disappeared, reality testing is falsified or, in serious cases, almost totally disrupted. Judgement of the outer world has vanished in favor of primitive wishful thinking, etc.

As so often happens in psychoanalysis, the study of pathology teaches us how normal development takes its course. We suppose, in the case of a serious neurosis or a psychosis, a regression of the drives accompanied by an ego regression. And we can understand what has happened. The pathogenic process has damaged the narcissistic position, which was either too weak because of its predisposition, or has been weakened by this process, or both. In the case of a character disturbance, we can observe the same process in a part of the ego. There are persons whose ego functions normally in several capacities, but who show pathological behavior at one single point; as regards one particular claim their judgement of reality may be disturbed and they project their own feelings onto the outer world. These persons, who can think very logically and who usually act absolutely correctly, form in certain situations the erroneous idea that the environment hates them and is trying to counteract their activity. I have called that the "personal delusion" of nearly normal individuals. Studying this phenomenon in ego analysis, one always arrives at a narcissistic injury in childhood which has produced the feeling of being powerless. We know this process very well from the little girl who lives under the wounding disadvantage of lacking a penis and who feels inferior and powerless because of it. However, the little boy, too, suffers from feelings of impotence toward the mighty father and in earlier stages even toward the mother who originally is almighty in his view. In this connection we must do justice to the old theory of Alfred Adler. His "will to power" is really an important tendency in the life of mankind, but it is merely a part of childhood development and by no means the only one. Moreover, Adler was unwilling to see the great part played by libidinal components in this longing for power, which has to strengthen or restore the narcissistic cathexis of the ego.

When we have the opportunity of studying so-called normal adults we realize that almost always survivals of primitive ego reactions are to be found. There are very few, if any, totally integrated persons whose synthetic function has succeeded in constituting a really harmonious personality, whose reality testing enables them to think and judge in each situation in an objective and rational way, and whose self-esteem makes them act according to their own needs as well as those of their fellow men. If we study the personality of the leader of a group we learn that his exceptional influence on others is based on a strong narcissistic cathexis. Unfortunately, this quality is often misused. His aggression is not sublimated into a socially advantageous activity but is used in a more or less primitive way for the satisfaction of his own craving for power.

There are still many questions and problems in this field of research open for study.

We might now look at the third part of the personality, the superego.

As part of the ego, the superego takes over some of the ego functions. In normal cases there is unity between them. However, we know how often a conflict exists. At earlier stages of human development this unity cannot yet be observed. Therefore it seems justifiable to turn our attention to the growth of the superego.

From analytic observation we must conclude that the superego develops in the same way as the id and ego. Still, there are some differences: the id is present from the very beginning of life; the ego develops from the infant's entry into the outer world, that is to say from birth on, though we had to assume the presence of an ego core in the id. The superego arisis only after some years, as an heir of the oedipus complex. As is well known, some analysts place its origin earlier, but I prefer to distinguish between the forerunners and the superego proper. A gradual maturation necessitates complicated processes of identification and introjection. So we must accept a developmental phase of which the superego is the main achievement. We assume that the construction and the mechanisms of the subsequent superego are to some extent predetermined. We observe, e.g., that the intensity with which infants take over the orders and prohibitions of their parents differs in different children. The acceptance of orders is primarily an imitation of parental behavior. By means of the mechanism of identification, however, it becomes an inner part of the psychic personality. Therefore, the capacity for identification is of paramount importance for the building up of the superego, and it certainly differs in nature in different individuals. Though the contents of the superego claims are dependent on the influence of the parents, the mechanism of identification is inherited. Moreover, we know from Freud that the severity of the punishing superego also depends upon the intensity of the child's hostility and his ability to turn aggression toward himself. Thus through this mechanism the superego is also partly independent of the parental image.[4]

Up to now we have spoken of the judging and punishing superego. But we must also consider another superego function, that of ideal formation. Observations teach us that this ideal formation occurs very early. As a matter of fact, in the harmonious adult these two parts of the superego, the ego ideal and the judging superego, are homogeneous and form a unity. But I think we must follow Alexander and some other authors, e.g., Fluger in *Man, Morals and Society* (1945), in separating them while we are studying their development. The ego ideal plays an important role in maintaining the narcissistic position of the ego organization. I have already mentioned that this position is indispensable for a well-balanced functioning of the personality. When the self-respect is wounded the child satisfies his narcissistic needs in creating and introjecting his ideal. At first it is formed after parental images. Later on, other examples are added to them, until finally social, moral, scientific, and religious ideals are created. It is important support for a man's mental balance if his ego ideal functions well, if its level is not too high but high enough to strengthen self-respect. Therefore the first identifications are of lasting significance for the entire development. Stimulating the process of identification without exaggerating it is an important educational method and may offer suitable ideals. The same principle holds for the formation of the judging superego. Here acceptable orders and prohibitions should be offered to the child. In describing the influence of education we must not forget the intrinsic force of the developing superego, as we know the mechanisms and the strength of the aggressive impulses to be inborn qualities. Moreover, the superego is intimately connected with the id, as it becomes fixated after the oedipal situation has passed. Therefore it not only revives ancestral images but also inherits part of the immobility and immutability of the instinctual drives. On the other hand, one can observe how changeable and unstable identifications can be in earlier periods of development, and it often

---

[4] According to a personal communication from Dr. Tibout, it is possible that the superego is established only after the aggression is turned inward.

happens that this instability remains throughout an entire lifetime. These antagonisms represents the two factors of Freud's complementary series: disposition and environmental influence. Many people remain at an early stage and do not succeed in developing an independent and adjustable superego.

So far we have spoken mainly about the mechanisms at work during the formation of the superego in the widest sense (thus including the ideal), as a psychic organ. But what about the creation of the contents? In the individual they are partly taken from the environment and therefore very much influenced by the family constellation and later on by the actual social, economic, and political circumstances. In so far as they are taken from inside — that means from the earliest identifications with norms and ideals of the parents whose own moral system was based on the requirements of an older generation — they contain precipitates of former superego formations and therefore represent residues of earlier periods and former cultures. The question arises whether phylogenetic laws exist in accordance with which morals and ethics have been built up. This question raises another one: are the tendencies of the superego inherent only in the id and ego mechanisms, such as the intensity of aggression, the mechanisms of identification and of turning aggression against the self, or is there also a specific factor inherent only in the superego? This is a wide and difficult problem for detailed research with which I cannot deal now.

We will make only two remarks in this connection: (1) in prohibitions the demand for the renunciation of satisfaction plays an important role. In this connection I am thinking particularly of aggression which disturbs the social relations of men. To check it, reaction formations against it have to be developed, e.g., overcompensation in loving one's fellow men. We know how often people fail and fall back upon open or hidden hostitlity. To use popular expression, the question is whether love can remain stronger than hatred. (2) In the creation of ethics and ideals the narcissistic need must be satisfied. At the same time the needs and interests of our fellow men have to be respected and included in our satisfactions. From a social point of view it is dangerous if men remain at the primitive phase of self-satisfaction and longing for power without adjusting their needs to a higher social level. It is also unfortunate if they try to compensate their lowered self-esteem by excessively worshiping another person, an idea, a deity. Can an equilibrium be achieved between self-assertion on the one hand and a due regard for the community?

It seems justifiable to suggest that well-balanced compensation of aggressiveness by love and acquisition of self-assertion through ideals are the driving forces of the religious, ethical, and scientific achievements of mankind.

9. The Origin and Development of Guilt Feelings

(1947)

In various discussions among psychiatrists and psychotherapists in Holland there has proved to be a confusing misunderstanding because of an insufficient differentiation between the concepts of "guilt" and "guilt feelings."

When trying to define the term "guilt" one enters the sphere of valuations. During the age-old history of the development of mankind a great number of normative systems, religious, philosophical, ethical, social, have come into existence. Different definitions of the words "guilt," "good and evil," are to be found in each system. It is very remarkable that within a given social or religious community definitions change in the course of time, from generation to generation, under the influence of economic, technical, geographical, and other conditions. Therefore one can speak of "guilt" (objective guilt) only within a certain community in a given space of time. Thus limited, the definition is useful and necessary in community life. In practice, each community needs norms and values in order to be able to protect itself against individuals or groups that might become a danger to its organization.

A psychologist who is working scientifically will put the question as follows: What are the causes of the development of *this* special conception of norms, in *this* very period in *this* very group of men? He will have to take into account social, economic, technical, geographical factors as well as biological and psychological ones in the light of their own development. It seems almost impossible for one single person to master all those sciences. The future will teach us whether modern teamwork will succeed in solving this problem. First and foremost the psychologist has to occupy himself with the psychological aspects, without neglecting the influence of the other factors mentioned above, of course.

In his daily work the psychoanalyst does therapeutic and research work with his patients at the same time. He is often accused by outsiders of being exclusively interested in the individual and of neglecting the urgent problems of mankind in distress. In my opinion this reproach is unjust. Each individual constitutes part of some community or other. Each community is composed of individuals. Without knowing the laws of psychic life of individuals one will never be able to get to the bottom of the problems of social psychology. It is unnecessary to emphasize that this does not imply that concepts and theories gained by exploring individual mental life should be applied to groups without further discrimination.

However, psychoanalysis has revealed many general human laws and trends which are of outstanding importance for sociology and social psychology. The pioneering work of Freud in this field is well known. Psychoanalytic science, however, is still penetrating more and more into the structure and dynamics of mental life, so that further contributions to social psychology are to be expected.

It is noteworthy that the very persons who disparage psychoanalysis as one-sided and narrow-minded expect it on the other hand to solve all the mental problems of mankind. The impossibility of realizing this expectation is in turn used as a reproach against psychoanalysis.

Reverting to the problem under discussion-guilt and guilt feelings: I have mentioned the divergence of views on "what is guilty" in various communities in different periods. Society defines "guilty" in its juridical laws. A person is "guilty" and therefore punished when he acts against these laws.

The normative systems, e.g., the religious ones, have created more or less dogmatic commands and prohibitions, norms of "good" and "evil." Within such systems a person acting in contradiction to the norms of "good" is considered to be "guilty."

Many dogmatists are convinced that they have the only real judgment of "good" and "guilt," referring to an inner feeling of evidence. Naturally a follower of another religious or ethical system is not satisfied by this statement, he himself pleading for his own conviction by a similar inner sentiment. Here the scientist can only make the highly interesting observation that in all of those different valuations similar mental processes are operating.

In the psychology of the individual, "guilt feelings" play an important role. The phenomenological description of those feelings is given in different terms, according to the religious, philophical, or ethical persuasion of the given person.

Some people speak of "sense of guilt," of "consciousness of guilt," of "an existential experience of guilt," of "a metaphysical guilt," and so on.

The psychoanalytic study of human mental life has taught us to describe "guilt feeling" as a (mostly unpleasant) tension within the personality. This tension is likely to become conscious as a feeling of being "bad," "guilty," as a feeling of discomfort, of dissatisfaction with oneself, as a shortcoming, as a vague anxiety, etc. We regard all of these feelings as falling into the group of guilt feelings, because they are tensions that come into being through similar inner processes, one being able to substitute for another.

This intrapsychic tension is localized between two parts of the psychic personality, the ego and the superego. The superego, it is well known, is a psychic structure that comes into existence during the development of man. The newborn infant has no function of conscience. He has many needs and wants: whenever these needs are statisfied the infant is tensionless and quiet (content, as the mother says); whenever they remain ungratified for a longer or shorter length of time, the baby shows an inner tension by being uncomfortable, by crying, etc. Not until the baby has achieved a psychic relationship, an attachment to the mother, does he begin to perceive what the mother desires, what she disapproves of, what she feels is "good" or "bad." In order not to lose the mother's love and approval, on which he is highly dependent, the young child will learn to renounce forbidden and bad wishes. The toddler, though already aware of the mother's valuations, quietly does forbidden things whenever there is no chance of his being punished or of losing the mother's love. In this period anxiety is the only factor to control the infant's behavior and to determine his being good or naughty. There is no inner voice of conscience, defining what is good or bad, and consequently we cannot speak of the infant's having guilt feelings in this phase.

Later on, the fear of punishment and of losing love is transferred to the father, educators, teachers, social institions, etc. It always remains part of the directives for behavior in the life of man, though variable in quantity in different persons.

However, older children and adults may feel guilty and renounce forbidden wishes when they need not fear punishment or loss of love and approval. These persons really have an inner conscience. There has been established an authority in their ego organization that judges good and evil. Sinning against this conscience produces a real feeling of guilt.

This newly organized part of the ego has come into existence through the process of identification with the parental images and their valuations. This process is a complicated psychic event and the final stage of the intensive and highly important development of the small child's instinctual and affective life. During this development the mechanism of identification comes into existence. At first it produces only unstable and changing trends in the child's ego. It is the same period in which the child becomes aware of the mother's demands and valuations and is influenced in his behavior by his fear of the mother's disapproval, as we described above.

However, at the end of the first developmental stage before entering the latency period, part of the child's ego produces a real, stable change by internalizing the parental images, claims, and judgements, and it thus creates the inner conscience, the superego. The parental judgements have now become part of the child's own mental inventory.

Sinning against the superego gives rise to guilt feelings and must be paid for by self-punishment in the form of the inner grief of self-reproach, self-torment, penance, and sometimes even self-mutilation. Guilt feelings develop out of the ego's fear of the superego claims and have their forerunner in the ego's fear of the claims of the environment.

In many persons the regulation of their social behavior occurs mainly through the fear of environmental commands, as already mentioned above. Other persons develop a severe superego and a strict conscience. Both regulating principles are always to be found, their mutual relations varying from case to case. It seems worth while to describe some peculiarities of the different types resulting from the various mixtures of the two principles.

Adults in whom the superego is poorly developed generally do not have a stable opinion about morals. They behave socially mainly out of fear of prison or some other punishment. They call "good" and "evil" what is defined as "good" and "evil" by the momentary authority in their environment. They know that they are "guilty" when they act against the law, but they do not *feel* guilty. Whenever another authority comes to power they easily take over the new opinions and act according to the changed laws. In this way they behave like small children. We may say that their mental development has been inhibited in the stage before the superego is stabilized. People with well developed superegos have acquired the ability te create opinions of their own. Originally, it is true, they have taken over the parental judgements. But maturation and mental growth involve development of the superego to more or less independence and originality. The persons in questions have their own opinions about morals and behave according to the inner voice of their conscience. When they act against their conscience, they become subject to real guilt feelings. When authority and law change, they keep their own valuations.

This description of independent development may be called too idealistic, it is true. However, I have already mentioned that in practice both regulating principles are always to be found. I have only described extremes in both directions. Another complication arises when an inhibition in development takes place not *before* the establishment of the superego as I described above, but soon after its formation. This inhibition can cause an arrest of the development of the superego. It becomes fixated to the parental opinions and remains rigid, unable to grow into independent personal mental structure. Extreme inhibitions in this direction are to be considered as belonging to the field of pathology. I shall come back to this later.

Next we will turn our attention to two striking peculiarities of guilt feelings.

(1) Some people suffer from an extraordinarily powerful sense of guilt without ever having done anything really bad. In these cases there are impulses to be observed which are labeled by the person himself as extremely bad ones. He judges himself as severely as a real judge would do when confronting a real delinquent. Here we encounter the remarkable unconscious phenomena of psychic identification of thought and deed, the "omnipotence of thought," usually found in primitives and children. I shall return to the origin of this primitive desire to be "almighty" later on.

(2) Some people deny every feeling of guilt (or the counterparts described above), although they behave as if they were guilty. They are constantly harming, punishing, tormenting themselves, or provoking harm and injury from others or from the state. We say these people are suffering from unconscious guilt feelings or, to put it more correctly, from an unconscious need for punishment. Evidently the conflict between ego and superego is repressed in these persons. However, it forces its way out into a neurosis or a neurotic attitude toward life. In both cases we enter the province of pathology.

The sound, integrated personality has established an equilibrium between the claims of reality and superego on the one hand and the needs, desires, and capacities of ego and id on the other hand. The diseased personality, however, has not been able to solve his inner conflicts and therefore has failed to find an equilibrium. Psychoanalysis tries to find out in which cases the pathological guilt feelings remain unconscious and where they force their way to the level of consciousness.

Now we encounter another important question: What is it that sometimes makes the superego so extremely powerful and tormenting? Where does this intensity come from? I mentioned above that the superego in its origin represents an introjected image of the parental behavior. It takes over the commands and prohibitions of the parents and at the same time the severity of their claims for obedience, but this process is not the only one. A very striking observation teaches us that many children with weak and idulgent parents develop a severe and sometimes cruel superego. This superego not only threats the ego as the parents used to treat the disobedient child; it also behaves toward the ego as the disappointed, vengeful child wished to behave toward the parents. How vengeful and destroying a child's wishes sometimes are can easily be observed in children who are educated in a free and not intimidating way. They ventilate the most harmful, damaging, and destructive fantasies toward siblings as well as toward the parents, either directly or in play activities. Severe disturbances like obsessional neuroses and melancholic depressions are characterized by the influence of an extremely severe superego. When analyzing patients suffering from these diseases we realize that these same destructive strivings existed in their infancies. An intolerant education of course furthers the process of repression in the infant and stimulates the inner process of self-punishment. On the other hand, I have already mentioned how often a mild attitude in the educators cannot prevent the building up of a pathologically severe superego. In order to understand this phenomenon we will consider the child's development in respect to these details.

Originally the infant regards himself as the center of the world. He does not know of any outer world but is exclusively aware of his own wants and needs. When he discovers a world outside of his "self" that does not afford direct satisfaction at every moment, he experiences disappointment and mortification, which provoke his hostility. The small, powerless child is unable to discharge his hostile, destructive impulses. On the one hand he must fear the parents' punishment, but when the parents are mild and tolerant the main point is that the hostile feelings come into an insolute conflict with strong love for them. We understand that the above-mentioned "omnipotence of thought" makes the child feel as if he really had damaged the parents, and therefore robbed himself of their protection and love. The child becomes afraid of his own destructive tendencies. This so-called "ambivalence conflict" leads to repression, to a turning against the self of the aggressive impulses. At the end of the period of the child's flourishing instinctual life, which, though only lasting for a few years, is very intense and of paramount importance to the full development of the personality, the attachment of the parents is definitely internalized and the parental images survive in the superego. However, this process is attended by an introjection of the hostile impulses toward them. One part of this aggressiveness is taken up by the superego, which now behaves in a severe and sadistic way with respect to the ego. The ego begins to fear the superego. The other part of the aggressiveness is drawn on by the ego, which becomes servile and masochistic in its relation to the superego. The tension between the two parts of the personality is perceived later on as a strong guilt feeling. These two processes always take place side by side but in various proportions. In pathological cases it is of importance for therapeutic success whether the greater part of the aggression is finally established in the ego or in the superego. Pathological guilt feeling (need for punishment) is always hard to influence. However, the masochistic ego is still more resistant to therapeutic attempts than is the abnormally cruel superego.

Summarizing, we are justified in stating that guilt feelings of adults, experienced in different ways and phenomenologically described in various terms, originate from the fear of the superego. They are differentiations of this superego fear.

I have already mentioned one of the forerunners in the child's development: fear of the claims of the environment. We now have to add a second one: fear of his own destructive impulses. Here I should like to face an old critical question. Is it really possible to fear one's instinctual drives? Perhaps the drive becomes a danger only through the prohibition of the environment? Many investigators (including some psychoanalysts) answer the second question affirmatively. The relations at issue are hard to penetrate indeed. The child works up each disappointment, each privation, into a penalty for a forbidden desire. However, it is obvious that there are situations in which a given ego constellation can be too weak to meet a cetain demand of a drive without fear. Here the ego can neither tolerate the discharge of the drive impulse nor master the striving in some other way. One may observe this in a small child if a given drive is provoked prematurely before the child is prepared to meet is, e.g., in cases of seduction by older children or grownups. This traumatic situation can apply to sexual as well as to destructive drives. It depends on the momentary relation between id forces and ego forces whether the trauma can be mastered normally or not. The destructive drives, however, involve another specific danger.

The imperative drive impulse of the infant and his actual helplessness cause his dependency upon the mother's love and care. The child has to love the mother in turn. Life as well as love are threatened by the destructive and hostile strivings. When the infant develops an impulse to damage or to destroy those whom he loves and wants to preserve, he must experience anxiety.

Fear resulting from the tension of the ambivalence conflict could be termed the biological root of guilt feelings. In the course of development, fear of the outer world comes into existence. Later on the fear of the superego is experienced as guilt feeling (or as one of the various equivalent sentiments described above). Here we encounter the socialpsychological background of guilt feelings.

We will turn now to the events provoking the infant's destructive tendencies. One group has already been mentioned above: disappointment, privation, unsatisfied longing for love provoke hostile impulses toward the object in question. There is another very important source to be found, however, from which aggressive strivings arise: injuries of self-esteem, of the craving for power, or to put in other words, primitive narcissistic injuries.

The newborn infant is originally unaware of an outside world; he imagines his "self" as the almighty center of the world. The discovery of his own lack of power is a shattering injury to his self-esteem. The infant tries to undo this injury by using the fantasy of the omnipotence of thoughts and wishes. However, this mechanism is foredoomed to failure and consequently it is followed by a wave of rage and aggression. At first the mother is made responsible for each sort of injury, and consequently the destructive forces of the child are directed toward her. Now the child's love of his mother is endangered, destructive tendencies have to be turned against the self, and the above-described process runs its course.

In our therapeutic work with patients we must know the sources of the fear of their own aggression (and guilt feelings); e.g., states of severe depression generally cannot be influenced without working through this early conflict of ambivalence.

Sometimes the view is met with in outsiders that psychoanalysis considers each guilt feeling as a pathological phenomenon. Another view often held is that psychoanalysis aims at destroying the patient's superego. Naturally both views are equally absurd. As soon as a community arises there is a need for laws and norms, the interests of individual and community often being in conflict. The internalization of the norms (the foundation of the superego) is a normal mental process in every child. It is one of the consequences, and a very important one, of the development of mental life in mankind. The superego not only represents the prohibiting authority; at the same time it enriches the personality with ideals, the mental and moral possession of men. In chapter 8 I expounded my view that it is advantageous to have a separate look at the development of the judging conscience (superego in a narrower sense) and at that of ideal formation. There are persons who develop a pathologically severe superego (they have to torment and punish themselves perpetually), but in whom ideals and ethics are on a low level. On the other hand, there are people of a high ethical and ideal standing who do not possess an excessively punishing superego. Guilt feeling is normal psychic phenomenon as well. It is an alarm signal of disturbed inner harmony between ego and superego, parallel to anxiety which signals the danger of a disturbed equilibrium between ego and id or ego and environmental claims. The forms and contents of the ideals as well as those of the prohibitions are borrowed from the outer world and therefore are as varying, multicolored, and changing as the different circumstances make community life. Which general function they are fulfilling in a given community at a given moment is a most interesting question within the psychological and sociological fields of research.

As already stated, the psychologist generally cannot possess the deep knowledge of other sciences (sociology, anthropology, history of religion and economics, etc.) necessary to answer this question. From the psychological point of view, a few remarks may perhaps be of value. As social and individual interests often collide, a community has to protect itself against possible individual opposition. Therefore it has to create prohibitive laws. Now, bodily and mental power are different in various persons. Thus it occurs that the prohibitive laws are more and more used by the persons or groups in power to protect their acquired authority (they call it their "rights") and to suppress the powerless people. This comes into conflict with the original purpose of the regulating and prohibiting measures, namely, to protect the survival of the community. The laws become more or less the servants of the needs and wants of a relatively small group of men in power. The result can sometimes be the desintegration of the given community. A similar process can be observed in regard to ideals and ethics. Various sources of suffering and misery make men grope for solace in religious and ethical pursuits. Strong ideals can cement the relations between the members of a community. But the men in power often begin using the idealistic force to dominate their weaker fellow men. They tend to rob them of their sources of consolation by threatening them with severe punishments before or after death when they refuse to be obedient. So religion and ideals may be degraded to weapons for suppressing fellow men. The oppressors are most successful when they manage to use both laws and ethical claims to fix their power.

We have been able to study the origin and development of guilt feelings in the individual. It is not surprising that, as usual, pathological cases were the first objects. However, the same psychic processes operate in normal development. It is decisive for the person whether he will succeed in creating and recreating an inner harmony between ego, superego, and id within his special invironment. When considering the almost immeasurable number of problems in the inner and outer worlds, one will understand how extremely difficult it is to grow into a harmonious integrated personality. One of these many problems is that of guilt feelings, the tension between ego and superego. We laid stress on the observation in our daily analytic work that pathological guilt feelings can be transformed into normal sentiments only by working through all the developmental stages without forgetting the underlying, biologically founded ambivalence conflict, i.e., the conflict between erotic and destructive strivings. Sometimes we encounter a tendency in therapists to deny or to devaluate the destructive drives in man. It would be easy and pleasant if they were actually lacking. Men would not have to suffer so much under the difficult task of solving the conflict of ambivalence. Moreover, one could ignore the unpleasant feelings of impotence that are raised by this conflict. One could feel "all good" and "almighty." However, denial has very seldom given a lasting solution to a conflict. It seems to be more appropriate to face the problem. The direct discharge of destructive and aggressive tendencies usually clashes with the claims of the migthy principle of life: love. Life itself offers numerous ways to transpose aggressive strivings into activity. The active mastering of the sources and forces offered to mankind in its struggle for life has created high technical achievements, mental and moral possessions of paramount importance. It is astonishing to observe how often people prove to be unable to grant each other and themselves the undisturbed enjoyment of these high values. But here we pass from the individual problem to one of the community.

Every community has to create moral norms, as mentioned above, for a variety of reasons. One of them, perhaps the most important, is that destructive and egoistic omnipotent strivings of the individual have to be suppressed (or at least greatly restricted) in order to produce security for the community. We need not emphasize again that the community up to now has shown very poor success in trying to do this. One out of many causes for this failure, however, is to be found in the denial (or at least the undervaluation) of the force of destructive tendencies and of wish for omnipotence. Denial excludes mastery.

When these destructive natural forces in mankind are recognized, accepted, and mastered, the conditions enabling man to create productive instead of destructive activity are given. Better social and economic circumstances may result from this process. Sublimating destruction into productive activity may satisfy part of man's craving for power and may simultaneously free the other partner in the conflict of ambivalence: love. Perhaps some of mankind's misery and grief could be reduced by the creative power of love.

10. Neurotics, Delinquents, and Ideal Formation

(1949)

It is a pleasure to contribute a paper in honor of the work of August Aichhorn, who opened new ways to our understanding and treatment of youthful delinquents. His famous book, *Wayward Youth* (1925) is not only an invaluable source of practical experience in dealing with problem children but also our first psychoanalytic orientation in the etiology and theory of delinquency.

Aichhorn considers delinquency the result of two types of faulty development in the child's libido structure. The first occurs in the process whereby the pleasure principle is converted into the reality principle. The second is a malformation of the ego ideal. Both are problems of libido and ego development.

According to Aichhorn, a characteristic symptom of the dissocial child is his inability to meet the demands of reality. His ego cannot give up the pleasure principle and he meets such demands of his environment with obsitnacy or revolt. This is the result of two extremes of faulty training, either of which may prevent him from an adjustment adequate to his age level. If he is treated with either excessive indulgence or excessive severity, the result may be the same. Our own clinical experience confirms this claim. Delinquent children all show the same inability to give up immediate gratification, and almost invariable they have been brought up by someone (parents of guardians) whose methods were extreme. Either they were too severe and did not compensate the child for frustrations of love or other gratifications, or they spoiled the child until he was incapable of bearing any disappointment, or they oscillated between the two attitudes so that the child became too confused to be able to make any adequate adaption.

But since these parental behavior patterns are found not only in the histories of delinquents but also in those of neurotics, the question arises what determines whether a child becomes neurotic or delinquent?

There has been much discussion of this point. Although psychiatric literature generally classifies waywardness and delinquency as psychopathies, a clear and uniform definition of this term is still lacking (see Rümke et al., 1947). It is very difficult to give such a definition because delinquent (psychopathic) behavior almost always reveals evidence of neurotic trends, and because both kinds of symptoms, delinquent and neurotic, show similar developmental disturbances. H. G. van der Waals (1943, 1946) in his studies on the problem of the psychopath distinguishes between "dispositional" and "developmental"

See chapter 8.

98

psychopathies, though he admits one must always allow for a complementary series of factors (Freud) in these as in the case of neurotics.

Although many psychiatrists tend to regard the neurosis as an acquired, the psychopathic state as a congenital disturbance, van der Waals concludes that "it is probable that the genesis of the psychopathic condition is identical in the main with that of the neurosis."

I agree with this author. The study of both neurotic and problem children usually reveals that their parents used faulty educational methods because of their own difficulties or neuroses. Therefore we tend to consider them responsible for the child's pathological development. Yet we sometimes meet cases of both categories whose parents were obviously normal and whose training was both understanding and free from the errors of extreme severity or indulgence. In such cases we are forced to postulate an abnormal dispostion, although we must still be cautious lest we have overlooked some influences of earliest childhood.

We would therefore say that the genesis of both neurotic dissocial disturbance lies in the interplay, in varying mixtures, of dispositional factors and environmental influences.

Yet this similar genesis should not blind us to the striking differences between neurotic and delinqent behavior. We must still be specific about these differences and attempt to find their causes.

Both neurotic and delinquent children show the same inability to harmonize their instinctual drives with the demands of their environment. We realize that in both cases it is a symptom of their faulty ego development. But the neurotic tries to solve the conflict by repressing id impulses while the delinquent ignores the social demands and acts out his primitive desires as far as possible. He refuses to give up immediate gratification and prefers to jeopardize his relation to his environment. In contrast, the neurotic's anxiety prevents him from risking a conflict in his relationship to his environment and so he has to bear the pain of giving up direct gratification. To put it differently, the delinquent's object attachment is not strong enough to act as a barrier against his instinctual needs and therefore his ego cannot achieve an adaptation to reality, whereas the neurotic is too dependent upon his object to permit the id more than a limited degree of instinctual satisfaction. Needless to say, we are using these quantitative terms in a relatively sense only.

The delinquent who has made himself relatively independent of his environment is then proportionately more dependent on the gratification of his instinctual drives.

Since the neurotic is able to free himself to some degree from the imperative demand for immediate gratification, he, in turn, is correspondingly more dependent on the love he receives from his environment. Thus we see that the neurotic's ego is strong where that of the delinquent is weak and vice versa.

Let us at this point return to Aichhorn's second type of faulty development in the child's mental structure, the malformation of the ego ideal.

During the course of its development, one of the functions of the child's ego is to take over the demands and prohibitions of his parents. Thus starts the development of the superego, which later becomes a part of the ego organization by the introjection of these parent images. This introjection if theoretically completed and the superego established with the beginning of the latency period[1].

The foregoing description of the neurotic's and the delinquent's reactions to their environment is now further complicated by the demands of the superego. An inadequate or disturbed relationship to the parents also disturbs the development of the superego, which manifests itself in a defective social adjustment.

Aichhorn (who uses the terms ego ideal and superego interchangeably) describes various types of delinquents whose behavior demonstrated their inability to form a socially acceptable ego ideal. He describes two groups.

In one group, the mechanism of the superego, or ego ideal, functioned well but the introjected parental norms were dissocial ones, that is, the parents were themselves criminal, so that the child who took over his standards from them inevitably came into conflict with society.

In the second group, it was the early relationship to the parents which had been disturbed, so that the process of ego ideal formation could not take a normal course but resulted in dissocial behavior.[2]

Let us specify at this point, parenthetically, that we consider an ideal social adaption one in which the inner equilibrium between ego, id, and superego enables the personality to realize its own needs and capacities without preventing others from doing the same. Since individual needs often differ from the interests of a group or society, this adaption is often hard to achieve.

Aichhorn, then, in discussing his second group of dissocial personalities enumerates various situations in early childhood which can cause faulty development of the ego ideal. Such is the case if a child is an orphan or semiorphan, or an illegitimate child who is placed in a succession of institutions or foster homes. He therefore has no one to whom he can form a sound and stable attachment or with whom he can make a real and lasting identification. In such cases there is either no way of establishing an ego ideal or it is defective and too weak to regulate conduct in later life.

Aichhorn describes other abnormal family situations that can have similar consequences, but they all demonstrate the same formula, namely, a defect or absence of object attachment causing a defect or absence of an ego ideal. Both a normal object relation and a sound ego ideal are necessary for an adequate social adjustment, and where either factor has been abnormal, delinquency may result.

Let us examine these same processes in neurotics.

The anamneses of neurotics also show disturbances in object cathexis and ego ideal formation. It seems probable that neglected children, who have not had a

---

[1] Following a proposition of Hartmann and Kris (1945), I shall, in order to make the terminology more precise, use the word "maturation" instead of "autonomous development" and reserve the term "development" for the processes of growth predominantly dependent on the environment.

[2] Here I should like to stress the fact that social adaption is not identical with uncritical submission to every passing demand of a given society. There can be and often really are circumstances in society which require a condemnation of prevailing norms and a rebellion against them.

mother's (or parent's) love seem more predestined to delinquency. Though my own experience with delinquency is too limited to justify an opinion, I am sure that lack of motherly love and severe frustrations can lead to a neurosis.

But this still does not illuminate our question about differential factors since most of the cases we meet show a combination of symptoms. The delinquent reveals neurotic trends, and our neurotic patients show tendencies toward more or less dissocial behavior. Therefore we have to confine ourselves to the quantitative aspect in making our diagnosis. Where the dissocial behavior predominates we speak of a delinquent with neurotic symptoms, and where there is a reversed balance of factors, we speak of a neurotic personality with (often concealed) delinquent features.

Although it is difficult to separate abnormal psychic manifestations from each other, careful observation sometimes enables us to gain insight into the origin of our patients' different behavior patterns.[3] Aichhorn describes types of delinquents who commit their dissocial offenses because of a need for punishment (an unconscious sense of guilt). Such cases force us to assume a severe superego (see Freud, 1916). Yet we repeatedly observe that a too severe superego causes neurotic symptoms. Can we discover what factors determine whether a strong and cruel superego leads to delinquency or to neurosis?

Since a punishing superego (like punishing parents in early childhood) makes one suffer, individual differences in the capicity to endure suffering, pain, or discontent must play a role in the problem. A person who cannot bear such tensions not only develops an inadequate adaption to reality but, unlike the neurotic, will not endure selfpunishment. He tries to escape it by mobilizing his rebellion against the outer world as a means of acting out the tension caused by his guilt feelings.

Why does the neurotic not do likewise? Perhaps his ability to endure suffering is greater, yet his means of relieving it would benifit him also. Must we conclude that his punishing superego is stronger than that of the delinquent? I do not believe so. The delinquents whose offenses are due to a sense of guilt show an intensity of purpose which hardly justifies this conclusion. It seems to me that another formulation may afford a deeper insight into this problem (see Chapter 8).

Up to this point, I have used the terms ego ideal and superego interchangeably as does Aichhorn. I now propose to make a distinction between them, as have Alexander, Flugel, and others.[4]

The superego is established through a dual process of development. The infant identifies himself early with both parents and wants to be or to become like them, and to incorporate their ideals as well. ("I want to be like my parent and have their ideals.") At the same time the child also takes over his parents' orders and prohibitions, and by introjecting them builds up the inhibiting (and

---

[3] Needless to say, we must always realize that clinically these various phenomena overlap and merge. Perhaps it will prove to be true that in each individual, whether "ill" or "normal," some trends of delinquency (psychopathy) are to be found.

[4] In the English translation of Aichhorn's book, *Wayward Youth* (1925), the translators also mention this tendency in psychoanalytic literature.

punishing) part of the superego. ("I must or must not do this or that.")

The ideal formation in the ego of the young child has a special function apart from that of social adjustment. It might be said to fortify the ego. These ideals serve the child as compensation whenever he feels hurt or incompentent in comparison with older children or adults. They strenghten his self-esteem by counteracting narcissistic injuries and frustrations. During maturation these ideals expand into all kinds of social, ethical, religious, and scientific norms. Even for adults, high ideals, if not exaggerated far beyond the personal level of attainment, are of great value to their self-esteem.

The young child's judging superego has the function of supervising his instinctual gratifications and curbing his passions through punishment whenever they threaten to conflict with external demands. This function of the superego, therefore, often injures the narcissistic position of the ego and hurts his self-esteem.

Where there has been a harmonious development, both parts of the established superego work together toward inner and outer equilibrium and finally form a unity. But if the development of either the ideal formation or the punishing part of the superego is disturbed, the two may diverge. We can understand this process better if we study the forces behind them.

We know from Freud that the severity of the superego does not correlate exclusively with the parents' attitude. The cruelty of the superego corresponds more closely to the strenth of the child's own aggressiveness. During the period when the child's superego is being established it uses the part of the child's aggressiveness which is turned toward the self. This takes place after the period of active instinctual life has terminated with the ending of its last phase, the oedipal situation.

When development is normal, the part of aggressive energy which is turned toward the self serves to secure the fulfillment of the ideals and thus strengthens the ego's self-respect. The remaining part of free, aggressive energy is used for mental, intellectual, and bodily activities in the outer world, for learning, adapting to, or changing the environment. It is "sublimated" into activity.

Unfortunately this difficult, complicated, and dual process is frequently disturbed. Often too much aggressiveness is turned toward the self. This aggression then becomes sexualized and the whole relation between superego and ego ceases to be a judging, regulating function in the service of normal adaptation. Instead it becomes a sadomasochistic relationship. The result is an obstinate tendency to self-punishment, an arrest and restriction of ego development and of the formation of the ego ideal.

On the one hand the ego is threatened by the cruel superego which has become as *triebhaft* as the id, and on the other the ego receives no support from the ego ideal because the ideal formation has been both damaged and restricted.

Moreover, when the two processes of the formation of an ego ideal and of a sadistic superego diverge, this divergence is itself another inhibiting force to the growth of the total personality.

When the aggressive energy used for developing normal activities cannot be adequately sublimated still another disturbance results. Either repression and inhibition are increased or the aggression is expressed in a direct, primitive manner. If it combines with sexual energy it can lead to various other forms of abnormal development.

Neurotics as well as delinquents may show a driving need for selfpunishment. I now claim that the differential factor between neurotics and delinquents is to be found in a developmental difference of their ego ideal and superego formations. Where there has been a strong ideal formation in early childhood which later was disturbed by an oversevere superego, its effect is to inhibit ego development and to prevent the sublimation of aggressive energy into activity. The strong ideals forbid the expression of any aggression toward the oudside world and it therefore turns toward the self. The result is the well-known vicious circle of the neurosis.

If in the young child there has been a weak ideal formation which later is disturbed by a sadistic superego, the result is self-punishment and also defective ego development. But in such cases the weak ideal formation is unable to prevent the aggression from discharging and the superego's aggression is acted out against the environment. This results in dissocial behavior or delinquency. There are interesting instances of mixtures of these two processes. Thus, for example, one may observe persons who, in one area of their lives have high ideals to which they may be either be making a good adjustment or if blocked in attaining them react with neurotic symptoms in this special field. But in other areas they may be utterly lacking in ideals and norms and behave quite dissocially. Careful examination of many delinquents often reveals a similar mixture in their personalities, with a few areas dominated by high norms and fine social feelings.

The ideal formation which begins in early childhood, and uses the mechanism of identification is probably a difficult and vulnerable process.

Since it would seem that almost everyone, be he as "normal" as possible in ordinary life, has a small "neurotic" nucleus and sometimes an almost undetectable "personal delusion," he probably also has a minor "psychopathic" spot in his makeup (Chapter 8).

I regret that the scope of this paper prevents me from presenting illustrative cases. Instead, I should like to discuss here two additional problems.

What are the prerequisites for a sound and lasting ideal formation? What is the source of this overpowering and ungovernable aggression which partly threatens the self and partly the environment?

I would say that there are two prerequisites for ideal formation. There must be a capacity for identification, innate and capable of being stimulated by experience. There must also be the right objects with which the child can identify. If these are lacking or inadequate, the process is correspondingly restricted.

There are children who succeed in building high ideals and norms in spite of having either no parents, or unsound or unstable parent figures. It may be that this astonishing achievement of some unloved children is the result of their need to compensate for the narcissistic unjuries which this lack of adequate object gratification caused them.

But when a child is not loved in his early years the more frequent result is an

impaired ideal formation. The child's narcissistic needs are then doubly frustrated through lack of love as well as through imperfect ideal formation. This
formulation brings us once more to an awareness of the importance of a child's
first love objects.

To return to our second point, namely, the source of the overpowering aggression: Observation of children convinces us that even a young child's aggression
can be and generally is mobilized by the frustration of a bodily or mental need or
wish.

The same is true in regard to sexuality. The infant at first seeks gratification of
his sexual urges through his own body (thumb-sucking, friction, anal play,
masturbation, etc.). It is the mother who introduces the child to sexual
pleasure. By offering her breast and by caressing the baby while nursing him,
she excites the baby and provokes his libidinal attachment. We know how
important maternal "seducing" proves to be for the child's sexual development
and how an excess of "seduction" may cause a variety of disturbances. It is true
that in normal development the baby's discharge of aggressive energy by means
of his own body is seldom noticed. The normal tendency toward the preservation of life ordinarily masks the signs of these aggressive urges. But occasionally
aggressive urges reveal themselves unmistakable in cases of self-damage (by
scratching, etc.).

In obviously pathological cases, however, severe self-mutilation has been observed.[5] But we hold to the truth of our previous statement, namely that acts of
aggression are in the main provoked by "frustration" as are sexual ones by
"seduction." These facts guide our educational procedures and make us say: A
child needs love but too much gratification may be experienced as seduction and
can be as harmful as lack of love.

Our knowledge that frustration stimulates aggression leads us to say: The child
must have opportunities for discharging a part of his aggression, but stimulating
his aggression by too much frustration will have damaging results. All of us who
deal with children are aware of this danger of steering from Scylla into
Charybdis.

Since too many frustrations provoke an excess of aggressiveness, the child must
be compensated by love so that he can make a sound love attachment and a
tenable ideal formation.

There seems a tendency in the literature to neglect the topic of aggressive,
instinctual urges in life, because of the fact that we only notice the aggression
which follows frustration. We would be in a similar position were we to ignore
the need for sexual object attachments because they arise only after stimulation. The fact that some authors have never observed acts of genuine aggression
hardly justifies this omission. In the same way, in the early days of
psychoanalysis, the existence of infantile sexual urges was indignantly denied by
the pediatricians, educators, and parents who had never observed them.
Although the analogous observation of aggressive urges is far more difficult, it
seems possible that further investigation will broaden the observer's views.

[5] See the case in W. Hoffer's paper on "Mouth, Hand, and Ego-Integration" (1949).

Some authors seem to neglect this topic of instinctual aggression because of their doubts about Freud's theory of a biologically founded death instinct. In my opinion, biology has not yet gone far enough either to affirm or deny Freud's hypothesis. Should it be proven erroneous, psychoanalysis must discard it. This would leave us without an answer as to the origin of aggressive energy until we can formulate a new and more tenable hypothesis. But meanwhile we cannot afford to overlook the manifestations of both sexual and aggressive drives in mankind.

From the social point of view it is virtally important that mankind does not deny the existence and intensity of genuine aggressiveness. Denial always leads to blindness and therefore to disturbed reality testing and adjustment. Some people seem to have a deep-rooted fear of admitting their own aggressive drives and therefore deny them in all human beings. Not until the role of the aggressive drives in the individual and in society has been accepted can we conceive of finding ways and means of overcoming the menacing manifestations of aggression and destructive behavior in mankind.

Among the major purposes of any educational program must be the aim of providing compensating love, constructive ideal formation, and suitable methods for sublimating aggression into fruitful activities.

In one chapter of his book (1925, pp. 167-185). Aichhorn describes an attempt to re-educate a group of juvenile delinquents in an institution. Their aggressiveness was so overwhelming as to segregate them from all other groups. Though he himself points out how, in his handling of this group, he was still groping for technique, and though today he might have used other methods, one is nevertheless struck by his intuitive understanding of their problems.

And we can recognize in this pioneer attempt at group re-education his awareness of the balance of factors and his endeavor to change the hitherto misdirected processes which have been the subject of this paper.

11. Some Remarks on the Development of Psychoanalysis During the Last Decades

(1950)

Psychoanalysis, like every science, has been continually developing during the more than fifty years of its existence. Development implies the possibility of enlargements and modifications of the original form. The object of psychoanalytic study is human psychic life, its theory is based on observations of the manifestations of this psychic life in both "normal" and "abnormal" persons. Since the observations have steadily increased and become greatly refined in the course of decades, the theory has gone through an evolution, has adjusted over and over again to the increase in knowledge, as is the case with all sciences. Where psychoanalytic psychology touches biology, notably where the biological substratum of the instinctual drives is concerned, the theory has for the time being, a more hypothetical character.

It may expected that a growing biological knowledge will either corroborate Freud's biological theory of the drives, or entail the necessity of modifying it. Psychoanalysis is often blamed for not being concerned with the socalles *Geisteswissenschaften*, which are engaged in the determination of values and norms (ethics), in philosophical speculations (such as, e.g., in the systems of Heidegger et al.), upon creeds, such as are to be found in the various religious systems, but − remarkably enough − on the other hand it is often said that analysis intends to affect or even to destroy norms and values, the "conception of life" of individuals and sometimes that of mankind itself.

Both reproaches are apparently rooted in a misappreciation of the empirical-scientific character of psychoanalysis. Psychoanalysis wants to observe, to gather knowledge, and to detect certain rules. Its relationship to the normative, speculative, and religious systems mentioned before can only be such as to take such systems − as manifestations of human emotional and mental life − for its objects of study, which has already been done by Freud and others. The objection that analysts do have a "view of life" and that consequently psychoanalysis has one too sounds very naïve. Every person who lives in community with others, and therefore the analyst too, needs values and norms, has a "conception of life." It stands to reason that enrichment of knowledge and extension of insight affect the conception of life and the determination of values. This has always been found to be true throughout the ages. Man, in our present civilization, no longer conceives of his genesis as a lump of clay which was molded, nor does he regard the earth as the centre of the universe. It would be a wrong way of thinking, which no longer needs to be refuted, to conclude from these facts that the conception of life and the determination of values of one or of a number of analysts proves that psychoanalytic *science* embraces a conception of life. It cannot and will not represent a conception of life.

I would like to discuss a condition which has often given rise to these errors in thinking. It lies in the fact that the analytic method of treatment is often mistaken for psychoanalytic science. Whenever two persons meet they will influence each other, however brief the encounter may be and even though the influence may be infinitesimal. An exchange of emotions may take place even without spoken words. If a patient applies to a doctor for help in combatting his neurotic symptoms, his psychic disturbances and disharmonies, and if the two of them decide upon a psychoanalytic treatment, they start upon this procedure with the conscious purpose of striving for a "value," which they have determined together, i.e., the patient's health. In doing so, the knowledge provided by psychoanalytic psychology is utilized, to wit, that neurotic symptoms or disturbances can sometimes be removed by tracing their genesis of which the patient is unaware.

By making the unconscious conscious, by reconstructing, remembering, and especially by once more *living through* and *working through* the conflicts that arose in previous developmental stages, a disturbed development can be modified and, if the patient is willing, it can be corrected.

In every encounter necessary for this purpose an exchange between analyst and patient takes place. Since the latter is usually helpless as a result of his illness and disequilibrium, he will be very susceptible to influence (unconscious or conscious), he will desire it and often even provoke it. The analyst, however, will try to utilize the patient's openess to influence for the sole purpose of making him accomplish the difficult psychic task, described above, which is a prerequisite for realizing the common goal (the "value"), i.e., to return to the patient his "health" and his own personality, if possible.

The analyst will regard every attempt at transferring the contents of his ethical, religious, or philosophical norms or concepts to the patient as taking advantage of the patient's openness to influence, a state which is temporarily raised by the therapeutic situation. Only with children, and with some adults who have remained very infantile and who have not developed a sufficiently normal personality, does one sometimes have to avail oneself of such a pedagogical influence in addition to the analytic treatment. Experience has taught us, however, that every such intervention is attended by a disturbance in the dynamic psychic process (to wit, the discovery and re-experiencing of the warded-off unconscious) which automatically arises in the analytic situation and the undisturbed course of which offers the best chances of recovery. Therefore one will avail oneself of these interventions as *rarely* and as *sparingly* as possible, and one will have to realize over and over again that in using them one runs the risk of adversely affecting the chances of recovery and development.

Now I have come to our subject proper: the development of psychoanalysis during the last decades. I want to distinguish three themes: (1) the development of the scientific theory; (2) the development of the technique and the therapeutic possibilities; (3) the influence of psychoanalysis on other branches of science, such as psychiatry, academic psychology, sociology, antropology, ethology, pedagogy, etc.

The development of psychoanalytic psychology

As has been said before, the psychoanalytic theory has been developed in the course of years and modified whenever necessary in the light of the experiences which increased owing to the growing refinement of the technique of exploration of mental life.

But Freud's fundamental discovery that neurosis arises whenever a psychic conflict cannot be solved in a normal way still maintains its validity. The neurotic patient displays, in a very obvious way, psychic phenomena (actions, thoughts, behavior) which are alien to his conscious personality. These observations made it necessary to accept a stratification or structuralization in the psyche and to distinguish between a conscious and an unconscious psychic life. This distinction could not be a merely descriptive one. Experience taught that one could make the unconscious conscious only by a certain psychic effort after overcoming the counteracting forces (resistance). Consequently one had to assume various systems in mental life, between which an interplay of forces takes place. Thus in addition to the topographic viewpoint, a dynamic viewpoint became necessary in the theory.

The study of hysterias and compulsion neuroses (and also the study of some paranoid states) soon revealed that certain startling events concerning the emotional life and certain urges, tendencies, and wishes which could not be tolerated or gratified by the conscious personality, were not only "forgotten," but were repressed to the unconscious, warded off, and by the mobilization of certain forces, prevented from entering consciousness; these are the very forces which, as I described before, manifest themselves as resistance in treatment.

The repressed urges were usually found to originate from the sexual sphere; and the starting events were found to be especially traumatizing when they occurred in early childhood, thus encountering a weak, undeveloped personality.

I will regard these early developmental stages of psychoanalysis as common knowledge and will leave it at this brief picture. I will only call to mind how the experiences on the instinctual and emotional life of the young child necessarily resulted in an extension of the concept of sexuality, which until then had practically been equated with adult sexual life. Adult love life turned out to be a final product of a long developmental course of sexuality from birth onward. This sexuality was found to go through a flourishing early period in the first years of life, during which it passes through various developmental stages (oral, anal-sadistic, and phallic phases), to flourish again in puberty after a latency period, and ultimately to result in adult life.

Certain traumatizations or excessive instinctual demands proved to be capable of disturbing this normal course of events, while the concominant object relationships were also disturbed and neurotic symptoms arose; now the dynamic viewpoint could also be better circumscribed in the theory. The interplay of forces was opposed by the sexual drives on the one hand and by the drives of self-preservation on the other. Quantitative factors required a third viewpoint in the theory: the so-called economic one. Quantitative relations between the various forces and in the various systems were decisive in regard to the final outcome of the conflicts in which constitutional factors and environmental influences were always found to play a part (Freud's "complementary series"). The biologically prescribed, autonomous development of infantile sexuality turned out to be subject to being influenced, stimulated, or inhibited by the attitude of the first love objects, originally the mother (or nurse), afterward also the father and other members of the family. At the heighth of the phallic phase a certain constellation of the object relatons is found, i.e., the so-called oedipal situation, consisting of a positive attitude (love for the parent of the opposite sex and rivalry and hate as far as the other parent is concerned) resulting in normal sexual development, and a negative oedipal situation (love for the parent of the same sex, rivalry with the other one), tendencies of which are gradually desexualized under normal conditions and sublimated into social relations. They may play an important role in pathology; however, I need not go further into this subject here. Freud's discovery that the oedipus complex constitutes the nuclear point of the neuroses can still be endorsed at present. We do know now, it is true, that the oedipal instinctual and emotional constellation is already the finished product of a greatly differentiated developmental process in the so-called preoedipal situation.

I will now briefly describe the developments that the various aspects of psychoanalytic theory have gone through. I will first examine (a) the structuralization of the mind, and then (b) the theory of the drives.

Topography or structure of the psychic personality

The division into conscious and unconscious psychic life (Freud's *Pcpt.-Cs.* vs. *Ucs.* systems) soon proved to be insufficient to allow the ever-increasing numbers of differentiated psychic phenomena to express themselves. It was found to be possible that processes which were at first counted as belonging to the system consciousness were repressed to the unconscious in a later developmental stage, etc. Freud suggested denoting the agencies between which the psychic processes take place as "id" and "ego." The id represents what has been carried in the germinal cells and comprises among other things the instinctual life (the drives); it is the source from which all subsequent features develop. In the id the so-called "pleasure-pain principle" prevails. Pleasure is striven for in an imperative, rigid way, and pain is avoided. The mode of action of the id is the so-called "primary process," well known from the study of a normal phenomenon, the dream, and extensively described in Freud's *The Interpretation of Dreams* (1900).

The ego is that part of the psychic personality which develops from the id under the influence of the outer world, and acts as an intermediary between the demands of the id and those of the outer world. To fulfill this task the ego develops a number of functions. It derives its power from the id and draws on the store of possibilities, capacities, and potentialities which are present at birth and are ever further developing. The ego modifies the pleasure-pain principle under the influence of the demands and restrictions imposed by the environment into the so-called "reality principle," which gives up the original rigidity, learns to tolerate pain to a certain extent and to renounce immediate gratification of pleasure. The mode of action of the ego is the so-called "secondary process"; in the mature ego this is an ordered, structured process, governed by thinking. As the ego gradually develops from the id, the development from pleasure principle to reality principle and from primary process to secondary process is a gradual one too, while transitions are always to be found.

As long as, for instance, the child's sense of reality has not yet developed, i.e., as long as the child cannot adequately distinguish between himself and the outer world, the reality principle cannot come to full development and action. In this case the mediation between the id and outer world is a deficient one for the time being, and the ego can respond to many stimuli and demands, both from the outside and from the inside, only by escape (repression, resistance, or denial) instead of by adequate handling and control.

Not only does the development of the sense of reality gradually take place but all functions of the ego have to be developed from a primitive stage. The possibility of observation of stimuli, perception, the formation of memory traces and memory images, the control of the steadily developing motility in order to make it subservient to the discharge of instinctual tensions and to the exploration and conquering of or adaptation to the outer world, the testing of reality — all these psychic functions the ego has to learn gradually. Intelligence, speech, and thinking also undergo a process of maturation from very primitive stages (see also the developmental psychology of Piaget).

At the same time the person needs not only discharge of instinctual tensions but also gratification of the strong desire for love, consequently a good relationship with the objects. These objects do help the child in the development of all his capacities, but on the other hand they make demands, impose restrictions upon the child, and cause frustrations the child is often unable to cope with. These difficulties can inhibit or even prevent the development of the various functions.

The ego produces mechanisms of defense and reaction formations against the instinctual tendencies which can become fixated and play a role in determining the character. Ultimately the ego strives for an inner unity and equilibrium. However, the synthetic function (integrative faculty) comes into existence comparatively late. From the very beginning this function can be damaged by disturbances in these infinitely complex, early, and labile developmental stages. In contradiction to academic psychology, psychoanalytic psychology has paid a great deal of attention to the dynamic processes. Both in the analytic exploration of the first years of childhood and in the direct observation of very young children it has found an abundance of material enabling the study of the effect of instinctual life on ego development. Without ulitizing this dynamic viewpoint the genetic psychology of the young child remains incomplete and results in a misconception of infantile psychic life.[1]

In neuroses and other faulty developments not only is a regression to an early fixation point of instinctual development to be found, but likewise a regression to an earlier stage of ego development. Inasmuch as reactive and defense mechanisms toward instinctual tendencies are concerned, there is a correlation with the corresponding libidinal stage. But all primitive ego attitudes may be mobilized again, and disturbances in certain functions occur in the various clinical pictures, such as hysteria, compulsion neurosis, paranoid states, etc.

I will now mention a very important process in ego development, described by Freud nearly thirty years ago, i.e., the formation of the superego. I may presume that it is well known that the superego is part of the ego, that arisis early in the latency period as a kind of precipitate of the oedipal object relationships which have been replaced by identifications. Through these identifications the modified part of the ego has assimilated the norms, commands, and prohibitions of the parents and at the same time the ideal images the child has made of them. Examples from the much wider social evironment are added later on. The superego has become, as it were, the conscience of the child: it exercises criticism, it demands and prohibits, and stimultaneously it has become the ego ideal (see chapter 10).

In normal development ego and superego harmonize with each other. The ego adapts itself to ideals, norms, and prohibitions, the superego adjusts its demands, if necessary, to the capacity of the ego. It is well known, however, how often this harmony is disturbed, leading to a gap arising between them.

The development of the superego is gradual, and correspondingly one also encounters precursors or, to put it otherwise, primitive developmental stages in the superego.[2]

The ego already uses the mechanism of identification at a very early stage, first, as a mechanism of defense against fear of loss of love, second (besides imitation), to learn from the object, to develop, and third, to form an ideal. By means of this form of identification the child also adopts prohibitions; this is very clearly observed in the anal phase of development. The child has already accepted, to a greater or lesser extent, what is permitted and what is not permitted; the ideal formation runs a parallel course. Normally a fusion of ideal ego and judging (prohibiting) superego is established only in the ultimate formation of a superego agency at the onset of the latency period.

This superego shows a further development throughout life and it obtains a greater or lesser autonomy by modifying the initial imperative parental norms in accordance with its own insight and experience. Nevertheless, in so-called normal people too, some residues of the infantile superego, acting in a compulsive way according to parental norms, are still to be formed. Furthermore, it is my opinion that an earlier precursor of the superego can be observed. In the earliest period of life, when the child begins to distinguish between "inside" and

---

[1] In the scope of this paper I cannot go into further detailed descriptions, and must refer to the analytic literature on these problems which has been published in various countries in the past few years (see Chapter 8; als A. Freud, 1936, 1945; A. Freud and D. Burlingham, 1942, 1943; Hartmann, Kris, and Loewenstein, 1946).

[2] For a different view of superego development, see Melanie Klein (1932, 1948).

"outside," the unpleasurable, the painful, the "bad" is projected onto the outside world. The pleasurable, the "good," remains inside. Later on "bad" and "good" obtain entirely different meanings, but in many people this primitive "What is within me, what I am, is good; the other is bad" is often found again in their subjective conviction that they have "the " thruth, know "the" revelation, advocate "the" good or "the" right, while misappreciating the subjective values of others. Here again a brief mention must suffice.

Many problems of ego and superego development are still unsolved, and so are their interrelations and their relations to various neurotic processes.

The development of the theory of the drives

Originally Freud was of the opinion that psychic conflicts, which can be studied most sharply in pathological phenomena in view of the larger dimensions assumed there, were caused by a clash between opposing instinctual drives which he conceived of as being linked with the two different systems, designated at that time *Cs.* and *Ucs.* He distinguished self-preservative or ego instincts from sexual drives. When, however, it was found that the ego too may become the object of sexual drives, that the ego has a libidinal cathexis, the so-called narcissistic cathexis, the distinction between the different groups of instinctual drives could no longer run parallel to the division into structural systems (or agencies). In the meantime Freud has also discovered that destructive and aggressive behavior could not be attributed to a certain transformation of the sexual drives, but that it was the manifestation of a destructive (or aggressive) drive which could be observed, being linked with and mixed with the sexual drives. In certain pathological cases, but notably in young children, an abundance of pertinent material is found on careful observation (see, e.g., A. Freud, 1949a). The new theory of the instinctual drives, which is still dualistic, distinguishes between erotic and destructive (aggressive) drives, which can act in conjunction (alloyed), but also separately.

Originally the drives are part of the id (in the widest sense). Aggressive drives accompany sexual ones on their way through the various developmental phases (oral, anal, phallic, and in adults the genital phases). In recent investigations attempts have been made to study the forms of expression of aggression in the various stages (see, for example, Hartmann, Kris, and Loewenstein, 1949). Especially in the first years of life one can observe how libido and aggression may be discharged simultaneously and separately. We meet, then, with instinctual ambivalence, which in turn entails emotional ambivalence. This ambivalence often continues throughout life; it may prevent the integration of the personality and may result in neuroses and/or character disorders.

During development the ego derives energy of both kinds of drive from the id. Partly the ego neutralizes or sublimates drive energy and it uses this neutralized energy for the many psychic functions and activities which it gradually develops during life. Yet a direct instinctual cathexis of the ego continues to exist throughout life. A certain level of narcissistic cathexis of the ego is found to be a precondition for normal functioning. Both excessive narcissistic cathexis, resulting in inadequate or faulty object relations, and a too small amount of narcissism may give rise to diseases or disorders. In the complexity of human existence in the present civiliation, an optimal condition does not seem to be easily attained.

Optimal sublimation of aggression into active control of outer world is also a difficult task. Far too often activities turn out to be more or less purely aggressive deeds. Here we are confronted with a new task of the ego. Besides the functions of acting as an intermediary between id and environment, developing its functions, developing defense and reactive mechanisms, and building up a harmonious unity with the superego the ego is also called upon to maintain a narcissistic cathexis, which is an indispensable basis for all its achievements. Injuries of this cathexis (so-called narcissistic injuries) also entail consequences for the development of the personality and may give rise to disharmonies (neuroses, deformities of character, etc.).

The legitimate need to find a biological basis for the forces that operate in psychic life (drives) caused Freud to construct a working hypothesis, in which he concieved of the vital process as an interplay of two different forces, the connecting (Eros) and the dissolving or destructive force. (The designations "life instinct" and "death instinct" are not a fortunate choice, in my opinion.) The erotic and aggressive drives, manifestations of which we observe in psychic life, would be expressions of the primal forces operating in all animate nature. This hypothesis is rejected by many people, among whom are psychoanalysts, although it may offer explanations for a number of phenomena for which a better or more elucidating hypothesis has not been advanced by any of its opponents. Such a speculative working hypothesis can never be proved from psychological knowledge, nor can it be refuted. It remains for biology to substantiate, reject, or modify this hypothesis.

The psychological theory of the drives, as it is presented to us today, is capable of explaining the dynamics of psychic phenomena fairly well. In this brief survey I cannot discuss the multiplicity and complexity of the various forms of expression to their full extent, of course.

The development of the psychoanalytic technique and the therapeutic possibilities

The increase in knowledge of mental life has greatly affected the technical process of psychoanalytic treatment. Conversely, the refinement of the technique has made us familiar with many more phenomena and has taught us to explain them more thoroughly.

Originally, Freud developed a technical procedure to make the repressed unconscious of a patient conscious because experience had taught him that neurotic phenomena sometimes could be removed by this process.

The discovery of the forces counteracting this process (resistances) made it necessary to go beyond making unconscious contents conscious and to find psychological means of handling these forces and to learn to control them. This required a finer technique and a slow working through of all positions, traumatic events, and fixation points in the past.

Our increased knowledge of the maturation and development of the ego gradually made it possible to develop a technique to treat not only the cases where the disturbance lays in conflicts between the instinctual life and a relatively intact, adult ego, but also those in which the ego had become involved in the disease and had been disturbed and inhibited in its own development. Not only were regressions to former stages of the libido made conscious, but ego regressions to early points of arrest in development were exposed, defense mechanisms and reaction formations were traced, inasmuch as they has assumed pathological forms, and thus the patient was given an opportunity to make up the deficiences in his ego development. Pathological reactions of the superego were also made conscious and worked through, owing to which morbid reactions of guilt feeling and tendencies toward selfpunishment would sometimes be abolished. Moreover, the knowledge of instinctical life makes it possible at present to remove not only disturbances in the sexual sphere but also pathological manifestations and modifications of aggression, which play so great a part in, for instance, inhibitions, disturbances of the capacity to work, depressions, etc. The discovery, referred to above, of the early history of the oedipus complex, the preoedipal attachment to the mother, and our detailed knowledge of the pregenital developmental states of the libido (Abraham, 1921, 1924a, 1924b, 1924c) enabled us to revive traumatic events of even the earliest childhood.

The psychoanalytic technique had to undergo a real change. The material from this primordial period does not rise to the surface in words, in memories, dreams, or fantasies, but by way of so-called acting out, the re-experiencing of infantile events, feelings, emotions, etc., in the analytic situation. Here again the modified and more refined technique provided us with new data on psychic events and on early ego development.

The increase in knowledge and the refinement of the technique have also widened the range of applications of psychoanalytic therapy. While at the onset only hysterias, complusion neuroses, and some paranoid states could be treated, at present we can also employ psychoanalysis in the so-called narcissistic neuroses, depressions, deformities of character, delinquency, developmental disturbances in children, and various mild psychotic states. Naturally this does not by any means imply that all these morbid states can always be entirely cured or that it is possible to make a perfectly harmonious, integrated personality out of every disturbed human being. Just like every medical therapy, psychoanalytic therapy has its limitations and restrictions. It is very remarkable that, in many people, even in doctors and psychiatrists, one encounters the idea, and the demand, that psychoanalysis must be able to remove all psychic disturbances. Although nobody blames a surgeon or a specialist on pulmonary diseases for not being able to cure a number of his patients after a careful and patiently continued therapy, a great fuss is often made when psychoanalytic treatment does not always yield the desired success.

In the event of a failure, the analyst can only take comfort in the idea that he has increased his knowledge by which other patients may benifit, and that he may have learned to realize where the limitations of therapeutic influence lie. I will not go further into this question here, since it would lead us too far from the subject under discussion. I will merely point out another field where the progress of psychoanalytic technique and science must be regarded as of importance.

There are many patients with whom one does not want or is not able to apply psychoanalytic treatment, for internal or external reasons. In order to make these patients fit for life, to a certain extent at least, one resorts to one of the forms of so-called "brief therapy." This used to be based (and this is still often the case) on an uncontrolled, so-called intuitive treatment of the patient. Our increased knowledge of psychic conflicts enables us occasionally (and probably will do so even more in future) to attack only certain conflicts or to displace them to fields where they are less disturbing in the patient's life situation.

Owing to our refined technique we are better able to see how we can and ought to utilize the relation between doctor and patient in order to help the latter in solving certain conflicts. The detailed elaboration of the technique of these "brief therapies" is still in the making, but it is being further studied by various analysts and in various institutions in Europe and the United States.

I want to point out one danger to which brief therapy is exposed to a much greater extent than is analysis. The improvement of the patient's condition arising in consequence of a displacement or of a merely partial solution of his disturbances can be undone again in later years. It very often happens that a patient, after having undergone one or more psychotherapies in the course of years, all of them attended with some success, ultimately does turn to the psychoanalyst, when middle-aged or older. The analyst then has to regard the chances for recovery in this period of life as much poorer than they might have been at an earlier time. It may even happen that an attempt to start an analysis has to be given up entirely, for instance, with women in the climacterium whose main talents lay in being a wife and mother and who would consequently not be able to do very much with their regained health.

As already indicated, I am of the opinion that psychoanalytic (and psychotherapeutic) treatment must remain a procedure which aims at tracing the causes of certain (mental) diseases and at trying to cure them.

An opinion which is often voiced at present, that the therapist should introduce a certain conception of life or of mankind into the treatment, is not only a nonmedical and unscientific one, but moreover limits to a great extent the group of people that can be reached. Experience has taught that with psychoanalysis one can help people of different races and nationalities, with the most divergent creeds, conceptions of life, and social convictions. Exercising influence in philosophical, religious, or political directions is the field of the philosopher, the pastor, the pedagogue, or the propagandist. When the psychotherapist is prepared to give up the narcissistic satisfaction of transferring his own values and convictions to his fellow men, he will be able to handle the human relation with his patients in order to restore the health of as large a number of people as possible.

The "ideal" that I am defending here is a medical-therapeutic one in the widest sense of the word.

Should it be indispensable in very infantile patients, as I remarked, to exercise more personal influence, one must always remain aware of the fact that one has added a second goal to the medical-therapeutic one. Our knowledge of psychic life enables us to make these finer distinctions and to dose the measure by which the patient is influenced.

The influence of psychoanalysis on other branches of science

Psychiatry and psychology have been more or less consciously adopting the discoveries of psychoanalysis for decades. This is denied by many, although one continually encounters the influence of analysis both in theory and in practice. This denial has undoubtedly affected psychiatry rather unfavorable. Sometimes psychoanalysis is said to be accepted. However, it often happens that this "acceptance" is limited to an injudicious and distorted utilization of technical terms, in which the unbiased observation of the phenomena has fallen into the background.

In practice one often encounters a conscious rejection together with an unconscious utilization of psychoanalytic psychology, which usually does not yield profit to the patient. The use of a method not mastered by the therapist may be very dangerous, as in every medical therapy. Where analysis is not consciously rejected, but where the therapist has not acquired the technique by personal experience in living through and working through his own conflicts, it is often observed that the so-called analytic treatment is limited to labeling certain conflict situations, preferably in theoretical terms. The dynamic character of the therapeutic process may be misjudged; the detection of his very individual experiences and the working through of his special conflicts in his own sphere and language may be withheld from the patient.

However, in view of the growing interest in psychoanalysis (especially in England and the United States but also on the Continent), it may be expected that a more objective, scientifically critical attitude of psychiatry will gradually prevail. Such an attitude would make a more judicious use of the findings of psychoanalysis and at the same time would further the efforts to fill the many gaps still present.

The influence of psychoanalysis on sociology and antropology[3] started very early. This influence began with Freud's own work, as is well known. (I merely refer to *Totem and Taboo* [1912-13] as a classical work.) During the last decades sociologists and anthropologists, especially in America, have often appealed to psychoanalysis. The analysts, too, have made attempts at elucidating sociological problems with the aid of analytic psychology. The difficulty is that in general sociologists are not sufficiently schooled in analysis, while analysts are not sufficiently in touch with the many facts to be found in the fields of sociology and anthropology.

Since a thorough knowledge of the development of the relations between men and of all aspects of mankind, social order, etc., does not seem to be possible

[3] In order to prevent misunderstanding, I will point out that "anthropology" is used here in the sense it had of old and still has almost everywhere in the United States, that is, the natural history of mankind, and not in the philosophical sense of Heidegger et al.

without a profound knowledge of the individual, one may assume that team-work will develop in the furure, as it is already operating in America on a small scale.

Analysis has been of great sifnificance in education, beginning at a very early date. Besides the application of the method to children, the so-called child analysis, it has greatly influenced the pedagogical attitude of adults, both in normal and in pathological cases, in connection with the enormous increase of knowledge regarding the development of the child.

I will not go further into this matter, but I want to stress the fact that the pioneer work of Aichhorn (1925) with dissocial and delinquent youth has been built up on the foundations of psychoanalysis.

Before concluding, I will point out that psychoanalysis, apart from the many discoveries it has made and the deep insight it has afforded into human psychic life, is still a growing science. Many psychic phenomena are not yet fully understood and further correlations and interdependencies must be studied.

In this brief survey I have endeavored to outline some trends and possibilities for the development of psychoanalysis, but I am fully aware of the fact that it is far from exhaustive.

12. Discussion on evolution and present trends in psychoanalysis

(1950)

The title of the subject under discussion embraces two different approaches to the developmental aspect of psychoanalysis. "Evolution" means organic growth, theoretical amplifications, and revisions as a consequence of the increase of empirically gained data, whereas "present trends" refer to applications to allied fields of work. In regard to psychoanalysis, applications both to other sciences and to therapeutic procedures are to be considered.

The four opening speakers give interesting illustrations of these two aspects.

Maurice Levine presents valuable examples of applied psychoanalysis. He gives an idea of the deep influence psychoanalysis has exercised on psychiatry, general medicine (psychosomatic medicine), social problems, child guidance, etc., and on some psychotherapeutic methods in America. (For a European analyst it is quite fascinating to learn the great extent to which psychoanalytic training is demanded in official psychiatric departments and medical schools of various American universities.)

But Levine does not fail to lay stress on possible dangers resulting from those applications. The penetration of psychoanalysis into the afore-mentioned disciplines is not, in the first place, due to an inner evolutionary process. It was born out of a need of those other fields of work, and that need sometimes gives rise to incorrect modifications of psychoanalysis for some practical purpose or other. Levine speaks of the danger of "dilution."

Real examples of evolution are brought forward by Anna Freud. She describes some modifications of theory introduced by Freud as a consequence of the process of internal evolution. The study of mental development during the first years of life produced advances in knowledge which led to a broader insight into: (a) the biological basis of psychic life, to wit, the interplay of two biological forces, the life force and the destructive force; (b) the development of the structured psychic life itself, to wit, the development of the ego organization (ego functions, defense mechanisms, superego, etc.).

Anna Freud advocates more experimental work, especially in child psychology, in order to stimulate further evolution.

The organic evolutional modifications of psychoanalysis naturally do not fail to influence the field of work to which it is applied. Conversely, data gained in related disciplines can be utilized for the development of analysis, *at least when the process of evolution remains undisturbed.*

In the course of applications, parts of analytic theory are lifted out of the whole structure over and over again. This method is a legitimate effort. However, it often occurs that the chosen parts gradually come to be handled as if they were representatives of psychoanalysis as a whole. In the allied disciplines they become isolated from the evolutionary process which takes place in analytic work, and then psychoanalysis is often attacked as a rigid, antiquated doctrine. A further consequence may be that other, essential parts of analytic theory are rejected or neglected.

Sometimes it is difficult to decide whether a proposal modification is correct or not. However, partial revisions that neglect essential knowledge based on observations, as for instance the knowledge of sexual development, cannot be fertile as far as evolution is concerned. They are bound to find their limits in themselves, and may lead to violation, mutilation, or "dilution" of psychoanalysis.

Levine and others are looking for the danger of "dilution" in the popularization of analysis among nonanalyzed research workers. However, similar events can be observed in psychoanalysts themselves. I should like to cite a few condensed examples out of the many that could be given.

A very interesting and far-reaching application is that to sociology. The topic lies beyond the scope of today's discussion. I only want to mention that several analysts working in this field tend to see the source of all personal as well as social misery in environmental influences, neglecting the importance of inner conflicts originating from the nature of the instinctual drives and the complexity of structures, both in individual and in social life.

But I must turn to a theme of today's discussion.

For the time being the work of Franz Alexander and his coworkers concerning so-called "brief psychotherapy" holds the limelight of therapeutic interest. Psychotherapy is as old as the history of mankind. Alexander's attempt to base brief therapy on a scientific, psychoanalytic theory deserves great interest and the appreciation of every socially minded therapist, since neuroses and mental disturbances are widespread maladies and severe dangers for men and society. It is undoubtedly a social disadvantage of psychoanalytic treatment that it can be performed only with a limited number of patients.

However, it is astonishing to see how, in order to recommend his therapy, Alexander has to make use of a devaluation and distortion of both analytic technique and knowledge.

The limited scope of this communication permits taking up only a few points: (1) Alexander proclaims as the aim of treatment a better adjustment of the patient to his environment, a "reconditioning," a practical, valuable goal indeed and sometimes attainable in brief therapy. But Alexander neglects the fact that the goal of analytic treatment goes further. It aims at liberating repressed forces originating from the instinctual life in order to enable the patient's ego to realize its capacities, making use of its own forces.

(2) It is perhaps in connection with this misunderstanding of the psychoanalytic goal that Alexanders considers practical arrangements, such as, for instance, daily sessions and the patient's being placed on a couch, etc., as the essential characteristics of analytic technique. Actually, they are merely tools promoting the dynamic analytic process.

(3) In my opinion, however, Alexander's greatest error is to be found in his reasoning for rejecting analytic treatment with very dependent patients. Too much dependency is caused not only by faulty education and wrong parental attitudes. It is the result of a strong infantile fixation on early levels of instinctual and ego development (passive-feminine attachment to the parents, oral fixation, conflicts with aggressive urges, etc., and imcomplete ego organization). That means that it is the result of an interplay of both *external and internal* factors.

Of course the therapist's active display of an attitude opposite to that of the patient's parents can have an influence, but it does not enable the patient to get through the psychic work necessary for a lasting change in his personality. Alexander does not seem to have noticed that he is merely substituting one form of dependency for another.

(4) A remarkable counterpart of the tendency to neglect the role of instinctual drives in therapy manifests itself in Alexander's new psychosomatic "surplus" theory of sexuality. The role of sexuality is reduced to a secondary one, a kind of waste of energy. The problem of where the energy of emotions and tensions comes from is eliminated. His theory has regressed to a preanalytic phase.

I now come to the report of Raymond de Saussure. It presents a most interesting research in the field of ego psychology and especially of the development of two ego capacities, (a) that of thought, and (b) that of mastering emotions. The attempt to connect psychoanalytic data with Piaget's findings is, in my opinion, a very stimulating evolutionary trend in our research work. I myself initiated this idea some ten years ago. It would be tempting to discuss the abundance of problems and suggestions stimulated by de Saussure's lecture, but time is lacking.

It is disappointing, however, to learn that de Saussure, too, could not escape the danger of overvaluing new points of view and mutilating analytic theory. For by proposing, for instance, "to oppose in psychopathology the prelogical or hallucinatory thinking to the rational or assimilated thinking rather than to preserve the opposition of the id, the ego, and the superego," it is clear (a) that de Saussure locates the origin of neurotic disturbances exclusively in ego development and eliminates the role of the instinctual drives, and (b) that he neglects the fact that prelogical thinking itself is already a complicated product of development. It is striking and interesting to see that in all the cases mentioned it is the theory of instinctual drives (sexuality) that is repudiated, just as happened in the earlier days of the psychoanalytic movement (Jung, Adler, and others).

I now come to the final question: What are the lines along which further evolution of psychoanalysis can be expected? For the time being I should like to make the following suggestions:

(1) In regard to the evolution of psychoanalysis proper: (a) In the field of instinctual life: developmental stages of aggressive (destructive) urges and their interplay with libidinal tendencies should be studied in detail. (b) The study of ego development, not only of thought but of all capacities and functions, including superego and ego ideal, requires further elaboration. Here wide fields

for research are still unexplored. (c) Finally, the interaction and mutural influence of instinctual development and ego (superego) development have to be studied in chronological order.

(2) In regard to applied psychoanalysis: (a) Continued application of scientific and therapeutic data to afore-mentioned fields of work. (b) Experimental research on young children in order to elucidate, verify, or, if necessary, revise psychoanalytic theory.

It should be kept in mind that the entire research work can be productive only if the tendency to take the part for the whole and to reject and neglect well-founded parts of the theory is counteracted and eliminated.

In summary: Evolution of psychoanalysis is still based upon experimental work. Neglect of present knowledge and well-founded theory has to be avoided. New insight has to be obtained, for instance (a) in the field of instinctual life (developmental stages of aggressive drives and their interplay with sexual tendencies); (b) in ego development; and (c) on the mutual influence of ego and instinctual development. Anna Freud presents examples of real evolution. In applications to other sciences or to psychotherapy, psychoanalytic theory is often mutilated when parts of its knowledge are treated as if they represented the whole theory. Alexander, for instance, in his application to therapy, underestimates the importance of the internalized conflicts and devaluates the role of the instinctual drives, aiming only at the patient's better adjustment to the environment. Alexander's attitude leads toward dilution of psychoanalysis. De Saussure, in his most valuable attempt to enlarge the knowledge of ego development, unfortunately also devaluates the role of instinctual life.

13. On Masturbation and its Influence on General Development

(1950)

I

In 1912, the Viennese Psychoanalytic Society published a symposium on the topic of masturbation. Freud (1912) concluded his own contribution with the statement: "For we are all agreed on one thing – that the subject of masturbation is quite inexhaustible" (p. 254). Today, after a lapse of thirty-eight years, I think this statement is still valid. However, we may be able to contribute some additional information to some of the outstanding points in the 1912 discussion. Freud summarizes, among other things, those points on which there existed a general consensus among the discussants and those on which opinions differed. The discussants agreed (a) on the importance and meaning of the fantasies accompanying or replacing masturbation, and (b) on the importance of the guilt feelings connected with masturbation.

Today we can confirm these findings; moreover, we are now better informed concerning the origin, development, and fate of the fantasies.

One of the points on which at that time opinions differed concerned the origin of the guilt feelings. This particular uncertainty has since disappeared; the various sources of the guilt feelings are now rather well known to us.

The other differences in opinion at that time centered, to be exact, around one question: "Can the masturbatory activity per se be harmful?" This question was answered, more or less passionately, by some discussants in the affirmative; by others in the negative as regards any direct somatic impairment.

To Freud, who belonged to the first group, this problem was inimately connected with his concept of the "actual neurosis." Freud maintained his first conception that a number of neurotic symptoms were caused by the toxic effects of undischarged or inadequately discharged quantities of instinctual energy, and thus created a nucleus for the psychoneuroses, caused by psychological conflicts.

The symptoms of neurasthenia – constipation, headaches, fatigue – were thought to be the consequence of (excessive) masturbation, the anxiety neurosis "at bottom a small fragment of undischarged excitation connected with coition" (p. 248). In the discussion at that time, Freud retracted his original idea that the "actual' symptoms" could not be influenced by psychoanalytic treatment (p. 249). However, he then considered the cure of those symtoms as a secondary effect of the treatment. He assumed that the psychoanalytic treatment effected a greater tolerance of the "current noxae" or that it enabled the patient, through alteration of the sexual regimen, to avoid these noxae. At what point and according to what mechanisms the direct organic (toxic) impairments of masturbation occur was not known, in Freud's opinion. He also emphasized at that time that one must separate these direct impairments from "those which arise *indirectly* from the ego's resistance and indignation against that sexual activity" (p. 253).

It would be wrong to conclude from these concepts that Freud always considered masturbation a harmful activity, although this conclusion frequently has been and may still continue to be drawn. Thus even at that time he pointed out that there are times in analysis when we must consider masturbation as a sign of therapeutic progress. He was referring to those cases, as in hysteria or compulsion neurosis, in whom, masturbation previously having been repressed for neurotic reasons, it then recurs during treatment.

At present we can neither prove nor disprove the existence of toxic impairment due to masturbation or frustrated excitation. On the one hand, we know how important a normal sexual life is for mental health and how greatly periods of life with physiologically increased instinctual demands, like puberty and menopause, predispose the person to psychological disturbances. On the other hand, our growing psychoanalytic experience has taught us how frequently neurasthenic complaints can be dissolved and how analogous they are in this respect, and also in respect to their causation, to hysterical or psychoneurotic symptoms.

It may be that today the question whether instinctual (sexual) energy could have a toxic effect (on the psyche) has lost its importance.

The investigation of the interaction between psychic and somatic disturbances has been very much in the foreground. It appears that certain organic pathological manifestations, asthma nervosum, colitis ulcerosa, ulcus ventriculi, skin diseases, hay fever, etc., may be caused by psychological conflicts similar to those underlying various psychoneurotic symptoms. Some of these somatic complaints have even been influenced, indeed cured, by psychoanalytic treatment (psychosomatic medicine). Careful observation has shown the frequency, even in healthy persons, of organic reactions to psychological stimuli — reactions, for instance, of the vascular system, of the intestinal tract, of the sensory apparatus. On the other hand, we have to presume an organic correlate as the basis for all psychic processes, even if its existence cannot be proved directly. It is improbable that this organic correlate is to be looked for only in the manifestations of sexuality. I will not elaborate on this interesting topic, or on the hopeful expectation that somatic and psychological therapy will be combined to an even greater extent when in the future our information about these interactions increases more and more.

I will return now to the subject of masturbation. I want to emphasize that so far my remarks have referred to the masturbation of adults. By masturbation I meant any manipulation of the genital apparatus (or of erogenous zones substituting for it) for the purpose of gaining pleasure. But we have to take into consideration that generally masturbation is indulged in from early childhood, at a time when any other discharge of instinctual tension is not yet possible because of physical and psychological immaturity. It has been ascertained that *all* children masturbate during their first year of life, that most of them masturbate during puberty, and that masturbation sometimes occurs during the latency period as well. By this means sexual as well as aggressive instinctual excitations are discharged.

I think we may describe masturbation as a normal activity of childhood for the purpose of discharging instinctual tension. It may fulfill the same function with adolescents or adults whenever the instinctual gratification of a physical and emotional relationship with a lover is not or not yet possible in a form more appropriate to adulthood. In the so-called civilized societies the latter situation frequently occurs, because the individuals have usually reached sexual maturity, physically and mentally, long before it is made possible for them to satisfy their emotional love needs in a permanent relationship and in the foundation of a family.

Masturbation may be accompanied or followed by neurotic disturbances of many kinds. There may be Physical ("neurasthenic") or emotional symptoms. The latter may consist of depressions, nosophobias, inferiority or guilt feelings, or self-torment. But whatever these manifestations, we are certain that the masturbatory act did not cause them but that we are dealing with neurotics who, as we know from psychoanalysis, acquired their disharmonies in early childhood and now connect their complaints with the masturbatory act. Therefore there is no sense in limiting the meaning of masturbation, either in psychology or in psychopathology, to the physical manipulations of the genitals or of the substituting erogenous zones. The decisive factor for health or sickness lies in the conscious or unconscious fantasies, feelings (guilt feelings), and impulses which accompany the masturbatory act.

This brings us to the two points mentioned above on which, according to Freud's summary, there existed a consensus among the Viennese discussants. However, we want to add that masturbation fantasies and (guilt) feelings not only are of importance but are of *essential* significance for psychic life.

Among the Viennese participants, Stekel more than anyone else argued against the concept of the injuriousness of masturbation. We are in accord with him as far as the physical actions are concerned.

On the other hand, we definitely dispute his statement that "all people masturbate" even if we take into consideration that Stekel includes herewith the disguised forms of masturbation. Emotionally healthy grownups will seek ways (and will usually find them) to satisfy their sexual needs in a normal love relation with a partner; they may occasionally use masturbation but only temporarily in periods of transition. Adults who *permanently* resort to masturbation (whether they choose it as the exclusive form of satisfaction or retain it in addition to sexual intercourse) are persons, more or less disturbed in their development, who have remained fixated or have regressed to that infantile form of sexual activity.

I now want to turn our attention to the psychological manifestations accompanying masturbation and trace certain vicissitudes of these fantasies, impulses, and emotions. Let me emphasize again that, when I speak of masturbation in what follows, I am referring to the *whole complex* of physical and emotional manifestations. We will see that both components may join in following the same path or may also be seperated. Wherever this separation occurs, psychoanalysis can always demonstrate that in the unconscious they belong together.

Masturbation, especially in young people, often gives rise to an oppressive burden of emotions. Feelings of anxiety, guilt, sin, inferiority, and depravity as well as fears of sickness, insanity, spinal disease, impotence, etc., may all be connected with masturbation.

It is well known that a very important source of all these horrors lies in various layers of society, in the attitude of those responsible for the child's upbringing. Parents, teachers, clerics, and often doctors too, in speech and writings, often very forcefully attempt to convince the young that masturbation is the most dangerous and sinful of vices.

Yet it is remarkable that in spite of these ominous threats and punishments so many people finally attain a normal sexual life. Whether in defiance of all intimidation they continue to masturbate until they achieve adult sexuality with a partner, or whether they give it up, the end result can be a healthy love life. On the other hand, there is a frighteningly large number of persons who react to these prohibitions and threats with mild or severe psychological disturbances. One encounters cases which range all the way from mild disturbances of potency, inhibitions or difficulties of adjustment, to severest impotence, neurosis, and impediments of development. Where there is no severe impairment, frequently simple reassurance about the harmlessness of the activity and enlightenment in case of ignorance may produce relief and may lead development into normal channels.

However, where such a procedure is of no avail, it is evident that the intimidations of the environment were not the sole cause of the neurotic illness, but that they affected an already sick or disturbed person, and that one has to seek for the causes in his childhood.

Masturbation, as I said before, already occurs during infancy. The infant plays with or rubs different parts of his body. In the beginning the mouth zone plays a very important role, sometimes perhaps in consequence of feeding, i.e., through stimulation by the breast or bottle. However, according to a number of observations by physicians and nurses, some infants, even before the first feeding, suck their fingers, which may lead to a facial expression of satisfaction and to quietly falling asleep. The sucking reflex seems to point the direction here. After some time various other body zones are rubbed and finally the genitals too. Some observations on infants up to the age of one seem to indicate that a kind of acme may be reached which could be considered as an early infantile form of orgasm. Perhaps more frequently this playing is quiet and uninterrupted, and seems to lead to a diffuse kind of satisfaction. In Spitz's interesting and important article, "Autoerotism," in which he records observations on 196 infants from birth to fifteen months, he calls such activity "genital play" instead of masturbation (1949).

A widespread opinion, already represented in the Viennese discussion in 1912, contends that the bodily care of the infant is in effect a seduction by the mother or nurse and that the child is led to genital activity in this way. In contrast to this view, Spitz believes that it is not the physical rubbing or friction which teaches the child the genital play but the emotional relation to the mother (1949).

I agree with the author when he writes in the introduction of his paper: "A really unimpeachable study would have to offer continuous 24-hour observation of the infant during the whole of the first year of life" (p. 85). It also seems to me that his experimental conditions – the observations of each child at *weekly intervals* during only *four hours per week* – are very far removed from the ideal conditions mentioned. I therefore think that the conclusions and hypotheses of Spitz, interesting as they appear to be, should be viewed with the greatest caution and that many observations under more favorable conditions will be nesessary to give them validity. Thus, for instance, I question whether the autoerotic gratification of rocking only occurs because the child is unable to establish an object relationship due to "the inconsistent, contradictory behavior of the mother." From a few but intensive observations I have gained the impression that rocking also occurs with a strong object relationship. (The latter can be neurotically tinged on the mother's part.)

On the other hand, it is a tempting hypothesis to assume that the infant's activity and thereby also his genital play is not only learned through mechanical stimulation but that the emotional relationship to the mother (or mother substitute) is an indispensable factor. It seems certain that infants treated without love (even though adequately nourished) deteriorate physically and are psychologically hampered in their development as well. Intelligence, emotional life, motility, instinctual life, and ego functions are interfered with in their maturational processes and show more or less retardation. From his observations, Spitz concludes: "When this [the mother-child] interrelation is at its best, genital play will be general in the first year of life and general development will surpass the average" (1949, p. 103). This is marvelously in accordance with Freud's concept, laid down in 1905 in his *Three Essays on the Theory of Sexuality* (1905c). In the section on object choice, Freud described that every object choice of the adult is a "refinding" and a continuation of the relationship of the infant to the mother (nurse) who not only stimulates and satisfies the child through his erogenous zones but also supplies him with emotions which originate in her own sexual life, etc. And further:

> As we know, however, the sexual instinct is not aroused only by direct excitation of the genital zone. What we call affection will unfailingly show its effects one day on the genital zones as well. Moreover, if the mother understood more of the high importance of the part played by instincts in mental life as a whole – in all its ethical and psychical achievements – she

would spare herself any self-reproaches after her enlightenment. She is only fulfilling her task in teaching the child to love. After all, he is meant to grow up into a strong and capable person with vigorous sexual needs and to accomplish during his life all the things that human beings are urged to do by their instincts. [1905c, p. 223].

Whether it results in an acme or in a diffuse gratification, masturbation plays a normal part in the development of a healthy infant's instinctual life, as well as supplying him with pleasurable activity of various bodily zones. A good, loving attachment (close relationship) is a precondition for sound development. What form this mother relationship takes is a different question. The emotional attachement develops gradually out of the biological, physical, mother-child unit. Just when or how this occurs, is, in my opinion, still unknow.

Melanie Klein concludes from her numerous and particularly impressive observations that during his first weeks of life, the infant already forms a wealth of complicated fantasies, of a loving as well as an aggressive nature. According to Klein, the infant wants to possess the mother, wants to penetrate her, wants to incorporate her and to dismember her, to rob her and to destroy her depending on his feelings about the mother as a "good" or "bad" object. The infant then supposedly is tormented by guilt feelings because of his bad fantasies and during the first months of life already has a severe and punitive superego (M. Klein, 1928).

It seems to me a large and arbitrary step to conclude that all these complicated fantasies are already present in the infant merely from the observations that satiated and contented infants smile at their mothers and that hungry ones or those suffering from painful sensations scream, struggle, or show expressions to be interpreted as anxious. It seems much more plausible to assume that intense primitive excitations, sensations, and impulses may exist in the infant which may be directed toward the mother, but that these are only elaborated into complicated psychic formations, as the above-mentioned fantasies, after the psychic apparatus reaches a certain level of development. We are aware that such excitations and impulses also exist in domesticated animals without concluding that they form similar fantasies. Ego development has not yet begun in the newborn child even though an innate nucleus of the ego exists. It still takes a rather long time before the infant develops his ego functions and before he is able to achieve an even primitive coordination of some of these functions. However, only after such an achievement is one justified in speaking of a primitive ego. The differentiation in the ego, which leads to the formation of the superego, belongs to an even later phase of maturation.

To make a simple equation between primitive id impulses and psychic formation involving ego and superego hardly seems a service to scientific attempts at clarification. This method ignores the fact that psychic life undergoes a process of development − of dynamic maturation. However, it would be premature to postulate more exact data for the individual stages of development. Let us console ourselves with the fact that many more thorough observations will be necessary for the clarification of these conditions.

However that may be, we may assume that the infant in his first year of life provides pleasure and gratification for himself by playing with various parts of his body, and that in this gratification the genital apparatus has an important role. Moreover, this gratification is closely connected with the mother-child relationship which accompanies and shapes the child's entire development.

When at the end of his first and in his second year the child enters the anal phase of libidinal development, this playing begins to be concentrated on the anal zone and its productions. It is quite certain that a high intensity of instinctual energy is disposed of here. But genital play and the stimulation of other body zones frequently continue during this period as they did during the preceding oral phase, although perhaps with less intensity. It is well known that Freud's classification of the three phases of infantile libidinal development is schematized and that an overlapping of the different phases occurs, with remainders of earlier phases coexisting with elements of later phases to a greater or lesser degree. In the final phase of early libidinal development, the phallic phase, the instinctual discharge occurs primarily via the genital zone. The sexual activity of the child now reaches its peak in masturbation, which may be accompanied by erections and which frequently culminates in an acme.

The fantasy activity, in the meantime, has blossomed along with the entire infantile personality. Intelligence, many ego functions, the forerunners of superego in ideal formation and moral demands, have taken shape. The child has learned to differentiate between his self and the environment to a greater or lesser degree; he has gathered knowledge of the external world and has developed a reality sense which sometimes is still incomplete, but which is frequently amazingly correct and keen. The fantasy life as the expression of intense instinctual and emotional strivings has followed its own course of development. That does not mean that the elementary force of the instincts has not exerted great influence upon infantile ego development. This influence may be a stimulus. Thus, for instance, the awakened sexual curiosity may lead to efforts at exploration and discovery which may foster the knowledge of reality. The child's craving for power arouses the desire to be big and, in his rivalry with the grownups, may support his intellectual unfolding and his desire to learn.

However, if for external or internal reasons the fantasy life constitutes a danger, a reverse influence may occur, resulting in an inhibiting and sometimes even destructive effect on the entire ego development.

It is well known that this second outcome occurs only too often, on the one hand because of the frequent and severe condemnation and punishment of infantile masturbation by persons in charge of the child, and on the other hand as a result of the many instinctual and emotional conflicts to which the child is exposed. As a consequence of these experiences we encounter neurotic disturbances, inhibitions of development, and character deformities. Before we take up the fate of the masturbatory activity and of the fantasies which initially, at least, accompany them, we will first say something more about the origin and content of fantasies during the anal and phallic phase.

The child's fantasies become well known to us as soon as he is able to verbalize them. This scarcely occurs before the age of one and a half or two years, even if one has learned to understand the child's primitive language. Yet we can hardly question the existence of a form of representation without words. This is proved by adult dreams in which desires, impulses, and emotional strivings find a plastic representation. We have learned from Freud's *The Interpretation of Dreams* (1900) that this representation is an archaic one belonging to the primary process. The primary process is the psychic mechanism which dominates psychic life of the young child before he is able to develop the secondary process. In addition, the one-year-old child, who has already developed certain psychological and physical abilities but not the ability to verbalize, demonstrates in his play and actions manifestations which we can only interpret as expressions of desires followed by symbolic gratification. In place of many illustrations I have only to cite Freud's observation of child play which he describes in *Beyond the Pleasure Principle* (1920a). This description also shows us the difficulty of interpreting such play and how cautious one has to be in interpretation since it is probable that many different impulses are discharged in a single action. The affectively charged games and activities of the one- or two-year-old child must be considered as the predecessors of fantasies at a later period which in the phallic phase are known to us as oedipal fantasies. Some times we are able to follow them through the latency period and watch them break through again with great intensity in puberty, even though they have been modified by development and the broadening of the world of experience.

Verbalized fantasies have become a dependable source of psychoanalytic knowledge. Sometimes the psychoanalytic treatment of adults yields us deep insight into the primitive forerunners of the fantasy world of the child. When a patient, during the psychoanalytic session, temporarily renounces his adulthood and presents the attitude, mimic behavior, crying, struggling, and stammering of a young child, he re-experiences, often with intense vividness, the impulses and sensations of this archaic period. Such an acting out resembles a real psychotic episode. The disadvantage of these observations during treatment in psychoanalysis compared with the direct observation of children lies in the difficulty of differentiating early from later material; this sometimes may represent a special task. However, the inner conviction with which, after this acting out, some patients are able to account for that immediate emotional experience is a valuable confirmation (or correction) and a pointer for the further task. The young child, of course, is unable to give such an account. Therefore the child observer lacks an important instrument for evaluating the correctness of his interpretations.

Let us now try to collect whatever we know so far about these primitive predecessors of fantasy life. From the beginning the child tries to get rid of unpleasant bodily tensions which are connected with imperative bodily needs (need for nourishment, excremental needs, etc.) and which are soon accompanied by psychic tensions or cause these tensions. Sexual and aggressive drives take part; passive and active strivings coexist; the impulses are awakened in the mother-child relationship and aim at the one and only object, the mother or her substitute. In rough outline there is a primacy of focus, shifting in succession from the mouth to the anal and finally the genital zone — although during all these phases there is also activity on various other parts of the body. Finally this whole complex of excitations, impulses, and emotions merges into the (relative) end phase of the oedipal constellation of instincts and emotions. This oedipal constellation lends to the whole personality a more or less stable structure, a pattern for the final shaping of the personality in adolescence.

In normal development the oedipus complex is distinguished by the fact that genital masturbation has become the only (or almost only) act of autoerotic gratification. At this point a boy's desires and instinctual impulses are expressed in fantasies whose abbreviated content is: "I want to take father's place with mother." The comparative simplicity of the strivings and fantasies in the oedipal situation is in contrast to the manifold diffuse impulses, strivings, and aims of the preoedipal period: However, on close inspection we notice that a great number of manifestations of the preceding period are preserved, in more or less disguised form, by the youthful Oedipus. These are just the ones which come to the fore in the infantile acting out of the patient during the psychoanalytic situation described above. Most striking are the strivings and desires with passive aims. The child desires to receive everyting passively from the mother, not only to be fed but also physical gratifications in forms of caresses, fondling, affection, and admiration, and all this with a child's well-known insatiability as the exclusive love object of the mother. These passive desires may be expressed in oral, anal, and phallic fantasies. During or after the oedipal phase these passive fantasies are displaced from the mother onto the father. Thus the passive-feminine father relationship (negative oedipus complex) develops in the boy, whereas in the girl it leads to the normal positive oedipus constellation which serves as a pattern for her later, grown-up femininity. Strangely enough, active as well as passive fantasies are discharged through masturbation.

Abraham (1924a) pointed out that in each of the three developmental phases one may distinguish two chronologically separate tendencies toward the object. These are the tendency to take in and to retain and its opposite, the tendency to expel and to destroy. They represent the instinctual and emotional ambivalence (libido-aggression and love-hatred). Abraham's work has greatly enhanced our understanding of the development of the child and of pathological conditions like melancholia, mania, compulsion neurosis, and paranoia. However, I believe that at that time not enough attention was paid to the coexistence of active and passive strivings. I also believe that in consequence the chronological succession postulated by Abraham becomes a schematization which does not completely correspond to observations. Tendencies to (passive) incorporation and (active) ejection always exist simultaneously during all three phases, although in individually different intensities.

In the newborn we find, together with the passive tendency to be nursed. also a clearly noticeable active tendency to search for the breast, to take possession of it, and to suck it. Even in the newborn one observes strong differences in *constitutional* activity and passivity. Furthermore, the personality and attitude of the mother – the other partner of the initial mother-child unit – has, of course, great influence on the further development of these strivings. During the anal phase also, active and passive attitudes coexist rather than succeed one another. One is always surprised anew by the observation that in psychic life passive experiences precipitate activity and active attitudes are followed by passive desires. Keen observation of healty adults reveals that they too show a succession of these alternating tendencies which are immediately evident in pathological conditions (most extreme in the manic-depressive).

The child's activity is initially to a large extent still an expression of instinctual ambivalence; i.e., discharge of the unsublimated aggressive or destructive drive, especially where it has been awakened by the frustration of passive desires. (The tendency to destroy the object in the cannibalistic phase and in the first part of the anal phase, as described by Abraham.)

The combining of aggression and libido and the sublimation of both drives results in the postambivalent phase, that of object relationship which Abraham presupposes, albeit as an ideal, for the final genital phase.

Marie Bonaparte, in "De la sexualité de la femme" (1949), broadens Abraham's scheme of early infantile instinctual development by giving great importance to the passive and active instinctual aims. Her extensice and very interesting report on female sexuality is particulary valuable. But in her description of early childhood processes, Bonaparte likewise presents as a chronological succession what, in my opinion, exists simultaneously. Though she acknowledges the phallic activity of the little girl, Bonaparte believes that the girl passes through a preceding passive phase during which she experiences pleasure sensations at the anal zone (called by the author "cloacal zone" in analogy to the biological embryonal development). The author also believes that these sensations attain a special "feminine" character through the fact that during clitoral masturbation the girl often accidentally reaches the introitus and thus becomes acquainted with her own vagina.

I agree with Bonaparte that the little girl may masturbate at the introitus and labia minora more often than had previously been assumed by Freud. We know that reddening and catarrh of the introitus have been observed in little girls and may have been caused by masturbation. However, it seems questionable to me whether these observations should be evaluated differently from similar anal play of the boy. It is absolutely certain that children of both sexes develop the most active aggressive games and fantasies with anal gratification; one could say with anal masturbation or masturbation of the introitus or of the labia. We also know that in the oedipal or postoedipal period, strongly passive-masochistic fantasies are discharged through penis – or clitoris – masturbation. I believe it is misleading to equate in a child vaginal masturbation with passivity or femininity and to identify phallic masturbation exclusively with activity and masculinity.

It seems improbable to me that a little girl is ever able to reach the fundus of her vagina at which the real orgasm of the adult woman originates. But even if this should sometimes occur, for instance after seduction, it has little significance in regard to the passivity or activity of the child's fantasies or experience. Passive and active forms of experience accompany the physical masturbatory activities of children of both sexes throughout the three main phases of development before the genital apparatuses actually gain primacy. In normal development, it is only after the recognition of the sex difference has had its effect that the active (penetrating) desire is tied to the male and the passive (receptive) desire is associated with the female organ. This occurs after the castration complex has taken effect. For the boy the passive-receptive organ is the "hole" which he has seen in the girl and which, in accordance with his anatomical knowledge and his own experience, can only be the anus. For the little girl it may be anus, labia, or introitus, but never the fundus vaginae.

Although the parallel drawn by Abraham between psychological and embryological physical development (a parallel also assumed by Bonaparte) is very interesting, one must not carry it too far.

In the first place, by the time psychic life begins, the sex of the person has long since been physically established. Secondly, the development of the highly complicated psychic processes is influenced by so many internal and external factors that it quite certainly also follows a course of its own.

To prevent misunderstandings I want to stress that it is far from my intention to prove that little boys and girls are identical in their psychological make-up. While the ratio between active and passive strivings varies in each person, it also certainly varies normally more in favor of activity in the male, and more in favor of passivity in the female child. Nor may one underestimate the importance of the parents' attitude. The mother ordinarily seeks to foster masculinity in the son, the father, femininity in the little daughter. However, in my experience the shaping of the sex does not take place in the individual child before the peak of the oedipal constellation has been reached. This is the very point when the development of boys and girls parts ways. In the boy the active sexual strivings will become victorious and passivity will be sublimated and becomes socially applied (of course, together with that part of activity which is withdrawn from direct sexual life). In the girl, activity is subordinated to passivity. Now at the end of the oedipal period, that forceful repression takes place (initiated in the boy under the pressure of castration anxiety) which leads into the latency period. All the restrictions and prohibitions of instinctual gratification which the child experienced from the mother (later from both parents) are now fused into one prohibition: you must not masturbate. This prohibition will be introjected and lead to the formation of the punishing part of the superego. The danger of castration as a threat to narcissism, the danger of losing the love of the parents and soon after the love of his own superego, cause the boy to renounce masturbation or at least to reduce it and to repress the accompanying fantasies. If he does not succeed in giving up masturbation, it will be practiced with anxiety and guilt feelings. Frequently the fantasies disappear from consciousness only to maintain a kind of isolated existence in the unconscious. Often, however, the opposite occurs: physical masturbation is renounced but a blossoming fantasy life persists.

The little girl's development runs a different course: the narcissistic injury due to her awareness of her being "castrated" causes enmity to the mother whom she holds responsible for this "defect." Her phallic activity toward her mother becomes unpleasurable and she turns toward the father with passive desires. The repression of instinctual life is not as imperatively effective, since castration anxiety is lacking. However, the repression-effecting threat of punishment by the parents (and the superego) is strongly reinforced by the very feeling of having an "inferior" genital with which one cannot really masturbate. And thus girls more often give up masturbation during the latency period than do boys. But then fantasy life (now most frequently directed toward the father) continues to flourish. Yet in girls also masturbation may break through the latency period, and be accompanied by conscious or unconscious fantasies.

Masturbation almost always re-erupts during a boy's puberty, less regularly in that of the girl. The fantasies frequently are real sexual images involving a partner; they may also be prolonged daydreams which begin to resemble stories or novels. Close inspection and analysis reveal more or less clear traces of the early infantile fantasy and impulse life.

I have given only a brief summary of the phallic-oedipal period of both sexes, since this phase and its importance for adult sexual life have been repeatedly and thoroughly described. I would now like to comment on the various vicissitudes both of the content of fantasies and masturbatory act, and finally on the influence of these vicissitudes upon character and personality development.[1]

In addition to the oedipal fantasies which are positive and active fantasies of taking possession of the mother, the boy in the phallic phase may also express other, more or less forceful, passive desires toward the father (negative oedipal constellation). These passive feminine (homosexual) strivings, which culminate in the desire to take the mother's place with the father, demand as a precondition the renunciation of the penis and are therefore dangerous for the child's masculinity.

If they cannot be sufficiently repressed, they frequently seek a way out in the return to the preoedipal object relation, in which the little boy lets himself be loved, taken care of, fondled, caressed, admired, fed, cleaned, even given an enema, and nursed by the mother. In this form of passive gratification the danger of castration no longer threatens him. Moreover, the mother herself particpates intensively in these kinds of gratifications, a fact which the child then experiences as permission or even seduction. Naturally, he also experiences many limitations and prohibitions, because the desires of the child are insatiable, and training and education demand adjustment to the norm, restraint, control, or renunciation of instinctual impulses altogether. The weaning from the breast, control of excretion, suppression of finger sucking, anal play, aggressive outbursts etc. may arouse anxiety which may become the forerunner of castratration anxiety. However, in comparison with castration anxiety, which concerns the most highly estimated part of the body, the penis, this anxiety is mild. Regression to the preoedipal period is mainly fostered by three factors: (1) a comparatively strong passive constitution; (2) forceful and extremely severe suppression of instinctual expression by the parents; (3) a dominating, aggressive mother who (because of her own penis envy) is not able to tolerate masculine activity in the boy and who seduces him into passive

---

[1] On its inhibiting influence which leads to neurosis, see chapter 4.

behavior, the child thus representing her own lacking penis which she unconsciously wants to fondle and caress (masturbate).

However, the *active* oedipal desires also may regress to the pre-oedipal phase. Castration threats, experienced or only expected, from the father arouse extremely intense anxiety if the child's aggressive drive is especially strong. Aggression becomes an internal danger through the attitude of severe parents (or a severe superego) as well as through the ambivalence conflict which makes simultaneous love and hatred, directed toward the same person, gradually intolerable. This aggression has to be suppressed and thus a sublimation of agression into constructive activity is prevented. The entire development falls back a step and the boy escapes to the preoedipal mother with both his active as well as his passive desires.

The interesting aspect of this is that the drives may or may not take part in this process. Where the drive participates, in some cases a permanent regression of instincts occurs, whereby (somethime only gradually) genital masturbation is given up completely and there is recourse to anal, oral, or other primitive discharge, sometimes in disguised or displaced forms. This for instance may be the case in compulsion neurosis, where the symptoms, the compulsive acts, may gradually replace masturbation. However, genital masturbation often continues without interruption up to adulthood, but the fantasies find expression in the language of preoedipal desires and experience. One finds this among hysterical neuroses, anxiety conditions, and phobias. But what is of greatest interest to us is the mode in which these fantasies, inhibited in their development, are built into the personality structure and into character formation.

In "The Preoedipal Phase in the Development of the Male Child" (Chapter 7) I described some forms of the love life of adults who have remained fixated to the preoedipal mother imago, or who returned to it, while their potency was only mildly disturbed. For instance, men who remain dissatisfied in their marriages and compulsively engage in one relationship after another are frequently looking for the image of the preoedipal mother from whom they demand the gratification of their infantile desires. Or men who compulsively devaluate and debase their wives may project on them the hatred belonging to the preoedipal ambivalent period, etc. I also mentioned in that paper the influence which the preoedipal mother fixation may have on superego formation.

In the same way we can also observe that a remaining with or returning to the preoedipal fantasy life may inhibit the *ego* (or parts of it) in its development. This leads to the so-called infantile personalities. Sometimes the development of intelligence is not inhibited but some of the ego functions may be partially or entirely arrested, as, for example, the sense of reality.

An adult who, in his unconscious fantasy, lives to be fed, indulged in, and cared for by his mother, expects the same situation in real life, demanding of his environment protection and affectionate handling, and will frequently be unable to realize and accept the sober reality and the necessity of building an independent life. The final outcome of this inhibition of development depends on the extent to which the sense of reality is impaired. If the greatest part of the ego remains in this infantile constellation, a psychotic condition may result. If a part of the reality sense remains intact, adjustment difficulties, inhibition of emotional contact with others, frequently even failure in work and professional life, will result. The objective evaluation of people, situations, political events will be impaired, because the formation of judgment is merely "self-related" and is tinged and distorted by narcissistic needs. A second important factor which leads to such defective evaluation of the real world lies in the fixation to the emotional ambivalence which is normal for the young child. In harmonious development, aggression and destruction are gradually bound by libido; they are partly sublimated and used for constructive activity and partly turned inward and used for self-criticism and self-control. If one or several of these mechanisms fail (e.g., in cases where frustration, disappointment, and injury are not overcome), the aggression may be indiscriminately turned against the external world. Then judgment and critical evaluation of the environment (persons, events, and situations) cannot be objective. The "other one" is bad and worthy only of contempt. From this description we also see that fixation and regression to the world of preoedipal experiences likewise inhibits another ego function, namely the synthetic (or integrative) one.

If one part of the personality, as for instance intellectual development, reaches the level of the actual chronological age, but the reality sense and the judgment formation connected with the inhibited emotional development correspond to the age of a young child, a disharmony, sometimes even a split, in the personality results.

Even the ego function of control and use of the motor apparatus may be impaired if the unconscious fantasy demands the gratification of being an infant with whom the necessary actions are performed by the mother. Some persons, because of anxiety due to their own aggression, either avoid any motor activity or at least inhibit it.

I have described some of the many inhibitions of development which may be caused by regression to the fantasy life of the preoedipal phase, and which in the male are due to the unconquerable anxiety of the oedipal situation, that is, to castration anxiety.

Similar infantile character formations may be found in the female who may take similar flight to the preoedipal mother. As we have said before, in the female the cause of this flight is not castration anxiety. It is the concurrence of her oedipal disappointment in the father with a sometimes insuperable narcisstic injury caused by her awareness of her own genital, which she considers defective.

This is the point, as mentioned before, at which the development of the two sexes takes radically different directions. Sex differences may have been noticeable before this time so far as differences in emphasis and intensity between active and passive attitudes go, but neither the physical modes of gratification not the fantasies showed essential differences.

Since I wish at this point to elaborate once more the different vicissitudes of the masturbatory act in boys and girls respectively, I have to make a brief recapitulation.

During the latency period the boy rarely gives up masturbation completely.

Masturbation will be suppressed, on the one hand owing to the comparative calm of the instinctual life, and on the other hand owing to the anxiety caused by the forbidden incestuous desires. But from time to time a discharge of the sexual urges through the masturbatory act may occur. The fantasies are concerned with being big and grownup; in the center of the fantasies is the ambition to be a powerful man both in a heroic love life and in all other life situations.

The maturation process, an active and progressing development, runs its course, to be most heightened in puberty and then gradually to merge into adult life. Masturbation, which was regularly practiced in puberty, gives place to normal sexual life; the ambitious narcissistic fantasies are replaced by full object love.

Disturbances of this course of development may occur if prohibitions and castration threats are so severe or have such a strong effect that masturbation is given up completely and the fantasies are completely repressed. These repressed fantasies may then lead their own life in the unconscious and, as mentioned above, may sometimes be cloaked in preoedipal forms. The instinctual life may regress.

Instead of elaborating on the neuroses thus caused, I wanted to present two other fates of such repressed fantasies.

(1) If a boy has developed a marked negative oedipal constellation based on a strongly bisexual constitution, and in consequence of a specific family constellation combined with specific experiences in early childhood, his castration anxiety will become exceedingly strong. For the gratification of these passive desires castration is a precondition, and therefore they are a threat to his masculinity. They enhance anxiety and force repression of both fantasies and the masturbatory act. At the same time they sometimes paralyze activity in other areas and inhibit the maturation process of the entire personality. Escape back to a preoedipal fantasy world and the preservation of the passive father attachment of the negative oedipus complex support each other in an inhibitory effect.

(2) The other important factor, which, in combination with the two just mentioned, may prevent normal maturation, is evident in those boys who turn inwardly an extreme amount of aggression during superego development; the passivity involved in this mechanism is then secondarily erotized and is turned into masochism. We thus encounter beating fantasies which have been extensively described in all their various phases and forms by Freud (1919). I will not elaborate on them but only mention that these fantasies are always of a sadomasochistic nature; i.e., the author of the fantasy always figures both as the beater and the beaten — while the act of beating is often replaced by fantasies of being overwhelmed, damaged, debased, or castrated. The nucleus of these fantasies is always the fantasy of parental coitus, regardless of whether or not it has been observed in reality. In this fantasy the child in turn plays the role of the father and the mother and the content is tied to the preoedipal fantasies. These sadomasochistic fantasies may increase both the fear of and the struggle against masturbating. Masturbation will seem more evil, forbidden, and dangerous than ever. I mentioned at the beginning of this paper that it is of utmost

importance to the adolescent whether the struggle against masturbation does or does not succeed. When it succeeds, it produces an enhancement of self-estimation which in pathological cases may range from an abnormal increase of ambition to megalomania. If the struggle fails, feelings of inferiority, depression, and pathological ideas of self-devaluation and self-abasement result. When these abnormal ideas of grandeur or of inferiority are chiefly the result of the threats of the adult world, they are frequently accessible to simple psychotherapy. Reassurance and enlightenment may be miraculously effective and may undo inhibitions in the development of the entire personality. But if the disturbancehad been caused by early inhibitions of development as a consequence of strong passivity, strong sadomasochistic tendencies and fantasies, preoedipal fixations and therefore defectively developed ego functions, the resolution of these developmental disturbances is very difficult and time-consuming and attainable, if ever, only by a correctly conducted psychoanalysis.

The difficulties on ego development are most intense in the area of maximum influence on ego development where consequently the disturbances of adjustment originated (A. Freud, 1949b). Let me select only a few from the many examples.

(1) A child who in his latency period completely gives up masturbation under duress of castration threats remains in a strong and mainly sadomasochistically tinged dependence on the adults. Whenever the urge to masturbate threatens, he has to reinforce his submission toward the prohibiting persons. In adolescence this process repeats itself and the young man is incapable of becoming independent. He remains, as we term it, an infantile personality.

(2) The complete suppression of masturbation due to external prohibitions may also lead to opposition against all adults. "Being good" in sexual matters is compensated for by indiscriminate "wanting everything different." This type always and everywhere desires the opposite of the environment as it is. The objective evaluation of other people and situations is also greatly impaired in such cases.

(3) The success in the struggle against masturbation by one's own power enhances self-esteem, but it may lead to feelings of grandeur, which then stamp the entire personality. A lack of self-criticism, overbearing behavior, and overestimation of the self then result. These qualities go back to the early infantile feeling of omnipotence, and they disable the personality in adjusting to the real world.

(4) If the struggle fails, self-accusations, self-torment, and inferiority feelings ensue which may impair the development of all other qualities and talents, and compulsive masturbation may paralyze all other activities of the person.

(5) Very frequently the struggle succeeds only partially with periodic breakthroughs of masturbation. Then we find a vacillation between megalomanic and inferiority fantasies, the one type always precipitating and increasing the other.

(6) Most frequent are the mixed forms of all these types. All of them lead to adjustment disturbances. In cases with more marked inhibitory tendencies, ego deformations and ego constrictions result in addition to neuroses. In cases in

which eruptions of instinctual impulses (primarily aggression) lead to external acting out, we encounter delinquency.

Only by the thorough presentation of individual life histories could one do justice to the manifoldness and intricacy of the various combinations of possibilities, a goal beyond the scope of this paper.

So far, I have mainly presented the various vicissitudes of the masculine developmental process. Naturally most of these phenomena are also found in the female. However, I want to draw attention to some particularities in female development.

I mentioned above that the complete suppression of masturbation during latency, and perhaps during puberty also, is a much more frequent occurrence in girls than in boys. This is the case even when the external prohibitions and the threats of punishment are the same for both sexes. The normal oedipal situation demands of the girl the renunciation of active-phallic desires, of the boy the renunciation of his passive strivings. It appears that with an equally strong bisexual constitution the subordination of passivity to activity is more easily effected than the reverse process. Instinctual life has an essentially active, driving, urging quality. Moreover, the danger of castration, which once had seemed to the boy overwhelmingly great, is and remains only an anxious fantasy which never becomes reality. If the passive constitution and with it the desire for castration is not too strong, the conquering of castration anxiety is effected without too great difficulty.

The girl, however, is convinced without redress, by her observation of the sex difference, that she will never obtain the once ardently desired male genital even though for a long time she still retains the fantasy that it will grow on her. This narcissistic injury is a decisive factor in taking the pleasure out of masturbation, and in renouncing it.

With a normal feminine constitution, these two processes, turning to passivity and the acceptance of the lack of a penis, are successfully accomplished either during latency or puberty. The active strivings are sublimated and employed for other ego functions as well as for intellectual development. However, this process remains more difficult than the analogous one in the boy.

The girl's passive situation in the oedipal father relationship seems to favor the renunciation of masturbation. At least, one can observe that it is the girl with a strongly bisexual constitution who fails in the struggle against masturbation. At first glance this appears strange, since it is the girl with strong active desires whom one might expect to be most injured and disappointed by her lack of a penis. One would expect her to withdraw from the manipulation of her "defective" genital at the earliest time. The explanation for the contrary fact is given by the fantasy world of these little girls. In the fantasy the lack of the male genital is regularly denied: it is hidden in the vagina and one day it will come out or will grow. The heroes of her daydreams of unconscious fantasies are frequently boys or young men and are easily recognizable as the ideal image of herself. Or the little girl repeats her fantasies of the parental sexual life (in various alterations, of course) whereby she simultaneously plays both roles, the active and the passive. Also, there is often a fantasy of being the father's penis or the penis of the phallic mother. Geleerd (1943) describes a case in which compulsive masturbation, which gravely inhibited the little girl's development, was accompanied by many such fantasies.

Frequently, also, manipulation of the genitals, whether clitoris or introitus, is given up and displaced onto other parts of the body (playing with the nose, mouth, ears, hair, breasts, rubbing of the legs, etc.).

A further particularity of the fantasies of the constitutionally active girl is that they are sadomasochistically tinged. In "A Child Is Being Beaten," Freud (1919) points to the fact that beating fantasies occur more frequently in women than in men. The passive "letting oneself be beaten" (letting oneself be over-powered) is, according to some authors, part of femininity. However, in normal femininity it plays a role only to the extent of a capacity for physical submission. If there exist strong sadomasochistic elements we are already dealing with a deformation of healthy femininity which is the consequence of a marked active-aggressive constitution. Aggression is partly turned inward; but where masochism is apparent psychoanalysis regularly reveals strongly sadistic fantasies. These fantasies substitute for the renounced masculinity and simultaneously take revenge on the envied male or on the mother-woman who is held responsible for the patient's sex.

Thus the active type of girl, like the boy, does not easily succeed in renouncing masturbation. Where the environment has enforced its prohibitions, the reactions and character formations are also similar; yet if the suppression of masturbation is forced by severe threats of punishment the girl, too, may develop into the "constant rebel" type, or she may remain the dependent child who cannot grow up.

Suppression of masturbation by her own efforts may also produce megalomanic ideas and overbearing behavior in the girl, whereas feelings of inferiority may be awakened by the temporary failure in this struggle.

For the development of sound femininity, the gradual renunciation or reduction of masturbation during latency seems to be most favorable, at least in our present civilization. A mild relapse during puberty with preference of introitus or vagina may serve the transition to adulthood. However, in many cases there is little or no masturbation at all in puberty. This may be an escape from the above-mentioned fantasies, originating in the masculinity complex; it may be caused by guilt feelings and anxiety, thus having a neurotic basis. But it may also be a preparation for the healty submission to adult sexual life, during which normal vaginal orgasm is experienced for the first time, and the remainders of the infantile fantasies are adjusted to adulthood and thus enter the realistic world of the woman, in her behavior in family life, and in her other social or professional tasks.

14. Re-evaluation of the Role of the Oedipus Complex

(1952)

During recent decades psychoanalytic research work has yielded a series of experiences regarding the development of the child in the first years of life. The significance of an undisturbed course of the preoedipal phase has been demonstrated by direct observations on children. Disturbances in the first mother-child relationship (which is based upon the biological mother-child entity) result in physical and psychical departures from normal, ranging from slight neurotic fears to grave inhibitions in instinctual, emotional, and ego development, to paucity of affect, pseudo debility, etc.

Study of the genesis of neurotic and developmental disturbances during analytic treatment has likewise shown, more and more clearly, that fixation points in the preoedipal phase, or regressions toward this developmental period, are responsible for the various symptoms or character anomalies or at least play a very important role in their genesis.

Such observations justify the question how we, equipped with our present knowledge, must evaluate the role of the oedipus complex. In the initial period of psychoanalysis Freud defined the oedipus complex (the "fateful" love attachment to the parent of the other sex and the hostile rivalry with the parent of the same sex in the phallic phase) as the central point of the healthy and the neurotic development, as the example for adult love life, both in the normal and in the abnormal. Freud's view was soon extended to cover the reverse feelings to the parents, which also belong to the oedipal situation. The concept of the oedipus complex has to include the negative oedipal constellation.

Can we still agree with this concept? Or does the stress at the present moment lie upon the preoedipal attachment to the mother in the anal or oral developmental phases? The oedipus complex does undoubtedly develop from the early attachment to the mother. We also know that each subsequent stage contains residues from earlier stages, that subsequent stages overlap, and that the "archaic" is elementary and powerful. On the other hand, what is the fatefulness by which Freud was struck at so early a date?

In order to answer these questions we propose (1) to consult our clinical material, obtained during the analytic process; and (2) to avail ourselves of the new theoretical insights regarding this problem.

Material supplied by the study of the analytic process

Although all persons go through identical developmental stages prior to attaining the capacity for becoming adult, stabilized personalities, we know from our experience how different a course the process of growing up may take in different persons. Two large groups of factors are responsible for this: (a) environmental influences; (b) the dispositional factors which determine the possibilities and limitations of the complicated structure of adult personalities. Psychoanalysis has pointed out from the very beginning how important are the attitude of the environment and the environmental factors for the child's development. The environment is supplied at first by the mother, who is herself likewise a product of her own environment. The influence of the family as a whole is soon added, and of its social conditions which are in themselves likewise dependent upon position, status, group relations, economic situation, national and racial peculiarities, etc. In the first phase of an analysis, these factors as well as the specific peculiarities and capacities of the individual himself come to the fore. They give the analyst an unforgettable impression of the variegation of the individual paths of life. Strangely enough, it is nevertheless possible to observe a more or less typical course in the analytic process. The general human problems begin to manifest themselves. This applies to the gravely neurotic patient who is presenting his unsolved conflicts, as well as to the approximately "healthy" analysand, who wishes to become acquainted with the special form and structure of his own personality. While endeavoring to bring to the fore some points of this typical course of the analytic process, we wish to point out with emphasis that, naturally, deviations from it may occur, and that they are not exceptional. *In psychic processes no rigid schematization is ever possible.*

The typical course of events is to be observed most clearly in analyses of children in the latency period. At this time of life the core of the personality has already been formed; the superstructure, however, is less complicated than it is in adults, the environment being still limited for the most part to family and school. A "typical" child analysis brings to the fore first the rivalizing attachment to the siblings: next, the phallic phase and the typical emotional relationship with the parents from the oedipal constellation. The oedipal tendencies and fantasies are linked to the problems of masturbation, sexual curiosity, and the infantile fantasies regarding the parents' love life. But they are charged with and distorted by pregenital representations. Not until then does that stage come up for analysis in which the early infantile attachment to the mother and the pregenital developmental phase indirectly repeat themselves, and can be dealt with.

On close scrutiny we shall be able, as we said above, to observe a similar course in most analyses of adults, although the persons of siblings and parents have been replaced by other persons and the rivalry will be acted out with friends, collaborators, colleagues, or superiors, and love will already have been directed toward spouse or lover.

The observation of the typical course here depicted is occasionally hampered during an analysis, because confusing periods, called by Helene Deutsch "chaotic" periods, occur in every analysis. In these chaotic periods divergent material from differing developmental stages is presented without logical sequence. It cannot be unraveled moment by moment. However, a correct psychoanalytic treatment is a *dynamic* process. If only we succeed in *accompanying* the analytic process and in supporting it by our interpretations of defense and content at the right moment without disturbing it by untimely interference, the typical phases mentioned above will gradually unfold themselves.

The most surprising feature is that, in an analysis which is running a favorable course, toward the end, a fourth phase begins to manifest itself. This is the convergent phase. The material which has led to working through and revising the early mother attachment is replaced by material converging once again toward the phallic phase and making possible another re-experience of the oedipal parent relationship, but now in a normal form, freed from pregenital fixations. In favorable instances a process of detachment from the parents and an afterdevelopment into normal, adult love life takes place. The latter yields an optimal therapeutic success.

Here we must stop for a moment and once more occupy ourselves with a question that has been asked repeatedly: How is it possible to recognize whether the material stems from the oedipal phase or from the period of the early mother attachment, the preoedipal phase?

We have already said that it is not always possible to answer this question in the chaotic period. In the convergent phase of clearing up, it is completely possible. The fact that a first light was not shed upon the preoedipal mother relationship of the little girl until in the late '30s clearly shows that this encountered great difficulties at the outset. Helene Deutsch and I were able to bring some typical facets to the fore. These observations were affirmed later on by Freud and others, and elaborated further.

Parallel studies on the rich variegation of the early mother attachment of the little boy were published afterward by Ruth Mack Brunswick and myself. In chapter 7 I presented some examples and also described some criteria for recognizing oedipal and preoedipal material. I will here repeat only two of these criteria, which are in my opinion the most important:

(a) In contradistinction to the oedipal material, often presented in fantasies and reminiscences, the preoedipal expresses itself exclusively in the form of *acting out*.

(b) When the analysand presents the preoedipal material, his personality changes during the analytical hour and his behavior greatly resembles that of an infant or very young child. It manifests itself in attitude,voice, behavior, motility, mimicry, and other primitive means of expression. As a matter of fact the patient re-experiences the prehistoric time of the first years of childhood (see chapter 13).

We will now occupy ourselves with a second problem.

Since we are so much impressed, during the analytic process, by the various typical phases in which the material presents itself and by the differences in the nature of the early mother attachment and the oedipal relationships, the residues of these differences must necessarily manifest themselves in the adult object relationships. Thus it is indeed. Out of the complexity and the many shades of these greater and lesser differences, I will select only a few in order not to exceed my time limits.

The adult woman orients herself in her love life with her male partner and in the problems of nursing and educating her children, basing herself for the most part on the example of her own child-father and child-mother relationships. Her husband inherits, as it were, the oedipal love for her father, the children receive the love she herself once got from her mother. We say that the normal woman finds her object relationships by way of the healthy identification with her mother. Her attitude toward her husband must, however, be different from her attitude toward her children.

Where a feminine surrender is indispensable for a healthy love life, the bringing up of children requires a strong activity, a harmonious blending of active and passive behavior. In other words, toward her husband the woman makes use of her identification with the oedipal mother image. She experiences love in the form of passive surrender, as she formerly did toward her father.

In regard to her children, who are in need of the activily and passively caring and loving mother, the woman utilizes the attitude resulting from identification with the preoedipal mother image. We can actually observe these various identifications expressing themselves in the family life. I need not say how often these relationships are disturbed because they are utilized inadequately. How far the family life is a harmonious one depends greatly on the right distribution of these two mother identifications.

In chapter 7 I described some cases in which the residues of the preoedipal and oedipal attachment to the mother clearly manifested themselves in the life of the adult man. In the normal development of men much less of the preoedipal relationship is left than in women. The little boy does not change the love object in the oedipal period as the girl is forced to do; it is only the nature of his love that changes in consequence of the process of growth. In the life of men a real repetition of the situation of the archaic child-mother entity never takes place, in contradistinction to the woman's life, wherein she becomes a mother herself. This may be the very reason why a neurotic fixation of the little boy on the early mother attachment often has a particularly disturbing effect on his adult love life.

I will add a few observations to the examples cited in the afore-mentioned paper.

Men who state that their married life is on the whole satisfactory sometimes complain that they occasionally experience obsessive impulses to visit prostitutes. Sometimes they merely speak to such women and leave it at that, or merely walk through the districts which prostitutes frequent; sometimes they look for an actual sexual outlet, yet without obtaining a real psychic satisfaction. Sometimes normal coitus does take place, but generally masturbation and various perverse acts are preferred. Analysis shows us that a split has taken place between the oedipal and the preoedipal mother image. The latter is occasionally longed for in an obsessive way. The prostitute unconsciously represents the preoedipal mother image, who actively gratifies all archaic (oral, anal, urethral, sadomasochistic) tendencies through the perverse acts and repeats the nursing and handling of the infant. If this archaic period is worked through in analysis, the preoedipal fixation may be removed and the two mother images united, thus bringing about the harmonious afterdevelopment and integration of the love life. One often hears the view expressed that man and woman cannot really understand one another in their love life. Many factors are responsible for this, but part of the explanation lies in this twofold origin of the object relationship. The wife cannot understand her husband's assurance to her that his infidelity has nothing to do with his love for her. The husband on the other hand cannot understand the grief of his wife, who has invested the whole of her capacity for love, coming from both the preoedipal and the oedipal phases, in marriage and family.

The typical course of the analysis, depicted here, shows us over and over again:

(a) how important is the preoedipal development for the ultimate formation of the oedipus complex;

(b) that the oedipus complex is the final product of the preoedipal development, but of a specific nature. Its ultimate shape is decisive for the normal as well as for the pathological love life of the adult;

(c) that disturbances in the preoedipal phase can cause abnormal shapes of or weaknesses in the oedipal constellation. Thus they further regressions toward early fixation points and give rise to neurotic and defective development.

When the fourth phase of the analytic process, the handling of the material which converges once more to the oedipus complex, is not at all or only partly successful, the therapeutic result of the treatment remains unsatisfactory. These failures have taught us which of the many responsible factors is the central one. It lies in the castration complex. If the castration anxiety of boys, which is linked to the oedipus complex (with girls it is the masculinity complex), cannot be overcome, a regression takes place toward certain fixation points in the preoedipal phase.

In the course of analytic work such regressive flights are repeatedly observed whenever a new quantity or intensity of castration anxiety is mobilized.

The preoedipal phase − as is well known − has its own sources and forms of anxiety. Whenever tensions arise because of ungratified needs, they are capable of producing anxiety reactions. As soon as the mother is recognized and loved as an object outside the self, fear of losing the mother's love will arise in the face of conflicts between instinctual life and the mother's wishes. An important source of anxiety is given in the ambivalence conflict. The child, simultaneously loving and hating the mother, finds himself in an *inner* conflict situation. Anxiety arises which can be diminished or reinforced, but not removed, by the mother's attitude. In the oedipal period love is directed toward one parent, whereas the other parent receives the child's hostility. Consequently the love for the mother obtains (in the boy) a much less varying and a more permanent character. The same applies to the rivalizing hostility toward the father. In this consolidation of the affect relationship lies part of the fateful nature of the love of the little Oedipus. The preoedipal forms of anxiety contribute to the formation and intensity of the castration anxiety in the oedipal period. However, the latter (anxiety over the possession of the penis in the phallic period) has a very exceptional character:

(a) as a result of the biological function of the sexual organ and its narcissistic significance for the self-esteem of the individual;

(b) because of the impossibility – acting as a narcissistic injury – of leading an adult love life, which is due to the immaturity of the child; and

(c) because of the bisexual disposition of all persons. In the boy the passive tendencies threaten his masculinity and are to a considerable extent the cause of his castration anxiety. In the girl the active (masculine) tendencies constitute the biological substratum of the factors deciding for normal or pathological developments and determining the form of the castration complex. The linking of the oedipal situation to the castration complex is a second facet of the fateful character of this period of life.

Here we must lay emphasis on the fact that especially in the girl the negative oedipus complex can be of the greatest importance in this connection. The question may arise whether there are cases in which the positive father attachment fails to develop.

We now arrive at:

The newer theoretical insights of the last few decades

Among these, the following are of importance for our theme: (a)our increased insight into the development of the instinctual life in the preoedipal phase; (b) our knowledge regarding the early ego and superego development.

(a) The instinctual life we now know to be an interplay of erotic and aggressive instinctual drives. The manifestations in the various preoedipal developmental phases bear the marks of both groups of drives. However, not sexuality alone passes through developmental stages; aggressive drives seem to do the same, and thus to influence the object relations. I will cite one instance out of many: The strivings for power and rivalry originating from the aggressive drives attain a certain acme in the anal period and color the object relationships. A great deal of them is preserved in later life, but in normal growth they are raised to a different level and merge, for instance, into a nondestructive ambition and a productive "trial of strength."

In the phallic phase the boy's relationship with the father is dominated by rivalry and aggression. However, the ambivalent relation develops and results in an identification with the father, and becomes the basis for normal masculinity. The girl emulates the mother; her identification with the oedipal mother image results in healhty femininity.

(b) Our knowledge of the early ego development is equally important for the understanding of the preoedipal and oedipal object attachments. The ego is still undifferentiated in the newborn. It gradually develops a number of qualities and functions. By means of some of these it becomes acquainted with the outer world; it learns to distinguish between within and without and to perceive the inner world. The ego must appropriate the control of certain instinctual demands as well as of other desires and needs, in order to bring them into harmony with the demands of the outer world. It must partly permit these needs and instinctual desires to be gratified, partly leave them unsatisfied or postpone their gratification or modify them in their ends. The ego must effect in part an adjustment to the outer world, in part it must try to modify the environment in accordance with needs and desires. In order to be able to accomplish all these tasks, the ego develops its intelligence, its thinking, its knowledge, etc. It produces reaction and defense mechanisms against intolerable instinctual tendencies and demands of the environment that cannot be satisfied.

It refines its capacity to distinguish between outer and inner world; it tries to intergrate wherever there are contradistinctions (see chapter 8).

The mutual influence of instinctual and ego development is discussed in another symposium at this Congress.

For our theme the following seems to be of importance:

Object attachments are the expression of instinctual needs that are related to a person or object in the outer world. Since the ego is the intermediary between inner and outer worlds, it is obvious that the nature of the object attachment is also determined by the developmental level of the ego. E.g., as long as the ego has not developed its faculty to distinguish between inner and outer worlds, an *object* love in a real sense, i.e., a love for the mother "on her own merits," is out of the question. The attachment to mother or to the mother's breast is still a biological and not a psychic one. The infant aims at satisfying his needs and expects this gratification from his mother in the same way as from his body. Therefore we call this earliest attachment a narcissistic one, in contradistinction to the real object attachment from later periods. It is well known that the growth of the narcissistic into the object-libidinal attachment is very gradual. Even if the object is already recognized as something outside the self, the character of the attachment is still for a long time predominantly "narcissistic." A great deal of this early attachment is preserved in the adult love relationships as well.

A certain amount of narcissistic gratification obtained from objects is indispensable for the health and the normal functioning of man. However, a sound relationship presents a considerable amount of actual love for the object, with respect and appreciation of the personality of the other. This latter form of object attachment seems to be prepared for during the preoedipal developmental phase, but it does not flourish until the phallic, oedipal period. In this period the ego has actually acquired a sense of reality, naturally in an interplay with the instinctual development and under the influence of the environment. The ego has overcome magical thinking and the magical attitude toward the outer world to a considerable extent; it has also developed its integrative powers to such an extent that ambivalent attitudes are no longer directed toward one single object, but can be divided between father and mother; it has formed the necessary reactive and defense mechanisms, which have transformed or warded off such instinctual tendencies as disturb the object relationship.

In the meantime, the *affective* life has also gone through an important development. Originally affects are attendant phenomena of instinctual manifestations. Before the period of differentiation between id-ego and inner-outer worlds, and thus before a primitive structuration of the personality, we can only attempt to describe the affects as diffuse phenomena. It is, however, part of the task of the growing ego gradually to get acquainted with the affects, to learn to register the instinctual processes of the id, to control the affects and ultimately to take possession of them. It is a triumph of the ego over the id, if, at last, the personality is capable of saying: "I feel something," and no longer "There is a feeling within me." This process, too, is not effected until a comparatively late stage, and it is never completely accomplished. The affects that are attendant upon the erotic drives are usually classified under the heading of love feelings. Affects covering aggressive drives are classed with the feelings of hate. In the infant the affects are not yet differentiated; they are elementary, passionate, and violent. Gradually a process of differentiation and refinement of the affects takes place.

In adults we find in the gamut of love a multiplicity of feelings, e.g., kindness, sympathy, friendship, compassion, admiration, adoration, etc. The series of feelings of hate comprises hostility, antipathy, spite, jealousy, revenge, contempt, and others.

The capacity for differentiating the affective life is dependent upon instinctual processes as well as upon the qualities of the ego. The greater the ability of the ego to understand the inner world, the more mature its knowledge of the outer world, its possibilities of learning from the environment, the richer will be the development of the affective life. This means that the affective life will present an increasing resemblance to that of the adult.

As the mother is the first example from which the child learns and with which he identifies himself, it is self-evident that the mother's personality is of paramount importance for the ultimate formation of the child's affective world. A healthy, loving, and emotionally balanced mother will be promotive of a normal affect relationship in the child. A sick or inharmonious mother will greatly interfere with the growth of the infantile emotional ties.

As long as the ego is undeveloped, however, this identification can only be a primitive one. It stands to reason that, after the first years of life, the personalities of the father, of other members of the family, and of persons outside the family, too, are of great importance for the affective development.

I have already pointed out that the *oedipal* object attachments and the love and hate *feelings* bear a very great resemblance to the adult love relationships.

The instinctual drives are directed toward the possession of the beloved person and the removal of the rival, just as in adult partners. However, the *shape* of the *sexual* representations is still an infantile pregenital one. The latter is connected with the somatic immaturity of the child as well as with the interruption of the instinctual development at the onset of the latency period, as already mentioned. In consequence of this interruption the instinctual development is one stage behind the affective maturation.

We will now turn to a particular developmental level in the construction of the ego, i.e., to the genesis of the superego.

As a result of the inhibition of the instinctual development at the onset of the latency period, the oedipus complex is repressed in its typical fateful shape, and it does not emerge until puberty, as a transition to adult love life.

Ego and emotional development proceed, but at a different level, no longer directly linked with a flourishing instinctual life. According to Freud's oldest formulations, the superego would arise as a residue of the oedipus complex, *an agency in the ego organization*. It takes over and represents the commands, prohibitions, norms, and ideals of the parents through identification with the oedipal objects. We have to face the question whether our knowledge of the prehistory of the oedipus complex does not require a revision of this concept regarding the genesis of the superego. We have already said that the process of identification plays an important role in the preoedipal phase, as regards both the ego functions and the growth of the affective life and the object relationships. It is obvious that in the preoedipal phase the child forms ideals through identification with an image of the admired parents. In the very period during which wishes for omnipotence and magical thinking are flourishing, ideal formation takes place. Disappointments at one's impotence and frustrations are compensated for by fantasies of omnipotence dealing with an ideal and identifying oneself with the "almighty" ideal. The formation of an ego ideal begins in the preoedipal phase. What about the judging and prohibiting superego, the conscience? In the beginning the young child puts up with restriction of his gratifications and disappointments for fear of punishments or of loss of the mother's love. Nothing of a judging agency or an inner prohibition can be perceived. When, however, the development has advanced so far that the child begins to identify himself with his mother, he also starts to take over her prohibitions and commands.

A differentiation takes place in the ego, owing to which the child learns what is permitted and what is not permitted. Now he is more or less able to determine his behavior himself, along these lines, so as to prevent painful experiences. This process bears a certain resemblance to the training of animals, and may obtain the character of the conditioned reflex. A good example is bowel training. Many children, trained in cleanliness, lose this acquired capacity rather easily under changed conditions: e.g. if the mother is absent or lessens her demands, or if in the inner relationship between the child's emotional life and his acquired ego functions new conflicts arise, which often occurs in consequence of the birth of a younger child, etc. According to a communication from Anna Freud it might also happen, however, that the internalized command of cleanliness can no longer be undone in the anal period, not even at the emphatic wish of the mother. If, for instance, the anxious mother should try to force her child, who is seriously ill, to deposit his urine and feces in bed, it may become obvious that the child is no longer able to do so. However, a conditioned reflex in an animal also continues to exist for a longer stretch of time, although it finally disappears. It might be interesting to investigate whether in the special group of children in the anal phase referred to by Anna Freud this inability to dirty themselves will continue to exist even if the demands of the educator are not renewed, or whether it would ultimately disappear. Such an experiment would be hampered by the progression of the development toward

148

the next, the phallic phase and the oedipal constellation, as a result of which the conditions are entirely different.

However this may be, the internalization of a certain command in the anal phase does not by any means appear to be identical with the existence of a conscience function, and a self-judging agency. The affects of the successfully trained child do not present — in a conflict situation — the differentiated character of the later guilt feelings. They rather resemble generally the primitive anxiety reactions of the animal that has dirtied the floor. It seems likely that here individual differences occur in connection with a more rapid or a slower maturation of the personality. Although we should not speak, therefore, in the anal preoedipal stage of a superego with the function of an inner conscience, we have to envisage this early, unstable internalization of commands as processes that constitute examples for the postoedipal identification processes resulting in the formation of the superego. They are — as it were — the precursors or primitive stages of the superego.

The superego itself displays a very definite structure that is not essentially changed even though the contents and the shapes of the norms are subject to modifications under the influence of growing up. The boy's ego ideal, which had been selected originally in accordance with the example of the mother (although it was the phallic mother) obtains more definitely the image of the father at the time of superego formation. The commands and prohibitions, mainly received from the mother, are attributed to the father and introjected in connection with the latter's person. Although archaic forms always persist — to a greater or lesser extent — the process of structuration and of conscience formation in accordance with the image of the father can be clearly followed in normal cases. In the girl it is the identification with the image of the preoedipal mother that causes the earliest ideal formation and the first internalization of commands. At the time of superego formation the imago of the oedipal mother, i.e., the mother as the father's wife and as the girl's rival, is the one to put its stamp upon the superego.

Formulating the matter in other terms, we may say:

During the preoedipal development primitive forms of ideals and internalized commands arise via identifications: they are consolidated in the oedipal phase into a superego and ego ideal of a structure, determined by the oedipus complex.

Summary

In the preoedipal phase a psychic object attachment to the mother develops from the biological mother-child entity. The form of this attachment is dependent (1) upon the nature of the mother; (2) upon the hereditary factors in the child; (3) upon the instinctual and ego development; (4) upon the maturation of the affects; (5) upon the early identifications (precursors of the superego); and (6) upon the mutual influence of all these different factors.

The structured and stabilized product of this varied and eventful development is the oedipus complex, which is to be placed in the phallic phase.

The oedipus complex is the example for the adult love life and, because it is linked with the castration complex, it is the starting point for the "coming into being" of neurotic disturbances in children in the latency period, adolescents, and adults. As the oedipus complex carries along with it its previous history, the preoedipal phase, the events of the latter period determine the shape of the oedipus constellation and thus play an important part in the ulitimate formation of the personality.

Severe preoedipal disturbances may *hamper* the process of ripening, *weaken* the phallic position, and distort the *oedipal* constellation. In such cases the infant's anxieties cannot be overcome, castration anxiety becomes overwhelming and causes regression toward preoedipal and pregenital positions and fixation points.

In conclusion we may say that:

Neuroses and other psychic disturbances may arise from several nuclei of maldevelopment, to be found in the oedipal *and* in the preoedipal phases.

15. Depression and Aggression

A contribution to the theory of the instinctual drives

(1953)

Differences in the pshychiatric and psychoanalytic approaches to the phenomenon of "depression"

In psychiatry, the term "depression" is often used in a diagnostic sense. A subdivision is made into different clinical pictures, such as reactive depression, psychogenic depression, hysterical depression, endogenic depression, etc.

Some authors distinguish between endogenic depression and melancholia, others seem to equate the two terms, but they all agree that endogenic (melancholic) depressions are constitutional diseases based on an innate predisposition.

Reactive depressions, on the other hand, are considered as reactions to external, traumatic events in otherwise almost normal persons, while the term psychogenic or neurotic depression is used for depressive disturbances developing in the course of life, on the basis of childhood neuroses.

From a descriptive point of view, these differentiations are justifiable. Many phenomenologists offer very fine and detailed pictures of the inner experiences of depressed patients.

As far as the psychoanalyst is concerned, however, the phenomenology is the starting point for his investigation. Some patients give as colorful and detailed a description of their depressive states as many phenomenologists have done in their writings. The analyst, however, wants to know far more. He is interested in the structure and genesis of the psychic deviations from normal; he searches not only for the immediate causes of the outbreak of the disease, but for the deeper causes as well. It is common knowledge that psychic disorders invariably arise from a conjunction of constitutional and developmental factors (Freud's complementary series). As regards the field of the depressive states, this implies that a fundamental separation of endogenic from exogenic depressions is impossible. *All* depressive clinical pictures contain endogenic and exogenic factors. Naturally, it is of practical, therapeutic importance to know at which end of the complementary series the syndrome in a given patient must be placed.

A psychotic patient presenting a grave melancholia with delusional ideas, having hardly any affective contact with his environment, is not amenable to psychotherapeutic or to analytic therapy in this stage. Yet Abraham (1924a) has

See also chapter 24, 26, and 27.

pointed out that, not infrequently, manic-depressive patients can be treated in the interval periods, sometimes even successfully.

It is my experience that there are cases of "endogenic" depressions where analysis is possible and, though the technique has to be slightly modified, rather significant results can be obtained. The periodic cyclothymic variations of mood mostly continue to exist, but the amplitude of the oscillations has decreased so much that they are sometimes hardly perceptible any more to the environment. Such experiences impel us to be very careful with our indications for shock therapy in depressions, the more so as the damage done by shocks to the subtle psychic functions can be very considerable.

The so-called reactive depressions may sometimes disappear spontaneously or with superficial therapeutic help. Whenever it is possible to observe them analytically, it becomes clear over and over again that they arise only in persons who have already gone through inconspicuous depressive changes of mood. The latter can regularly be tracked down into early childhood. Many of the differences between mild and grave depressive states, so great from the phenomenological viewpoint, prove to be based, genetically, on economic, i.e., quantitative, factors. The active psychic mechanisms are the same, however.

Psychoanalytic knowledge of depressive states

Psychoanalysis does not look upon depression as a separate disease but as a syndrome that may occur in nearly all neuroses. Fenichel speaks of "that most frequent and also most problematic mechanism of symptom formation, depression" (1945). And next: "To a slight degree, depression occurs in nearly every neurosis (at least in the form of neurotic inferiority feelings); of high degree it is the most terrible symptom in the tormenting psychotic state of melancholia."

We know that depressions occur in combination with hysterical symptoms, with obsessive-compulsive symptoms, with perversions, and also with all kinds of character deformities and developmental disturbances. The depressive mood is the expression of an injury to the selfesteem, ranging from slight inferiority feelings to a total loss of selfesteem. The latter is often attended by feelings of depersonalization; the patient has become estranged from his surroundings or from himself (once a patient used the expression: "I suddenly feel I have lost myself").

Sometimes an intense anxiety is experienced, sometimes it is suppressed, but during analysis it invariably manifests itself. This anxiety signals the great danger of the "ego loss," of the impoverishment in narcissistic libidinal cathexis, which is indispensable for a normal selfesteem.

It is also well know that self-reproaches may alternate with blaming others. The patient feels bad or guilty, the ego is no longer loved by the superego, as Freud puts it.

The ego tries to reconcile the superego by means of self-accusations, self-vexations, penances, etc., for the feeling of being loved again increases selfesteem. The latter also applies to the surroundings. In every possible manner, the patient demands that the persons in his invironment supply love, care, sympathy, help, etc., because he feels permanently wronged. To quote Fenichel: "These patients are love-addicts."

In other words, the patient's affective relationship with the environment as well as the relationship with his own person is not on an adult level; he does not love objects on the basis of their own merit; he has regressed to an infantile stage of love life.

The classic work of Abraham's referred to above moreover presents us, in a way still unsurpassed, with a picture of the regressive libidinal processes to be observed in depressions as well as in manic-depressive psychoses. The author found a combination with compulsion-neurotic phenomena in the mild forms of depression as well as in the interval of the manic-depressive psychosis. Therefore he was forced to accept a regression toward the anal phase. In the more severe and psychotic forms, however, the process of regression was found to have proceeded to the oral phase. Abraham holds this deeper regression responsible for the psychotic character of the disorder. In such cases, the representative of the object is introjected, in consequence of which the relationship with the environment gets lost. The more complete this process, the more deeply psychotic the patient becomes.

Abraham also assumes that such regressions may occur under the influence of traumatic events (e.g., the loss of beloved persons, etc.) in those persons who are predisposed by a fixation at the pregenital developmental stages. Constitutional factors may play a role here, but also the co-called "primal depression" of earliest childhood, which may arise from a lack of gratification of the primitive bodily needs as well as from a deprivation of love.

Abraham's subdivision of the three libidinal developmental phases (each of them further divided into two phases), explains some peculiarities of the ambivalent affective attitude of the depressive patient toward the environment. However, a number of questions remained open at that time, some of which can now be answered, in connection with the increase of our knowledge about the development of the ego and the development of the aggressive urges. Although Abraham's clinical material presents an abundance of aggressive and destructive reactions, both against others and against the own person, he speaks only of anal and oral sadism (or masochism), and no attempt is made to study the specific role of aggression.

At the present time we consider the following points as two of the most important problems of psychoanalysis: (a) how have we to envisage the coexistence of erotic and aggressive instinctual manifestations; and (b) what is the mutual influence of ego and instinctual development.

Concerning (a) I should like to recall to mind that no human relationship is free from ambivalence. In the greatest happiness of two loving partners a certain hostility, however deeply concealed it may be, is never entirely absent. One often gains the impression that living out a certain amount of aggression, provided that it is used in the right form and at the right moment, may increase the feeling of felicity. It is common knowledge that a wrong dosing or timing may disturb or destroy the entire experience of love. The very fact that erotic and aggressive feelings and urges are so closely interwoven renders our study much more difficult.

Concerning (b) I wish to recall to mind the fact that communications about instinctual urges only reach us via the ego. What we actually observe are instinctual derivatives in which we must recognize, by means of analysis, what portion was original instinctual urge and what modification this urge has undergone because of the responses of the ego. This is also valid when the whole of this conglomerate of drive-ego reaction has been repressed and, in the analytic work, has become conscious only after a resistance has been overcome. Uncontrolled, instinctual impulsive actions, in which the ego has been taken by surprise, provide us with a more direct picture of the instinctual event. This can become abundantly plain in certain psychoses. In more or less normal persons it is observed for instance in outbreaks of rage or under the influence of alcohol or other intoxicants. The observation of very young children who have developed only a very few ego functions is particularly instructive in this respect.

I am of the opinion that the study of the depressions may shed some light on the two problems mentioned under (a) and (b). Since analytic treatment of depressive patients can take place only with those patients in whom some of the ego functions have remained intact or, at least are functioning enough to permit cooperation of analyst and patient, we always have to contend with the difficulties mentioned above. Therefore we must be very cautious in our attempts at distinguishing the shares of the erotic drives,, the aggressive drives, and the ego functions in the psychic event. We are always dealing with a total personality. Observations of young children, such as were made by Anna Freud in the Hampstead Nurseries and such as are taking place in many American institutions, provide us with valuable, complementary data and corrections.

The role of aggression and of ego development in depressions

I shall present a few examples from the abundance and variety of the material gained from thorough personality analysis in order to illustrate the facets that are of significance to these two problems. The gloomy mood of a depressive patient, which he often accounts for by declaring himself to be inferior, bad, stupid, incompetent, figures prominently among his complaints.

We have already described that these complaints express an inner psychic conflict: the ego feels itself to be bad when confronted with a strict superego which acts condemning and punishing. But there is more to it: in every patient with strong inferiority feelings, analysis one day reveals the existence of superiority feelings, fantasies of grandeur and omnipotence.

The patient cannot love another human being on his own merit, because he is unable to give. He only wants the other *to be his*. In other words, the object is, to the patient, a complement, an extension of his own person. He can only love the other in the form of possessing him. It is a craving for power, an enlargement of his own power through that of another. In childhood, this wish for power is concerned with the parents who, in the child's fantasy, are omnipotent. In a certain phase of infantile development the feeling of omnipotence arises from an introjection of the images of omnipotent parents. The fantasies of omnipotence are well known in the obsessive-compulsive neurotic who performs "magic" in words, thoughts, and compulsive acts. In magical thinking and acting we recognize ego functions at a primitive level. However, these processes are, at the same time, manifestations of a twofold instinctual event. The need for love is satisfied through the union with the object, but at the same time the process serves as a means of increasing power. The existence of the object has become insignificant at the very moment the craving for power predominates. In some cases of depression the fantasy of devouring the object entirely (introjecting it) and destroying it gets the upper hand. Freud described this phenomenon in grave melancholias at an early date.

We are accustomed to linking the feelings of omnipotence which have to compensate for the experience of being powerless, so intolerable to many sensitive children, to the anal and oral phases of libidinal development. It is one of the earliest analytic discoveries that the young child's emotional attachment to the mother in the periods of breast feeding and bowel training is accompanied by a somatic sexual gratification and consequently by a discharge of libidinal tension. It did not become clear until much later, however, that the aggressive instinctual energy also may find an outlet in the struggle for power, in processes of conquering the object, wanting to possess it, keeping or destroying it.

The interrelationship of erotic and aggressive drives

Freud's original conception reads that, normally, we are dealing with a blending, a fusion of erotic and aggressive drives, while in pathologic cases a defusion can take place. This applies to the aggression turned against the outer world as well as to the aggression directed against the own person.

When observing an uncontrolled outbreak of anger or a temper tantrum in a child, we are struck by the enormous quantity of aggression that can be discharged. It is quite probable, to be sure, that such an event is accompanied by some discharge of libidinal energy. Freud pointed out, at an early date, that every important somatic process, such as, e.g., pain, may act as a sexual stimulus. However, in the outbursts of impotent rage the discharge of aggression is clearly predominant, in contradistinction to, for instance, what happens in a lust murderer, in whom sexual and aggressive (destructive) drives are discharged with nearly equal intensity. The latter also applies to the sadistic (and masochistic) masturbatory fantasies.

A patient suffering from depressive states, feelings of derealization and inferiority, once depicted the great difference in subjective experience. In the course of some years' analysis, an abundance of sadomachistic fantasies had been worked through. The early infantile material next emerged in acting out. Desperation and impotent rage manifested themselves in crying, yelling, trampling, kicking, and beating on the couch. In the subsequent discussions the patient was greatly impressed by the intensity of his destructive urge. When I tried to find a connection with his sadistic fantasies, in which he used to humiliate and beat his objects, he replied: "That's something entirely different;

with those fantasies, long drawn out in bed at night, I had erections and sexual gratification. What I experienced now was merely: 'wanting to smash, to bite, to destroy.' " I gained the impression that the patient was right.

After all, the patient had not really destroyed anything, neither myself, nor the furniture, nor some property of mine. What had put this destructive need in check prior to its realization?

In the analytic situation, the patient's ego had temporarily abandoned some of its functions, such as, for instance, self-control, but it was still functioning enough to preserve part of the reality sense and to leave part of the control of motility intact, and therefore actual destruction was given up. It goes without saying that this was due to a conjunction of various motives, e.g., under the influence of the moral system, of guilt feelings, and especially of anxiety.

We are interested, however, in the question of what happened here in the instinctual sphere. (a) Has the discharge of the aggressive energy simply been interrupted? (b) Has a fusion with libido, modifying the destructive urge, come about? (c) Has something happened to the aggressive instinctual drive itself, i.e., has it become an aim-inhibited urge, has a sublimation taken place?

Inhibition of the discharge has undoubtedly taken place, as is shown by direct observation. But surely more things have happened: as far as the processes of fusion with libido and of sublimation are concerned, the subsequent course of the analysis will shed some light on that. We might briefly describe this course as follows:

After an aggressive outburst such as the one described above, we see the patient regaining, more or less gradually, a positive attitude toward the analyst. At first this often occurs under the pressure of an enormous fear of retaliation on the part of the analyst, a fear of losing his love and appreciation. In this period of the analysis it is the analyst's often difficult task to deprive the patient, by a great deal of quietly waiting patience, understanding, and invariable kindness, of the possibility of rationalizing his anxiety by an actual danger situation.

He learns to understand that the danger was real in his early childhood but has overcome superannuated now and, in various circumstances, such as the analytic situation, no longer exists in reality. When the patient has repeatedly had this experience we see, after new aggressive explosions, the positive, libidinal attitude come into existence spontaneously, automatically as it were.

The more successfully the inner instinctual conflict is solved and the anxiety about the aggressive and destructive urge is overcome, the sooner the patient will be able to abandon his self-vexations, his raging against himself, i.e, his depressive symptoms.

I wish to add here that, naturally, this healing process can be accomplished only in some cases. As I discussed above, it is self-evident that one cannot embark upon an analysis in a grave melancholia where the representation of the object has been entirely, or almost entirely, introjected, where the patient has consequently turned nearly all aggression and destruction against his own person, and where there hardly exists any affective contact with the environment. In an interval, or with grave depressions on a more or less obvious endogenic basis, it is sometimes possible to bring about the process described above, although it may take many months and runs a monotonous course.

As I pointed out in the introduction, the result is often limited to a reduction of the amplitude of the oscillations; this however, may represent a very important improvement from the therapeutic viewpoint.

A practical difficulty may be encountered in the fact that, as is generally known, the self-destructive tendency may become so strong, in grave depressions, as to entail the danger of suicide. It is often very difficult, then, to decide whether the patient must be hospitalized or whether one may venture to continue the analysis. If the libidinal attachment to the analyst is strong enough to carry the patient over all aggressive and self-destructive tendencies, one may book a success in return for one's pains. But there are cases in which the analyst's courage, tact, and patience are of no avail.

I revert to the cases in which the healing process described does materialize. In addition to the aggressive discharges experienced by the patient as destructive urges, other forms of aggression can be observed in some cases. They are described by the patient as a wish to control, to get hold of, to gain possession of. In fantasies the object (the analyst) is belittled and humiliated, it is true, but it is not destroyed. These ideas and experiences, too, are clearly distinguished by some patients from their sadistic and masturbatory fantasies.

The events taking place here during the analytic process remind us in many respects of the observations of babies and toddlers by various authors, e.g., Anna Freud in the Hampstead Nurseries.

Anna Freud (1949a) describes the baby's first emotional contact as presenting the same characteristic quality of aggressive insatiable greediness that he displays toward food. And afterward: "In the oral stage the infant destroys what he appropriates (sucks the object dry, tries to take everything into himself)" (p. 40). She depicts the toddlers' "peculiarly clinging, possessive, tormenting, exhausting kind of love which they have for their mothers," etc. And, "We understand that on these pregenital stages it is not hate but aggressive love which threatens to destroy its object" (p. 40). The author describes elsewhere (1951) a form of "autoaggression" (head-knocking) as "the aggressive equivalent of autoerotism" and later on "as one of the rare representatives of pure destructive expression where fusion of the drives is incomplete, or after defusion has taken place" (p. 28).

Thus, in order to explain the phenomenon of "aggressive love," Anna Freud uses Sigmund Freud's theory of a fusion or mixture of the erotic with the aggressive drives. It is clearly distinctly observable that the infant, sucking, biting, laughing, and whining, is developing an erotic attachment to his mother's breast (and afterward to his mother). Tearing up and smashing toys, attacks on pet animals are, at the same time, the child's expressions of love just as the struggle for power and the toddler's wish to domineer are in the anal phase.

But it remains an open question whether this coexistence of aggression and erotic play is a real fusion of the two drives and whether, e.g., the substitution of a striving for power, or an urge to dominate, is to be solely attributed to an admixture with libido.

157

Another possibility urges itself upon us. Prior to going further into this object, I shall briefly discuss libidinal development. We readily follow Freud's conception that the sexual drives may have different aims. However, we must clearly keep in mind what we must understand by this concept. The general description given by Freud in "Instincts and Their Visissitudes" (1915) runs as follows:

> Tne aim of an instinct is in every instance satisfaction, which can only be obtained by removing the state of stimulation at the source of this instinct. But although the ultimate aim of each instinct remains unchangeable, there may yet be different paths leading to the same ultimate aim; so that an instinct may be found to have various nearer or intermediate aims, which are combined or interchanged with one another [p. 122].
>
> The aim which each of them [the sexual instincts] strives for is the attainment of 'organ-pleasure'; only when synthesis is achieved do they enter the service of the reproductive function and thereupon become generally recognizable as sexual instincts [pp. 125-126].

We can fully endorse the first sentence of this description. The aim of a drive is *gratification*, relief of tension, or, in other words, the personality aims at a discharge of tension (energy). The question remains, however, whether this discharge takes place at a body zone functioning as a specific source for a given instinct. We would rather assume that instinctual discharge takes place at different zones of the body, having an exceptional significance in certain developmental phases in relation to the body's needs, but not necessarily being the "source" of the instinctual energy.

These zones vary according to the person's maturation as well as his development under the influence of the environment (i.e., the educator's attitudes and demands).

We no longer speak, at present, of the instinct of self-preservation but regard the striving for self-preservation as an ego function. The first, most elementary need is the intake of food. The first libidinal discharge takes place at the mouth (the oral zone). Later on, it is the processes of digestion and excretion that are attended by sexual gratification (anal phase). Ultimately, in adult sexual life, an ejaculation of sperma, accompanied by an orgasm, provides a complete discharge of tension.

The "intermediary aims" are gratifications at the various erotogenous zones (apart from mouth, anus, and genital, the skin, the respiratory organs, and other parts of the body may also act as such). Thus we speak of organ pleasure, which is probably comparable to the more or less diffuse gratification the young child provides himself in masturbation and is undoubtedly different from the orgasm attending the ejaculation of the sexually mature male.

We shall now revert to our considerations of the aggressive drives. As far as they are concerned, we also assume that the ultimate aim is *gratification, discharge of tension*. Temper tantrums, etc., demonstrate this *ad oculos*. It does not seem unlikely, however, that the aggressive drives are not so rigid as Freud originally believed them to be, but that they, too, can reach the ultimate aim (gratification) by "various ways." A destructive or aggressive act can be directed against animate as well as against inanimate objects. The discharge of aggressive energy observable in an outburst of rage might be compared with the sexual discharge in a complete orgasm (see also Brunswick, 1940). It is my impression that "gaining possession of," conquering, mastering getting hold of an object should be regarded as variegated ways of discharge providing some kind of gratification. The object (animate or inanimate) is not incorporated (i.e., destroyed), then; its survival is tolerated and sometimes guanranteed. Gaining possession of the object serves the increase of the subject's own power. The problem of the aims of aggression has already been touched upon by Hartmann, Kris, and Loewenstein (1949). These authors write:

> What should we assume the aims of aggression to be? It has been said that they consist in total destruction of objects, animate or inanimate, and that all attempts to be "satisfied with less," with battle with or domination of the object or with its disappearance, imply restrictions of the original aims. It seems that at the present stage in the development of psychoanalytic hypotheses the question concerning the specific aims of the aggressive drive cannot be answered; nor is a definite answer essential [p. 67].

In my opinion, this formulation of the question is not the right one. As I said before: *the aim of a drive is gratification, discharge.* (The authors cited above assume, just as I do, that aggressive discharge per se may be experienced as pleasurable (p. 77) and that the pleasure does not necessarily arise from "narcissistic components.") *The ways by which discharge can be effected may differ*, but no one is "superior" or "inferior" to another. A given form of discharge is not a "restriction" of another form, either. Nor does an aim inhibition of the drive take place. The different modes of discharge are manifestations of *instinctual development.* The various ways of discharge can be used concurrently, e.g., an urge to gain possession of the object can be accompanied by a destructive urge. A specific mode can also be abandoned and replaced by another one. This is, e.g., clearly to be observed in a child as a reaction to the object's attitude. If, for instance, the mother resists the child's striving for power, if the child feels disappointed or hurt in some fashion or other, a tendency toward revenge will arise and provoke the destructive impulse.[1]

The question whether the *quality* and *intensity* are the same in the different forms of gratification should probably be answered in the negative. But in this respect there is no fundamental difference from the possibilities for sexual gratification.

---

[1] I feel justified in concluding from a personal communication of Hartmann's that he, personally, is inclined to accept a diversity of aims (perhaps he also means a diversity of modes of discharge?) of the aggressive drives.

The sexual gratification obtained at the oral or anal zones, or experienced by the little boy playing with his genital, certainly differs quantitatively, and probably also in intensity, from the orgastic experience attendant upon the ejaculation of the adult male, as I pointed out before.

We revert once more to the problem of the relation of libidinal and aggressive energy to certain *zones of the body*. Observation, especially of children, has taught that the sequence of oral, anal, and phallic developmental stages of the libido is not a constant one. For instance, genital stimulation takes place in the infant (masturbation in infancy), i.e., long before the phallic phase. Oral and anal phases overlap. The anal stage in particular is greatly subject to the influence of educational measures as regards its duration, form, and significance. In this connection I refer to a communication by Anna Freud in "Observations on Child Development" (1951) viz., that she was in a position to observe an extremely intense penis envy in one-and-a-half to two-year-old girls, following a particularly intimate bodily contact with little boys, such as perpetually occurs in nurseries.

According to many authors, the relation of the aggressive drives with certain parts of the body would be such that these organs are not places of stimulation, but serve as instruments of discharge of tension. Remarkably enough, one of the first organs to be used for the discharge of aggression is the mouth, the very organ where sexual stimulation and discharge takes place. I do not venture to discard the possibility that the stimulation of the mouth (lips and jaws) caused by sucking the breast may also be able to serve as a stimulant for the aggression, which is then discharged in "sucking out," biting, "swallowing up," and crying. When the musculature develops further, it is especially the muscles of arm and hand, in addition to the muscles of mouth and jaws, that become instruments for the discharge of aggression.

It is likewise an open question whether muscular tension per se may function as a stimulus for aggression (often in the form of an urge to gain possession of the object.) The so-called pleasure in functioning, i.e, the immense satisfaction a child may display when successfully utilizing muscular functions he has recently learned (e.g., walking), is certainly an expression of a saturated "possessive instinct" (power over his own body), apart from the sexual gratification it may represent.

Although differences in the development of libido and aggression cannot be discarded, we come to the conclussion that they are likely to be smaller than they appeared at first.

Aggression, ego development, and object attachments

We shall now turn to the following question: Under what conditions do the aggressive drives search for discharge in the one mode or in the other, by this or by that way?

It has become clear from the above that this depends upon the stage of maturation of the person, and upon developmental factors under the influence of the environment. The development of aggression partly follows libidinal development, partly the growth of the body, partly the psychic and emotional maturation, and it is especially correlated with the maturation of the ego.

In the process of growing, the ego gains mastery over motility, i.e., the use of the muscular apparatus which is the instrument for the discharge of aggression. In the oral developmental stage the object is captured and destroyed by "eating." It stands to reason that this does not imply, as is sometimes said, that the infant sucks the mother's breast "wishing" or "intending" to destroy it. As long as the baby cannot distinghuish a world outside his own self he cannot have a "wish" regarding such a world. He does not suck out of "love" or out of "hate" or because of his "wish to destroy." Sucking is a reflex movement stimulated by hunger. But this activity apparently offers, at the same time, a possibility for discharge of libidinal and aggressive instinctual tensions; therefore sucking is continued even if the stimulus of hunger is no longer operating.

A need, a wish for gaining possession of the object (the mother's breast) cannot arise until the child can distinguish an outside world from his own self, i.e., after a certain degree of ego development.

Only when the object is recognized as a prerequisite for the gratification of needs does a libidinal attachment come into existence. And only when the child has learned that destruction of an object means loss of what is indispensable (or beloved) will he replace the destructive urge by a striving to gain possession of the object, sparing its existence.

It is easy to observe this phenomenon in a toddler who smashes a favorite toy with blissful satisfaction, who is then surprised and unhappy on perceiving that it does not function any more, is broken or gone, and who ultimately learns to "possess" the beloved doll or animal while leaving it intact.

We mentioned above that disappointments and injuries may provoke destructive impulses again, e.g., in the form of a wish for revenge. In other words, part of the development of ego functions, e.g., the capacity to distinguish between outside and inside, acquiring a reality sense by means of experience, but also the magic form of thinking (the basis for fantasies of ommipotence and grandeur) are preconditions for being able to replace a certain mode of discharge of aggressive energy by another one.

A second process, the development of a psychic object attachment, also plays an important role. The object perceived at first as indispensable for the gratification of bodily needs becomes essential as a source of love later on. The feeling of being loved is a gratification of the self-esteem which is so easily hurt in the child, who feels utterly powerless when confronted with demands of the environment as well as in regard to his own wishes for power. The tragic conflict lies in the fact that being hurt or disappointed is likely to mobilize a destructive urge against the very person whom the child cannot do without as a love object. It is self-evident that the attitude of this person (at first the mother) may exert a great influence on the intensity of this conflict. Since, however, in consequence of the peculiar complexity of man, his protracted immaturity and dependence, a life without any frustration or feeling of impotence is impossible, the conflict is fundamentally unavoidable.

Thus we see alterations taking place in the forms of discharge of aggression, actuated by maturation and ego development on the one hand and consequent upon the libidinal object attachment on the other hand.

We shall now revert to our earlier question. Could this not be explained simply by the theory of the fusion of erotic with aggressive drives? Clinical observation leads me to regard this event, at least partly, as a developmental process of aggression which runs its course alongside the libidinal development, in addition to the process of fusion of aggression and libido.

I return to our depressive patients and the distinction, already described in their experiencing of sadomasochistic urges or fantasies and aggressive or destructive bursts of anger. The striking point is that a clear-cut difference between the therapeutic possibilities in regard to influencing the two phenomena can be observed. In sadistic and masochistic acts and fantasies, a fusion of libido and aggression is unmistakable. Hurting, humiliating, or destroying in perversions or masturbatory fantasies *is* gratification, and vica versa.

We all know how difficult it is therapeutically to affect the sadistic and masochistic perversions, as well as the morally masochistic attitude toward life. There are depressions, however, that are comparatively easy to cure and they are the very depressive states where there is less sadism involved but where one is chiefly concerned with aggressive (destructive) urges and with possessive tendencies. I have the impression that an intimate fusion with libido under special circumstances can fixate the aggressive drives in such a way as to render them invariable, whereas, remarkably enough, an aggressive urge operating more or less independently of the libido can be liberated from repression and eventually integrated into the personality. The nature of those special circumstances should be further explored.

The question how integration may take place leads to the problem of *sublimation*, which I have avoided so far and on which I will be brief.

Sublimation was described by Freud as an instinctual vicissitude of the libido. More than once I have expressed the view, and I am in agreement with many other authors, e.g., Hartmann, Kris, and Loewenstein, that aggression can likewise be sublimated (see chapters 8 and 10).

Possessive urges, besides sexual curiosity, provide an important contribution to exploring the world, acquiring knowledge, controlling nature, creating social achievements, etc. Such activities may become constructive for personality and fellow beings. Destructive tendencies, too, *can* be used in a constructive form; I refer to the well-known example of the surgeon who cuts up in order to cure; of the decomposition of substances in laboratories which can be used productively in chemistry and engineering; of analyzing man and social conditions, etc., etc. In the person himself, some of the sublimated aggression, together with sublimated (or desexualized) libido, is used for the structural differentiation of the psychic apparatus.

Hartmann prefers to speak of neutralized energy in this connection. Does it make sense to distinguish between neutralized and sublimated instinctual energy? Both expressions refer to aim-inhibited energy. However, to the term "sublimation" we attach the idea that the energy is drained off in actions valued as being "socially higher." Thus in distinguishing between the two terms we introduce the element of evaluation. Experience has thaught us how defective sublimations frequently are, both in the individual and in the community.

We now return to the therapeutic possibilities with depressive patients. Apart from the observation that it is difficult to affect libidinally fixated aggressive tendencies, we have to consider the greater or lesser capacity for sublimation (or neutralization) as playing a most important role in the therapeutic procedure, in addition to a number of other ego functions which I shall not discuss now.

Finally, however, I wish to stress the fact that the form of discharge of aggression predominantly present in a certain patient may be of importance. If the mode of *destruction* of the object prevails – i.e., if the instinctual regression to a very early stage has taken place, if, to cite Abraham's words, the "primal depression" is localized in the earliest years of childhood and caused or enhanced by traumatic events such as the mother's death or a particular lack of love on the mother's part, while moreover the patient's ability to neutralize energy is not very great – a grave melancholia is more likely to occur than in a patient in whom other possibilities for discharge of aggression have already come into existence, in whom no malign fixation has arisen from fusion with libido and in whom there are ampler and more extensive possibilities for sumblimation.

I feel justified, however, in mentioning one other experience. Though it is sometimes possible to cure a patient afflicted with a grave depression, it is definitely *not* possible to do so when one does *not* succeed in uncovering and bringing to consciousness the various ways used by his aggressive urges in the course of his development. For only this process, if successful, can offer the opportunity of effecting an afterdevelopment, of sublimating and of integrating those urges into the whole of his personality.

And only if this is done can a harmonious interplay of sexuality, aggression and ego achievements become possible. Such harmony seems to be a precondition for a constructive attitude toward environment and society as a whole.

16. Problems of Psychoanalytic Training

(1954)

It is remarkable that the four speakers of this symposion concentrate mainly on two fields of training activities: (1) the selection of candidates, and (2) the problems of training analysis.

The other part of the program, the theoretical and practical teaching in lectures and seminars and the supervision of treatment, are left out of consideration. This fact demonstrates that there is general agreement about the overwhelming importance of the candidate's personal analysis in the training procedure.

Though I share this opinion completely, I think that we should not altogether neglect the value of an efficiently composed program of courses on theory. Instead of giving positive suggestions, which would take up too much time, I want to mention only two difficulties which might impair the efficiency of the theoretical teaching, one on the part of the students, the second on the part of the teachers.

Many students join the courses expecting that they will be able to learn the whole of psychoanalytic theory during this teaching. I think it is necessary to fight this misconception by stressing over and over again the fact that courses are only able to stimulate the candidate to serious study of the analytic literature.

Some teachers tend, from the very beginning, to present to the students criticisms of and deviations from psychoanalytic theory. Such teachers seem to be afraid of being called "orthodox Freudians." They overlook the fact that the students usually become confused by this teaching. The Dutch Training Institute therefore decided to present to the students, in the first two years, the development of Freud's theory, the basic concepts and writings. Not until the last year are differences and deviations brought forward and broadly discussed.

Supervision, too, is an important part of training, not only to teach technique, but also as a means of judging the candidate's capacities and progress. I cannot go into further details here.

Before entering into the problems of the training analysis, I want to say a few words about the first point: the choice of candidates for admission.

Two of the four speakers in today's symposium take up the problem of the suitability of students.

Heimann presents us with seven criteria for the acceptance of candidates. I can

For the prepared papers, see M. Balint (1954), Heimann (1954), G. L. Bibring (1954), Gitelson (1954).

agree with all of them, though I share Balint's opinion that the rules of admission of training are rather vague, intuitive, and "haphazard," as he puts it. Nevertheless, I want to add one other (vague) point to Heimann's: in my opinion, integrity of character is indispensable for the future analyst. I am aware that I shall be blamed for bringing moral principles to the fore. However, as analysts are treating human beings therapeutically, their behavior has to be guided by medical ethics. It is a pity that we do not possess an objective criterion of a person's integrity. Our inability to define objectively the suitability of psychoanalysts for the profession is inherent in the nature of that profession, which works with feelings, needs, impulses, values, in short, with human mental processes.

Although only Heimann gives a list criteria for admission, all the speakers seem to be in agreement about the necessity for serious selection. Gitelson stresses the difficulty of the problem that in many Institutes a large and ever-increasing number of students are applying for training, wishing "to get through with it as rapidly as possible," and pretending to be "normal." Perhaps Grete Bibring is right in saying that this may be a more pronounced problem in America. Nevertheless, there are also European groups contending with the same difficulty and, as in some American Institutes, the temptation to capitulate to the pressure of the multitude of appicants is great. It seems highly questionble whether it is advisable to yield to this pressure. The Dutch Institute, for example, which originally welcomed the increase of applications, is experiencing more and more the disadvantages of having accepted candidates who later proved to be more or less unsuitable for analytic work. The Training Committee has now abandoned this mistaken attitude. For the sake of psychoanalysis as a science and as a therapy, as well as for that of the student himself, we prefer to reject an applicant rather than to educate inefficient persons. A small group of efficient workers is more valuable than a large group of mediocre ones.

We now come to the main theme of the symposium: the training analysis.

All participants in the symposion agree that the training analysis is the most important part of the training, but that it is full of difficult problems. There is also agreement on the three following points:

(1) The technique is in principle the same as in a therapeutic analysis.

(2) The training analysis has different aims. It does not terminate when neurotic symptoms are removed, as a therapeutic analysis usually does. It has to go further, "deeper," as Heimann puts it; it tends toward a "supertherapy," as Balint says; it must be a "character analysis," to use the words of Gitelson and Bibring.

(3) A special difficulty of the training analysis is that it takes place under conditions quite different from the well-known setup of the psychoanalytic situation. These conditions are consequences of two sets of circmstances: (a) the analysand occasionally meets his analyst in courses, seminars, and meetings, and he knows a good deal about his personal circumstances, peculiarities, and scientific convictions; (b) the analyst has to judge his analysand's suitability and capacities and decide at what point in time he can be allowed to start the theoretical and practical training.

In a lecture at the Amsterdam Institute, Anna Freud once presented a clear and colorful picture of the different ways in which the training analyst is bound to offend against the classic rules of technique.

Today's speakers also give their views on this difficult point, which undoubtedly has to be considered seriously.

I personally agree with Heimann and Bibring that the problems concerning the encounter of analyst and analysand outside the analytic situation are minor ones. It is more of a problem and a burden for the training analyst as it demands the latter's skill, self-knowledge, and self-control to help the analysand to overcome the resistances awakened by and attached to the extra-analytic encounter. The major difficulty seems to lie in the analyst's task of deciding on his analysand's status and progress in training. This problem was strongly felt by some members of the Dutch group as well. However, as the analyst's opinion of the student's capacities and personality proves to be indispensable for judging the candidate's suitability, the only possible way of meeting this problem seems to be its most careful and rightly timed handling in the analytic situation. It may happen that a candidate's distrust and oppositional hostility cannot be overcome. The analyst should then look for a disturbing element from his side and eventually send the analysand in question to another training analyst. In case of another failure with the second analyst, I think we are entitled to assume that the analysand is unsuitable for the psychoanalytic profession. We ought then to have the courage to reject him as a candidate.

I now come to the most problematical point: the special aims of a training analysis and its differences from a therapeutic analysis as a consequence of these aims.

Balint has pictured the changing claims made upon the future analyst's analysis during the development of psychoanalysis. Experience has taught that neither the curing of neurotic symptoms nor the additional demonstration of psychic mechanisms in a short analysis are sufficient preparation for the future analyst's task.

What more do we have to do? What does a "deeper" analysis, a "character analysis," a "research analysis" mean?

I suppose most of us have almost the same aims in mind, though the descriptions may be different. We are not content with merely liberating the warded-off instinctual and affective life of our analysand. In addition, we want to supply him with the most thorough knowledge of his personality structure, his capacities, peculiarities, and limitations. This means that we shall have to bestow great care on his ego analysis. We shall try to pursue the development of the ego, of its capacities, its reactions, its mechanisms of regulation, adaption, and defense in connection with the influence of the environment and the demands of the instinctual drives, both in the normal and the abnormal. We shall have to pay special attention to fixations on and regressions to early stages of ego development because these processes cause ego restrictions and disortions which often produce blind spots and handicaps in analytic work.

In this part of our training work we encounter a special problem, a magnified difficulty of ego analysis in general, already described by Anna Freud (1936). In analyzing id contents, the analyst can count on the patient's cooperation, because impulses and affects strive to penetrate into consciousness. In ego analysis, the patient begins to refuse each corroboration, defending the position of his reaction formations and defense mechanisms in order to protect himself against anxiety raised by inner and outer danger situations. In a therapeutic analysis we handle only the ego attitudes involved in the neurosis and constituting a hindrance to the patient's recovery. In the training analysis we have an additional task. We try to give the candidate insight into the development of all ego attitudes, peculiarities, and deformities of character, etc., even when he does not suffer from them. It is quite clear that without the stimulation of suffering, the resistance to cooperation with the analyst is still much stronger than it is in patients who suffer severely. Consequently, the analytic work in a training analysis may be more time-consuming, calling for still more patience and for uninterrupted contact within the analytic situation. Therefore the indications seem against reducing the number of weekly sessions or their length, as is sometimes recommended.

I am quite aware that I have put before you an ideal situation, and I think you will blame me for making such high demands on our poor students. It really seems necessary to reflect upon this situation, to ask ourselves whether it is advisable to run after ideals that will never be realized, and to question whether it would not be wiser to return to the period of pure instruction in the analyses of candidates.

Though this would certainly be the easier way, I think it is our duty not to yield to this temptation, but to continue to strive for a most thorough ego analysis in spite of the knowledge that an ideal solution will never be reached. A justification for this striving is found in our daily observation of our patients, or our students, of our control cases, and last but not least of ourselves.

Time and again we encounter failures in analytic work due to the circumstances that the analyst reacts to the analytic situation with unresolved conflicts of his own, with a blind spot resulting from unknown ego attitudes, fixated unconscious defense mechanisms, and the like. Those difficulties may present themselves as an uncontrolled countertransference, as pictured by today's speakers (and also by Annie Reich in a very interesting paper [1951]), or simply in a limited understanding or dull incomprehension of certain psychic events.

Every normal reaction formation and defense mechanism can grow into a pathological limitation of personality. One example, for instance, is to be found in the process of denial, so common a defense in a child exposed to strong anxieties. An analyst who has not mastered his own mechanism of denial is limited in his recognition of reality factors. Consequently he is unable to see his patient's lack of reality sense in its real proportions.

Instead of continuing the long list of ego limitations possibly disturbing to analytic work, I want to depict one other psychic situation that may lead to fateful failures.

A very frequent reaction to disappointments and narcissistic injuries in a child is the mobilizing of fantasies of grandeur and omnipotence. We call these fantasies normal mental products at a certain stage of development, the stage of magical thinking in ego development, corresponding with and reacting to the aggressive craving for power from the side of the id, in the preoedipal (anal) phase. The same is valid for the ambitious fantasies of puberty. Only when the infantile feelings of grandeur have become unconsciously fixated do they prevent an adult person from seeing reality and acting accordingly. The overvaluation of the self is then used as a defense mechanism not only against disappointments from the environment but also against inner feelings of inferiority. The fixated primitive form of this mechanism acquires the character of a delusion. The person in question feels offended, maltreated, persecuted, and reacts with hostility and aggression. When it covers only a part of the personality and leaves part of the reality sense intact, it causes no severe disturbance. But it remains a danger, as it usually strives for extension. This psychic process is especially dangerous for the analyst. I remind you of Freud's words: "Analyzing spoils the analyst's character." The analytic situation, in which the analyst is the leader, the patient's confidant, the object of the patient's love, admiration, and infantile adoration, is a real temptation to the analyst to mobilize his own feelings of grandeur and to overrate himself. Therefore it seems to be of extreme importance for the analyst to know his own personality in its actual proportions, his capacities as well as his limitations and his faults.

I have returned to the high demands made upon the training analysis of future analysts. In the meantime you will certainly have thought that these claims should not be addressed primarly to the students, but in the first place to the training analysts. I am in full agreement. In organizing our training we should first of all look for competent training analysts. The training analyst has to live up to the demands of self-knowledge as far as possible. Here I come very close to Bibring's remarks on this topic. She recommends that the training analyst should accomplish this task by means of a self-analysis. This is certainly good advice. However, I think we cannot expect too much from it. "The drawback of self-analysis is really the countertransference"; this means that self-love easily prevents us from seeing our own shortcomings. Each of us has his own particular blind spot.

In my opinion, training analysts would be wiser to hold to Freud's advice (in "Analysis Terminable and Interminable," 1937) to resume their personal analysis from time to time. In addition, and in cases where outer circumstances prevent the training analyst from resuming his own analysis, he should take every care to examine his own behavior, to recognize his wishful thinking, his strivings for grandeur, his character peculiarities, etc. By seeing his own limitations clearly, the training analyst on his part creates the most favorable situation for making the best of the cooperative work with the future analyst.

17. Group Discussions with Stepmothers

(1954)

At the time this communication was published in the Dutch periodical for mental health, an extensive literature on group discussions and group therapy was already available from the Anglo-Saxon countries as well as from the Continent, and had been studied by me. I did not refer to those publications, intending merely to survey my own observations and to present a few ideas stimulated by them. Therefore I do not claim any priority for the explanations and thoughts brought forward in this short article.

The data of my communication are derived from twenty-one weekly discussions with a group of nine mothers in whose families lived one or more stepchildren. The discussions lasted for one hour and fifteen minutes and continued for nine months. The mothers were clients of the Amsterdam Child Guidance Clinic (Prinsengracht 717), of the Youth Psychiatric Department of the Communal Health Service, and of the Child Guidance Clinic of the *Hervormde Stichting* (a Protestant institution) in Amsterdam. The staff members of these various institutions worked hard in searching for the most suitable cases. The discussions took place in the Psychoanalytic Institute of the Dutch Psychoanalytic Society.

The objective of these discussions were twofold: (1) a social one; (2) a scientific one.

(1) The social aim was to give support to the mothers, who had come to one of the three above-mentioned institutions for advice in connection with difficulties they experienced with the stepchildren in the family situation.

(2)The scientific aims were several. I wanted to try: (a) to investigate the special problems of the stepchild within a family constellation; (b) to gain some insight into the relation between educational problems specific for the stepchild and problems inherent in the upbringing of children in general; (c) to get some idea of the relation of group discussions on the one hand and group psychotherapy and individual psychotherapy on the other hand; (d) to find out what psychic mechanisms and dynamisms come to the fore in group discussions.

Concerning (1), I shall start with a brief survey of the course of the various sessions, fragmentary and incomplete as it will have to be.

During the first interviews all participants were present. Later on there were usually one or two absent as a consequence of their children's illness. The winter was cold and wet and many children got colds and minor diseases;

sometimes the mother herself was ill, and on some occasions she had not been able to find a friend or relative who could take care of one of the smaller children and babies. Usually there were five or six mothers present, occasionally only three. A few times a baby accompanied the mother when she had not been able to leave him elsewhere.

The complaints which had caused the mothers to seek help consisted of neurotic phenomena in the children, i.e., enuresis, anxieties, learning inhibitions, etc., as well as behavioral delinquent problems, i.e., "troublesomeness," tantrums, lying, stealing, pilfering, baiting and teasing, and "sexual misbehavior." The various institutions had prepared the mothers for our discussions. The first gathering served the purpose of getting acquainted with one another. The mothers did not know each other and I myself was a stranger to them. I started by welcoming them and stressing how difficult it is to handle and educate stepchildren. We were coming together in order to try to understand some of the problems and conflicts involved and to find out how to meet them. It was remarkable to observe how soon the ice was broken. After one mother had started, the others could scarcely wait for their turns to speak and to pour out their hearts. They told their troubles not only in connection with the stepchildren, but also with their husbands and their own children. In some families there were only one or two stepchildren, in others children from previous marriages of the father or the mother were present, as well as illegitimate ones and those of the present marriage.

During the first interviews I remained very passive. I listened and limited myself to a few words of understanding and encouragement in order to gain confidence. Later I had to answer questions and give explanations. After a short time most of the mothers became highly interested in the problems of the other members of the group. They tried to understand each other and then became eager to give advice.

The levels of intelligence and psychological insight were very different. After three or four sessions some of the participants left, either because the material was beyond their comprehension or because of a lack of emotional understanding. In this group were the "narcissistic" types. They demanded to be in the center of attention, they could not listen and were continually disappointed that their special problems were not always in the limelight. After the session they tried to have a personal talk alone with me. Usually I said a few words to them, trying to give some support. However, they were unable to enter into a group relationship, finally lost interest, and stayed away after some five or six sessions. The others came very regularly apart from the already-mentioned occasions of illness, and a strong group relationship was established.

The problems that gradually came to the fore could be divided into two groups: (a) general problems; (b) individual problems.

Prominent among the general problems was the never-failing fear of being a "real," that is, a "bad," stepmother as pictured in fairy tales. All the women were from the working class or from the lower-middle classes and without exception they had entered into the marriage with a strong intention of becoming a very good mother to the "poor" stepchild. The stepchild was to be pitied because his real mother had died after a long and painful disease, or because she had been a "bad" mother, neglecting her child and deserting the family. The stepmothers intended to replace the real mother completely, sometimes with a conscious or unconscious idea of surpassing her and of being a much better mother to the poor child. One of the participants had been a stepchild herself, and had suffered severely from her hostile stepmother. Now married for a second time, she favored her husband's little son strongly above her own little daughter whom she brought with her from her previous marriage. The little girl was by far the most disturbed in the family. The woman suffered so much from a fear of being prejudiced against her stepchild that she did harm to her own child. The discussion of this situation and the woman's experience of being understood by the group members brought her relief and she was able to become much more tolerant and much nicer toward her difficult little girl. I shall come back to these problems later on.

Another general problem centered on if and at what moment the stepchild should be told about his actual relation to his stepparent. Only one mother was in favor of withholding the truth from the child. All the others agreed about the desirability and even the necessity of speaking openly about the family relations, though some of them clearly showed a strong fear of actually doing so.

In connection with this point the difficulties of the stepchild himself were open for discussion. A good understanding was finally achieved of the suffering of a child deprived of his own mother, making for mistrust and suspicion in certain circumstances. The fact that a mother has a special bond to her own child, in connection with biological ties, which is lacking in the relationship to a stepchild was discussed repeatedly. With some of the group members it resulted in a more natural and softer attitude to the stepchildren's disturbances and behavioral difficulties which was then followed by a relief of tension in the total family. A number of friendships among the members emerged from the group discussions, which had a favorable result. Especially did the knowledge that all of them were struggling with identical problems bring great relief. I explained that though there are doubtless special problems in a family with stepchildren, the upbringing of children in an ordinary home is one of the most difficult tasks laid upon parents (at least in our society and culture). This explanation also provided reassurance.

I myself always tried to focus attention to the general problems of the stepchild. It was, however, remarkable to notice that from the second session onward the individual problems and the personal family situations came ever more to the fore. There were meetings where nearly every mother tried to present her own conflicts, normal as well as neurotic ones. In these cases the difficult or disturbed stepchild was not mentioned but the other family members and their reactions were discussed. It was especially the husband who was spoken of. A number of complaints about his behavior were put forward, i.e., "If my husband had not spoiled his child so completely . . ."; "If only my husband were not so hot-tempered toward the children . . ."; "If my husband has shown more understanding of my problems, and if he had only supported me, then . . ."; etc. Gradually a number of confessions about the mother's personal disturbances, as for instance anxieties, compulsive actions, frigidity, sexual abnormalities, tantrums, etc., were brought out.

The reader will understand that little by little we ended up in group *therapy* instead of group *discussion*. Though originally we had started with "discussions on the stepchild situation," I thought it better not to counteract the spontaneous course of development and to go along with the needs of the participants. Thus the "therapeutic" element could not be completely eliminated.

In using the word "therapy" I have to stress the fact that a real, uncovering (psychoanalytic) therapy was out of the question and was not even aimed at. From time to time a single neurotic symptom or mode of behavior was removed or diminished, sometimes bringing about a change in the mother's attitude toward the stepchild or toward other family members. Occasionally this led to a decrease of tension which influenced the children's difficulties to a certain extent. I shall present two examples.

Some of the mothers had been stepchildren themselves, as I have already mentioned. They had entered marriage with high ideals trying to support the poor stepchild and be a better wife to the widowed or deserted husband. However, every one had suffered disappointments with the consequence that she either tried spasmodically to regain the lost illusion, or unconsciously repeated her own childhood situation as a lonely and embittered stepchild. This state of affairs sometimes caused manifest or suppressed hostilities that disturbed the family bond and unfavorably influenced the neurotic or antisocial behavior of the stepchild. In the mother, strong guilt feelings, inferiority feelings, and anxieties were evoked.

A second example concerns a mother who in one of the later sessions confessed that she suffered from frigidity and sexual aversion. She had been brought up with great severity. In adolescence she had suffered from a suspicious mother who had prohibited every outing being afraid of her daughter's "going with a boy." In reality the daughter had been completely uninterested in boys. At the present time she could allow her fourteen-year-old stepdaughter scarcely any kind of freedom. In the long run the group succeeded in providing the woman with some kind of insight into her envy of the pretty young girl who was enjoying life, with the consequence that the sensitive woman tried very hard to change her attitude toward the handsome stepdaughter.

I cannot go into more examples. However, I shall try to summarize some of the unconscious mental mechanisms in the mothers which sometimes could be favorably influenced by our discussions to a certain extent. This brings us to a tentative and very incomplete answer to the questions formulated above.

Concerning (2a), the stepchild situation gave rise in some women to (1) an excessive neurotic guilt feeling; (2) a too strong feeling of being injured in connection with disappointed expectations and hostility aroused by them; (3) envy of the stepchild who was felt to have a much better life than the mother had had herself; (4) pathological jealousy toward the husband who was felt to favor his own child above his second wife, and jealousy toward the child; (5) some anxieties and mild neurotic symptoms.

It is well known that similar psychic factors may sometimes be influenced in individual (psycho) therapy. We have to consider whether some such brief therapy is to be preferred or whether one can expect a better result from group discussions or group therapy. This brings us to our next points:

Concerning (2c) and (2d): as far as my experience goes, I should like to formulate the following impressions:

The problems of neurotic guilt feelings can sometimes be discussed with relative ease and success in a group. Giving a hearing without prejudice to a participant's self-accusations may provide relief. However, the very fact that many other people in a group suffer from similar difficulties is even more releaving. One could say that "shared guilt is half of the guilt." In our group it was undoubtedly important that the leader-doctor was a mother figure, understanding, unprejudiced, listening, and explaining. However, of equal significance were the group bonds, sometimes developing into real friendships and actual mutual assistance. In connection with these interpersonal relationships some of the jealousy situations, disappointments, and injuries could be recognized and tolerated more easily, with the consequence that advice from other group members was accepted and assimilated to a higher degree.

A restriction of therapeutic possibilities in a group seems to lie in the fact that only the most superficial of anxieties and symptoms can be reached. Early and strongly repressed and warded-off material cannot be touched upon. Reaction formations and neurotic behavior patterns which have come about as a defense against fears and neurotic conflicts cannot be changed. If one tries to discuss or interpret a particular defense mechanism, the participant who is using this mechanism most intensively will put a limit to the explanations. If one goes beyond his capacity for using the explanation, the resistance can only become stronger with the possible consequence that one or more of the group members will run away. The group bond is then disturbed. Moreover, a similar interpretation may cause the mother to act out her conflicts in the family to a much higher degree than she did before, and the family may suffer considerably from this.

Concerning (2a) and (2b), I should like to comment: the special problem of the stepchild situation in regard to the mother lies in her recognition of the fact that (1) the tie to a stepchild is always different from that to her own child; (2) in connection with this state of affairs it is necessary to be sincere and to provide the stepchild with complete information. At the same time, the stepmother should have full understanding of the difficulty for a sensitive child to accept his position in the family and she should be loving and tolerant toward his behavioral disorders; (3) the stepchild situation is likely to provoke jealousy and rivalry in connection with the husband (father of the child) and the child's own mother, requiring a good deal of self-control on the stepmother's side; (4) her own children's upbringing is a difficult task as well; therefore the stepchild situation is *not* responsible for all of the conflicts and difficulties in the familiy.

Finally, I should like to make a few remarks on the question whether there was any success in the group discussions from the social side. Were our talks able to provide some support? A single experiment can merely give some tentative impressions. I myself think that one should not see the results either too optimistically or too pessimistically. Something undoubtedly happened in our group; tensions were relieved and displacements of conflicts occured within the family relations which sometimes influenced the family ties in a favorable way. However, fundamental changes did not take place, either in the mother or in the child. In cases where one or the other was severely disturbed, there was scarely any transformation, as was to be expected. It remains an open question whether the favorable influences have lasted and if so, for how long. However, the same problems are encountered in the infrequent (weekly or biweekly) contacts of individual mothers with, for instance, a psychiatric social worker, in casework, and even in "brief therapy." In a follow-up discussion with the staffs of the child guidance clinic and the other institutions, it became clear that some of the women who had originally benefited considerable from the discussions had come back after a longer period of time with the same or other complaints. Apparently the weekly active participation in the group had been a necessary condition for being able to keep to the changed attitude and to the improved family relationships.

This does *not* mean, however, that all of the affective ties to the group had been broken. I mention only one example out of many: more than a year after the termination of our meetings one of the participants asked my advice about a certain problem. She thanked me in a letter, in which she wrote in addition, "I was so impressed and grateful that you, Dr. Lampl. still knew the name of my stepdaughter. It is a proof of the fact that our discussions were extremely intimate . . . ."

Among the many questions raised in our final staff discussion, one should be mentioned particularly: "Are group discussions generally preferable to individual contacts, or is the reverse a better approach?" My tentative impression is that in cases where the mother is not severely hampered by her own neurosis the group ties may be so significant that they may make the group discussions more successful. For more gravely disturbed women, individual contact may be preferable.

18. The Theory of Instinctual Drives

(1956)

Freud's early libido theory, set forth as a working hypothesis in order to clarify certain problems of the genesis of neurotic disturbances, had to be enlarged and modified several times in connection with the increase of psychological material needing to be explained. A good survey of the development of Freud's theory of the instinctual drives is given by Edward Bibring (1936). The most exciting, remarkable, and at the same time disputed modification is known as the theory of the life and death instincts. It was first mentioned in *Beyond the Pleasure Principle* (1920). Some psychoanalysts were very much impressed by the new theory and embraced it enthusiastically, others rejected it more or less vehemently from the very beginning. A third group was skeptical and neither accepted nor rejected it. This conspicuous reception of the new hypothesis seems to prove that it was not welcomed objectively as a scientific contribution to be tested by further investigation, but was felt by many to be a disturbing and confusing burdening of human emotional life. Today, thirty-five years after Freud's first presentation, the attitude toward the theory of life and death instincts does not seem to have essentially changed. An affective response on the part of outsiders toward one or another theory of Freud's is quite familiar and understandable to psychoanalysts. But a similar reaction from analysts themselves calls for a serious inquiry into the phenomenon. Dous it prove that the theory itself is not a workable hypothesis? Or are there factors independent of its value to be held responsible for these various reactions?

First I want to make a few remarks on the second point: the attitude of psychoanalysts toward the "death instinct" theory. In an article in *Psyche*, R. Brun (1953) makes an attempt to prove its falsity. He gives, among other things, a review of the psychoanalytic literature on the topic, and draws the conclusion that most of the authors who originally accepted the theory as a valuable working hypothesis changed their minds at a later period (between 1931 and 1941). He states that thirteen authors (he mentions only twelve names) arrived at an "uncompromising rejection." One of the names mentioned is my own. Now for my own sake I must emphasize that the conclusion Brun draws from my paper "Masochism and Narcissism" (Chapter 5) is based on a misunderstanding or a misinterpretation. I tried to give some explanations of clinically observable phenomena of masochistic behavior, and I stated explicitly that in psychological events we are dealing with what is called secondary masochism. The so-called primary masochism, later on used by Freud as equivalent to the "death instinct," is not psychologically observable in clinical material. My paper does not in any way deal with the biological theory of drives. It is neither a proof nor a disproof of its correctness. I must confess that Freud's latest "drive theory" always impressed me as a far-reaching and consistent endeavor to form a connection between psychological and somatic biological data, in other words, to look for a biological basis of psychological phenomena. This endeavor was by no means the first in Freud's scientific life. In 1895 he wrote a manuscript (pubished in 1950, eleven years after his death), the "Project for a Scientific Psychology," in which he developed a highly interesting theory, trying to depict psychological events as quantitatively determined by conditions of material elements of the brain (see also Jones, 1953). Although Freud soon afterward discontinued his search for the brain-physiological basis of mental processes, he always used to say that at some time the connection between psychology and somatology-biology would need to be re-established. In chapter 22 I have tried to connect findings in modern brain physiology, cybernetics, and ethology with psychoanalytic data and theory. In today's presentation I must refer to many ideas laid down in that paper. There are remarkable analogies to be observed between Freud's ideas set forth in "Project" and many of the theories of the scientists working in those fields, though the terminology is different. I cannot pursue this interesting connection further here. However, in pursuing the train of though that seeks to find the somatic foundation of mental processes, we inevitably encounter the necessity of dealing with the underlying forces at work. In psychoanalytic psychology the forces providing mental energy were called *Triebe* (drives).[1] The drive energy undergoes different changes during growth and development. The fact that many interests of the individual as well as of the group run counter to a direct gratification of the instinctual drives brings about sublimation or neutralization of the drive energy. With some simplification we can say that the unconscious (mainly the id) works with direct, the conscious (mainly the ego) with neutralized drive energy.

From the very beginning Freud tried to localize the sources of the drives. He observed, e.g., oral, anal, phallic, and genital sources and components of the sexual drives. The source of the aggressive drives he localized in the musculature. With regard to the somatic, physiological processes from which the *forces* providing the mental energy originate, he confined himself to more general statements in his later works. In the *Outline* he says: "The forces which we assume to exist behind the tensions caused by the needs of the id are called *instincts* [Triebe]. They represent the somatic demands upon mental life" (1940, p. 19). In other places he speaks of "original forces" [*"Urkräfte"*]. In using the term "forces" Freud points to the physical origin of the drives. The same seems to be valid for his reformulation of the definition of *Trieb*. Originally the concept of *Trieb* was a psychological one. It covered the sexual needs of man and animal on the one hand and the need for self-preservation on the other (sexual and ego drives). In "Instincts and Their Vicissitudes" Freud explicitly

---

[1] Elsewhere I have proposed translating the word *Trieb* by "drive" and not by "instinct," because an "instinct" seems to be allready complicated behavior pattern. Animal instinct is perhaps a phylogenetic forerunner of human ego devices, as it deals with the outside world. Hartmann has dealt with the problem in a similar though slightly different way.

states that the theory is "merely a working hypothesis, to be retained only so long as it proves useful" (1915, p. 124). Though in this essay he repeatedly points to a somatic basis for the drives, e.g., to chemical processes underlying sexual functions, the somewhat different definition of the *Urtriebe* or *Grundtriebe* as derivatives of "forces" appears only in his later works.

Here Freud comes upon two forces, working in different directions. One force tends to bind, to constitute ever larger unities, the other to dissolve connections, to destroy unities. The question arises whether such forces operate only in the living world. The inorganic world was formerly considered to be eternal, indestructible; physics calls it a closed system, where a tendency toward increase of entropy reigns, and in which states of equilibrium are reached. But modern astronomy and physics teach us that in many parts of the universe unifying and resolving forces are at work. This holds true for atoms, molucules, and elements as well as for planets and stars. More complicated and higher elements and atoms originate from simpler ones, e.g., helium from hydrogen. In the solar system there is an augmentation of matter that may lead to organization and to the formation of new celestial bodies. On the other hand, a constant disintegration of matter and the disappearance of small and large bodies is observable. Unifying (constructive) as well as dissolving (destructive) forces are at work. I must emphasize that the words "constructive" and "destructive" are not used here in the sense usual in psychology, that is, charged with a connotation of *value* (good and bad, or desirable and undesirable, etc.). They indicate simply the *direction* of the forces at work in the process of unification and dissolution. Though the inorganic world as a whole is a closed system, it also contains open systems with decreasing entropy. From a scientific point of view we must consider living matter as having originated out of lifeless inorganic substance. According to biology, there exist particles, simple viruses, which can be crystallized, and are to be considered as transition phenomena between the inorganic and the living worlds. We are, it is true, still quite unaware of how the birth of life comes about. But it seems quite reasonable to expect that similar forces or tendencies are at work in both the inorganic and living world. A critical question arises here. In the nonliving world the dissolution or destruction of one body can be followed by the formation of another; one form of energy or matter is replaced by another; after destruction, new construction may occur. What of this in the living world? The individual life, it is true, is definitely destined to disappear. The phenomenon "life", however, does not disappear so long as certain environmental conditions are fulfilled. Life as we know it on our planet may be expected to cease when conditions of temperature, atmosphere, etc., change. It will certainly do so when the earth, perhaps after millions of years, comes to be destroyed as a whole. We do not know, however, whether life exists or will in the future exist on some other planet. In spite of our complete ignorance on this matter for the time being, we are, I think, entitled seriously to consider such a possibility. Be this as it may, as a matter of fact we see the opposed forces easily at work in somatic processes. In living cells and bodies we observe forces or tendencies directed toward binding and growth as well as forces or tendencies toward dissolution and decay. It is well known that metabolism provides the necessary energy (chemical, physical, and electrical) for these processes. We may find further support for these considerations in modern biology. The organic world is only *one* instance of an open system with decreasing entropy. Though total equilibrium is reached only in death, a tendency toward minimum entropy production, the so-called homeostasis or steady state, is at work in vital phenomena. But it is at work in every open system, and therefore in some inorganic systems as well. Ludwig von Bertalanffy (1950), e.g., states that the so-called equifinal behavior, considered by Driesch and others as "an extraordinary performance to be accomplished only by the action of a vitalistic factor and therefore a proof of vitalism," is *not* limited to vital processes. "Equifinality is found also in certain inorganic systems which necessarily are open ones." Prigogine is of the opinion that the second law of thermodynamics. formerly so defined as to apply only to closed systems, is an "admirable but fragmentary doctrine." He says: "It is necessary to establish a broader theory comprising states of non-equilibrium as well as those of equilibrium." This means a theory comprising organic as well as inorganic processes. To quote von Bertalanffy once more: "Not only must biological theory be based upon physics, the new developments show that the biological point of view opens new pathways in physical theory as well."

In our language we are accustomed to call the process of growth and organization in an organism "life", that of decay and disorganization "death." Now why should we not speak of life forces and death tendencies at work in the living organisms? We must certainly be aware of the fact that we cannot define the essence of the term "force." But in physics "force" is a hypothetical term as well. Enigmas are still to be found in the lifeless as much as in the living world. We will now turn to *mental* life, a very special and late developmental product of life, it is true, but still part of life. The assumption that representatives of the constructive and destructive biological forces are at work in psychic processes is inevitable, though we must be prepared to encounter them in a different shape. I think Freud had these points in mind when speaking of the necessity of a scientific psychology, of the physical basis of psychic events, and finally of a somatic-biological theory of mental forces.

We have now to ask the question: What is the psychical reflection of or correlation with these somatic processes? From a scientific point of view we have no reason to think of mental processes as mystical or supernatural events, entering into the human individual from outside, as do some philosophical and religious systems. Science considers body and mind as a single entity. I have earlier (Chapter 12) adopted this standpoint, though I explicity stated the limitations, for the time being, of physical and physiological approaches to mental events. Now, as Freud described the mental forces providing the energy for psychic processes as *Triebe* (drives), we come back to the question why it proves to be so difficult to see Freud's conception of Eros (life instincts) as the psychological *representatives* of the organic life forces and the destructive drives (or death instincts) as those of the organic destructive forces in the sense mentioned above. One of the most striking observable differences between the drives and the underlying forces seems to lie in the fact that the drives are charged with the psychic quality of sensations, feelings, affects, as I point out in Chapters 12 and 22. The feelings may be experienced as tensions (e.g., with needs), as pleasure and unpleasure, and in higher development in a variety of most differentiated and differently colored affects. It is well known from analytic observation that in the unconscious the drive representations do not lose their affective charge.

I should like to mention a few factors out of many that seem to me to be responsible for the difficulties of understanding Freud's latest drive theory, though of course they do not give us information about its validity. I ask myself whether some of the impassioned opponents may perhaps have failed to take into consideration the extension of the concept of drive inherent in the theory. Perhaps it may be called an omission on Freud's part not to havve announced this extension explicitly. Freud's rather humorous reference to a "mythology" in connection with the drive theory, too, may have promoted some misunderstanding. I wonder, however, whether the psychological concept of drive is any more mythological or mysterious than the concept of "force" in physics?

The earlier theory of the drives embraced the psychic manifestations and vicissitudes of the sexual drives. Sexuality, however, is only a part of the life process, though a very important one. The highly complicated development of the total psychic life seems to hamper the *observations* of connections with the bodily processes, not only for outsiders, but for analysts themselves. On the one hand we know for certain that the connections do exist, on the other we are aware of the fact that the underlying somatic forces are not observable directly and unchanged in psychic events. In these circumstances seem to lie many possibilities for a lack of understanding. I will mention one factor out of many: human beings, scientists included, tend to be proud of their highly complicated mental life. A deep-rooted narcissistic need often leads them to hold on (unconsciously) to primitive ideals and grandeur fantasies in one or another higher developed form. Where scientists do not embrace philosophical or religious systems, they can satisfy this need by (unconscious) glorification of some psychological theory or other. In our field the "drive theory" seems to be a very suitable one for this purpose. To see the drives as mysterious, supernatural powers seems to satisfy the pleasure principle in the form of a narcissistic gratification. In this connection I feel we should take Freud's above-cited remark about the drive theory as "mythology" as something of a warning against this pleasurable but unscientific tendency.

Be this as it may, a passionate uncritical adherence to the theory may be caused by such an affective need for idealization. But the reverse can occur as well. It is especially the part of the theory concerning the destructive drives, the death instinct, that may lead to an uncritical rejection, rationalized by the faulty supposition already mentioned that the death instinct has to be observable directly in clinical material. Brun, for instance, is of the opinion that the scarcity of suicides can be used as a proof against the theory. I will come back to this topic afterward. Flugel (1953) in his very interesting paper states: "The concept of the death-instinct is embarrassing not only emotionally but also intellectually, for its relations to the other more generally acceptable features of psychoanalytic theory are often far from clear." I wonder whether we really have to distinguish between emotional and intellectual embarrassment. What seems to be intellectual evidence may be in reality an overlooking of the extension of the concept of drive. Now the very fact of extending the meaning of a concept is nothing uncommon in psychoanalysis. More than half a century ago the concept of sexuality was enlarged by Freud to include the whole of infantile instinctual and affective life, an enlargement by now accepted by every psychoanalyst. The refusal to accept a similar extension of the concept of drive to make it embrace the underlying somatic forces as well is not likely to be based on intellectual, logical considerations, but rather on affective motives. Nevertheless, in order to facilitate the understanding of Freud's theory, we may propose a reformulation of the terminology used in the drive theory for practical purposes. From this practical point of view we suggest that the word "drive" be reserved for psychic phenomena, and differentiated from those forces or tendencies of a more general nature that underlie them and are closely related to them, in other words, that we distinguish between the purely psychological and the biological-physical concepts. While I accept Freud's idea of this close relatedness, the inclusion of both these series of factors under the same term may lead to ambiguities. Thus I propose to speak of sexual or constructive and destructive or aggressive *drives* on the one hand, and of life and death tendencies of *forces* of a more general nature on the other. Such a distinction carries in itself the danger of furthering the desire of many people to separate body and mind and to forget that in reality body and mind are one entity. However, as for the time being we are not able to indicate the organic correlate to each psychic event observed, we might accept the distinction until further notice and until progress in science enables us to unify the two theories in a less disputed form. We can benefit by this distinction in our practical psychoanalytic work. It at once becomes clear that in studying psychic phenomena we have neither the possibility nor the need to search for a "death drive." As Freud put it, the death instincts works silently. At the present time no human being is able to percieve psychically the metabolic processes of dissolution in the body cells. Neither can we experience the opposite processes of upbuilding. What we perceive are tensions, needs, longings, and so on. From the very moment of perception these phenomena are already psychic processes, though originally in a very primitive and simple form. That in the course of development they become complicated mental events and lead to a variety of refined reaction formations, etc., is sufficiently known. The ways by which the transformations and reactions take place are not always thoroughly clear. The investigation of these problems has to be reserved for future research.

I completely agree with Flugel and many others that a longing or wish for death is seldom experienced by human beings, whereas the wish to continue life is markedly more frequent. This observation does not prove anything in favor of or against a biological theory of the forces at work. It merely tells us that human individuals in their mental and affective life perceive the phenomenon of "life" as a property they want to preserve. This seems to be a particular developmental outcome of a special vicissitude of narcissistic drives. Where a longing to die is observable, it is the expression of complicated psychic processes, influenced by mental, bodily, and environmental factors.

Another striking phenomenon is a strong fear of death so often encountered in human beings. We know from our observations that it too has a complicated structure. Freud showed its close connection with castration fear. But it is obvious that this fear has other sources as well. Kurt Eissler (1955), in full acceptance of Freud's "thanatology," as he calls it, gives a number of highly interesting reflections on "death" as subjective experience, on the longing for and the fear of death. However, he does not differentiate adequately between the subjective experience "death" in the human mind and the biological organic forces terminating the individual life. I regret that I cannot discuss his valuable study here.

The very existence of the fear of death is perhaps a second factor responsible for the emotional embarrassment vis-à-vis the theory of the death drives, mentioned by Flugel. The use of the intellectual knowledge of the inescapability of death for each individual is so much hampered by the wish for eternal continuation of one's own personality and consequently by the fear of one's own death, that even scientific considerations of the origin of destructive mental forces are very difficult to pursue. If my ideas should prove to be correct, we should once more have an examplle of the well-known fact that emotional embarrassment can impair the intellectual judgment in scientific procedure. In order to avoid misunderstandings I must emphasize once more that the very fact of emotional involvement vis-à-vis the drive theory does not prove anything in favor of or against it. Whether it will finally be accepted or rejected as a workable hypothesis lies with future research.

A last remark here will concern another practical consequence for our daily psychoanalytic work. Freud was of the opinion that the understanding of the phenomenon of "aggression" was facilitated by the new theory. I think all psychoanalysts agree about the correctness of the observation that aggressive and destructive acts whether directed toward other persons or toward the self (in the most extreme form in homicide and suicide) are usually provoked by frustrations and severe disappointments. It seems much more difficult to search for the *forces* that enable men to commit murder and suicide. As Eissler puts it: "The . . . occurrence of suicide is not the decisive factor; rather, that every human being possesses during most of his lifetime the capacity of committing suicide should be made the center of investigation" (1955, p. 67). (See also the important contributions of Karl Menninger, and a footnote in his paper, "Regulatory Devices of the Ego Under Major Stress," 1954.)

From clinical observation we know that in a suicidal act many psychological factors are involved. Freud considers the fantasy or impulse to murder an ambivalently loved (or hated?) object as a very important determinant. Another fantasy may be equally decisive, namely the idea of returning to and being united with a once deeply loved dead person.

There are still other psychological factors which may be involved in suicide, and various forces have to work together in order to provide the energy neccessary for the performance of the act. As a matter of fact we frequently encounter suicidal fantasies and impulses, whereas the carrying out of the *act* occurs relatively seldom, at least in our Western culture (compare Brun). From this we must conclude that the tendency to live and the forces directed to the continuance of life are remarkably strong. On the other hand, whenever suicide actually takes place, it proves that the force directed toward the discontinuance of life is still stronger at that particular moment.

Many psychoanalysts cease their investigation after the statement that destructive actions are provoked by environmental circumstances. But the very fact that such a provocation can be successful points to the presence of forces providing the energy for the deed. And what sounds more plausible than to expect these to be psychological tendencies (or forces) attendant upon the somatic-biological forces constantly at work in the organism?

Summarizing, I would say:

(1) Science has to presume similar constructive (unifying) and destructive (dissolving) forces in the lifeless universe, in living bodies, and in mental life, though in different shapes.

(2) For practical purposes we can, for the time being, propose a terminilogical revision in the drive theory so as to reserve the term "drive" for psychological and the term "force" or "tendency" for the underlying somatic phenomena.

(3) Aggressive and destructive acts have to be studied psychologically as regards their various determinants, but the capacity to perform the acts is to be found in the underlying general forces.

In conclusion: Freud's theory of the "life and death instincts" (sexual and destructive drives), seen in *this* light, is no more "mystical" or "embarrassing" than any other hypothesis in any field of science. Further investigation will have to decide its value as a working hypothesis.

19. Psychoanalytic Ego Psychology and Its Significance for Maldevelopment in Children

(1956)

From the very beginning, the term "psychoanalysis" has had a twofold meaning. According to Freud, the term covered (a) a specific therapeutic method capable of curing or at least improving certain forms of psychoneuroses, and (b) a psychological theory which not only accounted for the genesis of neuroses but in addition was able to elucidate the dynamic, psychic processes in patients as well as in "normal" persons.

Observations on neurotics and on certain mental phenomena in "healthy" persons (e.g., dreams, parapraxia, etc.) necessitated enlargements, additions, and modifications of the theory. Conversely, theoretical deepening of knowledge gave rise to an extension of therapeutic possibilities. It goes without saying that psychotherapeutic and analytic influence both have their limits.

Psychoanalytic knowledge has proved to be of significance for other disciplines too. One of these areas is the bringing up of children. I want to start with a very short survey of the development of the psychoanalytic psychology of children. The newborn enters the world as an instinctual creature, as Freud put it. The infant has a variety of needs, originally of a somatic kind, which categorically demand satisfaction, originally of a somatic kind, which categorically demand satisfaction. Since the human child is completely dependent upon motherly care for a long period of time in order to survive, he soon makes an intense attachment to the mother. In addition to the bodily tie, a psychic tie comes about very early. The need for food is a particularly urgent necessity, but at the same time the needs for warmth, care, and bodily sensations demand immediate satisfaction. When a psychic tie to the mother has been established, this object relationship creates new needs and dependencies. The object bond provides new possibilities of gratification; however, it becomes a source of disappointments, frustrations, and suffering at the same time. Freud very early described the development of the child's sexual instinctual needs from birth to adulthood. I will not go into the different stages of sexual development here. Later, Freud pointed to the equal importance of aggressive drives and tendencies. In infants we observe love and aggression operating simultaneously and intermingled with each other, though sometimes separately as well. They may be directed toward objects as well as toward the self.

From the very beginning Freud opposed to the instinctual part of the personality, the id, another agency, the ego. He had observed the personality developing in and around conflicts. The ego, or ego organization, is the psychic agency which has an integrative (synthetizing) function; it mediates between inner and outer world. Later on the ego has to take into account the demands of the normative agency, the superego, as well. The superego, or conscience, comes into being in the little child when he encounters the demands and ideals of the parents and the wider environment. This process starts at an early age and consolidates in the fifth to sixth year of life, at the end of the phallic phase. However, the superego continues to develop throughout life with modifications of norms and ethics. The first principles of analytic ego psychology were laid down by Freud; they were further developed by a number of his coworkers after his death, e.g., by Anna Freud, Hartmann, Kris, this author, and many others. The extensions of ego psychology are still based upon observed phenomena. The hypotheses used to account for newly discovered material are re-examined and retested time and again. During the last decades a new field for research was found in direct observations of young children. The socalled "longitudinal life histories," observations from birth until adulthood, have provided very significant material and suggest the possible elucidation of many uncertainties and obscurities in the near future.

A short survey of present psychoanalytic child psychology

Before presenting the disturbed development of a three-and-a-half-year-old little boy, I want to give a short and necessarily incomplete presentation of the complicated ego development of the infant.

The newborn comes into the world with an archaic psychic heritage called by Freud "the id in a wider sense," by Hartmann "the undifferentiated phase." Out of these undifferentiated innate dispositions the different maturational stages of the instinctual drives (the id in a narrower sense) and the ego functions develop gradually during the first years of life. Some ego functions develop in a relatively autonomous way (Hartmann, 1939a), as a consequence of the general processes of growth and maturation. One example is the intellect. Academic developmental psychology describes the different stages of intellectual development of the little child (e.g., Bühler, Stern, Piaget). However, we know that many ego functions develop in interplay with and as reactions to drive processes. In mediating between the inner and outer worlds the ego makes use of adaptation mechanisms. It has to acquire knowledge of the environment, to learn to use it or to adapt to it. Many of these ego functions can become secondarily autonomous. This may happen after a certain amount of drive energy has become indifferent energy (according to Freud, sublimated or desexualized energy). Following Hartmann, we now speak of deinstinctualized or neutralized energy since observations have taught us that not only sexual energy but aggressive drive energy too can be neutralized (deaggressivized). However, all of these ego functions can again be instinctualized through certain experiences so that they revert to earlier modes of sexual and aggressive satisfaction, impairing the course of development. A clear example can be seen in many learning disturbances of young children. If, e.g., reading or counting secondarily regains a sexual or aggressive meaning, the further development of these achievements may become disturbed or paralyzed.

The infant's drives have to be tamed. Whether and in what way the feeble primitive ego succeeds in doing so or not is dependent upon a number of factors: (1) the nature of the drives, the instinctual disposition; (2) the capacities and inborn factors out of which the ego organization develops; (3) the demands and influences of the environment, the mother's attitude; (4) the continuous mutual interplay of the factors named under (1), (2), and (3). Observations on infants have revealed that a harmonious development is dependent not only on the nature of the mother's demands and educational measures, nor merely on their severity or leniency, but first and foremost on the developmental stage in which they are imposed upon the little child.

Though there exist individual differences of instinctual needs and ego capacities, we can nevertheless point to some factors which are not to be neglected in the endeavor to encourage a harmonious development: (1) in every developmental phase the little child should get a certain amount of direct drive satisfaction; (2) the possibilities for these satisfactions should be offered to the child for a certain (long enough) time. In the first year of life the infant is in need of a quantity of oral pleasure as well as of pleasure on other body parts, e.g., on the skin and on the motor apparatus, both in a passive and in an active way. Apart from the satisfaction of hunger, sucking at the breast provides pleasure, as do thumb sucking on other objects. Infantile sexual tensions are discharged by these activities. Skin erotism and passive needs as, for instance, being caressed, being lovingly handled, etc., have to be satisfied as well. In motoric movements, e.g., grasping, crawling, walking, etc., aggressive energy is discharged alongside libidinal energy. During the same period the infant's "ego" acquires knowledge of the outer world, it develops the functions of memory, of mastering motility and of using it for particular actions. Furthermore, the functions of differentiating between inner and outer worlds and of reality testing come into existence.

When the excreta come into the center of the child's interest, he experiences anal and urethral pleasure. If education in cleanliness is started too early, the result may be either a mechanical compliance at the cost of disturbed development, inhibitions, and anxieties, or a stubborn opposition followed by ego and character distortions. We assume the age of approximately one-and-a-half to two years to be the optimal one for starting training in our culture. Too frequent and too long-lasting soiling resulting from too much indulgence may cause similar developmental disturbances and inhibitions.

Similar considerations are valid in connection with masturbatory pleasure gain, in the infant as well as in the child in the so-called phallic phase, in which the manifold oedipal relationships to the parents emerge. The aggressive drives and their later derivatives, e.g., the urge to conquer, also must find an adequate discharge in movements, in the handling of objects, and in play (which is the child's "field of work").

The history of a little boy

Tonny is brought to a child guidance clinic by his mother at the age of three and a half years. The mother is very much worried because her son does not speak, never plays alone, and is not able to do anything at all. He usually sits down silently in a corner of the room, he wets and soils his pants. He is unable to put on or take off his coat. He cannot bring a spoon or fork to his mouth and has to be fed by his mother. He makes the impression of being a severely retarded child, nearly an idiot.

The first interview in the clinic seems to confirm completely the mother's statements. The psychologist trying to test the little patient is unable to make contact with him. After some time, however, she becomes aware of Tonny's casting a sudden glance at her and in saying good-by she gets the impression that he has perceived and retained some events. The former diagnosis of severe retardation is doubted and a longer period of observation is initiated.

The first interview with the psychiatrist starts in the usual way. Tonny sits down in a corner of the room and does not do anything. He is invited to play, there are trains, cars, dolls, little houses, etc. Tonny does not react and remains silent. The psychiatrist sits down himself and begins to play with the railroad cars, lets the train go in different directions, and does not pay any attention to Tonny. After some time he casts an inviting glance at the child, who does not react. The same situation is repeated without success. After some thirty minutes the therapist speaks to himself, saying softly, "I think Tonny fears that he is not *allowed* to play with the train. That is a pity, because the toys are here for Tonny to play with and it would be so nice if he would dare to do so." Tonny seems to listen, after some minutes he moves a little bit, very slowly. The therapist repeats his former words and looks at the boy encouragingly. Tonny sits down near the toys, stretches his hand in their direction, stops, and looks at the therapist inquiringly. Finally he seizes a car. He glances at the toy and at the therapist alternately and undecidedly. All of a sudden he puts the car down and lets it run. Tonny is playing. He gradually moves toward the other toys, hesistantly and with wooden movements, but with growing attention and finally with an unexpected intensity, which very much surprises the therapist. He lets Tonny go his way, does not interfere, and only answers the boy's inquiring gaze with a friendly smile. After fifteen more minutes the session is at an end. Tonny's pale face is flushed with excitement, he smiles and is happy. The moment the mother enters into the room, Tonny is pale and motionless again; only a slight angry twitching in his face is observable. The mother wants to put on his coat. He stares at her, suddenly he stands up, snatches his coat out of her hands and tries to put it on himself, in which he succeeds after some unsuccessful, clumsy attempts. This time the mother is startled. She says to the therapist, "But Tonny cannot put on his clothes all alone." The therapist calmly answers: "Apparently he can, Mrs. X." Then he makes another appointment with Tonny.

I cannot describe the course of Tonny's further treatment in detail, but wish to emphasize only this much: in every succeeding session the little boy starts to play more and more freely, he gradually becomes ever more skillful, and he initiates conversations with the therapist. In the beginning his childish speech is hard to understand, but in a remarkably short time the therapist and the patient are able to communicate with each other quite satisfactorily. Tonny listens with greedy interest to the therapist talking about Tonny's anxieties and fears, and every time it becomes clearer that Tonny has a good mental grasp and a correct comprehension of the doctor's explanations. The diagnosis of retardation is abandoned.

Though nearly all of Tonny's ego functions had been arrested in their development at a very early stage, most of them were afterdeveloped in an astonishingly short time. After six months of treatment Tonny was able to enter kindergarten and to adjust to the situation.

We must now concern ourselves with the question of what factors were responsible for the little boy's very severe developmental inhibitions. We once more let the mother narrate: Tonny had been a very normal, lively baby, feeding and growing well. Not until the end of his first year of life did the mother notice changes in his behavior; he became quieter, detached and absent. Crawling started late and walking was not learned until the age of two and a half years. Speech was never mastered; he merely stammered a few unintelligible sounds. He obstinately opposed bowel training.

Naturally the mother was asked several times whether something unusual or startling had occurred around his first birthday. She denied this and could not think of any extraordinary event. After several weeks, however, the mother, who came regularly for interviews, had gained more confidence and began to speak more intimately about her own problems. One day she related the following story. At the age of ten to eleven months Tonny had been a very lively, fidgety child. The mother, being very busy in her household, put him in a pen, often for many hours on end, to "protect him" against possible injuries. Once she found him playing with his genital and she was extremely frightened, thinking it was most dangerous. She pulled his hands away, hit it repeatedly, threatened the child, but nothing was successful. He continued his genital play. After the mother had heard about his supposed retardation, she was secretly convinced that this was the outcome of these terrible deeds. As prohibitions and punishment were of no avail, the mother fastened Tonny's hands to the pen's bars. She was convinced that she had saved her boy in "curing" him of masturbation. This procedure of fastening his hands continued for some six to eight weeks. Afterward Tonny did not masturbate any more. However, he was incapable of all other activities and motor actions, ordinarliy learned by a one-year-old. Tonny could not gain any pleasure satisfaction, neither an infantile sexual nor a motoric aggressive one. In addition the emotional tie to the mother became severely disturbed. We must assume that in this special period of life genital play was Tonny's main source of pleasure, as well as the basis for the unfolding of motor actions and activities in general. The complete suppression of pleasure gain and activity development, occuring at too-early age and too rigourously, had apparently paralyzed the growth of all ego functions. He was unable to learn anything new from that time on.

At the early age of ten or eleven months there is not yet any question of castration fear, which does not come to the fore until the phallic phase in connection with oedipal wishes and strivings. The little boy believes in the danger of castration only when he experiences his various oedipal conflicts and after he has observed that creatures (girls or women) without a penis do exist. With Tonny the genital play was merely a form of pleasurable activity. The mother's rigorous restrictions and punishments were the result of her own neurotic inhibitions and anxieties. To the infant a loving relationship with the mother is indispensable for his growth. As Tonny's mother attachment was so severly damaged, a stimulus from this side was lacking as well. Thus every progress in development had become impossible.

We had to come to the opposite conclusion from the mother's. It was not active masturbation which had caused Tonny's "illness," but the forceful impediment of the necessary activities which brought about the little boys' pseudo retardation.

In treatment the therapist gradually removed the prohibitions, with the result that the interrupted development was taken up again and could be continued more normally.

20. The Role of Identification in Psychoanalytic Procedure

(1956)

By the term "identification" we denote a normal mental process which leads a person in some way or other to become like another person. Identifications make use of the mechanism of "introjection" (or "incorporation"). The person "introjects" the image of the other person, he "takes over" some or many of the latter's characteristics. In normal growth "identifications" express themselves in different contexts during the various phases of maturation and development. In this short paper I have to limit myself to the description of only a few of them. As identification is a form of relationship with an object, it can only manifest itself after some (primitive) differentiation between self and object has come into existence.

In *Group Psychology and the Analysis of the Ego*, Freud defines identification as "the earliest expression of an emotional tie with another person" (1921, p. 105).

In normal development the process of identification serves different aims. I will mention three of them:

(1) Identification is one of the ways to secure the satisfaction of bodily and psychical needs, provided by the object.

(2) It finds a place in, and promotes, the process of learning. The little child acquires intellectual knowledge, he learns to speak, to read, to handle toys and tools, to test reality as well as to master emotional situations, and to adjust his instinctual life to the demands of the environment in large measure by identification with parents, siblings, and other persons. All these learned skills may be called ego achievements.

(3) Identifications form the base of the ego ideal. In the preoedipal, magic phase of development the little child identifies himself with the images of omnipotent parents in order to feel as powerful as they are imagined to be.

In normal development the ego ideal unfolds and widens its contents through new identifications with other persons, examples in social life, etc., a process continuing throughout the whole lifetime and constituting one of the normal outcomes of so-called narcissistic identifications.

It is a sign of maturity when ideals and norms are freed from primitive magic features; that means, when the person in question has learned to accept that neither omnipotent parents nor other almighty persons exist. However, every human being preserves remnants of early developmental stages. More of those relics persist in disturbed personalities such as our patients. This brings us to the question of what role identifications play in psychoanalytic procedure.

I shall try to depict some aspects of a patient's identification with the analyst during treatment. With a view to a clearer presentation I will distinguish between "normal" and "pathological" identifications, though in reality, of course, they are intermingled, and a clear-cut distinction is not always possible.

"Normal" identifications in analytic treatment

From the very beginning of treatment the analyst is an important person in the patient's life. No wonder that the patient tries to identify himself with that person as he does with teachers, superiors, authorities, heroes, celebrities, social or religious leaders, etc. The patient wants to know the ideas of the analyst, his outlook on life, his norms and ideals, his personal circumstances. But the analyst's task does not allow him to satisfy the patient's desire to obtain insight into the analyst's personal life and views.

There are two good reasons for this on the analyst's part:

(a) It is well known that psychoanalysis aims at furnishing the most favorable possibilities for the patient to develop his personality along the path of his *own* capacities and circumstances, and therefore at avoiding his being molded after the picture of the analyst.

(b) Only after the patient's desire to take over his analyst's views of life is frustrated does the uncovering of the infantile, archaic, pathogenic forms of identification become possible.

There is perhaps one limitation to the strict application of this rule, namely when the analysand is a future colleague. A "normal" "adult" identification with the analyst's professional personality may promote the acquisition of technical skill in the young analyst. However, as the first task of training analysis is always the removal of neurotic symptoms, blind spots, and other ego restrictions and distortions, we have to behave in the same way as we do with patients, at least for a considerabel part of the treatment. The danger that acquired technical knowledge may be used to ward off neurotic or archaic patterns is strong, especially with the candidate.

For the analyst a danger lies in the temptation to yield to his analysand's wish in trying to model him after his (the analyst's) own ideals.

"Pathological" identifications

We now come to what we may call "pathological" identifications.

(a) I mention only briefly the process of identification used by the ego's defensive organization as one of the various defense mechanisms, e.g. in hysterical symptoms.

Hysterical identifications are regressions of forbidden oedipal object relationships toward earlier forms of a bond with an object. An example is Freud's famous case of Dora. Some of the somatic complaints of this hysterical girl proved to be based on an identification with her father, to whom she was strongly attached with sexual fantasies. When analysis runs a favorable course the hysterical symptom and with it the pathological identification disappear after the interpretation and working through of the connected material, which is, at least partly, transferred to the analyst.

I will not go further into these forms of identification.

(b) I now turn to the so-called narcissistic identifications, of which we have to distinguish between (1) identifications in the ego ideal, and (2) ego identifications.

Identifications in the Ego Ideal

As suggested above, we have to deal in analytic treatment with the pathological parts of the ego ideal, that is, with its archaic features. Sooner or later every patient idealizes his analyst. This means that he projects upon him the persisting images of omnipotent parents, simultaneously, of course, with the reactive counterpart: extreme devaluation. Sometimes this is a regressive phenomenon; however, one often gets the impression of its being related to areas of the ego ideal that never reached a more mature level. They are fixated relics of the preoedipal magic phase. The usual interpretations reveal that the patient clings tenaciously to the images of omnipotent parents as well as to his own infantile fantasies of grandeur. Both groups of fantasies still have to compensate for the daily narcissistic injuries, once experienced by the child when he came upon his own powerlessness. They are still unconsciously at work in the patient's actual life circumstances and neurotic complaints. In many cases the analyst finds that analytical interpretations alone do not make for the patient's recovery. Here an aftergrowth, a re-education, sometimes has to take place.

In early days Freud remarked that psychoanalytic treatment comprises a kind of re-education. By this he did *not* mean to recommend the imprinting of new ideals and norms upon the patient's personality. On the contrary, we should avoid doing this. But what the analyst *can* do to stimulate the patient's maturation is to convince him of his unrealistic conception of the analyst's personality. It is sometimes difficult to show the analysand that the glorification of the analyst is a product of his (the patient's) own wishful thinking, that in reality the analyst is an average human being, to be esteemed for his merits, but with limitations and weaknesses similar to those of all other persons. It depends greatly on the attitude of the analyst whether the patient succeeds in forming a normal reality-adjusted ego ideal or not. Something similar is valid for our second point.

The archaic (pathological) ego identifications

When analytic procedure has liberated repressed forces by the undoing of the various warding-off practices, every patient has to find new ways to use those forces, and to revise many of his ego activities and reactions in life. Patients with a relatively well-structured ego organization (and, of course, with not too strong and rigid drive forces) find those ways spontaneously without too great difficulty. Patients with very unstable, primitive, archaic ego structures, however, not seldom prove unable to do so. They behave like children. Here analysis may take advantage of the afore-mentioned fact that the learning processes run very much along the path of identifications.

Needless to say, the analyst has *not* to deal with the patient's learning of intellectual and other skills. We are concerned here with the aftergrowth of the patient's emotional and instinctual life. The liberated drive forces have in part to be allowed to find direct gratifications, in part to be neutralized and used in sublimated activities. Where the inborn capacity for neutralization of drive energy is minute, psychoanalysis will have very little success.

In cases where the capacity for sublimation is sufficiently present, the patient has to learn how to provide enough direct gratification on the one hand and how to handle the neutralized energy on the other. He can make use of identifications with his analyst for the aftergrowth of his infantile emotional life. Once more I would repeat that this process is not accomplished through verbal suggestions for actual new activities, forced upon the patient. It depends considerably upon the analyst's attitude whether the patient can profit from his identifications or not.

Unconsciously by means of empathy the patient becomes aware of the analyst's tolerance and warm understanding, and of his firm and quiet mastery and control of affects and impulses, which the patient tries to provoke in the analyst through acting out.

The analyst's behavior, his timing of communications, his facial expressions, a number of imponderables, last but not least the tone of his voice, are extraordinarily important here, perhaps much more so than the words he actually uses. It seems of significance to mention one other special danger situation for the analyst himself. Empathy is necessary for the understanding of the patient. As empathy is based upon the identification mechanism, the analyst has to identify himself with his patient to a certain degree. Now the danger arises that the identifications with the analysand unconsciously become too strong or mixed up with old patterns from the analyst's own past life. Those identifications are bound to disturb instead of to further the favorable course of the patient's development.

Finally, I want to stress a particular point of great importance for the patient's recovery, though this may involve us in a number of difficulties. The point in question concerns aggression and the concomitant guilt feelings. It still seems uncertain whether aggressive energy is less suitable for neutralization than is libido. In every case liberated libido finds new ways for employment more easily than aggressive energy does. This holds true for the period of the upbringing of children as well as for that of the aftergrowth of our patients, at least in the circumstances of our culture, where very little aggression can be directly satisfied.

The analyst's attitude toward direct aggressive outbursts as well as toward more hidden aggression, as, e.g., in jealousy, rivalry, competition, etc., is of considerable value here. With many patients we get the impression that they will never master primitive aggressive impulses in a constructive way. They mostly have to turn them to the self, with many disastrous consequences. Sometimes, however, patients succeed in finally controlling and neutralizing aggression, in which process identification with the self-evident, natural behavior of the analyst can play a very stimulating part.

Time forbids my going further into this interesting area of exploration. Only one final remark to avoid misunderstanding:

The attitude of the analyst as here described is in no single way in contradiction with the classical technical rule of the so-called neutrality of the analyst. This rule is often misunderstood. The analyst, it is true, has to provide the patient with the possibility of projecting and transferring his (the patient's) own feelings and strivings onto a clear screen in the analystic situation. This does *not* mean that the analyst should be an absolutely neutral, emotionless creature. Apart from the fact that such a creature does not exist, it would be inhumane to try to live up to such an artificial automaton. Freud's technical devices clearly show that the rule aims merely at preventing the analyst's acting out of his own feelings instead of analyzing those of his patient and at guarding against his impressing his own stamp upon his analysand.

Freud used to stress the significance of the integrity of the analyst and of his being a humane, decent, and harmonious personality.

In this presentation I have tried to throw some light upon areas in analytic procedure where the patient's re-educational aftergrowth may go in a favorable direction under the influence of identification with an analyst, who is himself a well-balanced personality.

21. On Defense and Development: Normal and Pathological

(1957)

In studying the concept of defense one is confronted with much confusion in psychoanalytic literature about a great many problems. To name only a few of them:

(1) Is "defense" in itself a pathological phenomenon or are we entitled to speak of "normal" defense mechanisms and defensive processes?
(2) What is the relation of childhood neurosis to the defense mechanisms?
(3) We may turn our attention to the chronology of defense mechanisms.
(4) What is the role of defensive processes in the total ego organization?
(5) We could examine the different analysts' views regarding the practical question of whether or not every defensive process has to be dissolved during analytic treatment.

More questions could be raised. In this communication I shall limit myself to the presentation of only a few ideas on some of the points. I begin with the first problem mentioned above.

Can we speak of "normal" defense, or does every defensive process belong in the realm of pathology? What conception of defense is most fruitful in analytic theory and practice? There is no doubt that Freud first made use of the term defense in connection with psychopathology (1894, 1896). It seems that many authors tend to retain this early employment of the term and want to reserve it for neurotic and other forms of maldevelopment. They do so in spite of the fact that at later times, e.g., in *Inhibitions, Symptoms and Anxiety* (1926), Freud clearly showed the connection between "normal" and "pathological" defense mechanisms.

Speaking of the relation between "repression" and "defense," Freud (1926, p. 163) recommends the rehabilitation of the latter term as "a general designation for all the techniques which the ego makes use of in conflicts which may lead to a neurosis." "Repression" is to be viewed as one special defense mechanism.

In his contribution to the Symposium on Defense, Hoffer (1954) mentions this statement of Freud's, and further adds that many authors consider defense mechanisms to have "their own history and sources." He continues: "they [the defense mechanisms] may be traced back to their origin in the primary processes, e.g., in displacement and to the genuine mechanisms which the growing ego successively develops from inborn patterns, that is to the autonomous ego functions; they are often highly developed, very complicated structures of the mind" (p. 194).

Hartmann (1939b) has shown how important it is to view mental processes not only in their interplay with mental conflict but also from the point of view of the part they play in adaptation. Hoffer cites a number of other authors, who point out that defense mechanisms may be used "regressively" or "progressively"; they may "protect" the ego or "destroy" it (Eissler, 1953).

Nevertheless one repeatedly encounters the idea that defense mechanisms are pathological phenomena. Fenichel (1945) considers only sublimation to be a normal one and regards all others as pathogenic.

Anna Freud, in her book *The Ego and the Mechanisms of Defence* (1936), describes different defensive attitudes of which she says that they can also be seen in normal reactions. She includes them, however, under the heading "Preliminary Stages of Defence."

We should like to find a way out of these confusions. With this purpose in mind, I propose to examine two well-known defense mechanisms encountered in severe psychic illness: projection and identification.

Projection may be used in paranoid psychosis, identification (based on the mechanism of introjection) may, e.g., lead to severe symptoms in a melancholic patient.

When we turn to observations of infants, however, all of us assume that processes of projection and introjection play a considerable role in every infant's normal growth. None of us would think of a severe pathological process in this context. Therefore it may be confusing when Melanie Klein and others use certain terms taken from clinical psychiatry – e.g., "depressive position" or "persecutory anxiety" – to describe early processes in normal infants.

When we turn our attention to the newborn's behavior we see a somewhat different picture. The newborn responds at first merely somatically to outer and inner stimuli. To the shortness of oxygen during birth the infant reacts with putting into motion the respiratory organs, in order to "incorporate" oxygen. When hunger and thirst stimuli arrive the newborn will drink; this means he incorporates fluid food by sucking the mother's breast. Incorporation of oxygen and food as well as egestion of carbonic acid and excreta are normal regulative reactions to the metabolic processes tending to maintain a physiological homeostasis.

In this connection, experimental psychologists and ethologists speak of mechanisms of regulation and adaptation. There are other adaptive processes in the human newborn (though fewer than in newborn animals), e.g., the adaptation of the skin capillaries to stimuli of cold and heat, the closing of the eyelids when too strong a light stimulus reaches the eye, etc.

We assume that the first primitive awareness that inner and outer world are separate entities arises in connection with the different bodily responses to inner and outer stimuli.

It still is difficult to decide at what point we are entitled to begin to speak of psychic phenomena in the infant and at what moment the body "self" is enlarged with a mental "self." Among many factors the maturational state of the central nervous system apparently plays an important role. But we may take it for certain that the psychic life develops on the base of somatic reactions or, to put it more precisely, in interplay with them. This is one of the expressions of psychosomatic entity.

In a theoretical discussion in a small work group in Amsterdam, Bastiaans, referring to observations on psychosomatic patients, made the suggestion that every neurotic defense mechanism could be traced back to a normal somatic regulation or adaptation mechanism, and would represent a quantitative variation of the latter.

There is one early definition of Freud's (1905b) which points to what one could call a "psychosomatic" viewpoint. It runs: "Defensive processes are the psychical correlative of the flight reflex and perform the task of preventing the generation of unpleasure from internal sources" (p. 233). It points to the correlation of body reactions to dangerous stimuli (flight) and mental reactions guarded by the pleasure-pain principle.

When a little child projects unpleasurable drive stimuli and sensations upon the outside world and simultaneously introjects images of need-satisfying objects, the mechanisms of projection and introjection are not used merely for "flight" (and "fight"), but at the same time as regulative and adaptive processes.

A physically healthy child growing up under favorable circumstances, with a loving, understanding, and tolerant mother, presents himself as a friendly, gay, charming, and harmonious little creature. We are naturally aware of the fact that every person's growth proceeds on the basis of conflicts. But we should not overlook the fact that in these so-called "normal" children the conflicts result for the time being in a regulation of the emotional and instinctual needs and an adaptation to the outer world. I hasten to add that I am certainly not of the opinion that thereby these well-balanced little children would be prevented from acquiring neuroses in later times. There are too many examples of harmonious children finally developing more or less severely disturbed personalities.

What I wanted to suggest, however, is that we view the neurotic defense mechanisms as pathologically exaggerated or distorted regulation and adaptation mechanisms, which in themselves belong to normal development. One might raise objections and say that this formulation is merely a terminological variation. I do not think that is correct. I believe that apart from decreasing some of the confusions mentioned above, my formulation has the advantage of stressing the connection (or the continuum) of physiological-biological and psychic processes, both in the normal and in the abnormal. Last but not least, it may prevent us from overlooking normal developmental processes in our children as well as in our patients. I agree with Brierley (1947) and Hoffer (1954) that "our closer association with mental disease . . . has often hampered our dealings with normality" and that "the personal integrity of the patient [may be] impaired by the omission of the normal aspect of the rôle of defence in mental functioning." For the "normal aspect of the rôle of defence" I should like to substitute "the role of adaptation and regulation in all processes that deal with mental conflicts."

I realize that one could justifiably reproach me for speaking loosely of "normal" and "pathological" and of "health" and "disease," without giving clearer definitions. I cannot solve this problem in its complexity, and will remind you of the well-known, though stale statement that "normality" and "health" as well as "disease" are merely practical conceptions which so far defy scientific definitions.

We may nevertheless try to throw some light upon one special function which is indispensable for a person's psychic health – the synthetic or integrative capacity – precisely by using the viewpoint of the psychosomatic entity. The infant uses the inborn and the learned regulation and adaptation mechanisms to establish physiological homeostasis in metabolism. The little child does the same to attain psychic equilibrium. We know that it is the task of the ego to develop a synthetic, integrative, harmonizing ability.

The little child's growing, but still primitive and unstable, ego organization has to learn with the mother's help how to regulate its drives and affects, its needs, etc., as we mentioned before. In the first years of life the mother is indispensable for both normal *bodily and mental* growth. However, she remains indispensable much longer for mental development.

When the mother-child symbiosis succeeds in establishing and promoting a synthetic, regulative ego function and when in addition the mother is able to further the child's independence in the subsequent development, the outcome may really be a well-balanced personality. Or, examined from the reverse side, we may say: since every normal infant's instinctual needs come into conflict with the outside world, which can offer only limited satisfaction and always has to demand restrictions, the regulative ego functions cannot develop in a harmonious way when one or both of the partners of that early mother-child bond fail in the cooperative interplay. Such a failure impairs the normal growth of the still weak ego organization and threatens the ego with being overwhelmed by the drives and affects; thus inner conflicts are added to the outer ones, signaled by anxiety.

When the mother is aware of the child's emergency situations, she may be able to furnish the necessary support for the child's ego growth and a new balance may come into existence. When she fails to do so, the way is open for more or less severe neurotic disturbances in the child. The same may happen when the other partner in the mother-child relationship, the little child himself, falls short of his task in the cooperation, either through an unfortunate instinctual disposition (e.g., untamable drives, too much ambivalence, too strong clashes between libido and aggression or active and passive strivings, etc.) or through a lack of indispensable inborn ego capacities.

I will choose the process of identification to illustrate the pathological use of mental mechanisms. In normal development identifications play an important role in learning. When identification is used to ward off danger situations, it may go so far as to overwhelm the child's total ego organization. The child's personality "melts together" with the image of the mother. The resulting loss of one's own identity is experienced with strong anxiety and may lead to a severe damage of further development. I shall come back to this point later on.

Now I should like to give an example of a favorable collaboration between mother and child in a relatively normal boy of two years nine months. The boy was a lively, well-balanced child. Toilet training was accomplished in a quiet, natural way around the second year. After the birth of a new baby when the boy was two years two months old he wet his bed only two or three times. About half a year later the bed wetting suddenly reappeared. At first his mother did not understand what had happened. Nothing extraordinary could be discovered in the family situation. Then, however, the mother became aware of the fact that the boy was masturbating and having erections much more frequently than before.

On an appropriate occasion she spoke with her little son about his erections, apparently in a natural, reassuring way, with full acceptance of his masculinity and his right to pleasure and masculine pride. The next night everything was all right. After several weeks the enuresis came back, but only for a short time. Following this period it has never recurred up to the present time. The boy is now three and a half years old.

In the meantime, his ego development had also advanced in other respects, as I should like to demonstrate in an occurrence the explanation of which I owe to Anna Freud. When the boy was three years one month old he was taken on an excursion during which he traveled by car over a very long bridge. He admired it very much and was impressed by the many cars passing over it at the same time. Some hundred meters away lies a second, a railway bridge. When the boy was told that trains were running over this second bridge, he said: "But *cars* are running over it, *too*." To the answer: "No, that one is only for trains," he replied with the utmost conviction: "But *formerly* there were cars running over that bridge, too."

I did not understand the meaning of this statement, but Anna Freud gave a fascinating explanation of the event. She thought the boy wanted to say: "Formerly all pleasurable experiences were allowed to be made everywhere." She is of the opinion that the boy's statement indicated his readiness to accept limitations. This acceptance and the distinction between former and present times represent an achievement of the ego's development. Some months later this explanation was confirmed by a second experience.

The boy is the owner of a number of small toy cars. He is especially fond and proud of a Chevrolet. During another excursion the boy again traveled over the long bridge. This time a train was just passing over the railway bridge. He was happily excited and said: *"Formerly* when I was driving in my Chevrolet I passed by that bridge the way the train is doing now."

I would sum up the successive events in the following way. In the inner conflict, caused by an increase of masculine, genital sexuality that for a moment had threatened his inner balance, the still weak ego had made use of the mechanisms of regression to an earlier phase and produced the symptom of bed wetting. With the mother's support the ego succeeded immediately in discontinuing the regressive process. The boy returned to the former state of ego achievement in mastering again the excretory functions and in developing new ego capacities: the distinction between past and present and the acceptance of the different possibilities of satisfaction.

Such regressive phenomena occur very often during the period of the little child's growth, just as do other defensive attitudes in conflicts which provoke anxiety. Should we speak of a neurosis and of defense mechanisms in this connection? This question brings us to the second point I mentioned in the introduction of this paper: When should we speak of childhood neurosis and what processes have to be considered as normal developmental ones?

The answer apparently does *not* lie in the nature of the mental mechanisms used by the growing ego in its reactions to conflicts. We have already mentioned that projection and identification are normal regulative and adaptive mechanisms. By making use of them the ego learns to distinguish between inner and outer world, to develop reality testing, etc. Identifications especially play a paramount role in learning processes, in acquiring different skills, in learning how to handle emotional and instinctual needs.

Regressions and anxiety never fail to appear in normal development. Isolation of past and present events furthers the orientation in time and so stimulates the phase-adequate development. I think the answer is better to be looked for in the examination of the *ways* in which the different mechanisms are made use of by the child's ego.

If, at first with the help of a kind of auxiliary ego borrowed from the mother, the ego succeeds in making use of the various mechanisms in their regulative and adaptive aspect, the conflicts may be solved in a way that stimulates balance and growth. If, however, the ego has to fight too strongly against the drives, it has to use all available forces for the maintenance of its still weak, just established organization. In this case there is a greater opportunity for a lasting disturbance in balance and for an arrest in development.

This idea gives rise to the question of what causes the child's ego to go the one or the other way. I think that among the many ego capacities necessary for a favorable solution of these conflicts, there is one of the utmost, perhaps decisive, importance. It is the ego's capacity to deal with the child's aggressive drives. Or, in other words, the child's capacity to neutralize (and sublimate) aggression. I remind you of Freud's suggestion to view mental conflict in regard to aggression. Every conflict, whether between child and environment or between ego and id, provokes free aggression. And it is precisely aggression that is least tolerated in free discharge, that is most dangerous for the developing ego organization when turned inside, and that in many cases is more unsuitable for neutralization than is libido. Even in conflicts in the sexual sphere it might be the fate of the simultaneously provoked free aggression that becomes decisive for the final outcome.

In the analysis of one of my adult patients it ultimately became clear that the aggressive, mocking, and sneering way in which his mother had rejected the little boy's exhibitionistic genital wooing had provoked his own overwhelming aggressive response with the final result of a rigid standstill in his ego development.   .

Among other factors, the switching off of the normal learning processes by means of identifications, of which I spoke before, here played a decisive role. This little boy's sexuality was reduced to a passive surrender toward the father. He identified with the passive mother image to such a degree that he lost his

199

own identity. In his adult sexual life every approach to a woman meant a "melting together" with her. To escape the danger situation of losing his self he had to summon up nearly all his strength. The result was an inhibited personality with very restricted ego capacities.

Such observations point at the same time to the paramount importance of the mother's attitude toward the little child's aggression. In my patient every attempt to master aggression was counteracted by the mother. A well-balanced mother, on the other hand, is a well-suited object for identification and may thus come to be of very great help to her child in his effort to learn the controlling of aggression, to neutralize aggressive energy, and to use this energy in the building up of the ego organization.

Returning to our question of what constitutes neurosis in childhood, I should like to summarize as follows. Mental mechanisms, which may later be used as neurotic defense mechanisms in adult neuroses, are normal developmental mechanisms in early childhood as long as they serve and promote the ego's regulative and adaptive capacities.

I remind you here of Anna Freud's well-known statement (1945) that, in the assessment of childhood disturbances, we should make use of the criterion of an unimpaired advancement in ego development. In full agreement with this view, I should like to continue: regulative and adaptive functions of the so-called defense mechanisms are particularly endangered when the capacity for neutralization of aggression is not sufficiently present. Furthermore, we should speak of a real childhood neurosis only when the defensive function of the mechanisms outbalances the regulative function *and* holds up the continuation of the process of growth.

Here a critical remark is in order. In every child's development there is one phase in which the first condition – the prevalence of the defensive aspect of a special mechanism – is a regular and normal occurrence. This is the oedipal phase, in which the mechanism of repression predominates. In our culture every child has to repress his sexual and aggressive strivings inherent in the oedipus complex. However, after a more or less *"normal"* solution of this complex, the ego development receives a great impetus for further unfolding, and no neurosis develops. Precisely because the defensive function in repression of oedipal conflicts is indispensable, the preconditions for the coming into existence of a real neurosis become stronger in this phase. These considerations are in accord with Freud's very early view of the oedipus complex as the nucleus of the neuroses.

Perhaps we really could keep to this view for the average child. While preoedipal developmental disturbances may contribute to a particular unfortunate shaping of the oedipus complex, it is still the fate of the ego's development during and after the oedipal phase itself which decides whether a more or less fixed neurosis will originate or not. Only in infants who from the very beginning show severe disturbances, caused either by inborn factors or by serious deprivations, do we observe fixed neurotic symptoms in the preoedipal phase. We could assume in these cases that either the ego was lacking every possibility for advancement in development or that it was exposed to a precocious and therefore heavily endangered development, so that a regulative and adaptive use of the available mechanisms was eliminated from the beginning.

Be that as it may, in the preoedipal phase it is more often the mother's neurosis or other environmental circumstances that cause usually reversible disturbances in the little child. After the decline of the oedipal phase, when a preliminary shape of the child's personality and the establishment of his superego have taken place, the child's circumscribed neurosis takes a certain fixed shape.

In this context I merely want to mention the fact that an obsessional neurosis arises only in the latency period. If repression in latency and adulthood fails to be sufficient for defensive purposes, other mechanisms are used in the attempt to ward off the returning repressed contents; among them are mechanisms that formerly served regulation and adaptation, as for instance projection, identification, isolation, turning inside, etc. I will not name them all because they are well known from Freud's and Anna Freud's works.

It would be fascinating, however, to pursue the vicissitudes of the different mechanisms from the viewpoint of, on the one hand, their adaptive, regulative aspects, and on the other hand, their defensive aspects during the personality's development from birth to maturity. This brings us to our third point: the chronology of defense mechanisms. In following the chronology of specific mechanisms, we might really discover that all pathological defense mechanisms seen in the neuroses and psychoses of latency and adulthood are the very same mechanisms that served normal ego development in early childhood and that at a later stage were used simultaneously in a distorted way to ward off the re-emergence of the insufficiently repressed strivings. It is possible that some mechanisms become fixed only after the superego has been established, as for instance the turning of aggression against the self. The regulative, constructive side of this process furthers the consolidation of social norms and ethical values, whereas its defensive function operates in a destructive way and may lead to severe pathological guilt feelings and self-damage. Usually this mechanism of turning aggression inward is not observable in infants, though there are cases described of self-injuries in early childhood. However, it is probable that the ways in which defense mechanisms work in the service of the superego have their forerunners in relation to ego activities.

I leave this theme for further investigation and now turn to our fourth point: the place of the defensive processes in the total ego organization.

I speak here of defensive processes because in the course of development the ego, making use of different mechanisms, builds up a complicated defensive organization. From latency onward parts of this organization can be mobilized to ward off other parts of it. This may happen when the latter part proves to be endangered in new stages of development, in which additional demands are made upon the ego. I give one example out of many.

In the preoedipal phase the little boy's passive strivings toward the mother may be countered by the growing ego through a specific regulative and defensive mechanism, namely, through activation of active tendencies. In the oedipal situation the normally increased masculine urges may become a danger in connection with rivalry with the father. The boy now remobilizes passive strivings to ward off his masculine fantasies. Whether the boy finds a normal solution of his oedipal conflict or not depends upon the ego's capacity to save his active strivings from repression (or from being warded off) and upon the degree to which the ego succeeds in neutralizing energies and in sublimating these active strivings into constructive activities. In our neurotic patient this faculty of the ego proved to be too weak in relation to the instinctual urges, hence the result was a feminine sexual relationship to the father. In the course of further development such a father attachment can again be warded off and covered by a distorted, pseudo-masculine behavior in life.

It is clear from the foregoing that the ego's defensive activity constitutes a very important part − yet, it is true, only one part − of the totality of ego functions. Instead of examining in detail all ego activities and achievements, I will only stress once more the importance of considering the normal regulative-adaptive functions of the various mechanisms and processes, and their influence upon the development of other ego capacities, both on the intellectual and on the emotional level. I have illustrated this process in regard to the mechanisms of identification.

Finally, I want to mention again a specifically significant point. According to one of Freud's definitions, neuroses are disharmonies in the ego organization. Among the many factors that are responsible for those disharmonies, we have already referred to one of particular importance: the personality's capacity to neutralize aggressive energy. This capacity is dependent on the one hand upon the quality and intensity of the drives, and on the other hand upon very specific ego properties whose development may be stimulated or counteracted by objects in the environment.

Turning to our fifth and last point, I think we can do away with a frequent misapprehension expressed in the demand that psychoanalytic treatment should attempt to demolish the ego's defensive organization. For many of us it is self-evident that we should not, and even could not, succeed in our endeavors to live up to this "requirement." Nevertheless we often encounter pronouncements such as: "The patient's defense mechanisms have not disappeared, therefore he is not yet cured." Or: "You should aim at doing away with your patient's defenses," etc.

Keeping in mind that every defense originally has a regulative-adaptive function, we can correct these remarks. In analysis we should try to give the patient's ego the opportunity for abolishing the pathological, rigid employment of the mechanisms in the neurotic conflicts, and we should try to open ways for their regulative, constructive use in order to promote a harmonious afterdevelopment and unfolding of the total personality.

22. Psychoanalysis and Its Relation to Other Fields of Natural Science

(1959)

In this paper I shall endeavor to set forth some ideas on psychoanalytic theory, regarded in the light of findings in other branches of science. Freud developed his conception of the "complementary series" in the early stages of his study of neuroses. It is said that neuroses emerge from an interplay of innate dispositional factors and experiences, due to the environment, undergone during a lifetime. This conception may be extended to mental development in general. We already know a great deal about the processes of development from infancy to the adult stage; an increasing tendency toward tracing the earlier phases, to study the very young child and the newborn infant, may be observed in recent psychoanalytic research. In the course of these endeavors it is inevitable that we come up against innate factors. Several psychoanalysts, for instance Kubie, Masserman, Szekely, Ostow, Brun, and many others, have therefore in recent years turned their attention to predispositional factors. It is my impression that there are three particular fields of science which demand our special attention: (1) modern cerebral anatomy and physiology, which assist us in achieving a better understanding of the physical basis of mind; (2) modern physics and mechanics, which stimulate our knowledge of the way in which the brain functions; (3) animal psychology, especially ethology, as this teaches us a great deal about instinctive behavior and its development from the innate mechanisms of the various types of animal life.

In these branches of science I am myself a layman, and am therefore able only to develop a few tentative trains of thought which doubtless will require verification, revision, or both.

We all know that modern neuroanatomy, neurophysiology, and neurosurgery have taught us a variety of things about the construction of the central nervous system and its physical activities.

We know that the human brain contains approximately 10,000,000,000 neurones − nerve cells − and countless nerve fibres as well as afferent and efferent fiber tracts, which conduct stimuli into the brain and out of it. There are also the associative tracts which connect the different parts of the cortex. We know that the stimuli which activate the sense centers are carried on to other parts of the cortex. The same is the case with the inner stimuli, which reach the brain by means of the blood supply and the nervous pathways. Scientists tell us that the living brain contains electric potentials which are constantly at work and are able to vary their speed and rhytm: Adrian (1946), for instance, says that there is "constant transformation of energy in the brain." We have long been acquainted with the manner in which reflexes in the central nervous system operate (Pavlov); today, however, more particular research is being done into the origin and the working method of the so-called higher psychic functions, such as consciousness, thought, feeling, etc. Knowledge of these matters has been greatly stimulated by modern physics and mechanics, and especially by what is now known as cybernetics, a term which must be coupled with the name of Norbert Wiener (1949, 1954). I will discuss this presently, but first I would like to point out that, notwithstanding this imposing increase of knowledge, one constantly encounters among leading neurophysiologists and neuroanatomists the view that what actually takes place in the brain during the exercise of the higher functions is not known. Adrian, for instance, says: "The real trouble comes from the feeling that there may be an important part of the picture which can never be fitted in, however long we may work at it." Also: "It is a far cry from the nerve cell or even the cerebral hemispheres to the thoughts and desires of mankind." Sherrington says: "Aristotle, 2000 years ago, was asking how the mind is attached to the body; we are asking that question still." Le Gros Clark affirms that he has a "hunch" and wants to introduce time — "the time involved in the transmission of the impulses (travelling along nerve fibres), from one relay centre to another" — as a very important factor. But he continues: "The difficulty, however, is that the time intervals are so short — a matter of a thousandth of a second." He is more optimistic as regards the results of future research into the anatomical basis of the mind, but remarks all the same: "No more than the physiologists is he able to suggest *how* the physico-chemical phenomena associated with the nervous impulses from one part of the brain to another can be translated into a mental experience." W. Grey Walter, in *The Living Brain* (1953), relinquishes all attempts to localize the higher functions exactly in the brain.

I could quote further and similar pronouncements made by well-known neurophysiologists and neuroanatomists, but instead will concentrate on the significance of modern mechanical physics to brain physiology and therefore to psychology also. Here, as I have just remarked, cybernetics is more particularly important. It is chiefly the so-called feedback mechanism which Wiener and most of the neurologists bring into context with an analogous mechanism in the living organism. Wiener, generally speaking, compares the functioning of the modern, complicated automatic machine with that of the central nervous system. As a mathematician, he realized that cooperation between experts on various branches concerned with cybernetics was necessary. He got into touch, or cooperated in teamwork, with physicists, well-known physiologists, engineers, psychologists, and sociologists. To name a few: Rosenblüth, von Neumann, MacCulloch, Pitts, Goldstine, Bigelow, Lee, Cannon, Penfield, and others, both in the United States and in Mexico and Canada. We gain the impression that this teamwork by scientists with varied talents and possibly some degree of genius, which as well as in others may be suspected in Wiener himself, is bound to be very fruitful. It was moreover greatly stimulated by the distress caused by the Second World War. Physicists and mathematicians were compelled to pass on what they knew to engineers and technicians, to those engaged in the construction of automatic arms and weapons. When such weapons were put to use, it was found that man with his cerebral apparatus was an extremely important factor offering further possibilities of, and setting limits to, their use. A typical instance was that of Air Force pilots. Owing to the great plasticity, the result of the marked differentiation of the human organism and more especially of the mind, and by means of technical aids, these limits were considerably extended. We may think for instance of the special clothing which combats the effects of the cold at high altitudes: of the oxygen apparatus, which decreases or does away with the rarefied air; the training in resistance to irritation, shock, and fear. But notwithstanding these aids, there are limits to the pilot's powers of performance. This was doubtless one of the reasons for the construction of the so-called automatic pilot. Machines took on the tasks originally performed by the thinking and active human being, so that we have now begun to speak of the "thinking machine" and even of the "artificial brain."

Attempts were made on the other hand to explain the function of the human brain by means of physicomechanical terminology. Several authorities consider that these attempts have been but partially successful, as may be gathered from the excerpts quoted, and this gives us courage to continue the attempts by arguments of our own. To begin with I will try to give some description of the analogies between the working of the brain and that of the machine, following Wiener in doing so.

Simple calculating machines (digital machines) receive their information through human agency; by means of certain manipulations they can add up figures, and this they do more rapidly than the human brain. But the machine, too, is vulnerable. When, for instance, one particular part of one manipulation is wrong or faulty, the result goes wrong and the machine stops. Therefore, as a rule, rather more complicated machines are constructed; in these, one given element corresponds not only with one particular stage in the operation, but with several. Thus a selection process is taking place at every moment. As Wiener puts it, a "majority report" and a "minority report" result. That is to say all the (intact) parts of the machine (i.e., in a well-constructed machine the majority), are supreme and the machine can continue to function. The faulty (very small) part that gave the minority report had no influence on the current event, but warns, by means of the minority report, that there is a defect. The faulty part can then be replaced without interrupting the work. The automatic telephone, for instance, functions on this principle. There is, however, as Wiener remarks, a "critical level of failure." If an apparatus such as the automatic telephone is kept below this level, the machine will be found to function very efficiently, but as soon as this level is reached, the machine ceases to function. A "catastrophic traffic jam" may result.

I will now mention some of the coincidences between the events that take place in the machine and the processes involved in the functioning of the brain of a living organism. Again I follow Norbert Wiener. The machine obtains its information externally through the instructor or the person using it. This person can be replaced by an automatic instructor, as, for instance, in the case of a photoelectrical apparatus coupled to the machine. But the photoelectrical apparatus has previously received its information from its constructor. The central nervous system, too, receives information from without through the sense organs from the environment and through the afferent nerve fibers from the rest of the body by means of sensory irritation and through the blood by a physicochemical process. In the machine, electric wires and switches take care of communications, the relaying of the message. In the living organism communication is achieved by means of nerve fibers and the highways and circuits in the central nervous system. We have just described the control system contained in the machine: this is based on what is called a "feedback mechanism." A simple example of the feedback is the thermostat. When a heating mechanism has reached a certain temperature, a signal reaches the source of heat, and the supply is discontinued. There is, therefore, control and regulation of its activities. A similar thing occurs in the organism. Constant signaling from the periphery to the central nervous system attends each movement, each activity. Thus the action is regulated and normally leads to the result intended. By way of the electrical potentials in the nerve circuits and neurones, the various stimuli reach their appointed goal, as, for instance, the stimuli awakened by light, which arrive at the center of vision and so on. They are then conducted further until they reach the cortex, where they may lead to various psychic processes, motor action, behavior, etc. Connection is brought about in the synapses, and as neurones are in correspondence with a great many synapses, extensive areas of the central nervous system may become involved in the action. Very complicated psychic processes thus result.

The analogy between the complicated (thinking) machines and the brain is therefore that both are capable of receiving communications from the outside and that both have the means of transmitting this communication. According to the scientists, there are further analogies. One of the fundamental properties of the brain is memory. The machine, too, is capable of storing incoming information as a memory, for instance by means of photography, magnetic wires or tapes, etc. These fixed recollections are able in their turn to influence further actions, in the machine as well as in the human brain. Control in both systems is applied by means of the feedback system already mentioned.

But there are further analogies between the performances of the modern machine and of the human brain. The machine is capable of prediction and also of learning. The former characteristic, "prediction," was until recently thought to be solely a human characteristic, the second, learning, was attributed only to living beings, i.e. animals and man. But cybernetics and modern mechanics have conferred these capabilities on the machine as well. In many cases and under certain conditions prediction is achieved much more easily and rapidly by a machine than by man. Machines have been constructed which can calculate the future position of an airplane, flying on a given track at a given speed, far more quickly than a man could. Such machines can also compute the relative possibilities of eventual deviations and changes. The learning mechanism too can be constructed automatically. Wiener even indicates that it will in the future be possible to construct an automatic chess player. He adds, however, that such a machine would at best be able to cope with a mediocre human chess player, and considers the construction of an automatic chess expert as a further possibility. This is not the time to become involved any further in Wiener's extremely fascinating train of thought on this topic, or to discuss the remarkable opinions of Père Dubarle, who, in a review of Wiener's *Cybernetics,* proposes the question whether or not a "governing machine" could be constructed. This would have to be a machine by whose means peoples, states, or even mankind as a whole could be ruled in a direct and logical manner more so than actual governments and politicians manage to do it today.

All this sounds extremely fantastic, and to many people rather frightening. The fear of new technical inventions is not an unusual one. In former times people were equally frightened by the gun, the first steam engine, the electrical machine, the airplane, etc. The daily press presents us with terrifying stories about robots, machines which might come to rule over humanity. Luckily we also hear, even from the side of the scientists, pronouncements which put one's mind at rest. Even Wiener himself, in connection with Père Dubarle's ideas, has said that the "thinking machine" of today is unable to cope with more than onethousandth part of direct independent human behavior. There is therefore no danger that a machine could ever assume autonomous control over humanity. A Dutch physicist, Schouten, has presented the Dutch people with a reassuring picture: he suggests that if it were possible to build into the Amsterdam athletic stadium all the accessories, such as vacuum tubes, wires, switch elements, etc., appertaining to the modern machine, such a machine would possess the intelligence of a field mouse. But, he adds, this is not possible, for such a machine would explode, burn out, in fact, destroy itself. Apparently it is out of the question to construct a machine, even one the size of a room or a house, capable of completely imitating all possible actions of the ten billion neurones, with their synapses and nerve fiber connections, which exist together in the small human skull.

Not only the cyberneticists but also the brain anatomists and neurologists reassure us on this subject. And with a little consideration on our own part we, technical laymen, can reassure ourselves. After all, the modern thinking machine, the "artificial brain," has been invented by the "living brain," the brain of man. Without the latter, no machine can come into existence, let alone obtain power over mankind. The British anatomist Zuckerman has said: "The pattern of stimuli to which an artificial brain will respond is built into the machine by an external agency during construction. The patterns to which a real brain responds are, on the other hand, established through past experience. A living brain is thus self-organizing, establishing its own connections, its own pattern of memory, and the feedbacks necessary for the maintenance of equilibrium." And later, when discussing the machine which predicts the future position of a plane with high speeds, he adds: "It can do this only for one major task or run at the time. The run of a human brain lasts an entire lifetime."

The human brain is not only an extremely complicated switchboard, like the machine; it also embraces the switchboard operator, and this latter cannot, at any rate as yet, be defined and localized by anatomy or neurology. We might call this operator the creative mind, and that is something the machine lacks. Why then, is mankind anxious as a result of undreamed-of technical progress, and why has it taken fright at modern machinery? Wiener explains this as follows: "Its real danger is that such machines, though helpless by themselves, may be used by a human being or by a block of human beings to increase their control over the rest of the race, or that political leaders may attempt to control their populations by means not of machines themselves, but through political techniques as narrow and indifferent to human possibility as if they had, in fact, been conceived mechanically." The fear is, therefore, of the manner in which man may make use of his own inventions: fear that their use will not serve to increase the well-being of mankind, but lead to destructive activity which will bring discomfort, sorrow, or even annihilation.

Man's propensity to make his inventions serve widely contrasting ends can no longer be explained mechanistically. The physicochemical basis of processes such as memory, thought, reason, and so on, must be imagined as being localized in the extremely complicated network of our brain cells and circuits. We might possibly also imagine that the fact of certain circuits being open or closed forms the organic basis of a given psychic quality, as, for instance, conscious or unconscious. For the time being, at any rate, we are unable to comprehend how judgments, intentions, thoughts, resolutions, etc., could be arrived at by the location of circuits or neurones. Apparently there are forces or tendencies active in the life process which we cannot localize anatomically, even when we are aware that their source of energy resides in the physical processes of the living organism.

Generally speaking, life has a strange place in the scheme of things. We do not know whether it is confined to our earthly sphere or whether other planets have produced events analogous with life as we know it. In any case, life shows a tendency to differentiate, which is peculiar to only a given number of systems in the universe. Modern physics recognizes as the first law of thermodynamics that the total energy remains constant in a closed system, even when this energy is capable of changing its form. The second law lays down that in an open system there may be a general tendency toward increase of entropy, i.e., spontaneous gradual discharge of energy. In the universe there is a general tendency to the increase of entropy, in other words, to dedifferentiation, disorganization, chaos. But there are systems which show a tendency to decrease of entropy, and therefore an urge toward higher differentiation and organization. One of these systems is "life." To quote Wiener once again, "Organism is opposed to chaos, to disintegration, to death." And later: "Organisms (men) tend to maintain the level of their organisation as a local enclave in the general stream of increasing entropy, of increasing chaos and dedifferentiation. Life is an island here and now in a dying world." "The process by which we living beings respect the general stream of corruption and decay is known as homeostasis." According to Ludwig von Bertalanffy (1950), life is an open system. To perform work it must be, not in complete equilibrium, but tending to attain a steady state. It exchanges materials with the environment and, getting energy from importation of material from the outside world, it can avoid the increase of entropy. I cannot go further into these important theories here.

The tendency to higher organization and differentiation which is characteristic of life is met with in the evolution of lower organisms toward highly complicated beings. Among the higher mammals man is obviously the most differentiated, even when we consider that, in comparison with analogous ones found in anthropoid apes, some organs are declining; for example, the teeth (Bolk and others). In any case, the humain brain is the highest organized central nervous system known to us. It has even been able to invent mechanized systems – the above-mentioned thinking machines – which have defied the law of increase of entropy, at any rate for a series of actions. No other type of animal has ever achieved anything of the kind.

But mankind is part of the universe, and as such is subjected to the law of entropy. This is made plain by the fact that the single individual does become disorganized and dies. The power to live, and therefore to achieve higher organization, is transferred to the next generation through propagation.

Physics teaches us that highly differentiated systems are more vulnerable than simple ones, as with Schouten's machine in the Amsterdam stadium. There is a limit to the power of functioning. As we said above, every machine has its "critical point." When too great an influx threatens, the catastrophic traffic jam occurs and the machine no longer functions because vacuum tubes, switch elements, etc., have been eliminated. Wiener assumes there is also a limit to the human brain's capacity of functioning. A too severe psychophysical taxing would lead to defects of neurones, synapses, fibers, and circuits, and so induce psychopathological symptoms, such as insanity.

Here let us pause for a moment. We know of a number of mental disturbances founded on anatomical defects of the brain. But a study of our neurotic patients has revealed a number of psychic disturbances which prove to be reversible. It would be possible to imagine that, in such cases, the circuits have temporarily ceased to be thoroughfares, but such an event cannot be compared with the defect in vacuum tubes and switchboards. I imagine that we have now arrived at the point of which Adrian remarks that the brain physiologist and anatomist begin to flounder, and where, according to him, the psychologist can and must take over. Adrian here expects the aid especially of extended psychoanalytic psychology. He calls psychoanalysis "a new science which has gradually become an established part of our outlook on human behaviour."

I quote Adrian not only in order to justify my intention of co-opting psychoanalysis, but also because he defines analytic science as an "outlook on human behaviour." The opinion that psychoanalysis occupies itself solely or principally with subjective experiences happens to be widespread. But this is by no means the case. Even during the practical application of psychoanalysis, i.e. in therapy, the analyst does not confine his attention solely to the subjective experiences of the patient. A study of his behavior within and apart from the analytic situation has an important place in the therapy. A great many defense mechanisms which, for instance, have hardened into qualities of character and attitudes, can only be approached in this manner. Analytic science has always striven to study human behavior as a whole. The difference between it and the other branches of psychology is that it does not function only phenomenologically, i.e. observe phenomena in order to describe them. Analysis endeavors to trace the process of development of what it has observed; in other words, it has a genetic nature. Moreover, analysis studies the play of forces which takes place in the psychic process; it attempts to explain the psychic happenings genetodynamically. As a matter of course, analysis must continue to seek cooperation and augmentation by means of the other branches of psychological science and natural science of which I have spoken.

To sum up once again: brain physiologists and anatomists have partially discovered the physical basis of the mind. Modern physics and mechanics have enabled man to design machinery which copies certain functions and mechanisms of the brain. When and where we are as yet unable to explain certain manifestations of the mind by means of these disciplines, psychology must lend its help. An example is found in a phenomenon on which I have already remarked: the fear of its own creations which sometimes assails mankind. I repeat: why should man be afraid of the modern machine, the "robot" he has himself constrived? Apparently the living organism contains a number of principles of an active nature apart from the tendency to decrease entropy, to urge still greater differentiation and increased organization. This possibly is a point Wiener overlooked, or at least failed to describe sufficiently. He does draw attention to the principle of homeostasis, the search for a state of balance, inherent in the living organism. But the additional implications which this homeostatic principle brings in its train he does not mention. Homeostasis is the modern word used by Cannon, and is related to the constancy principle of Fechner. This principle, as we know, was applied by Freud to the psychic processes also. The homeostatic principle is founded physiologically in metabolism. The living cell and the organism strive for a certain constancy in the internal environment, i.e. the temperature of the body, the chemical composition of the blood, the pressure in the tissues, the acidbase ratio, the oxygen supply through breathing, etc. In psychic processes, physiological homeostasis is reflected by the tendency to retain certain tensions at their proper level. And this is the point where the experience factor counts. Freud described the pleasure-unpleasure principle as the psychic representative of the constancy principle. Tensions of a given intensity or a given rhythm may be experienced with pleasure; if the intensity increases or the rhythm is varied, they are experienced with pain. The mind urges toward the unloading, the discharge of the tensions. We assume that the pleasure-unpleasure principle is present in the higher types of animals as a regulating mechanism for the tensions. In the human being we encounter it in a far more differentiated form. Moreover we must not forget that the process of maturation is a much slower one in man than in animals (see also Hartmann). The patterns of behavior which are developed to obtain pleasure and avoid unpleasure we term instinctive behavior. In most animals these are coupled with the functions of seeking food, self-preservation, and propagation. Observations and experiments made by animal psychologists and ethologists such as Baerends, Lorenz, Tinbergen, and Kortlandt have proved that birds, for instance, develop extremely complicated patterns of behavior during the courting and mating period.

I should like to point out at this juncture that the instinctive patterns of behavior, which may be observed in the lower forms of animal life, such as insects (ants and bees), as well as in the higher animal types, are already highly complicated processes. In my opinion we should distinguish very sharply between the principles "instinctive behavior" and "drive." By "drives" Freud seems to mean, at any rate in his later theories of drives, the forces or tendencies active in the mind. Personally I feel that a better description or perhaps a reformulation of the psychoanalytic drive theory is required. This might make it possible to disentangle the disastrous confusion occasioned by the English use of "instinct" as the equivalent of the German *Trieb*. I will not say any more on this point at present. The instinctive patterns of behavior in animals, directed toward the search for food, the construction of the nest, courtship before mating, etc., result, as is generally accepted nowadays, from built-in mechanisms (innate release mechanisms), which, after birth and by means of the "learning mechanism," attain their final shape. The reflexes are also considered as built-in mechanisms. These also can be changed or conditioned, as Pavlov's experiments show. Zuckerman, too, remarks that "learning can occur in probably all organisms." When, for instance, a worm is put into a forked tube and given an electric shock every time it creeps into the left-hand fork, it will be observed after some time always to creep into the right-hand one. This, then, is conditioning, sometimes equated with learning. Ashby (1952) distinguishes between conditioning and learning. Both forms of adaptive behavior are based on "ultrastability of the organism" but in "learning" the feedback mechanism is activated, and this is wanting in "conditioning." Higher types of animals, such as monkeys, can be taught a great deal (Yerkes, Zuckerman, et al.). Monkeys can be taught to distinguish between quantities, one or more, and this not only when dealing with concrete objects. When monkeys are shown drawings, circles or squares, they will in the long run come to know the difference between a sheet of paper containing one and a sheet containing more figures. The thing we *cannot* teach these highly developed animals is to count, to abstract, to think abstractly, in short, to use symbols and signs which we humans use in our speech. The capacity of learning by insight is limited to man alone, whereas animals can only learn by "trial and error." Speech is a specifically human quality. Wiener says: "Speech is the greatest interest and most distinctive achievement of man." When discussing the remarkable fact that chimpanzees, who can learn a great deal, are never capable of learning to speak, he assumes that the human brain must possess a built-in power which enables man to "learn to speak." In the monkey this power is lacking. "The chimpanzee has no built-in mechanism which leads to speech." Later on Wiener remarks: "Speech seems to be an innate interest in coding and decoding, and this seems to be as nearly specifically human as any interest can be."

Now learning to speak, the use of language, and thinking are functions which the human young does not develop until quite some time after birth. The newborn child has very few reflex mechanisms at his disposal. The young bird is able to use instinctive patterns of behavior very soon after birth; these serve feeding purposes. The newborn human infant only disposes of a sucking mechanism where feeding is concerned. Ethology teaches us that geese, for instance, continue to follow the object that first brings them food. In the natural course of things, this object is the mother goose, but it can be replaced by another, a human object also. The innate release mechanism at this critical stage of the impression process is fixed by the learning mechanism, usually for life (Heinroth, Lorenz, et al.). The higher types of mammals, immediately after birth, are also dependent on the mother animal for food and for adapting themselves to the world around them for a while, but no newborn creature is so helpless and dependent for so long as the human child. Some children, just before birth, are apparently capable of sucking *in utero*, but on the other hand there are also newborn infants who do not suck when first applied to the breast: they have to "learn" even this. As we know, Freud considered that the child's helplessness and his long dependence were responsible for the intensity and complexity of the attachment of the human child to his mother (as well as the later attachment to other human beings). The adaptation by means of conditioning or learning during the human child's first few years may be compared to the analogous processes of learning in animals, as for example rats, cats, dogs, and monkeys. These animals are able to learn a variety of complicated reactions and mannerisms. Several reactions, such as fear raised by frustration, have been observed in animals. Szekely (1954), for example, writes in a very interesting article that fear in the infant is in origin very likely an inherited reaction to certain configurations (shapes) which can be replaced by dummies. These might then correspond to the "enemy scheme" in animals, the scheme which leads them to recognize dangerous enemies, such as beasts of prey. In the human being this danger might not be so much fear of a strange type of animal as a threat from a fellow man. The terrifying configuration was to consist of a movable two-eyes-and-forehead pattern (Kaila, 1932). This has also been determined by René Spitz, who studied the reactions of babies to a dummy consisting of two eyes and a forehead (1950). Here we have to remind ourselves of the interesting branch of psychology named the Gestalt (configuration) psychology (Koffka and Köhler).

We are prepared to accept that the earliest reactions and adaptation to the world outside are "learned" by man and animals (acquired through training) in an analogous manner, though by man at a slower speed because of his slow maturation, as already mentioned. However, from the moment that the specifically human capacity for learning to speak and think begins to develop an entirely new form of learning is added. Talking is gradually learned between the first and fourth year, though it passes through a great many stages. Developmental psychologists such as Bühler, Piaget, Rapaport (1951), and others have demonstrated that logical and abstract thought, which in the mature person is the basis for scientific practices and the enormous inventions which modern technical knowledge has produced, is developed over the course of many years and is capable of further development long after maturity has been reached. It seems as if the high organization and the subtle differentiation of the human brain take place at the cost of the instinctive behavior so highly developed in the higher animal species.

Neurophysiologists, cyberneticists, and possibly many other scientists in general recognize the specifically human in the flight of logical and creative thinking. The psychologists, and especially the psychoanalysts, know that there is another part of the spiritual life in man which has developed itself in a specific manner. This is the emotional life. From the first strong bond of love between the child and the mother an extremely rich and varied emotional contact is developed. Animals are able to become attached to others of their species; some birds for instance live in conjugal fidelity. But the subtly differentiated forms of affection, the feelings of sympathy, tenderness, respect, appreciation, admiration, and adoration, which develop from the original sexual love and erotism are not found among animals. It is the same with the feelings of hatred, envy, jealousy, contempt, etc., which we count among the aggressive tendencies.

While scientists therefore usually consider human intelligence and intellect as the qualities deserving most appreciation, others, artists for instance, set a still higher value on the subtler emotional expressions. Whatever our opinion on this score, we cannot deny that the strongly differentiated emotional life of man must be considered as typically human as his remarkable capacity for speech and thought.

Even less is known about the physicoanatomical basis of the human affective life than about the localization and the manner of functioning of the thought processes. That there actually is an innate somatic basis is made evident by the study of identical twins. Recognition of human thought and emotion, of human spiritual life, does not, to my way of thinking, imply that, because of our ignorance with regard to the physical basis of such processes, we must cling to supernatural, religious, or transcendental explanations. A psychology founded on the natural sciences should be able to accept the limits of its knowledge just as well as any other natural science. The frank recognition of its limits should become a stimulus to further research.

Neither do I consider it proper to use the fact of this higher differentiation and organization to feel excessive pride in man's performances and to feel ourselves elevated above our nearest companions in life: the animals. We are aware that man, living for so long in helpless dependence, has a strong urge to seek support from stronger and greater powers, such as he creates in the world of fantasy, the imagination. Religious and philosophic systems are our witnesses. The uncertain child who lives on in every adult is always attempting to hide his impotence beneath dreams of grandeur and power. Our spiritual life may indeed appear to us incomprehensible and miraculous, but is not life itself equally incomprehensible? Biochemistry teaches us the constitution of albumen, of the giant molecules which build up the living protoplasm of the unicellular organisms, but how and why and by what means living protoplasm can come into existence out of inorganic material is as great a mystery to us as is the manner in which the human mind develops. When we regard the mother of our life, the earth, and see it for what it is, one small planet in the solar system, and then remember that

that solar system is one among billions of others, it is but fitting that, notwithstanding our great knowledge of astronomy and physics, we should feel just as astounded. The actual secret of the world's order cannot be approached by even our boldest fantasy. We simply must have the courage to say: I do not know.

To return to our human world. We also know the reverse of our high differentiation. I have already remarked that a highly differentiated mechanical system is far more vulnerable than a simple construction. The complicated structure of our brain and the exceptional differentiation of our mental and emotional life make us human beings very unstable, spiritually and emotionally. It is very difficult, especially for man today, living in the extremely complicated and highly structured society of our time, to achieve and to retain inner harmony. Doctors and analysts are particularly impressed in this regard. In the course of their day's work they constantly meet people who are neurotic, psychotic, and psychosomatic patients who live at variance with themselves.

Here I would dwell for a moment on the problem of neurosis. In order to describe the analogies as well as the differences between human and animal development, I must return to the development of the child. In order to make a clearer picture of how such disharmony and inner conflict have arisen and how they act, psychoanalytic science uses certain dynamic and structural hypotheses. The structural theory presents the human mind as consisting of various systems, of several provinces, so to speak. Freud called these id, ego, and superego. These cannot as yet be localized anatomically, though Kubie and others have begun to attempt this.

I think that, following Freud's initiative, we must, when dealing with animals, at least with the higher types of animal, speak of a differentiation between id and ego too (of a primitive superego perhaps only in the case of domestic animals). The id of animals, as in human beings, embraces the drive needs. This does not mean that the contents of the animal id and the human id are the same. I agree with Hartmann's opinion that the id contents in the human being differ from those in animals, though the underlying biological forces may be identical. The animal ego, again as in the case of man, concerns itself with self-defense, self-preservation, and adaptation to the surroundings. It has, or develops in very little time, the necessary instinctive patterns of behavior. These deal with the food supply, warn against dangers, etc. After a short period of maturation the animal also uses instinctive reactions to achieve mating and the consequent external changes such as nesting, making a lair, etc. The young animal's ego is, as said above, relatively much more mature than that of the human infant. Relatively, too, it is soon at the end of its possibilities of development. Normally the pattern of behavior of the young animal is fixed after a short spell of learning and as a rule it will remain in this stark form of fixation for the rest of its life. The newborn human infant is relatively speaking much more of a "drive" creature than his animal counterpart. His ego needs much more time to develop the various functions and patterns of behavior; moreover, he cannot dispense with the relation to his mother and other external objects for a considerable time during the developmental process. We have said that the learning of language, in speech as well as in understanding, is out of the question without emotional contact with other people. But a number of other functions belonging to the ego, such as adaptation to the outside world, social demands (as, for example, bowel training), are also developed through object relations. The relative supremacy of the id (the vital urges) over the as yet primitive ego organization of the human young sets this ego an exceptionally heavy task during the complicated adapting and learning process. For, only too soon, education appears on the scene with demands no less exacting. It requires that the drive needs and impulses of the child must not be satisfied or indulged with unchecked immediacy. Practice has shown that the restraining of the id impulses is a wearing business. The as yet untamed drives form a menace to the primitive ego organization. The ego is forced to repress and to produce other defense mechanisms. The normal reaction and adaptive patterns may be used as defense forms against the id impulses. The defense process cannot, at any rate in our so-called cultural society, be called an abnormal process. For the development and maturation of the individual in his environment it is indispensable. It also permits the process of desexualization and neutralization of drive energy to take place. Thus the ego receives the necessary indifferent energy to achieve its performances (Hartmann et al.). The maturing processes of id and ego in their parallel courses take place amid constant interplay and mutual influencing. Environment at the same time applies unabated pressure through education, but also provides sources of satisfaction. During every stage and at any moment the harmonious unfolding may be disturbed. Too much repression of drive or too much indulgence may lead to mutilation of the ego functions, to a disordered adjustment to the environment. And a further complication arises when the superego is established as the third psychic agency, making fresh demands on the ego. The psychic growth of the child becomes yet more laborious owing to the specifically human events which accompany the late appearance of sexual maturity. Only in the human being do we encounter a recurring flowering of the drives. The latency period and puberty make their own demands on the maturing child. It is tempting but not possible here to go into some of the details of this growing process. But we understand that faulty developments of this complicated entity would lead to neurotic and other psychic disorders.

I feel, however, that I still owe an answer to the question: Why is humanity afraid of the self-constructed robots? The vulnerability of the highly differentiated ego organization quickly leads the ego into dangerous situations, menacing it from the outside as well as from the inside (i.e. from the id and the superego). Among the drive impulses the aggressive are especially important in this connection. The aggressive drives which cannot be used constructively in a sublimated form threaten to take the ego by surprise. Subsequent actions are then no longer determined rationally, but are directed against the individual and the outside world in a destructive manner.

Our previous arguments have brought us to the question: What are mental health and illness respectively? I feel that this question is exclusively a *practical* one. Scientific theory cannot determine just what is neurotic and what is healthy. Several psychoanalysts, such as Hartmann (1939b), and recently Kubie

(1954), have explained that the terms sickness and health are to a great extent dependent on the current opinion of a particular group of people at a given time. The meaning is variable, subject to changes under the influence of social, economic, and cultural factors. Although Kubie calls sufficient attention to these factors, he finally arrives at a very simplistic definition of the essence of neurosis. He feels, apparently, that unconscious, constrained action is neurotic, and conscious, flexible, free action is healthy. I cannot agree with these conclusions, which are too limited. They neglect our knowledge of the structured nature of the mind, the dynamic processes of defense and repression, and the genetic factors. They are descriptive, and may easily be proved wrong by means of examples. One might agree with Freud's definition: "Neuroses (and other psychic disturbances) are disharmonies of the ego." But the curious researcher will immediately ask: How, why, and when have these discords arisen? Personally I feel that we cannot do better than admit that we can only enumerate a number of factors which may direct the development in a healthy or disordered direction.

In summing up, I would return to Freud's conception of the complementary series I mentioned at the beginning of this chapter; every development, healthy as well as unhealthy, is ultimately the result of the interplay and mutual influencing of the built-in factors, experiences, and influence of environment. The built-in factors may be traced:

(1) In the disposition of the drives, i.e. the id in the narrow sense, in the relative relation of power between the drives, perhaps peculiarities in the rhythm and timing of the underlying forces. In view of this it is a matter of course that these factors are linked with and inseparable from somatic organic processes (metabolism, internal secretion, etc.)

(2) In the ego disposition (the ego nuclei) which indicate the possibilities and the limits of the ego functions, instinctive behavior, intelligence, thought, adjustment functions, reaction mechanisms, etc. Somatically these are linked with the central nervous system. At this point, therefore, we are assisted on our way by neurophysiology and anatomy. It is conceivable that the quantity or nature of the neurones, circuits, synapses, etc., will prove to be determining factors also. For the present, according to the neurologists and anatomists, we know too little of this subject.

Here peculiar innate organic qualities may be of great importance. But even if future research should teach us more about the physical basis of the ego functions, our knowledge would be increased with regard to only a few factors out of very many.

As the third group of dispositional factors I would mention:

(3) The mutual relative relation between built-in id potentialities and ego capabilities, possibly complicated by potentialities which color and direct the subsequent superego development. These relations, however, cannot at present be measured; they can only be deduced from a study of human behavior. The study of many life histories gives promise of fruitful help here.

With the other pole of the complementary series, the influence of the environment, I can deal briefly. I need not explain in detail here that, during the first

216

months and years of life, it is mainly the behavior of the mother which determines whether the child will develop healthily or inharmoniously, while later on the previously mentioned influences of wider environmental and social conditions in their various ramifications will be of particular significance.

I turn now to the question whether the abnormal behavior displayed by animals during laboratory experiments, when through frustrations etc. they are conditioned to given factors or taught to perform various unusual actions, may be compared with the human neurosis. Masserman (1953) draws a far-reaching comparison here. He speaks of neurotic animals and even mentions a therapy for their neurosis. For myself (in agreement with a number of other research scientists) I shall answer this question in the negative. Animals when experimented upon are able to demonstrate reactions such as fear, excitement, rage, etc., but the neurosis in the human being is something different. It comes into existence owing to a complicated defensive process which appears as a result of the interaction of external factors and internally active conflicts. The inner conflicts can only arise owing to the higher differentiation of the human psyche, which in animals is lacking. There is, possibly, a group of disorders of which a given number of built-in factors may be discussed a little more fully. These are the so-called psychosomatic disorders. We know that psychosomatic patients usually exhibit neurotic symptoms as well. Moreover, neurotic and psychosomatic symptoms often interchange and relieve each other. We note that patients suffering from psychosomatoses and neuroses usually have similar character structures and experienced similar environmental influences. Several researchers treating psychosomatic patients, such as Alexander, Groen, and others, have published schematic outlines of personality structures and behavior, coupled with certain family influences and stress situations which they considered to be typical for a certain type of psychosomatosis. But usually these schematic outlines can also be applied to psychoneuroses. It appears, however, to be definitely established that psychosomatic patients have certain built-in factors which can be isolated in the somatic situation; I refer to an ailment such as eczema of the skin. Here we must consider certain predispositional peculiarities of the skin. Diseases such as, for instance, ulcus ventriculi and duodeni, asthma, bronchitis, etc., show that the mucous membranes harbor factors which predispose the subject to these diseases. We are reminded of Freud's conception when he spoke of a somatic compliance when dealing with hysterical conversion symptoms. In the case of babies, where we cannot speak of hysteria, such a somatic, predisposed center may lead to the recognized eczema, bronchitis, pylorospastic syndromes, etc. It is more than possible that the very first experiences of the newborn infant, whose needs are somatically determined, play an important part in infectious diseases, alimentary disorders, etc. (see also Grinker). The attitude of the mother is bound to have an important influence on this somatic reacting of the infant.

Summing up, I would say that recent research in the fields of neurophysiology and anatomy together with cybernetics and ethology have greatly increased the scope of our knowledge of the physical basis of the mind and its earliest developments. In order to widen our outlook on the higher psychic functions and their unfolding in mankind we cannot, for the time being, do without psychoanalysis. The further development of this branch of science and its continued cooperation with the first-named sciences must not only be our constant hope, but, to my mind, is a definite necessity.

23. On Adolescence

(1960)

Adolescence is often regarded as a "stepchild" in psychoanalysis, in a theoretical as well as in a practical sense. A number of analysts consider the treatment of adolescent boys and girls to be very difficult, sometimes even impossible, though in some cases good results have been achieved, especially with inhibited, depressive, and compulsive-neurotic patients.

Many authors stress that our theoretical knowledge of adolescence is incomplete. I shall not review the literature in detail, but refer to the surveys of this subject by Leo Spiegel (1951) and by Anna Freud (1958).

Out of the many problems of adolescence, my paper will focus on two points: (1) a practical experience; and (2) some theoretical considerations, especially in connection with the formation of superego and ego ideal.

I

Anna Freud (1958) has reminded us of the fact that "our knowledge of the mental processes of infancy has been derived from reconstructions in the analyses of adults and was merely confirmed and enlarged later on by analyses or observations carried out in childhood." It is Anna Freud's opinion that in the treatment of adult cases one seldom succeeds in reviving their adolescent experiences in full force.

I think most authors will agree with this statement, and I have done so myself. However, a number of years ago two adult patients came to me for analytic treatment, a man and a woman, both in their early thirties, in whose analyses a wealth of adolescent experiences, real events as well as fantasies and impulses, came to the fore with remarkable liveliness and were accompanied by strong emotions and impulses. I hasten to add that this re-experiencing only emerged in the later phases of the analyses. In the beginning of treatment the adolescent material was brought forward merely as an account of the patient's life history in the way described by Anna Freud. The most interesting point was that the reliving of affects connected with this material did not become possible until the patient's childhood had been uncovered and reconstructed. Confronted with these observations, I recalled a statement which Freud made to me some thirty years ago. Freud told me about a young woman who had cooperated well in her analysis and whose childhood development had been fairly well reconstructed − but without a therapeutic result. Most of the patient's symptoms had persisted until she suddenly and vividly recollected a traumatic experience that had

219

occurred in her fifteenth year of life. After this traumatic situation and all the emotions involved had been worked through, the patient was cured.

My own observations led me to review a number of other cases, and I gained the impression that in some of them the failure or incompleteness of success might have been due to the lack of revival of the adolescent experiences. Of course I now had to ask myself what causes might have been responsible for the fact that in these cases childhood development could be reconstructed without difficulty and re-experienced with full emotional force, whereas the adolescent period remained deprived of a full affective conviction.

From the direct study of adolescent cases we are all familiar with the charged atmosphere in which the adolescent lives, with the intensity and depth of his feelings, the sudden and unexpected mood swings, the strength of his impulses, and the force of anxiety and despair. However, are we really entitled to assume that in small children feelings, impulses, demands, unforeseen swings from complete happiness toward deepest sorrow and desperation are less intense than similar phenomena in adolescence?

There is indeed a difference in the demands of the instinctual drives in childhood and in adolescence, because infantile sexuality is different from genitality, which has to become the leading factor in the adolescent and adult love life.

I have the impression, however, that it is not merely the intensity of feelings, impulses, and mood swings, but that there are other factors which are more responsible for the difficulties of reviving the adolescent mental processes. These factors seem to lie in ego and superego development.

The little child's ego, undeveloped as it is, has to rely upon the auxiliary ego borrowed from the mother in order to master outer and inner conflicts. The superego is not yet established as an independent mental agency in infancy. Norms and restrictions are imposed upon the child by the parents. Not until the oedipal phase does a structuration of the personality take place. In latency the child develops into a more or less individual personality, though he is still dependent upon the parents. Numerous ego capacities are established and mature during this period. In the sphere which is relatively free from conflict, intelligence, knowledge, special talents, and abilities are developed, whereas in the conflictual sphere, adaptations, reaction formations, and defense mechanisms gradually become character traits. The superego as an inner institution supervises the latency child's behavior to a large extent.

This brief outline of a child's development is very sketchy and incomplete, but it may suffice as a prelude to our considerations about adolescence.

When in puberty the instinctual drives make their new and intensified demands upon the youngster, they encounter a personality different from the one they encountered in childhood. The adolescent ego has many more ways and means of coping with the drives; in a certain sense, we could call this ego stronger. However, on the other hand, it lacks the support of the parents' auxiliary ego because the adolescent turns away from the parents. The loosening of the ties with the parents is a difficult and protracted process, often accompanied by genuine mourning, as Root (1957) and Anna Freud (1958) have pointed out. In this respect the adolescent ego presents itself as much weaker than the child's ego. A similar process is going on in the superego. On the one hand the adolescent superego is now established as an inner conscience; on the other hand its foundation is shaken by the very process of turning away from the parents and the parental norms and morals. The adolescent has to rely upon his own superego. The adult, looking back upon his life history, feels more responsible for his adolescent than for his infantile behavior; he feels more guilty and more ashamed about his adolescent conflicts, disharmonies, and oddities. As he usually remembers the factual events of adolescence, he tries to escape the revival of the accompanying guilt- and shame-burdened emotions, either by suppressing and denying every emotion of that period or by retreating to infantile experiences.

This is precisely what we often observe in analytic treatment. The patient brings us a wealth of infantile material, more and more, in different forms and associations, even when the childhood history has already been fairly well reconstructed and re-experienced. He clings tenaciously to infantile material; yet when we look at this material closely we realize that adolescent features have entered into the picture. The patient has used the infantile material in order to ward off adolescent experiences. The analyst must then analyze the defensive character of, and the underlying anxiety in regard to this material and confront the patient with his adolescent feelings of shame, guilt, hurt pride, etc. In a number of cases the result will be a real revival of the patient's adolescence in full force.

In trying to accomplish this task we encounter difficulties not exclusively due to the patient's reluctance to face his own adolescent problems, his unbalanced behavior, his extreme feelings, his extravagant emotions, and his oddities. We also have to cope with the analyst's reactions. The analyst is prepared to encounter the patient's acting out in the transference. When the patient transfers impulses upon the analyst from his childhood period and in an infantile form, it is much easier for the analyst to keep to his attitude of friendly understanding and neutrality. The adolescent has made use of all of his intelligence, capacities, and special gifts to ward off his forbidden impulses, his disappointments, and his conflicts. This is especially true in connection with his hostility toward parents and toward adults in general. Hence, in encouraging an adult patient to relive his adolescent experiences the analyst must cope with a refined form of the patient's aggression.

One can smile at a little child's direct form of aggressive behavior, but an adolescent's aggression is clothed in a much more irritating, tormenting, and sometimes nearly intolerable shape. It may happen that the analyst, being a human creature himself, is (unconsciously) inclined to follow the patient in his flight toward infancy in order to escape the patient's refined criticisms, reproaches, and hostile demands. In every adult, traits not only from the little child but also from the adolescent persist. This is especially true for our patients. They tend to excuse themselves for their accusations and tormenting attacks in taking for granted that the analyst is an omnipotent and therefore invulnerable person. The interplay between the patient's desire to relive his adolescent emotions and conflicts and the analyst's unconscious reluctance to bear the adolescent forms of aggression might be one of the causes of the difficulties we encounter in analyzing and working through an adult patient's adolescence.

II

I now come to my second point: some theoretical considerations, which, I hope, will contribute to our understanding of the practical difficulties just mentioned as well as of adolescent psychic life in general. In the scope of this presentation I can throw light upon only a few points. My assumptions are based partly on material gained in the treatment of adolescents, but mainly on reconstruction of adolescent experiences in adult cases.

A youngster's ego can react in an infinite variety of ways to the newly flourishing demands of his instinctual drives and to the newly arising social demands which are so different from those made upon the little child. The adolescent has on the one hand the ardent wish to be grown up because he usually imagines that adults are free, independent, and self-supporting, and he tries to use all his faculties in order to equal or even to better them. On the other hand, however, he wants to remain a little child in order not to have to relinquish his infantile ties with the parental objects. It is very well known how difficult a task this is. Having lost a beloved person or even having renounced the love of a still existing object is followed by a certain amount of "work of mourning" (see Anna Freud, 1958). Whether the outcome of the mourning process will be a relatively normal or a pathological one depends upon many factors, among them upon the amount of aggression originally directed toward the parents. We know that the little child holds his parents responsible for his distress and losses, and he responds to all sorts of pain with hatred and death wishes toward them. When in puberty the infantile object relationships are revived, the adolescent begins to react in a similar way. The more intense his archaic hostility, the more difficulties he will have in dealing with his death wishes. The mourning processes are colored by the aggression turned inward. The result may be a depressive neurotic disorder, psychotic reactions, acting out or antisocial behavior, or a combination of these various disturbances. Many authors have described several outcomes in clinical and theoretical papers.

I shall now turn to another problem of adolescence which is very different from childhood processes and nevertheless very closely dependent upon them. I mean the superego problems. I have already mentioned that in adolescence the superego has become an inner agency, whereas in early childhood behavior was directed by the parents' demands, prohibitions, and morals. The little child cooperates with them mainly in order to avoid loss of love or punishment. Only gradually does he internalize the parental norms, which subsequently become the content of the superego. Now in adolescence he must give up his old incestuous ties to the parents – a process partly equivalent to losing the love object. But in addition he must also give up a fundamental part of his superego content – those parts of the restrictions, norms, and ideals which, though internalized, are still closely linked to the incestuous object representations. The very fact that these superego contents are internalized implies that the adolescent must give up something that has become an essential part of his self. To turn away from a love object is a hard and painful process; to disengage oneself from a part of one's own personality is still more difficult to achieve.

In order to examine these events more closely I propose once more to distinguish between the superego in a narrower sense as the restricting and prohibiting agency and the ego ideal as comprising ethics and ideals. I have made this distinction in previous papers and it has, in my opinion, some advantages. The compliance with parental restrictions and prohibitions requires renunciation of direct pleasure, but this compliance is rewarded with love and approval from the parents. The formation of ideals, however, has an additional function and has already been on the way long before parental restrictions have become internal demands. The little child idealizes the parents and conceives of them as perfect, omnipotent creatures. He clings tenaciously to these ideas because he feels himself so extremely powerless. The introjection of the almighty and faultless parental image is a compensation for the feeling of helplessness; it begins in very early childhood and is a narcissistic satisfaction *par excellence*. These introjected images give rise to fantasies of grandeur and omnipotence, which in the magic phase of development are among the fundamentals of the child's self-esteem and self-maintenance. It is well known that part of the feelings of grandeur continue to exist, though unconsciously, throughout life.

The adolescent must bear not only the pain of losing love objects, of coping with the attending mourning, and of revising old patterns of restriction and prohibition. In addition to all these hard tasks, he must endure the narcissistic injuries caused by the experience that his self-esteem is being shaken in its fundamentals and therefore more or less lost. We know too well that a certain amount of narcissistic cathexis of the personality is indispensable for healthy development. When the basis of the ideal formation has gone to pieces, the youngster is utterly helpless. I hasten to add that the loss of love is of course partly felt as a narcissistic injury as well. The finding of a new love object raises the person's self-esteem, too. However, it seems to make a considerable difference when an essential part of the ego (ego ideal) is damaged or lost and has to be newly built up. New love objects are relatively easily found in adolescence in teachers, leaders, companions, etc. New ideals that compensate for the essential helplessness of human beings are more difficult to acquire (at least in our civilization). The youngster very well knows, and feels, that adults are not omnipotent but vulnerable creatures. With this acknowledgment, his ideals of perfect and omnipotent parents must collapse, and consequently his ego ideal is impaired. We find a confirmation of this assumption in studying those adolescents who do not respond to offers of love and guidance from a new object (relative, teacher, therapist, companion, etc.). These youngsters could not overcome the depth of their inner narcissistic injuries as a consequence of the disturbance of their ideal formation. They then are indifferent to supplies of love from the outer world. It is possible that a number of strange reactions, unexpected attitudes, and unpredictable mood swings are due to this basic disturbance in the economy of narcissistic libido and the ego's failure to restore it with another acquisition of ideals. Moreover, it is just the narcissistic injuries that are pre-eminently likely to give rise to aggression, and this hostility in turn diminishes a person's susceptibility to another person's loving assistance and to the offer of new ideals and norms.

In the transference during treatment we can observe that a patient's deep and refined hostility, severe criticisms of the analyst, reproaches that the analyst is impotent and worthless go side by side with an unconscious, archaic conviction of the analyst's omnipotence. The ideal image of almighty parents and analysts is not only indispensable for the youngster's maintenance of narcissistic cathexis, but is secondarily used to diminish the guilt feelings aroused by precisely this same hostile and aggressive behavior. It is as if the youngster says to himself: "Parents and analysts are omnipotent, consequently they are invulnerable; so I can scold, torment, and act out every aggression without having to feel guilty or reproach myself."

It would be tempting to illustrate these assumptions with detailed analytic material. However, in this paper, I merely wanted to emphasize the importance of the problems around the ego ideal in adolescence. The adolescent's clinging to the very archaic, idealized parental images makes it very difficult for him to cope with the narcissistic injuries occasioned by the disappointment of losing his infantile idealized images and by the necessity of having to give them up and finding new ideals in a more reality-adapted form. Furthermore, they need to hold on to this idealized picture because it also serves as a defense against guilt and shame engendered by the intense hostility.

Since many analysts agree that adolescent patients are often not suitable for analytic treatment, we must, in our attempts to understand adolescent psychology, rely mainly on observations and reconstructions of adolescence in adult cases. But even these reconstructions, as has been pointed out, are extremely difficult to achieve. This paper has endeavored to investigate some of the obstacles in the way of such reconstruction and to indicate means of overcoming them.

I believe that we might be successful in reviving adolescence in a number of cases if we made an effort to overcome our own resistances against the patient's adolescent forms of aggression, if we focused our and the patient's attention upon his hidden ideals and fantasies of omnipotence attributed to his parents and later on internalized, and if we supported the patient in enduring his narcissistic hurts and in giving up the defensive character of his archaic ideal. I believe that this effort is worth while.

24. Ego Ideal and Superego

(1962)

Originally the terms "ego ideal" and "superego" were used by Freud interchangeably. This fact can be explained historically. From the study of psychopathology, especially of melancholic disorders, Freud concluded that a part of the ego (a province within the ego) could oppose itself to the ego proper, making demands upon it and punishing it as formerly the parents had done. This means that through the process of identification the superego is formed as a substructure of the ego. In the course of development this process occurs at the end of the phallic phase (at the onset of latency) as a result of the solution of the oedipal object relationships. The superego is, according to Freud's formulation, the heir of the oedipus complex, and comprises the child's wish to be like the parents (ideal formation) and to comply with the parental restrictions and demands (superego in a narrower sense). These conceptualizations could account for and explain a variety of pathological phenomena in individuals (Freud, 1914, 1917, 1923b, 1924a, 1924b, 1925, 1931b) as well as in mankind (Freud, 1921, 1927b, 1930, 1937-39). In addition, they also explained normal psychological processes, e.g., humor (1927a).

Notwithstanding the gains in insight, there continued to exist a number of problems and inconsistencies which, according to Freud, were in need of further study and explanation. In recent years several authors have made contributions to the superego problems. For a more detailed review of the literature, I refer the reader to Sandler (1960).

From a structural point of view, I think we must adhere to Freud's conception of the superego as a special substructure in the human mind established at the onset of latency. Yet how are we to explain the difficulties and confusions around this concept which many authors have mentioned? Structuralization of the mind is a maturational and developmental process. The genetic point of view has brought about many clarifications of mental processes. I therefore propose to turn to the genesis of mental substructures of the ego in approximately normal development and to examine separately the ideal formation and the self-criticizing punishing agency.

The genesis of ego substructures

The genesis of the ego ideal
The child is born with an unstructured mind. The inborn potentialities out of which a structured mind is developed during growth are called by Freud the id in

225

a wider sense; Hartmann (1939a, 1950) speaks of the "undifferentiated phase." The newborn has vital needs which have to be satisfied sufficiently to guarantee survival and to ensure the reign of the pleasure principle. As long as the infant-mother unity is need-satisfying there is no stimulation for accelerating the maturational process. However, birth itself causes unpleasurable sensations and soon afterward the satisfaction of needs does not occur immediately and completely enough to avoid unpleasure. The experiences of alternate pleasure and pain stimulate development, and gradually a primitive structuralization of the mind comes about. A number of functions begin to develop: sensual stimuli are laid down in memory traces (structuralization of the brain), outside and inside are distinguished (object and self), testing of reality begins, etc. I do not need to mention all of them; they are well known as functions which later on will be organized. In the structured mind they build up the ego organization which must attempt to allow sufficient satisfaction of needs and wishes and at the same time to adjust to the necessities of life and to the demands of the environment.[1] I will now turn to a special function of the very primitive ego, already manifesting itself in the first months of life, because I think it has a bearing on our topic, the genesis of the later-established ego ideal.

When the little baby becomes aware of unpleasurable stimuli and tensions he is bodily still too immature to take appropriate action. He cannot produce food or warmth or comfort when he is hungry or cold or nearly overwhelmed by inner tensions. When the mother is not instantly available the infant takes refuge in "hallucinatory wish fulfillment," as Freud called it in earlier times.

I think these hallucinations already occur at a time when the function of distinguishing between self and outside world is not yet established. They appear during the narcissistic stage, when the mother (or the breast) is still part of the internal narcissistic milieu and not yet an object (Hoffer, 1950). However, as "hallucinating" does not abolish unpleasure in the long run, whereas the mother does, we may consider these processes as the starting point for the development of the distinction between inner and outer worlds.

As long as no object outside the self is recognized, these hallucinations are not yet fantasies centering around an object that provides pleasure or abolition or unpleasure. They are self-centered and, as far as they can temporarily alleviate discomfort, the gain is narcissistic satisfaction.

The reason why I dwell so long on this early and primitive ego function is that, in my opinion, we encounter here the basis of the ego ideal. In terms of structuralization we could speak of a forerunner of the ego ideal. According to this assumption, the genesis of the ego ideal is to be found in an ego function, which serves to provide pleasure and to undo pain, caused by frustrations. This latter function has already been described by me in Chapter 10. The ego ideal is an *agency of wish fulfillment*. If we pursue the further development of these primitive hallucinatory wish fulfillments, I think we find confirmation of this assumption.

---

[1] Modern ego psychology is so far advanced as to give us a fairly good insight into the development of a number of functions of the ego organization (Hartmann, 1939a, 1950; and many other authors).

When the infant has learned to distinguish between self and outer world he makes an object attachment to the breast and the mother, and he expects the mother to provide satisfaction. This object attachment is still a narcissistic one; the mother is loved not for her own sake, but merely as a need-satisfying object. During this period of differentiation between self and object new sources of unpleasure arise for the infant when the mother does not provide satisfaction and love as completely and as instantly as he wants them. Even the most loving and devoted mother is unable to fulfill every wish, to abolish every pain or discomfort in her child. There are always situations when the child feels disappointed, frustrated, and above all *powerless* because he is unable to bring about a change in this painful state of unpleasure. To deal with this condition, so dangerous for his self-esteem (his narcissistic equilibrium), the child develops alongside the primitive hallucinatory wish fulfillments his comforting fantasies of grandeur and omnipotence. Together with the formation of object relations (first need-satisfying attachments, and later on relations of object constancy), the fantasies of omnipotence and idealization of his self continue to exist. They can easily be observed in toddlers in the preoedipal phase.

I mention two examples, among many: little John, aged two years, ten months, told his mother his penis would grow to be as big as the garden hose; he would fill the ocean and a big steamer would take him overseas.

Little Ann (three years) said: "When my penis is as big as Dick's [her elder brother] . . . ." When her mother remarked: "But you are a little girl, only boys have a penis, why do you think you will get one?" Ann replied: "When I want it, I'll get it!"

The fantasies of grandeur are a narcissistic gratification and they heighten self-esteem. But gradually they begin to fail to do so because the child has the painful experience that they have no influence upon the actual events, and he feels his total powerlessness vis-à-vis reality. He then takes refuge in a second edition of fantasies which provide narcissistic gratification. He idealizes his parents and attributes to them omnipotence, in which he himself partakes. These images of ideal and almighty parents persist much longer, because the parents are, in comparison with the child, really much stronger and more powerful. These fantasies flourish especially during the oedipal phase in which the child identifies himself with the parent of the same sex in order to replace him (or her) with the other parent. In normal development the child at the end of the oedipal phase accepts reality more or less through recognizing his powerlessness and the impossibility of being the mother's (or the father's) lover. His attachment to the parents is desexualized and a more reality-oriented change takes place in his ego ideal. The contents of the ego ideal are no longer exclusively "I am as potent in sexual life and in other achievements as the parents." The ideals are partly transferred to attainable goals: learning, development of bodily and mental skills, understanding of reality and life in general. We know that even so-called "normal" adults sometimes take refuge in former fantasies of omnipotence in narcissistically frustrating situations. However, when they are able to live up to their own mature ideals and ethics, they experience a more lasting and much greater satisfaction. *The ego ideal*, even when developed into ethics and social ideals, *remains essentially an agency of wish fulfillment,* and it supports the ego in dealing with the inevitable disappointments and frustrations inherent in human life. In a way, it is still an ego function. However, just because it has its own contents and because it sometimes puts a distance between itself and the other organized ego functions, we can speak of an established substructure (or province) within the ego.

I shall next discuss the self-criticizing, prohibiting, and punishing agency which we could term "superego in a narrower sense" or "conscience."

The Genesis of the Superego

Before the infant distinguishes between self and outside world there is no question of "prohibitions, demands, or punishment." The infant merely experiences sensations of unpleasure. When the distinction between self and environment has been established the infant may experience restrictions of his needs and wishes from outside as prohibitions or demands. It seems plausible to assume that the earlier unpleasurable sensations form the basis of his experience of these restrictions. When he protests against complying with them, anxiety may arise. In order to avoid anxiety and to preserve the object (later on the love of the object), he will begin to try to live up to the demands.

The toddler may, to a certain extent, internalize the parental demands and even their punishments. The acceptance of the inevitable environmental claims leads to the establishment of an ego function which can be considered to be a forerunner of conscience and which thus is an *agency of restriction* imposed upon the little child from outside. The conflict is between child and environment and is likely to arouse anxiety but not yet guilt. Only at the end of the oedipal phase, when the child must give up his sexual wishes, do the environmental demands and restrictions become an inner property. The ego functions of renouncing certain wish fulfillments and of complying with parental demands can now be structuralized into the judging superego or conscience.

In normal development the superego and the ego ideal guide the ego in its double task, on the one hand of allowing the person to have sufficient satisfaction of drives, needs, impulses, etc., and on the other hand of modifying and sublimating parts of them in order to live up to the demands of the outside world and to cope with the inevitable restrictions.

Summary

The genesis of the ego ideal is different from that of the restricting superego or conscience. The ego ideal is originally and essentially a *need-satisfying agency,* whereas the superego (or conscience) is originally and essentially a *restricting and prohibiting agency.*

In the development of the ego ideal four phases can be distinguished:
(1) "Hallucinatory" wish fulfillment in the narcissistic phase (in which self and outer world are not yet distinguished).
(2) Fantasies of grandeur and omnipotence of the self after the infant has become aware of a distinction between inside and outside.

(3) Fantasies of the parents being omnipotent, and the child's sharing their omnipotence after experiencing his own powerlessness.
(4) Formation of ethics and ideals as attainable goals after disillusionment by the idealized parents.

In the development of the restricting superego, four phases can be distinguished:
(1) Experience of sensations of unpleasure.
(2) Renunciation of wish fulfillment and compliance with parental demands in order to preserve the parents' love.
(3) Internalization of single demands through identification with some parental demands during the preoedipal phase.
(4) Inner conscience and internal acceptance of restrictions and punishments imposed by the parents and the wider environment in order to guarantee a social relationship within a certain class or group or milieu.

Now the question arises, how was it that originally both ego ideal and restricting superego were seen as one single agency and one substructure within the ego? I believe it is because at the onset of latency their establishment is centered around the same object representations, the parental images, the purely narcissistic prestages having been abandoned. The content of the ego ideal, once the third phase of its development has been reached, could be expressed as follows: "I am like my parents (that is, in fantasy: omnipotent)." The content of the superego from an early stage of its development onward could be described in the following way: "I will live up to my parents' demands, and punish myself the way they punished me when I fail to do so (that is, in fantasy: I have to be obedient to avoid the loss of parental love)."
The ego ideal's content, "I am like my parents," implies taking over parental ideals and ethics. The superego's content, "I have to do what my parents require of me," implies taking over parental restrictions and prohibitions. Both institutions are marked by identification with the parents and the parental images. From the structural point of view, we can describe them as substructures within the ego, as a change of part of the ego through these identifications. If we examine their functions, however, they serve opposite ends. The ego ideal serves wish fulfillment and is a gratifying agency. The conscience (superego in the narrower sense) is a restricting and prohibiting agency. However, in this strictly schematic sense, this statement is true in childhood, but later on only in a very harmonious development. Because both agencies unite into one substructure after the passing of the oedipus complex, they may considerably influence each other's functions. The ego ideal's content, "I am like my parents," can acquire an imperative compulsive character: "I must be like my parents." Later on high ideals in general may be experienced as demands.
Even within the range of so-called "normality" there are many individual differences which can be explained in two ways: (1) we may assume a definite and rigid change of function after the establishment of the substructure superego in the wider sense; and (2) we may see them as individual variations

which already show a tendency toward inharmonious development. I myself am inclined toward the second explanation, because in a number of cases we clearly observe that living up to ethics, ideals, and norms is and remains a source of pleasure. It may provide real satisfaction through heightening self-esteem and self-assurance and so promote a number of gratifying ego activities. A strong compulsion to normative and ethical behavior (Kant's categorical imperative) points to an oversevere, judging superego, as is, for example, often found in persons with obsessional-neurotic characters. As in many other instances, the transitions between "normality" and "pathology" are fluid.

Be this as it may, the origins of both agencies can be traced back to infancy. In certain circumstances (most clearly in pathology), a disintegration of the one or the other, sometimes of both at the same time, takes place and regression to primitive, infantile stages occurs. Identifications with the mother and with the father naturally differ from one another. These as well as identifications made on different levels of development may again come to the fore and may cause splits in the entity of both agencies.

The visibility of structure in the mind

I now want to take up a problem which Freud mentioned on several occasions but to which other psychoanalysts have not paid sufficient attention. In the behavior of a "normal," well-integrated, harmoniously developed adult, we cannot always directly distinguish the different structures and substructures of the mind, because in this case the mind acts as a whole. When a person's ego has secured sufficient satisfaction of needs and impulses and when the ego is able to master the id strivings which cannot be satisfied, using their (neutralized) energy for constructive purposes, it is no longer possible to distinguish clearly what share the ego and id have in a number of activities. The same applies to a distinction between shares of the (judging) superego and the ego ideal in these activities. A person capable of living up to his inner ethics and ideals *and* capable of sound self-criticism, who can provide himself with sufficient gratifications in accordance with his own environment, acts as a whole, as an entity. The fact that the provinces of the mind were originally separate functional entities becomes apparent only in special circumstances. In "normal" persons this occurs in specific life situations which require a reorientation, e.g., in adolescence when the former balance between id and ego, ego ideal and superego has to be revised owing to the maturing sexuality, love life, and object choices. I described some of the problems involved in Chapter 23. In the menopause and in old age other problems arise. In these phases of relative unbalance the different structures of the mind and the various identifications may become much more visible until a new harmony is again achieved. It then becomes very clear that a variety of new contents has been added to the original ones.

In disturbed, inharmonious development which leads to neuroses, ego distortions, delinquency, psychoses, etc., the structuralization of the mind becomes much more observable. Partial and unequal regressions to earlier developmental stages of id, ego, ego ideal, and superego provide a clearer picture of how the mind is structuralized in the course of maturation and development.

For practical purposes we try to assess the nature and gravity of given disturbances and their accessibility to psychoanalytic (or other psychotherapeutic) treatment. Treatment aims at tracing back the disturbances to their origins in order to enable the mature ego to employ the mental energies in a different (and healthier) way. In this context it is necessary to look for criteria enabling us to assess the extent to which different parts of the structured mind have contributed to the disturbance. In its final outcome, the differences in the development of the superego and ego ideal may play an important role.

Some practical considerations in regard to psychopathology

The classical psychoneuroses
In hysteria, phobia, and obsessional neurosis a regression of libido and aggression to earlier developmental stages takes place in consequence of severe guilt feelings and strong castration anxiety. This early statement of Freud's can still be confirmed in our daily analytic work. The primary regression of the drives is sometimes followed by a secondary regression of a number of ego functions in connection with defensive processes, and of some rigid defense mechanisms.[2] We then speak of ego distortions. The functions of ego ideal and restricting superego may participate in these events. This is clearly observable in obsessional neurotics. Here the drives regress to the anal-sadistic phase and this regression is followed by a restriction of ego activities, e.g., of sublimated actions, and by a regression of the restricting superego, which becomes a very sadistic agency through sexualization and turning of aggression toward the self. The ego ideal secondarily regresses to the phase of fantasies of grandeur and omnipotence, and of magical thinking. These processes cause distortion of reality testing. Usually a part of the ego is still very well able to judge reality, while another part follows the regressed ego-ideal functions and adheres to a belief in the possibility of magically influencing the environment. Thus, splits in the ego and ego ideal have come about, and the patient feels torn apart.

In hysterical patients, the ego disturbance observable as a consequence of the regression of libido to the phallic phase seems to be less severe. It limits itself to an inhibition of some functions, e.g., of memory. The function of memory is more or less impaired through the defense mechanism of repression, which causes gaps in the patient's life history and may have a bearing on his judgment of reality factors.

Narcissistic neuroses, borderline cases, and psychoses
A different process seems to have occurred in these disorders. Here we may assume a regression of ego functions together with the libidinal regression. Both could be called primary regression. An alternative could be a disturbance

[2] The distinction between primary and secondary ego regression is used by Anna Freud in the assessment of childhood development.

of ego activities in the prephallic stage, an arrest of ego maturation, or a severe retardation in development already originating in the preoedipal phase. In narcissistic neuroses, it is sometimes difficult to decide whether we are dealing with an early arrest or with regression. In psychoses and borderline cases, there seems to be a closer tie to an early level of ego development. Concerning large areas of the restricting superego and of the ego ideal we clearly observe a position of an infantile nature. In these patients we see that the restricting superego has only partly reached the state of an inner voice, of a real conscience. These patients can submit only to the actual restrictions coming from outside, and then under the pressure of severe anxiety and primitive fears. The internalized part is limited mostly to self-punishment of a very sadistic, cruel, archaic nature. The contents of the ego ideal of borderline patients are still the primitive ideals of the little child, the fantasies of grandeur and omnipotence. A development toward adult morals and ethics is lacking or defective. Naturally, the interplay between the id and the defective ego and superego functions may cause further distortions of the ego ideal, and thus interfere with its normal functioning.

Delinquents

A special discordance of the superego and ego-ideal development is found in delinquents. In Chapter 10 I described some vicissitudes of the defective development of ideals and conscience. It is well known that delinquents often suffer from a severe, punishing superego, and that they often commit antisocial acts in order to satisfy their need for punishment. In many of these offenders we find a poorly developed ego ideal clinging to very primitive fantasies of grandeur. These pleasurable fantasies are retained in order to compensate for the pain experienced in the clash with the environment. The ego ideal has in principle preserved its original character as a wish-fulfilling agency. The superego in turn holds to its restricting and punishing function, though both are distorted and fail to function in an adequate way. The ego ideal's failure to provide real and adequate wish fulfillments creates new frustrations, which in their turn cause further regression to primitive fantasies of omnipotence.

These sketchy remarks on different developments, normal and abnormal, are necessarily oversimplified. We must never forget that the different stages of preoedipal development contribute to the genesis of the ego, the restricting superego, and the ego ideal. The archaic state of mind scarcely ever disappears completely. Even with minor disturbances an inharmonious growth of these agencies can come about. I have already mentioned that in approximately "normal" adolescence, disharmonies between the different parts and functions of the mind can be observed (Chapter 10). Within the ego-ideal functions proper, there may be unbalance as well. A person can have highly developed ideals and ethics in one area along with defective ones in other areas. One example out of many can be found in delinquency. A group of delinquents can adjust to a severe code of ideals within their own group while offending the ideals of the larger community and society. The same is valid for the restricting superego. Very severe demands and self-punishment in one area can exist side by side with refusal to accept inevitable restrictions in other fields, e.g., where property and interests of other people are concerned.

Summary

The ego ideal and the restricting superego originate alongside each other in primitive forerunners in infancy. They may be considered as special ego areas with their own functions. At the onset of the latency period they are centered around the parental images.

In harmonious development, they act together as a substructure within the ego organization, guiding the ego in its achievements. Throughout life the ego ideal remains essentially an agency of wish fulfillment. The superego is a restricting agency, necessary for living in a given community.

In abnormal development, traces of the origins of both ego ideal and superego can be observed as a consequence of fixations on and regressions to primitive developmental stages. The different identifications may be used as defense mechanisms in a pathological way and so add to the disharmony of the person.

25. On the Technique of Treatment of Female Neurotic Patients
Some remarks on the contributions of P.C. Kuiper and A. Mitscherlich

(1962)

P.C. Kuiper quotes as a rule that one should in psychoanalytic treatment pursue the life-history of the patient in reverse if possible. This quotation needs some clarification. The rule may be useful in many cases. However, this does *not* mean, that the analyst should or could be able to reconstruct and to make the patient relive and work through first the actual situation, then the adolescence, the latency period, later the oedipal- and the pre-oedipal period. That is often impossible. Experience shows, that material from the different periods of life can be used to ward off experiences from earlier or later periods. Two examples:

1. One often sees patients who already in the beginning of analysis tell about pre-oedipal experiences and conflicts, but without being able to really work them through. They use them unconsciously to keep far from becoming conscious of conflicts from later layers which are far stronger warded off and cathected with anxiety.
2. Many male patients show a marked masculine behavior and strong rivalry with father-images to ward off their passive feminine strivings. We interpret this behavior as pseudo-masculinity. The boy with male rivalry can only work through his real oedipal position after the anxiety for the passive sexual tie to the father has been solved.*

What was really meant, was that one should not be seduced to go deeply into the initial dreams and the early infantile material, which often breaks through in the first hours and weeks of analysis. The patient then is still very far from having an idea about the real meaning of this material. It should be taken as important information which gives the analyst some insight into the problems and the individuality of the patient. Then only one might try to find out what from the material can already be used for interpretation of content and what the patient needs and uses as a defence against the actual conflict.

Freud's still so very useful rule that one should go out from the present surface can be completed. Such a defence proces may be used as a defence of conflicts steming from totally different psychical layers, for instance from actual or puberal and latency periods.

As Kuiper in his contributions speaks mainly about the technique in the treatment of female patients, I will bring an example from the analysis of a young woman.

* See my article of 1952: Re-evaluation of the role of the oedipal complex, chapter 14.

The patient narrates in the first hours about the many boyish plays and romps she had during her fifth and sixth year of life. She narrates how she has always rivaled and romped with her two brothers – the one three years older, the second one and a half year younger – and how unhappy and angry she was that the older one could always beat her.

The young analyst interpreted this material as strong rivalry in relation to her (really intense) penis envy. The interpretation had of course only the result that the patient rejected the analyst with scorn and in a haughty manner. She reacted with silence during several hours now and then interrupted by scornful remarks. In the end the analyst said that at the moment she might not be too much concerned about her childhood and her brothers as worrying about some actual problems. She then confessed with great difficulty that she was very much concerned about her little five year old son. She loved him very much, however, she could not stand him. She had no idea at all how to educate him. At the same time he was the pride of herself and her much loved husband. A richness of much material from the present time followed. She told about the difficulty to give up her profession after marrying, about her mourning after the death of her idealized father, etc., etc.

The experiences from puberty were told, but without much affect or experiential quality. After a longer period she began to talk about her relation to her mother. At the age between six and ten she had rivaled very forcefully with her mother about the father's love. After a period of some months there followed material from the pre-oedipal phase and only after that some of her penis envy could be really talked about and experienced.

Only in the end it became possible to work through her stormy adolescence with real reexperiencing of her intensive affective mood swings.

The patient always uses material from one period of life to ward off conflicts from another period. Often it was far from easy to see what was defense and what the patient could really work through emotionally. Fortunally the gifted young colleague has learned gradually to the advantage of his patient and the analysis.

In surveying such a treatment one learns that though one needs certain rules, e.g. the one of interpreting defense before content, one should never rigidley adhere to a given rule. One should look at each patient as a unique individual and treat him accordingly. Flexibility of the analyst and an unprejudiced attitude toward each patient is the first condition for a constructive working-alliance.

Kuiper and A. Mitscherlich recommand another rule which to me seems very important, viz. to distinguish sharply between infantile passivity and sexual strivings with a passive aim. The latter form a condition for normal feminine love and sexual life. The satisfactions of the newborn are mostly of a passive nature. Strivings with an active aim can only be realized after a certain maturation of body and mind. This is the case for female as well as for male infants. The girl, however, should learn at the end of the phallic phase to subordinate her active sexual strivings to the passive ones. She has to surrender to the father as a love object in order to be able later on to have a harmonic adult love life.

In mature women, however, the kind of passive experience in the realm of the genital function has got other experiental qualities than the early infantile satisfaction of passive strivings can give.

It is quite right, as Kuiper stresses, that in boys a similar experience does not take place. In masculine adult sexual life active strivings should preponderate. However, we find the problem in the man in a somewhat different form. The infantile passive tendencies are used in healthy development in sublimated activities as well as in social relations as in various activities (work, creativity, etc.). When the strivings with a passive aim remain sexualized – or are secundarily again cathected with drive-energy – normal adult love life as well as work and creative activity are inhibited, or disturbed in another manner. In the man, too, passive tendencies from the early infantile period can find their very important place in normal development. The passive feminine sexual strivings, however, cannot be subordinated at the end of the phallic phase under the active ones and thus cannot be sublimated. They lead to pathological phenomena.

26. Symptom Formation and Character Formation

(1963)

To deal with this very broad topic in a single presentation seems impossible. It is not my intention to focus on one clinical constellation. Apart from theoretical reflection, there is a practical consideration, namely the fact that we hardly ever meet with a "simple" neurosis in our patients. I will therefore try to present a few aspects of the general theme. I do not intend to give a systematic presentation, and in order to make my points I shall elaborate upon themes not strictly falling under the title of this symposium.

It is true that Freud started his psychological investigations with hysterical patients. However, it soon became clear that most patients reveal a mixture of symptoms belonging to different neurotic pictures, for instance a combination of hysterical and obsessional-neurotic, of phobic and depressive constellations. Freud discovered that the foundation of obsessional neurosis was a childhood neurosis of the hysterical type, and established a close relationship between the symptoms of conversion hysteria and anxiety hysteria or phobia, as well as between those of phobias and obsessional neurosis. Moreover, in a number of cases that could be labeled as mainly hysterical neuroses we encounter character traits of a definite obsessional neurotic origin, and the reverse is encountered as well.

Other observations teach us that many patients cannot be classed in a special neurotic category. They show various disturbances: symptoms as well as inhibitions, depressive states, etc., which we usually term "neurotic disorders," not to mention those with more severe disturbances, such as borderline cases, psychotics, and delinquents. In the analysis of neurotic patients we often meet with psychotic mechanisms which manifest themselves, for instance, in a kernel of delusions. In addition, a mixture of symptoms and character distortions reveals itself in many cases.

In view of these various considerations, I intend to try to highlight some aspects of the processes involved in the genesis of symptoms and character traits, especially from the more recently developed structural-dynamic viewpoint. Before embarking on this endeavor, I want to point out a peculiarity of our topic. Symptom formation is a psychopathological phenomenon, whereas character formation is in itself a "normal" developmental process. However, as psychoanalysis has shown that there is an easy transition from "normality" to pathology, and that mental processes are more easily studied in the context of pathological phenomena, I will stick to the traditional line of using the manifestations of abnormal development in trying to describe some aspects of what may be termed a "normal" character formation and personality development.

Symptom formation

During the development of psychoanalysis, Freud used different terms for the description of symptom formation. I will cite a definition given in *Inhibitions, Symptoms and Anxiety* (1926, p. 91):

> The main characteristics of the formation of symptoms have long since been studied and, I hope, established beyond dispute. A symptom is a sign of, and a substitute for, an instinctual satisfaction which has remained in abeyance; it is a consequence of the process of repression. Repression proceeds from the ego when the latter – it may be at the behest of the super-ego – refuses to associate itself with an instinctual cathexis which has been aroused in the id.

Freud elaborates upon the subject in many very important directions. I mention only two of them.
(a) He points out that repression is only one of a variety of defense mechanisms, though it has a special place among them and a special relation to hysterical neuroses, without being the *only* mode of defense in this disease.
(b) He reconsiders the problem of anxiety, conceiving of it as an ego activity signaling a danger situation, from without as well as from within.
The first statement is an enlargement, the second a modification of former theories. Both have been of great significance for the stimulation of the development of ego psychology in more recent times.
When we now consider the coming into being of a symptom, we encounter Freud's early discovery of a conflict between the ego and an instinctual id impulse that cannot be satisfied. At that time the ego was conceived of as an entity opposing itself to the id because it had to mediate between the person's needs and the demands of the environment. In later periods Freud described the ego as an organization of different functions, and drew attention to the influence of the conflict on the ego organization. He spoke of an impoverishment, an impairment, a distortion, of the ego.
We often encounter the view that a conflict is a *pathological* phenomenon. I want to stress explicitly that conflict is a normal event in dynamics of living beings. It is inherent in the life process. Every creature experiences clashes with its environment which it has to cope with in order to preserve its own existence. In the highly differentiated and complicated structure of the human mind conflicts not only originate from an encounter with the environment, but to a great extent they take place between internal subareas. The process of development is centered around and stimulated by inner and outer conflicts. The decision whether a "normal" solution of a conflict is achieved or whether a symptom or some other pathological outcome finally emerges, depends upon the intactness of an ego capacity, the integrative or harmonizing ability. In Chapter 24 I called the original and basic function of the superego an agency of

restriction, that of the ego ideal an agency of wish fulfillment. I now want to add that I consider the basic function of the ego to be the synthetic or integrative one. The ability to achieve harmony is the outcome of a complicated process in ego development. A number of achievements are necessary in order to enable the ego to use the basic function in a satisfactory way. If the ego is capable of solving the conflicts, in synthesizing the different demands made upon the personality (the "self") from the inner as well as from the outer world, we speak of a "normal" psychic process. This means that the ego is able to allow the personality a sufficient satisfaction of instinctual and affective needs without disturbing the relation with the environment in agreement with superego and ego ideal demands and without impairing its (the ego's) own capacities. This is in accordance with the pleasure principle or its modified version, the reality principle. It does not mean that conflicts are eliminated forever from the mind. New conflicts continually arise, so that the integrative capacity has to come into action repeatedly. It is not a static but a dynamic process. Whether in a given situation harmony can be achieved through conflict-solving depends upon a number of factors, which can be brought under two headings: (a) the relative strength of the synthetic capacity (the economic aspect); (b) the mobility and the reversibility of the harmonizing process. The factors involved emerge from the different areas of the personality.

When we examine our patient's neurotic symptoms in the making, we observe an impairment of his synthesizing faculties. The patient starts by complaining of his symptoms, which he feels as alien intruders in his "self." He suffers from anxiety states, from obsessions, from depressive and other painful moods, and so on, which he is quite aware that he cannot escape. His incapacity to feel in harmony with his self is apparently a very painful experience. This state of mind does not imply that the capacity for integration is totally and forever eliminated; on the contrary, its working is apparent from the fact that in the long run the ego tries to integrate the symptoms into its organization. But it has failed to operate in a conflict-solving way. The conflict-causing id impulses had to be warded off (or repressed); they are now inaccessible to the ego, which is unable to influence them in any way. As the drive impulses constantly put pressure upon the ego demanding discharge, the latter agency must strengthen its anticathexis by using new defense mechanisms. The defensive procedures require energy that is withdrawn from other activities, including autonomous, ego-syntonic performances. The result is an inhibition, an impoverishment of the ego. A further consequence is a reduction of pleasure gain. A substitutive masochistic satisfaction from suffering and a secondary gain from illness are now the only modes of gratification available, so far as the diseased part of the personality is concerned.

Before turning to the examination of the defensive processes, the origin of the mechanisms of defense and their influence upon ego development, I want to indicate briefly the factors Freud made responsible for the failure to solve conflicts and to prevent neurotic conditions.

In analysis neurotic symptoms can invariably be traced back to an infantile neurosis. As the little child's ego organization is still in a state of immaturity, it is a "loose" and "feeble" agency which cannot deal appropriately with the demands of the drives. Drives and impulses are perceived as dangerous and have to be warded off. Anxiety is raised by the ego as a signal, indicating that a danger is present and that the ego has to take countermeasures. Though in principle a person can take refuge in "flight" before external dangers, such as oversevere demands and punishments, the child is too dependent upon his environment to do this. Therefore he has to undertake similar defensive action against both environmental and inner demands. When the parents' prohibitions have become internalized and laid down in the superego, the ego is still more intimately influenced by them and can take refuge exclusively in warding-off mechanisms. In connection with these facts Freud (1926) names three prominent factors that play a part in the causation of neuroses:

(a) A biological factor, the long period of helplessness and dependence during childhood.

(b) A phylogenetic factor, namely, the flourishing of the instinctual life in early childhood, followed by the interruption in the development of the drives during latency ("the biphasic onset of sexuality") which leads to a genuine incapacity for satisfaction of the needs and impulses in the first years of life.

(c) A psychological factor, the differentiation of the mental apparatus into id and ego (and superego), due to the necessity for dealing with the influence of the external world.

Here I would add that the third point (c) was later revised to show that the differentiation of id and ego is an inborn maturational factor affected and influenced by environmental stimuli.

I think we all adhere to Freud's statements when we examine the material presented to us by our patients. The three factors mentioned can help us to understand a good deal about the causation of symptoms, in so far as they explain the vulnerability of the child's mind. There are many children, however, who do not show neurotic symptoms in their first years of life or who "outgrow" their slight infantile neurosis and do not become neurotics in later life. We must therefore look for special factors which make for neurotic development or for "health." One important question is: What factors cause a lasting impairment of the ego's integrating capacity?

It is self-evident that we have to look for these factors among the three agencies of the structured mind and their dynamic interplay under the influence of the environment. Dynamics can only be understood when we consider genesis, course of development, and economic (quantitative) proportions. The magnitude of all these different relations is so confusing that we shall have to simplify by merely sketching some facets of the various processes.

Our knowledge is most advanced as regards the maturational process of the drives (the id). A smooth course for this process is certainly dependent on inborn peculiarities of the drives, for example their relative strength, which may lead to acting out and antisocial behavior, on the quantitative relationship between sexual and aggressive drives, their fusion and defusion, important in depressive and paranoid states, and perhaps on other factors, such as flexibility, rhythm, etc. However, the course of development is also strongly influenced by the attitude of the environment, by the way the mother responds to the infant's needs. The extent to which she is able to guide the development into favorable paths can be decisive.

The same is true with regard to the development of the ego functions and their organization into a structured part of the mind. Though psychoanalytic ego psychology has made great advances during recent decades (Hartmann, 1939a, 1950; Rapaport, 1958, and many others), it is still not far enough advanced to enable us to give an exact survey of the development of the different functions in chronological order. I will therefore limit myself to the description of some well-known facts and a few tentative suggestions.

Let us start by examining the "autonomous" ego functions (Hartmann, 1939a, 1950). Ego development is a maturational process dependent upon bodily growth as well as upon innate Anlage factors. At the same time it is a learning process influenced by the environment. The mother may stimulate the development of certain ego functions, as she stimulates drive development. On the other hand, she may hamper the developmental processes, in connection with peculiarities of her own personality and character, and her affective relationship with the child (see, e.g. Provence and Ritvo, 1961). The outcome can be a fortunate, smooth, as well as an uneven, disturbed growing up of the child.

We assume the mental ego to emerge from the "body schema" (or body ego) (Greenacre, 1960; Winnicott, 1960, et al.). According to Winnicott, the infant perceives his own body as a whole in the second half of the first year. So the basic function of synthesis is already present in the body ego at an early date, perhaps consequent on the binding, integrative tendency inherent in the life process. The differentiation between the self and the outer world probably begins in the first six months, though in a very incomplete way. Even when the child perceives his body as a whole, he still at times experiences a oneness with the mother. The newborn perceives stimuli from within as well as from without. So perception also is one of the first ego functions to develop. At what exact time memory traces begin to be laid down we do not yet know; probably as early as the first months.

Bodily sensations gradually give rise to motor activities, which develop into purposeful actions, e.g. crying, grasping, crawling, walking, etc. Memory traces, which in the beginning are laid down as images, begin to be connected with words after the child has learned to understand speech and gradually to use words himself, at the end of the first year and during the second. Learning starts with imitation. This is especially observable in the development of speech. Vocal communication without word symbols is present in the human infant as it is in the higher animals. But words can be learned only by *imitation*. In addition, connected with the *emotional* ties to the mother, the mechanism of identification begins to be used in the (normal) process of adaptation, precipitating the learning of speech as well as of other functions. Here we encounter an example of the mutual influence of emotional with autonomous ego development. During the first years of life a number of other adaptational mechanisms and

241

processes come into existence. The complexity of the different interrelationships makes the child's ego a vulnerable organization and often interferes with the process of integration. In addition, a complication arises when as an outcome of the oedipal situation the forerunners of superego and ego ideal are internalized into one substructure of the ego. In a "normal" case, however, we have to assume the existence of a basically integrated organization of the ego functions at the end of the oedipal phase. This does not, of course, mean that the learning (and developmental) processes have come to a standstill. Learning continues throughout life, and influences the dynamics of all vital processes. I now come back to the role of the ego in the various symptom formations.

During the preoedipal phase the growing, still "vulnerable" ego encounters a number of danger situations in which anxiety is experienced. "Dangers" come from the outer world in the shape of limitations of need satisfaction and of demands from the environment. They come from the internal world inasmuch as the child feels powerless to provide himself with sufficient satisfaction of needs. From the mother he fears punishment and loss of love; from the inner world it is the narcissistic injury of feeling powerless and threatened by id impulses that is experienced as an unbearable and inescapable danger. Now when the ego is not able to solve the conflict in a harmonious way, it has to take refuge in defensive measures, using several defense mechanisms.

We must, however, distinguish sharply between pathological neurotic defensive processes that lead to an inhibition and impairment of ego activities, and a sound conflict solution that may leave its imprint upon the ego, but without impairing the ego's autonomous functions (in the "conflict-free ego sphere," Hartmann). I suggest, therefore, the following formulation: If the capacity for integration *fails* to solve conflicts without damaging the ego, the impaired ego becomes unable to prevent several adaptation mechanisms from being drawn into neurotic defensive processes, and thus being employed as pathological defense mechanisms. The latter, then, may in their turn cause damage to the ego organization.

The following question here arises: What events are responsible for turning normal adaptation mechanisms into defense mechanisms, made use of in pathological processes? It may sometimes be difficult to decide whether we are dealing with a "normal" or a "pathological" process, because in a number of cases easy transition from a "healthy" to a "pathological" use of mental mechanisms is apparent. With hysterical symptoms, especially in conversion hysteria, a special defense mechanism, namely repression, is predominantly used. Is repression exclusively a pathological defense mechanism? We cannot confirm this. It is well known that (at least in our civilization) large parts of childhood experiences have become unconscious in persons whom we consider to be quite "normal." Memories are repressed. In hysterical neuroses, however, a number of autonomous ego functions have become involved and damaged; e.g., in hysterical conversion symptoms the employment of the motor apparatus may be paralyzed, or the sensorial functions are disconnected, in some instances perception is eliminated, etc. Furthermore, the symptoms cannot be removed without special measures in a treatment situation. Apparently the ego is using the mechanism of repression, which includes an anticathexis against the repressed impulses. It has not succeeded in mastering anxiety and danger situations sufficiently.

In phobias we encounter, among others, one special defense mechanism: avoidance. Do examples exist where we can consider avoidance of danger situations, signaled by anxiety, as a "sound" reaction? Apart from realistic dangers in the outer world which every "healthy" person will try to avoid, we encounter for example, persons living in special circumstances with whom certain id impulses, usually satisfied, have to be held in abeyance in consequence of these unusual circumstances. We do not call it pathological when the person in question avoids situations where these impulses are specially stimulated and apt to raise anxiety. All of us could give examples of such events, e.g. during wartime. In these cases, however, the avoidance remains restricted to the special situation, and as soon as the abnormal circumstances have ceased to exist, the avoidance will be removed also. Here too the mechanism served an adaptational process; it proved to be reversible, and did not involve other ego functions in a permanently damaging way. The phobic patient cannot give up the avoidance; in trying to do so, he is overwhelmed by anxiety and unable to have any kind of sound ego activity. Here, too, we have to assume an additional countermeasure against the id impulses from the side of the ego, that fixates the avoidance and makes it irreversible. The anti-cathecting activity of the ego is most clearly observable in obsessional neurotic symptoms (Freud, 1926). The immediate cause of this disease is the same as in hysteria, and exists in impulses of the oedipal situation which cannot be mastered by the ego. As repression does not succeed in keeping the drive impulses unconscious, according to Freud either because the genital drive organization was too feeble or because the ego began the struggle against the drives prematurely, namely during the anal-sadistic phase, the ego takes refuge in a number of other methods of warding off. First regression takes place, and impulses and fantasies now reveal themselves in an anal-sadistic shape. The ego defends itself against them with an anticathexis, e.g. in the form of reaction formations. Under continual pressure of the id the ego has to produce ever more defensive actions, using such mechanisms as turning against the self, isolation, undoing, denial, etc. Many of the defensive actions are initiated by a severe superego and serve self-punishment. In serious compulsion neuroses more and more ego functions become gradually involved and damaged. The impoverishment of the ego is partly a secondary result of the struggle with the id. But the ego not only *opposes* the id, it also *participates* in the regressive process, and thus falls back upon earlier, more primitive modes of action. This is clearly observable in a regression toward magic thinking and magical acting out. Removal of severe obsessional neurotic symptoms belongs to lengthy psychoanalytic work, and in many cases the symptoms prove to resist any recovery, especially when intellectual understanding of mental connections is isolated from emotional experiences and intellectualization is used in the defensive processes. We know that many of the reaction formations represent exaggerations and distortions of character traits. Cleanliness, orderliness, and economy are reaction formations against the pleasurable impulses to smear, to mess, and to waste. They are considered "normal" and valuable qualities. As we have already described character formation as a "normal" process, we have to look for the boundaries between "normal" and pathological reaction formations. I will come back to this point when embarking upon the study of character formation. Before doing so, I want to examine some more defense mechanisms. Apart from regression and reaction formation, we encounter, in obsessional neurotics, *isolation* and *undoing*. Isolation is a mental mechanism that finds its place in normality, e.g. in thought processes. Logical and scientific thinking has to isolate thought and to eliminate affect-laden representations ("wishful thinking") from abstract ideas. For abstract thinking neutralized energy is necessary; in wishful thinking drive-cathected energy is employed. Thus the two modes of thinking have to be separated, isolated from each other. Here too, however, the process (of isolation) can be abandoned at will, whereas in neurosis it has become rigid and unalterable. The same is valid for "undoing." "Healthy" people often consider an action, as well as a thought which is a trial action, as unjust, whereupon they will try to undo it by a counteractivity. In our neurotic patients the process of undoing has acquired a compulsive character, and is maintained in situations where it is no longer realistic and appropriate. With paranoid symptoms we encounter identification and projection as defense mechanisms. Both are "normal" adaptive methods in their origin. We have already mentioned the important role of identification in learning processes, as well as in mastering emotional situations. Projection is a "normal" way of dealing with unpleasurable sensations in the infant, and it promotes the distinction between self and outer world. In delusions, however, both mechanisms have become fixated, unchangeable models of reaction.

In defensive actions the ego may also make use of certain vicissitudes of the instinctual drives which come into existence in the course of development. The "turning inward" of drive impulses is a natural occurrence in the formation of the superego, when aggression is internalized. The process promotes adjustment to the environment. In pathological cases, however, the result is not a better adaptation but a masochistic mode of behavior in consequence of a strong need for self-punishment. Here quantitative factors are decisive. Reversal of drive impulses, e.g., from activity to passivity and vice versa, is continually occurring. The ego makes use of it in a number of adaptational processes. In learning, for example, a passive surrender to the objects and to verbal or written instruction is necessary. The constructive assimilation of what is learned needs a good deal of activity. Fixation of the one or the other tendency leads to pathology. Sublimation or neutralization of drives providing energy for a number of ego achievements is of special importance in many respects. I will return to this point later.

In summary, we may say: Adaptation mechanisms can be employed in neurotic symptoms as (pathological) defense mechanisms. We have to consider the outcome of the process as "health" if the mechanisms are made use of by ego activities in a flexible and changeable way. They belong to pathological phenomena if the process has become fixed and irreversible.

So far we have described merely neurotic disorders (the so-called transference neuroses). We assume that in these neuroses ego development has advanced more or less "normally" until the time of solution of the oedipal complex. In connection with traumatic events (e.g. an overwhelming castration anxiety) a danger situation emerges, resulting in a neurotic defensive attitude on the part of the ego. The formation of symptoms is the outcome of this struggle, together with an inhibition of ego functions. A *secondary* consequence may be regression of ego functions to points of arrest in earlier developmental stages. Symptoms are signs of and substitutes for instinctual satisfaction. This is above all apparent in compulsive actions which can, for example, be substituted for masturbatory acts. Furthermore, the pleasure principle reveals itself in a secondary gain of illness, in a narcissistic satisfaction by rationalization, magical thinking, and in fantasies of omnipotence, etc. The curtailed synthetic capacity comes to the fore in the attempt to incorporate the symptoms secondarily into the ego organization. But often the reverse takes place. Then the ego is secondarily drawn into the sphere of conflicts, sometimes under the impact of a severe superego, and it is invested with drive energy. The result is a paralysis of many of the ego functions including the harmonizing capacity, so that the ego can no longer mediate between the different demands from id, superego, and environment.

Character formation

In the introduction I recalled the fact that psychoanalytic theory has developed out of the study of ailments in our neurotic patients. Though character formation is a "normal" process in itself, I will keep to the line of including the influence of psychic disorders in our study of the development of character. I have already mentioned the reaction formations leading to a compulsive character that shows distortions of "normal" character traits. This is obvious in the case of exaggerated cleanliness, orderliness, and economy (the so-called "triad of compulsion neurosis"). Earlier, Freud described these qualities as reactions against anal drives which in "normal" development are methods of adaptation to the educational demands of the environment. They are called anal character traits. Similar processes find a place in connection with oral and urethral impulses. Outcomes of them are seen in certain qualities of well-adjusted persons, e.g. in eloquence, based upon oral tendencies, in productive ambition, developing out of urethral strivings, etc. In neurotic patients in whom the ego has failed to solve the anxiety-provoking conflicts in a harmonious way, the qualities become over-emphasized and rigid with more or less damage to other ego functions, including autonomous ones. There are, however, other factors to be examined. Since we see "character" as the usual (habitual) way in which a person deals with the inner and the outer world (Fenichel, 1945) it is clear that it comprises more than the ego's reactions to id impulses alone; we have to consider the vicissitudes of the development of the ego organization as well. In the "conflict-free sphere" the ego's autonomous functions come into existence. To begin with, the *inborn* potentialities out of which the ego will develop determine to a great extent the outcome of the process of growth. The amount of intelligence, of capacities of perception, reality testing, thought processes, etc., and last but not least the power of neutralization and sublimation, are decisive factors. If one or more of these natural abilities is lacking (or too feeble), the evenness of ego growth will be disturbed and the integrative process is likely to be interfered with, though the synthetic function itself may be normal. But even with a favorable innate disposition opportunities may arise for a maldevelopment of the ego from the very beginning of life. The disturbances may come from within as well as from without. I have mentioned the influence of an unfavorable drive disposition upon the coming into existence of mental disturbances. Especially is a disproportion between sexual and aggressive drives likely to disturb the course of maturation of the id as well as of ego functions, even in the first years of life, in the pregenital stages. Furthermore, the environmental influence is very important, because the ego, like the id, develops in the interplay of the mother's mind with the infant's mind.

Again we start by looking at pathological phenomena. The "simple" (transference) neuroses originate mainly in the oedipal phase in connection with uncontrollable castration anxiety. The origins of the more severe disturbances, such as borderline cases, psychoses, delinquency, and even so-called character distortions, are to be found in the preoedipal phase, and particularly in an early arrest of ego development. When a motherly object is not available, or when the mother herself is very disturbed, the conditions for a healthy development of ego functions in the infant are lacking. The autonomous functions and the learning processes through imitation and identification are in need of an example as well as of stimulation by love, support, and understanding. The mother's love is equally (or even more) indispensable for the infant's learning to cope with id impulses. Too much frustration hampers the ego's growth, resulting in an arrest on primitive levels and an inadequate manipulation of the requirements of the drives. In entering upon the oedipal situation the ego functions are poorly organized, with the consequence that the strong demand for a solution of the oedipus complex and for mastering anxiety leads to an incomplete solution and sometimes to a total disintegration. When, for example, an arrest took place in the phase where the body schema began to be developed (that is, in the phase where the infant perceives his own body as a whole, as different from external entities), the function of distinguishing between self and outer world cannot be formed adequately. In schizophrenic patients we often observe representations of parts of their own bodies as being separate from other parts, as well as a fusion of the boundaries between the self and the object world. In other words, there is a kernel of confusion between self-representations and object representations, and the need to be "one" with the mother cannot be adequately dealt with. A mother who, clinging to the child, is unable to let him develop his own personality, will promote the arrest of the child's ego development at this point (Sandler, 1962). A very disturbed mother, confused, egocentric, distracted, or rapidly changing from love to hate, does not provide the child with a stable image for identification. Consequently, the development of delineated object representations will be defective. The confusion between self and object influences the function of reality testing. A number of other ego functions may be drawn into this pathological process as well. The development of motor actions is dependent upon bodily sensations, including passively experienced movements. A disturbed, unloving mother is unable to hold and to carry around her baby with loving attention (see Winnicott's "holding position" [1960]). This can lead to a lack of satisfaction in the motor sphere, resulting in a poor development of motility in the child.

The lack of a suitable object with which to identify impairs the development of ego activities that have to be learned, such as speech, grasping, walking. In the emotional sphere the child is in need of a loving mother in order to advance from a need-satisfying object relationship toward object constancy. In order to deal adequately with id impulses the ego has to be equipped with a sound self-esteem which can only develop normally if there is a firm object tie.

The lack of a satisfactory love relationship may lead us to an arrest of ego ideal development in the magical sphere, where the fantasies of grandeur and omnipotence have to compensate for the various frustrations. In some cases the advance from magical wishful thinking toward realistic logical thinking is never adequately made. When a child with a similar early disturbance of development enters the phallic phase, his ego will certainly be unable to find a more or less harmonious way of solving the many problems involved in the various vicissitudes of the oedipus complex. The defective ego organization is not able to master castration anxiety, and alongside the regression of the drives to pregenital stages the arrested ego functions will overaccentuate the archaic, untimely modes of behavior.

I have already pointed to the differences in the genesis of the classical (transference) neuroses on the one hand and the manifestations of borderline and psychotic disorders on the other (see Chapter 24). In the first ailments the process of organization of ego functions has proceeded in an approximately "normal" way until the oedipal situation. The regressive ego phenomena emerged as a *consequence* of the regression of drives and in connection with the defensive processes provoked by this instinctual regression. In the second conditions, the process of organization of ego functions never reached the level normally belonging to the phallic phase. The ego defects are therefore of a primary nature.

What, now, is the impact of early arrests in ego development upon the formation of a person's character? Our former definition of character as the habitual way of dealing with the inside and the outside worlds can be reformulated in view of recent ego psychology as follows: Character is the habitual way in which integration is achieved, that is, in which a person's ego solves conflicts with the internal world (id and superego), conflicts with the environment, and conflicts within its own organization (between its various functions and capacities).

It is clear that an unevenness in the development of the organizational process, an arrest of some functions and a "normal" course for others, must give rise to conflicts within the ego organization which cannot be solved in a harmonious way. In addition, therefore, to the pathological reaction to needs and instinctual tendencies, to superego and environmental demands, borderline and psychotic patients will show an evergrowing inconsistency in their ego organization, leading to irreversible splits within their egos. The result may be a chaotic ego in which no synthesis is achieved. As a consequence the development of a "habitual way of reacting" is impeded, and stable character traits cannot come into existence. If we still wish to speak of the "character" of these patients, we can designate it only as an unpredictable mode of behavior. A further complication is due to the poor, unequal development of the ego ideal which stops, at least partly, at the stage of unrealistic omnipotent fantasies, provoking magical behavior. In connection with the unstable object relations, the internalization of parental demands gives rise to precarious contents in the superego. But as the "free-floating" aggression that the immature ego was unable to master is incorporated into the superego, the superego can become very sadistic toward the self, with the remarkable outcome that one of the very few habitual reaction patterns in these patients is a rigid masochistic behavior. Processes that will normally be accomplished by ego functions with the use of neutralized energy are in the patients "sexualized" and "aggressivized," that is, invested with deneutralized drive energy. In summary, pathological character formation could be classified under two main headings:

(1) Neurotically diseased persons show distorted character traits in consequence of defensive processes in which anticathexis and reaction formations have produced rigid and irreversible behavior patterns owing to a secondary regression toward stages in ego development of a primitive nature.

(2) Psychotic and borderline patients present a failure of character formation as a consequence of early arrests in ego maturation which could never be passed over and a primary defect in the organization of ego functions, ego ideal, and superego contents.

I want to stress once more that this grouping under two headings is made for the purpose of presentation. In practice we meet with transitions between the various phenomena. Neurotics, for example, may show psychotic mechanisms; obsessional neurotic patients may reveal paranoid traits, delusional and projective processes, etc.; psychotics may start with neurotic disturbances, and they may continue to employ neurotic mechanisms alongside psychotic reactions, depending on the different stages of development the various functions may have reached.

Let us now turn to the question of how we are to envisage the course of events that leads to the molding of a "healthy" character. So far I have placed the words "normal" and "healthy" in quotation marks. It is often said that normality and health are arbitrary concepts. This is certainly true in connection with the moral judgment of a person's behavior. In a given society or group of persons a certain line of conduct can be evaluated as "normal" or "healthy," whereas in another community it may be judged very "abnormal" and "sick." But from a scientific point of view we have, I think, to follow a different line. We speak of bodily health when the various organs of the body function in such a way that stimuli from inside as well as from outside can be assimilated and vital processes are not disturbed.

In psychology I think we should consider a person to be in psychic health when the different areas of the mind have reached a cooperation leading to optimum mental functioning. As the ego is the structured part of the mind that has the disposal of the capacities of action upon stimuli (needs) from the inside as well as upon stimuli (demands) from the environment, we have to look at the nature of the ego organization, and especially at the disposition of its synthesizing capacity, in order to decide between mental health or sickness.

"Character," being the habitual way of dealing with inner and outer worlds, is a property of the ego. "Habitual" implies some kind of constancy in a person's reaction patterns. We know, however, that life is not a static condition. Life processes involve change and fluctuations. The maturational processes reach a certain equilibrium (steady state) in adulthood, but they never come to a complete stop. Learning continues throughout life. Conflicts with the environmental demands and between the different substructures within the personality belong to the ordinary life processes. Therefore the ego organization and its synthesizing capacity have to possess some flexible qualities. We have already said that both id and ego develop out of inborn potentialities. The organization of the various ego functions gradually comes into existence in interplay with the drives in their maturational stages and with the simultaneous object relationships. Therefore character traits, though dependent upon innate qualities are largely the outcomes of adaptational processes. They represent the various adaptation mechanisms, among them reaction formations against id impulses. In addition, character formation develops in interaction with the objects, through imitation and identification. (I want to stress the fact that the concept of "adaptation" includes an active change of the environment whenever such an influence is appropriate and within the person's power.)

As the adaptational processes are in need of a certain amount of constancy in order to function well, we again come upon the fact that a harmonious development requires both constancy *and* mobility. In what way is this seemingly contradictory state of affairs to be achieved? We may compare the state of mind with the oscillation of a pendulum. The central point is to be found in the nature of the ego's synthesizing capacity. Its constancy is to be found in the well-known automatisms based upon innate factors, and developed during growth. When conflicts (from within or from without) arise, the ego is alarmed by signal anxiety and an integrating action is initiated. If a harmony or adaptation cannot be achieved, some defensive actions are provoked; regression, for example, can take place. But when it remains "regression in the service of the ego" (Kris, 1952) it will be only temporary. If the ego has at its disposal enough knowledge of the factors involved in the conflict (of demands from the id, from the environment, and from the superego as well as from the ego ideal), and if it has the power to master the different demands, the pendulum will swing from the one side (regression) back to the central point. Perhaps it will temporarily swing to the other side (a defensive compensation), but in the course of time the central point will again be reached. This means that a new equilibrium is achieved. Of course this description applies to an "ideal" concept of a "healthy" character. In practice this ideal will seldom be found. But slight deviations do not impair the person's performances and his well-being, and do not seem to be appreciable. However, an arrest in the pendulum on the one side or the other will cause disturbances of the integrative process, the flexibility having been abolished. Instead of describing more reactions and mechanisms subject to oscillations, I will now summarize as follows: it is a question of quantity (intensity) and of reversibility that decides whether a healthy or a pathological character development will take place. In other words, it evidently depends upon the intensity and the nature of the *energy* involved.

As the character develops in connection with the simultaneous interplay of ego and id, and as mental energy stems, at least largely, from the drives, we have to examine once more the conflicts involved in this interplay. Intensity of energy employed in adaptation and defense is correlated with the intensity of the drive demands in their maturational stage. Regarding the nature of the energy employed, it is decisive whether enough neutralized energy is available for the ego to build up its autonomous functions and to adjust to inner and outer worlds. I think the process of neutralization is dependent upon an inborn nature of the drives, but at the same time also upon an ego quality. This is most clearly seen in sublimation, an adaptation mechanism *par excellence*. Sublimated activities are performed with the use of neutralized energy, but they can only come into existence if the ego has specific talents and properties at its disposal. Logical, scientific thinking requires a special ego ability; artistic performances come about only if the ego possesses enough of the necessary talent.

When a person is gifted with a strong capacity to neutralize drive energy and at the same time with great talents and ego abilities, we may expect him to reach a high degree of integration. It often happens, however, that very talented people are subject to a rigid drive constitution which does not allow for much neutralization. In these cases the development of the ego is impaired in spite of its original gifts, with the result that no synthesis is achieved. The talents and abilities originally present shrivel up. A reduced personality emerges with neurotic symptoms and/of neurotic, rigid character traits. This is especially observable in cases with a lack of congruence between sexuality and aggression, that is, with exceptionally strong aggressive drives. In the struggle against aggression, there cannot be enough energy neutralized, and the surplus of free aggression is internalized into the superego. The sadistically deformed superego demands self-punishment and more restriction of pleasurable activities. It counteracts the development of the person's talents and of many other ego capacities. The rigidity of the masochistic character is well known, and does not need further exposition.

On the other hand, we often encounter a relatively poor ego equipment, and here the main cause for a disturbed development lies in the ego's incapacity to deal with the id, even when the distribution of the drives is not an unequal one. A variety of outcomes is possible, and transitions from a slight unevenness in some ego areas to total inhibitions of nearly every ego activity are observed.

I want to point once more to the fact that the concept of "health" does not cover the concept of "valuable performances." "Health" designates a state of mobile equilibrium of the psychic apparatus. It is a scientific concept and not applicable in a system of values. An interesting example is genius. A man of genius is gifted with great talents, with a high ability to neutralize energy, and with a flexibility of mental mechanisms. But he reveals a strong tendency to conflict. Integration can be achieved in the areas of his creative activities. In other areas of the personality, however, the conflict-solving synthesis may have failed. Here highly valued performances may go together with neurotic symptoms and/or character distortions.

As I cannot do justice to all the vicissitudes and outcomes of the various processes touched upon in this paper, I will present the following:

Conclusions

(1) Conflicts are normal manifestations in the processes of life.

(2) Conflicts stimulate development whenever a person is able to solve them without damaging his integrity.

(3) The solution of conflicts is one of the activities of the ego organization.

(4) The outcome of this solution depends upon a number of factors constituting the synthetic or harmonizing ability.

(5) The nature of this integrative capacity is decisive for a "healthy" as well as for a pathological result.

(6) The capacity to synthesize develops out of innate properties in connection with the other ego functions, in interplay with the development of the instinctual drives, and influenced by object relationships, by the environment at large, as well as by the nature of superego and ego ideal. In connection with object relations, identification is of special importance for the development of ego faculties.

(7) The properties of the instinctual drives, the distribution of libido and aggression, and especially the amount of possible neutralization (sublimation), have a strong bearing upon the final outcome of ego and personality development.

(8) Equally important for a harmonious growth is the ego's capacity to make use of neutralized energy in developing qualities in the conflict-free sphere and to undertake sublimated activities.

(9) Pathology emerges when the integrative process fails; neurotic symptoms are formed when the ego, in conflict with the id, cannot synthesize id impulses and the demands of superego and environment without the pathological use of defense.

(10) Character traits are formed as precipitates of mental processes. They originate in innate properties; they come into existence in the mutual interplay of ego, id, superego, and ego ideal, and the influence of object relations and environment.

(11) "Healthy" character traits allow the ego's synthesizing capacity to oscillate around a central point representing the character constancy. The

251

oscillations express the mobility of the character and permit of change and reversibility.

(12) "Pathological" character traits are exaggerations and distortions of a "normal" character; they are rigid and irreversible, and may lead to a hardening of the impaired ego organization and its various functions.

27. Superego, Ego ideal, and Masochistic Fantasies

(1963)

In this presentation I shall try to elaborate and enlarge on a few points made in previous papers. In Chapter 5 I raised the question what factors play a role in the persistence with which many patients cling to masochistic masturbation fantasies and moral masochistic behavior. In this connection I stressed the importance of narcissistic injuries inherent in the castration complex and penis envy. At that time (1937) I was concerned mainly with the drive manifestations. The essence of my point was that the pain of narcissistic injuries was more intolerable than the suffering from masochistic behavior and fantasies. I illuminated this point by citing the little girl's fantasy, originating in the phallic phase in connection with her penis envy: "I was once in possession of a penis; however I was deprived of it as a punishment for having masturbated." Apparently, masochistic satisfaction compensates for the narcissistically painful idea of having been inferior from the very beginning of life. I gave a few examples of male patients with a strong masochistic attitude in whom the idea − sometimes arising in connection with circumcision − of having an inferior genital organ in comparison with adults or older boys had led to a similar narcissistic wound. In addition, I pointed to the fact that after the establishment of the superego agency, guilt feelings and the need for self-punishment came into action, demanding suffering and reinforcing masochistic behavior. However, at that time I did not go into this problem any further, not yet being aware of the subtle differentiations within the ego and superego organizations.

At the present time our knowledge of the structuring of the mind has deepened, and I think we can enlarge our understanding of masochistic behavior and fantasies also by studying the phenomena from the viewpoint of ego psychology and the differentiation between ego ideal and superego proper.

In Chapter 24 I described the ego ideal as an agency that originally serves narcissistic wish fulfillment, with ideals developing out of wishful thinking and fantasies of grandeur and omnipotence. The superego was regarded essentially as an agency of restriction, originating from a lack of immediate need satisfaction, followed by the acceptance of environmental demands and curtailments. In addition, I pointed out that the contents of both ego ideal and superego are centered on the parental images during the oedipal phase. In this period ideals may be briefly described as: "I want to be like my parents" (as omnipotent as I imagine them to be). The superego imposes on the child compliance with parental demands: "I *must* behave as my parents want me to." The consequence of this centralizing process is not only that at the end of the oedipal phase both ego ideal and superego grow together into one substructure of the ego organization, but also that the functions of both agencies become strongly influenced by each other. The fantasies of the oedipal phase, latency, and even more those of adolescence bear the imprint of this mutual interplay.

Fantasies are mental products which compensate for unavoidable deprivations in life. Instinctual impulses can be satisfied directly only to a limited degree. Sexual as well as aggressive tendencies can find a certain discharge in masturbation or masturbatory equivalents during childhood and adolescence. However, the accompanying psychic needs have to find an outlet in fantasies as long as an adult love life with a partner is not yet available. This state of affairs is responsible not only for limited instinctual satisfaction, but may also cause narcissistic injuries at the same time. The experience of being powerless to fulfill sexual needs to a full extent hurts the person's self-love and self-esteem and may reinforce inferiority feelings connected with the little girl's wish for a penis and with the boy's idea of having too small a genital. Simultaneously, oedipal wishes and rivalry have produced conflicts, anxiety, and guilt feelings. Fantasies of grandeur that are to compensate for the feeling of powerlessness and inferiority become intermixed with the need for self-punishment in connection with guilt. Therefore, fantasies in latency and adolescence often reveal drive satisfaction mingled with punishment and pain. They result in sadomasochistic (masturbatory) fantasies, and sometimes in masochistic acts and behavior. In a patient suffering from masochistic perversions it is quite clear that being beaten, humiliated, or tormented provides him with masochistically deformed drive satisfaction. Usually this holds true only as long as the suffering does not go beyond a certain limit, though in very disturbed patients, such as many psychotics, the damage done to their own bodies and the accompanying masochistic excitement can rise to an astonishingly high level. The problem of masochistic pleasure gain is not yet fully understood, as Freud repeatedly stressed. Where no perversion is present and the situation of being beaten or tormented is merely fantasied, the imagined suffering can reach a great height as well. Yet this is less surprising than the actual self-mutilations of some psychotics.

Nevertheless, we feel entitled to wonder whether guilt feelings, the need for punishment on the part of the superego, and the attempt to deny the idea of having an "inferior" genital apparatus can sufficiently explain the origin of and the clinging to masochistic fantasies. We may ask whether other factors and modes of satisfaction may not be involved, especially when we see masochistic fantasies continuing to exist in our patients during analytic treatment even after the oedipal guilt feelings have diminished or been removed. Moreover, while the idea of a person's clinging to masochistic pain-pleasure to avoid the greater evil of a narcissistic hurt is descriptively valid, it still does not afford a satisfactory explanation of the tenacity with which masochism is retained.

It is my belief that the additional factor is to be found in part in the intermingling of the superego's demands for punishment with the ego ideal's fantasies of grandeur and superiority. Even if the latter feelings are not contained in the wording of the fantasy, the person may unconsciously derive a strong narcissistic satisfaction from them.

Here we have one of the causes that make the masochistic fantasy so persistent and sometimes so resistant to therapeutic influence. If we do not take our patient's communication of his masochistic fantasies at face value, but continue the analysis of those fantasies after bringing to consciousness their sexual and self-debasing meanings, we invariably come upon ideas of self-glorification. It is striking to observe how strongly many patients struggle against the unveiling of their fantasies of grandeur. It often happens that a patient renounces his resistance to oedipal strivings and the connected anxiety and guilt feelings, only to retire behind a nearly unconquerable stronghold of defense, so as to cling to his fantasies of self-aggrandizement. The patient feels himself to be a *unique, exalted person, an exception, superior to his fellow men, a martyr*. These ideas supply him with narcissistic gratification. *The tendency to experience punishment and suffering has become one of the patient's ideals,* his original ideals of being powerful and grand having been deformed into those of being pitiful and grand − *grand in martyrdom.* The severe superego has by now influenced the ego ideal and caused a distortion of its contents.

The first impression on examining masochistic patients might lead to the view that the ego ideal had completely given up its function of wish fulfillment because of the patient's loud and alarming complaints. However, as we have already seen, the idealization of his sufferings is a *hidden* but sometimes *strong source* of gratification. We might say that ideals that normally procure positive, constructive achievements, when guiding the ego in its actions, lead in these patients to negative, unproductive activities. In German we would say that he has become a *Tiefstapler* rather than a *Hochstapler* (a negative rather than a positive swaggerer).

Nevertheless, both forms provide satisfaction, although in the masochist the satisfaction is mixed with distress and pain.

A second mode of influence which a severe, punishing superego may exert on the ego ideal is to impart a compulsive quality to the ideals, which then become imperative demands. In such a case, the idea "I *want* to be as good and powerful as my parents" is replaced by "I *must* be as grand and almighty as my parents." The narcissistic pleasure gain of the fantasy of grandeur is now mixed with the unpleasurable feeling of having to yield to force, of being "unfree." The compulsive quality may now override the pleasurable experience of having a free choice of ideals.

Here I wish to make a point: the question whether a human being is a "free creature," whether a "free will" exists, has occupied the minds of philosophers throughout man's history. I do not intend to go into philosophical questions. It is undeniable that the forces of nature and the necessities of life limit man's freedom to experience pleasure and happiness. What I have in mind here is that the process of mental growth − in this case the development of gratification-providing ideals out of primitive fantasies of grandeur − is inhibited or disturbed by the interaction with a severe, sadistic, compulsive superego which makes for the feeling of inner unfreedom. That this neurotic process is either

the consequence of or attendant upon a drive regression toward earlier developmental states is a well-known fact.

The mutual influence of superego and ego ideal revealed in masochistic
manifestations comes to the fore in latency and still more clearly in adolescent
fantasies and behavior, as I have already mentioned (see also Chapter 23). In
psychoanalytic literature we find a wealth of descriptions of sadomasochistic
fantasies and fantasies of grandeur and omnipotence. The most beloved books
of many children in latency and prepuberty deal with tortured heroes and
martyrs, and we know how strongly their ardent readers identify with these
heroes. From both a theoretical and a practical point of view, I think it is
important to realize the genesis of the intermingling of those two kinds of
fantasies in the mutual influence of primitive ideals and the need for
punishment.

When we analyze the fantasies of adolescent patients or adults who are emotionally still in adolescence, we are impressed by the fact that it is just the
narcissistic gratification of the distorted ideals that makes the patient cling so
tenaciously to his masochism. The erotic pleasure derived from his surrender to
the torturers (originally parental figures by whom the child imagines he is loved
if he submits to punishment and pain) is generally easier to bring to consciousness and release from its pathological outlet than the narcissistic satisfaction of
being a great sufferer and a grand martyr. Whether one can succeed in freeing a
patient from these primitive ideals of heroic suffering, allowing them to develop
into attainable ideals which may provide realistic gratification, depends upon a
number of factors, of which I shall later mention three. First, I wish to present
some illustrations of my points from clinical material.

It is remarkable to note that we do not only encounter fantasies of grand
martyrdom in severely disturbed patients. We may find them in comparatively
"healthy" persons as well. I was much impressed by the highly significant role of
these fantasies in the mental make-up of a young man who was very successful
in his work. His marriage provided sexual satisfaction. However, he felt unable
to love and appreciate his wife as a human being of equal merit, as a real
companion for life. The patient was an ambitious, highly trained chemist,
suffering from strong rivalry with his colleagues. He developed a state of
excitement and anxiety whenever he had to demonstrate his capacities in
lectures or chemical experiments, though he was highly appreciated and praised
by his superiors. He could not escape a feeling of worthlessness and the
conviction of being a failure each time he stood before an audience. However,
once he had started his performance, everything would go well and he was very
successful.

A number of factors connected with his suffering came to the fore, such as
anxiety and guilt feelings related to his exhibitionistic tendencies; a strong need
for punishment; a fear of passive wishes to surrender to his employer; guilt
resulting from rivalry and death wishes toward his competitors; a wealth of
sadomasochistic masturbation fantasies; some anal character traits, etc. The
patient had been an only child until his tenth year of life, when a sister was born.
He had been strongly attached to both parents. His sister's birth had aroused a

considerable amount of rage and fury as a reaction to his jealousy and feeling of being rejected in favor of the baby. At the same time, he was very envious of his mother, who had produced a child, a performance he himself would never be able to achieve. During the analysis of this material, there was an improvement in his relationship to his wife, who had borne him three children, and he could be much more tender to her after he understood how strongly he had unconsciously been competing with her and his colleagues. But the anxiety states connected with his work did not subside. We had touched upon fantasies of omnipotence which had originated in early childhood. The patient remembered a strong desire to be grown up in order to be as omnipotent as he imagined both parents to be. However, he could not re-experience these fantasies emotionally. Only after many years of analysis did we discover the cause of his lack of emotion. Part of his fantasies were deformed in a masochistic way. He was no longer the almighty hero who could perform everything he wanted; instead, he imagined himself to be a poor, inferior, worthless, but suffering little child. However, he was an exception, different from any other child, and a grand martyr. This deformation of his fantasies of grandeur was due in part to an identification with his mother, who suffered from many fears and displayed self-pitying, masochistic behavior; in part it was the outcome of his inner ambivalence, later reinforced by guilt feelings and a need for punishment, and acted out in his relations to colleagues and superiors. Fortunately, the adult patient had been able to prevent a considerable part of his talents and abilities from being drawn into the masochistic behavior. He usually could master the compulsion to act out his martyr fantasies before really embarking upon his pursuits. Apparently, some of his ideals had developed into a mature striving for constructive productivity, others had persisted in (and regressed to) an infantile idealization of martyrdom. It was precisely this primitive area of his personality that was responsible for his inhibitions and anxieties.

The various processes described were vicissitudes of the patient's neurotic development, which I shall not discuss in detail. What is relevant to our theme is the nature of the patient's ego ideal, which to some extent regressed to a point of arrest in his early childhood development. In the preoedipal phase the child produces fantasies of omnipotence as a reaction to the narcissistic injuries caused by feelings of powerlessness and inferiority. In this patient, who had been alone with his parents for so long and who had always competed with them, these fantasies were deformed masochistically. Not being able to be "grown up" and as powerful as his parents, he had tried to protect his self-esteem (narcissism) by imagining himself to be a "grand" martyr. The ideal of martyrdom became part of his ego ideal. The *compulsive* character of this ideal was due to the influence of guilt and a severe superego. The very fact that a number of ego functions and some of his ideals had remained outside the neurotic development proved to be decisive for the patient's relative "health" and the final analytic success in mastering the infantile residues in his personality.

Unfortunately, not all cases follow a similarly favorable course in analytic treatment. I can think of another, equally intelligent and gifted male patient, who suffered from a more severe work inhibition, although in many life situations he apparently acted quite normally. His work disturbance proved to be a result of distorted ideals similar to those cited in the previous example. In addition to numerous guilt feelings and acts of self-punishment analysis revealed fantasies of grandeur deformed into the idea of being a "grand martyr." They were covered up, however, by the notion that all people besides himself were worthless and inferior. These notions had acquired a nearly delusional character. They were used as a defense against the distorted ideals of his being an exceptionally grand martyr, and may be considered another part of a "personal delusion" described by me in Chapter 8. There I drew attention to an observation made about individuals who functioned normally in several areas of life but who harbored deeply hidden ideas of being rejected and hated by their environment. At the present time I consider these imaginings to be only part of the delusional system. They are reversals of fantasies about other people being inferior and worthless, fantasies which in turn are used to hide the deeper layer of megalomanic "grand martyr fantasies." This patient succeeded only incompletely in mastering his delusional ideals. A core of them retained the delusional aspect, coming to the fore time and again, continuing to exist, and resisting every therapeutic influence.

We encounter these phenomena in female patients as well. At first glance we might be tempted to expect them to be of even greater significance because the little girl's feelings of inferiority are based on the anatomical fact that her genital is inside her body and not visible from the outside, as is the boy's organ. Her wish for a penis is the consequence of a biological datum that underlies her psychic reaction of feeling inferior and is "rock-bottom," as Freud pointed out in "Analysis Terminable and Interminable" (1937). However, we must take into account the fact that normal femininity requires surrender to a male partner and that feminine ideals do not necessarily have to cling to fantasies of grandeur and superiority. Only in so far as the active, masculine part of her personality is concerned, does a woman need fantasies of grandeur similar to men's. In female patients with a strong masculinity complex we do, as a matter of fact, come upon omnipotent fantasies comparable to those of men. I can remember a young woman who displayed an abundance of ideas about being inferior, worthless, and incapable of any achievement in spite of her intelligence and her professional standing. It was nearly impossible to convince her that fantasies of grandeur were hidden behind her self-depreciation. In defending herself against these (masochistically distorted) omnipotent ideas, she behaved as if she were feeble-minded. Finally, she could consider the possibility that fantasies of being a "grand martyr" were present in the hidden depths of her personality. However, she never succeeded in mastering them adequately and a core of a distorted ego ideal and some disturbed ego functions continued to exist.

I now want to re-examine a fantasy of one of the two women patients discussed in Chapter 1. At that time (1927) I wished to draw attention to the developmental stages of little girls prior to the establishment of the positive oedipal complex, the feminine attachment to the father. Some years earlier Freud had shown that this father relationship was initiated by the castration complex; that is, the little girl's discontent with her genital apparatus and her desire for a penis made her turn to a passive love for her father, the penis wish being replaced by a longing for a child from him. In my 1927 paper, I was able to demonstrate a still earlier developmental stage in which the little girl loves her mother actively and strives to possess her in a way similar to that of the little boy. This is the period in which the little girl has not yet accepted her own genital and the lack of a penis, and still believes that one will grow. In other words, the female negative oedipus complex precedes the castration complex, which in its turn initiates the positive oedipus situation. The negative form corresponds to the phallic stage of the preoedipal phase of development, the preoedipal mother attachment as it was called by Freud later on.

I return now to the fantasy of the young girl mentioned above. Her life history revealed a number of events, re-experienced in part in the transference situation, which seemed to prove the point in question. It came to the fore with particular clarity in a fantasy (Freud, 1919). Between her eight and tenth years of life my patient produced what she called her "hospital fantasy." I cite from my previous paper:

> The gist of it [the hospital fantasy] was as follows. A large number of patients went to a hospital to get well, but they had to endure the most frightful pains and tortures. One of the most frequent practices was that they were flayed alive. The patient had a feeling of shuddering pleasure when she imagined their painful, bleeding wounds. Her associations brought recollections of how her younger brother sometimes pushed back the foreskin of his penis, whereupon she saw something red, which she thought of as a wound. The method of cure in her fantasy was therefore obviously a representation of castration. She identified herself on one occasion with the patients, who at the end always got well and left the hospital with great gratitude, but generally she had a different role. *She was the protecting, compassionate Christ, who flew over the beds in the ward in order to bring relief and comfort to the sick people.*

The patient's further associations affirmed that the identification with Christ in the hospital fantasy depicted her possessive love for her mother, Christ having been born "without a father" and therefore being his mother's sole possessor. The idea of being her mother's lover was followed by castration (Christ's crucifixion), that is, by the patient's acceptance of the lack of a penis, leading then to a passive love for and surrender to the (God) father. The detail of flying around the ward is symbolic of masturbation.

In re-examining this fantasy now, we are immediately struck by the form it took. Alongside the sadomasochistic pleasure gain in the sphere of the instinctual drives, it provided the patient with a narcissistic gratification in the glorification of the self. It is a fantasy of grandeur *par excellence*. Apparently, it has to compensate for the narcissistic injury of the girl's conviction that her genital is "inferior." The Christ identification, however, reveals a special feature of the fantasy of grandeur. The omnipotent idea of being a God was cast into the form of being a *suffering* God, a crucified martyr, grand in power as well as in martyrdom. It is a perfect example of the deformed fantasy described above, which shapes and colors the ego ideal. Obviously, in our patient, too, the Christ-hospital fantasy had been absorbed by her ego ideal. However, at the time of her analytic treatment I did not realize this state of affairs. I did recognize the narcissistic satisfaction, but I did not see how strongly the patient's ideals were influenced by her fantasy. I now find proof of its active power in the patient's behavior after the termination of her analysis. In spite of the fact that she was an artist with remarkable talents, she decided to become a nurse, obviously being forced to act out the fantasy in life. Her ideal was now to care for suffering people, to tend and cure them. Of course the omnipotent facet of the fantasy could not be realized and this caused a permanent disappointment. After a year of nursing she came to see her error, gave up the hospital work, and returned to her artistic profession.

It would be interesting to speculate whether the acting out of the fantasy in real life might have been prevented if I had recognized during the analytic treatment the significance of the fantasy in the patient's ideal formation, its place in her ego organization and total mental make-up. Unfortunately, I cannot answer this question, as the relative proportions of the different processes and forces involved are not measurable.

However, in a number of more recently treated cases I have the impression that sometimes a thorough analysis of the deformed ideals may bring great relief and a better adjustment to reality and realistic ideals.

I now return to the earlier question what factors may be responsible for a person's production of primitive "grand martyr" ideals. I promised to mention three of them.

In the first place, the personalities and attitudes of the parents (and other idealized figures) are important. If both parents (or the one with whom the patient is most strongly identified) are themselves sadomasochistic characters, the primitive ideals will from the very beginning bear a masochistic imprint. In chapter 23 I pointed out how difficult it can be for a young person to give up his ideals formed through identification with parental images. Therefore it is sometimes almost impossible to induce an adolescent patient to exchange his infantile masochistic ideals, acquired from parents who are themselves sadomasochistic, for other, more suitable ideals.

A second factor is to be found in the patient's own personality; on the one hand, there is the nature of his drive equipment; on the other, there are the talents, the abilities, and the ego's capacity for sublimation, which the ego ideal can make use of in building up ideals with positive, constructive goals. Gifted persons, if freed from their inhibitions, masochistic symptoms, and guilt feelings, will have a much better opportunity for finding suitable ideals and realizing them to a certain extent than the majority of limited people. The endeavor to free a patient to such an extent that he can adjust his ideals to his innate and early acquired potentialities is a difficult but valuable enterprise.

To avoid misunderstanding I want to add that I do not have in mind "gifts," "talents," and "ideals" in the framework of a system of values. I mean only a more extended range of possibilities for neutralized activities, regardless of how they are valued by a given society, group or community. The milieu's value system is of importance only in so far as the person in question is dependent upon approval or disapproval from the environment. Complete independence rarely occurs, but degrees of dependency vary considerably.

This leads us to the third factor, which is provided by the person's wider environment in still another connection. The realizing of his ideals is determined not only by his own capacities. The environment must provide satisfactory opportunities for their realization, or it must be possible for the individual to change environmental circumstances according to his ideals. (Here emerges a sociopsychological problem with which I shall not deal.)

In conclusion, I want to make two additional points.

(1) Masochism is a mode of instinctual gratification that in itself need not be pathological. Up to a certain point, it finds a place in normal sexual life. It has a special relation to female sexuality, as Freud and others have pointed out on several occasions. In a sublimated form masochism can be helpful and even necessary for learning to bear the inevitable distress and pain inherent in human life, with its illnesses, natural catastrophes, and unavoidable misery of a social nature. With these "normal" events masochistic pleasure is not sought exclusively for its own sake. It enables the person to attain a certain resignation alongside productive activities in his personal and social life. In pathology, and especially in moral masochistic behavior, the person is restricted to masochistic pleasure, and his distorted ideals do not allow him to find satisfaction in constructive sublimated pursuits.

(2) My last point concerns an evaluation of recent ego psychology. It is often doubted whether the theory of the structuralization of the mind is of any value for the practical application of psychoanalysis. I have two answers to this question:

(a) A general one, which applies to every science: psychoanalytic theory always was and continues to be the outcome of a wealth of observations made on human beings, first by Freud and then by other psychoanalysts; it is constantly being enlarged and modified by new observations, the understanding of which has been made possible by theoretical knowledge.

(b) A specific one: our refined insight into the different functions of the structured mind, and their mutual interplay, enables us to support our patients in the comprehension and the mastery of their inner conflicts in a much more thorough and differentiated way than formerly.

I have presented this paper as a case in point, and I hope it has demonstrated the value of our theoretical knowledge for practical purposes. It is the suffering of our patients and of mankind in general that stimulates us never to give up our endeavor to deepen our knowledge of the functioning of the human mind.

28. Remarks on Genesis, Structuralization, and Functioning of the Mind

(1964)

In psychoanalysis the genetic approach to mental phenomena has proved its intrinsic value for the understanding of the human mind. For the explanation of adult behavior, normal as well as pathological, the tracing back to its origins in early childhood is a necessary procedure. However, the genetic approach is only part of the picture. Without taking into account the maturational processes, including the development of the different functions, the structuralization and the differentiation of the mind, the influence of the environment and the inner and outer conflicts which give rise to reactive and defensive processes, the explanation remains one-sided and incomplete.

I am aware of the fact that these statements are self-evident and generally accepted. The reason I mention them here lies in the fact that though they are common knowledge, they nevertheless are often neglected. I am referring to those authors who do not clearly distinguish between genetic determinants (to borrow a term of Hartmann's) and developmental end products of mental processes, especially in connection with the structuralization into id, ego, and superego with their different functions. This lack of distinction may lead to oversimplifications in two opposite directions. On the one hand, functions and activities of an adult's ego organization are sometimes described as if they were merely a defense against "oral," "anal," or "phallic" tendencies, which may be genetic determinants, but certainly do not cover the whole picture. This lack of a clear distinction between function and genesis was repeatedly stressed and criticized by Hartmann (1955), by Hartmann and Loewenstein (1962), etc. On the other hand, processes occurring in infancy are sometimes described in terms of an adult's (pathological) behavior (Melanie Klein, e.g.). Some authors speak, for instance, of an infant's or toddler's "schizophrenic ego split." It is quite clear that an infant's ego organization does not yet exist as a system and therefore cannot yet be "split." This kind of confusion was mentioned by me in connection with the antedating of the system superego in the infant's first months of life (Chapter 6). Thus I am in agreement with Hartmann that it is necessary to distinguish clearly between genesis and function and I think all psychoanalysts should take his warning to heart.

However, a number of questions arise in view of this general statement. I shall try to enter into a few of them. What happens to the different mental functions in the course of the maturation and development into adulthood? For the sake of clarity it seems preferable to examine the substructures of the mind separately, although I am quite aware of the fact that development occurs in a constant mutual interplay.

We begin by examining the id, the area of the instinctual drives. Freud pointed out at an early stage of psychoanalysis that the id functions according to the pleasure principle. The drives strive for instinctual gratification. This basic id function remains in existence during an individual's whole life. However, the shape of the drives changes in the course of the development. In infancy we observe the partial drives, oral, anal, and phallic, which gradually develop into the mature genital drive. I need not go further into this part of psychoanalytic theory which is well known and affirmed by numerous observations.

We next turn to the ego. Nowadays we prefer to speak of the "system" ego as an organization of a number of functions. In the earliest stages of psychoanalytic theory formation Freud used the term "ego" in different, not always clearly defined, ways. However, in *The Ego and the Id* (1923b) he definitely describes the ego as a structured part of the mind, as a "coherent organization of mental processes." It comprises consciousness, it controls partial processes, it is master of motility, and it is the agency which makes use of repression (and defense) in cases where instinctual strivings cannot be discharged or are not allowed to become conscious. The ego is that part of the mind which has direct contact with the outer world and acts according to the reality principle. Its basic functions are mediation between inner and outer world (passive and active), adaptation, and, finally, synthetization (or harmonization) of the various demands from inside and from the environment. The mature ego has developed a large number of singular functions, which may participate in the achievements of the basic functions of adaptation and integration. With Hartmann we distinguish between primary autonomous ego functions, e.g., perception, memory, reality testing, judging, etc., and other ego functions, which develop as reaction to or defense against instinctual tendencies and environmental demands. The latter group of functions may obtain a "secondary" autonomy if they are able to solve the conflicts with the id and the milieu and to enter into the "sphere free of conflict." However, both the primary autonomous and the secondary autonomous functions may be drawn into the sphere of conflict at a later stage and in pathological development the ego may not be able to get back its ability to master the conflicts, at least not without impairment of the ego organization itself.

We now return to our question: what happens to the different functions (and here we speak of ego functions) in the course of life? Ego functions are not yet present in the newborn child, though we assume with Freud and Hartmann that the individual potentialities out of which they are to develop are present in the archaic Anlage; but they come into being only after birth and under the influence of experience and learning processes. The infant is also in need of support of his mother's love and care in order to develop them in a favorable way. An organization of the ego functions into the system ego finds place only in a much later stage. In order to explain the great and obvious differences between the adult's and the little child's ego activities Hartmann has introduced the concept of "change of function," a very valuable concept indeed. However, I think we have to investigate to which ego functions this concept applies. In examining those ego functions which emerge in the conflictual sphere, e.g., in a conflict between instinctual tendencies and the ego, we have to accept that a change of function takes place if the ego succeeds in mastering the id striving that cannot be discharged directly. I shall give two examples out of many that could be described: (1) During the anal phase of instinctual development the little child has to learn to abandon the pleasure of messing and soiling himself, his clothes and his surroundings. The child's ego may reach this achievement by developing reaction formations of cleanliness, orderliness, and economy (the well-known "anal triad"). These reaction formations may gradually become character traits, automatisms. Later on these character traits, though originated as a defense against id strivings, may change their function and, for instance, enter into hygienic or economic activities which serve quite different purposes of a personal as well as of a social kind. They may have their share in processes of adaptation and organization and sublimated activities. (2) Compassion can genetically be traced back to a reaction formation to strong sadistic impulses. As a character trait in later childhood and adulthood it no longer functions as a defense, but it may serve social adaptation, integration, and contact with fellow men. At least, this state of affairs applies to "normal" development, where the ego's original defensive function may gain secondary autonomy. In pathological cases the conflict fails to be solved and the ego has constantly to ward off the pressing instinctual demands. To summarize: change of function in defensive processes can be observed in normal development; in pathology the defensive function persists.

In regard to the primary autonomous ego functions I think we observe the reverse situation. Perception and reality testing, for instance, continue to exist throughout life, though their contents may be enlarged by learning processes. More knowledge about the real facts of life may widen the scope of the fields covered; the functional side of the processes, however, need not be changed in "healthy" development. On the other hand, in pathological cases the autonomous functions may be drawn into the conflictual sphere with the consequence of a change of function, e.g., in being employed for defensive purposes. This is most clearly observed with psychotics. A case in point is a patient suffering from delusional jealousy. During a walk with his wife, he perceives an acquaintance greeting them and for a few seconds looking at his wife. This perception is instantly drawn into the patient's delusional system; it is used for accusing his wife of infidelity and functions as a warding off of his own impulses to commit adultery. The patient's reality testing is distorted in a way similar to his perception and both have changed their original function of learning about the real facts of life into the defensive function of warding off unacceptable instinctual tendencies.

Regarding the "basic" (or general) ego functions of mediating between the inner world and environmental influences, of adaptation and integration, I think we encounter a similar situation. In "normal," harmonious development those basic functions persist essentially unchanged throughout life. They merely become more consolidated and cover a larger field of knowledge through learning. In pathological conditions the functions may be changed, probably mainly to be used in warding-off processes.

If this train of thought should prove to be correct, we may summarize as follows: under "normal" conditions a change of ego functions takes place in the area of secondary autonomy, whereas the general, basic functions and the primary autonomous singular functions keep to their original aims. Under pathological conditions, however, every ego function is exposed to change by being drawn into the pathological process. It is decisive for the form and the severity of the mental illness how many and which functions share this fate. Here emerges the necessity for detailed, clinical research, which I cannot pursue at this time. A single tentative remark suggests that a contribution to the theme of "choice of neurosis" is to be expected from these considerations. In all mental disturbances the basic functions of adaptation and integration are affected, though in psychoses they are much more severely affected and lead to a more or less complete withdrawal from the outer world, whereas in neurotic disorders a certain contact with the object world is maintained.

Could it be that one important factor in these differences is to be found in the fact that in neuroses *secondary autonomous* ego functions lose their autonomy on re-entering the sphere of conflict and are subject to change, whereas in psychotic disorders the *primary autonomous* ego functions are impaired from the very beginning of the illness and therefore lose their original function? Several authors have described this process as occurring on the basis of an irregular, faulty, or interrupted development of ego functions in very early childhood and a regression to these points of arrest.

This seems to be the place to recall to mind an early paper of Freud's (1911) in which he describes how the pleasure principle, which originally governs the mental life, is gradually replaced by the reality principle as a reaction to disappointments and frustrations. At that time there did not yet exist a workable psychoanalytic theory of ego development. Now we know that the substitution of the reality principle for the pleasure principle occurs in connection with the growing organization of ego functions, a process which under normal conditions is stimulated by frustrations. We should not forget that in the same paper Freud states that this substitution does not abolish the pleasure principle. In fact, Freud says, the reality principle is its safeguard: an immediate, but in its consequences uncertain pleasure experience is renounced in order to gain a later, but certain one acquired along new paths. We may add: not only along new paths, but also with new means, new contents, and last, but not least, with a new mode of satisfaction. Though ways, means, contents, and modes of satisfaction change during the course of development, the original tendency to gain some kind of gratification is retained. Maybe we could assume that no mental action whatsoever is taken without the (often unconscious) expectation of acquiring some kind of gratification or of avoiding unpleasure. It is hardly necessary to recall that under the pressure of overpowering forces in the outside world it may happen that neither goal is attainable to the slightest degree. On the other hand, even neurotic suffering, which originates in the person's own mental life, contains some mode of satisfaction. In chapter 27 I give an example of "pleasurable" suffering in the shape of grandeur fantasies of being an exceptional and very great martyr.

This idea brings us to our next point, the examination of the third mental substructure: the superego and ego ideal system. In Chapter 24 I tried to investigate the precursors (or, to use Hartmann's term, the genetic determinants) of both conscience and ideals. I preferred to examine them separately because their original functions are opposite to each other, the conscience (superego in a narrower sense) coming into being as a restricting and prohibiting agency, whereas the ego ideal emerges as an agency providing satisfaction through hallucinating, magical wishful thinking, and fantasies of omnipotence. I also drew attention to the fact that in the course of development, that is, at the time of the passing of the oedipus complex, both agencies merge together in one substructure of the mind, the superego in a wider sense. This close contact necessarily provokes a mutual influence so that ideals may become "oughts" (you "ought" to live up to a certain ideal, instead of you "wish" to live up to it), and prohibitions may become ideals, e.g., complete obedience to the demands of an authority may be idealized. However, they show a compulsive character and are used as a defense against anxiety-provoking impulses. As far as they limit the person's inner freedom to choose his own ideals and restrictions, we are entitled to see them as having entered the realm of pathology.

In connection with the merging into one mental substructure of ideals and prohibitions during the passing of the oedipus complex Hartmann and Loewenstein (1962) prefer to speak of the superego system *tout court* and to distinguish between the idealizing and the self-criticizing functions of the superego. I agree with the authors, that their conceptualization is simpler, more in line with the concept of the ego, being an organization of functions and therefore more appropriate than the one, used by me so far, which conceived of the ego ideal and the restricting superego as two sides of the "superego in a wider sense."

In another context Hartmann and Loewenstein propose to apply the concept of "change of function," used in ego psychology, to the system superego as well. However, the authors do not indicate which functions are subject to such a change and under which conditions the changes take place. I shall try to make some remarks to this point in following a path similar to my previous one regarding ego functions. As a matter of fact it is quite obvious that a number of a "normal" adult's ideals are very different from the little child's grandeur and omnipotence fantasies and the idealization of his parental images, though we should not overlook the fact that much of the original magic and wishful thinking is still present in the conscious or unconscious mind of a "healthy" adult. Hartmann and Loewenstein also mention this fact.

However, I think we are entitled to put the question: *what* has changed in the more mature ideal functioning? Obviously the *contents* have changed, under the influence of the total personality as it increasingly takes reality factors into account. I also suggest that the mode of satisfaction provided by living up to the ideals has changed. Gratification drawn from thinking, from intellectual activities, from scientific and artistic, in short, from sublimated performances, is clearly different from direct instinctual satisfaction as well as from the narcissistic gratification provided by imagining oneself omnipotent.

But has the original *function* of procuring some kind of satisfaction really changed? I do not see that this is the case, at least not in harmonious development. Hartmann and Loewenstein (1962) describe as an example of a "change of function" in the superego system the more mature ego ideal's "striving after perfection," "a direction-giving function, which is relatively independent of the objects and relatively independent also of the instinctual precursors." I quite agree with the authors as to the description of the possible shape of an adult's ego ideal. However, is "striving after perfection" not a search for satisfaction? After all, as long as a person believes more or less that "perfection" can really be achieved by any human being, is it so far away from magic, wishful thinking? My notion is that the *basic* function of ideal formation — the aiming at narcissistic gratification and the attempt to guide the ego's activities in that direction — has not been changed in principle. The little child also, though not very successfully, tries to realize his wishes of being as powerful and perfect as he imagines his parents to be. What has undergone a transformation are the form and contents of the ideals and the paths along which the person attempts to gain satisfaction. The transformation, I think, has become possible in connection with the development of ego functions through learning and experience in contact with the outside world, in short, under the impact of the reality principle. Among the many special ego qualities which are of importance for this transformation process is the ego's capacity for neutralizing drive energy, which then may allow the superego system to make use of more or less neutralized energy. This point is more extensively elaborated by Hartmann and Loewenstein.

Under pathological conditions, however, e.g., in the above-described case where ideals have a compulsive character, the function may have changed from a pleasure-providing into a restricting one. In a similar way the "oughts" and "ought-nots" of the restricting superego which have become ideals may give satisfaction, but both processes, in adopting each other's original functions, have caused a distortion of the system superego and cannot be looked at as a harmonious developmental outcome.

Therefore I propose the following summary: if functions of the superego system are drawn into the sphere of conflicts for which the personality is unable to find a "sound" solution, pathological conditions have entered the picture with the consequence that a change of superego functions may take place. In harmonious development the *original* functions persist, though their *contents* and the *modes* of both gratification and unavoidable renunciation may be subject to transformations. This train of thought seems to be in line with Freud's statement that the superego is closer to the id than is the ego. This is valid not only as to the dynamics and economics in mental life, which are clearly described by Hartmann and Loewenstein in connection with aggression; it seems to apply also to the functions of *pleasure-seeking* and *renouncing* under the pressure of object relations. The superego has no direct contact with the real factors in the environment. It is only the ego that through its different functions, i.e., perception, action, reality testing, etc., can react to and act upon the outer world, and learns to store knowledge about all kinds of reality factors. And only through the mediation of the ego organization is the superego indirectly influenced by the environment, as is the id.

We here touch upon a field in need of thorough research, namely, on the influence which the mutual *interplay* between id, ego organization, and superego system exercises upon the various functions of the substructures of the mind as well as upon their contents and the modes of satisfaction. Many investigations in this field have already been carried out by Freud and others in a general way. However, more detailed research is still needed to gain a deeper insight into the manifold conditions which lead to the development of a harmonious personality or to pathological disturbances. I am quite aware of the fact that the propositions brought forward here are of a tentative nature and in need of either confirmation or substitution by more appropriate ones.

29. Heinz Hartmann's Contributions to Psychoanalysis

(1964/1965)

Introduction

It seems a very good initiative of the editors of this issue to publish in German some of the main works of *Heinz Hartmann* which have so far only appeared in English. *Hartmann* is not only a highly experienced analyst but also a scientist, a thinker and an outstanding theorist. It is not easy to do justice to the significance of *Hartmann* for the science of psychoanalysis as established by Freud, since his contributions are so rich and comprehensive.

They often link up with other disciplines which occupy themselves with human psychology and mental life. I can therefore only select a few facets and attempt to eludicate these.

The reader will notice especially, while studying *Hartmann's* works, that the author has taken up recommendations which *Freud* in writing and orally communicated to his pupils and staff. He has enlarged, supplemented *Freud's* work but also added original ideas. *Freud's* earlier theories, designed to put order in and to clarify his observations of psychological phenomena in healthy and ill people, have so often been confirmed by his own experiences and by those of other analysts that they are now recognized as regular events. They comprise the theories of the psychic unconscious, of the unsolved conflicts and of repression as the causes of the neuroses, the phasic development of infantile sexuality, the existence of the oedipus complex, etc. In the twenties *Freud* published his research on the instances, where repression and warding-off mechanisms are localised, namely, the "ego" and the "super-ego". These studies led him to complement and modify earlier theories, viz. the anxiety theory, but he had always stressed that they are incomplete and in need of completion by his successors. *Hartmann* did just that for Freud's ego-psychology and he has given us a deep insight in many functions of mental life which have influenced both our theoretical and our practical work favourably. Before I go deeper into this point, I will mention a second particularity of *Hartmann's* work. *Freud* has often stressed that psychoanalysis could and should become the basis of a general psychology. In the nineties he had made an attempt to attain this aim on a physiological basis in "Versuch einer Psychologie". He has, however, abandoned this attempt and concentrated on psychological categories. But he always fostered the thought of it. *Hartmann* then, took up this challenge. Even though he accentuates that there is not yet a complete, closed general human psychgology, he clearly indicates the ways which could lead to it.

It is only natural that he looks for connections with other disciplines and thinkers. He neither neglects the biological endowment in mental processes, nor the influences of the smaller and of the larger environment. That is how he also arrives at sociological problems and supports an interplay between analysis, psychyology, anthropology, sociology and biology which implicates cooperation with experts in these fields.

Three things stand out in these attempts of *Hartmann's* to follow Freud's initiatives and to develop, complement and if necessary modify his theories.

1. Like Freud, *Hartmann* is very careful in his formulations and repeatedly points out the gaps and limitations of knowledge;
2. *Hartmann*, as opposed to many other authors never succumbed to the temptation to accept parts of analytical theory and abandon other well-established and proven theories thereby devaluating *Freud's* discoveries;
3. He has contributed his own original ideas to psychoanalysis. It is these three points which, in my opinion, make *Hartmann's* work so valuable.

I now return to the narrower theme of psychoanalytical ego-psychology. In the literature some appreciation of Hartmann's work in this field can already be found.[1]

But *Hartmann's* works are too complicated and too difficult to understand. This objection could be valid for his style of writing. But the topic itself is very complicated. The differentiation of the mental apparatus in the course of maturation and development is a many sided and complicated process. The author has elaborated many aspects of this process very clearly, elucidated much and indicated lines for further research. Therefore I think that a serious study of his works is very rewarding and promising.

The second objection is more or less as follows: in the structural theory, the division of the psyche, by Freud, but especially by Hartmann, in id, ego and superego is a reification. What is meant is apparently that both authors want to regard the structure of the personality as material entities, as "things". In my eyes this criticism is based on a great misunderstanding. It is true that Freud occasionaly writes in metaphors in order to picture more clearly complicated psychic processes which are difficult to describe. However, time and again he stresses the point that "id", "ego" and "super-ego" are theoretical concepts which should help us to better understand the dynamic proportions in (neurotic and "normal") conflicts. *Hartmann* explicitly describes the various provinces of the personality as being defined by their functions and motivations. "Id" is the concept of the instinctual forces, aimed at satisfying drives and affects and at the preservation of the species. The function of the ego is to mediate between needs and reality, adaptation and synthesis. The super-ego functions as necessary restrictions and as the bearer of moral and ethics. If we understand *Hartmann* (and *Freud*) correctly this criticism will, I think, prove to be incorrect.

A third objection says: theory is not at all needed for practical analytical work. This is at the same time correct and false. It is correct in that we should *never* use

---

[1] *David Rapaport*, Die Struktur der psychoanalytischen Theorie, Stuttgart (Klett) 1963. George Klein in an article which has not yet been published.

theoretical considerations and terms with the patient (this rule is often trespassed upon, also by opponents of the ego-psychology). With patients we should only talk in normal every-day language. This objection is however wrong in that it is impossible to comprehend a patient fully and in depth without theoretical knowledge. New practical experiences have only become more comprehensible and clear in interaction with theory, and this not only with Freud. Every analyst who interprets to the patient a defence or an unconscious impulse uses (perhaps unconsciously or pre-consciously) his theoretical knowledge of the existence of the unconscious, of defense etc. Naturally, an analyst can only use the theory he really understands. Before I go deeper into *Hartmann's* contributions to psychoanalytic ego-psychology, I would like to mention briefly some of his works on general theory.

Hartmann's early psychoanalytical works appeared in German. In "Die Grundlagen der Psychoanalyse" (published in 1927) the author points out both the natural-scientific foundation of psychoanalysis and the connections with, and differences to other psychological and philosophical disciplines, the so called "Geisteswissenschaften" ("Mental sciences"). He demonstrates that psychoanalysis with fundamental concepts in regard to mental activity is moving in the direction of a general theory. In the chapter "Verstehen und Erklären" he convincingly illustrates that psychoanalysis is also an "understanding psychology", but at the same time he explains that the fact that "comprehension" of certain mental connections does not always provide the correct explanation for their origin. The evidence of "comprehension" can become a source of error. *Freud's* discovery of the unconscious and the dynamics in mental life made psychoanalysis a psychology pointing out causality and herewith being capable of correcting such errors. *Hartmann's* studies about identical twins (1934-1935) seems to me to be of particular importance in this respect.

I now leave out several excellent experimental works to arrive at the most fundamental early publication "Ich-psychologie und Anpassungsproblem" (published in 1939). Many of *Hartmann's* later works (including the ones published here) originate in this book. They contain elaborations, continuations and new formulations of what was written there, next to the original new thoughts and theories. *Rapaport* has included in his book "Pathology of thought" parts of "Ich-psychologye und Anpassungsproblem".

I will now follow *Rapaport's* communications from the depictions mentioned above: "Die Struktur der psychoanalytischen Theorie". He mentions a concept, newly introduced by *Hartmann*:

1. The undifferentiated phase

Hartmann attempts to elaborate the new thoughts initiated by *Freud* in "Die endliche und die unendliche Analyse".* These ideas claim that the genetic endowment includes genetic factors of the ego which are developing only after

* "Analysis Terminable and Unterminable".

271

birth. The "undifferentiated phase" therefore comprises all endowments and mental potentials with which a human being enters life. That means that not only everything instinctual is included but also all "Anlagen" (endowments) and nuclei from which the ego develops later-on in interaction with the drives and the environmental influences. *Freud's* widening of the "id" concept in "Abriss der Psychoanalyse" may perhaps cover this concept. The great advantage of *Hartmann's* new designation is that it prevents the interchange of the "id in a narrower sense" (that is of the exclusive instinctual), with the total mental endowment. It also puts the significance of the maturational processes which plays such an important part in the living nature, in the forefront. From this matrix of the undifferentiated phase, the drives (the id) develop and the organization of the ego-functions which have to relate to the exterior as well as to the interior world in continuous mutual influencing.

2. The autonomy of the ego and the "ego-apparatus"

These terms are I think often misunderstood. In the initial *Freudian* ego-psychology the ego was defined as a substructure in the mental apparatus, mainly according to one of its most important functions, viz. to the function of mediator in the conflicts between id and environment. One of the great merits of *Hartmann* is that he studied more closely the many ego-functions which develop in the maturational process and that he clarified their contribution to this task. He indicates the functions which develop while not in conflict with id or environment but are going through their own specific maturing process as primary autonomy of the ego. Functions like observation, memory, motoric control, judging, etc. belong to this. It is clear that *Hartmann* here makes a connection with the developmental psychology as the gradual maturing of these functions has been examined and described in detail by *Karl and Charlotte Bühler, Piaget*, and other developmental psychologists. *Hartmann* attempts to build-in the results of the developmental psychology into an analytical conceptual system.

The criticism expressed by some authors that *Hartmann* disengages the ego from the inner cohesion of the mind and "idealizes" it, seems to be perfectly unjustified. Again and again *Hartmann* stresses that the autonomous ego-functions can become engaged in the conflict sphere. These functions can be repressed, damaged or paralysed if in conflict with the drive-needs and/or with the environment. We can observe these processes in our patients. But ego-functions can sometimes also be stimulated by such conflicts. We can think for example of the observational function which can be strongly stimulated and sharpened through the growing sexual interest of the little child, but on the other hand be damaged and even paralysed through the prohibition to look issued by the environment that gives rise to anxiety for the drive-need. Neither can I agree with the objection that *Hartmann* is committed to "biologism". The autonomous ego-functions develop out of the genetic endowment partly tied to sense-organs (e.g. perception, speech, etc.), partly leaning towards sense-inprints (e.g. memory and later on judging) or also in connection with physical growth (e.g. motility). The later psychological development is again and again stressed and described by the author.

The primary autonomous ego-functions can be drawn out of the "conflict free sphere" by conflicts with id and environment. In the course of development they can however again be disengaged from the conflictual sphere and thus achieve a "secondary autonomy". *Hartmann* continuously emphasized that this process does not, or only incompletely takes place under pathological conditions. He also indicates that the succesful course in the development influences the ego-organization as well. In conflicts the ego has to apply defence mechanisms and the defensive processes have evoked changing of functions in the ego. This leads to the third introduction of a new concept in the theory:

3. The concept of change of function, which is also mentioned by Rapaport

According to *Hartmann* genesis should not be interchanged with the final shape of a number of ego-functions. Many ego-functions originate in childhood in conflict with, in reaction to and as a defence against drive impulses. In the course of development they can, however, attain the already mentioned "secondary autonomy" and no longer serve the drive-defence, but other functions, e.g. adaptation, integration or sublimated activities. The change of function then leads to a stabilized behaviour, to particular character qualities which end up in the final structuralization of the more mature personality through the continuously advancing differentiation. He calls these end-products "automatisms". Structuralized character stability is encountered in "healthy" people next to flexibility of the psychic apparatus which is indispensable in interior and exterior conflict situations. Hartmann never ignored the fact that we encounter in our patients morbid rigidity, e.g. in compulsive neurotics, as well as a lack of character stability, e.g. in acting-out patients.

A fourth contribution to the theory is *Hartmann's* concept of the

4. Process of adaptation

Adaptation, so important for life and mental "health" of a person, is one of the most essential ego-functions. *Hartmann* described this function already in his book: "Ego-psychology and problems of adaptation" very thoroughly. We will meet it again in the papers appearing in this issue. The concept of "adaptation" has been applied by many authors as a "passive" surrender to the requirements of the environment. This definition is not *Freud's* or *Hartmann's* and is not current in psychoanalytical literature. *Hartmann* explicitly describes that "adaptation" can also be an active process. This means that an individual can sometimes change his personal environment. He will either attempt to shape society in which he lives differently, which is naturally not always possible, or he will look for a different environment.

Sometimes the individual can create a suitable environment within a smaller personal circle, e.g. in the family constellation or at work. The criticism of Hartmann that he should deal with social problems only in an abstract and formal way, ignoring the fact that e.g. in the Nazi time in Central Europe even the most adaptation-willing analyst could not adapt himself, shows a fundamental misunderstanding and is also based on this too narrow passive definition of the "adaptive function". Most analysts have used at that time the active adaptation capacity, changing their environment by a certainly not easy emigration. In countries, occupied by Germany and from which it was impossible to emigrate, the small personal "environment" was changed in such a way that the officially prohibited analytical practice was continued "underground".

The adaptation process in healthy persons leads to an inner and outer balance. Hartmann describes how this balance rests on a different ego-function which we call the synthetic or organizing one. The mature ego has to satisfy drive needs, but also to solve conflicts, to face actively or passively the inevitable demands of the environment and of the conscience and to protect its own organization. *Hartmann* argues that for this task the capacity to synthesize is indispensable. I would like to comment briefly on one point of criticism by *Rapaport* which he adds to a very positive appreciation of *Hartmann's* work. *Rapaport* claims that in Hartmann's ego-psychology the theory of the primary and secondary ego-autonomy is not completely integrated with the existing theory of object-relations. It is true that *Hartmann* does not deal with the influence of object relations upon ego-development as laboriously as with description of the maturing of autonomous functions even though he does not exclude it. The author has never pretended to deliver a complete, final psychoanalytical scientific theory. He has modestly spoken about "contributions" to the theory. If we study these contributions seriously it seems however that they are major contributions to a comprehension of human mental life.

A final word about *Hartmann's* contribution to drive-psychology. Without his concept of neutralization of drive energy the ego-psychology would from the dynamic, energetic point of view remain incomplete and incomprehensible. He speaks of "neutralization" because the ego apparatus does not only work with desexualized energy but also with "neutralized" energy originating from the aggressive drives. The concept of "neutralization" indicates that drive-energy is not only used for immediate satisfaction of the drives, but can also be modified in such a way that it can provide the energy necessary for non-instinctual activities. This supposition is important firstly because we can sometimes really observe in our patients how this instinctual behaviour decreases while the patient gradually starts using his energy for "sublimated" activities, which can provide proper satisfactional albeit of a different nature. Secondly, this supposition of a neutralized drive energy also deepens our insight, explaining how "gifted" persons after having been lifted out of neurotic inhibitions have a better opportunity to recover and regain their inner balance than persons who lack this ability to neutralize.

In psychoanalytic literature *Hartmann* has quite rightly been recognized as the author who has contributed the most important and complete contributions to psychoanalytical ego-psychology.

Finally, I would like to point out *Hartmann's* interest in problems which play a very important role in human mental life. I mean the field of morals and ethics.

274

In his book "Psychoanalysis and Moral Values" (1960), the author deals with these problems looking at them from various angels. He convincingly argues that psychoanalysis as a science does not represent special values. Herewith he completes Freud's saying that psychoanalysis is not a "world philosophy" ("Weltanschauung") and its "value" is like that of every other natural science; namely the searching for laws and the striving for "truth". This does not contradict the fact that every analyst naturally has his own morals and ethics as an individual person. In this light does *Hartmann* explicitly represent *Freud's* personality as a "moral person" in as far as we know him from his books and letters which were published after his death. "Psychoanalysis and Moral Values" is a significant book; it shows us again the sharpness of *Hartmann's* intellect, his abundant knowledge in all fields regarding human mental life and his warm interest in the fate of mankind.

30. Some Thoughts on Adaptation and Conformism

(1966)

If we wish to distinguish between adaptive and conforming behavior, it is advisable to define the concepts "adaptation" and "conformism" as clearly as possible. In ordinary usage, these terms are often equated. Adaptive behavior is often viewed merely as surrendering to environmental demands and as completely in line with existing social laws, norms, and values. However, I believe that we should reserve the term "conformism" for this kind of compliant conduct.

In certain circumstances adaptive behavior does coincide with conforming to social demands. However, the concept of adaptation comprises much more than conformism and I shall try to define it in more exact terms later on in this paper. I shall begin my discussion by considering both adaptation and conformism as they apply to a person's behavior as a reaction to his environment.

The concept of adaptation originated in biology. Living organisms "adapt" themselves to the environment. If they do not, they cannot survive, either individually or as a species. In animals adaptation to the environment can occur through changes in the individual; e.g., in fur-bearing animals the thickness of the fur varies with the degree of heat and cold; in many amphibian species the color of the skin changes according to the coloration of the environment, etc. However, adaptation can also be achieved by changing the environment, by searching for and finding more suitable surroundings; e.g., migratory birds travel south in the winter to exchange their cold homeland for warmer countries; fish swim up a river to propagate in an environment suitable for their offspring; certain species of game migrate every year in order to find water and proper food, etc.

In human beings we encounter even more complex forms of adaptation. Freud speaks of autoplastic and alloplastic adaptation. In contrast to animals, human beings, by virtue of having evolved a differentiated mental life, have gradually changed their natural outer world into a complicated social environment. Therefore, they must "adapt" not only to guarantee survival and to protect their offspring; they must adjust to the society which generations of their ancestors have created and in which they are living.

As far as I know, Heinz Hartmann was the first analyst who systematically applied the concept of adaptation to psychological phenomena. He describes (1939) three forms of adjustment: (1) a change in the individual, i.e., a passive acceptance of the demands, norms, and laws of the environment; (2) a change of the environment by actively influencing it; and (3) a search for another environment where the norms and demands are more acceptable to the individual. The second and third forms could be described as active or creative adaptational processes, while in the first instance, the passive acceptance of social norms, the individual "conforms" to the environment.

While there is a limited parallel between psychological phenomena and biological processes, the complexity of man's mental life requires that the psychological concept of adaptation be extended to include the differentiated inner processes. The concept covers modes of behavior and is *not* merely a mental mechanism, in which sense it is sometimes used. Human "adaptation" comprises passive and active (creative) adjustment to the outer world as well as a synthesis of the forces at work in the different functional parts of the structured mind. It is well known that during growth, conflicts between id, ego, and superego functions arise and their solution involves a number of mental mechanisms. *Inner* adaptation requires a harmonious balance between instinctual and emotional needs, ego activities, and the person's moral system. I shall first deal with outer adaptation.

Outer adaptation

Whether a passive, conforming or an active, creative adaptation to the social milieu emerges is determined by a wealth of factors difficult to unravel. I shall try to highlight some aspects of the complicated processes involved.

Isaac Edersheim (1965) states that "adaptation" is ego *and* ego-ideal syntonic, whereas conforming conduct is ego syntonic but impairs the ego ideal.

Hartmann (1960), in describing how the ego's tendency to master inner conflicts can be curtailed by danger threatening from the environment, writes: the ego's "adaptive function will often overstep its integrative capacities. Thus in an environment where there is a high premium on conformism, the ego, still as a mediator, may well enforce the neglect or the suppression of personal moral valuation, even if they have, for the individual, a considerable integrative function. In such instances, social anxiety might have proved stronger than the demands of the personal moral system" (p. 32f.). This is certainly true of people who have been able to build up "a personal moral system"; that is, it is true of people who have grown up in a milieu which was not too authoritarian and which allowed some freedom at the time the child's superego was being established by introjection of parental norms and values. However, in cases where the integrative function is really overlaid with social anxiety, should we not speak of conforming behavior? We become aware of the necessity to distinguish between the *mechanism* of adaptation as a mental tool and adaptation indicating a behavioral attitude. Here I shall use adaptation in the second meaning.

Most children of parents who demand complete obedience and conformity do not acquire a nonconforming superego. Only exceptionally strong and gifted children can sometimes succeed in building up norms of their own which deviate from those of their parents. An impressive example of such an exception is described by Irving Stone (1961) in his novel about Michelangelo. Young Michelangelo was an obedient son to his authoritative father. At the age of 13, however, the boy, driven by an irresistible urge to become a sculptor, opposed his father's normative conviction that the Buonarroti were "noble burghers" and that labor and "work with the hands" were beneath their dignity. Michelangelo did not resist his father and uncle when they beat him severely, but he pursued his goal, becoming an apprentice first to the painter Ghirlandaio and later to the sculptor Bertoldo. His four younger brothers conformed to their father's demands. They all ended up as good-for-nothings, dependent upon the financial support of Michelangelo. It is interesting to note that Michelangelo's nonconformism led to a full unfolding of his forcefully driving talent and to his becoming one of the greatest sculptors of the Renaissance. He nevertheless paid for his disobedience to his father with a strong inner struggle and guilt feelings that forced him to live in poverty in order to meet the financial demands of his family.

There are, of course, less gifted persons with authoritarian parents who quietly develop nonconforming norms in childhood. However, their oppositional ideas often acquire a compulsive character very similar to those of the conformist, and this results in inhibition or paralysis of creative activities. Vladimir Nabokov, in *The Real Life of Sebastian Knight*, writes: "Well did he know that to flaunt one's contempt for a moral code was but smuggled smugness and prejudice turned inside out."

Throughout the history of man there have been periods when people lived and children were brought up under the pressure of authoritarian rulers and ruling classes, when conforming behavior was demanded on penalty of cruel punishment and on pain of death. In recent times the experiences in Nazi concentration camps during World War II are probably among the most striking examples. Many of the concentration camp victims had formed their norms and moral codes while living in freedom in democratic countries. When they were exposed to the most cruel and threatening authorities in the concentration camps, many of them could not adjust at all and soon died. A few of them managed to survive in spite of hunger, disease, exhaustion, and torture. Were these people able to conform only by ignoring or "suppressing" their personal moral values? There were undoubtedly many different individual solutions to this problem, but I would like to cite E. de Wind (1965), who is one of the very few survivors of the Auschwitz gas chambers. In a most impressive article he describes how a kind of adjustment took place by a "reversal of values." The high valuation of life, usually so common among human beings, had to be completely abandoned. The only thing to look forward to was death. The only "value" that mattered was how to escape or minimize the cruel treatment, how to die in the least painful way. The word "liberation" no longer meant being rescued from the Nazis; it meant "going the road through the chimney of the gas chambers" (de Wind, 1965). Persons who could not accept this new "norm" were felt to be threatening and they became outcasts. When rumors of German defeats began to circulate, the idea of a possible "real" liberation was confusing and even dangerous.

The general devaluation of life applied to the lives of everyone – one's own life and also the lives of wives, husbands, children, companions. "Compassion" for others had only one form: to smooth their way to death. Nevertheless, there must have been a deep unconscious clinging to life. It is possible that in these exceptional circumstances the paradox became true that a passive surrender to the idea of death was the only way to survive.

An even more difficult question to answer is whether and how the survivors of the concentration camps managed to readjust to their environments after their liberation. It is well known that some of them did not succeed, having become mentally or physically crippled personalities. Others did succeed, although the road from forced conformism and reversal of values to active (creative) adaptation was extremely difficult.[1]

However, people who live in more favorable circumstances, in a social milieu which allows for some kind of individual moral code, are also confronted with the problem of conformism versus creative adaptation, though in a different way. I shall describe two examples of conforming behavior and one example of nonconforming behavior.

1. Conformism in persons with defective superego development. In some persons the superego as an inner agency, an inner voice of conscience and value judgment, has not been fully established. These persons will easily conform to outer demands and let their behavior be guided by them. The causes for this may be a deficiency in the mechanisms of introjection and identification and unstable parental images, though several other factors may also be responsible (Freud, 1923, 1930).

2. Conformism in persons with strong inner anxiety. Some persons have developed a superego and nevertheless feel impelled to conform to a nonauthoritarian "social milieu." In this case we can assume that their "social anxiety" is due not so much to reality factors as to *inner* (neurotic) anxiety projected upon the outer world. Their conformism is used as a defense against their unsolved inner conflicts. Inner anxiety may have many sources, e.g., a clash between instinctual impulses and the ego organization. In delinquents the id tendencies have to some extent overwhelmed the ego which then has to "conform" to the id, thus causing these persons to oppose the environment. More often the outcome of the conflict is a neurotic condition in which the inner anxiety, under the guise of social anxiety, leads to conformism with the environment.

I would like to mention a special case which we often encounter in our analytic work. I am referring to persons with great ambitions and a strong competitive urge who are not gifted enough to realize most of their ambitions. This failure often mobilizes intense aggression toward rivals and in turn may lead to strong anxiety. Here again, conforming to outer demands may be used to cover up the inner fears and neurotic inhibitions, and eventually result in symptom formation. When patients suffer from their inability to live up to their personal moral code, we try to help them solve their neurotic conflicts and re-establish their own norms and values. A "healthy" development into harmonious personality

---

[1] Isaac-Ederheim (1965) describes similar situations in concentration camps in a slightly different context.

requires the capacity to integrate instinctual needs, moral and value codes, ego activities and talents, in interaction with the inevitable demands of the special social milieu. I have previously (1949, 1962, 1963) dealt with these complex processes, and Hartmann (1939, 1956, 1960) has contributed extensive and valuable propositions in regard to these problems.

3. *Nonconformism in persons with a strict and rigid superego.* During the structuralization of the mind, the superego, emerging in childhood as an inner deposit of infantile parental object relations, often retains the rigidity of primitive archaic processes. While some ego functions develop in the conflict-free sphere and are flexible enough to profit from new experiences, the superego functions often retain their original rigidity in spite of changes in content. This is particularly true when, at the time of the superego's emergence, aggression is turned inward and invested in the superego, a process that may be induced by, and ward off, anxiety provoked by aggressiveness. In order to keep this aggression under control, the superego must be very strict and often cruel in its demands. The person then experiences his individual moral code as a universal law and for this reason is intolerant of persons whose moral codes deviate from his.

People in authority sometimes use their fixed personal convictions to influence weaker persons to recruit followers and to keep them in obedience. The decision as to which norms and codes are indispensable to the maintenance and growth of a given society and which can be left to individual preference is a very difficult one. It is a question that belongs as much to the realm of sociology as to that of psychology. From the psychological side I would like to stress that this is a problem for both the ruler and the ruled. People in authority *can be* authoritarian, but it is *not necessary* that they demand unconditional surrender. They could try to encourage individual opinions and value judgments. This is desirable not only in sociopolitical fields but also in all areas of education. For instance, a scientist with a very wide knowledge of his field may either try to force his opinions on his students or he may stimulate the development of original thinking in them. The different outcomes will depend on the interaction of the personalities of teacher and students.

In summary, we may say that in general an individual who has been able to acquire some kind of a personal moral code will conform to his environment under the following conditions.

a. When the rulers are authoritarian and possess the material power to enforce complete obedience, the subjects may have to conform but they secretly retain their personal values. However, under extreme conditions such as occur in countries under dictatorships and in concentration camps, individuals must not only conform but also change and possibly reverse their moral systems. Here "social anxiety" is the response to *real* dangers.

b. When the leaders are nonauthoritarian and permissive in regard to differences of personal opinions and norms and the individual is an unharmonious (mentally disturbed) person who has projected his fears onto the environment, the individual usually changes his personal moral system according to what he thinks is expected of him. His original norms and ideals that are not completely in accord with expected environmental demands are either repressed or warded off, or they are more or less destroyed. Here "social anxiety" is a response to *psychic reality*, though from a *social* point of view the anxiety is *unrealistic*.

What I have described thus far are extreme positions. Actually, we often encounter mixed situations, e.g., milieus that are dictatorial in some respects and permissive in others; in these situations individuals are subject to a number of fears leading to conformism in some areas, but they retain a limited amount of freedom of personal judgment in other areas. It would be interesting to study the different outcomes of the various interactions (Mitscherlich, 1963).

Inner adaptation

In addition to the necessity for some kind of adaptation (active or passive) to the environment, the individual maturing under the impact of internal conflict must bring into equilibrium the various tendencies emerging from the different structures of the mind. The synthesis required for a "healthy" outcome is one of the functions of the ego organization. In order to achieve inner harmony, a number of other ego functions must remain unimpaired, e.g., the capacity to distinguish between inner and outer worlds, sound reality testing, and an undisturbed awareness of inner processes and faculties. To put it in other words: if a person is able to grant himself satisfaction of his instinctual and emotional needs to such an extent that it does not lead to an impairment of ego interests and his moral system, if he succeeds in developing his personal qualities and talents freely, and if his values and norms are shaped in such a way that they can be respected, we may speak of a well-balanced personality, in whom the process of "inner" adaptation has been carried out in a fortunate way. This description of the harmonious interaction of the functions of the different structured parts of the mental personality is an ideal picture. It presupposes the presence of an ego organization which can develop all of its potential faculties and talents, which has the instinctual and emotional impulses completely under control, and which is able to shape the moral system in accordance with those faculties and impulses. A person's inner harmony depends upon the intactness of the ego's basic functions of mediation and synthesis. This ideal picture is seldom realized. If it *is* realized, we can speak of an active adaptational process in the psychic inner world. If, on the other hand, the ego *fails* to master the id impulses (drives and affects) – the case with which we are only too familiar – the ego's defensive measures are accompanied and followed by inhibitions, ego impairments, and neurotic symptoms as compromises between id tendencies and ego interests. Furthermore, if the ego proves to be too weak to influence the moral system, it frequently surrenders to the superego demands, which results in similar restrictions and distortions of the person's faculties. In both cases we may speak of a passive adaptational process, which in these forms belongs to the realm of pathology. The threat of being overwhelmed by strong instinctual impulses or of being punished by a severe or cruel superego arouses anxiety that paralyzes some ego functions and forces the ego to give in to compromise formations. Sometimes both id and superego work together in endangering the autonomy of the ego organization, e.g., if the superego is secondarily sexualized and especially if the latter is invested with a great amount of aggression turned inward. However, passive adaptation is not always a pathological process. In certain circumstances it may promote inner balance and optimal functioning, especially if it alternates with active, creative adaptation. There is a really significant difference between a person who can *choose* to act in accordance with id and superego demands in order to achieve an optimum of unfolding faculties and of inner harmony and a person who out of fear must surrender to them with the consequence of impairment of capacities and equilibrium.

Returning to my proposal to distinguish between adaptation to and conformism with the environment, I would now like to suggest the extension of these definitions to the inner mental processes as well. *Inner* adaptation, then, could be defined as a creative process that brings forth a harmony between the various interests and needs of the different areas in the personality. A well-balanced mixture of their acceptance and their change will result in a synthesis and lead to an optimal functioning of the total personality. Conformism could be defined as a passive surrender to inner needs and demands – a surrender motivated by fear and resulting in impairment and restriction of the person's achievements.

Thus far I have presented some ideas on adaptive behavior (1) in regard to the outer world and (2) as a process of "inner" adaptation. This separation is, however, an artifact. In reality there is constant interaction between behavior directed toward the environment and processes mediating between the various tendencies of the inner world. Fear of the instinctual impulses is highly dependent upon prohibitions from outside. Fear of the superego has developed from parental demands and is still influenced by authorities and social norms. However, the more a person has achieved inner equilibrium by mediating and by creative adaptation to the different needs and demands from the inner world, the more he will be able to balance passive and active (creative) adjustments to the outer world.

I have already described situations of oppression in which an active adjustment cannot be achieved. Here the "creativity" must take refuge in inner changes, e.g., the reversal of ideals. The longing to be rescued was reversed into a craving to be "liberated" by death.

If one can subscribe to a common idea that the striving for survival is a "natural" and therefore a "normal" process, we must consider conformism to be the most "normal" attitude in a totalitarian society, although it greatly restricts the individual's mental growth. In a free and democratic society, the chances for creative adaptive behavior are considerable, and so are the possibilities for an unfolding of psychic faculties.

I must now point out another simplification I have made use of. In speaking of the ego organization I have not differentiated between the multiple ego functions which *may*, but very often *do not*, act together in the process of active adjustment. Some faculties and talents may function as an impetus to creative action, whereas other ego characteristics may act in an opposite way, restricting the person's free functioning. An example would be rigid character traits that developed as a result of conflicts, reaction formations, and defensive measures (Hartmann, 1956, 1960).

Finally, I would like to underline that the acquisition of inner and outer harmony of reality-directed creative inner and outer adaptation is dependent upon a multitude of complicated and vulnerable mental processes and is achieved only in rare cases. The ego organization must have special capacities to deal with a very strong drive endowment and with a moral system that may have become very rigid in the course of generations transmitting their norms and demands. The outcome will depend on the ego's consistency, on its faculties, and especially on its ability to neutralize energy and to use it for constructive activities.

Conclusion

1. A distinction should be made between adaptation as a mental mechanism and adaptation as a pattern of behavior.
2. A further distinction should be made between adaptation and conforming behavior.
3. Conformism should be defined as behavior characterized by passive surrender to inner and outer demands and norms and motivated by inner anxieties or social anxiety.
4. Adaptation should be defined as behavior directed by a creative assessment of inner and outer factors and leading to equilibrium and constructive action.

31. On Obstacles Standing in the Way of Psychoanalytic Cure

(1967)

Among the many unsolved problems in psychoanalysis I have chosen one that is of practical as well as theoretical importance. It was raised by Freud in 1937 in "Analysis Terminable and Interminable." He suggested that instead of investigating in which way psychoanalytic treatment accomplishes a cure (which is sufficiently known), we should ask ourselves: which are the obstacles standing in the way of achieving a cure? This question is still as interesting as it was thirty years ago. In the meantime, however, our experience and our theoretical knowledge have grown. These can be applied to work out some of Freud's points and to add new ones.

I shall not discuss untimely interruptions of analysis due to external circumstances, or the impatience or inexperience of the analyst, or unforeseen deteriorations in the patient's mental condition, e.g., the outbreak of severe psychosis, which demands discontinuation of analytic treatment and hospitalization. I shall limit myself to those situations in which the patient is sufficiently intelligent and able to cooperate, in which there is a good working alliance that has helped to uncover a considerable part of the unconscious conflicts, and in which the therapeutic effect has nevertheless failed to come about after patient working through in prolonged treatment.

Freud mentioned some of the factors responsible. Among them are the following:

1. A strong need for punishment that leads to the negative therapeutic reaction.
2. An incapacity to "tame" the instinctual drives and a particularly unfortunate relationship between sexual (libidinal) and aggressive drives.
3. An ego alteration or impairment which makes the patient incapable of coping with the instinctual demands in a favorable way; or, put in another way, an irregular development of ego functions.
4. A clash between passive and active tendencies, a repudiation of femininity in the sexual sphere.

I shall try to examine these different factors, especially in their interaction with each other.

Need for punishment

Freud discovered quite early that neurotic patients are not born as degenerates but are suffering from acquired illnesses that originate in childhood and are due to a failure to resolve the oedipus complex in a normal way. In this, traumatic experiences, e.g., the sexual use or seduction of small children by adults, play an important role. The uncovering of such repressed experiences was originally expected to result in mental health. The fate of the oedipal situation was seen as the core of neurosis.

The bringing into consciousness of the repressed oedipal conflicts did indeed sometimes lead to the expected recovery. In many cases, however, both analyst and patient were disappointed. The neurotic symptoms did not disappear or were replaced by others. The increased experience gained in analysis of adults and children, and especially by direct observation of infants, began to reveal the importance of the preoedipal phase of development, i.e., not only of the maturational processes of the instinctual drives, but also of the development of object relationships and of the gradual unfolding of ego functions. In the area of drive development, the recognition of the aggressive drives was of special significance. In the area of the ego functions, the gradual organization of the primary autonomous functions, the defense mechanisms, the structures leading to secondary autonomy, and the emergence of the superego as a subsystem of the ego organization greatly furthered the understanding of harmonious as well as disturbed mental development. Early object relations, the infant's first tie to his mother, proved to exert great influence on the course of further development in nearly every area. The mother-child dyad determines to a large extent the state of the infant's physical and mental well-being. Yet I do not believe that this increase in our knowledge has decisively added to the number of successes of analytic treatment during the last decades.

On the other hand, there has been a positive change in the type and range of psychic disturbances that we try to influence by psychoanalysis. We no longer limit therapeutic efforts to the "ordinary" (transference) neuroses. We analyze character neuroses, borderline cases, and even psychotics and delinquents, although these conditions may sometimes require the introduction of "parameters" in our technique (Eissler, 1953). This extension of the application of psychoanalysis has become possible through the increase in our knowledge. At the same time it has altered the goals and the expectations of the psychoanalytic procedure. We no longer are content with removing neurotic symptoms; we now look for character distortions and, if possible, try to alter disharmonies in the mental structure. This is especially necessary in training analyses.

Character traits are essentially shaped in the first years of life, in the preoedipal and the oedipal phases of development. It is true that they unfold on the basis of genetically determined factors inherent in drive equipment as well as in the potentialities out of which ego qualities, functions, and capacities gradually develop. It is the growing interaction of these given factors that can proceed harmoniously only if the mother-infant relationship provides the necessary favorable climate. For this reason we need to look into that archaic preoedipal phase, the period immediately following birth. We must examine the "prehistory" of patients who, suffering from a strong need for punishment, show the negative therapeutic reaction. This symptom is due to a very strict superego, which does not permit the enjoyment of a state of well-being. The superego, which becomes established as an internal system after the passing of the oedipus complex, has taken over the norms and the prohibitions of the parents. The severity of the superego partly mirrors the strictness of the parental demands, but these are not the only source of its cruelty. As is well known, this is to a large extent due to the turning inward of aggression that cannot be discharged in the outer world. This process, however, has its precursors in the preoedipal phase and it seems worthwhile to examine its fate during this period.

All of us have treated patients suffering from unconscious guilt and a strong need for punishment; we succeed in improving their condition by uncovering their adherence to the severe parental demands, thus enabling the mature person to choose his own norms and restrictions in a healthier way. However, this success, which sometimes already occurs in the initial phase of an analysis, is often followed by a regressive tendency and a renewed clinging to the feeling of inferiority and guilt-laden worthlessness. If we then try to unravel the superego *precursors* in the preoedipal phase, where single parental prohibitions were accepted and even internalized, we may be confronted with the child's overwhelming anxiety concerning his own *aggressive* impulses. After the superego demands have been attenuated, the sexual wishes are no longer experienced as quite so dangerous unless they are completely fused with aggression and have become transformed into sadistic fantasies and actions. But the *aggressive* impulses are, in any event, experienced as too dangerous. In the first place, the infant has at some time or other learned that an attack on or the destruction of some object or other, e.g., a pet or a toy, while originally providing intense joy and satisfaction, usually leads to loss or at least to damage of the object. This experience is especially threatening when the impulse is directed toward a living person, initially the mother. As a consequence of the child's magic thinking, he experiences his impulses as though they were real actions. The conflict between love and hate means to him: to keep or to destroy his mother, an unsolvable problem.

This brings me to a second source of anxiety. The little child's magic world includes the narcissistic fantasy of his omnipotence as well as that of his parents. His inability to solve the love-hate conflict is a severe threat to his inner equilibrium. In order to ameliorate the narcissistic injury he again clings to reinforced fantasies of grandeur, and a vicious circle emerges.

Some patients apparently find it less painful to keep their neurotic suffering in self-punishment than to face the primitive fear of their own aggressive drives and the destruction of their omnipotence fantasies. In other cases a real improvement in the patient's condition may occur, provided he is able to accept a certain *powerlessness*, as it exists in every human's life, and to find other ways of handling his aggressive impulses. Such a favorable outcome is by no means a regular occurrence. If we fail, we must ask ourselves: what other obstacles stand in the way of a patient's recovery?

Incapacity to tame the instinctual drives

My previous reference to a successful analysis of the preoedipal love-hate conflicts already implied that the infantile nature of the child's ego organization – i.e., his magical and wishful thinking – greatly influences his ability to deal with the drive impulses. We all know that it does not make sense to speak of the "strength" of the drives. What matters is the *relation* between the power of the drives and the forces available to the gradually developing ego functions, which will ultimately be organized in what we call the system ego. Quantitative considerations (which are often neglected) are of utmost importance, provided we realize that we are dealing with *relative* quantities or intensities.

What do we mean by the "taming" of the drives? It is not suppression, repression, or warding off of the instinctual impulses. Human beings cannot live and grow without a certain amount of direct satisfaction. However, living in a community with fellowmen demands considerable limitations of drive discharge. For this reason certain transformations of the *modes* of gratification are imperative. These must occur both in the original narcissistic state of the libido and its later investment in object relations and in the aggressive drive. We have conceptualized such transformations as processes of desexualization and desaggressivization or neutralization of the mental energy of the instinctual drives (Hartmann, 1964).

I am aware of the fact that the term "mental energy" may give rise to criticism on the part of psychologists, psychiatrists, and psychoanalysts. One of the arguments of those who oppose the concept of mental energy reads: the term "energy" is not applicable in mental life; it is borrowed from physics and therefore too mechanistic. I would counter this argument by maintaining that, as I see it, it may rather be the other way round. Since human languages have existed, words such as "force," "power," and "energy" have been used to designate certain activities and qualities of human beings. When the science of physics began to develop, from where did the physicists take their terminology? Is it not conceivable that they chose their terms for describing physical phenomena on the basis of an (unconscious) anthropomorphism? It is true that as analysts we cannot specify the sources of "mental energy," that we do not know whether its nature is chemical, hormonal, electrical, etc.; nor can we measure it. However, in psychology – as in physics and other sciences – there are many unknown areas and limitations of knowledge. As long as we do not have a better term to account for our observations, therefore, I see no advantage in discarding a concept that has proved to be of heuristic usefulness.

The "tamability" of drives seems to be dependent upon a certain degree of flexibility, which permits neutralization of a portion of their energy as far as the drives themselves are concerned. It is difficult to decide whether *aggression* is more inflexible and harder to neutralize than *libido* or whether the danger inherent in its destructive component is responsible for the strength of the countermeasures adopted against aggressive manifestations. Surveying man's history, one is strongly impressed by the numerous breakthroughs of violent, unneutralized, aggressive and destructive acts among fellowmen. The final outcome of the mental process that leads to a restriction of direct discharge is, however, equally dependent upon the qualities of the mediating and organizing ego organization. In early childhood the immature ego functions are not yet organized in a coherent system. The ego is therefore "weak" in relation to the imperative demands of the powerful drive impulses. In coping with them, the ego of the infant and the little child is strongly dependent on the mother's support.

Irregular ego development

The study of ego development is meaningful only if it is viewed in its interaction with drive development, because both ego and id develop out of an initially undifferentiated matrix. While the drives as well as the core of the gradually emerging ego functions are inborn, both developments are decisively influenced by the first experiences in the mother-child dyad and especially by the infant's reactions to external and internal stimuli. For theorizing in this field we cannot resort to information gained in psychoanalytic treatment but must turn to the careful observational studies on newborns and infants, such as those carried out by Spitz, Anna Freud, Bowlby, Margaret Mahler, Ernst and Marianne Kris, Winnicott, and many others.

I shall start with the observations made by Spitz, which he described in many papers but most comprehensively in his book *The First Year of Life* (1965). On the basis of many careful investigations Spitz depicts the newborn as having a high stimulus barrier which shields him against stimuli from the external world. His sensory organs begin to function only some time after birth. The newborn "receives" stimuli from inside, e.g., hunger, thirst, etc., and reacts to them with reflex movements, but he does not yet experience sensory *perceptions*. The *reception* of stimuli is accompanied by sensations of unpleasure; the removal of tensions provides pleasure. This original reception system is termed the *coenesthetic organization*. Later on the *diacritic organization* comes into being. The infant gradually develops his faculty of perception by way of making a "distance contact" with his mother. He now "recognizes" her face (or at least part of her face, a so-called Gestalt), and the diacritic organization begins to unfold. The mode of functioning of the coenesthetic organization is the primary process, whereas the diacritic organization gradually switches over to secondary-process functioning.

From the very beginning the reactions of individual infants differ remarkably. Some infants remain more or less passive, others seem to crave passionately for the satisfaction of their bodily needs, the gaining of pleasure and the removal of unpleasure. These observations highlight the constitutional differences in drive equipment. However, the infant's active behavior, manifested in his body movements, his crying, his grasping, etc., not only reveals something about his drives, it also indicates how and at what rate his ego functions of perception, memory, primitive awareness of an outer world, motility, etc., begin to develop. The individual differences in the timing and the speed of development point to inborn potentialities or qualities of the gradually emerging ego as well. It is well known that the infant's complete dependence on the mother's care for survival is complicated by the fact that he is also dependent on the mother's *love* for his physical and mental growth. If he is deprived of loving mothering, the infant is hampered or even totally disturbed in the development of the various functions. This is valid not only for the sensory functions and the active responses to stimuli (diacritic organization) but also for the passive receptive state of the earlier coenesthetic organization. In the course of development the diacritic mode of functioning more or less replaces and sometimes represses the earlier mode of functioning. Normally, however, both organizations continue to exist throughout life.

In one instance the coenesthetic organization is clearly revived, namely, in the healthy mother who is nursing her newborn child. The mother's coenesthetic way of functioning enables her to "understand" the newborn's signals which indicate his needs, to "respond" to them, to communicate with her baby in an adequate way. The question then arises: what is an *adequate way?* Since the newborn can function only in the passive receptive mode, that is what the mother must react to. However, the mother's understanding and furthering of the gradually developing diacritic organization are equally important. Her capacity to stimulate this unfolding is necessary as well. I believe we have to evaluate the "adequacy" of the mother's behavior in terms of a well-balanced interplay between the revived coenesthetic and the diacritic modes of reacting. We have always known that too much frustration as well as too much indulgence can lead to disturbed development. One explanation may be sought in an unharmonious relation of the two ways of functioning in the mother's personality. Apart from the fact that an infant's inborn passivity-activity pattern may be an unfortunate one, it seems to be highly dependent upon the nature of the "dialogue" between mother and child, upon the mother's competence to use both modes of functioning in accordance with the special needs of her baby. Spitz remarks that in many adults the coenesthetic organization is so deeply repressed or even abolished that it cannot be revived. If this is the case in a mother, her newborn will be frustrated from birth, with deleterious effects on his growth.

Spitz believes that the coenesthetic mode of functioning is retained not only in a healthy mother in her relation to the newborn but also in specially talented people, artists, musicians, composers, dancers, acrobats, etc. However, I believe that every person who in some way or other is performing original work must retain or reaquire the capacity to "regress" to the receptive mode of functioning, to the coenesthetic organization. This regression is a "regression in the service of the ego," to use Kris's concept (1952), a regression in the service of all nonautomatic functioning. Of course, the diacritic organization, the secondary-process functioning, must be developed as well, to arrange, regulate, and shape the person's final performance. In the last decades many authors have written about creativity and the related phenomena of intuition and empathy. I mention, among others, Bornstein (1948), Burlingham (1935), Greenacre (1957), Greenson (1960, 1966), Kohut (1966), Kris (1952), Olden (1958), Schafer (1959), and Spitz (1965). Greenacre draws attention to the "collective alternates," the talented child's "love affair with the world" in addition to the love for his mother. Kohut describes "transformations of narcissism," which he believes are responsible for creativity and empathy in connection with the development of a child's grandeur fantasies into adult ideals. Others stress the importance of the early mother-child relationship. Spitz especially points to the importance of both modes of functioning, the passive, receptive, and the active, ordering modality, which originate in the coenesthetic and in the diacritic organizations. In addition, Spitz draws attention to the observation that many highly creative persons exhibit disturbances in certain areas of their personalities, often in their emotional, sexual, and social life. Owing to the complex nature of mental development, it seems to be very difficult to achieve and to retain a harmonious balance between the two modes of functioning. On the one side derangements in the interaction between the processes of id and ego growth, and on the other side a lack of intensive support from the mother in this complicated interplay may lead to manifold disturbances in the child's development and the later adult disorders.

My special interest in this interplay concerns the case in which the mother fails to respond to the newborn's original coenesthetic mode of functioning, with the consequence that it is rigidly respressed and buried. For I believe that the capacity to revive the original receptive passive modality is of great significance in a variety of circumstances – *the psychoanalytic situation being one of them.* In psychoanalytic treatment a working alliance between analyst and patient is indispensable. It is a "dyadic" relationship in which both participants play their role.

It is well known that verbal communication between patient and analyst is not the only way in which they collaborate. Speech may suffice to uncover a patient's unconscious neurotic conflicts as they reveal themselves in the actual situation and can be traced back to their origin in the oedipal situation. The analyst's psychological knowledge, his technical skill, his adherence to the basic rule, his listening with free-floating (suspended) attention, and his self-knowledge enable him to avoid contamination of the analytic situation by his personal problems and peculiarities. These basic prerequisites may be sufficient to achieve the goal of working through the patient's *oedipal* conflicts. However, in the many cases in which development in the preoedipal phase was decisively distorted or hampered, nonverbal modes of communication become unavoidable. In these cases, I believe, the analyst's intuitive empathic understanding remains incomplete if he cannot revive his own coenesthetic organization. He must be able passively to receive signals sent out by the patient's behavior, his posture, his movements, his nonverbally expressed emotions and affects, his mimicry, his stammering, etc. This applies especially to those cases where the very first relation between newborn and mother was severely disturbed. Of course, the analyst must also be capable of alternatingly using the diacritic mode of functioning in order to verbalize what is going on in the patient's inner world. It is understandable that this verbalization may be difficult. Words can express inner experiences only approximately and often insufficiently. Attempts in this direction frequently proceed by trial and error. Sometimes the analyst's communication succeeds in reviving a patient's archaic personality residues and thus has a beneficial effect; sometimes it may fail to do so. But without the capacity to use the primitive receptive mode of functioning, the analyst cannot succeed.

This mode is, I believe, one of the deepest layers of empathy.

There is a parallel need for the *patient* to retain or revive his coenesthetic, receptive way of functioning. Although this capacity is based on innate factors, it may have been either furthered or impaired by the mother's intervention. If it has been suffocated at the very beginning, it may remain buried forever. In this case, the patient is unable to re-experience and to work through the very first conflicts, with the result that further conflicts affecting, in some cases, every area of the personality cannot be recovered. It is sometimes difficult to determine whether a failure in psychoanalytic treatment is due to the analyst's rigidity or to the patient's incapacity to overcome his resistance against the unearthing of his most primitive conflicts, because of the great amount of *anxiety* that has to be mastered. Initially the lack of the mother's response causes the infant unpleasure, but after a certain distance contact and a first narcissistic object relation have been established, anxiety comes into the picture. The development of the instinctual life, of the object relationships, and particularly of the primitive ego functions is hampered. The situation has become a traumatic one.

External events, provided they are not too life threatening, need not per se constitute an infantile trauma. They become traumatic when the infant's inner world has remained chaotic. In later phases, after ego functioning has been acquired, it becomes possible to determine whether an external event which was considered to be traumatic by the observer actually traumatized the child or not (Anna Freud and others). On the other hand, certain constellations usually have detrimental effects, especially a succession of states of unpleasure and lack of satisfaction which may arouse so much anxiety that a passive, receptive attitude is experienced as a danger. This may constitute the basis of the subsequent fear of passivity. In the phallic-oedipal situation, a passive attitude may acquire the meaning of passive *sexual* surrender. This implies, for the little boy, giving up masculinity and his male organ, in order to acquire his mother's position. The passive sexual wishes then engender great castration anxiety. If this meaning persists, every passive attitude may be experienced as a danger and may be repressed completely. Later in life, when passive receptivity is still indispensable in many situations, e.g., in learning processes, the maturing personality may become blunted to such an extent that the original capacities are more or less suffocated. As mentioned previously, this process is enhanced and reinforced by *aggressive* impulses, which are mobilized by experiences of unpleasure, lack of satisfaction, and disappointment. These are experienced as dangers during the phase of development in which the child is struggling with the conflict between love and hate, between the need to keep the love object and the wish to destroy it. If the latter predominates, every activity may be experienced as *destructive* aggression, with the result that the child is utterly dependent upon the mother's empathic understanding and her support in overcoming these anxiety-ridden inner conflicts. Whenever this support is lacking, *autoagression* is unavoidable.

This may be one of the factors underlying the resistances of some neurotics in whom "the instinct of self-preservation has actually been reversed. They [these patients] seem to aim at nothing other than self-injury and self-destruction. It is possible too that the people who in fact do in the end commit suicide belong to this group" (Freud, 1940, p. 180).

I shall now summarize what we have so far learned about the different obstacles standing in the way of a psychoanalytic cure. It has become clear that a strong need for punishment, leading to negative therapeutic results, has a prehistory in the very first days and years of life. In the analysis of patients suffering from this disturbance, we must look for this prehistory and attempt to revive their most primitive modes of experiencing and functioning, and help them find more favorable ways of acting and reacting. In doing so we also come up against the archaic drives, in their unmitigated intensity, especially the *aggressive, destructive* impulses and the concomitant clinging to the earliest omnipotent fantasies. As I mentioned before, I am far from optimistic about the therapeutic results that can be achieved in such cases. There are, e.g., patients whose mother-infant dyadic relationship was so disturbed and engendered so much anxiety that one does not dare to go too deep into the primitive, chaotic inner life and therefore cannot revive the oldest reaction patterns. We must then limit our therapeutic efforts to the improvements that can be attained by virtue of working through the actual and oedipal conflicts. All we can do in such cases is to continue to wonder about the chief causes of the failure: whether it was due to an inherent incapacity to tame the instinctual drives, to a lack of ego potentialities, unevenness of ego development, disturbed reality testing; or whether it was the mother's incapacity to "understand" the infant's needs and to respond to them in a well-balanced way. This also involves the question whether the analyst was capable of the necessary empathy to gain insight into the archaic mother-infant interaction. A psychoanalyst who has a rigid personality and who in his training analysis has not acquired the capacity to revive his own coenesthetic organization, his personal receptive mode of functioning, will be unable to carry out this special part of the treatment.

A further complicating factor lies in the fact that not only severe *frustrations* in the original dyad may lead to the burial of the archaic receptive mode of functioning and thus to a distorted development. As I mentioned before, too much giving in, "spoiling," may bring about a developmental disturbance as well. Too much and too instantaneous satisfaction of the infant in the receptive state may hamper the development of his active strivings and thus impair the coming into being of the diacritic, active functioning and result in similar disturbances of development. This outcome is less well described and understood than the pathogenic result of frustrations and lack of loving mothering. At first, it seems strange that love can have a deleterious effect. However, on second thought, we realize that a spoiling mother is an overanxious person who wards off her own unconscious hostile feelings in an active quasi-loving but domineering attitude. The infant then has no outlet for his own aggressive impulses, and his need to acquire some kind of independence is frustrated. Most of his active attempts are experienced as hostile attacks by both mother and child. In order not to lose the mother's love, the little child has to give up his strivings for independent activities and to cling to the passive modes of gaining

292

satisfaction. The resentment caused by the mother's suppression of his genuine need to become a person in his own right is firmly repressed. His diacritic mode of functioning may not develop adequately. According to Spitz, the outcome of a crippled diacritic development is much less frequent in our Western culture than the suffocation of the coenesthetic organization.

In connection with the psychoanalytic profession, Spitz therefore recommends that an investigation into a candidate's capacity to revive his coenesthetic organization should be a prerequisite for the decision whether to admit him to psychoanalytic training or not. Theoretically, I am in complete agreement with Spitz, but I do not know how to carry out this requirement. In the selection of candidates we try to evaluate a number of personality traits, among them a certain constancy, but also a certain flexibility of character. However, on the basis of a few interviews, it is extremely difficult to form a well-founded opinion of a candidate's suitability in this respect. Sometimes a person who has what appears to be a very rigid character profits a great deal from analysis and is then able to revive the necessary receptive empathy. In other cases, an intuitive person, who is apparently full of understanding and empathy, persists in clinging so tenaciously to a primitive, passive attitude that he becomes involved in acting out his own conflicts in the patient's analysis. In these cases it is only the personal analysis that can decide whether the necessary balance between the two modes of functioning will finally be achieved. I hope that at some time we shall be able to find more appropriate ways of evaluating the giftedness of the future analysts.

Reviewing the points I have raised so far, we can conclude that some of the obstacles to analytic cure mentioned by Freud can in part be traced back to the earliest developmental phases. The need for punishment and the unevenness of ego development are better understood if we view them in terms of the interaction of drive and ego growth and the mother's reaction to her infant in the dyadic relationship. The precursors of a cruel superego are to be found in the relative intensity and the fate of the *aggressive impulses*. If they cannot find appropriate outlets, initially in direct discharge and gradually in a more or less neutralized form, they will finally shape the superego into a sadistic, self-punishing agency. Although the innate properties of the drive equipment may be responsible for the fact that the drives cannot be tamed, other factors may also be of decisive significance: a deficiency in the possibilities for neutralization which depend on the interaction of certain drive properties with specific ego potentials, the presence or absence of a faculty for sublimated activities in the ego organization, and the influence of the mother on this process of interdependent development. The balance or imbalance that the mother has achieved between the two modes of functioning may further or hamper this threefold interaction. The same is true for the "clash" between passivity and activity. As we have already seen, passive and active tendencies are normal constituents of personality; they have their place in the mental life of healthy adults.

Repudiation of femininity

I now turn to the last point mentioned by Freud: the struggle between femininity and masculinity on the basis of innate bisexuality, the so-called anatomical "bedrock." Masculinity and femininity were originally more or less equated with activity and passivity. This view has been abandoned, although this has not always been made explicitly clear. I think we should make a very plain distinction. Passive and active modes of functioning manifest themselves in every human being from birth throughout life; both are indispensable for normal, harmonious development. Masculinity and femininity refer to *sexual* life and its derivatives in love life. Although the relation between the sexes is a model for many other performances in life, it coincides with active and passive behavior only when these behavior patterns are sexualized or, more accurately, invested with nonneutralized drive energy. Repudiation of femininity does not automatically imply repudiation of passivity. Freud's original idea that the psychic manifestations of bisexuality, the girl's wish for a penis and the boy's castration fear, were anatomically based (on the assumption that the clitoris is a rudimentary penis) has been disputed by more recent embryological discoveries. The female clitoris apparently is *not* a phylogenetically atrophied penis, since all mammalian embryos are morphologically female in the first days or weeks of their existence. The male-female struggle is genetically determined and unfolds hormonologically. The biological foundation of the woman's strong penis envy and the man's overwhelming castration fear − manifestations which we regularly observe in children and adult patients − must therefore be looked for in the genetic endowment and not in anatomy. However, the child's observation of the anatomical difference between the sexes is the trigger for the individual's sexual difficulties. In the treatment of male patients with intense castration fear, and in that of female patients who appear to be unable to conquer their penis envy and wish for a penis, we have to make the attempt to reach the forerunners of these phenomena in the preoedipal phase. In some instances we may be able to uncover the little child's intense fear not only of losing the mother's love but also, and sometimes predominantly, of losing his "own personality," his still unstable ego organization. The passive wish to "merge with the mother" may have become a severe danger to the gradually emerging need for independence. His growing, but still feeble self-esteem may have been threatened by the mother's domineering influence. It then may happen that in the phallic phase *every* passive wish is sexualized and acquires the meaning of sexual surrender, implying the acceptance of *castration*, as a consequence of which the faculties responsible for the neutralization of energy may become arrested. These faculties have to be freed and restored in the course of psychoanalytic treatment. If the analyst succeeds in supporting these processes, the patient may be able to conquer his current castration fear as a result of having worked through these primitive anxieties.

I want to stress once again that the increase in our knowledge of early mental development does not always bring us an increase in the desired therapeutic successes, but it enables us to make a more knowledgeable attempt. In training analyses, where we aim at liberating the future analyst's capacity for empathy, our effort cannot be confined to a mere attempt − its success is a prerequisite of our profession.

32. Cooperation Between Patient and Analyst in Psychoanalytic Treatment

(1967)

The following thoughts were stimulated by reading the book "The first year of life" by René Spitz (1965).

1. Introduction

The continuous development of psychoanalysis by the interaction of observation and theory formation has increased and stimulated our knowledge of the mental life of human beings and of our therapeutic capacity. At the same time, it has faced us with many new problems which for the greater part are still waiting for a solution. I would here like to tackle some problems occuring in the psychoanalytic therapeutic situation.

Analysis involves two persons. Both patient and analyst will have to make a contribution. These contributions differ but should be in tune with each other. Only when there is a continuous mutual influencing will this analytic process be favourable.

The fact that the two fundamental rules laid down by Freud at an early stage of his work on technique, the so-called basic rule for a patient to report everything that is in his mind without restricting criticism and the rule for the analyst to listen with "free floating attention", are tuned in to each other may be assumed to be known. In this way the logical, consciously criticising and selecting instance in both partners is eliminated. The logical, ordering ability should only be reemployed after the free associations of the patient converge with a sofar unconscious (pathogenic) conflict. The analyst uses his knowledge to summarize the interpretation of the material, the patient can increase his insight into the causes and connections of the sofar unknown conflict, which means a first step in the direction of a possible cure for his suffering. It is also known that these tasks for both members of the "therapeutic alliance" are far from easy. Often the patient has to begin to learn how to tolerate and conquer strong resistances and anxieties. The analyst will need inner harmony and inner stability to control his own emotions, conflicts and problems to such an extent that he can concentrate completely on the patient.

In spite of all the difficulties, experience has shown that analysis can guide a patient to recovery. The person involved is sometimes given access to the warded-off, unsolved, infantile conflicts which crystallized themselves in the oedipal situation as the essential core. This may help the patient to deal with his experiences in a better way. Inner tranquility to enable the analyst to observe the rule of freefloating attention is a prerequisite, in the same way as new insights are a first step in the direction of success for the patient who has to accomplish the much more difficult laborious task of dealing with conflicts, impulses, emotions, affects, etc. The analyst's inner tranquility should be accompanied by the ability to tolerate oppositional affects, demands, reproaches, in brief the patient's acting-out, which arises in the period of "working through". In addition the analyst should be able to assign them their legitimate place in the life-story of the patient.

Since "acting-out" occurs for the greater part in the "transference" (and quite rightly so) it is directed against the person of the analyst. Especially when seduction-fantasies and hostile, critical expressions of the patient hit upon a peculiarity or weakness of the analyst, he will find it difficult to control his reactions and only concentrate upon the patient. (Freud expressed his sympathy for the poor analyst of whom so much is demanded, in his own humorous fashion in his work "Die endliche und die unendliche Analyse" (1937), "Analysis terminable and interminable" St. Ed. *23*.)

I would like to make a few remarks on the concepts of transference and countertransference, which are sometimes misunderstood, and confusing.

2. Transference and countertransference

Kohut and Seitz (1963) use the concept "transference" in a metapsychological sense, originally used by Freud; transference thus means an inner process, namely the "influence of the Secondary Processes by the Primary Process" ("the penetration of unconscious psychic contents and powers in subconscious thoughts, feelings or desires").

In his later work on technique however, Freud used the concept "transference" for the process in which the patient transfers impulses, affects and conflicts of his infantile neurosis on the analyst. I will subsequently use the term in this sense. Here we meet already with an initial cause of the confusion which is so often encountered. Some analysts define all feelings of a patient towards the analyst as "transference". This usage does not make sense in analytic treatment. It is self-evident that a patient visiting a doctor has feelings, since affectionate rapport will evolve whenever two (or more) people meet. If the analyst is interested, understanding and prepared to help, the patient will have "normal" feelings of trust. If the analyst is uninterested, inhibited or cool, or if the patient has already had bad experiences with other doctors, he may be distrustful and reticent. All these feelings, which he naturally encounters in other situations in life, can, however, if handled properly by the analyst, be of benefit in carrying out the treatment.

The real analytical work is related to the repetition of affects and unsolved conflicts of the infantile neurosis, whether they show themselves directly in material from childhood or manifest themselves in a "new-edition" in a current neurotic conflict. In relation to the advancing analytic process it seems to make sense to use the concept "transference" in the latter sense.

Something similar applies to the concept of "countertransference". It does not seem to be appropriate to include all feelings of the analyst towards his patient in the analytical concept of countertransference. Natural, human interest and a preparedness to help the patient are necessary to start and continue an analysis. Feelings arising from the personal characteristics of the analyst must be controlled in sofar as they could disturb the analytical process. Sometimes feelings aroused in the analyst by the patient's acting-out, can be used as an indication of the conflict underlying the acting-out; they should therefore be regarded as a "red light", a warning signal. A real problem will only present itself if the analyst's own unconscious, unsolved conflicts and affects enter into the picture in the treatment.

Since no human being always knows himself and his unconscious completely, such a situation can occur. It seems appropriate to define only this set-up in the analytical treatment as "countertransference". It is one of the greatest difficulties of the "impossible profession" (Freud, 1937; Greenson, 1966). The analyst should always be aware of it, recognise the slightest indications of an inner lack of confidence or unrest and, if necessary, master them in his own analysis.

The variety of roles played by both patient and analyst means for the patient that to re-experience the childhood neurosis in the transference is the royal road to recovery whereas the carrying within of unsolved conflicts in the analytical situation on the part of the analyst (the countertransference) can only harm treatment, or even wreck it.

3. Empathy and intuition

So far, I have only dealt with work of the patient with the analyst involved in the treatment of neurotics. The core of their mental disturbance lays in the oedipal situation. The contact between patient and analyst in this treatment is mainly verbal. The patient communicates his ideas, thoughts, fantasies, dreams, he verbalizes his impulses, affects and emotions. It is relatively easy to verbalize the "material", produced in the form of behaviour, failure, symptomatic acts, etc. Insight, and gradually working through of quantities and intensities of feelings and drives, can lead to improvement. Elsewhere (Lampl-de Groot, 1952) I have explained that the Oedipal constellation is already a preliminary endproduct of the pre-oedipal developmental phases and that the material in a succesful analysis reconverges to the oedipal situation. Subsequently the pre-oedipal material can sufficiently be verbalized. From the side of the analyst interest, knowledge, technical ability and self-knowledge, as well as his control over his own conflicts, play a most important role. There are, however, restrictions. The above mentioned "ideal" situation does not occur as often as one wishes. When early infantile experiences and affects in the so-called "transference neurosis" emerge, it can sometimes take a long time until it is possible to verbalize the re-experiencing and to work it through. In that case the analyst needs more than mere theoretical knowledge about himself and others. In order to "understand" he needs empathy, intuition, "fine tuning", "Fingerspitzen Gefühl" or whatever you may want to call it. Much interesting material has been written about empathy and intuition in the past decades: Burlingham (1935), Greenacre (1957), Greenson (1966), Kohut (1966), Olden (1958), Spitz (1965) and others. I return to this problem because in my opinion these qualities are gaining more and more significance for the analyst since more and more patients request our help, patients who are much more disturbed than the "ordinary" neurotics and whose developmental disturbances began at a much earlier stage in life. These disturbances led to stagnation of the developmental processes of the drive-life, of the ego-functions and/or of the super-ego-formation at a very early age. I think that the latest book by René Spitz can make a significant contribution to the clarification of these phenomena. I do not mean to say that the origin of intuition or the ability to empathize can be explained. Talents and gifts are inborn potentials; it is, however, possible to follow partly their developmental possibilities or inhibitions in psychoanalysis. Something similar is valid for the related area of creativity.

I do not like to use the concept of creativity in relation to values, as often happens, for example when it is only related to artistic and scientific achievements. I prefer to define creativity as the ability to create something new or new contents, irrespective of the field of activity. A cook can be creative while composing and preparing dishes and meals, a carpenter can be creative in choosing wood, in moulding and in selecting colours when producing furniture, etc. A special ability (or a special "organ", a specific constellation), which is effective with only some people, not visible or tangible, is needed to expand these various, intuitive, emphatic, creative achievements.

Greenacre (1957) describes in a stimulating examination the "collective alternaties". According to her, the creative person (she refers only to artists and scientists) in his early childhood had an object-love not only to his mother but to many "objects", including lifeless objects. He had "a love relationship with the whole world". This love is the expression of a specific sensibility towards the exterior world and one of the foundations of the later creative achievements.

Kohut (1966), in his article "Forms and transformations of narcissism", carries back creativity and empathy to a specific development of narcissism. In this interesting work he shows how the development of ego-ideals which consist of grandeur-fantasies in childhood, formed according to the idealization of the parents, gradually continue and may lead to creative accomplishments in later life through transformations of narcissism. According to him, and I agree, Greenacre's concepts of "collective alternates" and of a "love affair with the whole world" are objects-attachments, for the greater part still belonging to the "narcissistic environment" of little children. Kohut however, mainly describes the drive-vissicitudes in development, and I agree that it is possible to "neutralize" narcissistic libido as well as object libido, which, however, originates from the narcissistic "reservoir". But it depends equally on the developmental potentials of the other parts of the personality and especially on those of the ego-functions, whether a "neutralized" (sublimated) accomplishment can come to the fore, or whether the grandeur-fantasies are retained in their primitive form of self-glorification.

Something similar is valid for empathy, and here we may, in my opinion, express some preliminary suppositions. They link up with the expositions made by Spitz (1965) about the way in which a newborn baby reacts upon stimuli and about the development of its functions of perception. Spitz has observed newborn babies and little children for decades. His findings and their theoretical treatment are laid down in his latest book. I can scarcely do justice here to the variety of observations and the wealth of thoughts and explanations. I only draw out what is appropriate to my theme. Spitz observed that a newborn baby possesses a high stimuli threshold. It is, as it were, shielded from exterior stimuli. It is not until some time after its birth that its senses start functioning. It receives interior stimuli, e.g. hunger and thirst and reacts to these with reflexes. The newborn receives stimuli from the inside e.g. hunger and thirst and reacts with reflexmovements. It "receives" stimuli, but does not, yet, know sensual perceptions. Spitz speaks of "reception of stimuli" as opposed to "perception". In his opinion, stimulus intake involves sensations of unpleasure, the lifting of tension involves sensations of pleasure (viz. when hunger has been satisfied). He defines this original "intake-system" for stimuli as the coenesthetic-organisation. In the diacritic organisation, which develops later, observations and the belonging sensations begin to play a part. The coenesthetic-organisation is expressed in physical sensations; the first contact with the mother is a direct skin-mouth contact (contact of the "oral cavity"). Only when the baby begins to get distance-contact, viz. when it learns to recognize the face of the mother, a diacritic organisation gradually comes into being.

The coenesthetic-organisation works like the primary-process, the diacritic one like the secondary-process. The latter will replace the first in the course of life, shield it, "repress" it. Both, however, will continue to exist during the lifetime, even though adults are not consciously aware of the coenesthetic faculty which sometimes is no longer operative. In the coenesthetic-organisation a "wholeness", a "Gestalt", is experienced; there are not yet differentiated sensations or affects available.

Spitz sees the survival of the coenesthetic processes confirmed in the way which a mother communicates with her infant. According to him, the old way of functioning emerges in the mother through this dual-relationship. This process may explain the fact that the mother "understands" her baby, that she unconsciously recognizes the signals indicating needs and that she can react upon them adequately through this "underground" communication. It is also well-known that an infant reacts quickly and vehemently to primitive changes of mood in the mother, often with physical symptoms. The diacritic way of functioning has not yet superseded the primitive one in this case. Adults who still possess the ability to receive coenesthetic signals are, according to Spitz, highly gifted persons (he mentioned composers, musicians, dancers, acrobats, painters, poets and others). They are at the same time, however, also tense, unbalanced personalities.

It appears from analyses that by impeding the secondary process by means of the primary process, strong disharmony may be the result. One might ask however, whether this must always be so, whether there could not emerge a certain balance between both organisations, as can be seen in the relationship of a healthy mother with her child. I think that the capacity of empathy, intuition or "fine-tuning", which is indispensable for the work of the analyst, has one of its origins in the coenesthetic functions. Mobilizing of the coenesthetic-organisation enables the analyst to "receive" and "understand" non-verbal material of patients and to empathize with their primitive affects, sensations, and tensions originating from the pre-verbal developmental phase. The analyst should naturally be able to work, at the same time or alternatively, "diacritically" with sense-perceptions, ordering and verbalizing. Spitz talks of regression when the coenesthetic way of functioning in adults is reactivated. In the analysis, however, a "regression in the service of the ego" is involved. If my supposition should prove to be true, this capacity for regression will even be a prerequisite for achieving an optimal analytic technique. Therefore one of the tasks for the analyst is to find the balance between both ways of functioning. If we had to agree with Spitz that only breastfeeding mothers and specifically gifted persons possess this coenesthetic mode of functioning, the implication would be that only mothers, dancers, musicians, acrobats, etc. could exercise analysis! It might however, be possible to open up the "receptive" faculty in certain people in their personal analysis so that they become capable of empathy. Men and women who have never experienced motherhood have all reacted in this way when they were infants. Of course we should not forget that newborns enter life with very varied potential gifts. But apart from the influence of innate differences in sensitive, affective reacting, we may suppose that the formation of the first mother-child-relationship plays an important part in the development of both ways of functioning. A healthy mother will give her child the opportunity in the "dyad" to deploy its coenesthetic faculty (and later on the diacritic one) and, if necessary, ease the reexperience of the first in the future. A disturbed mother will hamper the development of one (or both) ways of functioning and perhaps stifle the coenesthetic for ever.

The future analyst might, like the child "learning" much by identification with the mother, learn a new capacity for empathy from his teacher-analyst in the course of his training. Our considerations could also − at least partly − explain why rigid personalities, in whom coenesthetic functioning, intuition and empathy cannot be revived, are unfit to be analysts, or why they cannot progress any further in the treatment of patients than the understanding of later, verbally expressed conflicts. This means that they will never be able to help the pre-oedipal-fixated patients whose development was disturbed at a very early age. On the other hand we should not forget that, if the coenesthetic way of functioning dominates, this could lead to the analyst's acting-out together with the patient, to a disturbance of the secondary processes and to an impediment of the reality-testing. The analyst could be tempted by the analytical situation to linger too long and go too deeply in to the archaic way of functioning.

Many examples of such inflexible regression might be produced. I would only like to point out the specific danger of the analyst considering his primitive grandeur- and powerimpulses, which so easily can be raised through his work, not "diacritically", but experiencing them as a real power of his personality. I would like to recall here a remark of Freud that analysing could corrupt a character.

We have tried to use our increased knowledge of the development of mental life, this time in connection with the careful observations of infants by Spitz for our therapeutic efforts and an expansion of the analytic technique. The "part of the analyst" in the "dyad" of the analytical situation, has been described. Now I want to make some remarks about the patient's situation. This would link up with a suggestion of Freud's "Analysis terminable and interminable" ("Die endliche und die unendliche Analyse"): we should examine which factors are responsible for the failure of analysis because we know already sufficiently how a cure is achieved. A number of factors which we find in the patient, have by now long been known:

1. Too strong a need for punishment, which may lead to a negative therapeutic reaction;
2. An untamable drive-endowment;
3. An unfavourable relation between libido and aggression, between active and passive strivings;
4. An unbalanced development of ego-functions;
5. The coincidence and interference of one or more of these factors could make analysis of a patient impossible.

I would like to add one more possible factor:

6. A rigid defense, which cannot be influenced, to the coenesthetic way of functioning or its complete dissolution. When a patient whose disturbance is rooted in a very early period of life is no longer able to mobilize this primary functioning, the analysis will not succeed in making him relive his earliest affects and conflicts so as to finally conquer them.

Then the question arises which factors may lead to this rigid defense of the primary coenesthetic way of functioning. I already mentioned the attitude of the mother to her newborn child. When a mother does not "understand" the signals of her infant and is therefore unable to answer them, this faculty will soon shrivel up.

The "dialogue" between mother and child which Spitz speaks of, certainly provides the foundation for the development or crumpling-up of the receptive attitude of the child. It is here that the first and most profound faulty developments will come about. Of course, later experiences also may influence the progress of the development. Of the various factors involved I would like to point out just one, which in my view is very important and occurs quite often. Since the origin of the coenesthetic organisation lies in the "receptive" in-take, the satisfaction of needs requires a passive attitude towards the outer world, which for the newborn is about the only possibility. Passive strivings are thus satisfied. Only when a distance-contact between mother and child has been established can the child become active in, for example, searching for and reaching for the breast. Initially, active and passive strivings coexist peacefully. They will only give rise to an inner conflict when in later developmental phases the opposition between receiving and capturing begins to play a part.

The conflict will reach its climax in the phallic phase when in the child's representational world passive surrender postulates castration. It is well-known that castration-fear may lead to neuroses and developmental inhibitions. A girl's experience of dangers are evoked through the discovery of the anatomical difference between sexes and give rise to envy (penis-envy), not only directly of fear. They have already been described so often that I would like not to go over them here. In the analysis of adults we often encounter the great difficulty, or even an impossibility, of convincing the patient that passive strivings in their various forms and sublimations are needed throughout life. To detach them from sexuality and castration-images will only be possible through long and hard work and often not at all or only partly.

With a too rigid defense of the passive tendencies, the original receptive reactionmode cannot be experienced. This sometimes limits the psychoanalytical treatment definitely. If, however, a loosening of the defense finally takes place, not only the chances of recovery are better, but it sometimes results in an expansion of the personality and the liberation of potentially creative talents.

33. Thoughts on Advantages and Dangers of "One-sidedness" in Scientific Research*

(1968)

Introduction

It is certainly a commonplace to state that science has its limitations. No sensible person will dispute that all humans, including scientists, even if they are talented or right up to a genius, cannot pass over certain limits of their personalities and performances. Nevertheless one sometimes comes upon a notion or even a fear that these limits could be extended infinitely as a consequence of the enormous flight of science since the "Renaissance" and the "Enlightment". In view of the technical possibilities of our "atomic-age" such a fear is not ununderstandable. Nowadays, man possesses the means and instruments to destroy himself in the shortest span of time. However, most human beings want to live on. One reminds oneself of Goethes "Zauberlehrling" (sorcerers-apprentice). It seems that man has to pay for the high development of his intellect and "ratio" in the realm of irrationality, emotionality and affectivity, thus interhuman relationships.

As psychoanalysts we are interested in general psychology. So we ask ourselves *why* this has to be. However, we are aware of the fact how little we know. This short paper tries to express only some tentative thoughts.

I. Two areas of science

One can divide natural sciences in two large domains
1. the science of lifeless nature: physics, astrophysics, chemistry, mathematics, technology, and so on.
2. the science of living nature: biology with the subsection, antropology.

Natural science strives for objectivity. Some persons have the opinion that the pure objective research does exist, for instance in physics and allied disciplines. However, they overlook that science is devised by human beings and automatically includes subjective elements. This fact is convincingly demonstrated by Charles C. Gillispie, professor of the history of science at Princeton University, in his book: "The edge of objectivity, an essay in the history of scientific ideas". The author recalls to mind that the modern natural history of the sixteenth century was influenced by the philosophy of nature of the Greeks.

---

* Dedicated to Alexander Mitscherlich on the occasion of his sixtieth birthday

Physics of Aristoteles was part of Platonic philosophy. Until the age of the Renaissance and Enlightment science was permanently influenced by religious-mystical and romantic ideas. It is fascinating to follow Gillispie in his description of the *limits* of "objective" research, *not* of instruments, but of limitations inherent in human nature.

Science of living nature leads from Darwin to the knowledge of human nature. Psychoanalysts are best acquainted with human psychology. At the present time a general psychology is unconceivable without Sigmund Freud's Psychoanalysis, which has contributed most to the understanding of the human mind, of the *conscious* and *unconscious* forces, that underlie its functions or inhibit its achievements. Some researchers in the so-called exact sciences, have become aware of the influence of mental life on intellectual performances, as a matter of fact. I want to cite a few sentences from a lecture given in 1871 by the physicist *James C. Maxwell*, which is printed as an introduction in the above-mentioned book of Gillispie's: "The history of the development, whether normal or abnormal of ideas is of all subjects that, in which we as thinking men take the deepest interest. But when the action of the mind passes out of the intellectual stage in which truth and error are the alternatives into the more violently emotional states of anger and passion, malice and envy, fury and madness the student of science though he is obliged to recognize the powerful influence which these wild forces have exercised on mandkind is perhaps in some measure disqualified from pursuing the stuey of this part of human nature."

One admires the great physicist's insight in human nature and tend to despair, when one is just occupying oneself with that "part" of nature. However, a person's life-work does not let one go astray. So one continues to try notwith-standing successes and failures.

II. Thoughts on the development of the psychoanalytic science

Looking over Freud's life-work one discovers two important lines in succession. In the first decades of his psychological investigations, Freud limited himself to the study of pathological fenomena of their causes and of the interplay of forces in neurotic personalities. This brought about the discovery of the existence of an unconscious psychic life, a fact untill then denied by the academic, official psychology. In addition Freud found out that human beings may fall mentally ill, caused by unsolved conflicts, inner as well as environmental conflicts. These findings gave rise to the "Topical Theory" of the upbuilding of the mind and to the dynamic theory of the drives. As so many new discoveries were made Freud, at that time, restricted himself to the development of both theories: the topic one of mental instances and the dynamic one of the drives. In this regard Freud followed a word of Goethe's: "In der Beschränkung zeigt sich der Meister" ("Moderation makes the Master"). The poet himself, otherwise, did not keep to his own dictum in having a try in the field of exact science. But his "Farbenlehre" (theory of colours) is not at all free from subjective and mystical ideas. However, in "Faust" Goethe comes back to his knowledge of human limitations, where he lets "Frau Sorge" say: "Die Menschen sind im ganzen

Leben blind, nun Fauste, werd Du's am Ende" (Men are blind in their entire life, so Faust, should you be in the end). Then Faust loses his sight, but before dying he consoles himself with a magnificent grandeur fantasy by building "a paradisical country" for his fellow-men. He imaginesto see and exclaims: "Auf freiem Grund mit freiem Volke stehn . . . Im Vorgefühl von solchem hohen Glück geniess ich jetzt den höchsten Augenblick" (Standing on free ground with free people . . . With the foreboding of such a grand happiness I now enjoy the supreme moment).

The blind Faust cannot see that at this "supreme moment" the newly built houses and churches (built on sand by Mephisto far below the palace) crash down and go up in flame. Faust dies and Mephistofoles with his servants-devils try to capture Faust's soul. But finally Goethe creates celestial powers, which rescue Faust. In a genius, too, selfknowledge struggles with wishful thinking.

In former times many critics of psychoanalysis reproached Freud for being "one-sided", refering to the so-called "Pansexualism". This affectively coloured criticism reminds us of the above cited words of Maxwell. It affirms once more that from time to time "the action of the mind passes out of the intellectual stage into the more violently emotional states of anger and passion". Then "Truth and Error" are no more the valid criteria. In looking back towards the so-called "one-sidedness" of Freud's, we can only conclude that it has been beneficial. It brought about the second part of Freud's life-work in which the basic foundations to a general psychology of the human mind were laid down. In the later decades of his life Freud studied also the other realms of the psyche: consciousness, intellect, norms and ideals, as well as the interhuman relationships and the development of civilization. It is self-evident, that he did not find *"the"* absolute and *Final Truth*. He himself always stressed the general limitedness of human creations. However one may wonder what enabled Freud to make the step from the original "one-sidedness" to the gigantic widening of his understanding of mental life and human affairs. Maybe we cannot "understand" it and have to ascribe it to the essence of a man of genius and a grand researcher. A number of critics simply ignore the later development of Freud's work and still speak of the "pure pansexualism". Maybe they belong to the group, described by Maxwell, which is driven by "anger and passion, malice and envy". Be it as it may, I think the former "one-sidedness" of Freud's was a prerequisite for the later development of psychoanalysis in the direction of a general psychology of the individual, as well as of humanity at large.

III. Thoughts on the development of the so-called psychoanalytical movement

At the time that pupils and co-workers began to gather around Freud, psychoanalysis became no longer the work of one researcher. A "movement" came into being. It seems that the first pupils were very deeply impressed by the originality of the discoveries and of the fact that they came upon the affirmation of many of Freud's findings in their own work. It is well-known that a number of them produced important contributions to the theory and the practice of psychoanalysis. It is equally known that some talented pupils who in the beginning were attracted by the new "Sache" (Cause), turned away from it at a later date. Usually the turning-away proceeded gradually. In the beginning it was not always clear whether an author produced new and relevant contributions or whether he was looking for arguments to enfeeble findings which were already many times confirmed. It certainly was legitimate to start with detailed inquiries after Freud's example. However, these procedures often did not lead to additions and/or enlargements of the already verified theories, but to their rejection. We ask ourselves why that happened, where differences of opinion lead to "fighting". We use to look for an interaction of both parties, though the contribution of the fight maybe more extensive in one of the parties than in the other.

Critics of Freud's have reproached him to be "intolerant", "authoritative". It is true that Freud kept to those parts of the theory which had been affirmed in growing numbers of experiences. He wanted to preserve the "Sache" (the cause). However, the idea that Freud, as a human being and as a friend should have been more intolerant than his fellowman, can easily be contradicted by everyone who takes pains to read his personal communications and his letters to friends and colleagues. Whoever has known him personally could not help receiving the impression of a warm humanity and an open personality.

Freud himself has in a few articles written about the "dissentient movements". Among others he ventured the idea that some of the original adherents could, on the long run, not cope with their discontent with the significance of the sexual drives and especially of infantile sexuality for mental development. One denies and represses easily what is disagreeable. Of course this does not mean that dissidents never made good and important contributions. But if so, it included the negation of the sexual etiology of psychic disturbances. For instance: Adler has the, from psychoanalysis never disputed striving for power, described as the *sole* source of neurosis. Jung mystified love-life and disavowed the high importance of the underlying sexuality. Horney, Fromm, a.o. considered individual conflicts with the environment (which psychoanalysis has always taken into account) as the *only* cause of maldevelopments. One could give many more examples of the "one-sidedness" at the cost of "truth".

I now want to point to one general tendency in psychoanalytic development after Freud's death. Ego-psychology, part of Freud's conception of the structural theory first published in 1923 (in "The Ego and the Id") gradually became deepened and enlarged after Freud died in 1939. Many data were gained in analytic treatment of adults. They were widened and largely confirmed by observations on infants and children. These observations included the development of the intellect, of the different Ego-functions, of norms and ideals, ("Superego and Ego Ideal"). The interactions of the drives and the Ego-functions, the environment and the earliest object relations were studied and described in detail. The appraisal of the autonomous Ego-functions was very much emphasized. All of these discoveries promoted the understanding of the complicated mental life very much indeed. However, at the same time a number of authors more or less turned away from the biological base of life, from the vicissitudes and manifestations of the drives. The interplay of the different forces between the various psychic instances came into the background. The significance of the regulating pain-pleasure principle became neglected. Here is another example of the fact that one-sidedness maybe of advantage during a certain period, but can become a danger to the search for truth when the road to an all over survey of the mind has become blocked.

The refusal to acknowledge the drives and passions as a motor for normal as well as abnormal development became strenghened as Freud discovered that alongside the sexual drives we had to recognize the existence of aggressive drives, which underly destructive impulses and behavior in man. In the latest decades western civilization has become more tolerant toward sexual life. Living it to the full is more or less accepted in the modern world without societal sanctions. Aggressive needs of individuals and groups, even of mass-destructions, such as acted out in world-wars are still frequent events. However the fact that those actions derive their force from the energy of the biologically given aggressive drives seems to raise so much anxiety in many people, that they look for a variety of rationalizations in order to deny the natural forces. At present religions, claiming that human beings are essentially "good" and "evil" is not allowed to exist, have lost a good deal of their influence. Man has therefore taken refuge to other forms of denial and rationalization. How these processes have come about must be due to a multitude of factors, some still unknown. Perhaps we can venture to offer a presumption. The species "man" has in some respects developed far ahead of its relatives in the animal world. For instance: through the unfolding of intellect, verbal language and discovery of tools man became able to master parts of nature. These abilities provide human beings with a number of satisfactions and advantages. However, in emotional life they have brought out disadvantages, too. Power requires ever more power. In their conscious and unconscious fantasies people imagine to be all-powerful. Infants and small children, who in reality are powerless vis-a-vis the environment, take refuge in fantasies of grandeur and omnipotence. This is a normal event in the infantile inner world. The gradually development of *rationality* has failed with many adults to enable them to bring those fantasies up to the level of reality and attainable goals. They keep unconsciously to their omnipotence fantasy if confronted with their essential powerlessness towards many forces of nature. This phenomenon is to be found in the history of science as well.

The Greeks could not separate natural science from philosophy. They imagined the cosmos being centred around man. In modern science, too, we time and again encounter people who tend to devaluate achievements of singular genial researchers, who were able to reach "objectivity" upto a certain degree. Instead of adhering to the latter's obtained part of "truth", those people keep to wishful thinking and striving for omnipotence. Denial, repression, rationalization have in the long run, never brought about a real amelioration of man's fate, as psychoanalysis has tought us. Those reaction-formations more often cause catastrophes to individuals as well as to mankind. The "repressed" at some time or other, re-emerges from the unconscious, maybe in a different shape, into the active mental life. The denial of man's essential powerlessness against natural forces, especially the destructive ones, and the clinging to self-aggrandizement work as anaesthetics. However, what will happen if their effects have ceased? I have gradually entered into a field of science, in which I lack sufficient knowledge. The area of sociology and allied disciplines led to efforts for a better understanding and regulating of interhuman relations. I merely want to make a few remarks. Would it not be of advantage to look back to the origin of institutions which came into existence in mankind's societies through hundreds and thousands of years?

If we could gain a better understanding of those of the factors, that brought about the present forms, we perhaps could correct at least some of the worst mistakes. However, I think a special pre-condition is indispensable, e.g. the ability to submit to the natural forces manifesting themselves in mankind and to give up the illusion that human beings ever could become: "the omnipotent masters of the world".

34. Reflections on the Development of Psychoanalysis: Technical Implications in Analytic Treatment

(1969)

An invitation from the Editor of *The International Journal of Psycho-Analysis* to contribute to the commemoration of the journal's 50th anniversary challenges thought. But thinking about 'psychoanalysis past and present' arouses a considerable number of problems. The description of the growth of psychoanalysis as a science and as a therapeutic method, and of the increase in knowledge about the functioning of the human mind during the last 50 years would require the scope of a book. Thus the question is how to make a choice and which topic to elaborate upon for the present issue of the *Journal*. I have chosen two themes: (1) general remarks on the development of theory; (2) technical implications.

General remarks

Some 20 years ago I read a paper before an audience of psychiatrists and neurologists, entitled 'Some Remarks on the Development of Psychoanalysis during the Last Decades' (see chapter 11). After a few introductory remarks I spoke on three themes: (a) the development of the scientific theory; (b) the development of the technique and the therapeutic possibilities; and (c) the influence of psychoanalysis on other branches of science, such as psychiatry, academic psychology, sociology, anthropology, ethnology, pedagogy.

During the last 20 years a continuation of the expansion of psychoanalytic knowledge can be observed in all of the three fields mentioned. Its influence on psychology and sociology is specially seen in America and in Germany. Psychiatry is largely affected by psychoanalysis, for instance in America and in Holland. The same is valid for pedagogy in different countries, etc.

The therapeutic possibilities have been on the increase to include a wide range of mental disorders other than neurotic disturbances, either through application of psychoanalytic technique, with or without parameters, by means of so-called 'psychotherapy on analytic lines'. Finally, psychoanalytic theory has been extended in different areas.

Freud had already widened his original theory of infantile sexuality into a theory of the development of instinctual drives by including the aggressive drives. He presented a beautiful description of their manifestations in the object relations in the pre-oedipal phase, thereby emphasizing their importance for the shaping of the oedipal situation. Freud also expanded the topographic theory into the structural theory, deepening our understanding of the interaction of ego, id and superego conflicts leading to a normal or to a pathological developmental outcome. His later works have given us much insight into the psychology of mankind in the society at large.

In the last decades many authors have extended ego psychology.[1] The gradual unfolding of autonomous ego functions, the defensive measures of the ego against id impulses, which cannot be directly satisfied, as well as against outside demands, the secondary autonomy of a number of ego functions and the organization of all of these factors have been elaborated. Active and passive adaptation to inner and outer world were stressed by many authors. The development of superego and ego-ideal from their precursors in the pre-oedipal phase has been worked out. The role of the aggressive drives is better understood. Though aggression seems to be more rigid than sexuality, it is still liable to neutralization and sublimation to some degree. The events arousing aggressive manifestations are better known. We observe more clearly fusion and defusion of aggression and libido and their influence on the development of ego organization and the total personality. The mother-infant interaction from birth on during the very first years of life has been studied by many workers in analysis as well as in direct infant observations, etc. This summing up is merely an incomplete overall picture of well-known events. But I feel that we have the right to say that psychoanalytic psychology is nowadays one of the fundamentals of a general psychology of the human mind, normal and pathological, and that it contributes essentials to other branches of the humanities.

Thinking about the widened scope of psychoanalysis arouses great admiration for Freud's brilliant discoveries and for the further work of many of his successors. It would also give great satisfaction were it not that the gains in knowledge are accompanied by many losses. I will mention only a few of the latter. For instance, the influence of psychoanalysis on psychiatry has enriched the understanding of psychiatric syndromes to a considerable degree. However, it has also led to dilution of parts of psychoanalytic theory, which are well founded and based on numerous experiences and observations. One often encounters beautiful phenomenological descriptions of symptoms and behaviour. The dynamics may not be completely neglected, but they are often only described as they manifest themselves in the present state of the patient's disturbance. The genetic viewpoint, then, may be ignored. The maturational and developmental processes are not appropriately assessed and the origin of the disorder in an uneven psychic growth in childhood is neglected. A good superficial understanding, then, may prevent a deeper comprehension and occasionally deprive the patient of an adequate treatment. Psychoanalytic theory is reduced to a refined phenomenology, to be sure, but it is robbed of one of its most essential contributions to psychology, the genetic viewpoint. It seems to be one of the most difficult achievements to obtain an overall view of the processes of maturation and development from birth to adulthood.

A similar trend, it seems to me, becomes visible in the cooperation of psychoanalysts and psychologists. There is a general request for circumscription

---

[1] Started by Hartmann (1939, 1964), to whom psychoanalytic science is greatly indebted.

and clarification of psychoanalytic concepts. Such an effort is in itself very laudable. However, in many instances it leads to rigidity and impoverishment of analytic experience; for instance, when the cry for quantification of psychic processes prevails. In many psychological experiments which aim at investigating a given psychic situation of a testee a quantification of certain variables is in place. But dynamic maturational and developmental processes cannot be caught in a cross-section and are therefore, in the present state of our science, not quantifiable in numbers. I do not agree with the notion that a theory which cannot be quantified is therefore an unscientific one.

There is another group of authors who do not hold to quantification, but who try to clarify analytic concepts by using (consciously or unconsciously) philosophical ideas. Though reading philosophers can provide great and stimulating pleasure, I am not sure that philosophy contributes much to the understanding of dynamic and developmental psychic processes. Beautiful words and ideas very often tend to neglect the biological basis of mental functioning and of the human behaviour. For instance, in putting the question 'What is psychic energy?' they may bypass the observable fact that conflicting forces are operating in the human mind and that the outcome of conflicts, either in normal or in pathological mental acts, depends upon the *relative* energic strength of the conflicting parts of the mind. There is even no unity among scholars of other disciplines on the question what has to be called *science*.

Here I want to cite a passage from Popper's *The Open Society and its Enemies* (1952). Popper is a dissentient of psychoanalysis. But his criticism of Plato's essentialism (according to Plato the scientific 'essence' of things lies in 'forms' or 'ideas'), I feel to be applicable to a discussion of what science is in our field as well. Popper opposes methodological nominalism to methodological essentialism and writes

> Instead of aiming at finding out what a thing really is and at defining its true nature, methodological nominalism aims at describing how a thing *behaves* in various circumstances and especially whether there are any *regularities* in its behaviour. In other words, methodological nominalism sees *the aim of science* in the description of the things and events of our experience, and in an '*explanation*' of these events, i.e. their description with the help of universal laws. And it sees in our language and especially in those of its rules which distinguish properly constructed sentences and inferences from a mere heap of words, the great instrument of scientific description; words it considers rather as subsidiary tools for this task and not as names of essences. The methodological nominalist will never think that a question like '*What* is energy?' or '*What* is movement?' or '*What* is an atom?' is an important question for physics, but he will attach importance to a question like: '*How* can the energy of the sun be made useful?' or 'How does a planet move?' or 'Under what condition does an atom radiate light?' (pp. 32-3).

Popper then argues that he much prefers that

> modest degree of exactness which he can achieve by his methods to the pretentious muddle which the essentialists have achieved by theirs.

Is not Popper's attitude, after the abating of his emotional hostility, applicable with some correction to our psychological science as well? We cannot say what psychic energy *is*. But we need this concept in the explanation of human behaviour resulting from mental conflicts, though for the time being we do not know whether psychic energy is of a chemical, an electrical or some other nature. We can also understand the outcome of the conflicts in taking into account the relative distribution of the energy between the conflicting parts of the mind and their interaction with environmental forces. The neglect of the very fact that human beings are living organisms, and consequently open systems in which forces causing the growth as well as decay are operating, seems to promote with some authors certain descriptions of mental life in 'a mere heap of words'. Apparently the intercourse with the highly developed differentiated achievements of mental life and its refined world of ideas, affects, emotions and feelings stimulates neglect of the importance of the instinctual drives and the underlying biological forces governing the lives of all living beings.

Implications in the technique of psychoanalytic treatment

My foregoing remarks are born of experiences in psychoanalysis during a period nearly as long as the lifetime of the *International Journal*. Practice and theory have always fertilized each other. In the course of time the technique has undergone many changes. I select a special situation in which the analysis not only aims at removing neurotic disturbances, but where the analysand is in need of a thorough knowledge of his character structure, his abilities and limitations, his habitual reactions towards conflicts and his defensive measures to master the conflicts, because such knowledge is indispensable for his professional work. It concerns candidates in psychoanalytic training as well as workers in allied fields, in which understanding of and empathy with other human beings in distress is a prerequisite. For the sake of brevity, I will merely speak of character analyses with candidates in training. The reason why the latter are in need of a thorough character analysis is well known. A gifted analyst comes upon a personal difficulty in conducting his patient's analysis when the material brought to the fore by the patient touches upon the analyst's character peculiarities, which are still unknown to him as a consequence of unsolved infantile conflicts. As every human being has his abilities as well as his limitations, it is a matter of degree to what extent self-knowledge will be acquired.

As far as I myself have some skill in analysing deep-rooted character traits, I have not only learned from my own and others' experience with analyses of adults and children. I am very much indebted to those colleagues who have done systematic and thorough infant observations. They have not only confirmed analytic findings, but have provided us with a wealth of data about the budding personality of the newborn, his primary physical needs, his gradually dawning emotional attachment to the mother, the gradual unfolding of his ego functions and his grasp of the outer world during the first months and years of life.

In the past of psychoanalysis we already knew of character traits originating in the anal-sadistic phase and even of oral characters as described by Freud, Abraham and others. Those traits were found to be related to the successive phases of instinctual development. The role of the mother was merely seen in a global way. The particulars of the emergence of primitive ego functions were not yet known. Nevertheless we became soon convinced that many habitual behaviour patterns do have their origin in the infant's very first life experiences. One of the difficulties in unearthing those events lies in the fact that they originate in the preverbal stage, so the patient cannot communicate them in words. It was a kind of guesswork, more or less uncertain, to try to reconstruct them through signs and signals provided by the patient's behaviour, his moods, his attitudes, his wordless outbursts of distress or rage, his mimic and facial expression, his tears or his silence. At the present time I feel much safer in interpreting such behaviour, thanks to the support of the work of infant observers. From the many gains in this respect I will try to describe only a few.

I started by mentioning a category of analysands who are intelligent and gifted persons, who function well in many areas, but who are inhibited or disturbed in other fields.

For instance, a young person is doing very well in his job to his own satisfaction and to that of his environment, but who is discontented in his personal family life. Or the other way round: a happy husband and father has more or less severe problems with his work, though he is convinced of having chosen a suitable career. Another form of working disturbance reveals itself in the fact that the person's daily routine work is satisfactory, but that he is unable to perform original creative work, though he seems to have the necessary talent. He is unable to carry into effect a planned experiment or to write a thesis for which he has the raw material ready. There are many more part-disturbances which can be understood in terms of psychoanalytic ego psychology. Apparently the various ego functions have not developed in an even, balanced way; the ego organization is lacking in inner consistency. Sometimes a thorough analysis of his childhood neurosis, of his guilt-feelings and need for punishment in connexion with his competition with the parents and his siblings, centred on the oedipal and pre-oedipal situation, his castration anxiety and his fear of death as a reaction upon hostility and death-wishes, his feelings of inferiority caused by the disappointing experience that his grandeur fantasies are not to be realized, may bring the longed-for removal of his inhibitions and disturbances. However, in many cases the desired effect fails to come about. In some areas the functioning of the analysand's personality rigidly resists improvement and he feels restricted and unhappy, though the environmental circumstances prove to be favourable enough. A continuation of the analytic process points to very early disturbances in the development by means of the already described non-verbal communication, signs and signals. In some cases a first sign reveals itself in body-language. The analysand suddenly gets a severe headache, a painful abdominal tension, a paralysing sensation in one or some of his limbs, etc. I am not referring to conversion symptoms, which persist during stretches of time and which are neurotic disturbances originating in the phallic phase. The signs I have in mind are transitory and they come along mainly in the analytic session.

They point to an infant's reactions to stimuli, as originally the only way in which a baby is able to react upon frustration, pain, distress and anxiety is expressed in body language. The analyst, then, has to use his empathy and intuition in order to attempt the understanding of what the analysand is communicating in this non-verbal language. Metaphorically expressed, the analyst has to creep into the experimental world of the newborn or infant.

I found great support in this endeavour in the findings of René Spitz as an infant observer, finally laid down in his book *The First Year of Life* (1965).[2] It is well known that Spitz points to the fact that the newborn *receives* stimuli before he has learned to use his sense-organs for perception. This receptive way of functioning is called by Spitz 'the coenaesthetic organization'; it is a primary process functioning. Only later on does the 'diacritic organization', a secondary process functioning start to come into being, overlapping and sometimes outgrowing the receptive mode. A healthy mother automatically revives her coenaesthetic organization and responds to the baby's needs intuitively.

It is my experience that in order to understand the analysand's non-verbal signs as described above, the analyst has to be able to revive his receptive mode of functioning in a similar way to that of the normal mother. To be sure, the similarity to a mother's attitude ends here. Alternating with his listening to and receiving of the analysand's primitive signals, the analyst has to make use of his 'diacritic organization', his secondary process functioning in order to try to translate those signals into verbal language. Empathy and a certain distance to the material are both necessary to help the patient's reliving and working through of his infantile experiences (*Erlebnisse*). The words used by the analyst, the tone of his voice, the moment chosen to speak are of great importance indeed. This refinement of technique is vulnerable; it is a matter of trial and error.

If the attempt to establish this primitive form of interaction is successful, the joint efforts of analyst and patient sometimes reveal very early disturbances in the original mother-child relations. The mother proves to have misunderstood the bodily needs of the infant, his pains, his anxieties, his distress and his powerlessness, with the consequence of overwhelming stimuli and bouts of rage. With empathy and with the ability to bear the impact of primitive fits of fury on the part of the analyst, it sometimes is possible to have the patient work through and master these early faulty developmental events. It is a matter of fact that we have to be prepared to stand a failure in a number of cases. When success is not achieved, it can be due either to the analyst's limitations, or to the patient's overwhelming anxieties, or to both. But a successful outcome may be very rewarding.

I experienced further support in the work of another infant observer, Margaret Mahler. Her observations of the child's gradual development from the primary narcissistic phase (which she calls the state of primary autism) to the symbiotic relationship with the mother, in which the latter is still part of the 'narcissistic milieu', than into the separation-individuation phase, where there is a dawning

---

[2] I made my acknowledgement to Spitz in my 1967 paper, chapter 31.

awareness of the mother as a part of an outside world and where the infant is beginning to differentiate a self from the outside, are very revealing. In an analysis, which leads back to these early stages, we can sometimes recognize and reconstruct the development of the little child with the technique just described and we may come upon the happenings which disturbed the even growth. We observe our analysand in his symbiotic needs, in his wish to 'merge with the analyst' and the concomitant anxiety to lose his own individuality, very often warded-off by bouts of anger. We accompany him in his endeavour to separate, to withstand the mother's feared intrusion, and to establish a sound and more stable individuality. We may observe the return to the subphase of the 'practising period' in the patient's attempt to do the analysis alone by himself, alternating with a tendenty to *rapprochement* to regain the analyst's support and love. The fear of loss of love and the strong anxieties aroused by the little child's own aggression, as soon as the child has experienced that the destruction of an object results in losing the object, can sometimes clearly be relived in the analytic situation. The empathic accompaniment of the re-experiencing of these dramatic developmental events may in some cases allow the analysand to free his libidinal and aggressive energy from the fixation points in early childhood and to provide him with the freedom of using his forces in an age-adequate way. Whether the analysis will be successful or not, apart from the analyst's limitations in empathy and in toleration of fits of rage, depends largely upon the patient's capacity to bear anxiety and to neutralize aggressive energy for sublimated activities. In a number of former papers I pointed to the tremendous difficulties human beings have in accomplishing this.

In quite a few cases we are struck by the rigidity of the primitive aggressive and destructive impulses, which often come to the fore in a compulsive striving for power over other persons and situations and in a tendency to destroy whatever contradicts this striving. It is usually stiffened by primitive fantasies of grandeur and omnipotence, which tend to persist in the unconscious and to continue their hidden but forceful existence.

We do not only observe these tendencies in our analytic work. We meet them in mankind at large (see Lampl-de Groot, 1968). Competition, envy, the need to possess everything, the incapacity to share joy and happiness of other persons are among the most detrimental attributes of human beings. They tend to poison the life of human beings as well as human society at large. Our only hope can be that the capacity for constructive activities will gradually outweigh destructive needs, and finally that love may conquer envy and hate. Is it merely wishful thinking that, in case in the long run this hope should to some degree be fulfilled, the development of Freud's psychoanalysis may have contributed to bringing the ardently desired peace to mankind?

35. Extensions of Technique in the analysis of adult patients and adolescents in connection with the widened scope of experience and theoretical knowledge, highly influenced by child-analysis and infant-observations

(1971)

I. The analytic method originally depended largely on verbal communication in free associations in recounting dreams and fantasies. However, already at an early time, 1905 in the Dora case, Freud remarked that: "He, (the analyst) that has *eyes to see and ears to hear* may convince himself that no mortal can keep a secret. If his (the patient's) lips are silent, he chatters with his fingertips, betrayal oozes out of him at every pore. And thus the task of making conscious the most hidden recesses of the mind is one which is quite possible to accomplish." (pp. 77-78)

At the time Freud referred to the repressed events and unsolved conflicts of the patient's past pursuing them back from the present into the oedipal phase and the pregenital (anal and oral) stages of development. It is wellknown that the recollections of the patient can not be excact replica's of real events, but that they are new editions, revised and changed during the course of mental development. One very simple example: a patient starts the analysis with a childhoodmemory of his father being a crude, harsh and cruel person and his mother of a lovely, angelic nature, parental quarrels thus being exclusively the father's fault and the cause of the patient's illness. During the course of his analysis the picture changes: he remembers many nice and wonderful experiences with his father and a strong criticism and hatred of his mother.

II. Childhood memories, distorted as they may be can come back in the psychoanalytic situation in verbal communications. But very often they are not remembered in words, but expressed in behavior, gestures, and especially in somatic language, headaches, heartbeating, intestinal movements, pains, etc. The analyst then has to make 'reconstructions' of childhood experiences as Freud has pointed out (1937). These may contribute to a cure, if the patient confirms them by a feeling of evidence and conviction, either directly or at a later date.

The need for reconstructions is specially strong where pre-oedipal disturbances come into the picture. For instance: anal and oral material usually cannot be remembered because it goes back to a period in the little child's life where verbalization was not yet possible. A patient who later-on has learned from a member of the family that he has suffered from intestinal diseases or asthma in babyhood and was bowel-trained at the age of 1 or 1,5 year cannot remember these happenings, certainly not in words, because they occurred in the pre-verbal phase, or at least in a period where he only knew a few words but was not yet able to verbalize his impulses, emotions and feelings to himself, let alone to the analyst. The classical vehicle for overcoming resistance to remembering and reliving of childhood experiences, altered and distorted as they may be, is the transference. Transference was originally seen as the transfer of object-relations with the parents (and siblings) on to the analyst. This may hold true for the unearthing of the oedipal situation, and the toddler's pre-oedipal attachments. In the first years of life the bond with the mother is of a narcissistic nature, the budding ego emerges only gradually. What can sometimes be relived in the analytic situation is of a different nature from the later transference-experiences. To be sure, it is *not* an exact repetition of the baby's life, as some analysts maintain. It certainly is still more influenced and altered by the maturational and developmental processes than are the oedipal memories and later experiences. The very early unsolved conflicts, undigestable stimuli from outside, inner clashes between needs and between different drives and impulses, etc. persist in their primitive form in the unconscious. The vehicle that in some cases (certainly *not* in all) makes possible a kind of re-experiencing is, as far as I can see, *not* the classical transference. We perhaps could see it as part of the therapeutic alliance. The latter comes into being in the first phase of the analysis as a human contact from person to person, it is consolidated by the transference. The analyst reacts to the analysand's emotional life and instinctual, specially aggressive outbursts in a different way as did the environment in the past and still does in the present towards the patient's illness and character peculiarities. If the alliance between analysand and analyst has evoked trust the patient may be willing and able to follow the analyst picturing out the growing impulsive and emotional infant's life, his bodily needs, satisfactions and deprivations, his lust and his distress, his longing for 'good mothering', his rage and aggressive reactions. He responds with the above mentioned somatic feelings and communications. It then may extend the course which the psychoanalytic *process* is automatically running once it has started, well into the stage of narcissistic omnipotence. In some patients, who have retained enough flexibility, it may facilitate the acquirement of a better understanding of and grasp upon the unsolved pre-oedipal and oedipal conflicts as well as on their revival in adolescence. Our knowledge of the earliest period of life is partly gained in the analyses of very young children, who communicate mostly in behavior, play and action, partly it is strengthened by infant observations. I must refer here to a few of my former papers in which I stress the prerequisite of a special kind of empathy in both analyst and analysand (1967, 1969).

I originally came to this 'extended' technique more or less at hazard, or by a 'hunch', or whatever one may call it. I want to add that under certain circumstances it may be a dangerous enterprise, namely in case the analyst's fantasy goes astray. However, the same happens as with misinterpretations and misconstructions (see Freud 1937). Either the intervention has no effect at all, or the analysis stops, perhaps the patient runs away. With very infantile, dependent patients the analysis may become interminable, in this case due to the analyst's failure. The very fact that I saw a few, but impressive results, has encouraged me to present this contribution.

III. As the last point I want to go into a critical doubt some analysts express about the possibility and the usefulness of this endeavor of a technical extension. Among them is Anna Freud (1969). She 'feels doubtful about trying to advance into the area of primary repression, i.e. to deal with processes which, by nature, are totally different from the results of the ego's defensive manoeuvres with which we feel familiar' (pag. 39). And later: 'There is, further, the question whether the transference really has the power to transport the patient back as far as the beginning of life' (pag. 40). With the first pronouncement I am in complete agreement. The processes occurring in the undifferentiated phase are very different from the later ego's manoeuvres, though the latter are strongly influenced by them.

I think the differences of opinion rest on a number of factors, of which I will single out two.

1. The first concerns the second quotation of Anna Freud's paper: the role of the transference. I stressed already this point: my communication with the analysand in this respect does *not* find place on the base of the classical transference as long as there is no differentiation between self and object there can be no transfer from object-attachment onto the analyst. The first reaction of the patient is usually an intellectual interest in the events of the baby's earliest experiences, in the clashes between his needs and the unavoidable frustrations with the consequence of pain, distress and impotent rage. In case the patient responds with transient physical reactions an *emotional* understanding may follow and they sometimes point to special situations of his early experiences. In a favoral case this may contribute to a better understanding and emotional working-through of the later unsolved pre-oedipal (and oedipal) conflicts, which have partly become intrapsychic, when a primitive structuration has gradually come into being. Of special significance is the dealing with rage and in general with aggression, which are automatically raised by frustrations and experiences of powerlessness.

2. A second point of misunderstanding refers to the question of: what is reversible and what is irreversible? In my opinion this question is not appropriate here. Traumatic experiences can never be undone, neither the earliest in the narcissistic, undifferentiated phase, nor the later intrapsychic and environmental traumatic events. What matters is how far the analysand can become able to use the 'healthy' or more mature part of his personality to master them and to achieve some kind or other of inner and outer equilibrium. To repeat: whenever a result occurs it is *not* a result of the transference (which is not an aim in itself but merely a vehicle). It is perhaps only an extension (or a parameter) and as I see it a legitimate attempt to widen our technique in accordance with Freud's ever stimulating further research to study the obstacles standing in the way of psychoanalytic cure.

36. Vicissitudes of Narcissism and Problems of Civilization

(1975)

In this presentation I shall attempt to proceed along the path indicated by the founder of psychoanalysis. Freud repeatedly said that he had only made beginnings. He encouraged others to continue to extend psychoanalysis theoretically as well as practically and to apply it to other human sciences.

A psychoanalytic contribution to the problem of civilized societies can only be a limited one. Nevertheless, I feel that it might be worthwhile to venture a few ideas on this topic. As a psychoanalyst I shall start with observations made in the psychoanalytic treatment situation. In particular, I shall examine the genetic roots of the working alliance.

This term does not appear in Freud's writings. It is a concept that emerged in the psychoanalytic literature many years after Freud's death (Zetzel, 1956; Stone, 1961; Loewenstein, 1969; Greenacre, 1954, and in Greenson's work from 1965 onward). The term is used interchangeably with "therapeutic alliance." I believe the two terms cover the same phenomenon. A patient who has decided to work in an alliance with the analyst does so in order to obtain a therapeutic result, to be cured from his symptoms and his mental distress. Greenson uses, in addition, the term "real or nontransference relationship" between analyst and patient. This relationship is different from the working alliance. It concerns the analyst's attitude that in addition to being professional should also be humane – an important issue that has sometimes been neglected.

The concept of the working alliance

Working alliance is an appealing concept that must be studied carefully by every analyst. Yet, in going through the literature, I found that it is used rather loosely and with slightly different meanings.

There seems to be a consensus of opinion on the description of its starting point. Jack Novick (1970) summarized the common denominators as follows: "The core of the alliance is the patient's conscious, rational willingness to do analytic work. The motivation for such work is the awareness of suffering and the wish for cure. . . . The alliance becomes most apparent at times of heightened resistance and transference" (p. 236).

Even this generally agreed-upon formulation, however, raises questions. Experience has taught us that conscious motivation and rationality are overthrown when during the analytic process instinctual and emotional conflicts enter into the picture. If the *core* of the patient's alliance, his bond with the analyst, were no more than his conscious rational wish to be cured, he certainly would run away from the analysis at the very moment when this rational wish is no longer at his disposal. As a matter of fact, there are patients who stop the analysis at such a point. Every analyst has dealt at one time or another with this problem. However, in most of the cases the patient continues the treatment. We must therefore ask ourselves: what is the nature of the patient's tie to the analyst that enables the patient to stay in treatment notwithstanding strong resistances? What makes the patient continue despite his feeling that the analyst mistreats him, is an incompetent therapist, a bore, an inhuman person, or even a criminal?

In fact, Freud dealt with this problem in his early papers on technique. He believed that the affectionate, aim-inhibited part of the transference kept the analysis going in spite of strong resistances. This affectionate tie is part of the object relationship to the parents after the oedipal conflict (colored, of course, by the preoedipal factors) has passed away. At that time (1911-15) analysis was applied only to the transference neuroses, cases in which the core of symptoms centered on the unsolved conflicts of the oedipus complex. Later, when Freud also analyzed character neuroses and narcissistic personalities, he did not explicitly enlarge on his technical arsenal, though he was aware of the fact that these disorders originated in a much earlier phase of development, in the early mother-child relationship.

Narcissistic versus object-libidinal relatedness

Today we deal more frequently with analyses of character neuroses and narcissistic disturbances than with transference neuroses proper. This may be one of the reasons why the analyst feels the need for a separate term to distinguish the alliance with the analyst from the transference. The classical meaning of the term "transference" relates to the reemergence of the ambivalent object-libidinal tie to the parents in the analytic situation, while the working alliance is a *narcissistic* manifestation. It starts with a self-directed striving – the decision made by the relatively mature "normal" part of the personality to be freed from mental suffering. In view of the fact that the working alliance disappears at times of heightened resistances (which is convincingly described by Novick in his case presentation) but is nevertheless considered to become most apparent in precisely those situations, one has to wonder how these contradictory statements can be reconciled.

The transference of affectionate, object-directed, libidinal strivings is dynamically not sufficiently powerful to enable the patient to uncover and relive strong narcissistic, self-centered, infantile needs. What bond with the analyst, then, enables the patient to reexperience at least part of his unsolved conflicts of infancy and early childhood? One of the principles of psychoanalysis is the genetic approach to mental phenomena. I think we have to look for the genetic roots of that facet of the patient-analyst relatedness which is covered by the term "working alliance." They will be found, I am sure, in the very early bond of the infant with the mother, a bond that is exclusively narcissistic and self-centered. Its dynamics are dramatically powerful. The energy of impulses, drives, and needs is *relatively* much stronger in little children than in adults, because the ego develops only gradually and is still weak and vulnerable in childhood.

In the symbiotic phase the exclusively narcissistic nature of the mother-child dyad is self-evident. However, when the infant becomes aware that the satisfaction of his needs comes from the outside, his tie to the mother is still of a narcissistic nature. I venture the idea that here lie the genetic roots of the working alliance. I shall later describe the ways in which they may manifest themselves in the analytic situation. I continue with the description of the lines of development of the baby's experiential world.

The infant experiences the mother as an extension of his self. This is still the case in the individuation-separation phase (Mahler, 1968). However, the toddler who starts to crawl, to walk, to explore the world constantly meets with limitations, disappointments, and painful hurts. Even the most loving "good" mother cannot fulfill all of his needs immediately. She cannot prevent her little one from bumping himself against a piece of furniture. The little child feels lost, powerless, helpless. Such narcissistic blows are usually much more catastrophic than the physical pain of a scratch or a wound. The intensity of the injury to his self-assurance is often not understood by his mother, who usually has repressed her own infantile experiences and emotions. The little child then desperately tries to take refuge in his fantasy world. In order to compensate for his injured self-esteem he starts to create fantasies of grandeur and omnipotence.

In addition to a "grandiose self" (Kohut, 1971), he idealizes his mother and his parents, who in fact are less powerless than he is. At the time the little child is able to preserve the inner representations of the parents even in their physical absence — when he has reached object constancy — the cathexis of the object and its representation is still mainly narcissistic. The inner image of the parents serves as an extension of the child's self. Several years pass before the child is able to love his parents and other persons living in his small experiential world as personalities in their own right who have their own personal wishes, feelings, qualities, and peculiarities. In other words, it takes time for the child to invest his objects with object-directed libido. I think this kind of object relationship, which develops gradually alongside the narcissistic relatedness, usually becomes more or less settled in the oedipal situation. The precise point of time at which this happens, however, differs from individual to individual. On the one hand, it is dependent upon the infant's innate endowment in regard to drives and the gradually unfolding ego functions; on the other, it is greatly influenced by the kind of mothering and the emotional responses of the parents and other relevant persons in the little child's world.

In relatively "normal" development the object-directed libidinal ties grow during latency and diminish to some degree in puberty during which a relative increase of narcissism is a regular occurrence. In adulthood we consider as sound a durable love relationship in which both partners respect each other's personalities. However, the developmental line of object-libidinal ties (ambivalent as they may be) proceeds alongside the development of narcissism from its archaic, grandiose state into more realistic feelings of self-esteem, longings for self-satisfying achievements, and attainable ideals. A certain amount of self-love is a precondition for the capacity to love another person with empathy, respect, and appreciation.

I have tried to describe briefly the two lines of development of object-relatedness: the narcissistic one originating from the archaic mother-child dyad in the first years of life, and the object-directed libidinal relationship which grows out of it at a much later date.

This differentiation has a bearing on the understanding of the genetic origins of both the transference and the working alliance. To achieve the ability to invest the object with object-directed libido the child must have reached a certain degree of maturation. On the energetic side, drive development must at least in part have reached the phallic stage. On the side of the ego, a number of functions must have matured; for example, the child's reality sense must have reached the stage at which he is able to perceive the object not only as an instrument for fulfilling his bodily and emotional needs, but as another personality in his (or her) own right.

I see the working alliance as having its genetic roots in the very early narcissistic mother-child bond. Transference in the analytic situation is rooted genetically in the *object-directed libidinal* relationship. This sharp distinction is of course clouded in later stages of development. Then the two kinds of object ties become intermingled. In the preoedipal phase the narcissistic tie is prevalent. In the oedipal phase object-directed strivings acquire more impetus. During latency the aim-inhibited affectionate relationship begins to bloom. These various stages can be observed during the analytic process. The distinction between the genetic roots of working alliance and transference may clarify the statement stressed by most authors: that the working alliance is *not* transference, has to be distinguished from the transference, and is of equal importance. It may also explain the contradictory pronouncements that the working alliance disappears at times of heightened resistance, whereas it is supposed to become most apparent at those times. I believe that the solution is theoretically simple. The conscious rational wish to be cured disappears when overwhelming childhood conflicts are uncovered and relived, but the unconscious archaic root of the alliance, the narcissistic tie to the mother that is relived in the analytic situation, persists and is the "carrying power" for the continuation of the analytic process.

In practice the situation is not simple. It is often laborious and time-consuming for both analysand and analyst to disentangle transference manifestations, e.g., of the oedipal object relations, from the earlier narcissistic object ties.

Narcissism in psychopathology

With the classical transference neuroses the uncovering of the repressed oedipal conflicts, the object-libidinal love-hate relationships that are transferred onto the analyst, is sufficient to bring the strivings and affects under the matured ego's control. The neurotic symptoms can be cured by working through these conflicts. It is different with character neuroses and narcissistic personality disorders, in which an underlying fixation and/or regression to the archaic narcissistic tie to the object is responsible for the uneven development of ego functions.

In these cases the bond with the analyst is of a different nature. The analyst must therefore empathically enter into the experiential world of the infant and toddler. In the most severe disturbances, for example, with an autistic child or psychotics, this primitive narcissistic tie seems to be absent or too weak to be reached in the analytic situation. Infants who never experienced mothering care, e.g., institutional babies, either die or become very retarded children unable to reach a stage of narcissistic relatedness. I myself have no experience with the therapy of psychotics, but I worked a great deal with narcissistic disturbances. Such individuals generally have a primitive tie to a motherly person, unstable as it may be, because it was formed with a disturbed mother whose inconsistent behavior alternated between spoiling and neglecting the baby.

I have discussed some of the technical difficulties presented by these cases in earlier papers (1965, 1967, 1969). Kohut (1968, 1971, 1972) has devoted several publications to the analytic devices needed in the treatment of narcissistic personality disorders and demonstrated them in several case presentations. Kohut (1971) poses the question whether the therapeutic mobilization of the narcissistic structures (including the grandiose self and the idealized parent images) should be covered by the term transference. In a footnote Kohut mentions a comment of Anna Freud's, in which she points out that in these cases the patient uses the analyst not for the revival of object-directed strivings, but for the inclusion in a libidinal (narcissistic) state to which he has regressed or at which he has become arrested. She suggests to call that a "subspecialty of transference" (p. 205). Kohut himself adheres to the term "narcissistic transference."

From the foregoing it might have become clear that I prefer to reserve the term "transference," in its classical conceptualization, to the revival of object-directed strivings in the analytic situation. The term "subspecialty of transference" does not appeal to me. I would call this kind of relatedness *the narcissistic tie*. One of the reasons for my preference is the observation that this kind of bond differs qualitatively from the transference of object-directed strivings with their accompanying affects of love and hate. (In Europe we speak of a different color of this bond.) At the height of the transference neurosis, the analysand does not show concern with the analyst's personality. He is too much involved in his past conflicts. However, at other times he is able to take a certain distance from his childhood troubles and can perceive the analyst as a "real" person – that is, if the analyst is responsive to it. If he is unresponsive, such an inhuman attitude may disturb the patient and damage the course of the analytic process.

In contrast, when in an analytic treatment the stage of the very early *narcissistic* tie comes to the fore, the patient is completely absorbed in his own inner conflicts and *uses* the analyst merely as part of his grandiose self and omnipotent fantasy world. He feels that the analyst is the real, actual, and exclusive source of his complaints, his distress, his emptiness, his powerlessness, and he makes the analyst responsible for everything that threatens his narcissism. He really tries to use the analyst as an extension of his self, like the baby did with his mother.

In the experiential world of the little child the parent really *is* omnipotent and therefore responsible for every mischief. I agree with Kohut that the analyst should not interfere with the unfolding of the patient's idealized world of his self and of the analyst. Such periods may be prolonged and difficult because of the patient's intense anxiety, which he can overcome only with the assistance of the analyst who temporarily must accept the role of an omnipotent parental figure. This applies especially to cases where the actual mothering and parental understanding was absent or totally insufficient. In such situations the analyst needs a lot of empathy and an ability to put himself into the infant's and toddler's experiential world, which is so different from the adult's world. However, after an uncovering and at least a partial working through of the little child's idealized world, the analyst's task should become once more to represent reality to the patient. He should then point out to his analysand that the feelings and fantasies of grandiosity (of self and parents) are "normal" mental products in the magical world of the little child who in reality is small and powerless, but that they are not appropriate in the realistic adult's world. In adulthood one has learned to accept the realistic limitations of every human being as well as the fact that everyone is powerless in a number of life situations.

The working through of these disillusioning facts may be laborious and time-consuming as the earlier phase of uncovering the grandiose world. The patient often clings tenaciously to the omnipotent image of his analyst, on the one hand because he shares in the analyst's fantasied grandiosity and on the other hand because he can make the analyst responsible for everything. It is the duty of a godlike, almighty creature to fulfill every need and to undo all distress of the poor patient. This magical fantasy is a *creation* of the patient. The fact that it finally must break down may arouse nearly intolerable narcissistic injuries. It parallels in the *emotional world* the severe offense the little child experiences when the *bodily* performance of "creating" feces as a wonderful and originally admired product meets with its final devaluation by the mother, who throws it away as being dirty and worthless. If the mother has failed to accompany her child in his progressive move from one developmental phase into the next one with emotional understanding of his specific maturational course, abilities, and alternating progressions and regression, the analyst later on must try to serve as a *tool* for the patient in his attempt to catch up with this developmental lack. At this point the analyst has to become aware of the changed *quality* of the patient-analyst bond. It reveals itself in the patient's behavior, attitude, posture, tone of voice, stammering, temporary somatic complaints, body language, and other facets. Whether the final outcome of this working through will be a success or a failure depends upon the tact, empathy, and patience of the analyst and on the patient's endurance and special talents and proclivities.

324

Narcissism and "normality"

Following the psychoanalytic tradition of turning from pathology to normal development, I come back again to the fate of the original narcissistic tie to the parents and the object-directed strivings in so-called "normal" individuals. This problem is not only of theoretical interest; we also become involved in it with analysands who seek psychoanalytic treatment for reasons other than wanting to be cured from suffering, i.e., persons whose conscious motivation arises from their professional life. There are some scientists working in other fields of the humanities who do not intend to become psychoanalysts, but who want to know more about the unconscious sources of their own mental makeup. The problem is of course most apparent in the training analysis of psychoanalytic candidates. A certain amount of "normality" is indispensable for the professional task of an analyst. We consider mental health to be the outcome of inner and outer harmony, a well-balanced interaction between the forces of the drives, those at the disposal of the different ego and superego functions, and an *active* or *passive adaptation* to the outer world. This is only, if ever, acquired by a very few. A number of candidates function relatively well in certain areas – their work, their family relationships, their social contacts. If they are really motivated to become analysts, they gain awareness of the special goal of a training analysis – knowing as much as possible about their particular character structure and their personal peculiarities. Certain neurotic manifestations which are present in nearly every intelligent and sensitive person have to be removed first. Next the residuals of the infantile narcissistic experiential world may come to the fore. The rational part of an adult's personality may encounter great difficulties in recognizing a split in his personality and in accepting the persistence of an unconscious part adhering to the images of a grandiose self and idealized, omnipotent parents. If these unconscious, archaic fantasies are subjected to analytic work, the analysand may discover that they are still active and influence his behavior in many instances. They become apparent in the analytic situation by virtue of the different *quality* of the tie to the analyst, as described above. The analysand's resistances to this part of the analytic process can be extremely strong and sometimes they may become unsurmountable obstacles to a favorable outcome. Several factors account for such failures.

1. I have already mentioned the observation that for many people narcissistic injuries are unbearable and can lead to a breakdown of their self-confidence. They feel at a complete loss, empty, incapable of doing anything. The analyst should be on the alert and use his empathy either to forestall such a threatening situation, or to *help* the analysand to master it.

2. Another outcome may be a *secondarily* heightened feeling of grandiosity and an inaccessible delusional attitude. A vicious circle may come into existence. Many decades ago I spoke of "a personal delusion." By this I meant that a "core" of delusional formations remains present in everybody's unconscious, though its impetus varies individually. Whether this delusion will have a detrimental effect or lead to only minor impairment depends on its relative strength in relation to the other forces available to the "healthy," rational part of the personality.

3. It is a complicating factor in human development that the infantile gran-diosity will at some time or other inevitably clash with reality. We also know that disappointments and frustrations evoke, alongside feelings of being unloved, particularly strong narcissistic injuries. It is especially the impaired self-esteem that mobilizes great amounts of *aggression* and *destructive* feelings.

Narcissism and aggression

The theme of aggression has been widely discussed in the recent psychoanalytic literature. It was the main theme of the 1971 International Psychoanalytic Congress in Vienna as well as of many individual contributions too numerous to list here. I refer only to the study by Eissler (1971) who attempts to lend support to Freud's theory of the life and death drives. I agree with most of his reasoning, since I came to similar conclusions in 1955 (see chapter 18). In regard to the drive theory, however, I prefer to use the term "drive" for the psychological manifestations and speak of *biological forces* steering living organisms from birth to death.

Instead of discussing these highly interesting problems in this paper, I turn to observations of other living beings. It is most striking to observe the difference in the effect of both the libidinal and the aggressive forces in human beings and in other species of the animal kingdom.

I was immensely impressed when I saw large herds of all kinds of antelopes and other herbivores, grazing peacefully a few yards away from a group of lions and lionesses, sleeping under a tree in the East African bush and savannahs. Lions and other beasts of prey do not murder for the sake of murdering. They kill whenever they are hungry, or feel threatened, or if they have to defend them-selves against stronger animals.

In contrast, man may murder his fellowmen for very different purposes, not merely for survival. In certain circumstances, e.g., in wartime and especially in concentration camps as we know from the time of the Nazi regime, killing and murder may become sources of various shades of satisfaction. It is remarkable that young soldiers, who in civil life actively opposed the establishment, will obey their superiors with docility and sometimes with lust in murdering a civilian population. There are only a very few who refuse to do so. Millions of intelligent youngsters let themselves be lulled by such slogans as "defense of the fatherland" and the need to eradicate "inferior races." Would this be possible if there were no murderous impulses in every human being? Eissler (1971) ex-plains the difference in behavior between animals and man by pointing out that man's object relations are of an ambivalent nature. Together with narcissism they are the steering wheels for aggression. Eissler ends his essay with the dictum: "aggression, ambivalence, and narcissism become mankind's apocalyptic horsemen, when they ride together, as they always seemed to do" (p. 75).

Yet, is there no ambivalence in the animal world? I think there is, at least in the more highly differentiated animals. In animals lower on the evolutionary lad-der, destructiveness manifests itself in different ways and serves dissimilar purposes. I am thinking primarily of higher mammals. Jane van Lawick-Goodall (1971), who lived for many years in the bush of Uganda, has recorded her observations on chimpanzees, the closest relatives of men. Chimps live in family groups and keep very closely together. There is usually a strong bond between the members, "loving" each other as expressed, for example, in grooming activities and in the protection of the young and the weaker against dangers. They live in a hierarchical structure, the strongest male being the leader. Chimps are omnivorous and feed mainly on fruit and plants, only occasionally killing a smaller animal. The leader clearly is the first to feed. He can be very angry if a second-in-command tries to take his share. The others meekly wait for the remains, finally fighting each other to get part of the kill or the other food. There is a real ambivalent relationship between the family members, but they will not murder for any other motive than survival.

What then are the special human qualities that enable man to murder without being hungry or having to defend himself against a life-threatening danger? Is it narcissism? Is narcissism an exclusively human feature? There certainly is a biologically founded "body narcissism" in chimps, not unlike that in human beings. Chimps masturbate and they obviously have pleasant sensations in grooming themselves, but we cannot assume that they have a fantasy life and grandiose fantasies like human beings. Chimps communicate with each other by "shouts" or "screams," but symbolic language occurs only in human beings as far as we know. It is a human acquisition which enables man to shape his fantasy life verbally. The result is that fantasies continue to live on in the mind in word representations, though they may become unconscious. The clash between the archaic grandiose fantasies and reality evokes great amounts of aggression.

Another difference between humans and primates lies in the fact that human children grow through an extremely long period of dependence on their environment for survival. With higher mammals this period stretches over a few years. A chimp baby clings to his mother, first onto her tummy and later on riding on her back for some two years, until he is able to feed himself. It is different with human children. This is especially the case in civilized societies, in which the children's dependence on the adults usually extends far into adolescence or even into adulthood. A latency period in drive development is present in chimpanzees too, although it is of much shorter duration than in men. In some illiterate human societies, where a symbolic language in words *does* exist, children are much earlier able to provide for themselves than in civilized countries. They do not learn in schools, but from their parents, elders, and other children.

Jomo Kenyatta (1938) described this extensively in relation to the Gikuyu tribe in Kenya, East Africa, where he was born. According to Kenyatta, the upbringing of children usually follows a smooth course, with parents and child mutually understanding each other. As a result, the child early acquires work skills and independence. Of course, opposition and deviating behavior are not absent, but they are relatively scarce. Disciplining is taken over by the age group at a very early time. The severest punishment is to be considered as an outcast.

Another remark by Kenyatta concerns the tribal wars, which are fought solely for survival, for example, when cattle diseases and drought threaten the population with starvation. Even then no women and as few males as possible are killed. Murder for the mere pleasure of murdering occurs very rarely. This state of affairs was cruelly disturbed when the Western European countries felt compelled to impose their civilization on what they considered "savages." It led to a disruption of the original society. However, here I wish to stress that the early independence and the emotional understanding between parents and child further a more peaceful life.

There are of course other tribes and differently structured societies which exhibit far more violence, e.g., the Dogon and Agri tribes of Africa studied by Parin et al. (1971). But the authors are "Western foreigners" and the French-speaking tribes already "morbid groups of West Africans," according to some anthropologists. It would indeed be a fascinating topic to study different communities from the special point of view of how they deal with aggression. While there exists much more literature on African tribes and on ancient African culture, I cannot go into this interesting topic in this presentation.

Civilization and destructiveness

I return to the point concerning the destructive forces at work in civilized societies. We are in need of collaboration with various other disciplines, being concerned with human affairs in order to explain the reverse side of the medal in civilization. I mean we should not only be proud of the human achievements of conquering part of nature by science, art, and technology, but also study the drawbacks, the misuse of our achievements in individual, and largely in the joint acts of inflicting distress, humiliation, and destruction on each other. As a matter of fact, I do not intend to suggest that we abandon civilization and return to "primitive" societies, but I believe that we could learn something from their way of life. The European has robbed the Africans of their land and as Kenyatta (1938) says, "He is taking away not only their livelihood, but the material symbol that holds family and tribe together" (p. 317). The land was robbed to make money − for profit and *power*. The rifles and machine guns of the Europeans were superior and much more destructive than bow and arrow of the inhabitants. The conquerors murdered in order to satisfy their *craving for power* and secure submission.

I feel they were living out their personal fantasies of grandeur and omnipotence, with destructive urges breaking through. Is there not a parallel with the older generation in the civilized countries who, having lost contact with their children's world, try to subdue them to make them obedient, submissive, and tractable mass products? There were indeed periods in the history of civilization during which the ethical standards led to attempts to liberalize and to gain freedom for individual development. However, what has become of these endeavors? Time and again the striving for power and omniscience of some leaders has prevailed. Supported by sophisticated rationalizations, they wielded a new kind of power and acted out their unconscious omnipotent wishes, without shunning suppression, discrimination, torture, violence, murder, and war. At first the less sophisticated were subdued, but gradually they became aware of the injustice imposed upon them. Is one to wonder that with the spreading of knowledge by the mass communication media the younger generation resorts to opposition and violence?

As psychoanalysts, we have acquired knowledge about the period in human life when reason is not yet present. An infant's inner world is governed by needs and passions which are often sufficiently satisfied during the symbiotic phase in the mother-child dyad. As soon as he enters the next developmental phases, he becomes aware of his powerlessness, which disturbs his narcissistic equilibrium. Then, I repeat once more, his grandiose fantasies of self and parents have to compensate for the narcissistic injury. The little child's inner world is steered by his feelings of omnipotence and grandeur. When he has acquired speech and thinking, he has his own specific logic; he may, for example, say, "If I will be big, you mommy will be my child and I will wash your hands." Adults may laugh at him, but they usually do not understand the child's inner evidence and the damaging distress they impose upon him by their reaction. It is one example of the misunderstandings between the experiential worlds of children and adults. Being laughed at is one of the most severe damages to a sensitive child's self-esteem. He feels rejected and unloved and therefore inferior and powerless. This inner distress awakens aggression, destructive impulses, and once more fantasies of grandeur, but the latter now have to be kept secret. The conse-quence is a new estrangement from the parents, and an urgent impulse to live out aggression and destructive urges. Murderous impulses cannot be acted out by the child and are warded off by different maneuvers; but they live on in the repressed, unconscious part of the mind and are accompanied by anxiety and guilt.

The parents in their own infancy were subjected to similar injuries, which they had to ward off and relegate to oblivion. As a consequence they are incapable of empathizing with the child's experience and react with anger, rejection, and punishment. This alienation of the little child's world from the parents' seems to be most prevalent in the so-called civilized societies, in which the system of upbringing apparently fosters this process by laying stress on the intellectual development and sending the children to schools. It is well known that many children then feel abandoned and unloved by the parents. The school may provide new frustrations. The accumulation of distress may make it difficult for the child to adjust to this kind of education and his emotional life may become crippled or distorted. This educational system differs strikingly from the system of upbringing in some of the illiterate societies, e.g., in the Gikuyu and Masai tribes described by Kenyatta.

The smooth and playful learning from elders and one's own age group, without any pressure for intellectual work, seems to prevent or minimize alienation between children and the older generation to a great extent. The emotional life is allowed to express itself in plays, dances, and all kinds of festivities. In Western civilization, the repressed resentment of the lack of empathy in the parents, who fail to understand their little sons' and daughters' predicament of being powerless, creates hostile, self-centered disappointments and narcissistic injuries. Youngsters then may call for revenge and attempt to overthrow their elders' precepts and ethical norms. The clash between generations, with its recourse to more or less violent opposition, has come to the fore periodically during the history of mankind's social development, though in various forms and with different means.

Conclusion

I started this presentation by trying to uncover the early roots of the working alliance in analytic treatment. When I began to discover how difficult and time-consuming it is to undo the split in an adult's personality between his present and his past experiential world, I gained the impression that psychoanalytically obtained knowledge may eventually contribute to the world's problems of individual and social misery. It is man himself, after all, who through countless generations has created his social world. A change from the outside in hierarchical social structure is necessary in many respects, but the frequently voiced idea that this will solve all problems and remove all distress seems to be an illusion. Without a change of the inner emotional world of human beings the outcome of all social and economic corrections may prove to be short-lived and even provoke a reverse reaction.

It is normal for the little child to feel himself to be the center of the world, to have the right to demand all satisfactions, to expect that his "omnipotent" parents will undo every pain and misery, and to experience the impulse to kill whenever he is infuriated as a result of being confronted with his real limitations by the outside world.

In the inner world of an adult such an attitude is rightly considered to be a pathological delusion. Nevertheless, we meet with the reemergence of these repressed delusions in smaller and larger groups of people. In communities and small societies, competition, striving for power, self-aggrandizement, and destructive inclinations come to the fore time and again. Unfortunately, psychoanalytic societies are no exception. Perhaps, analysts should make a start, by trying to conquer the repressed childhood world and letting the hidden forces mature and add to rational behavior in adulthood. Whether this process will ever be achieved in smaller and larger groups and populations cannot be forecast at the present time. The renouncement of personal power, self-aggrandizement, and aggression seems to be a most difficult task, yet these proclivities are the most powerful enemy of the longing for understanding, unity with fellowmen, and love.

When Freud wrote *Civilization and Its Discontents* (1930), it was necessary for him to prove the universality of aggressive and destructive drives in man. Freud saw the destiny of mankind as dependent upon the question whether and how far civilization will finally be able to master the destructive and the self-destructive impulses. As mentioned above, Eissler (1971) added ambivalence and narcissism to the dangers threatening man's future.

I have tried to underline the alienation between the archaic primitive experiential world and the later sophistication as one other of the many factors involved. Civilization promotes rationality, unfortunately at the expense of empathy with the emotional life. Alienation between generations strengthens the lust for power to compensate for the original helplessness and evokes destructive acting out on both sides. This mutual estrangement often finds its way into society at large, with the disastrous outcomes of suppression, robbery, war, and all kinds of misery.

I close by questioning whether man will finally be capable of mastering the repressed residues of his archaic infantile experiential world, allowing its forces to mature and be utilized for more harmonious and peaceful purposes. Will lust for power and aggrandizement together with aggression and destruction prevail, or will loving empathy be recovered in the long run, tiding over the years of upbringing and the emotional gap between generations, countries, peoples, and the differently shaped communities?

37. Two Experiential Worlds: the World of the Child and That of the Adult

(1975)

"Children what are they?"
Prof. Dr. E.C.M. Frijling-Schreuder

There is no yesterday
there is no tomorrow"
M. Wertheim

"But understanding with reason is nothing compared to
understanding with feeling, with the heart"
M. Wertheim

In "Kinderen wat zijn dat?" (Children what are they?) Prof. Frijling gives a delicate description in simple language of the personality development. This development unrolls in a maturing process from birth till adulthood, in interaction of child and environment. The new born brings genetically determined potentials with it in the world. These determine the possibilities of physical and mental development. Initially, the inner world of the baby is centered round the satisfaction of physical needs and impulses. The mental and intellectual development will come later. The environment, initially the mother, reacts to the child from the own already shaped personality structure. Interaction between two different experientially worlds arises. The environment of the child expands gradually. The influences of the father, the members of the family, school and a wider social environment play a part in this development.
Dr. Frijling therefore pays attention to these influences. The subtitle of her book: "Verstandhouding en misverstand" (Understanding and misunderstanding) indicates that there are difficulties in the interaction of child and environment. She also devotes two chapters to "Essential misunderstandings between parents and children (schoolchildren and adolescents)". But she mainly describes the process of growth from the child's experience. I first thought to entitle my article, a modest addition to her book: "Adults, what are they?" But that would have been to pretentious. The psychic experiential world of grownups is so rich, so complicated and individually differentiated that we could write whole books about it. I will restrict myself and try to indicate some aspects of the differences between the experiential worlds of the very small child and the adult. It are after all these differences, which are the basis of possible later misunderstandings between parents and children. We could even add here, that

they provide psychological factors for the coming into being of the so-called "generation conflict".

Child psychiatrists and psycho-analysts repeatedly observe in their treatment and observations of family-interactions that many adults have no or little understanding for the "world" of the child. With this I do not mean an intellectual understanding. So much has been written about the psychology of the child that educators, psychologists, psychiatrists and all those who are involved with "well-being" can acquaint themselves with the mental growthprocess and can also grasp it rationally. But what I am driving at is *emotional* understanding, really *entering into* the world of the child. The empathic capacity is, of course, encountered with many people who have not been trained in one of the above mentioned professions and activities, e.g. with mothers and parents who may work in a completely different field. Artists in probably all field of art very often possess intuition and empathy. That is the reason, why I chose the second quotation on top of this article. The novelist M. Wertheim puts it so simple: "But understanding with reason is nothing compared to understanding with feeling, with the heart".

These words do not immediately apply to empathy into the experiential world of babies, but they concern his empathy with the irrational behaviour of his very intelligent daughter in her love life, with the problems, his older, lonely brother had with his own inner emotional emptiness and with emotional disturbances of many others, which have led to misery, unhappiness, gloom, inner disharmony and/or conflicts with the exterior world.

The author suddenly "felt" that reason goes completely different ways from emotions, needs, impulses and feelings. I may perhaps here recall a communication of Freud's. Summer 1910 when Freud stayed with his family in Noordwijk, he was approached one day by Gustav Mahler, who in extreme despair asked him for an interview. All day long Mahler told Freud of his conflicts and despair, walking up and down Breestraat in Leiden. Suddenly he stopped and exclaimed: "Now I understand why I have often been reproached for suddenly interposing a simple folksong when my symphonies reach emotional heights. As a little boy I deeply suffered from the many quarrels and violent scenes between my parents. I had the feeling that I had to protect my mother against my brutal father. At that moment the barrel organ in the street began to play a children's song. Apparently, I have never been able to forget. . .".

The great composer had regained apart of the experiential world of his childhood in a few hours (naturally with Freud's empathic help). Shortly afterwards Mahler had obligations in America and could not as he intended, continue his talks with Freud in analysis, because death surprised him.

As analysts we know that it can sometimes take months or even years before a patient is able to open the entrance to his early childhood experiences. All of us repressed this world, warded it off. A little child is powerless against its outside and inside conflicts; on the one hand it is completely dependent on its environment and it has only just been able to develop a tiny personality, ignorant of the emotional world of adults.

Since adults have hidden their own childhood experiences deep down, into the unconscious, they become split personalities without access to their own child-hood world. As a consequence they do not understand the child any more. Parents with good intentions can often no longer follow the struggling, emo-tional development of the child with empathy. This phenomenon can especially be seen in our western sophisticated culture. Other cultures show different patterns, though they, including the so-called "illiterate societies" have their problems as well.

I would like to give one example of a society where the course of development of children differed from those in our western society. I take this from the fascinating book: "Facing Mount Kenya", by Jomo Kenyatta. The author describes how the developmental processes ran its course in the days before western civilization forced its culture upon the illiterate Gikuya-tribe in Kenya. Initially by missionaries and later by conquerors. In old times, toddlers learned to speak because the mother was singing nursery rhymes for them. As soon as they could walk they participated in the activities of the parents, the girl was with the mother, the boy with the father. They could not "learn" in schools, which did not exist, but they did in the intimate association with the parents and adults so that as early as the age of 5 or 6 years they took part in all of the adult activities and became independent at an early age. Kenyatta does not conceal that there were difficulties but we get the strong impression that the emotional worlds of child and adult were very close and that a much greater harmony came into existance between young and old.

I have to leave this fascinating theme that I have already mentioned elsewhere. I move closer to our own society and I think of the big gap between the two experiential worlds in our culture. Analysts are repeatedly confronted with this gap, in the analytic treatment of children and of adults, in the observations of babies, infants and toddlers. The most disturbed children are naturally to be found in the child-psychiatric clinic. Sometimes they come from deeply deranged families but not always. It is often surprising to find a deeply disturbed child in a "good", more or less harmonious family. Naturally, we look for a physical cause, for example a prenatal deviation or a birth-trauma. Also post-natal diseases can disturb the developmental process in early childhood for example encephalitis, etc. But even when no somatic basis for a developmental disturbance or arrest can be found, the mental development of the child can be inhibited or distorted, even when family relations could be called "normal". Intelligent little children are usually also impulsive, passionate little creatures. This is a difficult problem for parents who try to educate their children to achieve the necessary adaptation. But parents can be equally disappointed by a less gifted or mentally deficient child, or as mentioned before by a physically handicapped child, with the consequence that they lose "empathy" in spite of their good intentions.

I will come back to that. The alienation between the experiential worlds of child and adult is extremely complicated and full of the most different aspects, even when the child is physically healthy. This forces me to simplify and generalize, knowing that words, especially written ones, can only approach a real, living process. Words are "tools" and often give rise to misunderstanding. We human beings are proud of our ability to write and to read but we should not forget that the extent to which we can depict the truly dynamic and emotional events is only limited.

Be it as it may: we have "to make shift with what we have". I choose two fields from the many possible misunderstandings between child and adult. These two are still closely linked in the child:

a. thinking

b. the impulsive, wishful, emotional life.

When the toddler learns words, he initially makes them "concrete". He plays with them as with his own body, his mother and his toys. Talking and thinking are still expressions of needs and impulses. The child's "logic" is one with its wishful world.

Adults have developed abstract thinking which has led to a completely different "logic". (I am not denying that logical thinking in the adult world all too often proves to be "wishful thinking!") I will come back to this later. I could give dozens, hundreds of examples of the "thinking" and speaking of little children which are logical within their inner world of impulses and wishes but which are not understood by adults. Out of many children's remarks I choose two: one by Molly and one by Francis:

Molly, three years old says: "Daddy, when my "*dicky* (penis) will grow it will become so long that it will reach the attic". This utterance betrays that Molly strongly wishes to posses like her brother and father a male genital. In her way of thinking this is a completely logical remark. She does not yet know that the genital difference is an anatomical fact which cannot be changed. She wants to have a *dicky*, that implies that it will grow and be even bigger than daddie's. Molly takes this for granted and she is serious about it. Her father who told me Molly's remark (and who himself is a very gifted analyst) laughed heartily and added: "we all made such fun of it!" But what about Molly? The "loving" laughing ("oh, how cute") hurt the little girl tremendously, she felt ridiculed and belittled.

To be mocked is one of the most hurting experiences for a sensitive small child. Molly was hurt, withdrew, silent and shy. Her self-confidence was injured. People often say in cases like these: "Alright, the child was a little sad at first, but next day it played as cheerful as ever". But when grown-up Molly for some reason starts analysis and after a long period encounters and re-experiences the event (or a similar one) in the transference situation, we see that these and similar experiences had made a deep impression, leading to developmental inhibitions, symptoms and unhappiness.

Francis is four years old, a clever town kid is in the country with his grandparents. He observes with great interest the various birds pecking for food but afterwards flying up to trees and faraway. Francis found himself a walking path to a farm and one day he wanted to take his grandfather there. This was arranged and they watched the various animals intensely. There were chickens and granddad used the word birds for chickens. Francis: "But granddaddy, chickens are not birds!" Granddad tried to explain to Francis but the little boy insisted: "Chickens are no birds". Granddad: "Well, Francis, when we come home we will call daddy to ask him whether it is true or not". Francis: "No, granddaddy, do not ask daddy". Granddad: "But whom shall we ask then?" Francis (with quiet conviction): "Me". In the way of thinking of a four year old complete logic reigns connected with the wish-world: birds fly high in the sky, chickens walk on the ground to peck seeds and can therefore not be birds. This little story naturally gives away that Francis' world was still influenced by a grandeur-fantasy. A very normal phenomenon for a four year old.

What about the impulsive, emotional world of our toddlers? Three year old Molly is apparently in the phallic phase of her drive-development. She seeks to approach her father and we may well suspect that she would like to be his "lover", his "wife". At the same time she wants to posses like him a very big genital to be equally powerful. Such a wish- and fantasyworld is normal for a three year old. Father's "laughing" doubly hurt Molly: her grandeur-feeling is injured; her father's attitude is, in her world, a fatal rejection: "He thinks I am small and worthless and he therefore does not love me". The self-confidence still strongly dependent on being loved, is doubly affected and she withdraws in her shell of misery and impotence.

Francis does not immediately reveal something about his sexual development but he demonstrates the "narcissistic" position, the grandeur-fantasy as a compensation for being small in reality.

What about adults and their way of thinking, their drive- and emotional life? History of mankind has taught us that thinking has greatly been expanded throughout the centuries. Word- and language development have strongly influenced action. Mutual communication and mastering of natural forces have led to group formation with ever growing social problems. Various cultures have reached high flowering periods, others went partly or completely back to ruin. Nowadays science and art have reached great heights. Knowledge of the natural forces and growth of the intellect have provided mankind with great power. Thinking has acquired a dimension of rationality and logic and testable laws concerning connections, causes and results have been laid down. But there is another side to the coin.

Repeatedly is said by many, also by Freud: "The cultural acquisitions partly came about at the expense of an impoverishment and restrictions of the drive- and emotional life". Alienation has arisen with people between their logical thinking and their spontaneous, natural, feeling. The original drives of human beings are indestructible natural forces, as long as life exists. They can however be reshaped. In our current civilization, the *basis* of love, in all its differentia-tions, the sexual drive, libido, has been substantially clipped and blunted. Libido has apparently also lost part of its capacity to restrain the other original force, the destruction. Aggression and destruction with the accompanying emotions of hatred, jealousy, hostility and lust of power nowadays reign unchallenged. All too often reason and logic are flooded by drive-impulses. This happens between people and social groups. But also between and in individuals. We analysts daily meet both an inner split in our patients and an emptiness and/or a being flooded by their drives. The often highly intellectually gifted individual has not been able to deal adequately with drive-impulses and especially the destructive ones in childhood and repressed them, warded them off. He then is often not able anymore to love an other individual and sometimes not even himself. He suffers from the inner struggle (which has become unconscious) between love and hatred, between acting constructively and destructively. Because of the defence and the resulting split many adults have no longer access to the spontaneous, natural emotional world of the child, in which a strong desire for love, sexual satisfaction and the lust "to destroy" are predominant. This can often be seen in the parent-child relationship. The result is a misunderstanding of feeling. This may sound very pessimistic. I do not intend to deny warm feelings for a child with "good" and "loving" parents. A "good" mother will be able to feed, to take care of and to hug the little one. But there comes a moment when the parent suddenly feels estranged after a particular utterance of the child, e.g., when the parent cannot understand the infantile logic, which described in Molly and Francis. He then, cannot take the child seriously anymore. The parent may react by becoming cool, indifferent or hostile. This may have desastrous results for the development of the child's personality. I described above the episodes of a 3- and 4-year old. The misunderstanding of feeling can, however, arise much earlier, at a time when the infant does not yet know words or cannot yet express his feelings in words. What can we know of this pre-verbal period of life of baby and toddler? Dr. Frijling puts it nicely: "How is a normal mother-child relation experienced by a new-born? Who can tell? The psychic life of a suckling is a delightful subject for speculation, because it cannot answer". How true! And still . . . does the suckling not answer? Certainly not in words, but there are other ways. It screams, cries, squirms and soon its features will change from quiet to smile, from rest to tense muscle contractions. Naturally our remarks such as: "the baby is cheerful, content, unhappy or angry" are "adultomorf". But we can sometimes draw certain conclusions from the mother's reaction. If the baby stops crying as soon as the mother takes it up and hugs it, a certain need has been satisfied, initially only a physical need, e.g., for warmth, for skin sensation, for movements, for satisfaction of hunger. Fortunately, there are still many mothers who intuitively perceive what their baby needs. Apparently, they have been able to retain some of the primal child behaviour, or to speak with René Spitz, the "receptive mode of reaction".

This modality is later overshadowed by the diacritic organization which reacts actively. The primitive receptive pattern can come to life again in a more or less harmonious mother who is happy with her child and can thus feel what her child needs at certain moments. But even the most loving mother repeatedly experiences the sorrow, that she cannot quieten her baby and does not know whether it is crying with hunger, pain, fear or something similar. It is impossible to satisfy every need immediately. Frustrations are unavoidable but a healthy and not too anxious mother soon knows how to cope with it. She will for example sing or hum a lullaby in a low voice if the baby is restless, even if its elementary needs are satisfied. How lovely when baby becomes quiet and falls asleep with an "angels" face. A loving mother knows too that eye-contact is very important, from the moment that the child becomes aware of the existence of an outer source of satisfaction.

If the mother looks indifferent while feeding and caring for the baby, because she is preoccupied with a problem of her own the baby will not quiet down. The "mother-child-dyad" has then been disturbed. Few adults are able to realize how much this influences the development of the baby. If the mother lacks empathy the baby may suffer too much deprivation which can form the basis of various later developmental disturbances. The tie between child and mother is in this period still a completely narcissistic one. The presence of the mother somewhere near is necessary for the sense of well being of the child. Mother's absence is felt as an eternal loss. The child lives for the "moment" and is ignorant of a future. In his inner world Wertheim's words are valid: "There is no yesterday, there is no tomorrow, *eternity is to-day*". Suffering from a frustration, no matter how briefly, is a difficult learning process and time consuming. An empathic guidance is extremely important. When the child begins to creep and walk and to actively explore the world a difficult period begins. Restrictions and prohibitions are necessary to protect it from dangers. But here again it is the way in which this happens and is guided with empathy that is so important.

Various authors have repeatedly written about this subject. Much attention has been paid to the period in which the child is toilet-trained. The toddler has to give up the autonomy over the drive-satisfaction which his body products provide. Initially, defecating and urinating are extremely lustful activities which he wants to do at his own time and in his own way. He is however deprived of this initiative, he has to adapt to his parents desires; they determine place and time and prevent him from throwing, eating and playing with his excrements. The inner experiential world of the toddler ("the self") is disturbed. Besides, his products which are part of him, are devalued, thrown away, which makes him feel worthless and rejected. All this is inflicted by his caring parental figures with whom he has a strong tie and whom he also needs. He feels that: "Only evil enemies can do this to him". The child lives in an inner confusion, he imagines to have lost his parents' love, is lonely, at a loss and powerless. In human life, deprivation, injuries and prohibitions automatically raise destructive impulses. The same accounts for the small child who has to face an inner conflict. To "keep" and to "destroy" the beloved parents at the same time is an impossibility. The child has to become "good" and to repress many of his impulses and wishes. But at what expense? A deep resentment can continue to exist in the repressed unconscious and be expressed in various ways in later periods of life. Are there no more salutary solutions for the toddler? Of course there are. The gradually growing personality can develop capacities to channel parts of his impulses and activities. "Childplay" is in his world serious "work" which can deal with many of his constructive as well as his destructive impulses. The intensity and the deep seriousness with which a toddler builds towers and next knocks them down, with which he draws and paints are phase-adequate "sublimations". It is however obvious how much "empathy" and guidance of this developmental process from the parent means. But how often is it lacking? Parents all too often experience a temper tantrum of a toddler as naughty, troublesome or evil and they suppress it strictly. The sweetness forced on the child can however again lead to inner insecurity and misery and eventually cause inhibitions and developmental arrest. In the next stage, the phallic phase, the child is not only confronted with the lack of understanding in the adults, who can no longer imagine the oedipal fantasy-world, but also with an unchanging reality. The three- to six year old is certainly in our culture "grown-up" in his mental life and fantasy-world. Physically he has not yet stopped growing and it is physically impossible to become mother's husband and/or father's wife. The long period, required for maturing is a natural hindrance for a harmonious unfolding. The impossibility to transform the sexual aggressive fantasies in a real love-relationship with the parents is a heavy psychic burden. Here again it is important for the adult to show empathy. I remember an old dutch nursery rhyme that meant that: children hinder, but the poet forgot that he had once been a child himself. How old-fashioned! And how up-to-date!

In this period a sensitive child again becomes extremely sensitive for the reactions of adults. To be "laughed-at lovingly" is one of the most desastrous experiences. People also tend to smile benevolently when the small child falls in love with a friend. A bright child may look for intellectual compensation and do well at school. But he will often be under the impression that his parents: "Only like my good marks, but not *me*". A very inhibited emotional life and inner loneliness could be the result.

The feelings of powerlessness can be compensated for in other ways as well, namely by the inner world of grandeur- and omnipotence-fantasies, in which also an idealized image of "omnipotent parents" in whose omnipotence the child shares, finds a place. With toddlers this fantasy world, as described in Mollie's and Francis' case, is quite normal. The fantasies of grandeur and omnipotence of "Self" and of idealized parents do, however, grow along in a more or less harmonious development. They then become ethical norms and ideals which can be realized in adulthood to a certain extent and lead to constructive activities. If this growth fails, the inner split is only reinforced. All people are in many situation in life powerless. This may lead to a regression to a re-experiencing of the repressed "absolute" grandeur world of the child. The sense of reality is then disturbed, relations with the surroundings can fall back to a more primitive level. Love-life for example regresses to the archaic "self-centered" (narcissistic) position. In work and social life the "absolute" is (unconsciously) again pursued and the individual falls victim to despair and failure. The revived hostility and destructivity can become desastrous for him and his environment. It seems to be impossible for us human beings to realize our potential where it is possible and to accept at the same time our essential impotence in other fields. We can imagine ourselves omnipotent in our fantasy-world. In reality and in society we often have to accept our powerlessness. An important facet of the essential impotence is death. In a well hidden world of wishes everyone wants to be immortal. In reality we have only a very limited power over the length of life and the moment of death. This may be one of the causes of *fear* of death, whereas *individual death belongs to life*. An unfortunate and well-known reaction to this fear of death can be a denial of fear and an acting-out of aggression in the mutilation and destruction of others.

I now come back to the theme of the two experiential worlds. First, I would like to make some brief remarks about the emotional "misunderstandings" between child and adult, which reappear in adolescence. Of course this occurs in different forms as the child has meanwhile developed a differentiated personality. The adolescent has acquired a great gamut of reaction- and defence organisations as a result of the growth of the ego-functions. But with the flowering-up of the drive- and emotional life in puberty, the old infantile patterns are reactivated. Many aspects of the alienation and the "misunderstanding" between youngsters and older people which can cause inner and outer rebellion in the young, originated in the early days of their life. The older generation often stares at the "sophisticated" attitude of youth with wonder, incomprehension and dislike. This essay does, however, not allow a closer and certainly necessary study of these problems. The reader will probably ask: what is the sense of all this information about psychological events, which are already often and aptly explained by many authors? Do not all of us know that the child lives and feels differently from an adult? My answer is: "Yes, we do know, but do we *really* know, feel and experience the child's inner world?

We all know the literature and the valuable analytical and psychological theories based on observations. We speak of the symbiotic phase, of individuation- and separationproblems, of anal stubbornness, of narcissistic injuries, of sadomasochistic fantasies, of the oedipal period, of the separation- and castrationanxiety, of latency, of puberty, of "normal" and pathological development etc. etc. But what do we *experience, feel?*

My answer is very personal and in addition I will give more general experiences. When I, more than fifty years ago, started a psycho-analytic practice I knew the then current literature fairly well. I had also been very privileged with my own analyst who never or rarely made use of a theoretical term. I learned a lot about my own, archaic past and also thought that my empathic capacity had been sharpened. Looking back I must however admit that it took many many years before I could really experience intensively the world of a child. I cannot evaluate how well I have succeeded and where there are still blind spots in my own personality. I do notice, however, that I daily acquire new dimensions in empathy. I will now turn to the more general experiences in my daily analytical work. I think of the patients who turned to me in confusion and extreme distress and with whom it appeared to be inevitable to help them revive and work through their earliest childhood experiences in order to regain a certain harmony, enjoyment of life and freedom for activities.

I especially think of the many patients who function more or less satisfactorily in different fields of life, in work, family, social contacts, but who struggle with certain inhibitions (especially in creativity), disrupting self-confidence.

It has always struck me how difficult and time-consuming it is to re-experience the earliest base of these disturbances in infancy in full intensity. It is equally hard work to deal with them in such a way that the originally repressed energy is released and can be used for constructive adult goals.

Just one example: sometimes old ressentiments of the child which have become unconscious and which were caused by the devaluation of his first body-products can inhibit the adult capacity to function productively. Then the pattern which was developed in the toddler repeats itself. The suppression and the devaluation of the child's achievements raised aggression and destruction and caused inner powerlessness and loss of self-confidence. Also anger can break through and destruction can take place, overwhelming reason. Destruction is turned outside and/or turned to the person himself. The latter takes place especially if later on (in the oedipal situation) a strict conscience with a need for self-punishment has been formed. The adult, sometimes very gifted personality is in that case unable to arrive at "sublimated" creative productivity. Sometimes family life will run smoothly but often alienation gradually comes about, a chilled relation with partner and/or children. Here, too, it is often necessary to re-experience the infantile injuries in order to gain inner freedom, in order to be able to love the other for his (or her) personality and no get stuck in the "self-centered" (narcissistic) requirement of being loved. A truly mature relationship is only stable if all persons involved can accept the peculiarities of the other with + and - signs. This naturally implies that the parent can guide with empathy his (or her) children in their special experiential world, relevant to each development stage, as I have tried to explain above.

It goes without saying that regaining the archaic experiential world of a child is not always or sometimes only partly possible. If it does succeed an inner release is experienced which can radiate over the person and his environment.

I would here like to prevent a possible "misunderstanding" between reader and author. The reader might think that according to me the psycho-analytic process could change a personality completely, almost "redo" it. I certainly do not foster this illusion. The idealized expectation of many, that analysis is omnipotent (or should be) is fiction, a remnant of the infantile form of grandeur-fantasies. Analysis can sometimes achieve a lot, sometimes a little, sometimes nothing.

Another criticism of analysis, quite rightly expressed by many authors runs as follows: "Analysis is a method to make unconscious conflicts conscious and thereby make it possible to 'work through' and integrate them. Before the differentiation between Self and Other comes about and before ego-functions, no matter how primitive came into existence, there are no conflicts and therefore the archaic baby-period cannot be attained in analysis". I agree with this.

Also inborn defects cannot be repaired. Innate capacities and talents can at most be released from inhibitions and be unfolded. It is highly likely that deposits of the earliest mother-child relation can neither be changed. It seems to me that here the relevant question should be *whether* and *how* the later personality learns to cope with this eventually unchangeable. The mature person can sometimes find a different and more satisfying method and puts up with the "impossible".

Events of the pre-verbal- and "archaic" time cannot be verbally remembered. I do, however, think that communication between analyst and patient does not take place exclusively in words. The attitude of the analyst, the way in which he welcomes the patient or takes leave, but *especially the tone of his voice* are varying dimensions of communication. When the patient talks about his childhoodexperiences one speaks with a different voice. If the analysis comes to a standstill when oedipal and pre-oedipal conflicts have been worked-through and some complaints still remain, an attempt could be made to describe something of possible very early developmental disturbances. One grasps and looks for words which could be suitable for this particular patient. If one is wrong the story is lost. This is of no importance if there is a good relationship, a reliable working-alliance. But sometimes it is after a shorter or longer period that the patient experiences a kind of "aha-experience" and "I feel something" which can lead to relief. A distortion in the earliest mother-child relationship can in that case be re-experienced with a feeling of evidence. This does not seldom come about via observations of one's own (or other people's) children. The patient suddenly notices how his mother deals with her grandchildren. "She will probably have done something similar with me", he will then exclaim. This often refers to a too early and too rigid toilet-training, but even grandmother's reaction to eating-disturbances and illnesses in the baby can give the patient the feeling of his own very early distortion of the mother-childrelationship.

I could give many other examples which may cause the evidence feeling described. But I will restrict myself to this one. If it succeeds, a sense of relief can occur. But one should always be able to accept failures.

It is often heard that psycho-analysis is much too time consuming and only achieves a little, for only a few people. We definitely should take this criticism seriously but I may perhaps mention the following problem: "The prevention". Parents, educators, psychiatrists, psychologists and all social-care-people who have acquired in themselves a harmony between needs, impulses, emotions and passions can perhaps transfer this to children and people in mental distress. All human beings live with "hope" for the better. I would like to end in a more optimistic vein. Let everyone work in his own field. Those who have succeeded in gaining a certain flexible balance within themselves, could perhaps in cooperation with others contribute to relieve the inner and outer distress in human beings. To think that we could get rid of this distress for ever would be a dangerous illusion. The only thing we can do is to be content with little.

Hoping this, I quote:

"Wer immer strebend sich bemüht
den können wir erlösen", Faust-Goethe

And I would like to apply this to our "earthly" and not to our "heavenly" life.

38. Mourning in a 6-Year-Old Girl

(1976)

The story of little Mary's bereavement is derived from her memories and from reconstructions in her analysis as an adult. Mary started psychoanalysis in her early 20s for professional reasons. She was a physically healthy and active person. She suffered from mild depressions which were transitory and of short duration, usually lasting one or two days.

Mary was the third of four children. Her parents were well-to-do, had many intellectual and artistic interests, as did Mary herself. The family life was relatively harmonious. Mary's depressions had never seriously interfered with her work. She had been a good student in school and at the university.

Very early in her analysis, Mary spoke of an important childhood event. A few days after Mary's sixth birthday the youngest child, 3½ her junior, fell ill. What seemed at first to be an ordinary childhood disease proved to be fatal. A few weeks later the little one died. During the last week of her sister's illness, Mary and her 2-year-older sibling stayed with their grandparents, because the mother was completely preoccupied with caring for the sick infant.

I shall let Mary describe the memories which had always been conscious, in her own words.

1. I had no idea of the seriousness of my little sister's illness. I was not unhappy staying with my grandparents, but one morning I woke up very early. I looked at the clock (I just had learned to read the clock), but I misread it. I thought it was an hour later and I was terribly upset because I would be late for school.

2. A few days later the headmistress came into my classroom and took me with her. She helped me into my coat and said something like, "Poor child, but do not forget that your little sister is now in heaven." I had no idea what she was talking about.

   Outside an uncle of ours was waiting for me and my two older siblings. I thought it a kind of adventure and hopped toward him. Then, suddenly I felt my uncle's earnestness and low spirits. Gradually I began to feel that something terrible must have happened. I felt at a loss, but understood that it concerned my baby sister. The uncle took us home. There the atmosphere was heavy and sad. I do not remember what was said, but I still feel my parents' distress, pain, and grief. My father had tears in his eyes and this confused and terrified me. After some time I went to the bookcase, fetched my favorite picture book, crawled into the farthest corner of the room and began to read.

After a long silence, Mary continued: There is a blank in my memory, a "nothing," only a vague feeling of heaviness and sadness. . . . Now another memory comes up. Some time later (it seems to me to be an endless stretch of time), I asked my mother, "Mommy, tell me, when one is dead, does one remain dead during one's entire life?" I do not recall mother's answer, but I have the feeling that I began to understand that I would never see my baby sister again.

After this conversation with her mother there followed a period in Mary's life of which she remembered very little. Her school years were uneventful as far as she could tell. Learning did not provide difficulties. A single recollection, dated by Mary approximately half a year after the baby's death, came to the fore relatively early in her analysis, actually after a half year of treatment. It was springtime. Mary was looking out of the window waiting for a band of street musicians who always came in spring; she was sad, but had a feeling of intense longing. Music played a special role in her life. The longing was for some relief from her sadness. When the musicians finally came, she wept and felt more relaxed. This is what Mary remembered about the death of her little sister.

I now turn to the reconstructions that gradually were made in the course of Mary's analysis. We had to understand this period of her life as the starting point of her depressive states. Mary was in the latency period when she lost her sibling. She had overcome her original jealousy and hostility by an intense maternal love. She used to protect and take care of the infant sister, who was a charming, beautiful, but weak child. Mary at first denied her bereavement. She felt bewildered by her parents' mourning, shaken by her father's weeping, and upset by her mother's depression. Of course, at the time she did not realize that her mother was in a depressive state, but in her analysis Mary recognized that her mother suffered from depressions more severe than her own. There were periods when her mother, who actually was a good and loving mother, was "absent-minded." Mary now realized that it was a withdrawal of affection, in part due to mourning, but more intense and of longer duration than in a "normal" mourning process.

Thus, at the time of her sister's death Mary had to deny both the loss of "her" child and the loss of her mother's loving attention. Hostility toward both could not be tolerated by the latency child, and she had to take recourse to denial and repression. Only much later did she understand the finality of the event, as is revealed in her question to her mother. This question is a logical one in the child's world. Death does not yet have any meaning for a child. "Forever," "eternal" are uncomprehensible words. "During one's whole life" represented Mary's idea of a very, very long time, but I do not think that it brought the notion of death any nearer to her. Her question contained an acceptance of absence, but at the same time denied the eternity of this absence and preserved the notion of "life."

Is this reaction very different from an adult's, who is confronted with death and especially with the death of a beloved person? Intellectually and cognitively, Mary's phrasing of her bewilderment is not that of an adult, but her emotional reaction is not very much at variance from that of an adult. Most people have great difficulties in accepting the finality and inevitability of individual death. They tend to deny it, though intellectually they "know." An intense fear of death can often be detected behind conscious rationalizations and may prove the emotional denial. For many people it seems to be an unbearable notion that individual death is part of life. The emotional acceptance of this fact would be too strong a narcissistic injury.

The 6-year-old latency child's affective reaction was not very different from that of an adult. Nor was her mode of mourning. What, then, were the underlying causes of Mary's depressive states? Her own grief and the subsequent process of mourning were greatly influenced by her mother's more severe depression. Mary had made a normal identification with her mother in the course of resolving the oedipal situation. The accompanying hostility toward her mother had already been repressed to a considerable extent, though unconsciously the hostility was reinforced by the lack of her mother's loving attention. Mary had already developed a more or less stable superego, and her unconscious guilt feelings had caused hostility and aggression to be turned inward. The analytic reconstructions of these events started with a similar reaction in her adult life. At a time when Mary was no longer living with her family, a second bereavement occurred. One of her older brothers died a few days after contracting a severe illness. Mary had loved and admired him very much and her grief was intense. Now, however, she also became aware of the extent to which her grief and mourning were influenced and aggravated by her mother's depression.

These early experiences of loss as well as other disappointments in life (e.g., a broken engagement with a young man) clearly were responsible for Mary's tendency to be depressed. In fact, she had to struggle very hard in order not to succumb to a genuine depressive state. The analysis finally released her from depressions.

Theoretical remarks

In the literature on mourning we encounter differences of opinion about the question whether children are able to mourn as adults do (see, for example, the discussion of Bowlby's paper [1966] by Anna Freud, Spitz, and Schur [1966]). It is not my intention to survey the literature in this short paper, nor to describe the various phases of the mourning process. I merely venture to present a few conclusions derived from my analytic knowledge of Mary.

It is likely that the controversies are in part due to terminological differences. There seems to be a more or less common consensus with regard to an infant's affective responses to the loss of the mothering person or that person's love. These affective reactions are called distress, grief, pain, and sometimes protest and anxiety. Actually, they leave lasting imprints on the child's physical and mental development. Some authors (e.g., Bowlby, Melanie Klein) equate these affective states with mourning and depression, and use these terms in a way that differs substantially from their original meaning. In Freud's terminology, "mourning" designates a complicated mental process. It is the reaction to loss, the working through of pain and grief, the loosening of the emotional and instinctual ties to the lost object and their gradual shifting toward new objects. In order to accomplish these tasks, a number of ego functions have to be developed, among them a sense of and a certain judgment of reality, an ability to take some distance from emotions which in the beginning are experienced as overwhelming, the capacity to bear pain and grief without deteriorating. In brief, the synthesizing or harmonizing function must be present to a certain degree. This implies that structuralization of the mind must have become established.

Similar considerations apply to the use of the term "depression." Originally it designated a highly differentiated mental disturbance in which one of the prominent reactive and defensive manoeuvers is the turning of object-directed aggression and destruction toward the own person. This also presupposes differentiation of the mind, the existence of an inner conscience, the superego. Some authors have the tendency to call every feeling of low spirits and sadness depression. It is, of course, permissible to redefine a term if we thereby clearly improve our psychological understanding of the underlying processes. However, in my opinion, this is not the case with mourning and depression. The equation of feelings and emotions that are complicated mental processes with primary, undifferentiated affective reactions is, I feel, an oversimplification, a dilution of our knowledge.

We cannot do without metapsychological viewpoints to understand our observations. (I am here in agreement with Anna Freud, Spitz, and Schur in their discussions of Bowlby's views.) Retaining the original meaning of the term "mourning" does justice to the processes of maturation and development of the human mind. We cannot imagine a child of 1 or 2 years to react to frustration and loss with anything other than immediate feeling response. In fact, we describe such a response in adult language, but the words at least indicate only feelings or affects. The infant's behavior entitles us to do so. But to ascribe to an infant the complicated processes of mourning and the neurotic disturbance of a depression seems to make no sense. The material we encounter in the analyses of older children and adults who have experienced the death of a parent or a sibling early in their lives is not their immediate and original reaction to this event – it is in all cases a secondary elaboration. The age at which a child is capable of "real mourning processes" varies individually, and is dependent upon the rate of maturation and developmental structuralization.

In Mary's case it was clear from her direct, never forgotten or repressed memories that she had already accomplished the differentiation of the mind that is normal in a latency child. She clearly understood after a short stretch of time the definiteness of the loss, though it was expressed in terms of a child's logic. She also worked through her grief and finally found other objects, at first via her longing for a musical consolation, then in shifting her attachment to an older sibling and to friends. In her later schoolyears and especially in high school, she was a gay and active child. Another characteristic reaction of a latency child who is already capable of "real mourning" was Mary's withdrawal into the corner of the room. But it differed from the withdrawal seen in infants whose original protest is unsuccessful in bringing back the baby and the mother's love. Mary's withdrawal was accompanied by a constructive activity. She used an already acquired ego capacity to read and to bear loneliness to a certain degree, though the underlying sadness did not fail to affect her. The intensity of her feelings came to the fore during her analysis in the tendency to repeat her original reaction to loss in later life. In her short periods of depressions, she would lie down on her bed and read all day.

We understood that her reactions were a flight from outer and inner dangers. The latter were her strong hostile and aggressive impulses, which had already been repressed and turned inward before her sixth year of life. They could be made conscious only during her analysis when her severe guilt feelings were mastered and her superego became capable of acquiring appropriate norms and adult ideals.

The incident of Mary's misreading the clock in her grandparents' house proved to be a displacement of her anxiety about the infant's illness and the "uncanny" home situation to the more unimportant fear of being late for school. The cause of this displacement was similar to the one that motivated her turning away from her parents' mourning. It was the hostility evoked by being sent away from home, from her parents, and from her sister (her child) – a hostility that was an intolerable evil and therefore had to be repressed.

I have described some of Mary's memories and their analytic reconstructions as one example out of many with which we are confronted in connection with the loss of beloved relatives. It was my intention to demonstrate the differences between an infant's reactions of helplessness and hopelessness and the response of individuals who have attained structuralization of the mind in their development. I should like to recommend that we reserve the terms "mourning" and "depression" for the complicated mental processes which are the outcome of inner, intrapsychic conflicts. This type of conflict may start at the onset of latency. However, we should take into account that the age at which the differentiation of id, ego, and superego is more or less accomplished differs from individual to individual. For an infant's responses to bereavement and loss of love, we should resort to terms that indicate feelings like overwhelming pain, distress, or grief, which cannot be mastered by the baby.

A further question arises: What makes the "normal" process of mourning following the loss of a loved person turn into a pathological one, a severe depression or a melancholia? In other words, what prevents a person from gradually loosening his ties to the deceased and turning his love to new objects? I think it is the ambivalence, the (unconscious) hostile part of the object attachment. It is well known that repressed hate and aggression may bind more strongly than love. This is the case especially when a severe superego and a concomitant need for punishment are present. These may prevent the mourner from becoming aware of and accepting the fact that every bereavement is accompanied by some sense of relief. A hidden triumph, "You are dead, I am still alive," is an extremely "evil" and forbidden experience and therefore must be warded off. The consequence is that a recovery and a new love investment cannot take place. Apparently, little Mary's mourning was more "normal" than her mother's, though in later life Mary had to struggle hard to recover from her tendency to succumb to depressions.

The loosening of the ties to the lost person does not mean that the deceased is completely forgotten. Memories are retained and usually the good and the happy experiences with the deceased predominate and allow for sad, but satisfying and happy remembrances. These may continue to enrich the personality.

I should like to end with words of Marcel Proust, which he addressed to a friend who seemed to be inconsolable after his mother's death. Proust himself had a lifelong attachment to his own mother. It was one of the reasons for his incapacity to attain a lasting relationship with a loved woman, though in his writings he denied this influence. His life story, however, cannot make us doubt the pathological intensity and ambivalence of his mother attachment. He developed a number of psychosomatic diseases, the most prominent among them his asthma attacks. He took a variety of medicines to fight them, sometimes in such quantities that he nearly killed himself. He was constantly freezing. When he attended parties, he always kept his overcoat on, to the astonishment and amusement of his hosts and friends. He shunned fresh air and lived in a stuffy airless room. In his sexual life he turned to homosexuality and finally to persons he himself considered to be "degraded" love objects, his drivers, his valets, and at last to male, and sometimes also female, prostitutes. His aggression was turned inward in a self-destructive way as a severe self-punishment.

Proust failed to make the "journey" he so beautifully recommended to his friend in his letter of sympathy (see Painter, 1965, p. 301):

> When at last the wound of separation [is] healed [your] mother [will] return, young and happy, and live for ever.
>
> Keep what I said to you for the day when you will be able to use it . . . at present my words are meaningless for you, and may perhaps contradict bitter thoughts; but you will find them true, consoling and strengthening *when you have made the journey from parting to memory, of which no one, alas, can spare you the cruel meanders.*

39. Personal Experience with Psychoanalytic Technique
and Theory During the Last Half Century

(1976)

Personal reflections

Although I believe that every psychoanalytic paper reveals some features of its author's personality, I want to present a few details of my own learning experiences which influenced my training and teaching activities. Every analyst gradually develops his or her personal style of technique. In the beginning, however, it is influenced by the experiences in his training analysis and consequently by the technical attitude of his analyst. I started my analysis in 1922. My analyst was Sigmund Freud. I learned from him how the psychoanalytic process evolves. I became acquainted with the emotional difficulties accompanying the uncovering of present and past repressed conflicts, with the resistances and the transference necessary to remove and to work through my neurotic symptoms; and finally I learned as much as possible about my special character peculiarities, limitations, and possibilities. But I learned more. At times of resistance I experienced my analyst's so-called neutrality (which he described in his early papers on technique [1911-15]) in order to facilitate the reliving of my old conflicts. However, at times of diminished tension after conflicts had been overcome, it became clear to me that alongside the transference situation a "real" relationship between analysand and analyst exists. It taught me, first, that Freud's early recommendations to the analyst – to remain neutral and to serve as a mirror onto which the patient can project his hidden conflicts – were primarily meant to forestall burdening the patient with the analyst's personal affects, problems, and conflicts. Secondly, I learned that this "real" relationship is one of the many prerequisites for the maintenance of a working alliance. In more recent times many analysts have stressed that a working alliance is as indispensable as the transference for a favorable outcome of the analytic process and the patient's cure.

In these "relaxed" periods Freud acted as a warm, helpful, humane man occasionally not shunning a personal communication of his own life experiences. I feel that Freud's carefully selected alternation of "strict neutrality" and human relatedness has definitely influenced my personal attitude and behavior as an analyst. After my analysis was completed, the relationship with Freud developed gradually into a warm friendship with him and his family.

In later times a real friendship with a few of my former analysands and colleagues also came into existence, although I am quite aware of the fact that such a relationship is possible and rewarding with only a few. One important precondition is the resolution of transference and countertransference to such a degree that idealization and competitive hostility are sufficiently conquered by both the analysand and the analyst. In addition, certain character traits, a like-mindedness, a not-too-different outlook on life, among others, are necessary for the formation of a "real friendship." One can analyze persons of a quite dissimilar background and philosophy of life, but a lasting friendship does not come into being in such circumstances. Therefore one has to be very careful in making choices, and not succumb to a disastrous attempt to maintain personal contact after the termination of an analysis with every analysand.

Another device I learned from Freud concerns the great value of a reanalysis after a few years. (I myself experienced the beneficial result of it in the early '30s and I was astonished how poignant that work was.)

This is not the place to give detailed examples of Freud's attitude and of our relationship. Instead, I shall briefly mention a few later influences on my person and on my work. In 1925 I went to Berlin, where at that time the Analytic Society and the Institute were flourishing. In Berlin I married Dr. Hans Lampl, also an analyst, and we, with our children, stayed there until 1933. During that time my husband and I learned very much from many older colleagues, among them Abraham, Sachs, Eitingon, Simmel, and from some younger ones, e.g., Fenichel, Alexander, and Rado. I mention especially Bernfeld, who at that time worked with social workers and educators. I joined his seminar and became a psychiatric consultant in a child guidance clinic. I think it furthered my outlook on life and profession very much indeed. From 1933-1938, when we again lived in Vienna, my experience was enriched by child analytic practice and by the lively seminars and discussions with Anna Freud and her co-workers and students. These experiences certainly proved fruitful in my teaching and training capacities at a later time, when the Dutch Institute of Psychoanalysis was founded.

Although in psychoanalytic practice I consider myself to be a "classical" analyst, I know that a number of colleagues may criticize my "unconventional" way of working. Be that as it may, I do not think I had more failures than others, and I feel I had a good number of successes as well. I am still convinced that a flexible and human attitude of the analyst is more beneficial in our work with patients. This attitude, in any event, gradually enabled me to develop my own style of analyzing and to contribute a few papers on psychoanalytic technique and theory.

Little by little I became aware of the immanent importance of the early "preoedipal" mother-child relationship for the shaping of the oedipal situation, which in its final form is still the core of later neuroses, character disturbances, and narcissistic personality disorders. I also was influenced by the development of ego and superego psychology, which in fact started in 1923 with Freud's *The Ego and the Id* and was greatly extended by Anna Freud's *The Ego and the Mechanisms of Defense* (1936). But the new discoveries captured me especially during World War II, when my family and I lived in Holland (my native country). Of course, I was much impressed when after the war I learned of the extensive contributions of Hartmann, Kris, and Loewenstein on ego psychology. We now analyze and interpret defensive manoeuvers on the part of the ego before or in conjunction with the interpretation of drive derivatives.

Unfortunately, new discoveries in our science are sometimes so exciting that earlier, well-established findings tend to be neglected by some workers in our field. As a consequence of the interest in ego psychology, for example, the importance of the warded-off content, the residues of the little child's vehement instinctual conflicts, are overlooked or minimized and "ego" disturbances are overemphasized. Or the early child-mother relationship may be drawn into the foreground, while the oedipal object relationships are not given the needed attention and are considered to be of lesser importance.

I myself have always tried to avoid such oversimplifications, though it is sometimes difficult to maintain an overall view of the analysand's psychic conflicts. This is, for instance, the case with patients who use intellectualization as a defense. They may understand intellectually, but they ward off feelings, emotions, and instinctual impulses. The analyst then has to be alert and not give in to the temptation of theorizing together with his patient, but to analyze the defense manoeuvers as such. One has to point to the "split" between the adult and the childhood worlds, a split which exists in every individual.

A special case in point concerns candidates in training, who usually have read much about and are expected to know psychoanalytic theories. They are as a rule intelligent. They have passed the selection procedure, which presupposes that their ego functions are reasonably intact. Yet, this very intactness may make the task of uncovering their repressed, unsolved infantile conflicts especially difficult, above all if they tenaciously cling to the special defense of intellectualization.

The child's experiential world

This observation can serve to introduce the ambiguous theme of the so-called narcissistic personalities. The term "narcissism" is used in an astonishing number of different meanings, above all in the recent literature. I venture the idea that this confusion has been caused by the fact that the term is charged with a value judgment. Many people perceive the statement: "He or she is hysterical" as meaning: "He or she is inferior or blameworthy." Equally, the term "narcissistic personality" often involves the notion of an unworthy or morally deficient person, who as a consequence, it may be rationalized, is unanalyzable. The term "narcissism" originated in Freud's libido theory. It designated the original position of the libido in the newborn child. Both self-love and object love gradually develop out of it. This theory has been enlarged by the inclusion of aggressive drives. Sexual and aggressive drives are present in every living creature. Sexual as well as aggressive *acts* and *fantasies* are developmental products and designate patterns of *behavior*. I feel we should clearly differentiate between drive or impulse and behavior. The latter involves a number of developing functions, including primitive ego functions. Many authors, however, use the term "narcissism" for "behavior" and do not clearly differentiate it from the underlying instinctual impulse. Finally, sexual impulses lead to love; aggressive ones, to acts of aggression and hate. Both love for the own person (self-love) and object love continue to exist during the whole life-span. The same is valid for aggressive behavior and hate.

If a person does not possess a certain amount of self-love, he cannot love another individual and vice versa. The question is how the available amounts of libido are distributed between the self and the object.

The fate of aggression requires a somewhat different outcome, as aggressive impulses often mean destruction of things and/or living beings. In this case, there is the additional question whether the person is able to make use of his aggressive impulses in a constructive, sublimated way instead of in a destructive one, doing harm to others and to himself. This developmental process is very difficult to achieve. Its success or failure depends on a number of inner capacities and outer circumstances. For the little child the outer world is usually the family situation. For the older child, the adolescent, and the adult it is the society at large.

During the last decades I have become more and more aware of the deep and essential differences between the experiential world of the little child and the experiential world of the adult. I learned much from my child patients, as well as from the work of infant observers, e.g., Margaret Mahler, René Spitz, and many others. The recognition of these differences is of paramount significance, especially in the analyses of the so-called narcissistic persons. Their ego-centricity, their feeling of importance, may be very well rationalized in their daily life. However, on careful scrutiny, the analyst may discover some inconsistencies in the analysand's communications. For instance, the patient may show off with his potency, but after some time the analyst discovers that the patient does not achieve psychic gratification in sexual intercourse, though the physical act is undisturbed. Or the patient recounts the success he had in his work. The wording and the overemphasis of his achievements alert the analyst. Acknowledging the value of the analysand's performances, the analyst may at some time prudently venture a slight doubt whether all of the patient's activities are completely satisfying. Then it may happen that the analysand becomes aware of some disappointments, e.g., he is very good in his daily routine work, but he longs to be creative in his chosen field of science or art. Here he feels an inhibition, though he apparently has the necessary gifts and talents. An inhibition of creativity may have many causes which vary from individual to individual, but here I want to stress a special one. The seeming self-assurance, a part of the so-called narcissistic attitude, proves to be a reaction formation against the disappointments, powerlessness, and desperateness the little child has experienced.

In such situations it may be rewarding to call to mind the infant's emotional experiences when he starts crawling, walking, and exploring the world around him. These reactions are of course well known, but I often meet with a phenomenon in colleagues and in supervisions which, I feel, has a bearing on our technique. The analyst's knowledge of the maturational and developmental processes in early childhood is often mainly an intellectual one, without sufficient empathy into the real emotional nature of the infant's and toddler's predicaments.

The infant is, normally, a passionate little creature with powerful instinctual needs, and his id and ego are not yet differentiated. Only gradually, small budding capacities develop sufficiently so that he can deal with the new world of the adults. In short, the baby's ego is still weak and not yet organized. He claims satisfaction of his sexual and aggressive impulses, but during his first year he also begins to strive for autonomy and for mastering the outside world. On both levels he constantly meets with restrictions and prohibitions. He is still unaware of real dangers. It is therefore unavoidable that he is prevented from touching the fascinating flame of the fire or from climbing the windowsill, from catching a teacup and throwing it down, or from tearing to pieces the parents' beloved pictures and books.

There are hundreds and thousands of similar calamities. It is very hard, indeed, for the little one to learn and accept the real need for these restrictions. They startle him because he does not yet understand them. They injure *his sense of self;* he may be bewildered, desperate, at a loss, and feel abandoned, rejected, unloved. They impair his activities, his explorations, and may inhibit his normal striving for independence. He has to take refuge to clinging anew to his mother or a nursing person, though the disappointments have mobilized his (normal) aggression and directed it toward the same person. Feeling unloved and misunderstood at the same time, he develops hate next to love and the well-known ambivalence in object relations becomes established.

Alongside the unavoidable restrictions vis-à-vis the exploration of the outside world, the little child is also exposed to curtailments of his instinctual impulses. Contrary to the prenatal situation, where normally all needs are fully satisfied, the baby in his postnatal life experiences intervals of a lack of immediate gratification. In the first months of life, the "oral phase," hunger, his need for comfort, warmth, cuddling, passive movements are not always satisfied at the very moment they are felt. In these periods the needed symbiosis with the mother is interrupted.

When the maturational process advances to the "anal phase," the toddler has to bear the restriction of his freedom to urinate and defecate whenever he feels the urge to do so. This period in growth is highly susceptible to influences by the environment. If the mother's (or father's) demands for cleanliness do not correspond to the child's inner readiness to give up his pleasure in wetting and soiling, it is much more difficult for him to comply with the parental demands. When he finally does so, however, it occurs at the price of a severe injury to the little child's self-esteem. This injury is further heightened by the fact that his products (parts of himself) are devalued by the environment as something dirty, worthless, to be thrown away.

He then feels misunderstood, alone, unloved, and powerless once more. The only compensation he can find is in the fantasy world. He takes refuge in omnipotent and grandiose fantasies and so retires to a self-centered ("narcissistic") world. Unfortunately, new disappointments follow in proportion to his growing reality sense. The child now finds another form of consolation. He begins to idealize his parents and to ascribe to them an omnipotence in which he can share. These fantasies also are his own products, his mental creations. He may then receive a staggering blow when he discovers faults and inconsistencies in the parental personalities. As a result, he not only loses trust in and love for his parents, he additionally suffers a new blow to his self-esteem. His psychic creations become devalued, as his bodily products had previously been. Nevertheless at a very early time in the little child's life, these grandiose fantasies of the self and the objects are legitimate and to some degree present in every individual. They are a quite *normal event* in the developmental process, though they are usually not recognized by the adult world and the parents themselves. The greater the estrangement between child and parent, the more the child's "narcissistic" *primitive* fantasy world will persist and become excluded from the normal integration into realistic ideals, norms, and ethics.

I believe that, at least in Western civilization, a part of the archaic grandiose experiential world continues to live on in the unconscious of every individual, though it is warded off, as are other parts of the preoedipal world. During maturation, above all in puberty and adolescence, the early object relations are revived, and so is the narcissistic self-esteem. Both of them have, however, undergone developmental changes. In the case of favorable growing up, the youngster and the adult will gradually find sound and harmonious relationships to other human beings, including a love partner. Their narcissistic world will be used in satisfying, productive activities in work, social and professional pursuits, according to their talents and ambitions. It is easy to describe an ideal development in words, but it is indeed difficult to achieve it. All of us fall short of the ideal. However, the ideal can serve as a level against which we can try to estimate the measure of deviation from it in a particular person. The residues of the primitive, archaic, grandiose world may influence a person's achievements and impair his logic and his judgment of himself and others. If they are too strong, they may also damage his object relations. If they overwhelm the person, a severe pathology emerges, ranging from "narcissistic disturbances" to borderline and psychotic illnesses.

Implications for technique

The fact that the residues of the infant's emotional world are split off from the adult's personality has a direct bearing on our technique, because especially in the so-called narcissistic personalities certain interventions may be necessary to bring the two worlds together again.

We may ask: is it really feasible for the analyst to introduce into the treatment situation the patient's primitive narcissistic grandiosity, which originates in the preverbal stage, in a phase in which a little child does not yet have the capacity to express his feelings and fantasies in words? This is an important question because at present we have to treat so many analysands who suffer from its residues or from a regression to this early stage.

A number of analysts answer this question in the negative. Some are of the opinion that conflicts which originate in the preverbal phase cannot enter into the analysis, because language is the main instrument of communication and interpretations rely on the patient's verbally expressed memories, fantasies, and experiences. However, we know that we do not only use interpretations, but very often have to utilize reconstructions. Even if the patient cannot confirm them with recollections, they can have a beneficial effect on the analytic process and the patient's recovery.

Other analysts take the stand that experiences of the symbiotic phase cannot be dealt with in an analysis. They argue that analytic treatment is devised for solving conflicts. A differentiation between self and mother and a certain structuralization of the mind must be present before outer and inner conflicts can arise. It is difficult to determine the exact age at which these processes come into being. Symbiosis, "oneness" with the mother, persists during a long stretch of time, even when a dim awareness of separation starts to enter the infant's inner world. There are transitions from one position to another as well as individual differences. They parallel the instinctual maturational and developmental processes which overlap. The vicissitudes of oral and anal impulses occur in the preverbal phase. They have to be reconstructed. With the exception of those analysts who ignore the biological basis of mental processes altogether, rejecting every theory of the instinctual drives, most analysts are convinced of the importance of disturbances in the oral and anal phases, and use reconstructions in their work with patients, in spite of the fact that these disturbances are founded in the symbiotic, primary narcissistic stage. As both object relations and self-love develop — and a person's sense of self and self-esteem are based on these — it is essential to examine their interplay meticulously.

While drive development and object relatedness were studied at an early date, the study of the subtleties of the development of secondary narcissism and self-love started only at a much later time (see chapter 36; Kohut, 1971). As injuries and frustrations influence both lines of development, we may investigate the reasons for this difference. Although lack of warmth and empathy from the mother damages the infant's well-being, it is my experience that an injury in his narcissistic world cuts deep into his inner equilibrium. It mobilizes the greatest possible amount of destructiveness for which there is not yet an object, not even in fantasy. Such injuries are deeply buried and seem to be inaccessible.

At this point I venture the idea that we might find a way to use the knowledge of this early period of life in our reconstructions or interventions. As object relatedness does not yet exist, this material cannot be transferred onto the analyst. As a consequence transference interpretations are inapplicable. Some analysts consider the analytic treatment process to be exclusively a development of a transference neurosis and its resolution by interpretation. I disagree with these authors. I even consider this definition to be dangerous. In my view the transference is a tool, albeit a very mighty one, but not an aim in itself. Viewing it as an aim may invite the analyst to focus only on the transference and to draw every communication of the patient into the transference. This tempts the analyst to overestimate the special meaning he has for the patient. Pleasant as this may be for the analyst, it may stimulate his own hidden grandiosity and prevent the countertransference from becoming conscious. In this case it often becomes an obstacle to the course the analysis should run.

I shall now describe briefly the ways in which I try to convey to the patient what and how an infant may experience unpleasure, powerlessness, and the frustrations of being abandoned. Such interventions are necessary only in those cases in which, after the fantasies of grandeur have been worked through, an integration of the infantile world into the adult personality is not achieved. It is essentially a matter of finding the appropriate attitude, tone, and empathy as one is forced to use "words" for communication with the patient. I avoid "baby talk," but an amount of warmth and emotional understanding of an infant's world is necessary. It is a process of trial and error. I tell the patient that my suggestion is tentative and that he might reject it or want to correct my wording. An analysand's first reaction is often surprise and rejection. He says, for instance, "Your talk does not mean anything to me" or "it is strange and I do not understand." Then I leave it at that. After a period of silence in which the patient is completely "absent," "plunged into thoughts," or has "feelings of emptiness," he may gradually resume speech. A dim recollection of his mother telling him that as a baby he suffered from severe diarrhea or that she had to leave him alone when she was ill or hospitalized may emerge. Or the patient suddenly observes his mother's demandingness and lack of understanding when she takes care of a grandchild or another infant. Or the patient may suddenly visualize himself crying and desperately shaking the bars of his cot in the parents' bedroom or in his playpen, when his mother has left the room. These are not memories, but elaborations of visions, accompanied by strong feelings of powerless despair. We do not know whether they were real events, but they loosen strong effects with a feeling of conviction.

There are many other events which possible have disturbed the analysand's well-being in his babyhood and left an imprint on which later traumatic experiences and fantasies are built. The latter, then, may draw the intensity and rigidity from the early imprints. Sometimes my interventions were unsuccessful, but in a number of cases the analysand responded with a kind of recognition, an "Aha" experience and relief. It certainly was not a "transference" experience of object relatedness, but an inner experience of a deeply buried self-centered world. I did not figure as a mother, father, or sibling image, but as an extension of the patient's archaic infantile personality experienced as a part of himself. I functioned as the other half of his symbiotic world. The original symbiosis with the mother cannot be altered as a matter of fact, nor can its disturbances be undone. However, the awareness and emotional understanding of a baby's vulnerability facilitate the mastering of later conflicts and distress, and even constitute "basic trust" that was unpaired in the original tie with the mother.

Such interventions in the analytic process differ from the usual interpretations and reconstructions of conflictual material, the working through of which becomes possible on the basis of a solid transference of earlier object relations. I consider them as an enlargement of the analytic technique. They are safely embedded in the usual analytic process and merely represent an attempt to reach a very early stage in the little child's development — a stage from which narcissistic problems, hurts, injuries, loneliness, primitive anxieties, and many other kinds of pain with the reaction formations of omnipotent and grandiose sensations and fantasies may emerge. If these interventions are successful, the return to the classic analytic situation takes place spontaneously. If the interventions are unsuccessful in their results, they are harmless and will simply be bypassed. I therefore consider them to be a legitimate addition to the analytic treatment technique. On the other hand, they constantly should be reconsidered and controlled in order to avoid a possible overemphasis of the preverbal mother-child relatedness because they might otherwise disturb the reconstructions of the preoedipal object relationships, including the significance of the father.

With a number of so-called borderline cases we may sometimes be able to achieve some relief or even success if we use a flexible technique, switching over, if necessary, from the classical analytic one to the interventions described above. If the analyst's empathic understanding of the infant's experiential world helps and enables the patient to recapture some rigidly repressed, narcissistically colored emotions and to advance to a primitive object relatedness, the result may be that we can then return to the classical technique. I end with a warning against overoptimism. Even if we work with much tact and patience, we have to accept the limits of our competence and the disappointment of our technical limitations.

Finally, I may be asked why I have not referred so far to metapsychological considerations. I have omitted this theoretical edifice on purpose. First, I think it is implicit in my presentation. The dynamic viewpoint reveals itself in the struggle between the instinctual drives and their vicissitudes and the ego and superego. The economic viewpoint comes to the fore in the overwhelming intensity of impulses and emotions in relation to the budding, still weak ego of early childhood. My emphasis on the gradual development of a differentiated mind stresses the importance of the structural as well as genetic viewpoints. The adaptive viewpoint is inherent in my description of the aims of our therapeutic interventions. My main reason for not going too intensively into metapsychology is another one: theory is too often used − I want to say misused − to intellectualize and to ward off empathy with and respect for the patient's and the child's emotional world. Yet, it is these attitudes which enable us to listen to the patient with free-floating attention. When we really understand a patient, our theoretical knowledge will then spontaneously guide our interpretations and interventions.

Here I meet once more with Freud and his brilliant recommendations, the starting point of my psychoanalytic career.

40. Can Psycho-analysis Contribute to the Alleviation of the Human Misery that Exists Today?

(1978)

I. Introduction

My honoured and dear friend Alexander Mitserlich has been engaged in psychoanalysis, social-psychology and politics for decades. He has given us numerous articles and books of great value and has taught us a lot about the significance of psychoanalysis for the understanding of group-interaction. I am pleased to make a small contribution to the "Festschrift" in his honour. I will not be able to contribute anything really innovative but merely some thoughts on power-relations and their relative intensities, determining both the individual and the group attitude.

II. Findings of Psychoanalysis

Sigmund Freud elaborated scientifically his discoveries concerning the significance of the unconscious mental life and the repressed infantile drive- and emotional life. He also supplemented and changed his theories if so required by new findings. Furthermore he formulated a first mass-psychology and he applied analytical depth-psychology when he was engaged with history, literature and human culture in general. I would like to mention here one of Freud's pronouncements: "I have only made beginnings, the younger generation should continue". That is precisely what Mitserlich did and there-with he deepened social psychology.

Other psychologists have also elaborated upon Freud's starting-points towards an ego- and super-ego psychology as laid down by himself in "Das Ich und das Es" (1923) ("The Ego and the Id"). I recall to mind the many works by Heinz Hartmann (1939) which he published mainly after Freud's death and partly in cooperation with Ernst Kris and Rudolf Loewenstein (1946). I also mention Anna Freud's "Das Ich und die Abwehrmechanismen", which appeared as early as 1936.

Biology has not (yet?) been able to explain the enigma of the origin of life and the evolution of micro-organisms into a human being ranking highest in the animal hierarchy. We know that a human baby enters life immature and that it needs its mother's care for a relatively long period in order to survive. In addition, in order to be able to unfold the specific human qualities such as the ability to communicate in language, in symbols, in words the child needs contact with the adult world. This also applies to the development of other cognitive faculties. This potential is given in endowment. The development depends, however, on the interaction with the environment (the mother figure). This interaction occurs in the first months and years. Our knowledge about the pre-oedipal stage has been widened and deepened in recent decades, on the one hand through child analysis and on the other hand especially through infant-observations (cf. Spitz, 1965; Mahler, 1968; Furer, 1964; the Kris-Yale-centre; Anna Freud's Hampstead Clinic and others).

I will not go further into the well-known description of the various developmental stages, the symbiotic, the individuation-separation phases, etc. We know the child's need for autonomy and at the same time the necessity of "rapprochement", i.e. a getting close to the mother for "refueling" of energy. This applies both to a favourable development of the infantile drive- and emotional life and for the unfolding of cognitive faculties.

I will go into two themes:

Firstly: in order to develop harmoniously and to move flexibly between progression and regression the infant needs a *loving, warm, empathic* relationship to the mother (and other persons in its environment). This is common knowledge.

Secondly: many adults, both laymen and professionals, have, however, an intellectual knowledge of the experiential world of the child whereby true empathy is lacking or insufficient.

I would like to deal more profoundly with this issue. Adults have repressed their own infantile experiences long before and are therefore no longer able to feel how far away their experiential world is from the child's world. Between parents and children a *misunderstanding of feelings* has come into being. Many mothers no longer know that apart from food a baby also needs body- and skincontact; that a warm smile, a tender address (where the words are not important, but where the tone is of extreme significance), the rocking "holding and the loving fondling are very important for growing up. When an infant starts to crawl and to walk the parents attitude needs to be very different. The infant does not know real dangers. It does not understand *why* the chair does not move out of its way when it bumps into it, *why* it cannot grab the teacup and throw it on the floor without hurting itself on the splinters, *why* the pretty flames burn his hand so painfully. It experiences strong anxiety which can sometimes turn into panic. The mother (parents) must here intervene. The child, however, experiences the restrictions and prohibitions as puzzling and "unfair" hostility of the mother. It feels lost, which in turn causes anxiety to be reinforced. The "ambivalence" of feelings so well known to us is here clearly shown. Many mothers find it hard to raise the necessary vigilance. Besides, they very often cannot sympathize with the child's need of independence; they cannot give up the "oneness of being" with their child. It is especially difficult for these mothers to experience the "backward and forward" movements of their child sympathetically. What I mean is the "away from mother" to explore and conquer the world, which alternates with the need to refuel, i.e. "back to mother" when the new world becomes too wide, too frightening or too painful. There are, of course "unsophisticated" mothers who can intuitively empathize with their child. But in our civilized world they are becoming more and more rare.

At the same time as the mother has to protect her child from dangers and prohibit certain things, there will be restrictions of the drive-needs. I refer for example to the necessary toilet training. Many mothers are proud when their child is toiled trained at the early age of 1 or 1,5. They do not know that any training might be a traumatic experience. Dependence and powerlessness will be reinforced and raise helpless rage. Children have different dispositions in the pace of their development. Many need more time to gradually give up the pleasure and pride they take in the body-products. By attending this process with loving understanding rather than coercion and severity the child is likely to shift its pride towards drive-control. It then will also learn to use the energy for sublimated, constructive activities, such as drawing, constructing and painting, etc.

The end result of the pre-oedipal development is, as was mentioned before, dependent on the endowment of the child and a growing-up in *interaction* with the parents. If the parent's attitude leads to a strong damaging of the child's sense of self, it will look for compensation by constructing grandeur- and omnipotency fantasies in order to repair its injured sense of self.

Since it is over and again confronted with its own impotence, it will transfer its idealising grandeur-fantasies to parents and other important persons. It still lives in the magic world of fantasy and, ignorant of reality, will therefore stick to its belief in the reality of its idealising fantasies for a long time.

In the oedipal stage it will "deify" one parent and it will imagine her or him as its lover. The other parent therefore becomes its rival and the hostility which was already raised at an early stage by frustrations is now transferred to the rival. The child is far more advanced in its fantasy- and emotional life than in physical growth. It cannot understand why it cannot be its father's lover or its mother's man, whatever it may imagine about the secret, exciting relationship between its parents. Naturally it is ignorant of adult sexual intercourse. Even after the child has received "sexual enlightenment" from the adults, it cannot comprehend emotionally the scope of the adult sexual relationships, differences in gender, their significance for propagation and the wider type of lovelife.

The child lives in its experiential world with its own fantasies and dreams. Drives are here *relatively* stronger than in the adult world since the child does not yet posses the capacity to sublimate the drives. Besides, it really lives in a magical inner world where wishes are experienced as real events, where it will not let itself be deprived of its "omnipotence". Its gradually developing sense of reality will for quite some time coexist with strong magical grandeur-fantasies about itself and the idealized parents, just as initially love and aggression of the infant directed towards one and the same person exist side by side. The opposing impulses, love and hate, directed towards the same love-objects do, however, no longer tolerate each other when the "integrating" (synthetic) function of the ego starts developing. I believe that the full unfolding of this ego-function is stimulated by the fact, which can no longer be denied, that the oedipal wishes in their infantile form and at their greatest intensity cannot be fulfilled. The child now has to repress one of its strivings and the accompanying fantasies. In the more or less "normal" development it wards-off the aggressive, destructive impulses and the death-wishes, the affectionate ties with the parents will evolve more clearly.

The grandeur- and omnipotence fantasies which are normal in the pre-oedipal phase are gradually replaced by norms which are more adapted to reality. They continue to exist however in the archaic form in the unconscious. The child enters latency in which the drive impulses are less imperative and in which many ego-functions develop gradually. We know how difficult this development is. Normally, regression and progression do alternate. At the same time an inner conscience is being formed. In the beginning the child adopts the parents' norms, which gradually become a real inner voice. The child learns to distinguish between reality and idealizations, which cannot be realized. It has to cope with the disappointment that the adults are not at all omnipotent or omniscient. This knowledge is a further severe blow to its self-confidence. The idealizing fantasies are after all the child's *creation* which are now gradually being destroyed. This process has its predecessors in the anal phase in which the initially admired body-products are thrown away as dirty and worthless.

I would like to give a brief example of an intelligent cheerful five-year old dutch boy, who was in the transition-stage between the experiential world of a small child and latency adapted to reality. He once expressed love and hate for a mother-substitute as follows: "Ik ga jou kwaadkozen". That means approximately: "I will fondle you with 'evil', mixed with 'love'." His announcement: "I am now a *small giant*" originated in his world of "omnipotence and grandeur". The experiential world of the infant in which ambivalence of feeling and grandeur-fantasies dominate must, as was mentioned above, be repressed in the unconscious. Adults, then, do not have access to it anymore, and they mostly become unable to have empathy with the childrens' world. The above mentioned "misunderstanding of feeling" arises. The psychoanalyst does, however, know that acts and behaviour are moreoften determined by the *unconscious* than by reason and logic. The intellectual capacities and the symbolic language of words have enabled people to develop a high level of culture, science, technology and art. This however, happened often at the expense of a substantial part of the world of affects and has in addition brought about a wide alienation of the world of early childhood. Emotional life has in fact impoverished especially with so many intellectuals and scientists. Great artists seem to have kept the talent to be influenced "intuitively", if unconsciously, by the child's world with its coexisting omnipotence fantasies and destructive impulses. I could give numerous examples from the history of civilisation of many thousand years, more or less known to us. I would like to restrict myself to a few, namely three brilliant poets and dramatists, Goethe, Schiller and Shakespeare.

In the person of the young Faust, with his inquiring mind, Goethe has given expression to his own unconscious, magic fantasies by letting him surpass all real limits of human life.

Faust can make a "Homunculus", he can fly, that means transgress distance and time. He is "omnipotent". However, Faust has to pay for it by selling his soul to Mephisto, thus relinquishing unconsciously part of his "Self" to the devil. We recognize that it is a destruction directed against the own person, as the soul is the essence of human kind.

This destruction will sometimes also be directed outward, i.a. against "Gretchen", whom he (not intentionally) leads to death. Faust is a personality wanting good, but ending up evil. When his death comes near, he orders Mephisto to reclaim land from the sea and to construct an immense city. "Frau Sorge" visits Faust, (again "magic") shortly before his death. This wise lady tells him: "People are blind throughout life, now you Faust shall become blind at the end of your life"*. She touches his eyes and he is blind. He then stands on a hill and images that he can see his newly created city. He says* "Traces of my earthly days cannot submerge in infinity / In anticipation of such glorious happiness / I now enjoy the highest sublime moment". Faust dies and at the same time the city falls to pieces with thundering noise. Mephisto built it on quicksands.

Mephisto symbolizes the "devilish" in Faust (Goethe) *and* in mankind, i.e. the *omnipotence-wishes* and the *destruction*. It becomes clear how much Goethe also desires "good", as he lets the soul of Faust be rescued by angels whereby "holy" Gretchen protects him in heaven. Is there a more wonderful picture of experiential world, the "secret", of children guessed by Genius, though it becomes repressed, but is still exercising its influence unconsciously during life? I recapitulate again: love impulses, destruction impulses, omnipotence and grandeur fantasies, magical experiencing belong to the inner world of the child. In adulthood they lead from the unconscious to the highest love to destructive acts and possibly to a real megalomania.

Schiller, too, knew intuitively of the hidden world and depicts the horror of megalomania. I quote a few lines from his poem "the clock"* * * :"It is dangerous to arouse the lion, pernicious is the tiger's tooth / the most awful horror however / is man in his delusion".

From Shakespeare I quote a few lines from "Julius Caesar". Caesar's friend Brutus justifies his murder of Caesar with the words:

"As Caesar lov'd me, I weep for him,
as he was fortunate, I rejoice at it;
as he was valiant, I honour him,
but as he was ambitious, I slew him".

In these lines we can discover a world of human qualities, which are also partly defence-measures against unconscious, repressed, conflicting impulses and feelings. Brutus shows friendly love and bewails Caesar's death. The fact that Brutus rejoices and honours his friend because he was happy and worthy is not merely adoration and love. These consciously experienced feelings conceal their opponents and make us guess that Brutus was unconsciously rivalling, envious and jealous and finally just as ambitious, if not more, than Caesar. Why

---

* "Die Menschen sind im ganzen Leben blind, nun, Fauste, werde Du's am Ende".

* * "Es kann die Spur von meinen Erdentagen nicht in Äonen untergehen / Im Vorgefühl von solchem hohen Glück geniess ich jetzt den hochsten Augenblick".

* * * "Die Glocke": Gefährlich ist's den Leu zu wecken, Verderblich ist des Tigers Zahn / Jedoch der schrecklichste der Schrecken / Das ist der Mensch in seinem Wahn.

else would he have killed him? Shakespeare also clearly felt that this hidden rivalry and the acting-out of his murder-impulses caused Brutus guilt feelings and the need for self-punishment because in the end he has him direct the destruction against himself by letting him commit suicide.

I now come back to the "ordinary mortals" who do not posses this mysterious, still unexplained brilliant talent to depict common-humanness in splendid works of art. There are of course also people who can to a lesser or greater extent regain empathy in the archaic world of infants. Mothers, who experience with the baby, the first physical and psychological contacts, are perhaps the first among them. However, a loving father may sometimes regain the needed empathy, through identification with the mother, as well. But, perhaps nobody possesses this gift completely. Psycho-analysts know a lot of things about early development. And a personal analysis may further an increase in the knowledge about the archaic experiential world. In spite of this we often encounter an incredible ignorance of a baby's behaviour, even with analysts and educators. I am thinking of one of Freud's sayings: "Two kinds of knowledge exist, one with the intellect and one with feeling".

It is of course striking how many analysts and psycho-therapists have acquired their intellectual knowledge by reading, but who can however in practice not raise sufficient empathy. It is not difficult to talk with a patient in technical terms and "jargon" about oral, anal, phallic phases, about grandeur-fantasies and aggression etc. It is however much harder to help a patient to enter again into his repressed experiential world of his infancy. We are especially faced with tremendous difficulties if the faulty development already took place in the very early, pre-verbal period. One needs *words* to communicate, but of course not baby 'language'. I try to indicate to an analysand how his earliest contact with his mother possibly may have been by means of already known facts of his life-history, his behaviour, his facial expression, his movements (or absence of them) and his occasionally primitive emotional outbursts. If one is able to empathize in the baby's world it is sometimes possible to find the right tone and words. In most cases the analysand is initially unable to find emotional access to what is communicated. I never insist that he "accepts" any of it, but I wait. One must be prepared that sometimes nothing is achieved, but time and again, it happens that the analysand has some sort of "aha-experience", that he can better deal with already known and worked-through memories and reconstructions of a later period, so that his emotional life somehow belatedly grows up. It may be of advantage for his understanding, if he is able to observe his mother's attitude towards his own (or other people's) children. The feeling: "Yes, that is how I could have felt rejected, abandoned, mocked and desperate", can bring relief (see chapter 36).

The question arises, why I went so deeply into the early experiential world of infants and its necessary repression. In my opinion "the emotional misunderstanding" is one of the numerous factors which have caused human misery, albeit an important factor. This leads me to the third point:

III. Can psycho-analysis contribute to the relief of this misery?

This question has already been dealt with at great length by Alexander Mit-serlich. He especially pointed out the aggression- and destruction drive, in-herent in human beings and their wrecking influence on social relations and society structures (1956 and 1958). I would like to make only one small addition. I think that the reactions of the primitive ego and the impossibility to realize in action the destructive drive-pleasure, reinforce the fixation of the archaic-drives and these reactionformations are often shaped in omnipotence- and grandeurfantasies. We can actually remark that with all people part of the archaic drive − and emotional − world of the infant will survive in the unconscious; this part may be smaller or greater, but it will never be absent. Since these early experiences are so violent, so frightening, the defence manoeuvers have to be strong and powerful. Man, then, becomes a "split" personality. He can not gain access to the archaic unconscious, denies it, but is unconsciously captured by it. The relatively strong drive-impulses, which lead from the initial powerlessness to the uncontrollable aggressions and destructions impulses cannot be satisfied. As reaction formations rigid omnipotence- and grandeurfantasies are formed, which in turn, are repressed from the unconscious, they can influence the intercourse with fellow-men.

This "split-off" constellation has not been able to grow and unfold with the rest of the personality but lives, as it were, its own life in the unconscious. It is however stirred-up by recent conflicts, by accidents, misfortunes and misunder-standing of the environment, by disappointments and injuries, from which no individual, no group, no nation, no part of the world is spared. Reactions are in that case not only determined by quiet consideration and adequate answer but also by the archaic world. Reason is often weaker than the archaic impulses and behaviour is then, guided more by the latter than by reason. This situation gets even more complicated by the question of "guilt". The already mentioned unconscious guiltfeelings – the need for punishment – are rooted in the infantile world. Whoever disturbs or misunderstands the child should "go away". "Gone" and "dead" are for the little child still the same. Only the inner conscience makes the individual feel guilty. Such an inner tension is hard to tolerate and the "guilt" is therefore laid at somebody else's door. He and the others should therefore be destroyed. This has repeatedly been manifested in history. In ancient time slaves could be killed at their master's liking. The Romans had the Christians thrown to the beasts in the arena. In the Middle Ages the Inquisition burnt witches, foreign people were treates as devils, etc. We only have to think of the "blacks" and of the "jews" in the Second World War.

The shuddering pitch of technical development has, at the present time, created the possibility of destroying all mankind. The panicky anxiety which has thus been raised in people is warded off by new aggressions, since it is always the other group or nation considered to be the "culprit". Often the guilt is (quasi objectively) attributed to the economic-social situations. This ignores the fact that for generations *people themselves* created these forms of society. Think of

Goethe's sorcerer's apprentice! A vicious circle! How to break it? Nowadays mankind is a pretty gloomy sight. Is it altogether possible to break this circle? We can almost say: "No and never". Looking at the evolution of human culture, however, we can see "ups and downs". Quiet periods alternate with periods of war, murder and manslaughter. Psycho-analysis can perhaps contribute to more sensible reflection, in the individual, as well as in smaller groups. Naturally it is impossible to change the whole world-situation, especially in the next future. This is not to much avail, since modern weaponry makes the matter urgent. We can only hope that people become more sensible and wise.

On a smaller scale one can imagine a very modest influence of psycho-analysis: not only future analysts, psycho-therapists and group-therapists should become aware of the significance of the archaic world of infancy for personality structures through their personal analyses, and therewith make the effort to work through archaic conflicts in such a way that they can catch up with the inhibited maturational processes. Sociologists, politicians and people in power should do the same so that mankind can be provided with more insight, reason and especially empathy.

You, the reader, will smiling (and angrily?) reproach me, remarking that this is merely a ridiculous illusion. You are right. Most of the people in authority, the politicians will never dream of undergoing analysis or of analyzing themselves. As long as they can afford to indulge in their lust for power, they (unconsciously) need the unbridled drives of the archaic period and the conviction of their own "grandeur". Failures are always due to the "others", are not they?

I would like to end with two somewhat less pessimistic points of view. Firstly, history provides examples of the occurence that the strong will of one person or of one small group in the end can dominate great masses and drag them along. This happened both in a good and an evil sense. In the "evil" sense I mention only Hitler's delusion which seduced millions. In the "good" sense: there have also been founders of religions and other great personalities who led various groups of people − even after having had to fight − to more peaceful ways of living.

Secondly, there is apart from hate, jealousy and the destructive tendency also *love*, which wants to preserve what it loves. No one can predict the future with any certainty. Who knows if love will triumph some time in the future? In the meantime every individual can only do his utmost in the smaller or bigger field of his activity. He should only beware of releasing his hidden megalomania but continuously try to sublimate his aggressive impulses and use them for constructive activities and actions.

41. Past, Present and Future of Psychoanalysis in a Bird's Eye View

(1978)

I. Introduction

I am thankful that the Dutch Psychoanalytic Society invited me, in spite of my being of old-age, to read a paper on Psychoanalysis at the occasion of the society's sixtieth birthday (1977).

II. The past

I was not present at the birth of the society in 1917. However, I am the only surviver who became a member of the society in its 8th year of life. In 1925 Dr. J. van Emden, who was one of the first dutch doctors, practizing psychoanalysis, asked me to become a member of the Dutch Society. I accepted this invitation with pleasure. I intended to settle down in Holland, having learned psychoanalysis in Vienna, but only after some 2 years of working at the Berlin psychoanalytic Institute to deepen my experience and knowledge. At the time the Berlin Society and Institute were the most lively and productive institutions where psychoanalysis was practized and teached. This early membership, however, was merely of a short duration. In Berlin I met Dr. Hans Lampl, a Viennese, who was a member of the Staff of the Institute. We decided to marry, and stay on in Berlin. My membership of the Dutch Society was transferred to the German Society.

In 1933 my family moved on to Vienna, and I became a member of the Viennese Society until 1938, when Hitler forced us to emigrate for the second time. We went to Holland (my native country) and I became once more a member of the Dutch Society, this time it lasts until today.

I intend to tell something about the development of psychoanalysis in general. Of course, that can be only done "in a bird's eye view". I want to describe a few essentials of the "childhood", the "Sturm und Drang"-period of adolescence with in between "Latency" and finally "Adulthood" of psychoanalysis as a science and as a therapy.

I do not belong to the very first pioneer-period of the early years of the twentieth century. In fact, I had taken note of Freud's "Traumdeutung" (The interpretation of dreams) in 1913, being a young medical student. I was fascinated (though of course I discovered in later times, how much of it I had not really understood at that early date). It happened not merely accidental, because I knew that Leiden's medical-faculty-society of students had invited

Sigmund Freud to give a lecture at the university. (In parenthesis: Leiden was the first university where psychoanalysis was accepted by the official scientists, among them especially Prof.Dr. Jelgersma, as the full Professor in Psychiatry). Freud had promised to come to Leiden in september 1914. It became impossible because of the outbreak of World-War I on August 1st, 1914. My interest in psychoanalysis fell more or less into the back-ground, but apparently it continued to exist in my unconscious or sub-conscious. For, after having become a M.D. in 1921, it was self-evident for me that I was going to learn psychoanalysis and that it had to be in Vienna. Only much later did I realize how privileged I have been that in 1922 circumstances allowed me to participate in the so-called second pioneer-period at the very birthplace of psychoanalysis. In addition I was accepted by Prof. Wagner-von Jauregg, ordinarius in psychiatry at the Vienna University to study neurology and psychiatry at his department. I can only briefly remind you of the situation of psychoanalysis in the first pioneer-period and of its scientific and technical level. The official sciences like psychiatry, psychology and philosophy considered mental life to be identical with conscienceness. Artists had already known since centuries that in man a great number of impulses, emotions and drives are living, which do not penetrate into consciousness. Authors and poets have described them since times immemorial. Freud was the first and for a long period the only scholar, who studied the unconscious psychic life scientifically. At first he made his observations in neurotic patients, whom he originally treated with hypnosis and suggestion, but later-on with the psychoanalytic technique. But also and especially in his self-analysis he discovered the differences between the mental processes running their course in consciousness and in the unconscious. In the "conscious" reigns logic, ordering of cause and effect, etc., the so-called "secundary process". The "unconscious" is "a-logical" and timeless. In this part of the mind the processes are subject to the "primary process"-functioning which seems to be absurd. However, Freud discovered that the "language" of the primary process can be "translated" into words full of meaning. He made these discoveries especially in the study of dreams and "Fehlleistungen". But they brought him much criticism and derision. A next discovery of Freud's however was rejected still more violently by the "official scientists". It contained his observations that adult sexual life has a pre-history in early childhood, where sexuality is already flowering. As the infantile sexual wishes and fantasies cannot be realized they become subject to repression. The criticists spoke of "desecration" of the "innocent" little child. Freud had to work in "splendid isolation" during the early decades. But in the beginning of this century a few persons, doctors and "laymen" became interested in his work. Gradually a small group of them came together and gathered around Freud. The happenings of this "first pioneer-time" can be red in the "Minutes of the Vienna Psychoanalytic Society" edited by Herman Nunberg and Ernst Federn and partly in Ernest Jones Freud-biography (1953).
I come now to the "second pioneer-period" in the twenties, in which I participated. In the meantime other analytical societies had been founded in Holland, Zürich, Berlin, Budapest, London, Paris and in the U.S.A. A number of

foreigners came to Vienna, mostly from England and America. The number of analysts in Vienna grew steadily. There was much interest and even enthousiasm for the "new" discoveries. As a scientist Freud had tried to "order" his observations and to look for explanations of "normal" psychic conflicts and of neurotic symptoms which he could lay down in theories. In the course of time with growing experience Freud has supplemented and sometimes modified some of the early theories. However, essential discoveries could be retained. I go into one of them, e.g. the so-called "Ergänzungsreihe" (Supplementary series). With this term Freud described that the development of every individual runs its course in an interaction of the person's endowment (given in the genes) with the environment. This is true for physical as well as mental development. Biology shows that this is the case in the total animal kingdom with all species. The biological basis of life comprises drive-impulses and instincts, which guarantee individual survival through the search for and the capture of food until death. They also secure propagation of the species until it eventually dies out. Most animals are able to provide for their own survival directly after birth or with "higher" animals after a relative short time. The human child is born as an "incomplete" creature. The human newborn is completely dependant upon the mother's care in order to survive. It lacks most of the instincts, which enable animals to secure their own survival. In human beings instincts are so to say "degraded" to *drives* (see K. Eissler). The life-forces are insufficient to keep the infant alive. The support of the environment is indispensable. The complete dependency of the baby on the mother's care leads gradually to the formation of an affective tie between baby and mother and finally to the development of mental life. The drives are the psychic representatives of the biological life-forces. The originally self-centered drive-impulses and emotional qualities lead finally to real object-relations. At the same time sensoric and intellectual potentials laid down in the genes, begin to develop, in addition the human's capacity to symbol-formation in words and language. We meet here with the essential difference between man and animals. The latter do have a communicative kind of "language" in sounds, gestures, behaviour of other forms, but they do not have the symbolic form in "words". It is unknown to us how this complicated development from "sign"-communication to "verbal"-communication has been achieved in nature. But I think we should know and accept the limitations of our human intellectual and affective development. We know for certain that man is a biological being with a complicated and differentiated mental development. We are acquainted with the drives and their maturational processes as originally described in Freud's libido theory (later widened into the theory of libidinal and aggressive-destructive drives.)

I now will try to summarize shortly the changes Freud made in his theories. The first one is the "Topographic" theory. It accounts for the fact that an unconscious and a conscious mental life exist side by side. They work along different laws (the primary and the secondary process). The unrealizable and forbidden drive-impulses, wishes and fantasies must be repressed. The conscious part (or "province") is called the W-Bw-system (Wahrnehmung-

Bewustsein, Perception-Consciousness). It mobilizes counterforces against the drive-impulses and thus prevents the system. Unconscious to penetrate into consciousness (resistance). The topographic theory is sometimes very useful to explain certain inner conflicts. However, more experience revealed the fact that it was not sufficient to account for other mental disturbances. For instance with some patients it became clear that the resistent, the warding-off manoeuvres could secundarily be repressed and then become subject to the timeless and a-rational mode of functioning of the system "unconscious". Then Freud developed the structural metapsychological theory of the Id, Ego and Superego as parts of the mind. The Id comprises everything inborn, the drives + the innate potential, out of which the different Ego-functions develop gradually during the maturational process. They comprise next to the defense reactions upon unrealizable drive-impulses, also those functions, which originally have not been involved in conflicts with the Id (and the environment), for instance sense-experiences, memory, reality-sense, capacity to form symbols and words, etc. That means: the cognitive abilities. The Superego comprises norms, ideals as well as prohibitions that are largely taken over from the demands and the attitude of the environment. They become a real "inner conscience" at the end of the oedipus-phase, when latency sets in. In the latency-period a relative quiet state, released from the urgent immediate satisfaction demanding wishes and fantasies, is more or less dominant.

I want to stress one point explicitly: metapsychology is not seldom misused by "reifeing" it, taken id, ego and superego as "things" instead of using the theory only as an "ordering model".

The up-growth of human beings is furthermore complicated by the unique event of the "Zweiseitige Aussatz der Sexualität" (the dual flourishing of sexuality). Humans are sexually mature only in puberty whereas the small child's passionate desires and grandiose fantasies are doomed to remain unsatisfied. In its fantasy-life it feels itself to be equal to the parents and adults. In reality it has to accept the fact of its powerlessness and of the impossibility to realize its sexual wishes to replace one of the parents in order to possess the beloved and desired other one. A favorable outcome of this difficult develop-ment leads to the adolescent (and adult) finding an adequate partner for sexual satisfaction and being able to overcome the infantile frustrations and making use of possible talents in sublimated activities. This theme brings us to another of Freud's extensions of his original libido theory. He introduced the term "narcissism" and defined it as the original source of drive-energy. Out of its biological base a libidinal cathexis of the self and later-on of the objects come into existence. Both are necessary for survival and for the satisfaction of basic needs and drives. Many authors use the term narcissism for a certain "behavior", which has led to a number of misunderstandings and confusions. Another extension of the drive-theory was given by Freud in naming and describing the aggressive-destructive drives. The bipolarity: libido-egodrives was replaced by libido-aggressive drives. The striving for self-preservation is an egofunction, the required energy comes from various sources. As already mentioned Freud, in studying the highly differentiated mental life, never forgot that the human species is a biological creature, one species in the world of living organisms. He also never denied the cosmic background of all events in nature. This comes to the fore in his hypothesis of Eros and Death-drive (the term "drive" seems to me not well-chosen in this connection. I myself have already proposed to make use of the term "force" (or tendency) many decades ago). Whether one looks at Freud's hypothesis with interest, or decides to reject it, immediately is a question of "personality". It is irrelevant in our practical work and in clinical theories.

An important gain in knowledge was Freud's modification of the anxiety-theory. Originally he conceived anxiety as a transformation of unsatisfyable libido. In the new theory anxiety is seen as an ego-function. In unsolved conflicts and in neurotic symptoms anxiety is aroused as a signal for the ego-organization to try to solve the conflict. This occurs in "normal" as well as in disturbed personalities.

Finally I draw attention to Freud's subtle description of the pre-oedipal phase. He supplemented his early construction of the developmental phases of infantile sexuality (the oral, anal and phallic phases) with detailed descriptions of object-relations, the original mother-child dyad, which form the basis for the oedipal-constellation and which experience a kind of "new edition" in adolescence. Freud described the significance of the pre-oedipal object-attachment especially for the female (and not for the male) development. He is often reproached for this fact. I will cite a dictum of Freud's: "I have only made beginnings, the younger generation should continue and if necessary make amendments". Though Freud made his original discoveries in the treatment of neurotic patients (and in his self-analysis), it is often overlooked that he has always been interested in the motivations and unconscious backgrounds of the works of great artists, e.g. poets and authors, as well as for social problems, for the influence of the various societal constellations, for mass-psychological events, in peace and in war, and for every natural happening in general. Already during Freud's lifetime other analysts applied his findings in different fields of human affairs. I mention August Aichhorn, who worked with delinquents, with extraordinary talent. Anna Freud (in Vienna) and Melanie Klein (in Berlin) started child-analysis. In Berlin Alexander and Staub tried to interest judges for the new psychology of crime. Ernst Simmel founded a hospital in Tegel-Berlin, where addicts were analytically treated. Unfortunately its lifetime was too short, as it was finished in 1933 by Hitler and the Nazi-regime. Another field where psychoanalytic insight was made use of was pedagogy. Siegfried Bernfeld (among others) first worked in Vienna and later in Berlin with pedagogues and social workers. Anna Freud led seminars with teachers and also with social workers. It was for me a fascinating experience to become acquainted with and to participate in these enterprises. Unfortunately shortness of time prevents me to go deeper into those various applications. I come now upon the theoretical enlargements and modifications after Freud's death (1939). During and after World War II it was especially ego-psychology which was studied and extended. I only name a few authors: Hartmann, Kris, Loewenstein and Rapaport, though there were many more. Hartmann (a.o.)

studied the affiliation with the cognitive psychology. I myself have used some of Piaget's work in my paper on "Ego and Superego" (read during the war in the Dutch Society and published afterwards). It concerned the early infantile development, that was studied in many different countries. In London Anna Freud and Dorothy Burlingham established the war-nurseries on behalf of orphaned infants, but where in addition many highly interesting studies were made. Their work continued after the war in the Hampstead Clinic. In New-Haven, U.S.A., a "Child-Centre" was founded at the Yale-University by Ernst Kris. After his death Marianne Kris, Lustman, Ritvo, Solnit and many others continued the very valuable studies. In Cleveland, too, a Child Centre came into existence under the leadership of Maurits and Anny Katan. A stimulating influence upon further research came from child-analysis and infant-observation. They also enriched analytic technique and theory-formation (I name among many authors René Spitz and Margaret Mahler with her co-workers). It is difficult and somehow hazardous to make use of observations of babies in the pre-verbal stage in analytic treatment of children and adults. Traumatic experiences in the pre-verbal time cannot be remembered in words and therefore not corrected in the treatment situation. Notwithstanding this difficulty I myself am of the opinion that an empathic understanding of that earliest developmental stage, and by picturing to the patient possible disturbing influences on a baby's growing up, can sometimes contribute to a better and more harmonious solution of later conflicts. The increase in knowledge has definitely furthered our technical abilities. I have advanced to the present in my exposition.

III. The present

How do we look upon psycho-analysis today? We do not restrict our treatment to neurotic disturbances anymore. We also analyze patients with character-disorders, early developmental disturbances and arrests, "borderline" cases and sometimes psychotic conditions (with or without additional pharmacological treatment).

It is well-known that it is not possible to learn the analytic profession merely from books and courses. It is a necessity for the future analyst to undergo a personal analysis, in order to solve as much as possible his own conflicts and to gain insight in his particular mental structure. Only then might he become able to understand emotionally:

1. his patient's "splitted" personality in conscious and unconscious parts, but also with "splits" in his ego-organization;
2. the fact that the disturbances originated in early childhood;
3. that an interplay of opposing forces finds place;
4. that the outcome of this interplay depends on the relative intensities of the forces available to the id (the drives) and to the ego and superego as the warding-off instances.

The theory of the first period is named the topographic viewpoint, the second is the genetic one, the third the dynamic and the fourth the economic point of view. Nowadays we add the adaptational one. When we speak of the principle of adaptation we have to consider its passive as well as its active mode of functioning. In regard to the superego we have to distinguish the restricting and inhibiting instance (the superego in a narrower sense) from the normative and ideal-setting part (the ego-ideal). A severe superego may have caused a strong need for punishment (and/or self-punishment) in the patient. In case the analyst has become aware of the shape and intensity of his personal peculiarities in the different areas, just described, and if he has solved his disturbing conflicts and more or less reached a certain inner harmony, he will have acquired the empathic and humanly sympathetic attitude, necessary for letting grow a working-alliance and a transference in his patients. In addition he will be able to make the suitable well-timed interpretations without too many mistakes. In the analytic treatment of "narcissistic personalities" it is of special importance that the analyst has acquired a good knowledge of his own structured mind, that he has conquered his infantile feelings of powerlessness, of being hurt and the reactive fantasies of grandeur and omnipotence. Otherwise the counter-transference may burden the course of analysis with the analyst's acting-out his personal problems, thus destroying the patient's chances of progress in the treatment situation. Of course there does not exist a completely "perfect" analyst. Everybody retains one (or more) "blind spots". But the analyst has to remain alert and to try to find and master them. A special weak spot is often found in the just mentioned archaic grandeur-fantasies. Here a passage in Goethe's Faust II comes to my mind. It reads as follows: The aged Faust philosophies on the "magnificent" deeds he has achieved with his "servant" Mephistopheles. In the end he has ordered Mephisto to reclaim from the sea and to drain a piece of land and to build a big city on it. It is clear to us that Faust lives in the world of his grandeur fantasies. Then "Frau Sorge" visits him. She says: "Die Menschen sind ihr ganzes Leben blind, so werde, Fauste, Du es jetzt im Sterben" (Man are blind throughout their total span of life, now, Fauste, you shall become blind in dying). She touches his eyes and he is blind. We hope that analysts in gaining self-knowledge, will become less blind for their grandeur-fantasies! Is it a vain hope? Who knows? Faust's end runs as follows: he stands on a hill above the city and fantasies that he still sees it. He exclaims: "Im Angesicht von solchem hohen Glück, geniess ich jetzt den höchsten Augenblick" (In anticipation of such glorious happiness, I now enjoy the highest sublime moment). At this moment the city tumbles down with a thundering tumult, it was built on quicksand by Mephisto. At the same time Faust drops dead. I think Goethe presents us here with a deep wisdom in a poetic form. The striving for grandiosity and omnipotence is one of the most significant factors that have brought misunderstanding, hostility, fight and unhappiness upon man. In the fantasylife of the small, powerless child these images do have a function in restoring part of its lost self-confidence. They may even promote maturation. However, time and again they bump against reality and are finally repressed. But part of them live on in the id, varying in scope and intensity with different individuals. In a number of patients we are confronted with too strong and persistent grandeur-fantasies, which cause a good deal of inhibitions and feelings of misery. In order to help the patient the analyst has to have the capacity to revive in himself the experiential world of the infant, which is so different from the adult's world; with empathy he might be able to support the patient in working-through the infantile disappointments and injured sense of self. Fortunately a number of younger analysts are interested in these problems and continue their personal analysis until they have mastered their own archaic fantasies of omnipotence with the distress and pain due to the loss of this "magic" world. As a matter of course, the technical attitude of the analyst asks for a new dimension in approaching the infant's experiential world. That does not mean that the original recommendation of Freud's have to be abandoned. For instance, the analyst should keep to the rules of

a. patiently listening (with the third ear)
b. avoiding acting-out together with the analysand
c. avoiding to burden the treatment with the analyst's own feelings and conflicts.

But a rapprochement to the baby's world asks for an empathy similar to a mother's intuitive understanding of her baby's needs. At the same time the analyst must keep his ability of distancing in order to communicate with the patient. He has to use words, but sometimes his behaviour, the tone of his voice, etc. are more important. After all, we also make use of a patient's non-verbal communication, his way of entering and leaving the consultingroom, his behaviour on the coach, etc., etc. It is difficult work for both patient and analyst. The latter has to realize his limitations and to accept failures, if unavoidable. Another special difficulty for both partners in the analytic process is given in the fact that frustrations and narcissistic injuries activate aggressive impulses. Apart from the moral judgement, present in many families that aggression is always "bad" and has to be "wiped out". It is often denied that in the infant's world aggression means destruction. A frustrated small child wants to destroy the source of its misery. In its world it is: "everything or nothing". But: "one cannot eat the cake and have it". The small child wants to keep the beloved parent and simultaneously to destroy him. It is an unsolvable conflict. So it is warded-off, especially because the intensity of the death-wishes may be overwhelming.

It is a hard time for both patient and analyst when the death-wishes become conscious in the analytic situation, where they are transferred to the analyst. Intense anxiety and guiltfeelings burst upon the patient. It is the analyst's task to support the analysand in mastering the conflict by pointing out the obliquity of the infantile impulses and the adult's possibility to "sublimate" them into constructive instead of destructive activities. With adolescents it provides a special difficulty as at that period the total personality is often in an upheaval with the return of the archaic infantile conflicts. In any case the analyst must have mastered and sublimated his own destructive impulses, in order to be able to endure the patient's verbal attacks. Many patients in their own narcissistic vulnerability have a faultless feeling for the analyst's weak spots, upon which they may fall with extreme refinement. Some people may have the impression that we know already very much of the development and the final shape of the mental life and of a method to alleviate or even to lift the misery of suffering.

Though I am not a pessimist I would say: "No, we know very little and there is still much to discover". Perhaps one could formulate it differently in the question: "Do we not make use of our knowledge, which is often expressed in complicated and grandiloquent terms, in a faulty way? In many analysts (and psychotherapists) a gap between "intellectual and emotional" knowledge still exists. Empathy into another person's inner world, that is analogue but not identical with one's own is often insufficient or even absent. I think this fact accounts at least partly, for the many differences of opinion and of theoretical formulations among psychoanalysts. Affective criticism of psychoanalysis has always been present. I pointed already to the emotional condemnation of Freud's findings in the early period at the turn of the century. But soon this trend was followed by adherents of the first pioneerstime. I merely name two well-known persons:

a. Alfred Adler, who maintained that neurotic and other psychic disturbances could exclusively be explained by the so-called "organ-inferiority" and the "will for power";

b. C.G. Jung, who made of psychology a kind of mysticism, of an unconscious "animo" and "anima" etc. It is noticeable that their originally accepted significance of sexuality was secundarily devaluated and denied by them, as well as by other "dissidents".

In the second pioneer-time it was a.o. Otto Rank, who made the "Birth-trauma" the cause of every disturbed development. With it he too denied the important role of sexuality. Gradually a group of analysts emerged, who maintained that the social milieu was the exclusive source of developmental disturbances, negating Freud's "supplemental series". Among them Wilhelm Reich was prominent. At *present* it is not so much the denial of sexual drives that is negated, "sex is in", but the genetic origin, the significance of the infantile aspect of the drive is neglected. The "here and now" is made responsible for disturbances, forgetting that maturational and developmental processes run their course from birth on. An example of it can be found with the behaviorists. The principle "pars pro toto" plays its role in all of these deviating disciplines. The rejected "parts" can be different ones. However, sometimes "old" ideas are taken up once more. For instance: we can recognize Jung's mysticism in a number of the "new" schools of thought, e.g. with those people who want to replace analysis through the theory of "action language". Here the importance of infantile life is not negated, but it is stripped of its basis on the drives. One gets the impression that many people are afraid of looking at humans as biological creatures and of excepting the astonishing unfolding of the incomplete new born into the highly differentiated adult in a few years time. Is it possible that man with his archaic fantasies of grandeur and omnipotence is not equal to tolerate "lack of knowledge"? Through centuries mankind has sought consolation for his limited knowledge in various religions, thus participating in the divine omnipotence.

Why are those people, who do not accept religion anymore, not able to acquire admiration for the events of nature, but also for the few human beings who possess the genius to make *real* new discoveries. Such an admiration can provide feelings of bliss. After all, everybody strives for happiness. It seems to be difficult to distinguish admiration from idolization. The latter stems from the magic world of little children who experience their over-idealizing of the parents as being "absolute". The warded-off remnants of this "absolutism" often still influence many people's behavior. In adulthood they may become a more or less extended delusion, whereby the person feels to participate in the omnipotence. I will cite a few lines of Schiller:

"Gefährlich ist es den Leu zu wecken
Verderblich ist des Tigers Zahn
Jedoch der Schrecklichste der Schrecken
Das ist der Mensch in seinem Wahn".*

Even a partial delusion side by side with "healthy" functioning can persist and than cannot be checked. It often raises "narcissistic rage" that may cause quarrel, accusation and suspicion even among analysts. As already mentioned many people consider society and milieu to be the only cause for deviating behavior. They opine that changes in society will solve all problems. They forget, however, that societal arrangements are made by mankind in the course of many generations. History tells us that through ages revolutions have brought about a flourishing of human abilities of science and art, after periods of violence and bloodshed. However, they were always succeeded by periods of ruin wherein lust for power, competition, hate and destructiveness reigned supreme. This happened in ancient times, in the middle ages, after the french and the russian revolution, with fascism and nazism.

Fortunately there are analysts who have extended and complemented the manyfold confirmed findings of Freud's in connection with more experience, without rejecting parts of them. However, as I already pointed out, others have done so, e.g. in denying unconscious mental processes, the genetic principle, infantile sexuality, the dynamic interplay of forces and the economical significance of relative intensities. Recently the repudiation of the importance of grandeur and the omnipotence fantasies and of destructive impulses (and acts) is predominant. One of its after-effects is to be found in the emergence of "new" forms of psychotherapy. It is self-evident that next to analysis other disciplines are needed to help people suffering mentally. Freud expressed this already in 1918 on the occasion of a Budapester Congress. Psychoanalysis has a special field of indication, like every medical treatment. It is time-consuming, difficult and accessible to merely a small number of patients. Some of them can be helped by supporting psychotherapy in their acute problems in a relative short period of time. Group treatment can also be of benefit in addition to a number of other forms of therapy. But it is remarkable that quite a number of therapists have the need to first attack psychoanalysis as "out-dated", "bourgeois", "Victorian" etc. In the mean time they do not have a well-founded theory of mental development. Whatever they use is borrowed from a half or total diluted

---

* For translation see pag. 362.

analytic theory. If one distinguishes clearly between "aim" and "technique" the new disciplines have to be welcomed. But mostly this distinction is lacking. A number of modern therapeutic disciplines promote an acting-out of affect and fantasy. Some inhibited persons, who have a more or less stable personality-structure, may profit from it in feeling more "free". However, with most of the participants in group-therapy (whether it is called "encounter", "sensitivity-training", "behaviortherapy", "screaming"- or "Gestalttherapy") it leads to being overwhelmed, prone to extreme anxiety and inner confusion. Usually the leader of the group does not notify and care for these after-effects.

Some "therapists" foster the idea that the unevitable frustrations of infants, still working in the patients, can be undone by living-out aggression and being physically satisfied by touching and caressing, with the consequence that the patients are "cured". Those therapists are mistaken, they overlook the fact that they are not dealing with babies and toddlers, but with individuals who have acquired a mental apparatus comprising reaction- and defensive manoeuvres and in whom this "making-up" for infantile experiences may mobilize strong conflicts in the adult personality. This negligence in the therapist may have many causes. But *one* factor seems to me to be of great importance, namely the absence of a thorough analysis of the own personality and especially of the archaic narcissistic injuries, which have evoked aggressive-destructive impulses and as reaction- and defense-manoeuvres the archaic omnipotence fantasies.

IV. The Future

About the future of psychoanalysis I can only speak briefly. In Austria we used to say: "Und es kommt immer anders als man denkt" (the outcome always differs from what one has expected). Nobody can predict the future with any kind of certainty. However, in the analytic literature we find many articles that speculate about the future. So, I will venture a few ideas. A number of authors are of opinion (or fear) that the "new" therapeutic disciplines will destroy psychoanalysis. How can we know? Nobody knows! However, in looking over the cultural processes in human history through centuries we always meet with "ups and downs". After periods of destruction, as already mentioned, revival of human constructive activities comes to the fore, e.g. of many works of art from ancient times merely remnants are still present. Much is destroyed by natural forces and by man, but maybe a hidden residue is retained in the depth of the mind of later generations. I think that the real values of Freud's discoveries and the later development of psychoanalysis at some time or another will regain meaning and influence and further human culture. Is it wishful thinking? I hope not. In any case I finish this lecture with this optimistic view, though maybe the younger generation will have to wait a longer stretch of time.

"Patience" is one of the many qualities a psychoanalyst has to acquire. "Perseverance" is a second, and "Love for fellowman" is a third one!

42. Flashes of Memory
On the development of psychoanalysis and the "Psychoanalytic movement" especially in the twenties and thirties

(1980)

Jaap van der Leeuw, to whom this Liber Amicorum is dedicated and I have had similar experiences in various fields of psychoanalysis and therefore share common interests. These fields of interest are the following:

Concerning theory we have both experienced that metapsychology is a useful means to order the many analytical observations and to give us insight in the genesis of psychic phenomena, in personality structure, in the dynamics, the interplay of forces in the various psychic instances and in the economic process, that is to say the relative intensities of the forces of which these instances can dispose. Metapsychology is a tool used by the analyst and/or the psychotherapist to realize and form a clear idea of the disorders in psychic and emotional development of his patients which have caused symptoms, character-deformities, anxieties and inner suffering. Naturally, theoretical terms should not be used in interpretations and interventions. At best, they are unnecessary, but they all too often confuse the patient, reinforce resistances and disturb the analytical process.

A second point of shared interest is the significance of pre-oedipal development for the formation of the oedipal constellation and thereby in the end for the adult personality. Van der Leeuw has paid special attention to pre-oedipal experiences of the male child which have not been described in detail by Freud, but which are also of great significance for the expansion of analytical technique.

I will now come to my actual theme which again interests us both: *the history* of the development of analysis and the so-called "Analytische Bewegung" (the Psychoanalytic Movement). Those who have read Van der Leeuw's article about Freud-Jung (1977) will have noticed how intensely he dealt with the earliest period of the "Movement". There are more authors who are interested in the earliest period, of which a number of followers and co-workers of Freud's gathered together. I have met no-one who has understood the *real* significance of the relation between Freud and Jung so clearly and correctly as Van der Leeuw.

As a matter of fact I was not yet present during the first 'pioneer period' of psychoanalysis. However, I attended the 'second pioneer period' of analysis which covers approximately the twenties and the thirties. Of course I have heard quite some things about that first period. There were no doubt many intelligent and courageous people among those who took part in the "Mittwochabende" in Freud's house. Since the official 'academic' world rejected the

377

new psychology, psychoanalysis, with great hostility it took courage to belong to this group. It is striking that Freud's Traumdeutung which appeared in 1900 was greeted with appreciation and sometimes enthusiasm by the *literary* world which prospered at the turn of the century in Vienna. It is well known that in this first period some secessions took place (nowadays we would call the persons 'dissidents'). I call to mind Adler, Jung, Stekel, Wittels and others. They partly formed a 'school' of their own. These 'schools' differed and carried the mark of the person who had founded them. But one thing sticks out. They all share the fact that they rejected one of the most fundamental discoveries of Freud or at least attributed it a subordinate place. It is of course Freud's discovery that sexual life in human beings does not originate in puberty but that sexual drives are active from birth on and flower in the first years of life, finally determining the shape of adult sexuality. It was precisely 'infantile sexuality' which was stigmatized by official science under the mask of 'moral indignation' as objectionable rubbish. We could be inclined to ascribe this phenomenon to Victorian 'bourgeois' morals of the last century. If we, however, study later and more recent 'dissidents' or/and adherents to a "New Psychology" we will make a remarkable discovery. Infantile sexuality is no longer directly denied but the *biological* basis of every human functioning is denied or at least minimized. I choose two examples.

1. There are currents which *exclusively* ascribe disturbances in mental life of human beings to the "social environment". It goes without saying that the environment has a great influence on the development of the newborn into adulthood. Freud always mentioned it, and he spoke of an "Ergänzungsreihe" ("the complementing series"), indicating that inner fateful occurences such as innate factors plus environmental influences and pain, illness, disasters etc. determine whether a child will grow up to a 'normal' or a 'disturbed' personality.

2. The ego-psychology, initiated by Freud and after his death widely expanded, has induced a number of analysts to minimize the significance of the drives (sexuality and agggression). The words 'libido' and 'aggression' may be mentioned occasionaly but the eminent significance of the drives is swept under the carpet. This is the more striking as it is precisely the knowledge of the pre-oedipal phase which has extended partly through the so-called infant observations. But many describe this phase mainly as the mother-child dyad as if it were already an *object*-relationship. No analyst will deny the significance of the mother for her baby. But it is often ignored that the primary significance of a mother for her baby is a 'biological' one. The mother has to satisfy the bodily needs of the baby so that it can survive. Only when the baby has been able to make a distinction, be it a very primitive one, between its 'self' and the 'other' we can talk of an *object*-relationship, even if this is still merely directed at need-satisfaction in favour of the *life-forces* which rule the total living world. The newborn does not differ much from a little animal. We get the impression that mankind which is so proud of its highly differentiated mental- and emotional development must deny its animal origin. Why is it that so many people must feel so superior to their animal brothers? If we look at what people with their

378

gigantic achievements, for instance in the technical field, have done and still do, we can only regard their haughty pride with scepticism. The destructive- and life-forces which reign in the living nature, have led to aggressive and libidinal drives in the development of the human species, which resulted in great achievements in sublimated forms in the maturing process of child into adulthood. But much aggression continued to exist in its original destructive form and may, either or not mixed with love, lead to disastrous actions. One of the many confusions which denial of the biological basis has caused is often encountered in the use of the term 'narcissism'. This term is used by Freud to indicate the *position* of libido in the newborn, therefore it is based on the biological tie with the mother. I already mentioned that only when the baby can distinguish between 'itself' and 'something outside' we can speak of a psychic tie. This is archaic and initially exclusively centered on the 'self'. It takes weeks or sometimes even longer, partly through the attitude of the mother in the interaction with her baby, before such a psychological tie can emerge. It is then still a 'narcissistic tie'. An object-relationship in which the object is acknowledged as a separate being with a special personality emerges much later, usually at the age of 2-5 year, in the oedipal constellation.

In modern literature the term 'narcissism' is often used for relations which expect and demand in deed and/or in fantasy satisfaction of the 'self', of one's own needs and drive impulses, while there is already a differentiation between self and object. This involves *behaviour* which presupposes a differentiation of 'drive' and 'ego' as well.

I now return to the situation of psychoanalysis in the so-called "second pioneer period" in the twenties and thirties of this century. The most radical secession-movements took place before the first World War (Jung e.g. in 1913). During that war contact between Freud and a number of his co-workers was often thwarted or very limited. A number of those who had started their education in Switzerland turned their backs on Jung and followed Freud. I mention Abraham and Eitingon who went to Berlin; Van Ophuysen who returned to the Netherlands and several Swiss, e.g. Meng, Sarasin, both Oberholzers, Pfister and some others. Many had to do military service, e.g. Simmel and Ferenczi. Sporadic contact by letterwriting was sometimes possible. However, after the war psychoanalysis began to flourish again. Freud originally thought as a consequence of his self-analysis that others would be able to do the same and that theoretical knowledge and sporadic talks with a few dream interpretations would be enough to make them become good analysts. This proved to be a mistake. Freud overestimated the capacity of his co-workers to carry through their self-analysis and he underestimated his own genius. This was, as far as I know, first understood by Nunberg who at the Budapest Congress in September 1918 (before the armistice) raised the issue of the necessity of a training analysis. A second important suggestion at this congress came from Freud. Several psychiatrists-analysts (i.a. Simmel) had treated soldiers who suffered from a traumatic war-neurosis with a form of brief psychotherapy, based on analytical knowledge and experience and they had achieved important successes (if necessary even hypnosis was used). Freud's famous reaction in

Budapest ran as follows: "Apparently in some cases it is possible to mix the gold of analysis with the brass of psychotherapy". He also pleaded for the set-up of possibilities to cure those who were financially less well off and could not afford private treatment of their neurosis with analysis or analytical therapy. The first psychoanalytic Institute was established in 1920 in Berlin by Eitingon. Patients could be treated analytically free of charge. The institute also became a training institute where candidates (realizing Nunberg's proposal) could undergo a personal training analysis, where they could attend courses and seminars and analyze patients under supervision. Eitingon received support from Abraham, Simmel, Horney and others. Soon Hans Sachs from Vienna came to Berlin as training-analyst.

Young candidates like Fenichel, Hans Lampl, Bernfeld from Vienna, Loewenstein and a little later Rado, Melanie Klein and Alexander from Budapest took care of consulting hours and took part in all activities. The Berlin Institute became very prosperous in a few years time. In 1921 Vienna followed the Berlin example. The so called 'Ambulatorium' came into existence. The town of Vienna made localities available on the condition that all patients had to be examined and treated free of charge. Hitschmann was in charge. Analytical societies also arose in other countries such as England (Jones came to London from Toronto), Holland, Switzerland, France and the United States of America. They were however less well-organized and their members less well trained. In the twenties many of them came to Berlin and Vienna to learn psychoanalysis and deepen their knowledge and abilities. The enumeration of names is certainly incomplete since it concerns recollections of times long gone by. When I arrived in Vienna in 1922 there were, apart from young Viennese candidates, a number of foreigners who were eager to acquire analytical knowledge. They were mainly Americans and British people. Most of them had regrettably only a limited period to go through their own analysis. Quite a number of them could merely afford one year leave from their job at home. This was too short a period for a thorough analysis of their own personality as a matter of fact. Some were analyzed by Freud: I remember the names of Sarasin from Basel, Asch, Ruth Mack-Blumgart (later called Ruth Mack-Brunswick) and others from America. Many were analyzed by other analysts like Federn, Helene Deutsch, Rank, Hirtchmann etc. Other foreigners went to Berlin where especially Abraham had acquired great fame by his analytical writings. Unfortunately, Abraham died much too early (December 1925).

Among the foreigners were Jones, Van Ophuysen and the already mentioned Viennese and Hungarian young people. Also Simmel, Eitingon, Horney and Josine Muller did, amongst others, training analysis. The Viennese Society had in the meantime organized courses and seminars as well. There was great enthusiasm for the 'new' analytical science and technique. We attended courses and seminars at least three evenings a week. Helene Deutsch's, Bernfeld's, Federn's, Wilhelm Reich's (who was then still a good analyst) and Theodore Reik's lectures impressed me most. We candidates also attended the scientific meetings of the Vienna Society.

In 1922 and the first half of 1923 Freud was president and I have unforgettable memories of his leadership and especially of his final discussion and summaries. The first paper I attended was Rank's on "Don Giovanni" (1922). It was excellent indeed. I was also greatly impressed by Anna Freud's maiden speech (1922) which she spoke by heart. And young Waelder's contribution whose erudite way of presenting challenged great admiration (he was the only one who delivered his speech standing up).

Unfortunately, Freud had to give up his presidency of the Society in the second half of 1923 because of an extensive jaw-operation caused by a cancerous process. When he took up his practice again in January 1924 we, his analysands, soon got used to the impedement in his speech. He acted once more as president at a meeting in January but the large audience could not hear him well enough and he never did it again. Federn took over. The above mentioned enthousiasm was hardhit in 1923. Otto Rank who was engaged in writing his book "Das Trauma der Geburt" (The Birth-Trauma) told us in his course of the analysis of a female patient whom he had treated for a period of nine months (mainly by means of dreams). According to Rank she had conquered her "Birth-trauma" in that period, was "born anew" and released as healthy. Anna Freud and I, who attended his course, did not understand and shared our doubts about Rank's success. Naturally, we both talked it over with Freud. I will never forget how Freud who had done so much for Rank and had great expectations about him told us to be patient. "Warten wir ab, vielleicht ist noch etwas daran" ("We have to wait and see, perhaps there is something in it") he said. After Ranks return from a trip to America, Freud had a long, analytical, conversation with him. Freud with his famous optimistic tolerance supposed that everything was allright. But soon he became aware of the contrary. As is known, Rank turned his back on psychoanalysis. He established himself in Paris and made his own "school". These adversities had unfavourable repercussions in the Vienna Society. In the meantime the Berlin Society flourished more than ever. Much young talent had been unfolded there. I decided to take advantage thereof to further my own analytical development.

Early 1925 I went to Berlin (partly on Freud's advice). I intended to work there for a few years and to settle in Holland afterwards. Fate ordained things differently. I got to know Dr. Hans Lampl and we decided to get married and to raise a family. I therefore stayed in Berlin and worked with patients of the Eitingon institute.

I have never interrupted my analytic work for a longer period; naturally I did limit it when I had both my children in order to spent a great deal of "their" day together with them.

Life in Berlin in the 1925-1931 era was extremely rich and stimulating. As far as culture was concerned, theatre and film from the Soviet Union which were prohibited in Paris, London, Amsterdam and the whole of the "western" world flourished in Berlin. Cabarets were abundant and offered great talent. It was delightful meeting many of the gifted artists late at night in the artists' cafés and restaurants.

But back to the psychoanalytical Society. Often scientific meetings were fascinating and inviting to stimulating discussions. After a few years I also began

381

to teach, giving courses and supervisions. Besides I took part in courses and seminars for pedagogues which were set up by Bernfeld and Steff Bornstein. During a couple of years I worked weekly in the Prenzlauerberg-district as psychiatrist at the "Jugendberatungsstelle" (a sort of child guidance clinic). There I learned a lot about children, adolescents and the child-parent relationships. My participation in the above mentioned course for pedagogues benefitted from this. Bernfeld was also a highly gifted analyst and an excellent speaker. A completely different but interesting set-up came from Otto Fenichel. He was the leader of the so-called "Kinderseminar"; this did *not* deal with child-patients but with "youthful" analysts and candidates. It was a pleasure to attend it.

There were also analysts in Frankfurt/M among whom Karl Landauer, Frieda Fromm-Reichmann and Erich Fromm. They would occasionally attend the Berlin meetings. Groddeck from Baden-Baden would once in a while deliver a lecture and provided us with his original ideas on what we nowadays would call psychosomatic illnesses. I already mentioned the fact that foreign analysts came to Berlin for a personal analysis. This contributed to a wider view on analysis and the "Bewegung" (the Movement). I also mentioned that around 1931 things changed as a consequence of the political situation. The Weimar Republic had not succeeded in restoring the bad economy in Germany which had lost World War I. Politics moved in a "right-wing" direction and Nazi's became more influential. Several analysts accepted invitations from England and America to further and lecture analysis over there. Melanie Klein had already gone to London (on request of Ernest Jones). Horney, Alexander and Rado went to America. Loewenstein had left earlier for Paris. All this had its repercussions on our society-life. When Hitler came to power in 1933 we understood that the prospering of analysis was over and done with. There was also much personal misery for young "left-wing" oriented colleagues and candidates.

Initially, socialists and communists were arrested and tortured, later this fate also befell the Jews. The fact that the news about the awful torture was considered to be "Greuel Propaganda" in the west, did not only surprise but also appalled us and led us to despise this easy-going blindness. My husband and I stayed in Berlin to assist our patients as much as possible until the summer of 1933 (being Austrians made us foreigners in Germany so that we personally did not suffer). Thereafter we went to Vienna, Hans' native town. Only some non-jewish analysts stayed on in Berlin. Hans Sachs had left much earlier for America, Simmel joined him, when his creation, the psychoanalytic clinic in Tegel which took in deeply disturbed and addicted patients for analytic treatment, had to be closed. In 1934 Eitingon settled in Jerusalem, then still Palestine. We strongly rejected the suggestion of some non-jewish colleagues, shortly after Hitler had come to power, to report the Berlin Society to the authorities for the so-called "Gleichschaltung". That meant: "purification of jewish persons". To our dismay and annoyance this resistance was to no avail. Felix Böhm and Carl Müller-Braunschweig did negotiate with the government and joined the Society for Psychotherapy led by Göring (a cousin of Hermann).

382

Psychoanalysis was forbidden, Freud's works were burnt and it was forbidden to mention his name. A sad end of a glorious era! But psychoanalysis itself continued to prosper. The scene moved from Berlin to Vienna, where in the meantime much had changed. When our family arrived in Vienna in the summer of 1933 we were soon taken up in a circle of extremely gifted, productive and enthusiast analysts. Freud himself continued to work a lot, in spite of his suffering and the many operations he had to undergo. He no longer attended the regular meetings of the Society but from time to time invited group members to Berggasse 19 to give papers and to have discussions. It was a sort of revival of the "Mittwochabende" of the first pioneer period. But how much experience and knowledge had been acquired! I cannot give full information but I mention a number of names which became well-known in analytic literature: Heinz Hartmann, Ernst and Marianne Kris, the Bibrings, the Waelders, the Hoffers and the Deutsch' who had formed a circle of friends into which we soon were accepted. There were the Sterba's, the Isakovers and last but not least August Aichhorn. Anna Maenchen who came from Berlin became soon a member of our circle too. Bernfeld stayed in Vienna for a brief period but then moved to the South of France and next to San Francisco. A special place in this history is naturally reserved for Anna Freud. She had started analyzing children in the second half of the twenties. She could not only confirm many analytical findings in adults but also contribute new data on child development as well as a special child analytic technique. She also cooperated with the very original Aichhorn, who dealt especially with juvenile delinquents, but who at his consulting hours in the city of Vienna also had to deal with neurotic children. Through him, we all received child-patients. Apart from that, Vienna had a great influx of foreigners who came to be analyzed, which also meant that they took their children with them, who not seldomly needed analysis as well. They were mostly Americans, but also British, French and a few Dutch people. Analysts were never short of patients in this period, neither of adults nor of children. Anna Freud led a childanalytic seminar and a seminar for pedagogues and teachers (mostly *female*). My husband and I were involved in training analyses and supervision courses and seminars. My husband worked a lot for the analytical institute which was finally established in the Berggasse (I think nr. 7). This was where the "Psychoanalytische Verlag" was put up, as well as the library.

I would like to go deeper into two points which I think are important. The first concerns the international psychoanalytical congresses. *Four* took place *before* World War I, *eleven* after, until World War II. The one but last was in Marienbad (Czechoslovakia, 1936). Otto Fenichel had emigrated to Prague from Berlin and formed an active analytical group. The Marienbad Congress was very successful although the political threat from Hitler-Germany became more and more perceptible. My second point concerns the so-called "Vierländertagungen" ("Conferences for four countries"), which had been organized in the meantime. These included exchanges of experiences and ideas between Vienna, Budapest, Prague and initially still Berlin. After 1933 they became more or less "Dreiländer meetings". There was a lot of contact between analysts in Vienna, Budapest and Prague. Hungarian analysts (for adults *and* for children) often came to Vienna and vice versa. Friends from Prague too came to Vienna and I myself went several times to Budapest and Prague. In Budapest there were the Balints, Hollos and Hermann and many young people. In Prague the active group around Fenichel functioned excellently. They were always mutually stimulating contacts. Naturally we could not ignore the political situation. The murder of Dolfuss in 1934 was a bad omen. The "Vaterländische Front" of Schnussnig seemed to me to be in a very weak position.

I used to visit Freud weekly at a certain hour. Naturally we discussed analytical problems (we had each one partner of an unstable marriage in analysis) but the political situation at the time was equally (if not more) important. Freud was more optimistic than I. He had expectations of the "Vaterländische Front". I saw Hitler, who after his successes in the Rhineland and Saarland and with the "Inexplicable blindness" of the Western world which cheered "Chamberlain with the umbrella" for his so-called agreement in Munich, take his opportunity in Austria. Hitlers invasion of Austria in 1938 was nevertheless a great shock to us. It also meant the end of a short existence of the "Edith Jackson Kindergarten", a daycenter for infants and toddlers. Anna Freud and Dorothy Burlingham were in charge and Edith Jackson financed it. It only existed for two years but was nevertheless a relief for a number of children of very poor Viennese parents and at the same time an opportunity to follow and study childrens' behaviour. It was no doubt a precursor of the "War nurseries" which were founded by Anna Freud and Dorothy Burlingham during the war in London and of the current nursery which is connected with the Hampstead Clinic.

After the "Anschluss" (Hitlers invasion of Austria) the Viennese analysts were considered to belong to the "death enemies of the 'thousand year'-Reich". They therefore had to leave which was not simple. It was very fortunate that many foreign colleagues and friends were very cooperative. I just mention a few names: Marie Bonaparte, Ernest Jones, and from America Muriel Gardner and Bullit. All assisted us greatly. Jones supplied many visa and work-permits. Freud and his family went to London as did the Krisses, the Bibrings with their children. During the war the Krisses and the Bibrings moved to the United States where the Bibrings ended up in Boston and the Krisses in New York. The Hoffers stayed on in London. The psychoanalytical situation in London was not simple because of the controversy between Freudian analysis and the deviating theories of Melanie Klein and her changed technique. Replacing the Oedipus complex and the super-ego formation at practically near the moment of birth does in my view deny once again the biological basis of every living creature, including human beings.

There are some interesting ideas in the works of Melanie Klein and her followers. The coexisting curriculi in the British Society might be confusing for young candidates (there is an A = Kleinian, a B = Freudian course and an intermediate group). Controversies continue to exist. However, Anna Freud recently (1979) expressed her gratitude to Ernest Jones in her speech on his centennial, *and* to the British Society for its hospitability in 1938 to so many analysts.

Most other analysts ended up in the United States, some after wandering about France, Scandinavia, Switzerland etc. This caused a high development of analysis in the United States of America, not only in numbers but especially in productive and creative work. There was still one international congress before World War II, summer 1938 in Paris. I would like to refer to a special event which had great repercussions for the "Analytische Bewegung" (the analytical movement). An "Internationales Ausbildungs-Komitee" (international education committee) had existed for years. Its aim was to make fit in the training requirements in the various "component societies" as much as possible with each other. Eitingon was president, Anna Freud secretary. But opinions differed about pre-education. Most american analysts consider analysing as a purely *medical* profession. Non-medical persons with a solid analytical training could not become a member of the American Psychoanalytical Association. An American diploma was even required for doctors. European medical emigrants had to do American training courses inclusing "internships" before becoming a member of the APA and via this a member of the International Psychoanalytical Association (only a few older persons who were internationally renowned received "Direct Membership" of the APA. This was also applied for lay-analysts who had never been accepted as an APA-member). The APA's attitude had always clashed with the European attitude. At the aforementioned Paris congress the Europeans did not succeed in making the Americans change their point of view. Therefore the international education committee was dissolved. Most other requirements such as personal analysis, courses, seminars, supervision etc. were however accepted in the curriculum to be sure. But even now an analyst who is not medically trained cannot become a member of the APA. The core of the "Movement" had clearly moved to the USA, with both favourable and unfavourable aspects. War ended the flourishing time of psychoanalysis in Central-Europe. It was only many years later that psychoanalysis was revived in Germany, as far as I know in Berlin first on a small scale, in Heidelberg and Frankfurt where Mitscherlich created the Sigmund Freud Institut. Vienna too has woken up again. The Sigmund Freud House, Berggasse 19 deserves attention and support. In England, analysis continued during the war but the "Blitzkrieg" and post-war austerity were a handicap. The war nurseries of Anna Freud and Dorothy Burlingham accomplished very much indeed. They assisted orphan children and extended and refined the science of developmental psychology. The occupied countries went through a difficult period. All work on training in Holland went underground. In 1946, the "Instituut van de Nederlandse Vereniging voor Psychoanalyse" (Institute of the Dutch Psychoanalytical Society) was founded. Van der Leeuw was deeply involved in all of these activities. On an international level he functioned later as President of the IPA. This episode is described elsewhere. I would like to end in expressing my gratitude for the great amount of work that Van der Leeuw has done for psychoanalysis and for us.

43. Psychoanalysis: Frame of Reference for Training

(1980)

Introduction

It is *easy* to present the regulations for training in Psychoanalysis, as laid down by the International Psychoanalytical Association. It is very *difficult* to picture the Value of Psychoanalysis both as a scientific theory and as a method of psychotherapy *and* of the training for the profession in the short span of time of 35 minutes. Therefore I will omit the description of the regulations. Everyone, interested in the curriculum can ask for information at the Central Office of the Association in London. My contribution to the second, difficult theme will be incomplete, in a birds-eye view.

The frame of reference for training is obviously the psychoanalytic theory. The original one was named by Freud:

The topographical theory

I want to underline explicitly that it is not a *preconceived* theory. It is originated from *observations* of human mental life. It was always and still is a flexible theory, open to change and enlargements, whenever new discoveries are made. The topographical theory is the theory of the unconscious psychic life. The study of the neurotic symptoms of his patients revealed to Freud that the causes of the mental disturbances were completely unknown to the patient. They could only come to consciousness by a special procedure which allowed the patient to overcome strong resistances, due to repression of vehement guilt-feelings, anxieties and other affects. The first methods of treatment were hypnosis and suggestion, as Freud had been much impressed by Charcot's hypnotic experiments. But Freud had to abandon hypnosis, as many patients were not hypnotizable and/or the eventual results were transitory. He, then, developed the analytic method of free associations. The uncovering of repressed conflicts invariably led back to earlier life-experiences, in adolescence and basically in early childhood. The infant is a creature with bodily needs and of passion. He demands immediate satisfaction from the motherly caretaker on whom he is completely dependent. His sexual-aggressive instinctual drives are predominant at birth. Intellectual and cognitive functions develop only gradually. The little child's oral, anal, phallic (and later-on genital) imperative demands are not completely realizable and have to be restricted. His preoedipal and oedipal object-relationships undergo the same fate. The adult environment has usually lost the empathy with the child's inner world and reacts upon his strivings, wishes and fantasies with prohibitions and punishments. An *emotional "misunderstanding"* between child and adult is the result. Some mothers' intuition may find a way to accompany the child's upgrowth with empathy and tolerance. Unfortunately this is rather the exception, at least in our "civilized" world. The study of dreams, parapraxis etc. in healthy individuals made it clear that there is a split between the "consciousness" and the "unconscious" in all human beings. In the system "Unconscious" reigns the primary-process-functioning. It is a-logic, it is timeless, and to the innate endowment the repressed impulses, wishes and fantasies are little by little added. They become subject to processes of condensation, shifting, symbolization etc. In the system "Perception-Consciousness" the secondary-process functioning holds sway. It is in contact with the outer world, in that it develops logical, intellectual and cognitive functions, it acquires words, language and speech. It finally represses and wards-off the forbidden sexual-aggressive impulses and fantasies. The outcome of an individual's upgrowing mental life is always determined by an interaction between his specific endowment and the environment. In this context Freud spoke of a "complementary series" ("Ergänzungsreihe"). I stress this point explicitly, because a number of critics still maintain that psychoanalysis negates and even rejects the paramount importance of environmental influences. This is an error, based on insufficient knowledge. The topographical theory comprises the genetic point of view. It may be still of use in describing conflicts. But new discoveries made corrections and extensions necessary. I pass a number of corrections and come to the more elaborated theory: the metapsychology.

Metapsychology

This term has given rise to much criticism, even among psychoanalysts. Why did Freud choose this word, which for some people became associated with the word metaphysics, or some other magical mystics? Well, I think it had not any mystical connotation for Freud. He only came to the conclusion that the increase of gained material about the complexities of mental life, normal as well as pathological, needed a theoretical frame of reference going far beyond the different academic psychologies, even beyond the topographical theory. Metapsychology accounts for the dynamic, structural and economic peculiarities of psychic life. The dynamic viewpoint stresses the fact that mental manifestations are the outcome of an interplay of forces. The structural theory describes the different systems of the mind, to which forces are available in situations of conflicts. The economic principle points to the *relative* intensities of those forces that were at the disposal of the various systems, called: "id, ego, superego and ego-ideal". The content of the id is approximately the same as that of the system "Unconscious" in the older theory. The "ego" is the heir to the system: "Perception-Consciousness", but enlarged by an expanded study of the developmental processes. The ego develops skills, for instance motoric functioning and others, to deal with the surroundings. It builds up defence manoeuvres against the unrealizable and forbidden impulses.

A very important innovation in the theory resulted from Freud's becoming aware of a separate instance in the ego, the superego, arising at the end of the oedipal configuration, holding the internalized parental prohibitions. The Ego-ideal represents the incorporated norms and ideals. Freud made it explicit that the terms did *not* apply to parts of the brain. They are theoretical concepts, facilitating our understanding of conflicts and their origin. Unfortunately a number of analysts still *reify* the concepts and thereby bereave themselves of a deeper notion of psychic functioning. As a matter of fact metapsychology is *not* used in the treatment situation. It is only of assistance in ordering observations for the analyst's own help. In a "healthy" person the different parts of the psyche are in harmony with each other and therefore not or hardly discernible. The developmental changes from early childhood through adolescence towards adulthood are flexible and *adapt* to a wider environment, either in a passive or in an *active* way. The upgrowth is impeded in neurotics and otherwise disturbed persons. This may lead to rigidity, accompanying the symptoms. Especially severe super-ego demands can cause hardly changeable guiltfeelings and the need for punishment. An increase in experiences brought Freud to describe the eminent importance of the pre-oedipal objectrelations for the shaping of the oedipal constellation.

After Freud's death (1939) a number of analysts enlarged psychoanalytic psychology in various ways.

Ego-psychology was extended, morals, ethics and values were deeply explored. Attention was payed to the problems of adaptation. Childanalysis and infant observations provided a wealth of material, widening the scope of analytic knowledge and promoting the treatment of early disturbances, as did the study of narcissism, leading to the so-called: "Psychology of the Self". I refrain from citing prominent authors in the various fields, due to the shortness of time. Instead I turn to psychoanalytic therapy.

Psychoanalytic treatment, its value, advantages and disadvantages

As a prelude I want to draw attention to the fact that the word "psychoanalysis" is used in a double sense. Some analysts consider this to be a matter for regret. The term designates "a particular therapeutic method and it has become the name of a science – the science of unconscious mental processes" (Freud, 1925).

I now cite from John Bowlby's *recent* article: "Psychoanalysis as art and science" (1979) the following passage: "As practitioners we use theory as a guide; as scientists we challenge that same theory. As practitioners we accept restricted modes of enquiry, as scientists we enlist every method we can".

Bowlby, originally an ethologist, tells us that: "when I (= Bowlby), qualified in psychoanalysis in 1937, members of the British Society were occupied in exploring the fantasy world of adults and children, and it was regarded as almost outside the proper interest of an analyst to give systematic attention to a person's real experiences. – Almost by definition it was assumed that anyone interested in the external world could not be interested in the internal world, indeed was almost certainly running away from it".

388

Well, I think his dictum may not have concerned all members of the Society. It certainly was not adhered to by Freud (remember his "Ergänzungsreihe") and neither by the members of the Viennese Society. The Vienna Society was in the thirties the most advanced and prominent one in the analytical world. Bowlby probably related to Melanie Klein's followers. Klein's level of theorizing was far below her therapeutic aptitude. She may have been misunderstood by her pupils. Be that as it may, I cite this episode as one example of quite a few others, where psychoanalytic theory was reduced by taking "pars pro toto". This phenomenon can be observed during the whole history of psychoanalysis. At the present time there are still too many examples to be enumerated. Returning to the first quotation of Bowlby's interesting article I am in agreement with his statement that as practitioners we use theory as a guide. I disagree with him that we have to accept restricted modes of inquiry. On the contrary I think we have to make use of all knowledge of functioning of the mind. Though the psychoanalytic situation was and still is the royal road to acquire such knowledge, we use information from other sources as well. I pointed already to the enrichment of our knowledge from infant-observations. We utilize their findings to enrich our treatment-arsenal, especially of early (narcissistic) characterdisorders. I add the importance of the work of a number of sociologists, providing us with relevant knowledge about the influence of smaller and wider environments and of social milieus upon the upgrowth of human beings from birth to adulthood and old age.

It is exactly one of the true *values* of psychoanalytic treatment, that it enables the analyst to incorporate into his choice of interventions all and everything known. This is an ambitious statement, but an ideal to strive after, knowing our limitations and the fact that ideals are never completely realizable. We all have to avoid the danger of overestimating our capacities and of giving in to wishful thinking and fantasies of grandeur, pleasant as they may be.

The *advantages* of analytic treatment over other therapeutic methods lies in its *aim*, i.e. the uncovering of *all* of the factors, in *all* of the different stages of the patient's development responsible for his mental suffering and disturbed upgrowth. In principle, if the patient has the capacity to overcome his resistances with the analyst's help, it may lead to a cure, because then the *causes* originating in early childhood, can be removed. The traumatic events of infancy and childhood may be mastered and the liberated forces can then be used in a constructive way, personally as well as socially. A succesful analysis can lead to *structural* changes of the personality. This differs from other forms of psychotherapy, which deal with actual conflicts and may achieve merely shifts of symptoms, sometimes helpful sometimes harmful. They may be overpowering, giving rise to enormous amounts of anxiety, which could only have been mastered in daily analytic sessions.

Like every mode of therapy analysis has its semi-successes and failures as well. Therefore a careful and thorough examination of the patient has to be made before indicating that analytic treatment is the method of choice. There are more practical disadvantages of analytic treatment. It is a difficult enterprise for both patient and analyst. The patient has to be motivated for a painful and long-lasting task. It is hard work to overcome strong resistances and to work through the distress, strong anxieties, feelings of being lost, unloved and rejected, of vehement guilt-feelings and the need for punishment in connection with masturbatory sado-masochistic fantasies, that originated in childhood and continued unconsciously in adolescence and adulthood.

Apart from the patient's conscious motivation there must at least exist a minimum of more or less intact ego-functions with which the analyst can cooperate in order to assist the patient in enduring the pain of solving his conflicts. The examiner will point out the difficulties to the patient, though the latter can only *experience* them in *doing* analysis. If the recommendation for analysis as the method of choice for a particular patient is made very carefully, then analysis may be the most *economic* method of treatment, as a really cured patient will be no longer a financial burden for the community.

There are cases for which another mode of therapy may be indicated. Psychotherapy on analytic lines (though not reaching the deeper layers of the disturbances), short, supportive therapy, group-therapy and a few others, can be of help for solving actual problems with a number of patients, sometimes to the latter's contentment.

Presently you will hear about: "grouptherapy", "behavior therapy", "client centered" therapy, a.o. A few words about some "new" methods come in order now.

It is remarkable and rather amusing to witness the re-emergence of pre-analytic, abandoned methods, for instance in so-called screaming therapy, primal scream, hit- and haptic therapy a.o. They promote and even *order acting-out* of impulses, affects and especially violent aggression. This reminds us of Breuer and Freud using so-called "abreaction" of dammed-up affects. Freud did not only abandon this mode of treatment because of its lack of *continued* relief, he disliked the overpowering of a person's rational, moral and ethical standards to the extreme. In addition, quite a few patients are not able to endure such a procedure. They become confused and disintegration may be the outcome. To the personal misery, then, is added a great economic waste for the community. I come now to the:

Training in psychoanalysis

I want to start with a short digression of this theme. Why do I use the word "patient" for a person seaking help for mental suffering, instead of the word "client", as has become the modern custom? "Client" derives from the latin "Clients". In the ancient roman world it meant something life "Serf". Though not a complete possession of the master, as were the slaves, the "serf" was said to be free, but in reality he was totally dependent on his master's whims. I feel it to be a gross failure to use this word in a therapeutic relationship.

I always wonder why many people consider the word "patient" as degrading. I have met lots of people with neurotic and other psychic problems, who are of much more value to mankind than many so-called "normal" persons. The fact that they seriously seek help for their suffering and problems is to be admired instead of despised.

I turn now to the proper theme of training.

Why is the candidate's personal analysis the first and most important part of his training? To begin with: the candidate has to get rid of his neurotic symptoms, which, at least, in our civilization are never lacking, minor as they may be. Thereby he experiences that mental conflicts exist, that it demands an effort to overcome resistance against the uncovering of repressed impulses, memories and fantasies. He becomes aware of the origin of his conflicts in childhood, of his preoedipal and oedipal objectrelations, of their influence upon his present lifesituation, his mature relationships, his values, his work and his social behavior. He learns the significance of transference and countertransference in the developing analytic process. In contradiction to the treatment of a patient, who may feel content if he has lost his symptoms, the future analyst has to do more. It is of great importance that he becomes familiar with his own, particular structured mind, his abilities and talents, his peculiarities and his *limitations*. As the structuring of the mind starts already in early childhood he has to acquire knowledge of his narcissism and to *relive* with feeling tones his infantile fantasies of omnipotence and overvaluation of the surroundings that play such a prominent role in the life of the little child. If the candidate remains unaware of the importance of this early development, he may be unable to master his *therapeutic ambition*, thereby doing unjustice to his patients. In my opinion one of the most intrinsic values of the analytic treatment lies in the possibility for the patient to find and to recover his own, singular individuality. The candidate has to learn that this aim is only to be reached, if the analyst is willing and able to show respect for his patient and to *accept* the patient's singularity, *avoiding* to burden him with the analyst's own outlook and convictions. It needs empathy, tact, self-knowledge, a love of human beings, of truth, patience and modesty. In addition the analyst has to have a real inquiring mind, a deep interest in psychic development and the necessary endurance to search after his personal inner mental life, as far as possible for any human being.

People may laugh at this long range of requirements, including value-judgments. They may label it: old-fashioned, out-dated, Victorian, bourgeois or with any other depreciatory connotation. Perhaps it is the privilege of old age and of many decades of work in the field to keep to one own's valuation of the uniqueness of every human being and of the necessity to respect this uniqueness likewise in patients and in candidates.

This implies that the striving for *perfectionism* is unacceptable. Everyone, training analyst, the analyzand-candidate, as well as the patients have to accept their limitations. However, some candidates are more gifted for the specific analytic profession than others. In the selection procedure the senior training analyst tries to assess the giftedness of a possible future candidate. Unfortunately it is also one of the most difficult features for assessment. The measure of giftedness is often only coming to the fore during the candidate's analysis. As a consequence of this difficulties, failures in the selection procedure are unavoidable. They are reflected in the different criteria adhered to in the various component societies of the International Association. One of those criteria is labelled "analyzability". Even this word is often differently defined. In my experience the presence of minor neurotic symptoms and character-peculiarities like, for instance, feelings of inferiority alternating with superiority-feelings and grandeur fantasies, is not in itself decisive. They are analyzable in principle. What counts more are endurance and motivation. With some groups of psychiatrists, psychologists, a.o., it has become "fashionable" to be an analyst. In other groups analysis is utterly despised. If someone lets himself be guided by such prejudices and/or by the idea that analysts earn a lot of money and his principle motive is to become rich, he is not *really* motivated for the profession. Whether the above mentioned *real* values are present in an applicant is exactly what is so hard to assess. After all, quite a few really gifted applicants are accepted for training. They will be the candidates, who profit most from the training procedures. They will be interested in the theoretical courses and seminars, provided as a stimulus for further personal study.

When the candidate starts analyzing patients, supervision is necessary as a help to overcome initial insecurity and anxiety. A good working alliance between supervisor and supervisee promotes the young analyst-to-be to handle transference and counter-transference adequately. If he becomes aware of "blind spots" he will bring them in his own analysis. A special problem for the candidate is the handling of his patient's violent aggressive outbursts, because they may threaten his self-esteem. He, then, may need the supervisor's support to endure the narcissistic injuries in order to help his patient. He needs to remain friendly, not to loose his patience and to await calmly the right moment for an intervention. The analyst's attitude should be an interested and a *humane* one, as no human being (and therefore no patient) can reveal his innermost secrets to a distant, "wooden" person.

The psychoanalytic training is a rather long and heavy load of work. So, every applicant should be extensively informed and not at all be pressed to start the extensive curriculum. If he is really motivated he will probably benefit much from it, for himself, for his patients and also for his ability to make the right choice of therapy for his patients. I think, a personal analysis for everyone, who wants to do any kind whatever of psychotherapeutic work, should be a requirement. His archaic omnipotent- and grandeur fantasies, hidden behind his ambition to help patients, should be mastered by himself, to avoid the possible overpowering of the patient's unique personality.

After all: psychoanalysis, both as a science and as a therapeutic method, is fascinating and stimulating. Moreover it enriches one's outlook on mankind and one's way of life.

44. On the Influence of Early Development Upon the Oedipal Constellation

(1980)

Introduction

In observing little children of approximately 4-6 years, we notice a number of similarities in their behavior, but perhaps still more differences. One of the earlier discoveries of Sigmund Freud in treating mentally disturbed patients was the very fact that their symptoms proved to be longstanding and reaching back far into the patient's childhood. The inhibitions and disturbances of their love lives, as well as their working capacities, already had their forerunners in childhood. The events of that period, however, were nearly completely forgotten, repressed, and warded off. They were merely able to come into consciousness through a special procedure, at first by hypnosis. Soon this technique was replaced by the psychoanalytical technique. The patient was requested to communicate his free associations, and the psychoanalyst, making use of his knowledge, tried to find origins of the patient's suffering in interpreting the material, in collaboration with the patient himself. The theoretical outcome of Freud's observations was formulated in his statement that the core of neurotic symptoms lies in the Oedipus complex. In studying "normal" personalities, Freud discovered that every human being passes through an oedipal constellation in his mental development in the period of 3 or 4 to about 6 years of life. He described it, as is well known, in the following terms: A little boy wishes and has fantasies to replace his father in becoming his mother's lover (like Oedipus). A little girl's strivings produce the fantasy of being father's beloved one instead of mother. The fate of this early fantasy life is complicated by the fact that in both boys and girls the negative oedipus constellation is present alongside the positive one. Passive, sexual strivings in the little boy bring about the fantasy of being father's beloved one. In the little girl, active sexual urges lead to the wish to be mother's lover. In "normal" development the positive oedipus constellation will prevail. From the repressed unconscious it influences in some way or other the final love life of the adult.

We can still adhere to Freud's statement that the Oedipus constellation is the core of later neuroses and also of more or less "healthy" sexual love life, only with the addition that the Oedipus complex is already a kind of outcome of most complicated maturational and developmental processes in the pre-oedipal phase (see chapter 14). The study of the latter was initiated by Freud but further elaborated by other analysts, and infant observers, partly after Freud's death (Freud, 1909, pp. 97, 111, 206; 1931).

393

Children, ages 4-6 years

Physically healthy newborns with an "average-normal" anlage of the instinctual drives and the potentialities for ego-function development, when adequately mothered in babyhood and educated with understanding love in the family situation, show an active and lively type of behavior in the oedipal phase. The little boy may say "When I will be big I will marry you, mommy." His rivalry and hostility toward daddy will finally be repressed and gradually give way to admiration and love. He will identify with daddy and strengthen his masculinity. His passive strivings will be sublimated and lead to an ability for learning, accepting knowledge from adults, and communicating with his peers, in latency. In puberty and adolescence the revival of the old oedipal bonds with the parents will not show more than the usual upheavals and lead to a more or less healthy adulthood.

The little girl will go through similar developmental lines, which encompass flexible progression and regression without fixations for both boys and girls (Freud, A. 1965). For the girl, however there is an additional developmental problem in the fact that she has to give up her original love object (the mother), provoking a stronger hostility. This situation makes it more difficult to arrive at a sublimated positive relationship and a female identification with the mother. However, both sexes have to cope with the physical impossibility of realizing the heterosexual bond with the partner, and both have to do away with the hostility and death wishes toward the parent of the same sex. Nevertheless healthy children live up to the necessities of human life.

Up to now I have described the so-called "normal" development, more or less from a macroscopic viewpoint, and mentioned a number of preconditions which are rather ill defined and vague. I mentioned physical health. As a matter of fact, gross bodily defects cause a number of mental developmental disturbances as well. Here I put the question whether bodily intact newborns are all alike (as quite a few people and doctors sometimes maintain) in their behavior and activities. I go back to experiences of my own, dated more than 50 years ago, when I worked in the obstetrical ward of the Amsterdam University as a young medical student.

It sometimes happened that two to five babies were born in the same night under similar circumstances. That is, the deliveries were "normal," without artificial intervention and of an average duration of the mother's labor pains and work. The mothers seemed to enjoy having their babies and wanted to have them near their bodies to cuddle and feed. I shared the mothers' happiness, but I marveled about the wonders of nature. (I hasten to add that, as a matter of fact, I also encountered disturbed childbirths, with artificial interventions, sometimes successful, sometimes unsuccessful, with many tragedies for the mother and other relatives.) If the baby was "intact," one could sometimes console a mother who had suffered too much. If the baby was abnormal with severe physical and/or brain damage, one wondered whether it was not an inhuman attitude to try to keep it alive with the knowledge that it could never be a "normal" human being.

394

But here I want to come back to the healthy baby. Though at the time I knew nearly nothing of psychology and psychoanalysis, I was nevertheless fascinated by the observation of *how different* the newborns were. Some of them, after their first cries had started the breathing process, became very quiet, passive babies, sleeping much and being slow in taking up the mother's breast (or the bottle, for that matter). On the whole, these babies develop gradually into "normal" babies. Other newborns reacted quite differently after birth. They seemed to be very active, looking around, though I knew they could not yet focus on a special object because the myelinization of the nerves was not yet completed. Nevertheless they displayed a very different behavior. They were quick in finding the nipple of mother's breast and sucking energetically. The early fascination of these observations made me try never to forget the importance of anlage factors. Of course, no psychoanalyst will deny that anlage plays a role in developmental processes. Yet one not infrequently meets with authors who neglect or forget about its importance.

I have already mentioned the anlage of the instinctual drives. An imbalance between the sexual, libidinal, and the aggressive-destructive drives may have important consequences for the developmental processes. An innate excessive degree of aggression is more often mentioned in the literature than an innate weakness of libidinal drives. Maybe such a weakness is present in the above described passive, slow newborns. After the anlage of the drives, I mentioned the innate potentialities for the development of ego functions. They include intelligence, cognitive functions, sense perception, integration, etc., which come into being only at a later period of development. But they also comprise reaction formations, defense mechanisms, and defense manoeuvers. I also pointed to an adequate mothering of the baby as a precondition for healthy growth. This brings us to one of the most important factors: the gradual unfolding of object relations. The human newborn is completely dependent upon mother for survival. He has to be fed and cared for in order to survive. In contrast to the intra-uterine life, where there is a constant supply of everything needed, the baby experiences periods of lack of satisfaction of his needs. He is dependent on the quality of the mothering whether the privations are of a short duration or an intolerably long one. We speak of an infant-mother dyad, a symbiotic bond, and of mother being a part of the infant's narcissistic milieu.

(I interrupt for a moment the description of the little child's development to digress on the meaning of the terms narcissism and narcissistic. They are used in so many different meanings that much confusion results. The term "narcissism" originated in Freud's libido theory. It designated the original position of the sexual drive (libido) in the newborn child. Later on the aggressive (destructive) drives were included. Both sexual and aggressive *drives* are present in every living creature. However, sexual, as well as aggressive *acts* and *fantasies*, are developmental products and designate modes of *behavior*. I think we should clearly differentiate between *drives* and *behavior*. Many authors use the term "narcissism" for "behavior" (and often in a depreciating way) not differentiating it from the underlying drive. *Behavior* is already a developmental product, including (primitive) ego functions. Finally, sexual impulses lead to love, aggressive ones to hate and *acts* of aggression. Both self-love and object-love continue to exist during the whole lifespan. The same occurs with aggressive behavior and hate.)

I return to the child's maturational and developmental growth processes. In the first weeks and months of life the infant's physical needs are satisfied by a "good-mothering" person. As long as the baby is breast fed, it is the real mother who is needed. However, not every mother has the capacity for good mothering – many are not aware of the fact that providing food and clothes is not enough for a healthy growing up. Love and warm feelings with empathy are as necessary as bodily care. From observations of babies who grew up in an institution or who were often hospitalized for long stretches of time, we know that they may become retarded children; in some instances they even die (see Spitz 1965). A baby is greatly in need of being fondled, cuddled, laughed with, spoken to, and moved around. Only when this really happens the little child can gradually develop an awareness of the motherly person being a separate individual, of what is called "object-constancy" (the capacity to hold on to the bond with the temporarily absent object), and finally to a "real" object-love, accepting the object as his (or her) own right. I will not describe in detail the various phases of development of the object-relatedness from the symbiotic to the separation-individuation phase with its subphases of rapprochement, etc. because they are so aptly studied and fully published by infant observers. I refer here especially to the work of Mahler (1968, 1972, 1975). Instead I want to mention two other problems, a theoretical one and a practical one.

I think we should most clearly correlate the development of object relatedness with the phase-specific states of the so-called oral, anal, and phallic phases. In the oral phase the infant lives in symbiose with the mothering object. We know that in the oral phase, satisfaction is not only acquired by being fed and stimulated on the zone of the mouth and the oral cavity, but is also dependent on the just-mentioned facial, acoustic, skin-contact, and movement gratifications. When the little child begins to crawl and to walk, his need for autonomy and for individuation-separation coincides with the anal phase of the drives. In this period the cleanliness training usually starts. It is well known that here the wishes of the adults very often run counter to the desires for anal lust in the little child. The object bond is the child's need for autonomy combined with a need for "refueling" (nearness of the motherly object) which is frequently grossly disturbed through badly timed and too severe demands of the adults for compliance with their regulations concerning cleanliness. This state of affairs may lead to a severe opposition, to subbornness and hostile feelings. As the little child is powerless, he has to submit, sometimes at the expense of loving capacities and of a disturbance of his sense of self. His aggressive impulses have to be repressed, but residues of his resentment and unhappiness remain in the unconscious and may influence the next developmental phase, the phallic one, where normally the object relations take the shape of the oedipal constellation.

The developmentally normal progression from one phase to the next is never a smooth, even one. Regressive tendencies are still present. If these are flexible, the progression will proceed. If, however, a fixation has become too strong, the "normal" oedipal constellation may be impaired.

A practical problem of recent times: The modern quest for "emancipation" with adolescents and young adults has many and varied consequences. I will only go into a few. Both partners of a couple have an outside job; they decide to have a child. Pregnancy and birth are normal. What to do after the leave of absence is over? The baby is a few weeks old, and the question arises how to proceed. Both partners want to go ahead with their jobs. The solution is: "Well, there is a 'creche' in the neighborhood." The baby is brought to the creche from 8 a.m. until 6 or 7 p.m. We assume that the workers in the creche are decent people and take care of the baby's needs. The baby is confronted with many different caretakers. He scarcely sees his parents. He was a healthy, active newborn. The parents wonder why their baby gradually becomes passive, sad, and unresponding to their kindness, and sometimes unmanageably aggressive. They are absolutely unaware of what they have done to their child. We understand the baby's reaction, as a basic trust experience is lacking; good mothering is a first requirement for a healthy development into a lively little child.

In another situation, a young mother, some weeks after the birth of her child, insists on resuming her work. The father, being very proud of his son or daughter, may reduce his working time (or be unemployed) and is happy to care for his child. He becomes the mothering person. Instead of speaking of the mother-child dyad, we should in this case use the expression father-child dyad. The only thing father cannot do is to breast-feed the baby. In other modes of caretaking he sometimes may be the more motherly person. If the mother does not completely neglect her baby, the triad is already originating long before the child enters into the oedipal situation.

Another very important problem centers around the little child's sexuality. I have already mentioned the need for oral and anal satisfaction. The attitude of the parents vis-a-vis masturbation is of great significance. The so-called "old-fashioned" parents condemn the child's masturbatory activities with more or less severity. Either the child gives them up, or he feels anxious and guilty and absorbs his fantasies into his guilt and inferiority feelings. The "modern" parents who claim sexual freedom may "seduce" their child by showing their naked bodies, taking the little child into their bed, and letting him witness their sexual intercourse. They are unaware of the possibility that the child is being overstimulated and unable to cope with such overwhelming excitement at this early age. Aside from the parents' attitudes, the little child is unable to actualize his oedipal desires, so frustrations are unavoidable.

As the child feels helpless and powerless, he takes refuge in fantasies of grandeur and omnipotence. In healthy development, the grandeur fantasies may develop into norms and ideals which may give a beneficial direction to the adult's strivings and activities (see chapter 36). In my experience, a residue of the original grandeur lives on in the unconscious in everyone. However, the relative intensity is decisive for the later outcome in the adult's life. If the parents are unaware of the child's inner world (which is the usual situation), the "emotional misunderstanding" between children and adults becomes a fact. The little child's experiential world is very different from the adult's. The little child's passionate demands for drive satisfaction are relatively much more powerful than the adult's because their ego functions are not yet established; they have still to grow and are very vulnerable. They live according to their need for drive gratification; they are yet unaware of reality factors and of the calamities of the wider world that make demands upon the parents and therefore also on themselves. Most grownups have forgotten (repressed) their own infantile experiential world, and lack of empathy with their little children is the consequence.

From both sides ambivalence comes into being. The toddler, who cannot understand why he has to abstain from so many lustful activities, feels abandoned, unloved, and worthless. His awakened aggression cannot be discharged; his powerlessness (as mentioned earlier) finds sole consolation in fantasies of grandeur. The unresponsive parents may feel deceived and disappointed. They have the power to act out their hostility and to punish the child. A vicious circle may arise, and the emotional estrangement between parents and child only augments. Luckily this gloomy situation does not always come to the fore. But I think, in principle, it happens more often than is usually assumed. In any case we understand that it is deleterious for the child entering into the phallic phase and the oedipus constellation. In extreme cases the latter is not arrived at at all. Sometimes the positive oedipus complex is distorted, or it is reversed, and the negative constellation prevails. Masturbation, if not completely abandoned (which is seldom the case), may give rise to severe guilt feelings and a need for (self) punishment. The fantasies often begin to lead a life of their own, and they become very sadomasochistic.

Correlations of an abnormal oedipus constellation with disturbances in the pre-oedipal phases of development

I am aware of the fact that I gave only a simplified and sketchy account of the possible distortions in the developmental processes during the first 3 or 4 years of life, resulting in an abnormal oedipus situation. Trying to correlate deficiencies in the pre-oedipal phase of development with disturbances in the oedipus constellation will be equally fragmentary. I venture the following remarks.

If an infant during the first year of life, though physically normal at birth, is not adequately "mothered," there is a big chance for a severely disturbed growth. The real mother may be absent, or she herself may be mentally disturbed and unable to display any warm interest and feeling for her baby. A substitute motherly person may bring a favorable outcome, but often this person is not a steady companion to the infant. This situation may impair the normal development of the instinctual drives, which are dependent on a warm object relatedness. The budding ego will not be able to develop its innate potentialities, and a (at first primitive) structuration of the baby's mind will not occur. The object relatedness remains in the symbiotic shape. Object constancy is not achieved. With severe neglect the child may become a psychotic, a borderline, an addict, or a delinquent.

The baby who has not suffered too severe neglect in his first year of life may have reached a (though sometimes fragile) kind of object constancy. Then a failure on the part of the parents to accompany empathically the special tempo of the toddler's developmental processes, for instance, in connection with his readiness to comply with the demands for cleanliness, may disturb his maturational proceeding. A consequence may be a fixation in the anal phase, accompanied by strongly ambivalent object relations, an insufficient fusion of aggression and libido, severe envy and rivalry with parents and siblings, and a persistence of the archaic form of the grandeur fantasies with the magic feelings of omnipotence alternating with the sense of inferiority. It is clear that this state of affairs predisposes for a neurotic development, especially for the acquisition of an obsessive, compulsion neurosis, often becoming manifest in latency and/or in adolescence or early adulthood.

If in the phallic phase castration anxiety is too strong, the oedipal object relations may be impaired. For instance, a little boy may have given up masturbating together with his masculine fantasies out of fear of retaliation by his rival (the father), by whom he expects to be bereft of his penis. By giving up masturbation he (unconsciously) castrates himself, so to speak, in order to prevent father from doing it. The boy may then turn to passivity, which may or may not extend to other areas, e.g., to learning inhibitions, difficulties in friendship with his peers, etc. As a reaction formation to his fears, outbursts of aggression, uncontrollable rage, and/or self-damage may arise. Usually, hysterical symptoms are linked to the disturbances of the phallic-oedipal phase. In any case, the boy is unable to form a "real" object relation — love for another person on his own merits. The little girl, reaching the phallic phase, has to cope with a special problem, namely her feeling of being discriminated against and handicapped as compared with little boys, who are allowed and even ordered to touch their genitals in urinating. The little girl often tries to copy the boys but she feels inferior in having to sit down in order to urinate and in not being able to compete with the boy's games in producing far-reaching jets of urine. In her so-called penis envy she makes her parents responsible for her imagined inferiority. It is usually said that she resents her mother for this "handicap." In my experience, it may be the father as well, especially when father feels very much attracted toward his young daughter and in a certain way starts to flirt with her. As he finally leaves her alone and prefers mother in the bedroom, the little daughter may feel betrayed and full of resentment. In any case, it is difficult for the girl to enter into the "normal" oedipal relationship. Both boys and girls have to fight against special motives for envy. The girl has to struggle with her penis envy. The boy may be intensely envious of mother and other women who can produce wonderful, living, and beloved babies, whereas the boy's "products," the excrements, which at first are admired, end by being called "dirty" and "worthless" and are thrown away.

It is little consolation for the girl when she is told that she herself will later on bear a child of her own, which is never possible for her brother. A 5- or 6-year-old child lives in the present time and cannot yet imagine a distant future. The little boy of this age has to find solace in his becoming a father in the distant future, though he will never have a baby in his belly and will never give birth to one. Nor is he told that his future wife will need his semen to become pregnant. Anyhow he does not know what that means, even if the parents try to explain it to him. And the 6-year-old boy is as incapable of visualizing a distant future as is the girl.

Here we come upon a special feature in *human* development, different from the growth toward maturity of our brothers in the animal kingdom. Many newborn animals are able to survive without being dependent on the parents' care. With our next of kin, the chimpanzees, we differ in the length of time of dependency. Chimps need their mothers' care for some 2 years, and after a short adolescence they are mature and able to realize their own family life. The human child at 5-6 years of age is much further advanced in his emotional and fantasy world than he is in his physical development. He must wait some 8-10 years more before he reaches physical maturity.

Human beings have developed a number of intellectual capacities that are usually considered of inestimable value, one of the most valued being the acquisition of a language in symbols and words, the human's privilege. Over millions of years human beings have acquired a great number of qualities, equipping them for conquering forces of nature, for developing science, technology and art. Most humans are very proud of these acquisitions and the attending civilization. However, the question arises whether they are strong enough to bear the *emotional* burden this rapid development of knowledge and technique has brought with it.

I have tried to describe the affective misunderstanding between children and grownups, leading to psychopathology, to competition, envy, hate, aggression, as well as to inhibitions, inertia, and addictions. It seems to me that comparable processes find place in larger unities than a single family. Social groups, countries, continents are fighting each other, not only in words but with deadly weapons. Lust for power, envy, competition, and hate provoke violence with often lethal outcome.

I started to describe a healthy development of little children into adulthood. One of the necessary clues is the final prevailing of love over hate and destruction. Let us hope that similar constructive processes will come into being in the world at large.

45. Notes on "Multiple Personality"

(1981)

The similarity of the concepts, splitting and "multiple personality", has been generally overlooked. Both are originally present in all human beings, both have pathological connotations in clinical usage, but both may actually be obserbed in a wide variety of "normal" psychological phenomena. Some residues of each development phase are preserved in the depth of the mind. These remnants are the constituents of the multiple personality of human beings.

I Introduction

Many psychoanalysts have gained their knowledge of human development mainly by treating patients in their psychoanalytical practice. Thus they became acquainted with *psychopathology*, with *disturbances* in the growth of the human from birth through the various developmental phases into adulthood.

Even at an early stage Freud drew attention to psychic phenomena present in both 'normal' and 'abnormal' people – for instance: dream, parapraxes, the successive phases of the development of the drives, etc. He also stated that there is no *essential* difference between 'normal' and 'abnormal' persons. Whether a human will be "healthy" or "mentally ill" depends upon a variety of factors, among others the interaction of individual endowment of the drives and the potentialities for later ego and superego development, with the influence of the specific environment.

Many psychoanalysts have followed Freud's lead in looking for "normal" psychology and for the various complicated interactions leading to "health" or "sickness". Nevertheless, in a number of instances special phenomena have been described only as "abnormal". In recent times an example is found in descriptions of *"splits" in the personality* and especially in *"multiple personality"*.

The purpose of this paper is to draw attention to my experience that both "splitting" and "multiple personality" are originally present in all normal humans. I will also try to outline some factors which play a role in the final shape of a person's mental functioning, "normal" or "abnormal". I will draw a parallel to another mental phenomenon, which I described (1963) in the pre-published paper I presented at the Stockholm International Congress, "Symptom Formation and Character Formation". In that contribution I was concerned with defense mechanisms and defensive processes. These have usually been seen as leading to psychopathology, whereas I ventured the idea that genetically they are "normal" reactions to conflicts which the little child is unable to resolve. Conflicts are part of all human life. But the question is which are the unsolvable ones in infancy. Here we come upon safe ground. The human infant is completely dependent upon a mothering person for the satisfaction of his bodily needs. However, of equal importance for a smooth development is the gratification of his needs for the mother's love, empathy, and emotional understanding, especially when he has to curb or abtain from the direct satisfaction of part of his drives, his sexual and aggressive impulses. In the little child of one to three years the reactions to the necessary abstaining from the satisfaction of some drives and wishes can promote the progress to the next developmental stage. However, progression may fail because of an unfortunate endowment, because of the lack of the mother's empathic support, or, as is so common, because of a combination of both factors. A fixation to a given phase of drive development and/or an arrest in ego development may occur. The normal progression from one developmental stage to the next one has been very aptly described by Anna Freud in her studies on "the developmental lines"; so I do not need to repeat them in detail. I wish only to stress two points. First, progression is never complete, and under certain circumstances a temporary regression may take place (e.g., when the child is very tired or in distress). Thus a residue of an earlier phase is retained. My second point is that the reaction-formations can become unconscious, but in "normal" development they do not share the rigidity of the pathological defense mechanisms and defensive processes.

II Multiple Personality and "split" personalities

Before going into the factors which determine whether multiple personality is a normal facet of human behavior or a psychopathological phenomenon, I want to say a few words about "normality" and "abnormality". I placed these terms in quotation marks because they are arbitrary designations. First, we have to consider that their objective and subjective meanings may coincide, but often enough they are at variance with one another. Their meaning also differs in various groups and societies, as well as in terms of historical times. I will give a few examples.

1. A psychoanalyst may observe a little child, aged two, who may behave toward a newborn sibling in one moment with tenderness, but may the next moment hit the baby forcefully on the head. The analyst knows that the toddler has not yet progressed from the pleasure-unpleasure principle to the reality principle. Therefore, the observer is not alarmed and considers the behavior "normal", whereas the parents may be very alarmed and afraid that their child is going to be an abnormal person. The child himself experiences his deed completely as a matter of fact.

2. In some societies it is normal to wean a baby after a number of months of breast-feeding and to put him in his crib after feeding, separated from the mother. In other societies the baby is carried on the mother's body for several years and breast-fed on demand, often ten or more times a day. This approach

may be viewed by the parents in more modern societies as one that spoils the baby and harms his development.

3. In ancient Egypt it was a king's duty to marry his sister, whereas at other times incest was considered to be a sign of pathology. In ancient Greece it was a knight's duty to introduce young adolescent boys to sexual life, whereas at other times homosexuality has been seen as abnormal. Some homosexuals may experience their sexual life as completely normal, although others may feel it as a disturbance of their love-life and suffer from it.

4. Another example is the definition of murder. In peacetime a murderer is seen as an abnormal person, whereas in wartime the soldier is ordered to kill another human being and even punished if he refuses to do so.

It is apparently impossible to define normal behavior only from sociological and historical viewpoints. Therefore I return to the study of multiple personality in our time and in the narrower realm of the Western world's definitions. I will give a few examples of actions of persons who feel themselves to be normal and are judged by the environment in the same way, but who reveal that "different" personalities are parts of their make-up. In other words, these persons are capable of making use of an inner, though often unconscious multiplicity of behaviors.

Physicians or psychoanalysts must be different persons when they are working with patients than they are when they are playing with their children at home, are involved with their spouses, or are attending scientific meetings, dinners with colleagues, concerts, the theater, etc. The same is valid for other people, e.g., for teachers who are "different" with their pupils from the way they are at home or in a meeting; or for a workman who behaves in one way at the factory and quite differently when at home or attending a protest meeting with other workmen.

Of course, similar attitudes are present in females, who behave in a completely different way at work – in a factory, as a secretary of a businessman, or as a scientist – from the way they behave in being "good companions" to their men friends or in being loving wives and mothers at home. Sometimes males and females can be very "awkward" persons: for instance, "bad" parents or citizens who are hateful toward the environment.

A number of people complain of feeling psychically unhappy, inhibited, prone to anxieties, suffering from neurotic symptoms or from other more or less severe mental disturbances. They consider themselves (or are considered by their environment) as mentally ill. However, many others feel themselves to be quite "normal" and are experienced by their narrow and wider environment as mentally "healthy" individuals. As mentioned before, this does not mean that the latter have no conflicts and are free from mental pain. But they manage in some way or other to solve their problems and to function to their own satisfaction, perhaps just because they have "multiple personalities" which provide them with various methods of solution. The issues I address here are broader than what can be encompassed by the term "ego-syntonic", because I try to include a view of the totality of the human mind. Why do many psychoanalysts consider "multiple personalities" (and, for that matter, "splits" in a person's mind) per se as indications of illness and/or abnormality? The psychoanalytic profession confronts psychoanalysts continually with disturbed patients. Maybe in their secluded situaton they tend to overlook the majority of human beings who do not feel any need to consult an analyst and who are able to solve their problems without professional help.

We have now come to the question of what factors make human beings mentally "healthy" or mentally "disturbed". In *theory* the answer is a simple one. We know that many ego functions develop gradually during maturation from infancy towards adulthood. A special function is the integrative one (sometimes also called the synthesizing or harmonizing function). If a person is capable of integrating the various demands of his mental inner world and of making a *passive* or *active* adaptation to the outer world, he will feel himself satisfied and "healthy". In *practice* it is a very complicated process to achieve this state of mind. So we have to search for the multitude of factors which may cause failures of the integrative function.

To do so, I turn to metapsychology. Freud used this term to connote a psychology which went beyond the academic psychology of his times, because that psychology equated all psychological phenomena with consciousness. He meant metapsychology to stand for the theory of the unconscious. To this I add the genetic and adaptive viewpoints.

Freud recognized even in his early writings (e.g., Breuer and Freud, 1893-1895; Freud, 1887-1902, 1905, 1909) that the mental disturbances of his adult patients arose in childhood. Dynamic forces actually emerge in early infancy when the demands of bodily needs and for the satisfaction of drives are preponderant. To achieve pleasure and to avoid unpleasure, the infant is dependent on a motherly person. As satisfaction is not always immediately forthcoming, a "split" in the infant's inner world occurs. The conflict between demands and dependency upon the mother promotes the gradual development of ego functions out of innate potentialities. So the conflicts gradually become partly inner conflicts. Psychic structure formation has begun. It is, however, still vulnerable. A number of cognitive functions are developing, and reaction formations against unsatisfied impulses come into being. They evoke resentment and aggression against the mother, who has provided the little child with satisfaction and love as well. Conflicts between need for love and hostility come to the fore. We designate the energy working in the human mind as the economic factor. The amount of energy available to id demands versus the amount of energy at the disposal of the gradually developing ego organization begins to play a major role. However, love and hate, sexual demands, and the necessity imposed by the mother to curb the expression of drives remain side by side for a longer stretch of time. The maturational growth of id, ego, and later on superego and ego ideal asks for a certain harmony, which eventually can be attained if the integrating function is a strong one.

However, progression is not an even, ongoing process. It alternates with regressive attitudes, as is well known. Some *residues of each developmental phase* are preserved in the depth of the mind. *These remnants are the constituents of the multiple personality of human beings.* But what factors make for "normality" or "pathology"?

I will first mention a few examples of the use of multiple personality in a beneficial (normal) way.

1. If a mother, nursing her baby, is able to revive (unconsciously) the normally repressed experiential world of her own babyhood, she will treat her child with empathy and react to his needs in a way that is beneficial for him. If she returns to older children, grown-ups, or work, etc., she will be able to use another facet of her personality and react according to the requirements of those encounters. Apparently it is essential for her well-being *and* for the baby's "basic trust" that the multiple facets of her personality have remained *flexible*.

2. An adult playing with a toddler has to return to the reliving of his own state of mind as a toddler: for instance, to the emotional understanding of the toddler' need for autonomy as well as for closeness (refueling) to make the play enhancing for the little child's development.

3. A teacher who is able to swith from his adult attitude to the still retained facets of his own latency or puberty will promote his pupils' *capacity for and wish to learn*. Here, too, *flexibility* is the essential condition for an optimal functioning as a teacher and educator.

The people mentioned above are normally functioning individuals in many areas of their lives.

I therefore question why many psychoanalysts consider "multiple personality" to be the expression of severe psychopathy. Indeed, in its most flagrant forms, it is so. But are we not failing to recognize that the phenomenon is present in all human beings? Maybe the daily work with *patients* who suffer from a lack of flexibility in regard to continuously re-emerging conflicts that they are unable to meet and to solve makes the analyst overlook the ubiquity of the phenomenon. Moreover, the "splits" in a severely disturbed patient have become *fixed* patterns of behavior, manifested continually and to a more penetrating degree, therefore more recognizable to the analyst. It is one of the patient's tragedies that his integrating ability has been inadequate to further his developmental processes and that he has lost the *flexibility* of switching from one stage of development to the next one and thus from one facet of his personality to another. The patient's "splits" have become structurally and dynamically *"split-off's"*, *fixed* parts of his personality, making him suffer from various symptoms and mental disturbances. Anxieties about feelings of being "split", "fragmented", "torn to pieces", etc., reinforce his disturbances. Often a vicious circle emerges, which cannot be broken through. The gap between his adult personality and the *fixed* patterns of behavior from childhood may make him suffer in the extreme.

Finally, we come to the question: What accounts for a person's ability to retain *flexibility* and what makes a person fixated to archaic modes of behavior leading to unremovable "split-off's" and severe psychopathology?

I mentioned earlier the common knowledge that psychic development is determined by the interaction of the inborn potentials of the drives and ego qualities with the influence of the environment. It is remarkable that in spite of this knowledge there are (and have been) always a number of psychoanalysts who tend to take *pars pro toto*. That means in this case that they either stress the patient's innate inadequacies for a "normal" development, minimizing the influence of the environment, or the other way around. The latter makes merely (or mainly) the mother and the wider environment responsible for the "normal" or "pathological" development of the child.

In wider circles of psychotherapists and workers in the field of mental health it is often taken for granted that all mental disturbances are caused by the milieu, by the wrongs of the present society. A change of society should make all human mental suffering disappear. These people overlook at least two points:

1) that societies are man-made, developed through many generations into the present shape; and

2) that in these "faulty" societies a great number of normal people are living.

These mental health workers have no idea of and therefore ignore the maturational processes through which human beings grow up from infant to adult. They ignore, too, the complicated interactions between the individual's inner world and the outside world, including the fact of the "multiplicities" of all personalities. Possibly they are able to ignore some fixations to early patterns of behavior and the incapacity for flexibility by ascribing every discomfort to bad societal influences. It is well known that through the centuries artists have been quite aware of splits in their persons. I think of Goethe's saying: *"Zwei Seelen wohnen, ach, in meiner Brust"* ("Two souls live within my breast"); of Henry Moore's sculpture of a human being actually split into two parts; of Picasso, who gives expression to multiple personality in many of the portraits he painted. I do not know much of the early development of these (and many other) artists. Perhaps they had "neurotic" problems and some irregularities with fixations in their development. But they were very successful in their artistic lives, able to use the flexibility of switching from one mental state to another. So in many instances they could give expression to their multiple-personality aspects in a constructive way.

Until now I have spoken of multiple personality in a global way. But we must distinguish those aspects of multiple personality from the implications imposed by psychic structure and the consequence of "splits" for the intersystemic functioning of id, ego, and superego. In every human there exists a "split" between the conscious and the unconscious, as the larger part of the little child's experiential world is repressed. This may lead to "normality" as well as to "pathology". However, there may also occur "splits" in the ego organization. Here it is important that, among other factors, the *integrative function* is maintained and not included in a "fixed immobility". Furthermore, splits in the superego and between superego and ego may occur. If this develops without any flexibility, these splits may give rise to severe self-punishment and masochistic behavior. We encounter this in an analysis as the negative therapeutic reaction, so refractory to change. Splits may also occur in the ego ideal and between ego ideal, superego, and ego, preventing the person from creating his own reliable norms, ethics, and ideals.

Although genetically and essentially all humans are "multiple personalities", I think we should take into account that many are "normal" people. We should therefore leave the decision of whether a person is normal or pathological to the person himself (at least as long as he does not do great harm to his fellowmen). If someone feels himself to suffer from his "split" personality, from anxieties of feeling estranged from himself, etc., we should consider psychotherapy if he comes for help.

III Analyzability of Multiple Personality

This brings me to the practical question of the analyzability of "split" personalities. A number of colleagues are of the opinion that, for instance, severe anxieties, strong sadomasochistic fantasies, and/or fantasies of omnipotence alternating with overvaluation of parental figures are contraindications for psychoanalytic treatment. In my experience the reverse is true. Those disturbances can *efficiently* be treated *only* by psychoanalysis. It may prove to be rewarding if the analyst has enough empathy with the experiential world of the infant and the little child. In my opinion analyzability depends upon *some* ego functions, especially the integrative one, being available and more or less flexible, although other functions may be stalled in the "split-off" part of the patient's ego. It is often not easy to conclude from a few interviews whether the ego functions are flexible enough to tolerate mood swings, anxieties, etc., and to establish a working alliance with the analyst. I abstain from using psychiatric diagnosis in cases where an average (or a high) intelligence is present and where there are no signs of severe schizophrenia, senility, idiocy, etc. Labeling, such as "character neurosis", "borderline", etc., often leads to rigidity on the part of the analyst, tying him to some prejudice. In my experience quite a number of multiple personalities are analyzable. In dubious cases one has to take into account: *first*, that a prudent scanning is necessary; *second*, that *patience* is *essential*; *third*, that the analyst must have the empathic capacity for a feeling understanding of the experiential world of the infant. If this capacity is lacking or insufficient, the analyst's unconscious anxiety will make him unable to tolerate a *temporary* regression in himself toward the archaic level of functioning; this may hamper the analytic process so that it cannot emerge and run its course in a favorable direction for the patient. Among others, the archaic modes of aggressive behavior, which are of a complete destructiveness, belong to the most difficult ones to master for the analyst as well as for the patient.

If the analysis is successful the patient's fixed patterns of behavior may gradually be loosened and freed. Then his integrative capacity may improve and a more or less satisfying, harmonious life may be opened up.

46. Thoughts on Psychoanalytic Views of Female Psychology 1927-1977

(1982)

The stimulus for this article was the publication of *Female Psychology: Contemporary Psychoanalytic Views*, a volume edited by H. Blum (1977) which contains eighteen articles written by twenty-three authors on a subject which has concerned me for half a century.

My very first psychoanalytic paper was titled, "The Evolution of the Oedipus Complex in Women" (1927) In it I referred to a negative oedipal situation: the girl attempts to win the mother's sexual love and wishes to take her father's place with the mother, just as a boy does in his positive oedipal situation. In "normal" development she has to accept the anatomical fact that she lacks the male organ, and this recognition thrusts her into the positive oedipal position. At the time of writing that paper I was still a very young analyst with barely five years of experience. How did I dare to write the article? The courage to do so was given to me by Sigmund Freud. In 1925 I went to Berlin to work at the Institute of Psychoanalysis after the termination of (the first part of) my personal analysis. In saying goodbye, Freud added this to his good wishes: *"Und jetzt sollten Sie Ihre eigenen Erfahrungen niederschreiben"* ("And now you should write of your own experiences"). I felt "flabbergasted" and said: "Oh no, that is impossible. You yourself have already written everything." Freud laughed and answered: *"Ich habe nur Anfänge gemacht, Ihr solltet fortsetzen"* ("I have only made beginnings, the younger generation should continue").

In reading and rereading Freud's work, I realized that in 1905 he had described the oral, anal, and phallic phases of the child's sexual development, but that object relations, while mentioned, were not elaborated upon in equivalent detail for the preoedipal phases. I wondered about this lack because in my own analysis I had experienced and worked through my very early bonds with parents and siblings. It is worthwhile mentioning here that in the early twenties there were still no practicing child analysts. Hug-Hellmuth did some analytic work with children (although not with the very young) and, as far as I remember, this was more educational than analytic. Melanie Klein and Anna Freud had just started to develop child analysis. The only published case was the "indirect" analysis of Little Hans by Freud (1909). Systematic infant observation started much later, mainly after Freud's death. The only observation of a small child was published by Freud in *Beyond the Pleasure Principle* (1920, pp. 14-16): the now famous description of a one-and-a-half-year-old boy's playful reaction to his mother's absence.

Freud's statement that he knew much more about the development of the male child has caused many people, including psychoanalysts, to overlook his remarkable contributions to the understanding of the development of the little girl. He himself had grown up in what is called a "paternalistic" environment. And certainly his female patients were particularly burdened in childhood with sexual taboos which contributed to creating severe (unconscious) guilt feelings in connection with every kind of drive manifestation. Masturbation and the accompanying fantasies in early childhood were "sins" and were severely punished. In puberty the larger society underlined the threatening consequences by attributing to masturbation such terrible bodily illnesses as destruction of the spinal cord. In the meantime the youngster had acquired a severe and cruel superego, often under the additional influence of religious strictures. The prohibitions and punishments affected *both* sexes. Yet, it seemed that girls were more inhibited than boys. What were the reasons for these differences? Freud described the more complicated oedipal situation in girls compared with that in boys. Girls had to change their love object (from mother to father) and, according to Freud, also the phallic (genital) zone of sexual stimulation (from clitoris to vagina).

It is a well-known but nevertheless remarkable fact that Freud in the early thirties wrote two articles about the *preoedipal phase* of the *girl*, giving an extensive description of the love-hate bond with the mother, the longings and the frustrations in normal and pathological development (Freud, 1931, 1933). He never did the same for the male child. We do not know Freud's intentions in this respect. Perhaps he felt that *the similarities and the differences* between male and female development in the preoedipal phase were self-evident.

By the 1920's a number of analysts, most of them female, began to investigate the prehistory of the oedipus complex in the female, with special emphasis on object relations.[1]

When one compares these early papers with the group collected in the 1977 volume edited by Blum, one immediately notices that the *contents* of the papers have different thematic emphases. In the intervening fifty years psychoanalytic knowledge has advanced in many areas. Today we know much more about the development of the instinctual drives and their biological sources, about object relationships throughout life, about normal and pathological ego, superego, and ego ideal, about special pubertal maturational factors, as well as those in later periods of the life cycle. Moreover, rapid changes in cultural and social mores and in the mass media of communication have altered norms and value systems and have been of significant influence upon the psychic and even the physical development of the human species.

It is remarkable that in both periods a number of authors have expressed their criticisms of Freud's works, often *not* in an objective, scientific way, but with more or less violent emotional attacks. Most of them were female analysts, and there were more of them in the first period (the 1920's) than in the later one.

---

[1] These contributors include Karen Horney (1923, 1926, 1928), Josine Müller (1931), Helene Deutsch (1925, 1930), and Melanie Klein (1928, 1932). I wrote the article mentioned above in 1927 and a second one, "On the Problems of Femininity" in 1933. One of the male analysts who wrote about female sexuality was Ernest Jones (1927, 1935).

The main issue on which controversies (and criticisms) centered in the 1920's concerned Freud's description of the phallic-oedipal phase. In Freud's formulation the girl's sexual involvement turned toward the passive feminine love attachment to the father consequent upon her accepting the lack of the male organ. This change was accompanied by a strong *"Penisneid,"* penis envy, and an increase of hostility toward the mother, whom the girl made responsible for her "inferior" organ. In the oral and anal phases of development the girl behaved "like a little man," according to Freud. However, this last postulation gives rise to serious questions. The equation of masculinity with activity and of femininity with passivity is based on adult sexual behavior, human as well as that of other higher species in the animal kingdom. For instance, with many mammals the male springs upon the female in the reproductive act. Sperm is actively discharged into the vagina (or cloaca) that "receives" it. However, in the nonreproductive behavior of human beings, both males and females show both passive and active aims and actions with few clear-cut distinctions of the kind Freud's formulation implied. In my 1927 paper I followed Freud's view. But soon I became aware of the richness of the earlier preoedipal phase in which girls do display much active behavior. In my second paper I corrected my former formulation. Freud himself had already expressed doubts about equating male with active and female with passive (though in his later writings he sometimes returned to this idea). The importance of penis envy has been demonstrated again and again. However, there are differences of opinion regarding its origin. Authors like Horney, Josine Müller, and others reported observations of girl infants who masturbated on the vulva and in the vagina in addition to stimulating the clitoris at the age of one and a half years. According to these authors, this meant that "femininity" and "feminine identity" were already being experienced at that early age. They repudiated Freud's statement that although infantile genital play takes place, it is penis envy and the "masculinity complex" at the phallic-oedipal stage of development which make the girl, from approximately three to five years, feel "feminine," at least in *normal* development. Their conclusion, briefly summarized, was that penis envy at the phallic period is a "secondary" product. I could not, and still cannot, agree with their argument.

I have not made systematic infant observations, but I have observed many infants during my lifetime. I think it is true that infants experience pleasure from stimulation of many parts of the body. In the oral phase the mouth and the oral cavity play a special role. In the anal phase the anus and the nearby genital zones are centers for pleasure-seeking. But during the pregenital-preoedipal phases, the *whole body*, including the genital area, if stroked and manipulated, provides sexual pleasure in both boys and girls. If not intimidated by adults, male and female infants and toddlers display activity and passivity in similar ways. In my experience, there are in these early stages more *individual* differences than gender variations. Of course a girl toddler may be interested in the fact that her brother's or her playmate's way of urinating is so different from her own. But curiosity is present in both sexes. Equally important, envy, competition, and jealousy play a central role in the lives of little children (in adults as well, for that matter!). When one toddler is playing peacefully with blocks and another with motorcars, each will invariably try to grab the other's plaything with passion. Still more passionate is the fight over mother's (or father's) attention, love, and approval.

A toddler's "love," whether the child is a boy or a girl, is self-centered; it is called "narcissistic." The possibility of *sharing* affection and even materials is not yet present. Variations in behavior provoked by frustrations, envy, and rivalry are influenced by innate endowment, especially of the force of aggressive drives. Of course the adult's attitude toward the little one is of paramount importance as well. I will come back to this factor later on.

From my experience, I must conclude that the "real" violent, "fateful" penis envy comes to the fore only in the phallic-(genital-)oedipal phase. Now the child's fantasy life centers on rivalry with the parents. It is well known that the child's fantasies are always of a sadomasochistic nature. The "fateful" disappointment the little girl experiences when she learns that in reality she is unable to compete with her father and to take his place in "possessing" mother strikes a hard blow to her self-esteem. In "normal" development she gradually adjusts to this impossibility and turns to the father as her love object. That means that in her fantasies she renounces sexual activity and tries to obtain father's love with passive surrender. Of course, in other areas of her life there is opportunity for activity, for instance in play in kindergarten and in school as latency sets in and in many kinds of sublimated performances.

Although the girl's oedipal situation is more complicated than the boy's, the development of *envy* in the boy is similar to that in the girl. In the overlapping of the anal and phallic developmental stages, the little boy's envy is directed toward mother (and women in general). One can observe rather often a little boy playing at being with child, for instance, by inserting a pillow into his pants and proudly announcing that he is going to make a baby. His own products (feces) have been devaluated and thrown away during toilet training. And now he observes that mother's "product" is highly valued, admired, and loved. He is envious of her and feels jealousy toward the "product" as well. On his part, then, he must renounce his fantasies of being equal to mother in her sexual and propagative capacities. Normally, the little boy imagines himself as his mother's lover, and as he identifies with the father-figure he moves further toward a masculine identity, a strengthened superego, and more attainable ideas. His passive strivings are sublimated and may participate in his acceptance of non-sexual social relationships, as well as in the incorporation of the knowledge presented to him by teachers, books, etc.

It is well known how easily deviations from the healthy course of development may occur. In the genital-oedipal phase the main obstacle is the difficulty of overcoming the castration complex. For the girl this means switching over to the feminine attitude in her sexual fantasy life and channeling her active strivings into sublimated performances. The boy must master castration anxiety, which has two sources: his fear of his father's retaliation in connection with the positive oedipus, and, even more persistent, his fear in the negative oedipal position derived from his passive (feminine) strivings. Of course, the prerequisite for becoming his father's sexual partner is the renunciation of his genitals. Although the girl's growing up is usually seen as a more difficult process in connection, for instance, with the change of the love object, I should not dare to minimize the problems of the boy in mastering his anxieties. In recent years I have often been asked: "Why don't you write about femininity and female sexuality after a half-century of experience?" My answer, up to now, has always been: "Because female sexuality does not interest me more than does male sexuality. It is more fascinating for me to try to look at the differences as well as the similarities of the maturational processes in both sexes." Moreover, my interest became gradually more focused on wider aspects of human mental development and of man's interactions with specific environmental influences (see chapters 7, 14, 31, 34, 37).

Here I have to venture an opinion about the authors of the 1920's who expressed their newly found observations of female infants not only in objective ways, but often with passionate hostility, accusing Freud of being a misogynist. I myself never experienced any special hatred of women in Freud. I should like to cite a letter of Freud's published in a volume edited by Ernst L. Freud (1960). Freud adds to his congratulations at the birth of our first (girl) child: "I . . . am even inclined to think that with today's attitude toward the sexes it doesn't make a great difference whether the baby is manifestly male or female. Especially as a clear predominance in one direction can be compensated to your liking by the results of future experiments" (p. 365). I can only guess that the hostile criticisms, especially from female authors, are based on their value system. They seem to feel the terms "penis envy" and "female passivity" are degrading to the female sex, forgetting the equally intense envy in male children, especially in regard to their desire to produce a *living* product, a child. The difficulty of all of us human beings, female and male, in dealing adequately with the calamities inherent in the oedipal situation as a consequence of the long dependence on adults and the dual flowering of sexuality (childhood and puberty) makes for unconquered residues of castration anxiety and penis envy. As I mentioned earlier, the shape of the oedipal situation is strongly influenced by the events of the preoedipal phase and thus by the attitudes and conventions of the child's milieu.

This brings me to the second period, the 1970's, in which another mass of publications on female sexuality and femininity has appeared. During the intervening decades, not only had the number of psychoanalysts increased, but so had the number of places in the world where analysis is practiced. Emigration from Vienna and Germany in the years before World War II had enlarged the British Society. Still more analysts had settled in the United States, while Latin America was also a beneficiary of the exodus from Europe. With this territorial and numerical expansion came extensions of theory as well.

In the study of female development, major contributions have come from work in the allied fields of biology and physiology and from new appreciation of the influences of environmental factors and of the social milieu.

Biological research has revealed that the genitals start to develop in the embryo under the influence of hormones some seven weeks after conception. Some authors, Sherfey (1966) for example, have drawn the conclusion that all embryos start by being female. This is an apparent error, since whether an individual will become male or female has already been determined by the chromosomes in the fertilized egg. Sherfey and others who "use" biology for polemical purposes present new forms of the old opposition to the "supposed" "inferiority" of woman. Their approach is to try to make her "superior"!

Masters and Johnson's (1966) work represents another current approach to the experimental study of sexuality. In their examination of physiological processes in sexual behavior, in coitus as well as in masturbation, they observed that female orgasm involves the total genital apparatus, including the pelvic muscles. It can start with stimulation of the clitoris, but also of the vulva and the vagina. In childhood the nerve endings of the vagina are not yet excitable. This process starts only in puberty. So full vaginal (and pelvic) orgasm is possible only in adolescence and adulthood. But there exist very many individual differences in the way orgasm is reached. The widespread idea that clitoral orgasm in adulthood is "abnormal" is untenable, as it may be part of a female's complete mature sexual satisfaction. Although Masters and Johnson's studies were "laboratory experiments," I can confirm their statements from quite a number of interviews with "healthy" women.

Such additions to our knowledge can be valuable stimuli to the further growth of analytic theory and to more accurate clinical observations by analysts. Freud's early theory that sexual excitability has to be *transferred* from the clitoris to the vagina needs revision in the sense that deep vaginal orgasm is *added* to the clitoral one in puberty. Analytic theory must also take account of the fact that the total genital region takes part in the adult's orgastic experience. As for the second source of new knowledge, the influences of environmental factors and of the social milieu, the principle of these influences was already acknowledged by Freud (1920, pp. 239-240) in the so-called "complemental series" (*die Ergänzungsreihe*). But clinical studies of the preoedipal phase, combined with the findings of child observers (like Anna Freud and her co-workers, René Spitz, Margaret Mahler, and others), have provided us with an extensive picture of the infant's and the toddler's experiential world and their rich object relationships.

Some authors conclude from the observation of little girls aged one to one and a half years, who discover their vulvas and their vaginal orifices, that they develop a "female identity" at this time, especially if the mothers address them as "my girl." I think these conclusions are "adultomorphisms." First, the pleasure gained from rubbing the entrance and lower part of the vagina is not much different from that of rubbing other parts of the body, from mouthing and sucking, or from stimulating the anus, etc. If the little girl envies a little boy's penis, the envy is not much different from the envy of other possessions of the boy, his toys, etc. Little children aged one to one and a half of *both* sexes are unaware of what the implications of sex differences will be at later ages. The term "identity" is used in different and confusing contexts in the literature. I myself prefer to speak of the "sense of identity," by which I mean the awareness of "I am I," in some way separate from other persons. I think that "sexual identity," in the sense we ordinarily mean, develops in the phallic-oedipal phase and is characterized by fantasies in which boys and girls "identify" with adults in their sexual lives as little children imagine them.

Second, at the early age of twelve to eighteen months the *words* "girl" and "boy" do not mean much to infants in connection with sex differences. Of course, the attitude and feeling tones with which parents use the words do have an impact on the child. If the parents pronounce them with love and tenderness, the child will feel accepted on his/her own. If a disappointed parent uses the words with animosity or hostility, children of both sexes will feel rejected and worthless. In these ways the shape of preoedipal object relations will influence the outcome of the oedipal situation to a high degree. We confront here the importance of a little child's environment (the family or its substitute) upon his or her growing up. In our sophisticated (Western) world, most adults have lost much necessary empathy with the experiential world of the little child which is so different from the adult one. In early childhood the idea of "relative" satisfaction or frustration does not yet exist. The infant expects that its bodily needs will be *immediately* and completely satisfied, as will the demands of its libidinal and aggressive drives. Its object attachment is still of a "narcissistic" nature. Every disappointment and frustration is experienced as a blow to its sense of self, a loss of self-esteem. As a compensation, it gradually develops a primitive fantasy life of grandeur and omnipotence. Because these fantasies invariably collide with reality, the child feels powerless anew. Then, he or she starts to overidealize the parents. But the child again meets with disappointment on beginning to discover the imperfections of grown-ups. For the little child every event is an "al or nothing" experience.

Disappointment gives rise to aggressive behavior and may contribute to "temper tantrums" for which the child is scolded and punished. The child then feels unloved and powerless and may cling anew to grandiose fantasies. This state of affairs may impair the "normal" unfolding of the oedipal situation. A "real" object relationship in the sense that the object is loved in his or her own right (and not exclusively as a need-satisfying object) does not develop adequately. These developmental vicissitudes apply equally to girl and boy.

If the parents *do* have the necessary empathy with the infantile experiential world, they can accompany the different stages of their child's development with loving care and tolerance, but also with necessary support when their child meets with inevitable restrictions. I agree with those authors who are of the opinion that the oedipal situation occurs at an earlier age than Freud originally thought. Many children reach this stage of development at two and one half to four years. There are, however, many individual differences, dependent upon endowment and environmental influences. It is astonishing to observe the rapidity with which a "normal" and intelligent newborn acquires emotional as well as intellectual capacities in a short period of time. The oedipal child imagines himself or herself capable of replacing one of the parents in his or her love and sexual life even though the *real* facts of adult sexuality are not understood. It is a severe blow for the child's self-esteem when he or she realizes the impossibility of fulfillment of these desires.

To recapitulate what I outlined earlier, the girl's difficulty is greater because her development is more complicated. She not only has to change her love object from mother to father, she has the additional problem of accepting receptivity and the change in her sexual role in her fantasy life. It is well known that a good deal of active wooing may be used to effect a (passive) feminine orgasm and a satisfying love-life. As the girl becomes aware of the role of the male organ, having often observed and envied the little boy's pleasure in the way he can use his penis to urinate, her penis envy reaches its peak. At the same time she has to overcome her increased hostility to the (also loved) mother, whom she makes responsible for her lack of the male organ. The difficulties of the little boy's oedipal situation are often overlooked or minimized: he has to overcome his *"Gebährneid,"* his envy of the female capacity to bear children (to produce a "living" product), as well as his castration anxiety. However, it seems that nature has made it more difficult for an active and sensitive child to give up *active* sexual strivings and to change the sexual love object, as the girl has to do, than it is to solve the problems in the reverse situation, as the boy must do. Maybe this state of affairs accounts for the greater animosity and hostility among adult females, especially the "feminists," to the idea that the inner mental development and the sexual life of both sexes is predestined by biology. However, analysts do, in fact, recognize the paramount importance the environment plays in every developmental phase in the maturation of human beings.

In the postoedipal and latency period the child's environment is greatly widened. In addition to the family, the kindergarten and school milieus exercise their influence, from the side of the teachers as well as from the peer group. So much depends on the emotional atmosphere created by the school staff. If the child has gone through a fortunate development in the preoedipal and oedipal phases in regard to the drives, object relationships, and ego development, he or she usually will reach a kind of "healthy" mixture of passive and active adaptation to the demands of the new environment. It goes without saying that an early disturbed development may lead to maladaptations and learning disabilities.

I will now turn to the girl's specific postoedipal problems. Residues of her early competition with boys may come to the fore in "tomboyishness." I would not call this an "abnormal" event unless it persists into adolescence and adulthood. Then, it may lead to a disturbed feminine love-life. A number of traumatic happenings may hamper a child's development from birth on. These commonly include: jealousy of a younger sibling, illnesses of the child and of family members, deaths of parents or siblings, etc. The girl's vulnerability of early childhood may be reawakened in adolescence. A kind of repetition of early childhood experiences takes place. Since in the meantime she has acquired a critical superego and an ego ideal, her reactions to traumatic events are much more complicated. The physical maturation into womanhood requires new ways of dealing with herself as a female, physically as well as psychologically. Normally, a girl is proud of her menstruation and of the growth of her breasts. However, many pathological developments may interfere with this desirable maturational direction. For example, a girl may have given up masturbation, repressed her "feminine" fantasy life, and in the aftermath of unresolved early envy of the little boy and infantile resentment of the mother, she may feel no pleasure in her developing female body and may transfer her revived resentments against her mother to the male sex. The manifold and confusing upheavals of adolescent girls are well known and beyond the scope of this paper.

Instead, I will now turn to the general social outcomes of the female's inability to accept the feminine role in her love-life when, in addition, she cannot find adequate use for her active strivings in intellectual, artistic, or other "sublimated" activities. Anthropologists tell us that once, in ancient times, matriarchy ruled societies. In historical times, patriarchy prevailed, at least in the "civilized" world. In earlier centuries a number of singular women, perhaps also small groups of them, revolted against male domination. But in general it was accepted that women gave birth to children, looked after them, and attended to the household.

In more recent times major social and political movements ask for "equal" rights for females and males in modern societies. Insofar as women and men are *human beings* equipped with equal intelligence and with similar capacities for acquiring knowledge in contributing to scientific, artistic, and other activities, as well as for understanding and working in all human and societal affairs, "emancipation" has to be accepted. This means that the achievements of equal merit of both sexes should be valued and rewarded to the same extent. In many societies female labor, for instance, is still underpaid in comparison to the man's. This state of affairs is in need of correction. However, some radical feminist groups do not ask only for social equivalence, they claim superiority of females over males. Some of the "feminists" even keep to the "fantasy" that they can "produce" children without a male. I know, for instance, of cases where women have had intercourse with a number of men, one shortly after another. Since nobody knows who the father of the child is, the woman can enjoy the (infantile) fantasy of having "made" the baby all alone. In other cases two women living in a lesbian relationship believe they can obviate the need for a father for the growing child. They undertake the upbringing of the child, imagining they are doing it *better* than the real father could do. Psychoanalysis can account for this belief and conduct. The attitude of these feminists is built on a reaction formation to an (unconscious) feeling of *inferiority*. Individually it reflects residues of the little girl's penis envy which were insufficiently overcome. It is rationalized by pointing to the actual social suppression of women's activities during long stretches of history. I would emphasize that there is an important distinction between emancipation, insuring that society grants and preserves equal rights, and the radical feminist movement, insofar as it claims superiority of females over males.

Feminists, female and male, find support in the modern general tendency to attribute all human suffering only to the present shape of society. These adherents of a political position neglect the complicated psychical development of individuals, and of smaller and larger groups, in their complex interactions

416

with manifold economic, political, and other factors which finally shape each individual society. It is my hope that social psychologists will be able to look at societal problems with a broad view of all the factors involved.

Returning to the theme of female psychology, I want to stress once again that the special difficulties of the little oedipal girl in accepting a feminine passive attitude in sexuality, while retaining her active strivings for sublimated performances, are once more activated in puberty and adolescence. But now she has obtained an inner conscience, a superego directing her conduct and an ego ideal giving her moral and ethical ideals. Her sense of "female identity" can now be consolidated in "healthy" development. She has acquired the capacity for *"real, adult"* love, which means she has become able to add to a mature sexual satisfaction various refined forms of loving her partner as another individual. Tenderness, appreciation, comradeship, etc., are of the utmost importance in adult love life. It is a special capacity of human beings to be able to enlarge a sexual relationship with this wide scope of differentiated feelings. It goes without saying that an "ideal" situation is hardly reached. However, even an approximation may enhance the lives of the woman and her family. If the woman wants to combine family life with work outside, she must face realistic problems of coordinating and apportioning her energies and time, without doing harm to the children while functioning well in the work situation. Many "modern" women leave their babies in day-care facilities, sometimes for a whole day, not realizing how much harm this may do to the baby's development. It requires an emotional understanding and empathy with a little child's experiential world, combined with well-balanced deliberations between both parents to achieve a reasonable, effective result in bringing up a child. A deep self-knowledge of her talents and of her limitations and her "healthy" sense of feminine identity are indispensable if the mother is to combine the two tasks. It is also necessary that she be aware of the fact that a change in the society will *not* bring "paradise" on earth, that it is only *one* of the factors for a necessary improvement in the world of human beings. The "working" woman is in principle neither superior nor inferior to a man. The same applies to her sisters who devote themselves to family life, without having the wish or the opportunity to do other work as well. Also, those women who do not want to have children and are not suffering from a neurotic inhibition should not be considered either "inferior" or "superior." Why should not a woman be free to make her own choice? However, a woman who decides to remain without child deprives herself of a natural experience of satisfaction, happiness, and joy available to the human species.

Unfortunately, the "striving for power" and the sometimes "dictatorial" attitude of the so-called social reformers often tend to maintain in both males and females the idea that females are not equal to males. Psychoanalysis has invariably found that it is competition, envy, jealousy, and aggression that threaten "love" and may damage "harmony" in human relationships, among individuals as well as with the society at large. While much has changed, this recognition has been kept steadily through all the decades of the twentieth century.

47. On the Process of Mourning

(1983)

In 1922, when I came to Vienna to be trained in psychoanalysis, I met Marianne
Rie, who then was still a medical student. We soon became friends. Marianne
was a warm, lovely young girl, perhaps a little shy. But so was I at that time.
Later on I moved to Berlin to gain more experience at the Berlin institute,
which was then the best and most flourishing psychoanalytic training center. I
married Dr. Hans Lampl and, in 1933, when Hitler came to power, we again
settled in Vienna, Hans's birthplace. In the meantime the psychoanalytic scene
had changed. The Vienna psychoanalytic society and institute had become
prominent, with a number of young, bright, and gifted analysts working there
productively. Whereas in my Berlin days Marianne and I had met only occasionally, we saw much of each other in the '30s. Marianne, too, had married. As
a wife and mother, she had become a mature woman, as lovely and likable as
she had always been. Moreover, having completed her training, she became a
valued colleague.

We were separated again in 1938 when Hitler overran Austria. Our friends
emigrated mostly to England and the United States, as did the Kris family. We
went to Holland, my native country. Good fortune allowed us to survive the
German occupation. After the war, in 1946, Hans and I were invited by our
friends to the States, where we renewed our friendships and saw a good deal of
Marianne once more. We also continued to meet at congresses and other
analytic scientific meetings.

After both of us were widowed, Marianne in 1957 and I in 1958, the two of us
became even closer. We always got together whenever I went to New York or
she came to England. In the '70s we were together quite a few times with Anna
Freud and Dorothy Burlingham. The "four old ladies" had many a good time
together.

On the mourning process in children

In 1976, I wrote a paper on "Mourning in a 6-Year-Old Girl" that originally was
written in honor of Marianne on the occasion of her 75th birthday. Marianne
wrote to me that she liked it very much, especially because she agreed with me
that a child who has achieved some structuralization of the mind is capable of
mourning the death of a beloved person in a way that is not much different from
an adult's reaction, whereas many authors continue to deny a child's capacity to
mourn.[1]

---

[1] See Furman (1974) for a comprehensive review.

This is in sharp contrast to the overuse of the term "mourning" that has become prevalent in recent years. Some analysts describe the reaction to disappointments, frustrations, loss of love, the experience of powerlessness, feeling injured, etc., as mourning. For example, a younger colleague asked me how a postoedipal child copes with his "mourning." I think that this extended use of mourning blurs the precision of a valuable psychoanalytic concept. In analytic theory (Freud, 1917), mourning is a *process* that includes the gradual coping with the distress and pain caused by the *death* of a beloved one and the bereaved person's ability finally to invest another object with "libido" (as Freud called it originally, but later on widened to "drive energy").

In my 1976 paper I suggested the idea that an infant and preoedipal child lack the capacity to do just that. The very young child may feel bewilderment, pain, longing, distress, etc., but he or she is not able to cope with the finality of death and to shift libido to another object. The infant's reaction to death does not yet differ from his response to a parent's brief absence, or to being reprimanded by an angry mother, because the very young child has not yet acquired a cognitive notion of "future."

The postoedipal child, the adolescent, and the adult, however, *have* learned that absence of a love object does not mean "forever," whereas death does. Thus, if the oedipal disappointment of the child is referred to as "mourning," the term is misused. The postoedipal child does not actually *lose* the parent whom he wants to be his sexual love object. A relationship continues to exist, though a much more ambivalent one, sometimes with more hostility and hate than sublimated love. In fact, individual reactions may differ very much; but one can observe that the actual death of a beloved one – parent, sibling, or grandparent – usually has a more traumatic impact than the estrangement caused by disappointments and frustrations due to lack of fulfillment of infantile sexual desires and fantasies.

Latency children, adolescents, and adults know intellectually that a dead person never returns; emotionally they all more or less deny this fact. In pathological cases, the denial cannot be corrected. If it overwhelms the personality, some circumscribed delusions may take hold of part of the personality and continue to exist in the unconscious. In extreme cases, a delusional psychosis may be the outcome. Various inner and outer factors determine whether a mourning process will lead to a "normal" or to a "disturbed" mental life. Among the many factors I draw attention to three: (1) a person's ability to master his unconscious guilt feelings and his need for punishment due to repressed infantile death wishes toward the deceased parent or sibling; (2) the overcoming of his unconscious triumph over the deceased: "You are dead, I am alive" – the survivor guilt; (3) the capability to sublimate destructive impulses into constructive activities.

Mourning in adult life

In our middle years we encounter some age-specific life crises and losses, but I believe that here too we should not speak of mourning unless the event involves the death of a beloved person. Women in the menopause around age 50 may feel depressed, worthless, and weak. In my opinion, this is a neurotic reaction, as many women cope very well with the normal physiological process that ends the period of propagation and the ability to give birth to a child. Much depends upon their wish and capability to find other fields of activity.

With men one also speaks of "menopause." Some men feel distressed when their physical strength diminishes. They may become conscious of a fear of death and an anxiety about the prospect of their sexual potency diminishing. The latter, too, is a neurotic overanxiety. Sexual potency can be retained into old age. A depressive state of mind points to the reemergence of a neurotic disposition. Of course, if a life partner, a child, or another beloved relative dies, we expect a mourning process to start, but it may run the "normal" course already described.

Another typical distress that needs to be overcome during this phase of life is presented by the fact that children become independent adults and leave the parental home. But this belongs to the normal course of life as well. Much joy and satisfaction can be found in a grandparent's position, as well as in work and social activities, whether it is housework such as cooking and sewing and carpentry, or intellectual and artistic occupations, or a job performed outside the home.

As we grow older, other tasks confront us. One of the main ones concerns retirement from work. Most institutions in Western countries set a mandatory retirement age around 65 to 70 years. At present, however, there is a trend in many countries toward increasingly lowering the age of retirement – a trend that is dictated by economic and political factors rather than a person's ability to perform his job. From a psychological point of view, it is remarkable to observe the many differences in people's reaction to forced retirement. Some feel relieved, especially if their work was unsatisfactory or performed in an unpleasant environment. They may feel even "younger" and busy themselves with hobbies, ranging from painting and redecorating their house, gardening, taking trips, reading, studying, writing, to pursuing many forms of art. Others are distressed, desolate, angry, or depressed, and feel themselves to be real old-agers. They may even look many years older and become prone to hypochondriasis and fantasied physical illnesses or in fact undergo a rapidly accelerated aging process.

Old age – and I leave open the question when it starts – brings other important losses. The strength of the body declines; many organs fail to function well; mobility may be restricted; in some instances memory and other psychological functions may be diminished. All these contribute to a sense of loss of a self that cannot be regained. While I personally believe that the term mourning should be restricted to the actual loss of a love object, others might be inclined to include narcissistic considerations and extend the term mourning to parts of the self that have indeed been irretrievably lost, though here too interests may be channeled into new directions, comparable to a bereaved person's investment of new objects.

But old-agers not only have to confront the decline of their own capacities.

They have usually lost, and continue to do so, very many persons dear to their hearts — parents and other relatives, marital partners, possibly children or grandchildren, and usually very many, more or less intimate friends. How can one cope with so many bereavements? How can one master the pain and distress, the feelings of loneliness and abandonment? How can an old-ager shift not only his or her libido but also the need for warmth, closeness, sharing thoughts and interests, etc., to new objects?

Some people even in their 80s and 90s might find new outlets and interests and under favorable conditions actually do. The individual variations of the mourning process are great indeed. But with declining age the opportunities for finding new love objects actually decrease. Perhaps what old people cathect instead are the memories of their past positive and satisfying relations. Retaining fine and happy memories is a wonderful blessing. Marianne left me many of them, for which I am very thankful.

Bibliographical Notes

(i.)   The Preface is edited by Bess Bernstein.
(i.i.)   The Chapters of the Development of the Mind are in this edition indicated with numbers. 1 up to and included 28. Only 25 is inserted for chronological reasons.
(i.i.i.) Foreword of the Development of the Mind, written by Anna Freud. London, March, 1965.

The author of this book belongs to a small but prominent group of psychoanalysts who served their apprenticeship in Vienna in the twenties of the century and who are now, one after the other, approaching, celebrating, or looking back on their 70th birthday.

The members of this group were fortunate in their professional career in several respects. They entered the analytic field late enough to be spared many of the setbacks, hardships, and attacks by a hostile world to which the pioneering generation had been subjected. They were early enough, on the other hand, to be taught by the originator of psychoanalysis himself, and to develop their ideas in lively interchange with him. They entered the Vienna Society when scientific life there was at its height. And, when this Society broke up, they dispersed all over the world, to become the mainstay of analytic branches elsewhere, valued teachers in new analytic Institutes, editors of or contributors to analytic journals, and guiding figures in the International Psycho-Analytical Association. Jeanne Lampl-de Groot is conducting her life as an analyst in conformity with this exacting tradition. In practical terms this implies that she does a great deal of hard work with minimal interruptions; that she carries out as many analytic treatments herself as she supervises therapy done by others; that by means of training analyses, seminar and lecture work, she cooperates in producing succeeding generations of well-informed and capable representatives and teachers of psychoanalysis. It implies above all that she extracts from her activities the insights needed to break new ground and increase the volume of psychoanalytic knowledge, a task to which she brings considerable acumen, conscientiousness, prudence, and complete scientific integrity. That her interest embraces a wide range of psychoanalytic problems and that, with her, theoretical deduction never appears divorced from clinical experience, is borne out by the scope, the quality, and the variety of papers presented in this book.

(i.v.)   Introduction of The Development of the Mind, written by the author. Amsterdam, February, 1965.

In this volume have been assembled most of my contributions to psychoanalysis written between 1927 and 1964. Many of them appear here in English for the first time and several chapters have never been published before. They are presented in chronological order and almost entirely in the original form. Though at the present time I probably would formulate some of the phenomena and ideas put forward in the earlier papers in a slightly different way, I preferred to present the original text because I feel that in this way a certain development of my understanding of human mental processes comes to the fore more naturally.

Like every psychoanalyst I am greatly indebted to Sigmund Freud, and I always tried to start my contributions from observations and from the body of theoretical concepts he presented to the world. I was encouraged by Freud to enlarge and to modify some of his hypotheses and conceptualizations whenever newly gained material made it necessary. As psychoanalytic theory is still a growing body of science, there will have to be more extensions and modifications in the future. The essential discoveries, however, we owe to Freud. His basic finding of the existence of an unconscious part of the mind, not only in a descriptive sense but as a system separated from the conscious part by mental forces (countercathexis), stimulated my therapeutic endeavors. It became fascinating to try to find regularities and irregularities in the dynamic course of a psychoanalytic treatment, to become aware of its possibilities and limitations, and to struggle with the many difficulties involved in the treatment of mentally disturbed patients.

Freud's discovery of the importance of the early developmental stages in the infantile instinctual life stimulated me to study the negative oedipal situation and the preoedipal phase first in little girls and later on in little boys as well.

Freud's refined description of the structured mind, the mutual interplay of forces at work in the id, the ego, and the superego influenced by environmental factors and the relations to the parents, enabled me to go further into the substructures of ego organization, into the different origins of the superego proper and the ego ideal, and into their influence on each other. Furthermore, I became interested in a variety of factors responsible for a harmonious ("normal") as well as for a pathological outcome of the processes of mental growth. I tried, too, to highlight some of the special events leading to the different forms of mental illness.

More and more it became clear that a study of the genesis (development) of the interplay of forces (dynamics) working between the various (structured) parts of the mind, including the quantitative (economic) viewpoint, is indispensable for a better understanding of mental processes.

A great number of other psychoanalysts, friends and colleagues, have influenced and stimulated me as well. I am greatly indebted to them indeed. I cannot name all of them; the list would be too long. I want, however, to thank Anna Freud warmly for her willingness to write a few lines to accompany this publication.

February, 1965

The articles of this book:

1. was originally published as "Zur Entwicklung des Oedipuskomplexes der Frau" in the Internationale Zeitschrift für Psychoanalyse, 13: 269-282, 1927. The English translation appeared in The International Journal of Psycho-Analysis, 9: 332-345, 1928, and was reprinted in The Psychoanalytic Reader, ed. R. Fliess. New York: International Universities Press, 1948, pp. 207-222.

2. was originally published as "Zu den Problemen der Weiblichkeit" in the Internationale Zeitschrift für Psychoanalyse, 19: 385-415, 1933. The authorized English translation by Irmarita K. Putnam appeared in The Psychoanalytic Quarterly, 2: 489-518, 1933.

3. was originally published as a review of Rado, S.: Die Kastrationsangst des Weibes in the Internationale Zeitschrift für Psychoanalyse, 21: 598-605, 1935. It is for the first time published in English in the Development of the Mind.

4. was originally published as "Hemmung und Narzissmus" in the Internationale Zeitschrift für Psychoanalyse, 22: 198-222, 1936. It is for the first time published in English in the Development of the Mind.

5. was read at the Fourteenth Congress of the International Psycho-Analytic Association, Marienbad, 1936. It was originally published as "Masochismus und Narzissmus" in the Internationale Zeitschrift für Psychoanalyse, 23: 479-489, 1937. It is for the first time published in English in the Development of the Mind.

6. was originally published in The International Journal of Psycho-Analysis, 20: 408-417, 1939.

7. was originally published in The Psychoanalytic Study of the Child, 2: 75-83. New York: International Universities Press, 1946.

8. was originally published in The International Journal of Psycho-Analysis, 28: 7-11, 1947. It was reprinted in The Yearbook of Psychoanalysis, 4: 50-60. New York: International Universities Press, 1948.

9. was presented in a slightly different version at a meeting of the Nederlandse Vereniging voor Psychotherapie, October 18, 1947. It is for the first time published in English in the Development of the Mind.

10. was originally published in Searchlights on Delinquency, ed. K.R. Eissler. New York: International Universities Press, 1949, pp. 246-255.

11. was read before the annual meeting of the Nederlandse Vereniging voor Psychiatrie en Neurologie, December 11, 1948. It was originally published in Folia Psychiatrica, Neurologica, et Neurochirurgica Neerlandica, 53 (1): 18-31, 1950. It is for the first time published in English in the Development of the Mind.

12. was read at the Symposium ,,The Evolution and Present Trends in Psycho analysis", Congrès International de Psychiatrie 5, Paris, 1950. It is for the first time published in English in the Development of the Mind.

13. was originally published in The Psychoanalytic Study of the Child, 5: 153-174. New York: International Universities Press, 1950.

14. was the opening paper in the Symposium on "Re-evaluation of the Role of the Oedipus Complex" at the Seventeenth Congress of the International Psycho-Analytical Association, Amsterdam, August 5-9, 1951. It was originally published in The International Journal of Psycho-Analysis, 33: 335-342, 1952.

15. was originally published in Drives, Affects, Behavior, ed. R.M. Loewenstein. New York: International Universities Press, 1953, pp. 153-168.

16. was the introduction to the discussion in the Symposium on "Problems of Psycho-Analytic Training" at the Eighteenth Congress of the International Psycho-Analytical Association, London, July 28, 1953. It was originally published in The International Journal of Psycho-Analysis, 35: 184-187, 1954.

17. was originally published as "Groepsbesprekingen met Stiefmoeders" in Maandblad voor Geestelijke Volksgezondheid, 9: 305-312, 1954. It is for the first time published in English in the Development of the Mind.

18. was read at the Nineteenth Congress of the International Psycho-Analytic Association, Geneva, July 24-18, 1955. It was originally published in The International Journal of Psycho-

Analysis, 37: 354-359, 1956. It was also published as "Anmerkungen zur psychoanalytischen Triebtheorie" in Entfaltung der Psychoanalyse, ed. A. Mitscherlich. Stuttgart: Klett, 1956, pp. 194-204; and in Psyche, Heidelberg, 10: 194-204, 1956.

19. was originally published as "Psychoanalytische Ich-Psychologie und ihre Bedeutung für die Fehlentwicklung bei Kindern" in Acta Psychotherapeutica, Psychosomatica et Orthopaedagogica, 4: 195-202, 1956. It is for the first time published in English in the Development of the mind.

20. was a contribution to the Symposium on "The Theory of Technique" held at the Centenary Scientific Meetings of the British Psycho-Analitic Society, May 5, 1956. It was originally published in The International Journal of Psycho-Analysis, 37: 456-459, 1956.

21. was originally published in The Psychoanalytic Study of the Child, 12: 114-126. New York: International Universities Press, 1957.

22. was originally published in The International Journal of Psycho-Analysis, 40: 169-179, 1959.

23. was read at the Twenty-First Congress of the International Psycho-Analytical Association, Copenhagen, July, 1959. It is was originally published in The Psychoanalytic Study of the Child, 15: 95-103. New York: International Universities Press, 1960.

24. was read at the Twenty-Second Congress of the International Psycho-Analytical Association, Edinburgh, August, 1961. It was originally published in The Psychoanalytic Study of the Child, 17: 94-106. New York: International Universities Press, 1962.

25. was originally published as: "Zur Behandlungstechnik bei neurotischen Patientinnen (Einige Bemerkungen zu den Beiträgen von P.C. Kuiper und A. Mitscherlich)" in Psyche Heft II XV, 1962.

26. (Chapter 25 in The Development of the Mind) was the subject of a discussion at the Twenty-Third Congress of the International Psycho-Analytical Association, Stockholm, July-August, 1963. It was originally published in The International Journal of Psycho-Analysis, 44: 1-11, 1963.

27. (Chapter 26 in The Development of the Mind) was there published for the first time.

28. (Chapter 27 in The Development of the Mind) was originally published in The Psychoanalytic Study of the Child, 19: 48-57. New York: International Universities Press, 1964.

29. was originally published as "Heinz Hartmann's Beiträge zur Psychoanalyse" in Psyche Heft 6/7, XVIII, 1964/1965.

30. was originally published in "Psychoanalysis, a general Psychology". Essays in honor of Heinz Hartmann. International Universities Press, 1966 (N.Y.).

31. was originally published in the Psychoanalytic Study of the Child, vol. 22, 1967.

32. was originally published as "Die Zusammenarbeit von Patient und Analytiker in der psychoanalytischen Behandlung" (Übertragung, Gegenübertragung, Einfühlung und Intuition) in Psyche, Heft 1-3, XXI, 1967.

33. was originally published as "Gedanke über Vorteile und Gefahre der Einseitigkeit in der wissenschaftlichen Forschung" in Psyche 9-11, XXII, 1967.

34. was originally published in The International Journal of Psycho-Analysis, vol. 50, 567-572, 1969.

35. was a contribution to the meeting of the members of the American Association for Child Psychoanalysis on July 25th, 1971 in Vienna.

36. was originally published in the Psychoanalytic Study of the Child, 30, 1975.

37. was originally published as "Twee belevenswerelden, die van het kind en die van de volwassene" in: "Opstellen uit de Kinderpsychiatrie". Van Loghem Slaterus B.V., Deventer, 1975.

38. was originally published in the Psychoanalytic Study of the Child, 31, 1976, written in honor of Marianne Kris on occasion of her 75th birthday.

39. was originally published in the Psychoanalytic Study of the Child, 31, 1976.

40. was originally published as "Kann die Psychoanalyse zur Linderung des heutigen menschlichen Elends beitragen?" In: Provokation und Toleranz. Festschrift für Alexander Mitscherlich zum siebzigsten Geburtstag. Suhrkamp Verlag, Frankfurt, 1978.

41. was read as a lecture on the occasion of the 60th anniversary of the Dutch Psychoanalytic Society in 1977, under the title "Verleden, heden en toekomst van de psychoanalyse in vogelvlucht". A slightly different version was read at the Psychiatric Department of the Nijmegen University in 1978.

en de psychoanalytische beweging in de twintiger en dertiger jaren. In: Psychoanalytici aan het woord. Van Loghem Slaterus B.V., Deventer, 1980.

43. was originally published in: Psychotherapy: research and training. W. de Moor and H.R. Wijngaarden eds. Elseviers/North Holland Biomedical Press, 1980.

44. was originally published in The Course of Life. Psychoanalytic Contributions Toward Understanding Personality Development. Vol. I: Infancy and Early Childhood. S.I. Greenspan and G.H. Pollock, eds. NIMH, 1980.

45. was originally published as "Notes on Multiple Personality" in the Psychoanalytic Quarterly, L, 1981, as a contribution to the Jubilee Issue of this Journal and the honouring of Jack Arlow.

46. was originally published in the Psychoanalytic Quarterly, LI, 1982.

47. was originally published in the Psychoanalytic Study of the Child, 1983.

Bibliography

Abraham, K. (1920), Manifestations of the Female Castration Complex. Selected Papers. London: Hogarth Press, 1927.

Abraham, K. (1921), Contributions to the Theory of the Anal Character. Selected Papers. London: Hogarth Press, 1927.

Abraham, K. (1924a), A Short Study of the Development of the Libido, Viewed in the Light of Mental Disorders. Selected Papers. London: Hogarth Press, 1927.

Abraham, K. (1924b), The Influence of Oral Eroticism on Character Formation. Selected Papers. London: Hogarth Press, 1927.

Abraham, K. (1924c), Character Formation on the Genital Level of Libido-Development. Selected Papers. London: Hogarth Press, 1927.

Adrian, E.D. (1946), The Mental and the Physical Origins of Behaviour. Int. J. Psycho-Anal., 27.

Aichhorn, A. (1925), Wayward Youth. New York: Viking Press, 1944.

Alexander, F. (1923), The Castration Complex in the Formation of Character. Int. J. Psycho-Anal., 4.

Ashby, W.R. (1952), Design for a Brain. New York: Wiley.

Balint, M. (1954), Analytic Training and Training Analysis. Int. J. Psycho-Anal., 35.

Bibring, E. (1936), The Development and Problems of the Theory of the Instincts. Int. J. Psycho-Anal., 22, 1941.

Bibring, G.L. (1954), The Training Analysis and Its Place in Psycho-analytic Training. Int. J. Psycho-Anal., 35.

Blum, H.P., ed. (1977), Female Psychology: Contemporary Psychoanalytic Views. New York: International Universities Press.

Bolk, L. (1918), Hersenen en Cultuur. Amsterdam: Scheltema en Holkema.

Bolk, L. (1926), Das Problem der Menschwerdung. Jena: Fischer.

Bonaparte, M. (1949), De la Sexualité de la Femme. Rev. Franc. Psychanal., 13.

Bornstein, B. (1948), Emotional Barriers in the Understanding and Treatment of Young Children. Amer. J. Orthopsychiat., 18: 691-697.

Bowlby, J. (1960), Grief and Mourning in Infancy and Early Childhood. This Annual, 15: 9-52.

Bowlby, J. (1979), in: The International Review of Psychoanalysis, vol. 6, Part 1.

Breuer, J., Freud, S. (1895), Studies on Hysteria. Standard Edition, 2. London: Hogarth Press, 1955.

Brierley, M. (1947), Psycho-Analysis and Integrative Living. Trends in Psycho-Analysis. London: Hogarth Press, 1951.

Brun, R. (1953), Über Freuds Hypothese vom Todestrieb; eine kritische Untersuchung. Psyche, 7.

Brunswick, R.M. (1940), The Pre-Oedipal Phase in Libido Development. Psychoanal. Quart., 9.

Burlingham, D.T. (1935), Die Einfühlung des Kleinkindes in die Mutter. Imago, XXI, 1935. Wien (Int. Ps. Anal. Verlag), 429-444.

Deutsch, H. (1925), The Psychology of Women in Relation to the Functions of Reproduction. Int. J. Psycho-Anal., 6: 405-418.

Deutsch, H. (1930), The Significance of Masochism in the mental Life of Women. Int. J. Psycho-Anal., 11: 46-60.

Eidelberg, L. (1935), Das Problem der Quantität in der Neurosenlehre. Int. Z. Psychoanal., 21.

Eissler, K.R. (1953), The Effect of the Structure of the Ego on Psychoanalytic Technique. J. Amer. Psychoanal. Assn., 1.

Eissler, K.R. (1955), The Psychiatrist and the Dying Patient. New York: International Universities Press.

Eissler, K.R. (1960), The Efficient Soldier. The Psychoanalytic Study of Society. 1. New York: International Universities Press.

Eissler, K.R. (1971), Death Drive, Ambivalence, and Narcissism. The Psychoanalytic Study of the Child, 26: 25-78.

Elias, N. (1937), Über den Prozess der Zivilisation. Basel: Falken, 1939.

Fenichel, O. (1926), Identification. Collected Papers, First Series. New York: Norton, 1953.

Fenichel, O. (1945), The Psychoanalytic Theory of Neurosis. New York: Norton.

Fliess, R., ed. (1948), The Psychoanalytic Reader. New York: International Universities Press.

Flugel, J.C. (1945), Man, Morals and Society. New York: International Universities Press, 1947.

Flugel, J.C. (1953), The Death-Instinct, Homeostasis and Allied Concepts. Int. J. Psycho-Anal., 34 (Suppl.).

Freud, A. (1922), The Relation of Beating-Phantasies to a Day-Dream. Int. J. Psycho-Anal., 4, 1923.

Freud, A. (1936), The Ego and the Mechanisms of Defence. New York: International Universities Press, 1946.

Freud, A. (1945), Indications for Child Analysis. The Psychoanalytic Study of the Child, 1, ed. R.S. Eissler, A. Freud, H. Hartmann, M. Kris; currently 19 volumes. New York: International Universities Press, 1945-1964.

Freud, A. (1949a), Aggression in Relation to Emotional Development: Normal and Pathological. The Psychoanalytic Study of the Child, 3/4.

Freud, A. (1949b), Certain Types and Stages of Social Maladjustment. In Searchlights on Delinquency, ed. K. Eissler. New York: International Universities Press.

Freud, A. (1951), Observations on Child Development. The Psychoanalytic Study of the Child, 6.

Freud, A. (1952), The Mutual Influences in the Development of Ego and Id: Introduction to the Discussion. The Psychoanalytic Study of the Child, 7: 42-50.

Freud, A. (1958), Adolescence. The Psychoanalytic Study of the Child, 13.

Freud, A. (1965), Normality and Pathology in Childhood: Assessments of Development. New York: International Universities Press.

Freud, A. (1969), Difficulties in the Path of Psychoanalysis. New York: International Universities Press.

Freud, A., Burlingham, D. (1942), War and Children. New York: International Universities Press, 1943.

Freud, A., Burlingham, D. (1943), Infants Without Families. New York: International Universities Press, 1944.

Freud, A., Schur, M., Spitz, R.A. (1960), Discussion of Dr. John Bowlby's Paper. The Psychoanalytic Study of the Child, 15: 53-94.

Freud, E.L., ed. (1960), Letters of Sigmund Freud. New York: Basic Books.

Freud, S. (1894), The Neuro-Psychoses of Defence. Standard Edition, 3.

Freud, S. (1895), Project for a Scientific Psychology. The Origins of Psychoanalysis: Letters to Wilhelm Fliess, Drafts and Notes: 1887-1902. New York: Basic Books, 1954.

Freud, S. (1898), Further Remarks on the Neuro-Psychoses of Defense. Standard Edition, 3.

Freud, S. (1900), The Interpretation of Dreams. Standard Edition, 4-5.

Freud, S. (1905a [1901]), Fragment of an Analysis of a Case of Hysteria. Standard Edition, 7.

Freud, S. (1905b), Jokes and Their Relation to the Unconscious. Standard Edition, 8.

Freud, S. (1905c), Three Essays on the Theory of Sexuality. Standard Edition. 7.

Freud, S. (1909a), Analysis of a Phobia in a five-year old Boy. Standard Edition, 7.

Freud, S. (1909b), Notes upon a Case of Obsessional Neurosis. Standard Edition, 10.

Freud, S. (1909c), Two case Histories. Standard Edition, volume 10. London: Hogarth Press, 1955.

Freud, S. (1911), Formulations on the Two Principles of Mental Functioning. Standard Edition, 12.

Freud, S. (1911-1915), Papers on Technique. Standard Edition, 12: 85-171.

Freud, S. (1912), Contributions to a Discussion on Masturbation. Standard Edition, 12.

Freud, S. (1912-1913), Totem and Taboo. Standard Edition, 13.

Freud, S. (1914), On Narcissism: An Introduction. Standard Edition, 14.

Freud, S. (1915), Instincts and Their Vicissitudes. Standard Edition, 14.

Freud, S. (1916), Some Character-Types met with in Psycho-Analytic Work: Criminals from a Sense of Guilt. Standard Edition, 14.

Freud, S. (1917), Mourning and Melancholia. Standard Edition, 14: 237-260.

Freud, S. (1918 [1914]), From the History of an Infantile Neurosis. Standard Edition, 17.

Freud, S. (1919), A Child is Being Beaten. Standard Edition, 17.

Freud, S. (1920a), Beyond the Pleasure Principle. Standard Edition, 18.

Freud, S. (1920b), The Psychogenesis of a Case of Homosexuality in Woman. Standard Edition, 18.

Freud, S. (1921), Group Psychology and the Analysis of the Ego. Standard Edition, 18.

Freud, S. (1923a [1922]), A Seventeenth-Century Demonological Neurosis. Standard Edition, 19.

Freud, S. (1923b), The Ego and the Id. Standard Edition, 19.

Freud, S. (1923c), Das Ich und das Es. Gesammelte Werke, Bd. 13. London: Imago 1941, 235-289.

Freud, S. (1924a), The Economic Problem of Masochism. Standard Edition, 19.

Freud, S. (1924b), The Dissolution of the Oedipus Complex. Standard Edition, 19.

Freud, S. (1925a), Some Psychical Consequences of the Anatomical Distinction between the Sexes. Standard Edition, 19.

Freud, S. (1925b), An autobiographical Study. Standard Edition, 20.

Freud, S. (1926), Inhibitions, Symptoms and Anxiety. Standard Edition, 20.

Freud, S. (1927a), Humour. Standard Edition, 21.

Freud, S. (1927b), The Future of an Illusion. Standard Edition, 21.

Freud, S. (1930), Civilization and Its Discontents. Standard Edition, 21.

Freud, S. (1931a), Libidinal Types. Standard Edition, 21.

Freud, S. (1931b), Female Sexuality. Standard Edition, 21.

Freud, S. (1932), New Introductory Lectures on Psycho-Analysis. Standard Edition, 22.

Freud, S. (1933), New introductory lectures on psycho-analysis. Lecture 33: Femininity. Standard Edition, 22: 112-135.

Freud, S. (1937), Analysis Terminable and Interminable. Collected Papers, 5. London: Hogarth Press, 1950.

Freud, S. (1937-1939), Moses and Monotheism. New York: Knopf, 1947.

Freud, S. (1940 [1938]), An Outline of Psychoanalysis. New York: Norton, 1949.

Freud, W.E. (1975), Infant Observation. The Psychoanalytic Study of the Child, 30: 75-94.

Furer, M. (1964), Some developmental aspects of the superego. Int. J. Psycho-Anal., 1967, 48, 277-280.

Furman, E. (1974), A Child's Parent Dies. New Haven-London: Yale University Press.

Geleerd, E. (1943), The Analysis of a Case of Compulsive Masturbation in a Child. Psychoanal. Quart., 13.

Gitelson, M. (1954), Therapeutic Problems in the Analysis of the "Normal" Candidate. Int. J. Psycho-Anal., 35.

Greenacre, P. (1954), The Role of Transference. J. Amer. Psychoanal. Assn., 2: 671-684.

Greenacre, P. (1957), The Childhood of the Artist. The Psychoanalytic Study of the Child, 12.

Greenacre, P. (1960), Considerations Regarding the Parent-Infant Relationship. Int. J. Psycho-Anal., 41.

Greenson, R.R. (1960), Empathy and Its Vicissitudes. Int. J. Psycho-Anal., 41: 418-424.

Greenson, R.R. (1965), The Working Alliance and the Transference Neurosis. Psychoanal. Quart., 34: 155-181.

Greenson, R.R. (1966), That "Impossible" Profession. J. Amer. Psa. Assn., 14: 9-27.

Greenson, R.R. (1967), The Technique and Practice of Psychoanalysis. New York: International Universities Press.

Hartmann, H. (1939a), Ego Psychology and the Problem of Adaptation. New York: International Universities Press, 1958.

Hartmann, H. (1939b), Psychoanalysis and the Concept of Health. Essays on Ego Psychology. New York: International Universities Press, 1964.

Hartmann, H. (1948), Comments on the Psychoanalytic Theory of Instinctual Drives. Essays on Ego Psychology. New York: International Universities Press.

Hartmann, H. (1950), Comments on the Psychoanalytic Theory of the Ego. Essays on Ego Psychology. New York: International Universities Press, 1964.

Hartmann, H. (1952), The Mutual Influences in the Development of Ego and Id. Essays in Ego Psychology. New York: International Universities Press.

Hartmann, H. (1955), Notes on the Theory of Sublimation. The Psychoanalytic Study of the Child, 10.

Hartmann, H. (1956), Notes on the Reality Principle. Essays, 241-267.

Hartmann, H. (1960), Psychoanalysis and Moral Values. New York: International Universities Press.

Hartmann, H., Kris, E. (1945), The Genetic Approach in Psychoanalysis. The Psychoanalytic Study of the Child, 1.

Hartmann, H., Kris, E., Loewenstein, R.M. (1946), Comments on the Formation of Psychic Structure. The Psychoanalytic Study of the Child, 2.

Hartmann, H., Kris, E., Loewenstein, R.M. (1949), Notes on the Theory of Aggression. The Psychoanalytic Study of the Child, 3/4.

Hartmann, H., Loewenstein, R.M. (1962), Notes on the Superego. The Psychoanalytic Study of the Child, 17.

Hartmann, H., Kris, E., Loewenstein, R.M. (1964), Papers on Psychoanalytic Psychology. [Psychol. Issues, Monogr. 14]. New York: International Universities Press.

Heimann, P. (1954), Problems of the Training Analysis. Int. J. Psycho-Anal., 35.

Hoffer, W. (1949), Mouth, Hand and Ego-Integration. The Psychoanalytic Study of the Child, 3/4.

Hoffer, W. (1950), A Reconsideration of Freud's Concept "Primary Narcissism". Unpublished Ms.

Hoffer, W. (1954), Defensive Process and Defensive Organization: Their Place in Psycho-Analytic Technique. Int. J. Psycho-Anal., 35.

Horney, K. (1923), On the Genesis of the Castration Complex in Women. Int. J. Psycho-Anal., 5, 1924.

Horney, K. (1926), The Flight from Womanhood. Int. J. Psycho-Anal., 7.

Horney, K. (1928), The problem of the monogamous ideal. Int. J. Psycho-Anal., 9: 318-331.

Horney, K. (1932), The Dread of Woman. Int. J. Psycho-Anal., 13.

Isaac-Edersheim, E. (1965), Unpublished speech for the Dutch Psychoanalytical Society.

Jones, E. (1927), The early development of female sexuality. Int. J. Psycho-Anal., 8: 459-472.

Jones, E. (1935), Early female sexuality. Int. J. Psycho-Anal., 16: 263-273.

Jones, E. (1953), The Life and Work of Sigmund Freud, vol. 1. New York: Basic Books.

Kaila, E. (1932), Die Reaktionen des Säuglings auf das menschliche Gesicht. Annal. Univ. Aboensis, 17.

Kenyatta, J. (1938), Facing Mount Kenya. London: Secker-Warburg, 1961.

Klein, M. (1928), Early Stages of the Oedipus Conflict. Int. J. Psycho-Anal., 9: 167-180.

Klein, M. (1932), The Effects of Early Anxiety-Situations on the Sexual Development of the Girl. The Psycho-Analysis of Children, New York: Norton, p. 268-325.

Klein, M. (1940), Mourning and Its Relation to Manic-Depressive States. Contributions to Psycho-Analysis, 1921-1945. London: Hogarth Press, pp. 311-338.

Klein, M. (1948), Contributions to Psycho-Analysis, 1921-45. London: Hogarth Press.

Kohut, H. (1966), Forms and Transformations of Narcissism. J. Amer. Psa. Assn., 14: 243-272.

Kohut, H. (1968), The Psychoanalytic Treatment of Narcissistic Personality Disorders. The Psychoanalytic Study of the Child, 23: 86-113.

Kohut, H. (1971), The Analysis of the Self. New York: International Universities Press.

Kohut, H. (1972), Thoughts on Narcissism and Narcissistic Rage. The Psychoanalytic Study of the Child, 27: 360-400.

Kohut, H., Seitz, P.F.D. (1963), Concepts and Theories of Psychoanalysis. In: Concepts of Personality; hrsg. v. Wepman und Herne. Chicago (Aldune).

Kris, E. (1951), The Development of Ego Psychology. Samiksa, 5.

Kris, E. (1952), Psychoanalytic Explorations in Art. New York: International Universities Press.

Kris, E. (1975), The Selected Papers of Ernst Kris. New Haven-London: Yale University Press.

Kubie, L.S. (1948), Instincts and Homeostasis. Psychosom. Med., 10.

Kubie, L.S. (1954), The Fundamental Nature of the Distinction Between Normality and Neurosis. Psychoanal. Quart., 23.

Kubie, L.S. (1958), Some Implications for Psychoanalysis of Modern Concepts of the Organization of the Brain. Psychoanal. Quart., 27.

Laslett, P. (1950), The Physical Basis of Mind. Oxford: Blackwell.

Lawick-Goodall, J. van (1971), In the Shadow of Man. New York: Houghton Mifflin.

Loewenstein, R.M. (1957), A Contribution to the Psychoanalytic Theory of Masochism. J. Amer. Psychoanal. Assn., 5.

Loewenstein, R.M. (1969), Developments in the Theory of Transference in the Last Fifty Years. Int. J. Psycho-Anal., 50: 583-588.

Lorenz, K. (1950), The Comparative Method in Studying Innate Behaviour Patterns. Symp. Soc. Exp. Biol., 4.

Mahler, M.S. (1968), On Human Symbiosis and the Vicissitudes of Individuation. New York: International Universities Press.

Mahler, M.S. (1972), On the First Subphases of the Separation-Individuation Process. Int. J. Psycho-Anal., 53: 333-338.

Mahler, M. S. (1975), On the current status of the Infantile Neurosis. Journal of the American Psychoanalytic Association, 23(2): 327-333.

Masserman, J.H. (1953), Psycho-Analysis and Biodynamics: An Integration. Int. J. Psycho-Anal., 34 (Suppl.).

Masters, W.H., Johnson, V.E. (1966), Human Sexual Response. Boston: Little, Brown.

Menninger, K.A. (1954), Regulatory Devices of the Ego Under Major Stress. Int. J. Psycho-Anal., 35.

Mitscherlich, A. (1956 + 1958), Aggression und Anpassung. In: Aggression und Anpassung in der Industriegesellschaft. Frankfurt: Suhrkamp, 1969, 80-127.

Mitscherlich, A. (1963), Auf dem Weg zur vaterlosen Gesellschaft. München: Piper.

Müller, J. (1931), A Contribution to the Problem of Libidinal Development of the Genital Phase of Girls. Int. J. Psycho-Anal., 1932, 13: 361-368.

Nabokov, V. (1941), The Real Life of Sebastian Knight. Norfolk, Conn.: New Directions, 1959.

Novick, J. (1970), The Vicissitudes of the 'Working-Alliance' in the Analysis of a Latency Girl. The Psychoanalytic Study of the Child, 25: 231-256.

Nunberg, H. (1932), Principles of Psychoanalysis. New York: International Universities Press, 1955.

Olden, C. (1958), Notes on the Development of Empathy. The Psychoanalytic Study of the Child, 13: 505-518.

Ostow, M. (1954), A Psychoanalytic Contribution to the Study of Brain Function. Psychoanal. Quart., 23.

Painter, G.D. (1965), Marcel Proust: A Biography. Vol. 2. Boston: Little, Brown.

Parin, P., Morgenthaler, F., Parin-Matthey, G. (1971), Fürchte deinen Nächsten wie dich selbst. Frankfurt: Suhrkamp.

Penfield, W., Rasmussen, T. (1950), The Cerebral Cortex of Man. New York: Macmillan.

Piaget, J. (1936), The Origins of Intelligence in Children. New York: International Universities Press.

Piaget, J. (1937), The Construction of Reality in the Child. New York: Basic Books, 1954.

Popper, K.R. (1952), The Open Society and its Enemies. Vol. 1. London: Routledge-Kegan Paul.

Provence, S., Ritvo, S. (1961), Effects of Deprivation on Institutionalized Infants. The Psychoanalytic Study of the Child, 16.

Rado, S. (1926), The Psychic Effects of Intoxication: Attempt at a Psycho-analytic Theory of Drug Addiction. Int. J. Psycho-Anal., 7.

Rado, S. (1933), Fear of Castration in Women. Psychoanal. Quart., 2.

Rapaport, D., ed. (1951), Organization and Pathology of Thoughts. New York: Columbia University Press.

Rapaport, D. (1958), A Historical Survey of Psychoanalytic Ego Psychology. In: Psychological Issues, 1. New York: International Universities Press.

Reich, A. (1951), On Countertransference. Int. J. Psycho-Anal., 32.

Root, N.N. (1957), A Neurosis in Adolescence. The Psychoanalytic Study of the Child, 12.

Rümke, H.C., Carp, E.A.D.E. (1947), article in Psychiat. Neurol. Bladen 5.

Ruyer, R. (1954), La Cybernétique et l'Origine de l'Information. Paris: Flammerion.

Sandler, J. (1960), On the Concept of Superego. The Psychoanalytic Study of the Child, 15.

Sandler, J. (1962), Psychology and Psycho-Analysis. Brit. J. Med. Psychol., 35.

Schafer, R. (1959), Generative Empathy in the Treatment Situation. Psa. Quart., 28: 342-373.

Sherfey, M.J. (1966), The Evolution and Nature of Female Sexuality in Relation to Psychoanalytic Theory. J. Amer. Psychoanal. Assn., 14: 28-128.

Simmel, E. (1930), Zum Problem von Zwang und Sucht. Bericht v. allgem. ärzt. Kongress Psychotherapie, Baden-Baden.

Spiegel, L.A. (1951), A Review of Contributions to a Psychoanalytic Theory of Adolescence: Individual Aspects. The Psychoanalytic Study of the Child, 6.

Spitz, R.A. (1949), Autoerotism. Some Empirical Findings and Hypotheses on Three of Its Manifestations in the First Year of Life. The Psychoanalytic Study of the Child, 3/4.

Spitz, R.A. (1950), Anxiety in Infancy, a Study of its Manifestations in the First Year of Life. Int. J. Psycho-Anal., 31.

Spitz, R.A. (1957), No and Yes: On the Beginning of Human Communication. New York: International Universities Press.

Spitz, R.A. (1965a), Vom Säugling zum Kleinkind. Stuttgart: Klett, 1967.

Spitz, R.A. (1965b), The First Year of Life. New York: International Universities Press.

Stone, L. (1961a), The Agony and the Ecstasy. New York: Doubleday.

Stone, L. (1961b), The Psychoanalytic Situation. New York: International Universities Press.

Szekely, L. (1954), Biological Remarks on Fears Originating in Early Childhood. Int. J. Psycho-Anal., 35.

Tinbergen, N. (1951), The Study of Instincts. Oxford: Clarendon Press.

Van der Waals, H.G. (1943), Aanleg en Ontwikkeling. Mensch en Maatschappij, 19(4).

Van der Waals, H.G. (1946), [On the Rorschach Test]. Psychiat. Neurol. Bladen, 49.

Van Ophuijsen, J.H.W. (1918), Contributions to the Masculinity Complex in Women. Int. J. Psycho-Anal., 5, 1924.

Von Bertalanffy, L. (1950), The Theory of Open Systems in Physics and Biology. Science, 111.

Waelder, R. (1936), The Problem of the Genesis of Psychical Conflict in Earliest Infancy. Int. J. Psycho-Anal., 18, 1937.

Walter, W.G. (1953), The Living Brain. London: Duckworth.

Weiss, E. (1932), Bodily Pain and Mental Pain. Int. J. Psycho-Anal., 15.

Wiener, N. (1949), Cybernetics. New York: Wiley.

Wiener, N. (1954), The Human Use of Human Beings. New York: Double-day.

de Wind, E. (1965), Voor wie aan Auschwitz ontkwam gaat de Bevrijding door. Nieuwe Rotterdamse Courant, January 23.

Winnicott, D.W. (1960), The Theory of the Parent-Infant Relationship. Int. J. Psycho-Anal., 41.

Zetzel, E.R. (1956), Current Concepts of Transference. Int. J. Psycho-Anal., 37: 369-376.

Index

434

residue of early phases 404
normal versus abnormal 322, 394, 401-406
see also Child development
De Wind, E. 278
Diacritic organization 288, 337
Difference between sexes 412
Discharge 398
Disciplining by age groups 327
Dissidents 374
Dream parapraxis 401
Displacement 115, 194, 344-347
Driesch, H. 178
Drives 32, 81, 109, 145, 147, 177, 369, 378, 386, 395
defusion of 22-24, 29, 62, 155, 157, 240
demands of, in adolescence 220
destructive, see Death force
discharge of 48, 110, 112, 123-124, 158-162, 239-264
disposition of 216
erotic, see Life force
fear of 94
fusion of 155, 161-163, 240
intensity of 43-48, 55, 108, 250
interrelationship of erotic and aggressive 155-160
organic nature of 58, 236
satisfaction 402
theory of 16, 19-28, 106, 112-116, 121, 151-163, 175-182, 211
topography of 47-50
versus instincts 211
see also Aggression; Id; Libido
Dubarle, Père 207
Economic (-social situation) 364
Education 105, 117, 120, 133, 215
Ego analysis 166
Ego functions 40-45, 56, 63, 81-87, 109-110, 113, 126, 127, 134-137, 154, 158, 161, 184, 187, 202, 215, 216, 225-228, 231, 241, 245-249, 262
autonomous 241, 242, 246, 263-264, 267
development 246, 263, 272, 288, 402
disturbances (impairment) of 42, 50-51, 55, 231, 238
restriction of 43
see also Adaptation; Memory; Motility control; Perception; Reality testing; Synthetic function
Ego ideal 87-88, 90-103, 111-112, 148-149, 189, 219, 222-224, 239, 242, 247-261, 265, 267
Ego ideal (continued)
genesis and formation of 87, 95, 98-105, 128, 148, 225-228, 266-267

identifications in 190-191
and superego system 101, 225-233
see also Superego
"Ego loss" 152
Ego organization 40-42, 45, 53, 56, 91, 100, 109, 120, 148, 183, 191, 226
in adolescence 220-221
animal 241
body ego 83, 195, 241
in borderline and psychotic patients 247-248
development of 22-23, 34-35, 71, 81-88, 98, 111, 113-114, 118, 127-128, 134, 145, 154-155, 160-163, 166-167, 184, 197, 199-200, 220, 241-242, 244-245, 247-248, 266
differentiations within 253
disposition of 216
in infants 262
nature of, in determining mental health 249-250
qualities of 147
in symptom formation 242-245
vulnerability of 216
Ego paralysis 47
Ego psychology 82, 120, 183-188, 209, 226, 253, 261, 266, 271-273, 378
Ego strength 44-45, 56
Ego weakness 53, 94
Eidelberg, L. 44
Eissler, K.R. 181, 195, 326, 330
Eitingon, M. 380
Elias, N. 81
Emancipation 397
Empathy 192-193, 291, 333, 341, 359-387
Entropy 208-210
Eros
see Life force
Ethology 195, 203, 210, 212, 217
Equation of different concepts 346
Experience 349-357
Experiential world 321, 324, 325, 332-342
Failure (of analytic treatment) 342
Fantasy 127-130, 181, 226, 254-255, 259
in adolescence 253-256
of curing 80
in infancy 71, 127-128
in latency 253-254
see also Beating fantasy; Castration fantasy; Grandeur and omnipotence fantasy; Masochistic fantasy; Masturbation fantasy; Punishment fantasy, etc.
Feces 324
Fechner, G. 20, 210
see also Constancy principle
Federn, P. 77
Feedback mechanism 206-207, 211